Introductory Econometrics for Finance

This bestselling and thoroughly classroom-tested textbook is a complete resource for finance students. A comprehensive and illustrated discussion of the most common empirical approaches in finance prepares students for using econometrics in practice, while detailed case studies help them understand how the techniques are used in relevant financial contexts. Worked examples from the latest version of the popular statistical software EViews guide students to implement their own models and interpret results. Learning outcomes, key concepts and end-of-chapter review questions (with full solutions online) highlight the main chapter takeaways and allow students to self-assess their understanding. Building on the successful data- and problem-driven approach of previous editions, this third edition has been updated with new data, extensive examples and additional introductory material on mathematics, making the book more accessible to students encountering econometrics for the first time. A companion website, with numerous student and instructor resources, completes the learning package.

Chris Brooks is Professor of Finance and Director of Research at the ICMA Centre, Henley Business School, University of Reading, UK where he also obtained his PhD. He has diverse research interests and has published over a hundred articles in leading academic and practitioner journals, and six books. He is Associate Editor of several journals, including the Journal of Business Finance and Accounting, the International Journal of Forecasting and the British Accounting Review. He acts as consultant and advisor for various banks, corporations and professional bodies in the fields of finance, real estate, and econometrics.

Introductory Econometrics for Finance

THIRD EDITION

Chris Brooks

The ICMA Centre, Henley Business School, University of Reading

CAMBRIDGE
UNIVERSITY PRESS

CAMBRIDGE
UNIVERSITY PRESS

University Printing House, Cambridge CB2 8BS, United Kingdom

Cambridge University Press is part of the University of Cambridge.

It furthers the University's mission by disseminating knowledge in the pursuit of education, learning and research at the highest international levels of excellence.

www.cambridge.org
Information on this title: www.cambridge.org/9781107661455

© Chris Brooks 2014

First published 2002
Second edition 2008
Third edition published 2014

Printed in Spain by Grafos SA, Arte sobre papel

A catalogue record for this publication is available from the British Library

Library of Congress Cataloguing in Publication data
Brooks, Chris
Introductory econometrics for finance / Chris Brooks, The ICMA Centre, Henley Business School, University of Reading. – Third edition.
   pages   cm
Includes bibliographical references and index.
ISBN 978-1-107-03466-2 (hardback) – ISBN 978-1-107-66145-5 (pbk)
1. Finance – Econometric models.   2. Econometrics.   I. Title.
HG173.B76   2014
332.01'5195 – dc23   2013049908

ISBN 978-1-107-03466-2 Hardback
ISBN 978-1-107-66145-5 Paperback

Additional resources for this publication at www.cambridge.org/brooks3

Contents

Figures

Tables

Boxes

Screenshots

Preface to the third edition

Sales of the first two editions of this book surpassed expectations (at least those of the author). Almost all of those who have contacted the author seem to like the book, and while other textbooks have been published since in the broad area of financial econometrics, none are really at the introductory level. All of the motivations for the first edition, described below, seem just as important today. Given that the book seems to have gone down well with readers, I have left the style largely unaltered but changed the structure slightly and added new material.

The main motivations for writing the first edition of the book were:

- To write a book that focused on *using and applying* the techniques rather than deriving proofs and learning formulae.
- To write an accessible textbook that required no prior knowledge of econometrics, but which also covered more recently developed approaches usually only found in more advanced texts.
- To use examples and terminology from finance rather than economics since there are many introductory texts in econometrics aimed at students of economics but none for students of finance.
- To litter the book with case studies of the use of econometrics in practice taken from the academic finance literature.
- To include sample instructions, screen dumps and computer output from a popular econometrics package. This enabled readers to see how the techniques can be implemented in practice.
- To develop a companion web site containing answers to end of chapter questions, PowerPoint slides and other supporting materials.

What is new in the third edition

The third edition includes a number of important new features:

(1) Students of finance have enormously varying backgrounds, and in particular varying levels of training in elementary mathematics and statistics. In order to make the book more self-contained, the material that was previously buried in an appendix at the end of the book has now been considerably expanded and enhanced, and is now placed in a new chapter 2. As a result, all of the previous chapters 2 to 13 have been shunted forward by a chapter (so the

previous chapter 2 becomes chapter 3, 3 becomes 4, and so on). What was the concluding chapter in the second edition, chapter 14, has now been removed (with some of the content worked into other chapters) so that there are also fourteen chapters in the third edition.

(2) An extensive glossary has been added at the end of the book to succinctly explain all of the technical terms used in the text.

(3) As a result of the length of time it took to write the book, to produce the final product and the time that has elapsed since then, the data and examples used in the second edition are already several years old. The data, EViews instructions and screenshots have been fully updated. EViews version 8.0, the latest available at the time of writing, has been used throughout. The data continue to be drawn from the same freely available sources as in the previous edition.

(4) Two of the most important uses of statistical models by students in their courses tend to be the methodology developed in a series of papers by Fama and French, and the event study approach. Both of these are now described in detail with examples in chapter 14.

(5) New material has been added in the appropriate places in the book covering panel unit root and cointegration tests; measurement error in variables; unit root testing with structural breaks; and conditional correlation models.

Motivations for the first edition

This book had its genesis in two sets of lectures given annually by the author at the ICMA Centre (formerly ISMA Centre), Henley Business School, University of Reading and arose partly from several years of frustration at the lack of an appropriate textbook. In the past, finance was but a small sub-discipline drawn from economics and accounting, and therefore it was generally safe to assume that students of finance were well grounded in economic principles; econometrics would be taught using economic motivations and examples.

However, finance as a subject has taken on a life of its own in recent years. Drawn in by perceptions of exciting careers in the financial markets, the number of students of finance grew phenomenally all around the world. At the same time, the diversity of educational backgrounds of students taking finance courses has also expanded. It is not uncommon to find undergraduate students of finance even without advanced high-school qualifications in mathematics or economics. Conversely, many with PhDs in physics or engineering are also attracted to study finance at the Masters level. Unfortunately, authors of textbooks failed to keep pace with the change in the nature of students. In my opinion, the currently available textbooks fall short of the requirements of this market in three main regards, which this book seeks to address:

(1) Books fall into two distinct and non-overlapping categories: the introductory and the advanced. Introductory textbooks are at the appropriate level for students with limited backgrounds in mathematics or statistics, but their focus is too narrow. They often spend too long deriving the most basic results, and

treatment of important, interesting and relevant topics (such as simulations methods, VAR modelling, etc.) is covered in only the last few pages, if at all. The more advanced textbooks, meanwhile, usually require a quantum leap in the level of mathematical ability assumed of readers, so that such books cannot be used on courses lasting only one or two semesters, or where students have differing backgrounds. In this book, I have tried to sweep a broad brush over a large number of different econometric techniques that are relevant to the analysis of financial and other data.

(2) Many of the currently available textbooks with broad coverage are too theoretical in nature and students can often, after reading such a book, still have no idea of how to tackle real-world problems themselves, even if they have mastered the techniques in theory. To this end, in this book, I have tried to present examples of the use of the techniques in finance, together with annotated computer instructions and sample outputs for an econometrics package (EViews). This should assist students who wish to learn how to estimate models for themselves – for example, if they are required to complete a project or dissertation. Some examples have been developed especially for this book, while many others are drawn from the academic finance literature. In my opinion, this is an essential but rare feature of a textbook that should help to show students how econometrics is really applied. It is also hoped that this approach will encourage some students to delve deeper into the literature, and will give useful pointers and stimulate ideas for research projects. It should, however, be stated at the outset that the purpose of including examples from the academic finance print is not to provide a comprehensive overview of the literature or to discuss all of the relevant work in those areas, but rather to illustrate the techniques. Therefore, the literature reviews may be considered deliberately deficient, with interested readers directed to the suggested readings and the references therein.

(3) With few exceptions, almost all textbooks that are aimed at the introductory level draw their motivations and examples from economics, which may be of limited interest to students of finance or business. To see this, try motivating regression relationships using an example such as the effect of changes in income on consumption and watch your audience, who are primarily interested in business and finance applications, slip away and lose interest in the first ten minutes of your course.

Who should read this book?

The intended audience is undergraduates or Masters/MBA students who require a broad knowledge of modern econometric techniques commonly employed in the finance literature. It is hoped that the book will also be useful for researchers (both academics and practitioners), who require an introduction to the statistical tools commonly employed in the area of finance. The book can be used for courses covering financial time-series analysis or financial econometrics in undergraduate or postgraduate programmes in finance, financial economics, securities and investments.

Although the applications and motivations for model-building given in the book are drawn from finance, the empirical testing of theories in many other disciplines, such as management studies, business studies, real estate, economics and so on, may usefully employ econometric analysis. For this group, the book may also prove useful.

Finally, while the present text is designed mainly for students at the under-graduate or Masters level, it could also provide introductory reading in financial modelling for finance doctoral programmes where students have backgrounds which do not include courses in modern econometric techniques.

Pre-requisites for good understanding of this material

In order to make the book as accessible as possible, no prior knowledge of statistics, econometrics or algebra is required, although those with a prior exposure to calculus, algebra (including matrices) and basic statistics will be able to progress more quickly. The emphasis throughout the book is on a valid application of the techniques to real data and problems in finance.

In the finance and investment area, it is assumed that the reader has knowledge of the fundamentals of corporate finance, financial markets and investment. There-fore, subjects such as portfolio theory, the capital asset pricing model (CAPM) and arbitrage pricing theory (APT), the efficient markets hypothesis, the pricing of derivative securities and the term structure of interest rates, which are frequently referred to throughout the book, are not explained from first principles in this text. There are very many good books available in corporate finance, in investments and in futures and options, including those by Brealey and Myers (2013), Bodie, Kane and Marcus (2011) and Hull (2011) respectively.

Acknowledgements

I am grateful to Gita Persand, Olan Henry, James Chong and Apostolos Katsaris, who assisted with various parts of the software applications for the first edition. I am also grateful to Hilary Feltham for assistance with chapter 2 and to Simone Varotto for useful discussions and advice concerning the EViews example used in chapter 11.

I would also like to thank Simon Burke, James Chong and Con Keating for detailed and constructive comments on various drafts of the first edition, Simon Burke for suggestions on parts of the second edition and Jo Cox, Eunyoung Mallet, Ogonna Nneji, Ioannis Oikonomou and Chardan Wese Simen for comments on part of the third edition. The first and second editions additionally benefited from the comments, suggestions and questions of Peter Burridge, Kyongwook Choi, Rishi Chopra, Araceli Ortega Diaz, Xiaoming Ding, Thomas Eilertsen, Waleid Eldien, Andrea Gheno, Christopher Gilbert, Kimon Gomozias, Cherif Guermat, Abid Hameed, Ibrahim Jamali, Arty Khemlani, Margaret Lynch, David McCaffrey, Tehri Jokipii, Emese Lazar, Zhao Liuyan, Dimitri Lvov, Bill McCabe, Junshi Ma, David Merchan, Victor Murinde, Mikael Petitjean, Marcelo Perlin, Thai Pham, Jean-Sebastien Pourchet, Marcel Prokopczuk, Guilherme Silva, Jerry Sin, Andre-Tudor Stancu, Silvia Stanescu, Yiguo Sun, Li Qui, Panagiotis Varlagas, Jakub Vojtek, Henk von Eije, Jue Wang and Meng-Feng Yen.

A number of people sent useful e-mails pointing out typos or inaccuracies in the first edition. To this end, I am grateful to Merlyn Foo, Jan de Gooijer and his colleagues, Mikael Petitjean, Fred Sterbenz and Birgit Strikholm.

Useful comments and software support from Quantitative Micro Software (QMS) (now IHS Global) are gratefully acknowledged. Any remaining errors are mine alone.

1 Introduction

Learning econometrics is in many ways like learning a new language. To begin with, nothing makes sense and it is as if it is impossible to see through the fog created by all the unfamiliar terminology. While the way of writing the models – the *notation* – may make the situation appear more complex, in fact it is supposed to achieve the exact opposite. The ideas themselves are mostly not so complicated, it is just a matter of learning enough of the language that everything fits into place. So if you have never studied the subject before, then persevere through this preliminary chapter and you will hopefully be on your way to being fully fluent in econometrics!

Learning outcomes

In this chapter, you will learn how to
- Compare nominal and real series and convert one to the other
- Distinguish between different types of data
- Describe the key steps involved in building an econometric model
- Calculate asset price returns
- Deflate series to allow for inflation
- Construct a workfile, import data and accomplish simple tasks in EViews

The chapter sets the scene for the book by discussing in broad terms the questions of what econometrics is, and what the 'stylised facts' are describing financial data that researchers in this area typically try to capture in their models. Some discussion is presented on the kinds of data we encounter in finance and how to work with them. Finally, the chapter collects together a number of preliminary issues relating to the construction of econometric models in finance and introduces the software that will be used in the remainder of the book for estimating the models.

> ## Box 1.1   Examples of the uses of econometrics
>
> (1) Testing whether financial markets are weak-form informationally efficient
> (2) Testing whether the capital asset pricing model (CAPM) or arbitrage pricing theory (APT) represent superior models for the determination of returns on risky assets
> (3) Measuring and forecasting the volatility of bond returns
> (4) Explaining the determinants of bond credit ratings used by the ratings agencies
> (5) Modelling long-term relationships between prices and exchange rates
> (6) Determining the optimal hedge ratio for a spot position in oil
> (7) Testing technical trading rules to determine which makes the most money
> (8) Testing the hypothesis that earnings or dividend announcements have no effect on stock prices
> (9) Testing whether spot or futures markets react more rapidly to news
> (10) Forecasting the correlation between the stock indices of two countries.

1.1   What is econometrics?

The literal meaning of the word econometrics is 'measurement in economics'. The first four letters of the word suggest correctly that the origins of econometrics are rooted in economics. However, the main techniques employed for studying economic problems are of equal importance in financial applications. As the term is used in this book, financial econometrics will be defined as the *application of statistical techniques to problems in finance*. Financial econometrics can be useful for testing theories in finance, determining asset prices or returns, testing hypotheses concerning the relationships between variables, examining the effect on financial markets of changes in economic conditions, forecasting future values of financial variables and for financial decision-making. A list of possible examples of where econometrics may be useful is given in box 1.1.

The list in box 1.1 is of course by no means exhaustive, but it hopefully gives some flavour of the usefulness of econometric tools in terms of their financial applicability.

1.2   Is financial econometrics different from 'economic econometrics'?

As previously stated, the tools commonly used in financial applications are fundamentally the same as those used in economic applications, although the emphasis and the sets of problems that are likely to be encountered when analysing the two sets of data are somewhat different. Financial data often differ from macroeconomic data in terms of their frequency, accuracy, seasonality and other properties.

In economics, a serious problem is often a *lack of data at hand* for testing the theory or hypothesis of interest – this is sometimes called a 'small samples problem'. It might be, for example, that data are required on government budget deficits, or population figures, which are measured only on an annual basis. If the methods used to measure these quantities changed a quarter of a century ago, then only at most twenty-five of these annual observations are usefully available.

Two other problems that are often encountered in conducting applied econometric work in the arena of economics are those of *measurement error* and *data revisions*. These difficulties are simply that the data may be estimated, or measured with error, and will often be subject to several vintages of subsequent revisions. For example, a researcher may estimate an economic model of the effect on national output of investment in computer technology using a set of published data, only to find that the data for the last two years have been revised substantially in the next, updated publication.

These issues are usually of less concern in finance. Financial data come in many shapes and forms, but in general the prices and other entities that are recorded are those at which trades *actually took place*, or which were *quoted* on the screens of information providers. There exists, of course, the possibility for typos or for the data measurement method to change (for example, owing to stock index re-balancing or re-basing). But in general the measurement error and revisions problems are far less serious in the financial context.

Similarly, some sets of financial data are observed at much *higher frequencies* than macroeconomic data. Asset prices or yields are often available at daily, hourly or minute-by-minute frequencies. Thus the number of observations available for analysis can potentially be very large – perhaps thousands or even millions, making financial data the envy of macro-econometricians! The implication is that more powerful techniques can often be applied to financial than economic data, and that researchers may also have more confidence in the results.

Furthermore, the analysis of financial data also brings with it a number of new problems. While the difficulties associated with handling and processing such a large amount of data are not usually an issue given recent and continuing advances in computer power, financial data often have a number of additional characteristics. For example, financial data are often considered very 'noisy', which means that it is more difficult to separate *underlying trends or patterns* from random and uninteresting features. Financial data are also almost always not normally distributed in spite of the fact that most techniques in econometrics assume that they are. High frequency data often contain additional 'patterns' which are the result of the way that the market works, or the way that prices are recorded. These features need to be considered in the model-building process, even if they are not directly of interest to the researcher.

One of the most rapidly evolving areas of financial application of statistical tools is in the modelling of market microstructure problems. 'Market microstructure' may broadly be defined as the process whereby *investors' preferences and desires are translated into financial market transactions*. It is evident that microstructure effects

> **Box 1.2   Time series data**
>
> | Series | Frequency |
> | --- | --- |
> | Industrial production | Monthly or quarterly |
> | Government budget deficit | Annually |
> | Money supply | Weekly |
> | The value of a stock | As transactions occur |

are important and represent a key difference between financial and other types of data. These effects can potentially impact on many other areas of finance. For example, market rigidities or frictions can imply that current asset prices do not fully reflect future expected cashflows (see the discussion in chapter 10 of this book). Also, investors are likely to require compensation for holding securities that are illiquid, and therefore embody a risk that they will be difficult to sell owing to the relatively high probability of a lack of willing purchasers at the time of desired sale. Measures such as volume or the time between trades are sometimes used as proxies for market liquidity.

A comprehensive survey of the literature on market microstructure is given by Madhavan (2000). He identifies several aspects of the market microstructure literature, including price formation and price discovery, issues relating to market structure and design, information and disclosure. There are also relevant books by O'Hara (1995), Harris (2002) and Hasbrouck (2007). At the same time, there has been considerable advancement in the sophistication of econometric models applied to microstructure problems. For example, an important innovation was the autoregressive conditional duration (ACD) model attributed to Engle and Russell (1998). An interesting application can be found in Dufour and Engle (2000), who examine the effect of the time between trades on the price-impact of the trade and the speed of price adjustment.

1.3   Types of data

There are broadly three types of data that can be employed in quantitative analysis of financial problems: time series data, cross-sectional data and panel data.

1.3.1   Time series data

Time series data, as the name suggests, are data that have been collected over a period of time on one or more variables. Time series data have associated with them a particular frequency of observation or frequency of collection of data points. The frequency is simply a measure of the *interval over*, or the *regularity with which*, the data are collected or recorded. Box 1.2 shows some examples of time series data.

A word on 'As transactions occur' is necessary. Much financial data does not start its life as being *regularly spaced*. For example, the price of common stock for a given company might be recorded to have changed whenever there is a new trade or quotation placed by the financial information recorder. Such recordings are very unlikely to be evenly distributed over time – for example, there may be no activity between, say, 5 p.m. when the market closes and 8.30 a.m. the next day when it reopens; there is also typically less activity around the opening and closing of the market, and around lunch time. Although there are a number of ways to deal with this issue, a common and simple approach is to select an appropriate frequency, and use as the observation for that time period the last prevailing price during the interval.

It is also generally a requirement that all data used in a model be of the *same frequency of observation*. So, for example, regressions that seek to estimate an arbitrage pricing model using monthly observations on macroeconomic factors must also use monthly observations on stock returns, even if daily or weekly observations on the latter are available.

The data may be *quantitative* (e.g. exchange rates, prices, number of shares outstanding), or *qualitative* (e.g. the day of the week, a survey of the financial products purchased by private individuals over a period of time, a credit rating, etc.).

Problems that could be tackled using time series data:

- How the value of a country's stock index has varied with that country's macroeconomic fundamentals
- How the value of a company's stock price has varied when it announced the value of its dividend payment
- The effect on a country's exchange rate of an increase in its trade deficit.

In all of the above cases, it is clearly the time dimension which is the most important, and the analysis will be conducted using the values of the variables over time.

1.3.2 Cross-sectional data

Cross-sectional data are data on one or more variables collected at a single point in time. For example, the data might be on:

- A poll of usage of internet stockbroking services
- A cross-section of stock returns on the New York Stock Exchange (NYSE)
- A sample of bond credit ratings for UK banks.

Problems that could be tackled using cross-sectional data:

- The relationship between company size and the return to investing in its shares
- The relationship between a country's GDP level and the probability that the government will default on its sovereign debt.

1.3.3   Panel data

Panel data have the dimensions of both time series and cross-sections, e.g. the daily prices of a number of blue chip stocks over two years. The estimation of panel regressions is an interesting and developing area, and will be examined in detail in chapter 11.

Fortunately, virtually all of the standard techniques and analysis in econometrics are equally valid for time series and cross-sectional data. For time series data, it is usual to denote the individual observation numbers using the index t, and the total number of observations available for analysis by T. For cross-sectional data, the individual observation numbers are indicated using the index i, and the total number of observations available for analysis by N. Note that there is, in contrast to the time series case, no natural ordering of the observations in a cross-sectional sample. For example, the observations i might be on the price of bonds of different firms at a particular point in time, ordered alphabetically by company name. So, in the case of cross-sectional data, there is unlikely to be any useful information contained in the fact that Barclays follows Banco Santander in a sample of bank credit ratings, since it is purely by chance that their names both begin with the letter 'B'. On the other hand, in a time series context, the ordering of the data is relevant since the data are usually ordered chronologically.

In this book, the total number of observations in the sample will be given by T even in the context of regression equations that could apply either to cross-sectional or to time series data.

1.3.4   Continuous and discrete data

As well as classifying data as being of the time series or cross-sectional type, we could also distinguish them as being either continuous or discrete, exactly as their labels would suggest. *Continuous* data can take on any value and are not confined to take specific numbers; their values are limited only by precision. For example, the rental yield on a property could be 6.2%, 6.24% or 6.238%, and so on. On the other hand, *discrete* data can only take on certain values, which are usually integers (whole numbers), and are often defined to be count numbers.[1] For instance, the number of people in a particular underground carriage or the number of shares traded during a day. In these cases, having 86.3 passengers in the carriage or $5857\frac{1}{2}$ shares traded would not make sense. The simplest example of a discrete variable is a *Bernoulli* or binary random variable, which can only take the values 0 or 1 – for example, if we repeatedly tossed a coin, we could denote a head by 0 and a tail by 1.

---

[1] Discretely measured data do not necessarily have to be integers. For example, until they became 'decimalised', many financial asset prices were quoted to the nearest 1/16 or 1/32 of a dollar.

1.3.5   Cardinal, ordinal and nominal numbers

Another way in which we could classify numbers is according to whether they are cardinal, ordinal or nominal. *Cardinal* numbers are those where the actual numerical values that a particular variable takes have meaning, and where there is an equal distance between the numerical values. On the other hand, *ordinal* numbers can only be interpreted as providing a position or an ordering. Thus, for cardinal numbers, a figure of 12 implies a measure that is 'twice as good' as a figure of 6. Examples of cardinal numbers would be the price of a share or of a building, and the number of houses in a street. On the other hand, for an ordinal scale, a figure of 12 may be viewed as 'better' than a figure of 6, but could not be considered twice as good. Examples of ordinal numbers would be the position of a runner in a race (e.g. second place is better than fourth place, but it would make little sense to say it is 'twice as good') or the level reached in a computer game.

The final type of data that could be encountered would be where there is no natural ordering of the values at all, so a figure of 12 is simply different to that of a figure of 6, but could not be considered to be better or worse in any sense. Such data often arise when numerical values are arbitrarily assigned, such as telephone numbers or when codings are assigned to qualitative data (e.g. when describing the exchange that a US stock is traded on, '1' might be used to denote the NYSE, '2' to denote the NASDAQ and '3' to denote the AMEX). Sometimes, such variables are called *nominal* variables. Cardinal, ordinal and nominal variables may require different modelling approaches or at least different treatments, as should become evident in the subsequent chapters.

1.4   Returns in financial modelling

In many of the problems of interest in finance, the starting point is a time series of prices – for example, the prices of shares in Ford, taken at 4 p.m. each day for 200 days. For a number of statistical reasons, it is preferable not to work directly with the price series, so that raw price series are usually converted into series of returns. Additionally, returns have the added benefit that they are unit-free. So, for example, if an annualised return were 10%, then investors know that they would have got back £110 for a £100 investment, or £1,100 for a £1,000 investment, and so on.

There are two methods used to calculate returns from a series of prices, and these involve the formation of simple returns, and continuously compounded returns, which are respectively

Simple returns	*Continuously compounded returns*

$$R_t = \frac{p_t - p_{t-1}}{p_{t-1}} \times 100\% \qquad (1.1)$$

$$r_t = 100\% \times \ln\left(\frac{p_t}{p_{t-1}}\right) \qquad (1.2)$$

Box 1.3   Log returns

(1) Log-returns have the nice property that they can be interpreted as *continuously compounded returns* – so that the frequency of compounding of the return does not matter and thus returns across assets can more easily be compared.

(2) Continuously compounded returns are *time-additive*. For example, suppose that a weekly returns series is required and daily log returns have been calculated for five days, numbered 1 to 5, representing the returns on Monday through Friday. It is valid to simply add up the five daily returns to obtain the return for the whole week:

Monday return $r_1 = \ln(p_1/p_0) = \ln p_1 - \ln p_0$
Tuesday return $r_2 = \ln(p_2/p_1) = \ln p_2 - \ln p_1$
Wednesday return $r_3 = \ln(p_3/p_2) = \ln p_3 - \ln p_2$
Thursday return $r_4 = \ln(p_4/p_3) = \ln p_4 - \ln p_3$
Friday return $r_5 = \ln(p_5/p_4) = \ln p_5 - \ln p_4$

Return over the week $\ln p_5 - \ln p_0 = \ln(p_5/p_0)$

---

where: R_t denotes the simple return at time t, r_t denotes the continuously compounded return at time t, p_t denotes the asset price at time t and ln denotes the natural logarithm.

If the asset under consideration is a stock or portfolio of stocks, the total return to holding it is the sum of the capital gain and any dividends paid during the holding period. However, researchers often ignore any dividend payments. This is unfortunate, and will lead to an underestimation of the total returns that accrue to investors. This is likely to be negligible for very short holding periods, but will have a severe impact on cumulative returns over investment horizons of several years. Ignoring dividends will also have a distortionary effect on the cross-section of stock returns. For example, ignoring dividends will imply that 'growth' stocks with large capital gains will be inappropriately favoured over income stocks (e.g. utilities and mature industries) that pay high dividends.

Alternatively, it is possible to adjust a stock price time series so that the dividends are added back to generate a *total return index*. If p_t were a total return index, returns generated using either of the two formulae presented above thus provide a measure of the total return that would accrue to a holder of the asset during time t.

The academic finance literature generally employs the log-return formulation (also known as log-price relatives since they are the log of the ratio of this period's price to the previous period's price). Box 1.3 shows two key reasons for this.

There is, however, also a disadvantage of using the log-returns. The simple return on a portfolio of assets is a weighted average of the simple returns on the individual assets

$$R_{pt} = \sum_{i=1}^{N} w_i R_{it} \tag{1.3}$$

But this does not work for the continuously compounded returns, so that they are not additive across a portfolio. The fundamental reason why this is the case is that the log of a sum is not the same as the sum of a log, since the operation of taking a log constitutes a *non-linear transformation*. Calculating portfolio returns in this context must be conducted by first estimating the value of the portfolio at each time period and then determining the returns from the aggregate portfolio values. Or alternatively, if we assume that the asset is purchased at time $t - K$ for price p_{t-K} and then sold K periods later at price p_t, then if we calculate simple returns for each period, $R_t, R_{t+1}, \ldots, R_K$, the aggregate return over all K periods is

$$R_{Kt} = \frac{p_t - p_{t-K}}{p_{t-K}} = \frac{p_t}{p_{t-K}} - 1 = \left[\frac{p_t}{p_{t-1}} \times \frac{p_{t-1}}{p_{t-2}} \times \ldots \times \frac{p_{t-K+1}}{p_{t-K}} \right] - 1$$

$$= [(1 + R_t)(1 + R_{t-1}) \ldots (1 + R_{t-K+1})] - 1 \tag{1.4}$$

In the limit, as the frequency of the sampling of the data is increased so that they are measured over a smaller and smaller time interval, the simple and continuously compounded returns will be identical.

1.4.1 Real versus nominal series and deflating nominal series

If a newspaper headline suggests that 'house prices are growing at their fastest rate for more than a decade. A typical 3-bedroom house is now selling for £180,000, whereas in 1990 the figure was £120,000', it is important to appreciate that this figure is almost certainly in *nominal* terms. That is, the article is referring to the actual prices of houses that existed at those points in time. The general level of prices in most economies around the world has a general tendency to rise almost all of the time, so we need to ensure that we compare prices on a like-for-like basis. We could think of part of the rise in house prices being attributable to an increase in demand for housing, and part simply arising because the prices of all goods and services are rising together. It would be useful to be able to separate the two effects, and to be able to answer the question, 'how much have house prices risen when we remove the effects of general inflation?' or equivalently, 'how much are houses worth now if we measure their values in 1990-terms?' We can do this by *deflating* the nominal house price series to create a series of *real* house prices, which is then said to be in *inflation-adjusted terms* or *at constant prices*.

Deflating a series is very easy indeed to achieve: all that is required (apart from the series to deflate) is a *price deflator series*, which is a series measuring general price levels in the economy. Series like the consumer price index (CPI), producer price index (PPI) or the GDP Implicit Price Deflator, are often used. A more detailed discussion of which is the most relevant general price index to use is beyond the

	Nominal	CPI	House prices	House prices
Year	house prices	(2004 levels)	(2004 levels)	(2013) levels
2001	83,450	97.6	85,502	105,681
2002	93,231	98.0	95,134	117,585
2003	117,905	98.7	119,458	147,650
2004	134,806	100.0	134,806	166,620
2005	151,757	101.3	149,810	185,165
2006	158,478	102.1	155,218	191,850
2007	173,225	106.6	162,500	200,850
2008	180,473	109.4	164,966	165,645
2009	150,501	112.3	134,017	173,147
2010	163,481	116.7	140,086	167,162
2011	161,211	119.2	135,244	155,472
2012	162,228	121.1	133,962	165,577
2013	162,245	123.6	131,266	162,245

Table 1.1   How to construct a series in real terms from a nominal one

Notes: All prices in British pounds; house price figures taken in January of each year from Nationwide (see appendix 1 for the source). CPI figures are for illustration only.

scope of this book, but suffice to say that if the researcher is only interested in viewing a broad picture of the real prices rather than a highly accurate one, the choice of deflator will be of little importance.

The real price series is obtained by taking the nominal series, dividing it by the price deflator index, and multiplying by 100 (under the assumption that the deflator has a base value of 100)

$$real\ series_t = \frac{nominal\ series_t}{deflator_t} \times 100 \tag{1.5}$$

It is worth noting that deflation is only a relevant process for series that are measured in money terms, so it would make no sense to deflate a quantity-based series such as the number of shares traded or a series expressed as a proportion or percentage, such as the rate of return on a stock.

Example: Deflating house prices

Let us use for illustration a series of average UK house prices, measured annually for 2001–13 and taken from Nationwide (see Appendix 1 for the full source) given

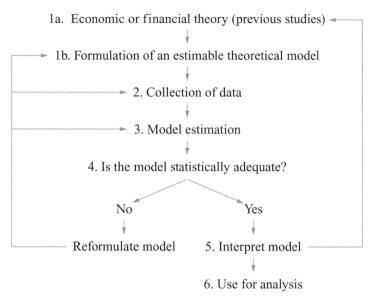

Figure 1.1　Steps involved in forming an econometric model

in column 2 of table 1.1. Some figures for the general level of prices as measured by the CPI are given in the third column. So first, suppose that we want to convert the figures into constant (real) prices. Given that 2004 is the 'base' year (i.e. it has a value of 100 for the CPI), the easiest way to do this is simply to divide each house price at time t by the corresponding CPI figure for time t and then multiply it by 100, as per equation (1.5). This will give the figures in column 4 of the table.

If we wish to convert house prices into a particular year's figures, we would apply equation (1.5), but instead of 100 we would have the CPI value that year. Consider that we wished to express nominal house prices in 2013 terms (which is of particular interest as this is the last observation in the table). We would thus base the calculation on a variant of (1.5)

$$real\ series_t = \frac{nominal\ series_t}{CPI_t} CPI_{reference\ year} \tag{1.6}$$

So, for example, to get the 2001 figure (i.e. t is 2001) of 105,681 for the average house price in 2013 terms, we would take the nominal figure of 83,450, multiply it by the CPI figure for the year that we wish to make the price for (the reference year, 123.6) and then divide it by the CPI figure for the year 2001 (97.6). Thus $105,681 = \frac{83450}{97.6} \times 123.6$, etc.

1.5　Steps involved in formulating an econometric model

Although there are of course many different ways to go about the process of model building, a logical and valid approach would be to follow the steps described in figure 1.1.

The steps involved in the model construction process are now listed and described. Further details on each stage are given in subsequent chapters of this book.

- *Step 1a and 1b: general statement of the problem*   This will usually involve the formulation of a theoretical model, or intuition from financial theory that two or more variables should be related to one another in a certain way. The model is unlikely to be able to completely capture every relevant real-world phenomenon, but it should present a sufficiently good approximation that it is useful for the purpose at hand.

- *Step 2: collection of data relevant to the model*   The data required may be available electronically through a financial information provider, such as Reuters or from published government figures. Alternatively, the required data may be available only via a survey after distributing a set of questionnaires, i.e. *primary data*.

- *Step 3: choice of estimation method relevant to the model proposed in step 1*   For example, is a single equation or multiple equation technique to be used?

- *Step 4: statistical evaluation of the model*   What assumptions were required to estimate the parameters of the model optimally? Were these assumptions satisfied by the data or the model? Also, does the model adequately describe the data? If the answer is 'yes', proceed to step 5; if not, go back to steps 1–3 and either reformulate the model, collect more data, or select a different estimation technique that has less stringent requirements.

- *Step 5: evaluation of the model from a theoretical perspective*   Are the parameter estimates of the sizes and signs that the theory or intuition from step 1 suggested? If the answer is 'yes', proceed to step 6; if not, again return to stages 1–3.

- *Step 6: use of model*   When a researcher is finally satisfied with the model, it can then be used for testing the theory specified in step 1, or for formulating forecasts or suggested courses of action. This suggested course of action might be for an individual (e.g. 'if inflation and GDP rise, buy stocks in sector X'), or as an input to government policy (e.g. 'when equity markets fall, program trading causes excessive volatility and so should be banned').

It is important to note that the process of building a robust empirical model is an iterative one, and it is certainly not an exact science. Often, the final preferred model could be very different from the one originally proposed, and need not be unique in the sense that another researcher with the same data and the same initial theory could arrive at a different final specification.

1.6   Points to consider when reading articles in empirical finance

As stated above, one of the defining features of this book relative to others in the area is in its use of published academic research as examples of the use of the various techniques. The papers examined have been chosen for a number of reasons. Above all, they represent (in this author's opinion) a clear and specific

> **Box 1.4 Points to consider when reading a published paper**
>
> (1) Does the paper involve the development of a theoretical model or is it merely a technique looking for an application so that the motivation for the whole exercise is poor?
> (2) Are the data of 'good quality'? Are they from a reliable source? Is the size of the sample sufficiently large for the model estimation task at hand?
> (3) Have the techniques been validly applied? Have tests been conducted for possible violations of any assumptions made in the estimation of the model?
> (4) Have the results been interpreted sensibly? Is the strength of the results exaggerated? Do the results actually obtained relate to the questions posed by the author(s)? Can the results be replicated by other researchers?
> (5) Are the conclusions drawn appropriate given the results, or has the importance of the results of the paper been overstated?

application in finance of the techniques covered in this book. They were also required to be published in a peer-reviewed journal, and hence to be widely available.

When I was a student, I used to think that research was a very pure science. Now, having had first-hand experience of research that academics and practitioners do, I know that this is not the case. Researchers often cut corners. They have a tendency to exaggerate the strength of their results, and the importance of their conclusions. They also have a tendency not to bother with tests of the adequacy of their models, and to gloss over or omit altogether any results that do not conform to the point that they wish to make. Therefore, when examining papers from the academic finance literature, it is important to cast a very critical eye over the research – rather like a referee who has been asked to comment on the suitability of a study for a scholarly journal. The questions that are always worth asking oneself when reading a paper are outlined in box 1.4.

Bear these questions in mind when reading my summaries of the articles used as examples in this book and, if at all possible, seek out and read the entire articles for yourself.

1.7 A note on Bayesian versus classical statistics

The philosophical approach to model-building adopted in this entire book, as with the majority of others, is that of 'classical statistics'. Under the classical approach, the researcher postulates a theory and estimates a model to test that theory. Tests of the theory are conducted using the estimated model within the 'classical' hypothesis testing framework developed in chapters 2 to 4. Based on the empirical results, the theory is either *refuted* or *upheld* by the data.

There is, however, an entirely different approach available for model construction, estimation and inference, known as Bayesian statistics. Under a Bayesian approach, the theory and empirical model work more closely together. The researcher would start with an assessment of the existing state of knowledge or beliefs, formulated into a set of probabilities. These prior inputs, or *priors*, would then be combined with the observed data via a likelihood function. The beliefs and the probabilities would then be updated as a result of the model estimation, resulting in a set of *posterior probabilities*. Probabilities are thus updated sequentially, as more data become available. The central mechanism, at the most basic level, for combining the priors with the likelihood function, is known as Bayes' theorem.

The Bayesian approach to estimation and inference has found a number of important recent applications in financial econometrics, in particular in the context of volatility modelling (see Bauwens and Lubrano, 1998, or Vrontos *et al.*, 2000 and the references therein for some examples), asset allocation (see, for example, Handa and Tiwari, 2006), portfolio performance evaluation (Baks *et al.*, 2001).

The Bayesian setup is an intuitively appealing one, although the resulting mathematics is somewhat complex. Many classical statisticians are unhappy with the Bayesian notion of prior probabilities that are set partially according to judgement. Thus, if the researcher set very strong priors, an awful lot of evidence against them would be required for the notion to be refuted. Contrast this with the classical case, where the data are usually permitted to freely determine whether a theory is upheld or refuted, irrespective of the researcher's judgement.

1.8 An introduction to EViews

The number of packages available for econometric modelling is large, and over time, all packages have improved in breadth of available techniques, and have also converged in terms of what is available in each package. The programs can usefully be categorised according to whether they are fully interactive (menu-driven), command-driven (so that the user has to write mini-programs) or somewhere in between. Menu-driven packages, which are usually based on a standard Microsoft Windows graphical user interface, are almost certainly the easiest for novices to get started with, for they require little knowledge of the structure of the package, and the menus can usually be negotiated simply. EViews is a package that falls into this category.

On the other hand, some such packages are often the least flexible, since the menus of available options are fixed by the developers, and hence if one wishes to build something slightly more complex or just different, then one is forced to consider alternatives. EViews, however, has a command-based programming language as well as a click-and-point interface so that it offers flexibility as well as user-friendliness. Three reviews that this author has been involved with, that are relevant for chapter 9 of this text in particular, are Brooks (1997) and Brooks, Burke and Persand (2001, 2003). As for previous editions of this book, sample instructions and output for the EViews package will be given. This software is employed because it is simple to use, menu-driven and will be sufficient to estimate most of the models required for this book. The following section gives an introduction to this software and outlines the key features and how basic tasks are executed.

1.8.1 Accomplishing simple tasks using EViews

EViews is a simple to use, interactive econometrics software package providing the tools most frequently used in practical econometrics. EViews is built around the concept of objects with each object having its own window, its own menu, its own procedure and its own view of the data. Using menus, it is easy to change between displays of a spreadsheet, line and bar graphs, regression results, etc. One of the most important features of EViews that makes it useful for model-building is the wealth of diagnostic (misspecification) tests, that are automatically computed, making it possible to test whether the model is econometrically valid or not. You work your way through EViews using a combination of windows, buttons, menus and sub-menus. A good way of familiarising yourself with EViews is to learn about its main menus and their relationships through the examples given in this and subsequent chapters.

This section assumes that readers have obtained a licensed copy of EViews 8 (the latest version available at the time of writing), and have successfully loaded it onto an available computer. There now follows a description of the EViews package, together with instructions to achieve standard tasks and sample output. Any instructions that must be entered or icons to be clicked are illustrated through out this book by **bold-faced type**. The objective of the treatment in this and subsequent chapters is not to demonstrate the full functionality of the package, but rather to get readers started quickly and to explain how the techniques are implemented and how the results may be interpreted. For further details, readers should consult the software manuals in the first instance, which are now available electronically with the software as well as in hard copy.[2] Note that EViews is not case-sensitive, so that it does not matter whether commands are entered as lower-case or CAPITAL letters.

Opening the software

To load EViews from Windows, click the **Start** button, then **All Programs**, **EViews8** and finally, **EViews8** again.

Reading in data

EViews provides support to read from or write to various file types, including 'ASCII' (text) files, Microsoft Excel '.XLS' and '.XLSX' files (reading from any named sheet in the Excel workbook), Lotus '.WKS1' and '.WKS3' files. It is usually

---

[2] A student edition of EViews 7 is available at a much lower cost than the full version, but with restrictions on the number of observations and objects that can be included in each saved workfile.

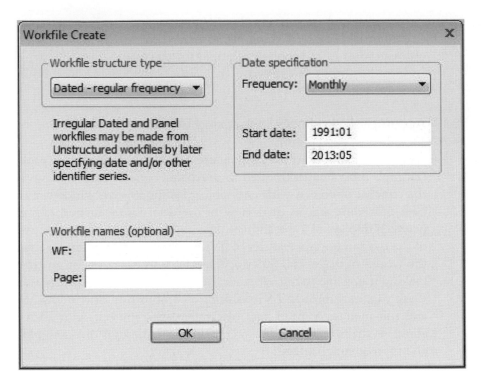

Screenshot 1.1   **Creating a workfile**

easiest to work directly with Excel files, and this will be the case throughout this book.

Creating a workfile and importing data

The first step when the EViews software is opened is to create a *workfile* that will hold the data. To do this, select **New** from the File menu. Then choose **Workfile**. The 'Workfile Create' window in screenshot 1.1 will be displayed.

We are going to use as an example a time series of UK average house price data obtained from Nationwide, which comprises 269 monthly observations from January 1991 to May 2013.[3]

Under 'Workfile structure type', keep the default option, **Dated – regular frequency**. Then, under 'Date specification', choose **Monthly**. Note the format of date entry for monthly and quarterly data: YYYY:M and YYYY:Q, respectively. For daily data, a US date format must usually be used depending on how EViews has been set up: MM/DD/YYYY (e.g. 03/01/1999 would be 1st March 1999, not 3rd January). Caution therefore needs to be exercised here to ensure that the date format used is the correct one. Type the start and end dates for the sample into the boxes: **1991:01** and **2013:05** respectively. Then click **OK**. The workfile will now have been created. Note that two pairs of dates are displayed,

---

[3] Full descriptions of the sources of data used will be given in appendix 1 and on the web site accompanying this book.

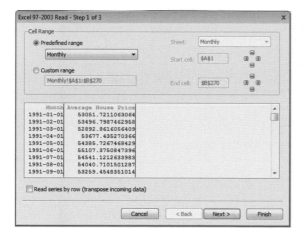
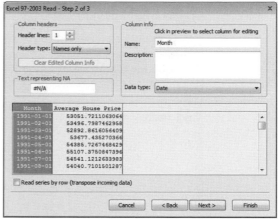
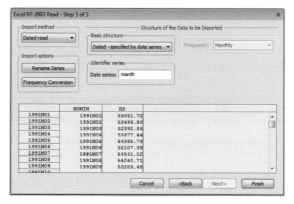

Screenshot 1.2   Importing Excel data into the workfile – screens 1 to 3

'Range' and 'Sample': the first one is the range of dates contained in the workfile and the second one (which is the same as above in this case) is for the current workfile sample. Two objects are also displayed: C (which is a vector that will eventually contain the parameters of any estimated models) and RESID (a residuals series, which will currently be empty). See chapter 3 for a discussion of these concepts. All EViews workfiles will contain these two objects, which are created automatically.

Now that the workfile has been set up, we can import the data from the Excel file UKHP.XLS. So from the File menu, select **Import** and **Import from File**. You will then be prompted to select the directory and file name. Once you have found the directory where the file is stored, enter **UKHP.XLS** in the 'file name' box and click **Open**. You are then faced with a series of three screens where it is possible to modify the way that the data are imported. Most of the time it is not necessary to change any of the default options as EViews peeks inside the data file and identifies the structure of the data, whether there is a header row containing the names of the series etc. The three screens are shown in screens 1 to 3 of screenshot 1.2. In the third screen, click **Rename Series** and in the box that appears, type **AVERAGE_HOUSE_PRICE HP** and

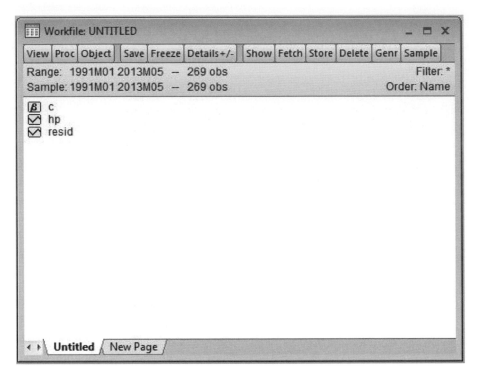

this will change the name of the series to 'HP', which is a bit easier to deal with!

Click **Finish** and the series will be imported. The series will appear as a new icon in the workfile window, as in screenshot 1.3. Note that EViews has sensibly not imported the column of dates as if it were an additional variable.

Verifying the data

Double click on the new hp icon that has appeared, and this will open up a spreadsheet window within EViews containing the monthly house price values. Make sure that the data file has been correctly imported by checking a few observations at random.

The next step is to save the workfile: click on the **Save As** button from the **File** menu and select **Save Active Workfile** and click **OK**. A save dialog box will open, prompting you for a workfile name and location. You should enter XX (where XX is your chosen name for the file), then click **OK**. EViews will save the workfile in the specified directory with the name XX.wf1. I have called my file 'ukhp.wf1' You will also be prompted to select whether the data in the file should be saved in 'single precision' or 'double precision'. The latter is preferable for obvious reasons unless the file is likely to be very large because of the quantity of variables and observations it contains (single precision will require less space) so just click **OK**.

The saved workfile can be opened later by selecting File/Open/EViews Work-file . . . from the menu bar.

Transformations

Variables of interest can be created in EViews by selecting the *Genr* button from the workfile toolbar and typing in the relevant formulae. Suppose, for example, we have a time series called Z. The latter can be modified in the following ways so as to create variables A, B, C, etc. The mathematical background and simple explanations of these transformations, including powers, logarithms and exponents, will be discussed in detail in the following chapter. Some common transformations are:

$A = Z/2$	Dividing
$B = Z*2$	Multiplication
$C = Z\hat{}2$	Squaring
$D = LOG(Z)$	Taking the logarithm
$E = EXP(Z)$	Taking the exponential
$F = Z(-1)$	Lagging the data
$G = LOG(Z/Z(-1))$	Creating the log-returns

Other functions that can be used in the formulae include: *abs*, *sin*, *cos*, etc. Notice that no special instruction is necessary; simply type 'new variable = function of old variable(s)'. The variables will be displayed in the same workfile window as the original (imported) series.

In this case, it is of interest to calculate simple percentage changes in the series. Click **Genr** and type **DHP = 100*(HP-HP(-1))/HP(-1)**. It is important to note that this new series, DHP, will be a series of monthly percentage changes and will not be annualised.

Computing summary statistics

Descriptive summary statistics of a series can be obtained by selecting **Quick/Series Statistics/Histogram and Stats** and typing in the name of the variable (**DHP**). The view in screenshot 1.4 will be displayed in the window.

As can be seen, the histogram suggests that the series has a slightly longer upper tail than lower tail (note the *x*-axis scale) and is centred slightly above zero. Summary statistics including the mean, maximum and minimum, standard deviation, higher moments and a test for whether the series is normally distributed are all presented. Interpreting these will be discussed in subsequent chapters. Other useful statistics and transformations can be obtained by selecting the command *Quick/Series Statistics*, but these are also covered later in this book.

Plots

EViews supports a wide range of graph types including line graphs, bar graphs, pie charts, mixed line–bar graphs, high–low graphs and scatterplots. A variety of options permits the user to select the line types, colour, border characteristics, headings, shading and scaling, including logarithmic scale and dual scale graphs. Legends are automatically created (although they can be removed if desired), and customised graphs can be incorporated into other Windows applications using copy-and-paste, or by exporting as Windows metafiles.

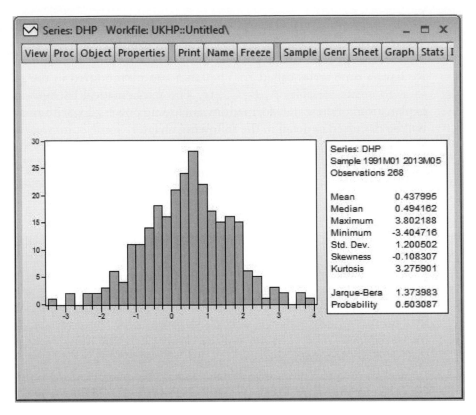

Screenshot 1.4   **Summary statistics for a series**

From the main menu, select **Quick/Graph** and type in the name of the series that you want to plot (**HP** to plot the level of house prices) and click **OK**. You will be prompted with the 'Graph Options' window where you choose the type of graph that you want (line, bar, scatter or pie charts, etc.) and also control the layout and style of the graph (e.g. whether you want a legend, axis labels, etc.). Choosing a line and symbol graph would produce screenshot 1.5.

It is always useful to plot any series you are working with to get a feel for the basic features of the data. It is clear that in this case house prices appreciated quickly to reach a peak in October 2007 before falling sharply until early 2009, after which a partial recovery began. It is possible to identify any value on the chart and its timing by simply hovering the mouse over it. Double-clicking on the graph will revert back to the Graph Options menu.

As an exercise, try **plotting the DHP** series – you will see that the volatility of percentage change series makes their graphs much harder to interpret, even though they are usually the form of the data that we work with in econometrics.

Printing results

Results can be printed at any point by selecting the *Print* button on the object window toolbar. The whole current window contents will be printed. Graphs can

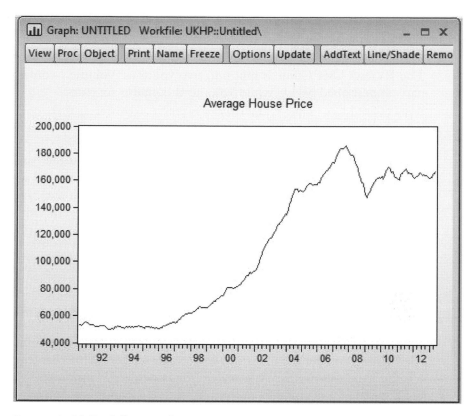

Screenshot 1.5   **A line graph**

be copied into the clipboard if desired by right clicking on the graph and choosing *Copy to clipboard*.

Saving data results and workfile

Data generated in EViews can be exported to other Windows applications, e.g. Microsoft Excel. From the main menu, select *File/Export/Write Text-Lotus-Excel*. You will then be asked to provide a name for the exported file and to select the appropriate directory. The next window will ask you to select all the series that you want to export, together with the sample period.

Assuming that the workfile has been saved after the importation of the data set (as mentioned above), additional work can be saved by just selecting *Save* from the *File* menu. The workfile will be saved including all objects in it – data, graphs, equations, etc. *so long as they have been given a title*. Any untitled objects will be lost upon exiting the program.

Econometric tools available in EViews

Box 1.5 describes the features available in EViews, following the format of the user guides for version 8, with material discussed in this book indicated by *italics*.

Box 1.5   Features of EViews

The EViews User Guide is split into two volumes. Volume I contains four parts as described below, while Volume II contains six parts.

PART I (INTRODUCTION)

- Chapters 1–4 contain introductory material describing the basics of Windows and EViews, *how workfiles are constructed* and how to deal with objects.
- Chapters 5 and 6 document the basics of working with data. *Importing data into EViews, using EViews to manipulate and manage data* and exporting from EViews into spreadsheets, text files and other Windows applications are discussed.
- Chapters 7–10 describe the EViews database and other advanced data and workfile handling features.

PART II   (BASIC DATA ANALYSIS)

- Chapter 11 describes the series object. Series are the basic unit of data in EViews and are the basis for all *univariate analysis*. This chapter documents the basic *graphing* and *data analysis features associated with series*.
- Chapter 12 documents the group object. Groups are collections of series that form the basis for a variety of *multivariate graphing* and *data analyses*.
- Chapters 13 and 14 provide detailed documentation for the production of various types of graphs.

PART III   (CUSTOMISING OUTPUT)

- Chapters 15 to 17 continue to describe the creation and customisation of more advanced tables and graphs.

PART IV   (EXTENDING EVIEWS)

- Chapter 18 describes in detail *how to write programs using the EViews programming language*.

PART V   (BASIC SINGLE EQUATION ANALYSIS)

- Chapter 19 outlines the basics of *ordinary least squares (OLS) estimation* in EViews.
- Chapter 20 discusses the *weighted least squares, two-stage least squares* and non-linear least squares estimation techniques.
- Chapter 21 covers approaches to dealing with simultaneous equations including *two-stage least squares*.
- Chapter 22 describes *single equation regression techniques* for the analysis of time series data: *testing for serial correlation, estimation of ARMA models*, using polynomial distributed lags and *unit root tests* for non-stationary time series.

- Chapter 23 describes the fundamentals of using EViews to *forecast from estimated equations*.
- Chapter 24 describes the *specification testing* procedures available in EViews.

PART VI   (ADVANCED SINGLE EQUATION ANALYSIS)

- Chapter 25 discusses *ARCH and GARCH estimation* and outlines the EViews tools for *modelling the conditional variance* of a variable.
- Chapter 26 covers *singe-equation models for cointegrated variables*.
- Chapter 27 documents EViews functions for estimating *qualitative and limited dependent variable models*. EViews provides estimation routines for *binary or ordered (e.g. probit and logit), censored or truncated (tobit, etc.)* and integer valued (count) data.
- Chapters 28 to 31 discuss more sophisticated modelling approaches for single equations, including *robust estimation, allowing for structural breaks* and *switching regressions*.
- Chapter 32 discusses the topic of the estimation of *quantile regressions*.
- Chapter 33 shows how to deal with the log-likelihood object, and how to solve problems with non-linear estimation.

PART VII   (ADVANCED UNIVARIATE ANALYSIS)

- Chapter 34 discusses various univariate analysis that can be undertaken, including *unit root testing, panel unit root testing* and use of *the BDS test*.

PART VIII   (MULTIPLE EQUATION ANALYSIS)

- Chapters 35–6 describe *estimation techniques for systems of equations* including *VAR* and *VEC* models.
- Chapter 37 presents state space models and their estimation via the Kalman filter.
- Chapter 38 offers a more general discussion of how to set up and estimate various types of models in EViews.

PART IX   (PANEL AND POOLED DATA)

- Chapter 39 outlines tools for working with *pooled time series, cross-section data* and estimating standard equation specifications that account for the pooled structure of the data.
- Chapter 40 describes how to structure a panel of data and how to analyse it, while Chapter 41 extends the analysis to look at *panel regression model estimation*; *panel cointegration* is considered in Chapter 42 and other panel issues in Chapter 43.

PART X   (ADVANCED MULTIVARIATE ANALYSIS)

- Chapters 44 and 45, the final chapters of the manual, explain how to conduct *cointegration* and factor analysis in EViews.

1.9 Further reading

EViews 8 User's Guides I and II – IHS Global (2013), Irvine, CA.
EViews 8 Command Reference – IHS Global (2013), Irvine, CA.
Startz, R. *EViews Illustrated for Version 8* IHS Global (2013), Irvine, CA.

1.10 Outline of the remainder of this book

Chapter 2

This covers the key mathematical and statistical techniques that readers will need some familiarity with to be able to get the most out of the remainder of this book. It starts with a simple discussion of functions, and powers, exponents and logarithms of numbers. It then proceeds to explain the basics of differentiation and matrix algebra, which is illustrated via the construction of optimal portfolio weights. The chapter then moves on to present an introduction to descriptive statistics and probability distributions.

Chapter 3

This introduces the classical linear regression model (CLRM). The ordinary least squares (OLS) estimator is derived and its interpretation discussed. The conditions for OLS optimality are stated and explained. A hypothesis testing framework is developed and examined in the context of the linear model. Examples employed include Jensen's classic study of mutual fund performance measurement and tests of the 'overreaction hypothesis' in the context of the UK stock market.

Chapter 4

This continues and develops the material of chapter 3 by generalising the bivariate model to multiple regression – i.e. models with many variables. The framework for testing multiple hypotheses is outlined, and measures of how well the model fits the data are described. Case studies include modelling rental values and an application of principal components analysis to interest rate modelling.

Chapter 5

Chapter 5 examines the important but often neglected topic of diagnostic testing. The consequences of violations of the CLRM assumptions are described, along with plausible remedial steps. Model-building philosophies are discussed, with particular reference to the general-to-specific approach. Applications covered in this chapter include the determination of sovereign credit ratings.

Chapter 6

This presents an introduction to time series models, including their motivation and a description of the characteristics of financial data that they can and cannot capture. The chapter commences with a presentation of the features of some standard models of stochastic (white noise, moving average, autoregressive and mixed ARMA) processes. The chapter continues by showing how the appropriate model can be chosen for a set of actual data, how the model is estimated and how model adequacy checks are performed. The generation of forecasts from such models is discussed, as are the criteria by which these forecasts can be evaluated. Examples include model-building for UK house prices, and tests of the exchange rate covered and uncovered interest parity hypotheses.

Chapter 7

This extends the analysis from univariate to multivariate models. Multivariate models are motivated by way of explanation of the possible existence of bi-directional causality in financial relationships, and the simultaneous equations bias that results if this is ignored. Estimation techniques for simultaneous equations models are outlined. Vector autoregressive (VAR) models, which have become extremely popular in the empirical finance literature, are also covered. The interpretation of VARs is explained by way of joint tests of restrictions, causality tests, impulse responses and variance decompositions. Relevant examples discussed in this chapter are the simultaneous relationship between bid–ask spreads and trading volume in the context of options pricing, and the relationship between property returns and macroeconomic variables.

Chapter 8

The first section of the chapter discusses unit root processes and presents tests for non-stationarity in time series. The concept of and tests for cointegration, and the formulation of error correction models, are then discussed in the context of both the single equation framework of Engle–Granger, and the multivariate framework of Johansen. Applications studied in chapter 8 include spot and futures markets, tests for cointegration between international bond markets and tests of the purchasing power parity hypothesis and of the expectations hypothesis of the term structure of interest rates.

Chapter 9

This covers the important topic of volatility and correlation modelling and forecasting. This chapter starts by discussing in general terms the issue of non-linearity in financial time series. The class of ARCH (autoregressive conditionally heteroscedastic) models and the motivation for this formulation are then discussed. Other models are also presented, including extensions of the basic model such as GARCH, GARCH-M, EGARCH and GJR formulations. Examples of the huge number of applications are discussed, with particular reference to stock returns. Multivariate GARCH and conditional correlation models are described, and applications to the estimation of conditional betas and time-varying hedge ratios, and to financial risk measurement, are given.

Chapter 10

This discusses testing for and modelling regime shifts or switches of behaviour in financial series that can arise from changes in government policy, market trading conditions or microstructure, among other causes. This chapter introduces the Markov switching approach to dealing with regime shifts. Threshold autoregression is also discussed, along with issues relating to the estimation of such models. Examples include the modelling of exchange rates within a managed floating environment, modelling and forecasting the gilt–equity yield ratio and models of movements of the difference between spot and futures prices.

Chapter 11

This chapter focuses on how to deal appropriately with longitudinal data – that is, data having both time series and cross-sectional dimensions. Fixed effect and random effect models are explained and illustrated by way of examples on banking competition in the UK and on credit stability in Central and Eastern Europe. Entity fixed and time-fixed effects models are elucidated and distinguished.

Chapter 12

This chapter describes various models that are appropriate for situations where the dependent variable is not continuous. Readers will learn how to construct, estimate and interpret such models, and to distinguish and select between alternative specifications. Examples used include a test of the pecking order hypothesis in corporate finance and the modelling of unsolicited credit ratings.

Chapter 13

This presents an introduction to the use of simulations in econometrics and finance. Motivations are given for the use of repeated sampling, and a distinction is drawn between Monte Carlo simulation and bootstrapping. The reader is shown how to set up a simulation, and examples are given in options pricing and financial risk management to demonstrate the usefulness of these techniques.

Chapter 14

This offers suggestions related to conducting a project or dissertation in empirical finance. It introduces the sources of financial and economic data available on the internet and elsewhere, and recommends relevant online information and literature on research in financial markets and financial time series. The chapter also suggests ideas for what might constitute a good structure for a dissertation on this subject, how to generate ideas for a suitable topic, what format the report could take, and some common pitfalls. Detailed illustrations of how to conduct an event study and how to use the Fama-French approach are presented.

> ## Key concepts
>
> The key terms to be able to define and explain from this chapter are
>
> - cardinal, ordinal and nominal numbers
> - financial econometrics
> - time series
> - panel data
> - continuous data
> - real and nominal series
> - geometric mean
> - continuously compounded returns
> - cross-sectional data
> - pooled data
> - discrete data
> - deflator

Self-study questions

1. Explain the difference between the following terms:
   (a) Continuous and discrete data
   (b) Ordinal and nominal data
   (c) Time series and panel data
   (d) Noisy and clean data
   (e) Simple and continuously compounded returns
   (f) Nominal and real series
   (g) Bayesian and classical statistics
2. Present and explain a problem that can be approached using a time series regression, another one using cross-sectional regression, and another using panel data.
3. What are the key features of asset return time series?
4. The following table gives annual, end of year prices of a bond and of the consumer prices index

Year	Bond value	CPI value
2006	36.9	108.0
2007	39.8	110.3
2008	42.4	113.6
2009	38.1	116.1
2010	36.4	118.4
2011	39.2	120.9
2012	44.6	123.2
2013	45.1	125.4

   (a) Calculate the simple returns
   (b) Calculate the continuously compounded returns
   (c) Calculate the prices of the bond each year in 2013 terms
   (d) Calculate the real returns

2 Mathematical and statistical foundations

Learning outcomes

In this chapter, you will learn how to
- Work with powers, exponents and logarithms
- Use sigma (Σ) and pi (Π) notation
- Apply simple rules to differentiate functions
- Work with matrices
- Calculate the trace, inverse and eigenvalues of a matrix
- Construct minimum variance and mean-variance efficient portfolios
- Compute summary statistics for a data series
- Manipulate expressions using the expectations, variance and covariance operators

This chapter covers the mathematical and statistical building blocks that are essential for a good understanding of the rest of the book. Those with some prior background in algebra and introductory statistics may skip this chapter without loss of continuity, but hopefully the material will also constitute a useful refresher for those who have studied mathematics but a long time ago!

2.1 Functions

2.1.1 Straight lines

The ultimate objective of econometrics is usually to build a model, which may be thought of as a simplified version of the true relationship between two or more variables that can be described by a *function*. A function is simply a mapping or relationship between an input or set of inputs, and an output. We usually write that y, the output, is a function f of x, the input: $y = f(x)$. y could be a linear function of x, where the relationship can be expressed as a straight line on a graph, or y could be a non-linear function of x, in which case the relationship between

Table 2.1 Sample data on hours of study and grades	
Hours of study (x)	Grade-point average in % (y)
0	25
100	30
400	45
800	65
1000	75
1200	85

the two variables would be represented graphically as a curve. If the relationship is linear, we could write the equation for this straight line as

$$y = a + bx \qquad (2.1)$$

y and x are called *variables*, while a and b are *parameters*; a is termed the *intercept* and b is the *slope* or *gradient* of the line. The intercept is the point at which the line crosses the y-axis, while the slope measures the steepness of the line.

To illustrate, suppose we were trying to model the relationship between a student's grade point average y (expressed as a percentage), and the number of hours that they studied throughout the year, x. Suppose further that the relationship can be written as a linear function with $y = 25 + 0.05x$. Clearly it is unrealistic to assume that the link between grades and hours of study follows a straight line, but let us keep this assumption for now. So the intercept of the line, a, is 25, and the slope, b, is 0.05. What does this equation mean? It means that a student spending no time studying at all ($x = 0$) could expect to earn a 25% average grade, and for every hour of study time, their average grade should improve by 0.05% – in other words, an extra 100 hours of study through the year would lead to a 5% increase in the grade. We could construct a table with several values of x and the corresponding value of y as in table 2.1 and then plot them onto a graph (figure 2.1).

We can see that the gradient of this line is positive (i.e. it slopes upwards from left to right). But more generally, in other situations it is also possible for the gradient to be zero or negative. Note that for a straight line, the slope is the same along the whole line; this slope can be calculated from a graph by taking any two points on the line and dividing the change in the value of y by the change in the value of x between the two points. In general, a capital delta, Δ, is used to denote a change in a variable. For example, suppose that we want to take the two points $x = 100$, $y = 30$ and $x = 1000$, $y = 75$. We could write these two points using a coordinate notation (x,y) and so $(100,30)$ and $(1000,75)$ in this example. We

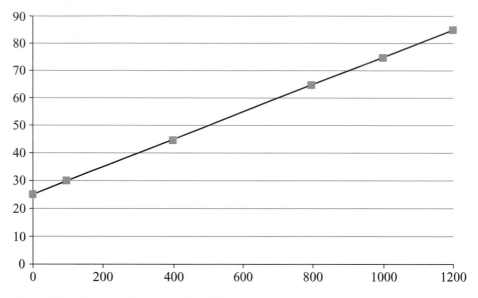

Figure 2.1   A plot of hours studied (x) against grade-point average (y)

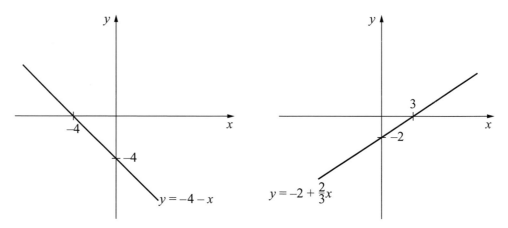

Figure 2.2   Examples of different straight line graphs

would calculate the slope of the line as

$$\frac{\Delta y}{\Delta x} = \frac{75 - 30}{1000 - 100} = 0.05 \qquad (2.2)$$

So indeed, we have confirmed that the slope is 0.05 (although in this case we knew that from the start). Two other examples of straight line graphs are given in figure 2.2. The gradient of the line can be zero or negative instead of positive. If the gradient is zero, the resulting plot will be a flat (horizontal) straight line. If there is a specific change in x, Δx, and we want to calculate the corresponding change in y, we would simply multiply the change in x by the slope, so $\Delta y = b\Delta x$.

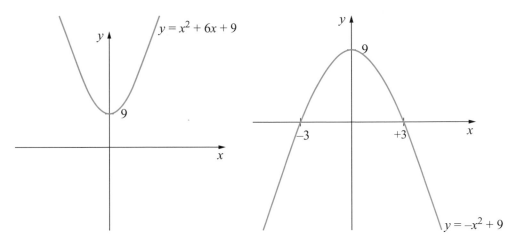

Figure 2.3   Examples of quadratic functions

As a final point, note that we stated above that the point at which a function crosses the y-axis is termed the intercept. The point at which the function crosses the x-axis is called its *root*. In the example above, if we take the function $y = 25 + 0.05x$, set y to zero and rearrange the equation, we would find that the root would be $x = -500$. The equation for a straight line has one root (except for a horizontal straight line such as $y = 4$).

2.1.2   Quadratic functions

A linear function is often not sufficiently flexible to be able to accurately describe the relationship between two variables, and so a quadratic function may be used instead. We could write the general expression for a quadratic function as

$$y = a + bx + cx^2 \tag{2.3}$$

where x and y are the variables again and a, b, c are the parameters that describe the shape of the function. Note that a linear function only has two parameters (the intercept, a and the slope, b), but a quadratic has three and hence it is able to adapt to a broader range of relationships between y and x. The linear function is a special case of the quadratic where c is zero. As before, a is the intercept and defines where the function crosses the y-axis; the parameters b and c determine the shape. Quadratic equations can be either ∪-shaped or ∩-shaped. As x becomes very large and positive or very large and negative, the x^2 term will dominate the behaviour of y and it is thus c that determines which of these shapes will apply. Figure 2.3 shows two examples of quadratic functions – in the first case c is positive and so the curve is ∪-shaped, while in the second c is negative so the curve is ∩-shaped. Box 2.1 discusses the features of the roots of a quadratic equation and shows how to calculate them.

> ## Box 2.1   The roots of a quadratic equation
>
> - A quadratic equation has two roots.
> - The roots may be distinct (i.e. different from one another), or they may be the same (repeated roots); they may be real numbers (e.g. 1.7, -2.357, 4, etc.) or what are known as *complex numbers*.
> - The roots can be obtained either by *factorising* the equation – i.e. contracting it into parentheses, by 'completing the square' or by using the formula
>
> $$x = \frac{-b \pm \sqrt{b^2 - 4ac}}{2c} \tag{2.4}$$
>
> - If $b^2 > 4ac$, the function will have two unique roots and it will cross the x-axis in two separate places; if $b^2 = 4ac$, the function will have two equal roots and it will only cross the x-axis in one place; if $b^2 < 4ac$, the function will have no real roots (only complex roots), it will not cross the x-axis at all and thus the function will always be above the x-axis.

Example 2.1

Determine the roots of the following quadratic equations

1. $y = x^2 + x - 6$
2. $y = 9x^2 + 6x + 1$
3. $y = x^2 - 3x + 1$
4. $y = x^2 - 4x$

Solution

We would solve these equations by setting them in turn to zero. We could then use the quadratic formula from equation (2.4) in each case, although it is usually quicker to determine first whether they factorise.

1. $x^2 + x - 6 = 0$ factorises to $(x - 2)(x + 3) = 0$ and thus the roots are 2 and -3, which are the values of x that set the function to zero. In other words, the function will cross the x-axis at $x = 2$ and $x = -3$.
2. $9x^2 + 6x + 1 = 0$ factorises to $(3x + 1)(3x + 1) = 0$ and thus the roots are $-\frac{1}{3}$ and $-\frac{1}{3}$. This is known as repeated roots – since this is a quadratic equation there will always be two roots but in this case they are both the same.
3. $x^2 - 3x + 1 = 0$ does not factorise and so the formula must be used with $a = 1$, $b = -3$, $c = 1$ and the roots are 0.38 and 2.62 to two decimal places.
4. $x^2 - 4x = 0$ factorises to $x(x - 4) = 0$ and so the roots are 0 and 4.

> ### Box 2.2   Manipulating powers and their indices
>
> - Any number or variable raised to the power one is simply that number or variable, e.g. $3^1 = 3$, $x^1 = x$, and so on.
> - Any number or variable raised to the power zero is one, e.g. $5^0 = 1$, $x^0 = 1$, etc., except that 0^0 is not defined (i.e. it does not exist).
> - If the index is a negative number, this means that we divide one by that number – for example, $x^{-3} = \frac{1}{x^3} = \frac{1}{x \times x \times x}$.
> - If we want to multiply together a given number raised to more than one power, we would add the corresponding indices together – for example, $x^2 \times x^3 = x^2 x^3 = x^{2+3} = x^5$.
> - If we want to calculate the power of a variable raised to a power (i.e. the power of a power), we would multiply the indices together – for example, $(x^2)^3 = x^{2\times3} = x^6$.
> - If we want to divide a variable raised to a power by the same variable raised to another power, we subtract the second index from the first – for example, $\frac{x^3}{x^2} = x^{3-2} = x$.
> - If we want to divide a variable raised to a power by a different variable raised to the same power, the following result applies
>
> $$\left(\frac{x}{y}\right)^n = \frac{x^n}{y^n}.$$
>
> - The power of a product is equal to each component raised to that power – for example, $(x \times y)^3 = x^3 \times y^3$.
> - It is important to note that the indices for powers do not have to be integers. For example, $x^{\frac{1}{2}}$ is the notation we would use for taking the square root of x, sometimes written $\sqrt{x}$. Other, non-integer powers are also possible, but are harder to calculate by hand (e.g. $x^{0.76}$, $x^{-0.27}$, etc.) In general, $x^{1/n} = \sqrt[n]{x}$, the nth root of x.

Note that all of these equations have two real roots. If we had an equation such as $y = 3x^2 - 2x + 4$, this would not factorise and would have complex roots since $b^2 - 4ac < 0$ in the quadratic formula.

2.1.3   Powers of numbers or of variables

A number or variable raised to a power is simply a way of writing repeated multiplication. So for example, raising x to the power 2 means squaring it (i.e. $x^2 = x \times x$); raising it to the power 3 means cubing it ($x^3 = x \times x \times x$), and so on. The number that we are raising the number or variable to is called the *index*, so for x^3, 3 would be the index. There are a few rules for manipulating powers and their indices given in box 2.2.

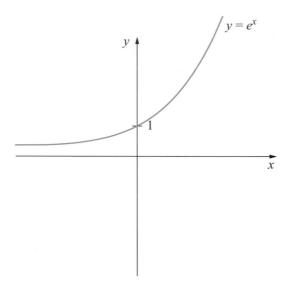

Figure 2.4   A plot of an exponential function

2.1.4   The exponential function

It is sometimes the case that the relationship between two variables is best described by an *exponential* function – for example, when a variable grows (or reduces) at a rate in proportion to its current value, in which case we would write $y = e^x$. e is a simply number: 2.71828. . . . This function has several useful properties, including that it is its own derivative (see section 2.2.1 below) and thus the gradient of the function e^x at any point is also e^x; it is also useful for capturing the increase in value of an amount of money that is subject to compound interest. The exponential function can never be negative, so when x is negative, y is close to zero but positive. It crosses the y-axis at one and the slope increases at an increasing rate from left to right, as shown in figure 2.4.

2.1.5   Logarithms

Logarithms were invented to simplify cumbersome calculations, since exponents can then be added or subtracted, which is easier than multiplying or dividing the original numbers. While making logarithmic transformations for computational ease is no longer necessary, they still have important uses in algebra and in data analysis. For the latter, there are at least three reasons why log transforms may be useful. First, taking a logarithm can often help to rescale the data so that their variance is more constant, which overcomes a common statistical problem known as *heteroscedasticity*, discussed in detail in chapter 5. Second, logarithmic transforms can help to make a positively skewed distribution closer to a normal distribution. Third, taking logarithms can also be a way to make a non-linear, multiplicative relationship between variables into a linear, additive one. These issues will also be discussed in some detail in chapter 5.

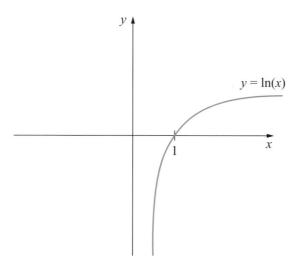

Figure 2.5   A plot of a logarithmic function

Box 2.3   The laws of logs

For variables x and y:

- $\ln (x\,y) = \ln (x) + \ln (y)$
- $\ln (x/y) = \ln (x) - \ln (y)$
- $\ln (y^c) = c \ln (y)$
- $\ln (1) = 0$
- $\ln (1/y) = \ln (1) - \ln (y) = -\ln (y).$
- $\ln(e^x) - e^{\ln(x)} = x$

To motivate how logs work, consider the power relationship $2^3 = 8$. Using logarithms, we would write this as $log_2 8 = 3$, or 'the log to the base 2 of 8 is 3'. Hence we could say that a logarithm is defined as the power to which the base must be raised to obtain the given number. More generally, if $a^b = c$, then we can also write $log_a c = b$. If we plot a log function, $y = log(x)$, it would cross the x-axis at one, as in figure 2.5. It can be seen that as x increases, y increases at a slower rate, which is the opposite to an exponential function where y increases at a faster rate as x increases.

Natural logarithms, also known as logs to base e, are more commonly used and more useful mathematically than logs to any other base. A log to base e is known as a *natural* or *Napierian* logarithm, denoted interchangeably by $\ln(y)$ or $\log(y)$. Taking a natural logarithm is the inverse of a taking an exponential, so sometimes the exponential function is called the *antilog*. The log of a number less than one will be negative, e.g. $ln(0.5) \approx -0.69$. We cannot take the log of a negative number (so $ln(-0.6)$, for example, does not exist). The properties of logarithmic functions or 'laws of logs' describe the way that we can work with logs or manipulate expressions using them. These are presented in box 2.3.

2.1.6 Sigma notation

If we wish to add together several numbers (or observations from variables), the *sigma* or summation operator can be very useful. Σ means 'add up all of the following elements'. For example, $\Sigma(1 + 2 + 3) = 6$. In the context of adding the observations on a variable, it is helpful to add 'limits' to the summation (although note that the limits are not always written out if the meaning is obvious without them). So, for instance, we might write $\sum_{i=1}^{4} x_i$, where the i subscript is again called an index, 1 is the lower limit and 4 is the upper limit of the sum. This would mean adding all of the values of x from x_1 to x_4. It might be the case that one or both of the limits is not a specific number − for instance, $\sum_{i=1}^{n} x_i$, which would mean $x_1 + x_2 + \ldots + x_n$, or sometimes we simply write $\sum_i x_i$ to denote a sum over all the values of the index i. It is also possible to construct a sum of a more complex combination of variables, such as $\sum_{i=1}^{n} x_i z_i$, where x_i and z_i are two separate random variables.

It is important to be aware of a few properties of the sigma operator. For example, the sum of the observations on a variable x plus the sum of the observations on another variable z is equivalent to the sum of the observations on x and z first added together individually

$$\sum_{i=1}^{n} x_i + \sum_{i=1}^{n} z_i = \sum_{i=1}^{n} (x_i + z_i) \tag{2.5}$$

The sum of the observations on a variable x each multiplied by a constant c is equivalent to the constant multiplied by the sum

$$\sum_{i=1}^{n} c x_i = c \sum_{i=1}^{n} x_i. \tag{2.6}$$

But the sum of the products of two variables is not the same as the product of the sums

$$\sum_{i=1}^{n} x_i z_i \neq \sum_{i=1}^{n} x_i \sum_{i=1}^{n} z_i \tag{2.7}$$

We can write the left hand side of equation (2.7) as

$$\sum_{i=1}^{n} x_i z_i = x_1 z_1 + x_2 z_2 + \ldots + x_n z_n \tag{2.8}$$

whereas the right hand side of equation (2.7) is

$$\sum_{i=1}^{n} x_i \sum_{i=1}^{n} z_i = (x_1 + x_2 + \ldots + x_n)(z_1 + z_2 + \ldots + z_n) \tag{2.9}$$

We can see that (2.8) and (2.9) are different since the latter contains many 'cross-product' terms such as $x_1 z_2$, $x_3 z_6$, $x_9 z_2$, etc., whereas the former does not.

If we sum n identical elements (i.e. we add a given number to itself n times), we obtain n times that number

$$\sum_{i=1}^{n} x = x + x + \ldots + x = nx \tag{2.10}$$

Suppose that we sum all of the n observations on a series, x_i – for example, the x_i could be the daily returns on a stock (which are not all the same), we would obtain

$$\sum_{i=1}^{n} x_i = x_1 + x_2 + \ldots + x_n = n\bar{x}. \tag{2.11}$$

So the sum of all of the observations is, from the definition of the mean, equal to the number of observations multiplied by the mean of the series, $\bar{x}$. Notice that the difference between this situation in (2.11) and the previous one in (2.10) is that now the x_i are different from one another whereas before they were all the same (and hence no i subscript was necessary).

Finally, note that it is possible to have multiple summations, which can be conducted in any order, so for example

$$\sum_{i=1}^{n} \sum_{j=1}^{m} x_{ij}$$

would mean sum over all of the i and j subscripts, but we could either sum over the j's first for each i or sum over the i's first for each j. Usually, the inner sum (in this case the one that runs over j from one to m would be conducted first – i.e. separately for each value of i).

2.1.7 Pi notation

Similar to the use of sigma to denote sums, the pi operator (Π) is an operator that is used to denote repeated multiplications. For example

$$\prod_{i=1}^{n} x_i = x_1 x_2 \ldots x_n \tag{2.12}$$

means 'multiply together all of the x_i for each value of i between the lower and upper limits.' It also follows that $\prod_{i=1}^{n} (cx_i) = c^n \prod_{i=1}^{n} x_i$.

2.2 Differential calculus

The effect of the *rate of change of one variable on the rate of change of another* is measured by a mathematical derivative. If the relationship between the two variables can be represented by a curve, the gradient of the curve will be this rate of change.

Consider a variable y that is some function f of another variable x, i.e. $y = f(x)$. The derivative of y with respect to x is written

$$\frac{dy}{dx} = \frac{df(x)}{dx}$$

or sometimes $f'(x)$. This term measures the instantaneous rate of change of y with respect to x, or in other words, the impact of an infinitesimally small change in x. Notice the difference between the notations Δy and dy – the former refers to a change in y of any size, whereas the latter refers specifically to an infinitesimally small change.

2.2.1 Differentiation: the fundamentals

The basic rules of differentiation are as follows:

1. The derivative of a constant is zero

$$\text{e.g. if } y = 10, \frac{dy}{dx} = 0.$$

This is because $y = 10$ would be represented as a horizontal straight line on a graph of y against x, and therefore the gradient of this function is zero.

2. The derivative of a linear function is simply its slope

$$\text{e.g. if } y = 3x + 2, \frac{dy}{dx} = 3.$$

But non-linear functions will have different gradients at each point along the curve. In effect, the gradient at each point is equal to the gradient of the tangent at that point – see figure 2.6. Notice that the gradient will be zero at the point where the curve changes direction from positive to negative or from negative to positive – this is known as a *turning point*.

3. The derivative of a power function n of x

$$\text{i.e. } y = cx^n \text{ is given by } \frac{dy}{dx} = cnx^{n-1}.$$

For example

$$y = 4x^3, \frac{dy}{dx} = (4 \times 3)x^2 = 12x^2$$

$$y = \frac{3}{x} = 3x^{-1}, \frac{dy}{dx} = (3 \times -1)x^{-2} = -3x^{-2} = \frac{-3}{x^2}.$$

4. The derivative of a sum is equal to the sum of the derivatives of the individual parts. Similarly, the derivative of a difference is equal to the difference of the derivatives of the individual parts

$$\text{e.g. if } y = f(x) + g(x), \frac{dy}{dx} = f'(x) + g'(x)$$

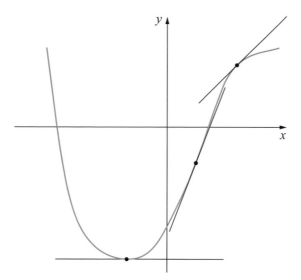

Figure 2.6   The tangents to a curve

while

$$\text{if } y = f(x) - g(x), \quad \frac{dy}{dx} = f'(x) - g'(x).$$

5. The derivative of the log of x is given by $1/x$

i.e. $\dfrac{d(\log(x))}{dx} = \dfrac{1}{x}$.

6. The derivative of the log of a function of x is the derivative of the function divided by the function

i.e. $\dfrac{d(\log(f(x)))}{dx} = \dfrac{f'(x)}{f(x)}$.

For example, the derivative of $\log(x^3 + 2x - 1)$ is given by

$$\frac{3x^2 + 2}{x^3 + 2x - 1}.$$

7. The derivative of e^x is e^x. The derivative of $e^{f(x)}$ is given by $f'(x)e^{f(x)}$. For example, if $y = e^{3x^2}$, $\frac{dy}{dx} = 6xe^{3x^2}$.

2.2.2 Higher order derivatives

It is possible to differentiate a function more than once to calculate the second order, third order, ..., nth order derivatives. The notation for the second order derivative (which is usually just termed the second derivative, and which is the highest order derivative that we will need in this book) is

$$\frac{d^2y}{dx^2} = f''(x) = \frac{d(\frac{dy}{dx})}{dx}$$

To calculate second order derivatives, we simply differentiate the function with respect to x and then we differentiate it again. For example, suppose that we have the function

$$y = 4x^5 + 3x^3 + 2x + 6$$

The first order derivative is

$$\frac{dy}{dx} = \frac{d(4x^5 + 3x^3 + 2x + 6)}{dx} = f'(x) = 20x^4 + 9x^2 + 2.$$

The second order derivative is

$$\frac{d^2y}{dx^2} = f''(x) = \frac{d(\frac{d(4x^5+3x^3+2x+6)}{dx})}{dx} = \frac{d(20x^4 + 9x^2 + 2)}{dx} = 80x^3 + 18x.$$

The second order derivative can be interpreted as the gradient of the gradient of a function – i.e. the rate of change of the gradient.

We said above that at the turning point of a function its gradient will be zero. How can we tell, then, whether a particular turning point is a maximum or a minimum? The answer is that to do this we would look at the second derivative. When a function reaches a maximum, its second derivative is negative, while it is positive for a minimum.

For example, consider the quadratic function $y = 5x^2 + 3x - 6$. We already know that since the squared term in the equation has a positive sign (i.e. it is 5 rather than, say, -5), the function will have a $\cup$-shape rather than an $\cap$-shape, and thus it will have a minimum rather than a maximum. But let us also demonstrate this using differentiation

$$\frac{dy}{dx} = 10x + 3, \frac{d^2y}{dx^2} = 10.$$

Since the second derivative is positive, the function indeed has a minimum. To find where this minimum is located, take the first derivative, set it to zero and solve it for x. So we have $10x + 3 = 0$, and thus $x = -\frac{3}{10} = -0.3$. If $x = -0.3$, the corresponding value of y is found by substituting -0.3 into the original function $y = 5x^2 + 3x - 6 = 5 \times (-0.3)^2 + (3 \times -0.3) - 6 = -6.45$. Therefore, the minimum of this function is found at $(-0.3, -6.45)$.

2.2.3   Partial differentiation

In the case where y is a function of more than one variable (e.g. $y = f(x_1, x_2, \ldots, x_n)$), it may be of interest to determine the effect that changes in each of the individual x variables would have on y. The differentiation of y with respect to only one of the variables, holding the others constant, is known as *partial differentiation*. The partial derivative of y with respect to a variable x_1 is usually denoted

$$\frac{\partial y}{\partial x_1}.$$

All of the rules for differentiation explained above still apply and there will be one (first order) partial derivative for each variable on the right hand side of the equation. We calculate these partial derivatives one at a time, treating all of the other variables as if they were constants. To give an illustration, suppose $y = 3x_1^3 + 4x_1 - 2x_2^4 + 2x_2^2$. The partial derivative of y with respect to x_1 would be

$$\frac{\partial y}{\partial x_1} = 9x_1^2 + 4$$

while the partial derivative of y with respect to x_2 would be

$$\frac{\partial y}{\partial x_2} = -8x_2^3 + 4x_2$$

As we will see in chapter 3, the ordinary least squares (OLS) estimator gives formulae for the values of the parameters that minimise the residual sum of squares, given by $L = \sum_t (y_t - \hat{\alpha} - \hat{\beta} x_t)^2$. The minimum of L (the residual sum of squares) is found by partially differentiating this function with respect to $\hat{\alpha}$ and $\hat{\beta}$ and setting these partial derivatives to zero. Therefore, partial differentiation has a key role in deriving the main approach to parameter estimation that we use in econometrics – see appendix 3.1 for a demonstration of this application.

2.2.4 Integration

Integration is the opposite of differentiation, so that if we integrate a function and then differentiate the result, we get back the original function. Recall that derivatives give functions for calculating the slope of a curve; integration, on the other hand, is used to calculate the area under a curve (between two specific points). Further details on the rules for integration are beyond the scope of this book since the mathematical technique is not needed for any of the approaches we will employ, but it will be useful to be familiar with the general concept.

2.3 Matrices

Before we can work with matrices, we need to define some terminology
- A *scalar* is simply a single number (although it need not be a whole number – e.g. 3, −5, 0.5 are all scalars)
- A *vector* is a one-dimensional array of numbers (see below for examples)
- A *matrix* is a two-dimensional *collection or array of numbers*. The size of a matrix is given by its numbers of rows and columns.

Matrices are very useful and important ways for organising sets of data together, which make manipulating and transforming them much easier than it would be to work with each constituent of the matrix separately. Matrices are widely used in econometrics and finance for solving systems of linear equations, for deriving key results and for expressing formulae in a succinct way. Sometimes **bold–faced type** is used to denote a vector or matrix (e.g. **A**), although in this book we will not do so – hopefully it should be obvious whether an object is a scalar, vector or matrix from the context or this will be clearly stated. Some useful features of matrices and explanations of how to work with them are described below.

- The dimensions of a matrix are quoted as $R \times C$, which is the number of rows by the number of columns.
- Each element in a matrix is referred to using subscripts. For example, suppose a matrix M has two rows and four columns. The element in the second row and the third column of this matrix would be denoted m_{23}, so that more generally m_{ij} refers to the element in the ith row and the jth column. Thus a 2×4 matrix would have elements

$$\begin{pmatrix} m_{11} & m_{12} & m_{13} & m_{14} \\ m_{21} & m_{22} & m_{23} & m_{24} \end{pmatrix}$$

- If a matrix has only one row, it is known as a *row vector*, which will be of dimension $1 \times C$, where C is the number of columns

  e.g. $(2.7 \quad 3.0 \quad -1.5 \quad 0.3)$

- A matrix having only one column is known as a *column vector*, which will be of dimension $R \times 1$, where R is the number of rows

  e.g. $\begin{pmatrix} 1.3 \\ -0.1 \\ 0.0 \end{pmatrix}$

- When the number of rows and columns is equal (i.e. $R = C$), it would be said that the matrix is square as is the following 2×2 matrix

  $\begin{pmatrix} 0.3 & 0.6 \\ -0.1 & 0.7 \end{pmatrix}$

- A matrix in which all the elements are zero is known as a zero matrix

  e.g. $\begin{pmatrix} 0 & 0 & 0 \\ 0 & 0 & 0 \end{pmatrix}$

- A symmetric matrix is a special type of square matrix that is symmetric about the leading diagonal (the diagonal line running through the matrix from the top left to the bottom right), so that $m_{ij} = m_{ji} \ \forall \ i, j$

  e.g. $\begin{pmatrix} 1 & 2 & 4 & 7 \\ 2 & -3 & 6 & 9 \\ 4 & 6 & 2 & -8 \\ 7 & 9 & -8 & 0 \end{pmatrix}$

- A diagonal matrix is a square matrix which has non-zero terms on the leading diagonal and zeros everywhere else

  e.g. $\begin{pmatrix} -3 & 0 & 0 & 0 \\ 0 & 1 & 0 & 0 \\ 0 & 0 & 2 & 0 \\ 0 & 0 & 0 & -1 \end{pmatrix}$

- A diagonal matrix with 1 in all places on the leading diagonal and zero everywhere else is known as the identity matrix, denoted by I. By definition, an identity matrix must be symmetric (and therefore also square)

$$\text{e.g.} \quad \begin{pmatrix} 1 & 0 & 0 & 0 \\ 0 & 1 & 0 & 0 \\ 0 & 0 & 1 & 0 \\ 0 & 0 & 0 & 1 \end{pmatrix}$$

- The identity matrix is essentially the matrix equivalent of the number one. Multiplying any matrix by the identity matrix of the appropriate size results in the original matrix being left unchanged. So for any matrix M

$$MI = IM = M$$

2.3.1 Operations with matrices

In order to perform operations with matrices (e.g. addition, subtraction or multiplication), the matrices concerned must be *conformable*. The dimensions of matrices required for them to be conformable depend on the operation.

- Addition and subtraction of matrices requires the matrices concerned to be of the same order (i.e. to have the same number of rows and the same number of columns as one another). The operations are then performed element by element

$$\text{e.g.} \quad \text{if } A = \begin{pmatrix} 0.3 & 0.6 \\ -0.1 & 0.7 \end{pmatrix} \quad \text{and} \quad B = \begin{pmatrix} 0.2 & -0.1 \\ 0 & 0.3 \end{pmatrix}$$

$$A + B = \begin{pmatrix} 0.3+0.2 & 0.6-0.1 \\ -0.1+0 & 0.7+0.3 \end{pmatrix} = \begin{pmatrix} 0.5 & 0.5 \\ -0.1 & 1.0 \end{pmatrix}$$

$$A - B = \begin{pmatrix} 0.3-0.2 & 0.6--0.1 \\ -0.1-0 & 0.7-0.3 \end{pmatrix} = \begin{pmatrix} 0.1 & 0.7 \\ -0.1 & 0.4 \end{pmatrix}$$

- Multiplying or dividing a matrix by a scalar (that is, a single number), implies that every element of the matrix is multiplied by that number

$$\text{e.g.} \quad 2A = 2\begin{pmatrix} 0.3 & 0.6 \\ -0.1 & 0.7 \end{pmatrix} = \begin{pmatrix} 0.6 & 1.2 \\ -0.2 & 1.4 \end{pmatrix}$$

- More generally, for two matrices A and B of the same order and for c a scalar, the following results hold

$$A + B = B + A$$

$$A + 0 = 0 + A = A$$

$$cA = A c$$

$$c(A + B) = cA + cB$$

$$A0 = 0A = 0$$

- Multiplying two matrices together requires the number of columns of the first matrix to be equal to the number of rows of the second matrix. Note also that the ordering of the matrices is important when multiplying them, so that in general, $AB \neq BA$. When matrices are multiplied together, the resulting matrix will be of size (number of rows of first matrix × number of columns of second matrix), e.g. $(3 \times 2) \times (2 \times 4) = (3 \times 4)$. In terms of determining the dimensions of the matrix, it is as if the number of columns of the first matrix and the number of rows of the second cancel out.[1] This rule also follows more generally, so that $(a \times b) \times (b \times c) \times (c \times d) \times (d \times e) = (a \times e)$, etc.
- The actual multiplication of the elements of the two matrices is done by multiplying along the rows of the first matrix and down the columns of the second

e.g. $\begin{pmatrix} 1 & 2 \\ 7 & 3 \\ 1 & 6 \end{pmatrix} \begin{pmatrix} 0 & 2 & 4 & 9 \\ 6 & 3 & 0 & 2 \end{pmatrix}$

$(3 \times 2) \quad (2 \times 4)$

$$= \begin{pmatrix} ((1 \times 0) + (2 \times 6)) & ((1 \times 2) + (2 \times 3)) & ((1 \times 4) + (2 \times 0)) & ((1 \times 9) + (2 \times 2)) \\ ((7 \times 0) + (3 \times 6)) & ((7 \times 2) + (3 \times 3)) & ((7 \times 4) + (3 \times 0)) & ((7 \times 9) + (3 \times 2)) \\ ((1 \times 0) + (6 \times 6)) & ((1 \times 2) + (6 \times 3)) & ((1 \times 4) + (6 \times 0)) & ((1 \times 9) + (6 \times 2)) \end{pmatrix}$$

(3×4)

$$= \begin{pmatrix} 12 & 8 & 4 & 13 \\ 18 & 23 & 28 & 69 \\ 36 & 20 & 4 & 21 \end{pmatrix}$$

(3×4)

In general, matrices cannot be divided by one another. Instead, we multiply by the inverse – see below.

- The transpose of a matrix, written A' or A^{T} is the matrix obtained by transposing (switching) the rows and columns of a matrix

e.g.   if $A = \begin{pmatrix} 1 & 2 \\ 7 & 3 \\ 1 & 6 \end{pmatrix}$ then $A' = \begin{pmatrix} 1 & 7 & 1 \\ 2 & 3 & 6 \end{pmatrix}$

If A is of dimensions $R \times C$, A' will be $C \times R$.

---

[1] Of course, the actual elements of the matrices themselves do not cancel out – this is just a simple rule of thumb for calculating the dimensions of the matrix resulting from a multiplication.

2.3.2 The rank of a matrix

The rank of a matrix A is given by the maximum number of linearly independent rows (or columns) contained in the matrix. For example,

$$\text{rank}\begin{pmatrix} 3 & 4 \\ 7 & 9 \end{pmatrix} = 2$$

since both rows and columns are (linearly) independent of one another, but

$$\text{rank}\begin{pmatrix} 3 & 6 \\ 2 & 4 \end{pmatrix} = 1$$

as the second column is not independent of the first (the second column is simply twice the first). A matrix with a rank equal to its dimension, as in the first of these two cases, is known as a *matrix of full rank*. A matrix that is less than of full rank is known as a *short rank matrix*, and such a matrix is also termed *singular*. Three important results concerning the rank of a matrix are:

- $\text{Rank}(A) = \text{Rank}(A')$
- $\text{Rank}(AB) \leq \min(\text{Rank}(A), \text{Rank}(B))$
- $\text{Rank}(A'A) = \text{Rank}(AA') = \text{Rank}(A)$

2.3.3 The inverse of a matrix

The inverse of a matrix A, where defined, is denoted A^{-1}. It is that matrix which, when pre-multiplied or post-multiplied by A, will result in the identity matrix

i.e. $AA^{-1} = A^{-1}A = I.$

The inverse of a matrix exists only when the matrix is square and non-singular – that is, when it is of full rank. The inverse of a 2×2 non-singular matrix whose elements are

$$\begin{pmatrix} a & b \\ c & d \end{pmatrix}$$

will be given by

$$\frac{1}{ad - bc}\begin{pmatrix} d & -b \\ -c & a \end{pmatrix}$$

The expression in the denominator above to the left of the matrix $(ad - bc)$ is the *determinant* of the matrix, and will be a scalar. If this determinant is zero, the matrix is singular, and thus not of full rank so that its inverse does not exist.

Example 2.2

If the matrix is

$$\begin{pmatrix} 2 & 1 \\ 4 & 6 \end{pmatrix}$$

the inverse will be

$$\frac{1}{8}\begin{pmatrix} 6 & -1 \\ -4 & 2 \end{pmatrix} = \begin{pmatrix} \frac{3}{4} & -\frac{1}{8} \\ -\frac{1}{2} & \frac{1}{4} \end{pmatrix}$$

As a check, multiply the two matrices together and it should give the identity matrix – the matrix equivalent of one (analogous to $\frac{1}{3} \times 3 = 1$)

$$\begin{pmatrix} 2 & 1 \\ 4 & 6 \end{pmatrix} \times \frac{1}{8}\begin{pmatrix} 6 & -1 \\ -4 & 2 \end{pmatrix} = \frac{1}{8}\begin{pmatrix} 8 & 0 \\ 0 & 8 \end{pmatrix} = \begin{pmatrix} 1 & 0 \\ 0 & 1 \end{pmatrix}$$

$= I$, as required.

The calculation of the inverse of an $N \times N$ matrix for $N > 2$ is more complex and beyond the scope of this text. Properties of the inverse of a matrix include:

- $I^{-1} = I$
- $(A^{-1})^{-1} = A$
- $(A')^{-1} = (A^{-1})'$
- $(AB)^{-1} = B^{-1}A^{-1}$

2.3.4 The trace of a matrix

The trace of a square matrix is the sum of the terms on its leading diagonal. For example, the trace of the matrix

$$A = \begin{pmatrix} 3 & 4 \\ 7 & 9 \end{pmatrix}$$

written $\text{Tr}(A)$, is $3 + 9 = 12$. Some important properties of the trace of a matrix are:

- $\text{Tr}(cA) = c\text{Tr}(A)$
- $\text{Tr}(A') = \text{Tr}(A)$
- $\text{Tr}(A + B) = \text{Tr}(A) + \text{Tr}(B)$
- $\text{Tr}(I_N) = N$

2.3.5 The eigenvalues of a matrix

The concept of the eigenvalues of a matrix is necessary for testing for long-run relationships between series using what is known as the Johansen cointegration test used in chapter 8. Let Π denote a $p \times p$ square matrix, c denote a $p \times 1$ non-zero vector, and λ denote a set of scalars. λ is called a *characteristic root* or set of roots of the matrix Π if it is possible to write

$$\underset{p\times p}{\Pi}\underset{p\times 1}{c} = \lambda\underset{p\times 1}{c}$$

This equation can also be written as

$$\Pi c = \lambda I_p c$$

where I_p is an identity matrix, and hence

$$(\Pi - \lambda I_p)c = 0$$

Since $c \neq 0$ by definition, then for this system to have a non-zero solution, the matrix $(\Pi - \lambda I_p)$ is required to be singular (i.e. to have a zero determinant)

$$|\Pi - \lambda I_p| = 0$$

For example, let Π be the 2×2 matrix

$$\Pi = \begin{bmatrix} 5 & 1 \\ 2 & 4 \end{bmatrix}$$

Then the characteristic equation is

$$|\Pi - \lambda I_p|$$

$$= \left| \begin{bmatrix} 5 & 1 \\ 2 & 4 \end{bmatrix} - \lambda \begin{bmatrix} 1 & 0 \\ 0 & 1 \end{bmatrix} \right| = 0$$

$$= \begin{vmatrix} 5 - \lambda & 1 \\ 2 & 4 - \lambda \end{vmatrix} = (5 - \lambda)(4 - \lambda) - 2 = \lambda^2 - 9\lambda + 18$$

This gives the solutions $\lambda = 6$ and $\lambda = 3$. The characteristic roots are also known as *eigenvalues*. The eigenvectors would be the values of c corresponding to the eigenvalues. Some properties of the eigenvalues of any square matrix A are:

- the sum of the eigenvalues is the trace of the matrix
- the product of the eigenvalues is the determinant
- the number of non-zero eigenvalues is the rank.

For a further illustration of the last of these properties, consider the matrix

$$\Pi = \begin{bmatrix} 0.5 & 0.25 \\ 0.7 & 0.35 \end{bmatrix}$$

Its characteristic equation is

$$\left| \begin{bmatrix} 0.5 & 0.25 \\ 0.7 & 0.35 \end{bmatrix} - \lambda \begin{bmatrix} 1 & 0 \\ 0 & 1 \end{bmatrix} \right| = 0$$

which implies that

$$\begin{vmatrix} 0.5 - \lambda & 0.25 \\ 0.7 & 0.35 - \lambda \end{vmatrix} = 0$$

This determinant can also be written $(0.5 - \lambda)(0.35 - \lambda) - (0.7 \times 0.25) = 0$ or

$$0.175 - 0.85\lambda + \lambda^2 - 0.175 = 0$$

or

$$\lambda^2 - 0.85\lambda = 0$$

which can be factorised to $\lambda\,(\lambda - 0.85) = 0$.

The characteristic roots are therefore 0 and 0.85. Since one of these eigenvalues is zero, it is obvious that the matrix Π cannot be of full rank. In fact, this is also obvious from just looking at Π, since the second column is exactly half the first.

2.3.6   Portfolio theory and matrix algebra

Probably the most important application of matrix algebra in finance is to solving portfolio allocation problems. Although these can be solved in a perfectly satisfactory fashion with sigma notation rather than matrix algebra, use of the latter does considerably simplify the expressions and makes it easier to solve them when the portfolio includes more than two assets. This book is not the place to learn about portfolio theory *per se* – interested readers are referred to Bodie, Kane and Marcus (2011) or the many other investment textbooks that exist – rather, the purpose of this section is to demonstrate how matrix algebra is used in practice.

So to start, suppose that we have a set of N stocks that are included in a portfolio P with weights $w_1, w_2, \ldots, w_N$ and suppose that their expected returns are written as $E(r_1), E(r_2), \ldots, E(r_N)$. We could write the $N \times 1$ vectors of weights, w, and of expected returns, $E(r)$, as

$$w = \begin{pmatrix} w_1 \\ w_2 \\ \ldots \\ w_N \end{pmatrix} \quad E(r) = \begin{pmatrix} E(r_1) \\ E(r_2) \\ \ldots \\ E(r_N) \end{pmatrix}$$

So, for instance, w_3 and $E(r_3)$ are the weight attached to stock three and its expected return respectively. The expected return on the portfolio, $E(r_P)$ can be calculated as $E(r)'w$ – that is, we multiply the transpose of the expected return vector by the weights vector.

We then need to set up what is called the variance-covariance matrix of the returns, denoted V. This matrix includes all of the variances of the components of the portfolio returns on the leading diagonal and the covariances between them as the off-diagonal elements. We will also discuss such a matrix extensively in chapter 4 in the context of the parameters from regression models. The variance–covariance matrix of the returns may be written

$$V = \begin{pmatrix} \sigma_{11} & \sigma_{12} & \sigma_{13} & \ldots & \sigma_{1N} \\ \sigma_{21} & \sigma_{22} & \sigma_{23} & \ldots & \sigma_{2N} \\ \vdots & & & \vdots & \\ \sigma_{N1} & \sigma_{N2} & \sigma_{N3} & \ldots & \sigma_{NN} \end{pmatrix}$$

The elements on the leading diagonal of V are the variances of each of the component stocks' returns – so, for example, σ_{11} is the variance of the returns on stock one, σ_{22} is the variance of returns on stock two and so on. The off-diagonal elements are the corresponding covariances – so, for example, σ_{12} is the covariance between the returns on stock one and those on stock two, σ_{58} is the covariance between the returns on stock five and those on stock eight, and so on. Note that this matrix will be symmetrical about the leading diagonal since $Cov(a, b) = Cov(b, a)$ where a and b are random variables and hence it is possible to write $\sigma_{12} = \sigma_{21}$ and so forth.

In order to construct a variance-covariance matrix, we would need to first set up a matrix containing observations on the actual returns (not the expected returns) for each stock where the mean, $\bar{r}_i$ $(i = 1, \ldots, N)$, has been subtracted away from each series i. If we call this matrix R, we would write

$$R = \begin{pmatrix} r_{11} - \bar{r}_1 & r_{21} - \bar{r}_2 & r_{31} - \bar{r}_3 & \cdots & r_{N1} - \bar{r}_N \\ r_{12} - \bar{r}_1 & r_{22} - \bar{r}_2 & r_{32} - \bar{r}_3 & \cdots & r_{N2} - \bar{r}_N \\ \vdots & & & & \vdots \\ r_{1T} - \bar{r}_1 & r_{2T} - \bar{r}_2 & r_{3T} - \bar{r}_3 & \cdots & r_{NT} - \bar{r}_N \end{pmatrix}$$

So each column in this matrix represents the deviations of the returns on individual stocks from their means and each row represents the mean-adjusted return observations on all stocks at a particular point in time. The general entry, r_{ij}, is the jth time series observation on the ith stock. The variance-covariance matrix would then simply be calculated as $V = (R'R)/(T - 1)$ where T is the total number of time series observations available for each series.

Suppose that we wanted to calculate the variance of returns on the portfolio P (a scalar which we might call V_P). We would do this by calculating

$$V_P = w'Vw \tag{2.13}$$

Checking the dimension of V_P, w' is $(1 \times N)$, V is $(N \times N)$ and w is $(N \times 1)$ so V_P is $(1 \times N \times N \times N \times N \times 1)$, which is (1×1) as required.

We could also define a correlation matrix of returns, C, which would be

$$C = \begin{pmatrix} 1 & C_{12} & C_{13} & \cdots & C_{1N} \\ C_{21} & 1 & C_{23} & \cdots & C_{2N} \\ \vdots & & & & \vdots \\ C_{N1} & C_{N2} & C_{N3} & \cdots & 1 \end{pmatrix}$$

This matrix would have ones everywhere on the leading diagonal (since the correlation of something with itself is always one) and the off diagonal elements would give the correlations between each pair of returns – for example, C_{35} would be the correlation between the returns on stock three and those on stock five. Note again that, as for the variance-covariance matrix, the correlation matrix will always be symmetrical about the leading diagonal so that $C_{31} = C_{13}$ etc. Using the correlation instead of the variance-covariance matrix, the portfolio variance given in equation (2.13) would be

$$V_P = w'SCSw \tag{2.14}$$

where C is the correlation matrix, w is again the vector of portfolio weights, and S is a diagonal matrix with each element containing the standard deviations of the portfolio returns.

Selecting weights for the minimum variance portfolio

Although in theory investors can do better by selecting the optimal portfolio on the efficient frontier, in practice a variance minimising portfolio often performs well when used out-of-sample. Thus we might want to select the portfolio weights w that minimise the portfolio variance, V_P. In matrix notation, we would write

$$\min_{w} \; w'Vw$$

We also need to be slightly careful to impose at least the restriction that all of the wealth has to be invested ($\sum_{i=1}^{N} w_i = 1$), otherwise this minimisation problem can be trivially solved by setting all of the weights to zero to yield a zero portfolio variance. This restriction that the weights must sum to one is written using matrix algebra as $w' \cdot 1_N = 1$, where 1_N is a column vector of ones of length N.[2]

The minimisation problem can be solved to

$$w_{MVP} = \frac{1_N \cdot V^{-1}}{1_N \cdot V^{-1} \cdot 1'_N} \tag{2.15}$$

where MVP stands for minimum variance portfolio.

Selecting optimal portfolio weights

In order to trace out the mean-variance efficient frontier, we would repeatedly solve this minimisation problem but in each case set the portfolio's expected return equal to a different target value, $\bar{R}$. So, for example, we set $\bar{R}$ to 0.1 and find the portfolio weights that minimise V_P, then set $\bar{R}$ to 0.2 and find the portfolio weights that minimise V_P, and so on. We would write this as

$$\min_{w} \quad w'Vw \quad \text{subject to} \quad w' \cdot 1_N = 1, \, w'E(r) = \bar{R}$$

This problem is sometimes called the *Markowitz portfolio allocation problem*, and can be solved analytically as expressed above. That is, we can derive an exact solution using matrix algebra. However, it is often the case that we want to place additional constraints on the optimisation – for instance we might want to restrict the portfolio weights so that none are greater than 10% of the overall wealth invested in the portfolio, or we might want to restrict them to all be positive (i.e. long positions only with no short selling allowed). In such cases the Markowitz portfolio allocation problem cannot be solved analytically and thus a numerical procedure must be used such as the Solver function in Microsoft Excel.

---

[2] Note that $w' \cdot 1_N$ will be 1×1 – i.e. a scalar.

Note that it is also possible to write the Markowitz problem the other way around – that is, where we select the portfolio weights that maximise the expected portfolio return subject to a target maximum variance level.

If the procedure above is followed repeatedly for different return targets, it will trace out the efficient frontier. In order to find the tangency point where the efficient frontier touches the capital market line, we need to solve the following problem

$$\max_{w} \quad \frac{w'E(r) - r_f}{(w'Vw)^{\frac{1}{2}}} \quad \text{subject to} \quad w' \cdot 1_N = 1$$

If no additional constraints are required on the stock weights, this can be solved fairly simply as

$$w = \frac{V^{-1}[E(r) - r_f \cdot 1_N]}{1'_N V^{-1}[E(r) - r_f \cdot 1_N]} \tag{2.16}$$

2.3.7   The mean-variance efficient frontier in Excel

This section will now describe how to construct an efficient frontier and draw the capital market line using a three stock portfolio with Microsoft Excel. Although EViews is used for conducting the empirical work throughout the rest of the book, it is more natural to tackle these sorts of problems within a standard spreadsheet environment. It is assumed that the reader knows the standard functions of Excel – for those who need a refresher, see the excellent book by Benninga (2011).

The spreadsheet 'efficient.xls' contains the finished product – the plots of the efficient frontier and capital market line. However, I suggest **starting with a blank spreadsheet, copying across the raw data and starting to reconstruct the formulae again** to get a better of idea of how it is done.

The first step is to construct the returns. The raw prices and T-bill yields are in columns two to six of the sheet. These series are identical to those used in the example in the following chapter on estimating the CAPM. We will not need to use the S&P index or Oracle share prices since we are going to assume a three asset portfolio. However, all of the principles outlined below could be very easily and intuitively extended to situations where there were more assets employed.

Since we are dealing with portfolios, it is probably preferable to employ simple rather than continuously compounded returns. So start by **constructing three sets of returns** for the Ford, General Electric and Microsoft share prices in columns H to J, and head these columns 'FORDRET', 'GERET' and 'MSOFT-RET' respectively. Column K will comprise the weights on a portfolio containing all three stocks but with varying weights. The way we achieve this is to set up three cells that will contain the weights. To start with, we fix these arbitrarily but later will allow the Solver to choose them optimally. So **write 0.33, 0.33 and 0.34 in cells N12 to N14 respectively**. In cell N15, **calculate the sum of**

Screenshot 2.1   **Setting up a variance-covariance matrix in Excel**

the weights as a check that this is always one so that the all wealth is invested among the three stocks. We are now in a position to construct the (equally weighted) portfolio returns **(call them 'PORTRET')** in column K. In cell K2, **write =H3*$N$12+I3*$N$13+J3*$N$14** and then **copy this formula down the whole of column K until row 137**.

The next stage is to construct the variance-covariance matrix, which we termed V in the description above. So first, **click on Data and Data Analysis** and then select Covariance from the menu. **Complete the Window so that it appears as in screenshot 2.1** with input range $H$3:$J$137 and output range $M$3:$P$6 and **click OK**.

Now **copy the covariances** so that they are also in the upper right triangle of the matrix, and also **replace 'Column 1' etc. with the names of the three stocks in the column and row headers**.

We now want to calculate the average returns for each of the individual stocks (we already have their variances on the leading diagonal of the variance-covariance matrix). To do this, in cells M9 to O9, **write =AVERAGE(H3:H137), =AVERAGE(I3:I137) and =AVERAGE(I3:I137)**.

Next, we can construct summary statistics for the portfolio returns. There are several ways to do this. One way would be to calculate the mean, variance and standard deviation of the returns directly from the monthly portfolio returns in column K. However, to see how we would do this using matrix algebra in Excel, for calculating the average portfolio return **in cell N18, enter the formula =MMULT(M9:O9,N12:N14)** which will multiply the returns vector (what we called $E(r)'$) in M9 to O9 by the weights vector w in N12 to N14.

In cell N19, we want the formula for the portfolio variance, which is given by $w'Vw$ and in Excel this is calculated using the formula **=MMULT(MMULT(Q13:S13, N4:P6),N12:N14)**.

M	N	O	P	Q	R	S	T
Variance-Covariance matrix, V							
	FORD	**GE**	**MSOFT**				
FORD	293.02	61.55	42.90				
GE	61.55	66.90	25.79				
MSOFT	42.90	25.79	50.05				
Stock Returns							
1.31	0.24	0.39					
Portfolio Weights, w			**Portfolio weights transposed, w'**				
FORD	0.33			**FORD**	**GE**	**MSOFT**	
GE	0.33				0.33	0.33	0.34
MSOFT	0.34						
	1.00	<<< sum of weights					
Portfolio Statistics							
Mean	0.64						
Variance	73.80						
Std Dev.	8.59						

Screenshot 2.2   **The spreadsheet for constructing the efficient frontier**

Effectively, we are conducting the multiplication in two stages. First, the internal MMUL is multiplying the transposed weights vector, w' in Q13 to S13 by the variance-covariance matrix V in N4 to P6. We then multiply the resulting product by the weights vector w in N12 to N14. Finally, **calculate the standard deviation of the portfolio returns in N19 as the square root of the variance in N18**.

Take a couple of minutes to examine the summary statistics and the variance-covariance matrix. It is clear that Ford is by far the most volatile stock with an annual variance of 239, while Microsoft is the least at 50. The equally weighted portfolio has a variance of 73.8. Ford also has the highest average return. We now have all of the components needed to construct the mean-variance efficient frontier and the right hand side of your spreadsheet should appear as in screenshot 2.2.

First, let us calculate the minimum variance portfolio. To do this, **click on cell N19**, which is the one containing the portfolio variance formula. Then **click on the Data tab and then on Solver**. A window will appear which should be **completed as in screenshot 2.3**. So we want to minimise cell $N$19 by changing the weights $N$12:$N$14 subject to the constraint that the weights sum to one ($N$15 = 1). Then **click Solve**. Solver will tell you it has found a solution, so **click OK** again.

Note that strictly it is not necessary to use Solver to evaluate this problem when no additional constraints are placed, but if we want to incorporate non-negativity

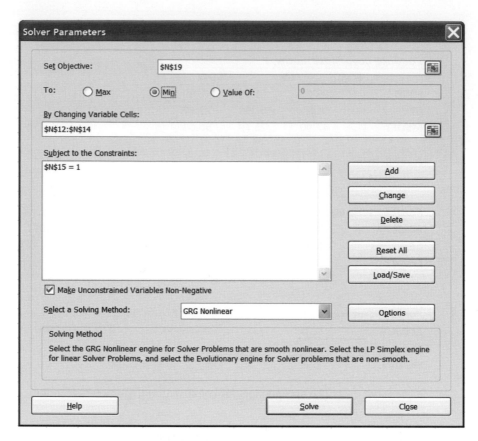

Screenshot 2.3   **Completing the Solver window**

or other constraints on the weights, we could not calculate the weights analytically and Solver would have to be used. The weights in cells N12 to N14 automatically update, as do the portfolio summary statistics in N18 to N20. So the weights that minimise the portfolio variance are with no allocation to Ford, 37% in General Electric and 63% in Microsoft. This achieves a variance of 41 (standard deviation of 6.41%) per month and an average return of 0.33% per month.

So we now have one point on the efficient frontier (the one on the far left), and we repeat this procedure to obtain other points on the frontier. We set a target variance and find the weights that maximise the return subject to this variance. **In cells N25 to N40, we specify the target standard deviations from 6.5 to 17, increasing in units of 0.5**. These figures are somewhat arbitrary, but as a rule of thumb, to get a nice looking frontier, we should have the maximum standard deviation (17) about three times the minimum (6.5). We know not to set any number less than 6.41 since this was the minimum possible standard deviation with these three stocks.

We **click on the cell N18** and then **select Solver** again from the Data tab. Then we use all of the entries as before, except that we want to **choose Max** (to maximise the return subject to a standard deviation constraint) and then **add an additional constraint that $N$20 = $N$25**, so that the portfolio standard

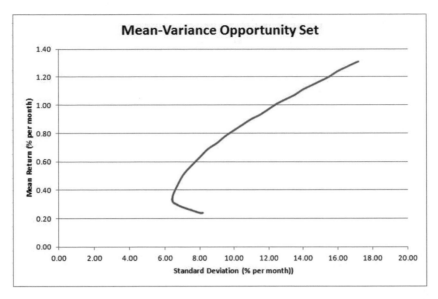

Screenshot 2.4   **A plot of the completed efficient frontier**

deviation will be equal to the value we want, which is 6.5 in cell N25. **Click Solve and the new solution will be found.** The weights are now 4% in Ford, 30% in GE, and 66% in Microsoft, giving a mean return of 0.38% and a standard deviation of 6.5(%). **Repeat this again for the other standard deviation values from 6.5 through to 17**, each time noting the corresponding mean value (and if you wish, also noting the weights). You will see that if you try to find a portfolio with a standard deviation of 17.5, Solver will not be able to find a solution because there are no combinations of the three stocks that will give such a high value. In fact, the upper left point on the efficient frontier will be the maximum return portfolio which will always be 100% invested in the stock with the highest return (in this case Ford).

We can now plot the efficient frontier – i.e. the mean return on the y-axis against the standard deviation on the x-axis. If we also want the lower part of the mean-variance opportunity set (the part where the curve folds back on itself at the bottom), we **repeat the procedure above** – i.e. targeting the standard deviation of 6.5, 7., . . . , but this time we **minimise the return rather than maximising it**. The minimum return is 0.24 when the portfolio is 100% invested in GE. The plot will appear as in screenshot 2.4. The line is somewhat wiggly, but this arises because the points are insufficiently close together. If we had used standard deviations from 6.5 to 17 in increments of 0.2, say, rather than 0.5 then the plot would have been much smoother.

The final step in the process is to superimpose the capital market line (CML) onto the plot. To do this, we need to find the tangency point, which will be the point at which the Sharpe ratio of the portfolio is maximised. So first we need to **calculate the average of the T-bill series** (dividing it by twelve to get the monthly rate for comparability with the stock returns, which are monthly), putting

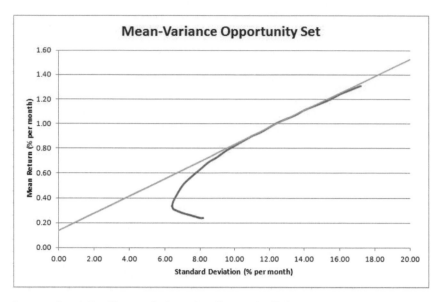

Screenshot 2.5   **The capital market line and efficient frontier**

this in cell N55. We then **calculate the risk premium in N56**, which is the risky portfolio return from N18 less the risk-free rate in N56. Finally, **the Sharpe ratio in N57** is the risk premium from N56 divided by the portfolio standard deviation (N20). We then get Solver to **maximise the value of N57 subject to the weights adding to one** (no other constraints are needed).

The tangency point has a mean return of exactly 1% per month (by coincidence), standard deviation 12.41% and weights of 66%, 0% and 34% in Ford, GE and MSoft respectively. We then need **a set of points on the CML to plot** – one will be the point on the y-axis where the risk is zero and the return is the average risk-free rate (0.14% per month). Another will be the tangency point we just derived. To get the others, recall that the CML is a straight line with equation $return = R_f + Sharpe\ ratio \times std\ dev$. So all we need to do is to **use a run of standard deviations and then calculate the corresponding returns** – we know that $R_f = 0.14$ and Sharpe ratio = 0.0694. The minimum variance opportunity set and the CML on the same graph will appear as in screenshot 2.5.

2.4   Probability and probability distributions

This section discusses and presents the theoretical expressions for the mean and variance of a random variable. A *random variable* is one that can take on any value from a given set and where this value is determined at least in part by chance. By their very nature, random variables are not perfectly predictable. Most data series in economics and finance are best considered random variables, although there might be some measurable structure underlying them as well so they are not purely random. It is often helpful to think of such series as being made up of a fixed part (which we can model and forecast) and a purely random part, which we cannot forecast.

The mean of a random variable y is also known as its expected value, written $E(y)$. The properties of expected values are used widely in econometrics, and are listed below, referring to a random variable y

- The expected value of a constant (or a variable that is non-stochastic) is the constant, e.g. $E(c) = c$.
- The expected value of a constant multiplied by a random variable is equal to the constant multiplied by the expected value of the variable: $E(c\,y) = c\,E(y)$. It can also be stated that $E(c\,y + d) = (c\,E(y)) + d$, where d is also a constant.
- For two independent random variables, y_1 and y_2, $E(y_1 y_2) = E(y_1)\,E(y_2)$.

The variance of a random variable y is usually written var(y). The properties of the 'variance operator', var$(\cdot)$, are

- The variance of a random variable y is given by $\text{var}(y) = E[y - E(y)]^2$
- The variance of a constant is zero: $\text{var}(c) = 0$
- For c and d constants, $\text{var}(c\,y + d) = c^2\,\text{var}(y)$
- For two independent random variables, y_1 and y_2, $\text{var}(c\,y_1 + d\,y_2) = c^2\text{var}(y_1) + d^2\text{var}(y_2)$.

The covariance between two random variables, y_1 and y_2 may be expressed as cov(y_1, y_2). The properties of the covariance operator are

- $\text{cov}(y_1, y_2) = E[(y_1 - E(y_1))(y_2 - E(y_2))]$
- For two independent random variables, y_1 and y_2, $\text{cov}(y_1, y_2) = 0$
- For four constants, c, d, e, and f, $\text{cov}(c + d\,y_1, e + f\,y_2) = df\,\text{cov}(y_1, y_2)$.

The data that we use in building econometric models either come from experiments or, more commonly, are observed in the 'real world'. The outcomes from an experiment can often only take on certain specific values – i.e. they are discrete random variables. For example, the sum of the scores from following two dice could only be a number between two (if we throw two ones) and twelve (if we throw two sixes). We could calculate the probability of each possible sum occurring and plot it on a diagram, such as figure 2.7. This would be known as a *probability distribution function*. A *probability* is defined to lie between zero and one, with a probability of zero indicating an impossibility and one indicating a certainty. Notice that the sum of the probabilities in the figure is, as always, one.

Most of the time in finance we work with continuous rather than discrete variables, in which case the plot above would be *probability density function* (pdf). The most commonly used distribution to characterise a random variable is a *normal* or *Gaussian* (these terms are equivalent) distribution. The normal distribution is easy to work with since it is symmetric, and the only pieces of information required to completely specify the distribution are its mean and variance, as discussed in chapter 5. The normal distribution is particularly useful because many naturally occurring series follow it – for example, the heights, weights and IQ-levels of people in a given sample.

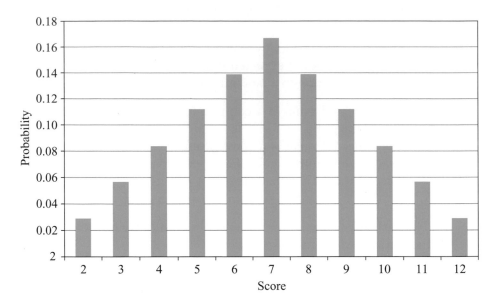

Figure 2.7   The probability distribution function for the sum of two dice

The normal distribution also has several useful mathematical properties. For example, any linear transformation of a normally distributed random variable will still be normally distributed. So, if $y \sim N(\mu, \sigma^2)$, that is, y is normally distributed with mean μ and variance σ^2, then $a + by \sim N(b\mu + a, b^2\sigma^2)$ where a and b are scalars. Furthermore, any linear combination of independent normally distributed random variables is itself normally distributed.

Suppose that we have a normally distributed random variable with mean μ and variance σ^2. Its *probability density function* is given by $f(y)$ in the following expression

$$f(y) = \frac{1}{\sqrt{2\pi}\sigma}e^{-(y-\mu)^2/2\sigma^2} \tag{2.17}$$

Entering values of y into this expression would trace out the familiar 'bell-shape' of the normal distribution described in figure 2.8.

A standard normally distributed random variable can be obtained from this by subtracting the mean and dividing by the standard deviation (the square root of the variance). The standard normally distributed random variable would then be written

$$Z = \frac{y - \mu}{\sigma} \sim N(0, 1)$$

It is usually easier to work with the normal distribution in its standardised form.

We can use the pdf to calculate the probability that the random variable lies within a certain range – e.g. what is the probability that y lies between 0.2 and 0.3? To obtain this, we would plug $y = 0.2$ and then $y = 0.3$ into equation (2.17) above and calculate the corresponding value of $f(y)$ in each case. Then the difference between these two values of $f(y)$ would give us the answer.

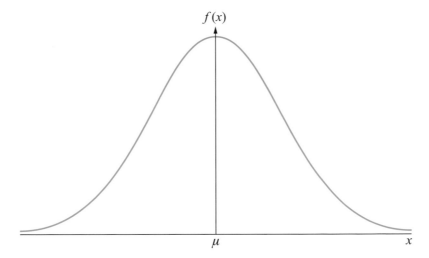

$f(x)$

μ

x

Figure 2.8   The pdf for a normal distribution

Note that for a continuous random variable, the probability that it is *exactly* equal to a particular number is always zero by definition. This is because the variable could take on any value – for example it could be exactly 1 or 0.99999 or 1.01 or 1.0000001, etc.

More often, rather than wanting to determine the probability that a random variable lies within a range, we instead want to know the probability that the variable is below a certain value (or above a certain value). So, for example, what is the probability that y is less than 0.4? Effectively, we want to know the probability that y lies between $-\infty$ and 0.4. This information is given by the *cumulative density function* (cdf), which is written $F(y)$. Thus the probability that y is less than (or equal to) some specific value of y, y_0, is equal to the cdf of y evaluated where $y = y_0$

$$P(y \leq y_0) = F(y_0)$$

The cdf for a normally distributed random variable has a sigmoid shape as in figure 2.9. Table A2.1 in appendix 2 at the back of this book presents what are known as the critical values for the normal distribution. Effectively, if we plotted the values on the first row, α against the values in the second row, Z_α, then we would trace out the cdf. Looking at the table, if $\alpha = 0.1$, $Z_\alpha = 1.2816$. So 10% (0.1 in proportion terms) of the normal distribution lies to the right of 1.2816. In other words, the probability that a standard normal random variable takes a value greater than 1.2816 is 10%. Similarly, the probability that it takes a value greater than 3.0902 is 0.1% (i.e. 0.001). We know that the standard normal distribution is symmetric about zero so if $P(Z \geq 1.2816) = 0.1$, $P(Z \leq -1.2816) = 0.1$ as well. Note that there are also alternative versions of the normal distribution table that present the information the other way around, so that they show many values of Z_α and the corresponding values of α – i.e. for a given value of Z, say 1.5, they

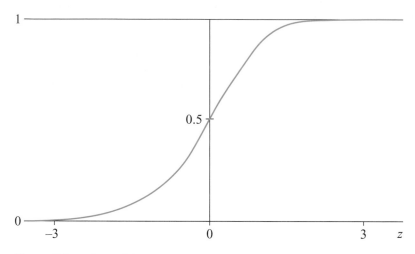

Figure 2.9　The cdf for a normal distribution

show the probability of a standard normally distributed random variable being bigger than this.

2.4.1 The central limit theorem

If a random sample of size N: $y_1, y_2, y_3, \ldots, y_N$ is drawn from a population that is normally distributed with mean μ and variance σ^2, the sample mean, $\bar{y}$ is also normally distributed with mean μ and variance σ^2/N. In fact, an important rule in statistics known as the *central limit theorem* states that the sampling distribution of the mean of any random sample of observations will tend towards the normal distribution with mean equal to the population mean, μ, as the sample size tends to infinity. This theorem is a very powerful result because it states that the sample mean, $\bar{y}$, will follow a normal distribution even if the original observations $(y_1, y_2, \ldots, y_N)$ did not. This means that we can use the normal distribution as a kind of benchmark when testing hypotheses, as discussed more fully in the next chapter.

2.4.2 Other statistical distributions

There are many statistical distributions, including the binomial, Poisson, log normal, normal, exponential, t, chi-squared and F, and each has its own characteristic pdf. Different kinds of random variables will be best modelled with different distributions. Many of the statistical distributions are also related to one another, and most (except the normal) have one or more *degrees of freedom* parameters that determine the location and shape of the distribution. For example, the chi-squared (denoted χ^2) distribution can be obtained by taking the sum of the squares of independent normally distributed random variables. If we sum n independent squared normals, the result will be a χ^2 with n degrees of freedom. Since it comprises the sum of squares, the chi-squared distribution can only take positive values. Unlike the normal distribution, the chi-squared is not symmetric about its mean value.

The F-distribution, which has two degrees of freedom parameters, is the ratio of independent chi-squared distributions, each divided by their degrees of freedom. Suppose that $y_1 \sim \chi^2(n_1)$ and $y_2 \sim \chi^2(n_2)$ are two independent chi-squared distributions with n_1 and n_2 degrees of freedom respectively. Then the ratio will follow an F distribution with (n_1, n_2) degrees of freedom

$$\frac{y_1/n_1}{y_2/n_2} \sim F(n_1, n_2)$$

The final, and arguably most important, distribution used in econometrics is the t-distribution. The normal distribution is a special case of the t. The t-distribution can also be obtained by taking a standard normally distributed random variable, Z, and dividing it by the square root of an independent chi-squared distributed random variable (suppose that the latter is called y_1), itself divided by its degrees of freedom, n_1

$$\frac{Z}{\sqrt{y_1/n_1}} \sim t(n)$$

The t-distribution is symmetric about zero and looks similar to the normal distribution except that it is flatter and wider. It will be discussed in considerable detail in chapter 3 onwards.

2.5 Descriptive statistics

When analysing a series containing many observations, it is useful to be able to describe the most important characteristics of the series using a small number of summary measures. This section discusses the quantities that are most commonly used to describe financial and economic series, which are known as *summary statistics* or *descriptive statistics*. Descriptive statistics are calculated from a sample of data rather than assigned based on theory. Before describing the most important summary statistics used in work with finance data, we define the terms *population* and *sample*, which have precise meanings in statistics, in box 2.4.

2.5.1 Measures of central tendency

The average value of a series is sometimes known as its *measure of location* or *measure of central tendency*. The average value is usually thought to measure the 'typical' value of a series. There are a number of methods that can be used for calculating averages. The most well-known of these is the *arithmetic mean* (usually just termed 'the mean'), denoted $\bar{r}_A$ for a series r_i of length N, which is simply calculated as the sum of all values in the series divided by the number of values

$$\bar{r}_A = \frac{1}{N} \sum_{i=1}^{N} r_i \tag{2.18}$$

Box 2.4   The population and the sample

- The *population* is the total collection of all objects to be studied. For example, in the context of determining the relationship between risk and return for UK stocks, the population of interest would be all time series observations on all stocks traded on the London Stock Exchange (LSE).
- The population may be either finite or infinite, while a sample is a selection of *just some items from the population*. A population is finite if it contains a fixed number of elements. In general, either all of the observations for the entire population will not be available, or they may be so many in number that it is infeasible to work with them, in which case a *sample* of data is taken for analysis.
- The sample is usually *random*, and it should be *representative* of the population of interest. A random sample is one in which each individual item in the population is equally likely to be drawn.
- A *stratified sample* is obtained when the population is split into *layers* or *strata* and the number of observations in each layer of the sample is set to try to match the corresponding number of elements in those layers of the population.
- The *size of the sample* is the number of observations that are available, or that the researcher decides to use, in estimating the parameters of the model.

The two other methods for calculating the average of a series are the *mode* and the *median*. The mode measures the most frequently occurring value in a series, which is sometimes regarded as a more representative measure of the average than the mean. Finally, the *median* is the middle value in a series when the elements are arranged in an ascending order.[3] If there is an even number of values in a series, then strictly there are two medians. For example, consider a variable that has taken the values listed in order: $\{3, 7, 11, 15, 22, 24\}$, the medians are 11 and 15. Sometimes we take the mean of the two medians, so that the median would be $(11 + 15)/2 = 13$.

Each of these measures of average has its relative merits and demerits. The mean is the most familiar method to most researchers, but can be unduly affected by extreme values, and in such cases, it may not be representative of most of the data. The mode is arguably the easiest to obtain, but is not suitable for continuous, non-integer data (e.g. returns or yields) or for distributions that incorporate two or more peaks (known as bimodal and multi-modal distributions respectively). The median is often considered to be a useful representation of the 'typical' value

---

[3] A more precise and complete definition of the median is surprisingly complex but is not necessary for our purposes.

of a series, but has the drawback that its calculation is based essentially on one observation. Thus if, for example, we had a series containing ten observations and we were to double the values of the top three data points, the median would be unchanged.

The geometric mean

There also exists another method that can be used to estimate the average of a series, known as the *geometric mean*. It involves calculating the Nth root of the product of N numbers. In other words, if we want to find the geometric mean of six numbers, we multiply them together and take the sixth root (i.e. raise the product to the power of $\frac{1}{6}$).

In finance, we usually deal with returns or percentage changes rather than prices or actual values, and the method for calculating the geometric mean just described cannot handle negative numbers. Therefore, we use a slightly different approach in such cases. To calculate the geometric mean of a set of N returns, we express them as proportions (i.e. on a $(-1, 1)$ scale) rather than percentages (on a $(-100, 100)$ scale), and we would use the formula

$$\overline{R}_G = [(1 + r_1)(1 + r_2) \ldots (1 + r_N)]^{1/N} - 1 \tag{2.19}$$

where $r_1, r_2, \ldots, r_N$ are the returns and $\overline{R}_G$ is the calculated value of the geometric mean. Hence what we would do would be to add one to each return, then multiply the resulting expressions together, raise this product to the power $1/N$ and then subtract one right at the end.

So which method for calculating the mean should we use? The answer is, as usual, that 'it depends'. Geometric returns give the fixed return on the asset or portfolio that would have been required to match the actual performance, which is not the case for the arithmetic mean. Thus, if you assumed that the arithmetic mean return had been earned on the asset every year, you would not reach the correct value of the asset or portfolio at the end.

But it could be shown that the geometric return is always less than or equal to the arithmetic return, and so the geometric return is a downward-biased predictor of future performance. Hence, if the objective is to summarise historical performance, the geometric mean is more appropriate, but if we want to forecast future returns, the arithmetic mean is the one to use. Finally, it is worth noting that the geometric mean is evidently less intuitive and less commonly used than the arithmetic mean, but it is less affected by extreme outliers than the latter. There is an approximate relationship which holds between the arithmetic and geometric mean, calculated using the same set of returns

$$\overline{R}_G \approx \bar{r}_A - \frac{1}{2}\sigma^2 \tag{2.20}$$

where $\overline{R}_G$ and $\bar{r}_A$ are the geometric and arithmetic means respectively and σ^2 is the variance of the returns.

2.5.2   Measures of spread

Usually, the average value of a series will be insufficient to adequately characterise a data series, since two series may have the same mean but very different profiles because the observations on one of the series may be much more widely spread about the mean than the other. Hence, another important feature of a series is how dispersed its values are. In finance theory, for example, the more widely spread are returns around their mean value, the more risky the asset is usually considered to be.

The simplest measure of spread is arguably the *range*, which is calculated by subtracting the smallest observation from the largest. While the range has some uses, it is fatally flawed as a measure of dispersion by its extreme sensitivity to an outlying observation since it is effectively based only on the very lowest and very highest values in a series.

A more reliable measure of spread, although it is not widely employed by quantitative analysts, is the *semi-interquartile range*, sometimes known as the *quartile deviation*. Calculating this measure involves first ordering the data and then splitting the sample into four parts (*quartiles*) with equal numbers of observations.[4] The second quartile will be exactly at the half way point, and is the median, as described above. But the interquartile range focuses on the first and third quartiles, which will be at the quarter and three-quarter points in the ordered series, and which can be calculated respectively by the following

$$Q_1 = \left(\frac{N+1}{4}\right)^{th} value$$
(2.21)

and

$$Q_3 = \frac{3}{4}(N+1)^{th} value$$
(2.22)

The interquartile range is then given by the difference between the two

$$IQR = Q_3 - Q_1$$
(2.23)

This measure of spread is usually considered superior to the range since it is not so heavily influenced by one or two extreme outliers that by definition would be right at the end of an ordered series and so would affect the range. However, the semi-interquartile range still only incorporates two of the observations in the entire sample, and thus another more familiar measure of spread, the *variance*, is very widely used. It is interpreted as the average squared deviation of each data point about its mean value, and is calculated using the usual formula for the variance of a sample from a variable y

$$\sigma^2 = \frac{\sum(y_i - \overline{y})^2}{N-1}$$
(2.24)

[4] Note that there are several slightly different formulae that can be used for calculating quartiles, each of which may provide slightly different answers.

Another measure of spread, the standard deviation, is calculated by taking the square root of the variance formula given in the previous equation

$$\sigma = \sqrt{\frac{\sum (y_i - \overline{y})^2}{N - 1}}. \tag{2.25}$$

The squares of the deviations from the mean are taken rather than the deviations themselves to ensure that positive and negative deviations (for points above and below the average respectively) do not cancel each other out.

While there is little to choose between the variance and the standard deviation in terms of which is the best measure, the latter is sometimes preferred since it will have the same units as the variable whose spread is being measured, whereas the variance will have units of the square of the variable. Both measures share the advantage that they encapsulate information from all the available data points, unlike the range and quartile deviation, although they can also be heavily influenced by outliers (but to a lesser degree than the range). The quartile deviation is an appropriate measure of spread if the median is used to define the average value of the series, while the variance or standard deviation will be appropriate if the arithmetic mean constitutes the measure of central tendency adopted.

Before moving on, it is worth discussing why the denominator in the formulae for the variance and standard deviation includes $N - 1$ rather than N, the sample size. Subtracting one from the number of available data points is known as a *degrees of freedom correction*, and this is necessary since the spread is being calculated about the mean of the series, and this mean has had to be estimated as well. Thus the spread measures described above are known as the *sample* variance and the *sample* standard deviation. Had we been observing the entire population of data rather than a mere sample from it, then the formulae would not need a degrees of freedom correction and we would divide by N rather than $N - 1$.

A further measure of dispersion is the *negative semi-variance*, which also gives rise to the *negative semi-standard deviation*. These measures use identical formulae to those described above for the variance and standard deviation, but when calculating their values, only those observations for which $y_i < \overline{y}$ are used in the sum, and N now denotes the number of such observations. This measure is sometimes useful if the observations are not symmetric about their mean value (i.e. if the distribution is *skewed* – see the next section).[5]

A final statistic that has some uses for measuring dispersion is the *coefficient of variation*, CV. This is obtained by dividing the standard deviation by the arithmetic mean of the series:

$$CV = \frac{\sigma}{\overline{y}} \tag{2.26}$$

CV is useful where we want to make comparisons across series. Since the standard deviation has units of the series under investigation, it will scale with that series.

---

[5] Of course, we could also define the positive semi-variance where only observations such that $y_i > \overline{y}$ are included in the sum.

Thus, if we wanted to compare the spread of monthly apartment rental values in London with those in Reading, say, using the standard deviation would be misleading as the average rental value in London will be much bigger. By *normalising* the standard deviation, the coefficient of variation is a unit-free (*dimensionless*) measure of spread and so could be used more appropriately to compare the series.

2.5.3 Higher moments

If the observations for a given set of data follow a normal distribution, then the mean and variance are sufficient to entirely describe the series. In other words, it is impossible to have two different normal distributions with the same mean and variance. However, most samples of data do not follow a normal distribution, and therefore we also need what are known as the *higher moments* of a series to fully characterise it. The mean and the variance are the first and second moments of a distribution respectively, and the (standardised) third and fourth moments are known as the *skewness* and *kurtosis* respectively. Skewness defines the shape of the distribution, and measures the extent to which it is not symmetric about its mean value. When the distribution of data is symmetric and unimodal (i.e. it only has one peak rather than many), the three methods for calculating the average (mean, mode and median) of the sample will be equal. If the distribution is positively skewed (where there is a long right hand tail and most of the data are bunched over to the left), the ordering will be *mean > median > mode*, whereas if the distribution is negatively skewed (a long left hand tail and most of the data bunched on the right), the ordering will be the opposite. A normally distributed series has zero skewness (i.e. it is symmetric).

Kurtosis measures the fatness of the tails of the distribution and how peaked at the mean the series is. A normal distribution is defined to have a coefficient of kurtosis equal to 3. It is possible to define a coefficient of excess kurtosis, equal to the coefficient of kurtosis minus 3; a normal distribution will thus have a coefficient of excess kurtosis of zero. A normal distribution is said to be *mesokurtic*. Denoting the observations on a series by y_i and their variance by σ^2, it can be shown that the coefficients of skewness and kurtosis can be calculated respectively as

$$skew = \frac{\frac{1}{N-1}\sum(y_i - \overline{y})^3}{(\sigma^2)^{3/2}} \tag{2.27}$$

and

$$kurt = \frac{\frac{1}{N-1}\sum(y_i - \overline{y})^4}{(\sigma^2)^2} \tag{2.28}$$

The kurtosis of the normal distribution is 3 so its excess kurtosis (*kurt* − 3) is zero.[6]

---

[6] There are a number of ways to calculate skewness (and kurtosis); the one given in the formula is sometimes known as the moment coefficient of skewness, but it could also be measured using the standardised difference between the mean and the median, or by using the quartiles of the data.

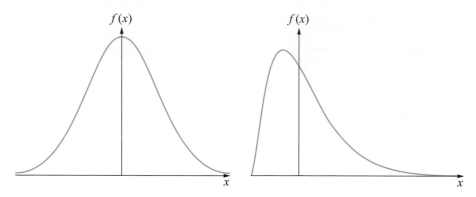

Figure 2.10   A normal versus a skewed distribution

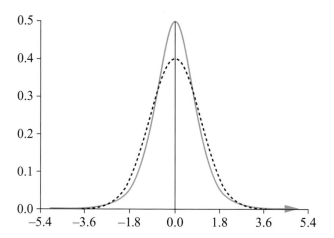

Figure 2.11   A normal versus a leptokurtic distribution

To give some illustrations of what a series having specific departures from normality may look like, consider figures 2.10 and 2.11. A normal distribution is symmetric about its mean, while a skewed distribution will not be, but will have one tail longer than the other. A leptokurtic distribution is one which has fatter tails and is more peaked at the mean than a normally distributed random variable with the same mean and variance, while a platykurtic distribution will be less peaked in the mean, will have thinner tails, and more of the distribution in the shoulders than a normal. In practice, a leptokurtic distribution is more likely to characterise real estate (and economic) time series, and to characterise the residuals from a time series model. In figure 2.11, the leptokurtic distribution is shown by the bold line, with the normal by the faint line. There is a formal test for normality, and this will be described and discussed in chapter 5.

Unfortunately, this implies that different software packages will give slightly different values for the skewness and kurtosis coefficients. Also, some packages make a 'degrees of freedom correction' as we do in the equations here, while others do not, so that the divisor in such cases would be N rather than $N - 1$ in the equations.

Screenshot 2.6   **Sample summary statistics in EViews**

Calculating summary statistics in EViews

We will now re-use the house price data from chapter 1 to examine the summary
statistics of the returns (the percentage changes in the logs of the house prices).
So **re-open the house price EViews workfile** and **click on the DHP series**
to bring up the spreadsheet view. Then **click View/Descriptive Statistics &
Tests/Stats Table** to see screenshot 2.6 containing some simple summary statistics. We can see that the mean house price is around 0.44% per month while the
median is slightly larger at 0.49%. The highest monthly price increase was 3.8%,
while the biggest fall was 3.4%. The standard deviation is 1.2%, which is quite
small compared with stocks (see the next chapter) and reflects the smoothness of
house prices over time. The series has a negative skew so it has a slightly longer
lower tail than the upper tail. The series is also leptokurtic and so has fatter tails
than a normal distribution with the same mean and variance; there are a total of
268 return observations. EViews also tells us whether the series shows significant
departures from normality which in this case it does not (more on this in chapter 5).

If we wanted to calculate less well known statistics including the interquartile
range, coefficient of variation and so on, it would be easier to do this using
the functions built into Excel. For example, to get the interquartile range of the
percentage returns we would first need to **construct a column of returns**
and then use the QUARTILE function twice to get the third and first quartiles.
We would write =**QUARTILE(C3:C270,3)–QUARTILE(C3:C270,1)** if the

returns data were in column C. Similarly, we could easily calculate the coefficient of variation using the standard deviation of returns divided by their mean using the formula =**STDEV(C3:C270)/AVERAGE(C3:C270)**. If we calculated these for the house price returns we would get $IQR = 0.685$ and $CV = 2.78$.

2.5.4 Measures of association

The summary measures we have examined so far have looked at each series in isolation. However, it is also very often of interest to consider the links between variables. There are two key descriptive statistics that are used for measuring the relationships between series: the covariance and the correlation.

Covariance

The *covariance* is a measure of linear association between two variables and represents the simplest and most common way to enumerate the relationship between them. It measures whether they on average move in the same direction (positive covariance), in opposite directions (negative covariance), or have no association (zero covariance). The formula for calculating the covariance, $\sigma_{x,y}$, between two series, x and y is given by

$$\sigma_{x,y} = \frac{\sum (x_i - \bar{x})(y_i - \bar{y})}{(N - 1)} \tag{2.29}$$

Correlation

A fundamental weakness of the covariance as a measure of association is that it scales with the standard deviations of the two series, so it has units of $x \times y$. Thus, for example, multiplying all of the values of series y by ten will increase the covariance tenfold, but it will not really increase the true association between the series since they will be no more strongly related than they were before the rescaling. The implication is that the particular numerical value that the covariance takes has no useful interpretation on its own and hence is not particularly useful. Therefore, the *correlation* takes the covariance and standardises or normalises it so that it is unit free. The result of this standardisation is that the correlation is bounded to lie on the $(-1,1)$ interval. A correlation of 1 (-1) indicates a perfect positive (negative) association between the series. The correlation measure, usually known as the *correlation coefficient*, is often denoted $\rho_{x,y}$, and is calculated as

$$\rho_{x,y} = \frac{\sum (x_i - \bar{x})(y_i - \bar{y})}{(N - 1)\sigma_x \sigma_y} = \frac{\sigma_{x,y}}{\sigma_x \sigma_y} \tag{2.30}$$

where σ_x and σ_y are the standard deviations of x and y respectively. This measure is more strictly known as *Pearson's product moment correlation*.

Copulas

Covariance and correlation provide simple measures of association between series. However, as is well known, they are very limited measures in the sense that they are linear and are not sufficiently flexible to provide full descriptions of the relationship between financial series in reality. In particular, new types of assets and structures in finance have led to increasingly complex dependencies that cannot be satisfactorily modelled in this simple framework. *Copulas* provide an alternative way to link together the individual (*marginal*) distributions of series to model their joint distribution. One attractive feature of copulas is that they can be applied to link together any marginal distributions that are proposed for the individual series. The most commonly used copulas are the Gaussian and Clayton copulas. They are particularly useful for modelling the relationships between the tails of series, and find applications in stress testing and simulation analysis. For introductions to this area and applications in finance and risk management, see Nelsen (2006) and Embrechts *et al.* (2003).

Key concepts

The key terms to be able to define and explain from this chapter are

- functions
- turning points
- sigma notation
- quadratic equation
- inverse of a matrix
- eigenvalues
- mean
- skewness
- covariance
- population

- roots
- derivatives
- logarithm
- conformable matrix
- rank of a matrix
- eigenvectors
- variance
- kurtosis
- correlation
- sample

Self-study questions

1. (a) If $f(x) = 3x^2 - 4x + 2$, find $f(0)$, $f(2)$, $f(-1)$
   (b) If $f(x) = 4x^2 + 2x - 3$, find $f(0)$, $f(3)$, $f(a)$, $f(3 + a)$
   (c) Considering your answers to the previous question part, in general does $f(a) + f(b) = f(a + b)$? Explain.

2. Simplify the following as much as possible
   (a) $4x^5 \times 6x^3$
   (b) $3x^2 \times 4y^2 \times 8x^4 \times -2y^4$
   (c) $(4p^2 q^3)^3$
   (d) $6x^5 \div 3x^2$
   (e) $7y^2 \div 2y^5$

(f) $\dfrac{3(xy)^3 \times 6(xz)^4}{2(xy)^2 x^3}$

(g) $(xy)^3 \div x^3 y^3$

(h) $(xy)^3 - x^3 y^3$

3. Solve the following
   (a) $125^{1/3}$
   (b) $64^{1/3}$
   (c) $16^{1/4}$
   (d) $9^{3/2}$
   (e) $9^{2/3}$
   (f) $81^{1/2} + 64^{1/2} + 64^{1/3}$

4. Write each of the following as a prime number raised to a power
   (a) 9
   (b) 625
   (c) 125^{-1}

5. Solve the following equations
   (a) $3x - 6 = 6x - 12$
   (b) $2x - 304x + 8 = x + 9 - 3x + 4$
   (c) $\frac{x+3}{2} = \frac{2x-6}{3}$

6. Write out all of the terms in the following and evaluate them
   (a) $\sum_{j=1}^{3} j$
   (b) $\sum_{j=2}^{5}(j^2 + j + 3)$
   (c) $\sum_{i=1}^{n} x$ with $n = 4$ and $x = 3$
   (d) $\prod_{j=1}^{3} x$ with $x = 2$
   (e) $\prod_{i=3}^{6} i$

7. Write the equations for each of the following lines
   (a) Gradient $= 3$, intercept $= -1$
   (b) Gradient $= -2$, intercept $= 4$
   (c) Gradient $= \frac{1}{2}$, crosses y-axis at 3
   (d) Gradient $= \frac{1}{2}$, crosses x-axis at 3
   (e) Intercept 2 and passing through $(3,1)$
   (f) Gradient 4 and passing through $(-2,-2)$
   (g) Passes through $x - 4, y = 2$ and $x = -2, y = 6$

8. Differentiate the following functions twice with respect to x
   (a) $y = 6x$
   (b) $y = 3x^2 + 2$
   (c) $y = 4x^3 + 10$
   (d) $y = \frac{1}{x}$
   (e) $y = x$
   (f) $y = 7$
   (g) $y = 6x^{-3} + \frac{6}{x^3}$
   (h) $y = 3 \ln x$
   (i) $y = \ln(3x^2)$
   (j) $y = \dfrac{3x^4 - 6x^2 - x - 4}{x^3}$

9. Differentiate the following functions partially with respect to x and (separately) partially with respect to y
   (a) $z = 10x^3 + 6y^2 - 7y$
   (b) $z = 10xy^2 - 6$
   (c) $z = 6x$
   (d) $z = 4$

10. Factorise the following expressions
    (a) $x^2 - 7x - 8$
    (b) $5x - 2x^2$
    (c) $2x^2 - x - 3$
    (d) $6 + 5x - 4x^2$
    (e) $54 - 15x - 25x^2$

11. Express the following in logarithmic form
    (a) $5^3 = 125$
    (b) $11^2 = 121$
    (c) $6^4 = 1296$

12. Evaluate the following (without using a calculator)
    (a) $\log_{10} 10000$
    (b) $\log_2 16$
    (c) $\log_{10} 0.01$
    (d) $\log_5 125$
    (e) $\log_e e^2$

13. Express the following logarithms using powers
    (a) $\log_5 3125 = 5$
    (b) $\log_{49} 7 = \frac{1}{2}$
    (c) $\log_{0.5} 8 = -3$

14. Write the following as simply as possible as sums of logs of prime numbers
    (a) $\log 60$
    (b) $\log 300$

15. Simplify the following as far as possible
    (a) $\log 27 - \log 9 + \log 81$
    (b) $\log 8 - \log 4 + \log 32$

16. Solve the following
    (a) $\log x^4 - \log x^3 = \log 5x - \log 2x$
    (b) $\log(x - 1) + \log(x + 1) = 2\log(x + 2)$
    (c) $\log_{10} x = 4$

17. Use the result that $\log(8)$ is approximately 2.1 to estimate the following (without using a calculator):
    (a) $\log(16)$
    (b) $\log(64)$
    (c) $\log(4)$

18. Solve the following using logs and a calculator
    (a) $4^x = 6$
    (b) $4^{2x} = 3$
    (c) $3^{2x-1} = 8$

19. Find the minima of the following functions. In each case, state the value of the function at the minimum
    (a) $y = 6x^2 - 10x - 8$
    (b) $y = (6x^2 - 8)^2$
20. Construct an example not used elsewhere in this book to demonstrate that for two conformable matrices A and B, $(AB)^{-1} = B^{-1}A^{-1}$.
21. Suppose that we have the following four matrices

$$A = \begin{bmatrix} 1 & 6 \\ -2 & 4 \end{bmatrix}, B = \begin{bmatrix} -3 & -8 \\ 6 & 4 \end{bmatrix}, C = \begin{bmatrix} 1 & 2 & 3 \\ 4 & 5 & 6 \end{bmatrix}, D = \begin{bmatrix} 6 & -2 \\ 0 & -1 \\ 3 & 0 \end{bmatrix}$$

   (a) Which pairs of matrices can be validly multiplied together? For these pairs, perform the multiplications.
   (b) Calculate $2A$, $3B$, $\frac{1}{2}D$
   (c) Calculate $\text{Tr}(A)$, $\text{Tr}(B)$, $\text{Tr}(A + B)$ and verify that $\text{Tr}(A) + \text{Tr}(B) = \text{Tr}(A + B)$
   (d) What is the rank of the matrix A?
   (e) Find the eigenvalues of the matrix $(A + B)$
   (f) What will be the trace of the identity matrix of order 12?
22. (a) Add

$$\begin{bmatrix} 2 & -1 \\ -7 & 4 \end{bmatrix} \quad \text{to} \quad \begin{bmatrix} -3 & 0 \\ 7 & -4 \end{bmatrix}$$

   (b) Subtract

$$\begin{bmatrix} -3 & 0 \\ 7 & -4 \end{bmatrix} \quad \text{from} \quad \begin{bmatrix} 2 & -1 \\ -7 & 4 \end{bmatrix}$$

   (c) Calculate the inverse of

$$\begin{bmatrix} 3 & -1 \\ -4 & 2 \end{bmatrix}$$

   (d) Does the inverse of the following matrix exist? Explain your answer

$$\begin{bmatrix} 3 & 2 \\ 3 & 2 \end{bmatrix}$$

23. Expand the parentheses as far as possible for the following expressions
    (a) $E(ax + by)$ for x,y variables and a,b scalars
    (b) $E(axy)$ for x,y independent variables and a a scalar
    (c) $E(axy)$ for x,y correlated variables and a a scalar
24. (a) Explain the difference between a pdf and a cdf
    (b) What shapes are the pdf and cdf for a normally distributed random variable?
25. What is the central limit theorem and why is it important in statistics?

26. Explain the differences between the mean, mode and median. Which is the most useful measure of an average and why?
27. Which is a more useful measure of central tendency for stock returns – the arithmetic mean or the geometric mean? Explain your answer.
28. The covariance between two variables is 0.99. Are they strongly related? Explain your answer.

3 A brief overview of the classical linear regression model

Learning outcomes

In this chapter, you will learn how to

- Derive the OLS formulae for estimating parameters and their standard errors
- Explain the desirable properties that a good estimator should have
- Discuss the factors that affect the sizes of standard errors
- Test hypotheses using the test of significance and confidence interval approaches
- Interpret p-values
- Estimate regression models and test single hypotheses in EViews

3.1 What is a regression model?

Regression analysis is almost certainly the most important tool at the econometrician's disposal. But what is regression analysis? In very general terms, regression is concerned with describing and evaluating the *relationship between a given variable and one or more other variables*. More specifically, regression is an attempt to explain movements in a variable by reference to movements in one or more other variables.

To make this more concrete, denote the variable whose movements the regression seeks to explain by y and the variables which are used to explain those variations by $x_1, x_2, \ldots, x_k$. Hence, in this relatively simple setup, it would be said that variations in k variables (the xs) cause changes in some other variable, y. This chapter will be limited to the case where the model seeks to explain changes in only one variable y (although this restriction will be removed in chapter 7).

There are various completely interchangeable names for y and the xs, and all of these terms will be used synonymously in this book (see box 3.1).

Box 3.1   Names for y and xs in regression models

Names for y	*Names for the xs*
Dependent variable	Independent variables
Regressand	Regressors
Effect variable	Causal variables
Explained variable	Explanatory variables

3.2   Regression versus correlation

As discussed in chapter 2, the correlation between two variables measures the *degree of linear association* between them. If it is stated that y and x are correlated, it means that y and x are being treated in a completely symmetrical way. Thus, it is not implied that changes in x cause changes in y, or indeed that changes in y cause changes in x. Rather, it is simply stated that there is evidence for a linear relationship between the two variables, and that movements in the two are on average related to an extent given by the correlation coefficient.

In regression, the dependent variable (y) and the independent variable(s) (xs) are treated very differently. The y variable is assumed to be random or 'stochastic' in some way, i.e. to have a *probability distribution*. The x variables are, however, assumed to have fixed ('non-stochastic') values in repeated samples.[1] Regression as a tool is more flexible and more powerful than correlation.

3.3   Simple regression

For simplicity, suppose for now that it is believed that y depends on only one x variable. Again, this is of course a severely restricted case, but the case of more explanatory variables will be considered in the next chapter. Three examples of the kind of relationship that may be of interest include:

- How asset returns vary with their level of market risk
- Measuring the long-term relationship between stock prices and dividends
- Constructing an optimal hedge ratio.

Suppose that a researcher has some idea that there should be a relationship between two variables y and x, and that financial theory suggests that an increase in x will lead to an increase in y. A sensible first stage to testing whether there is indeed an association between the variables would be to form a scatter plot of them. Suppose that the outcome of this plot is figure 3.1.

In this case, it appears that there is an approximate positive linear relationship between x and y which means that increases in x are usually accompanied by

---

[1] Strictly, the assumption that the xs are non-stochastic is stronger than required, an issue that will be discussed in more detail in chapter 5.

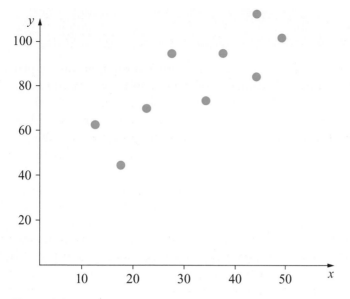

Figure 3.1   Scatter plot of two variables, y and x

increases in y, and that the relationship between them can be described approximately by a straight line. It would be possible to draw by hand onto the graph a line that appears to fit the data. The intercept and slope of the line fitted by eye could then be measured from the graph. However, in practice such a method is likely to be laborious and inaccurate.

It would therefore be of interest to determine to what extent this relationship can be described by an equation that can be estimated using a defined procedure. It is possible to use the general equation for a straight line

$$y = \alpha + \beta x \tag{3.1}$$

to get the line that best 'fits' the data. The researcher would then be seeking to find the values of the parameters or coefficients, α and β, which would place the line as close as possible to all of the data points taken together.

However, this equation ($y = \alpha + \beta x$) is an exact one. Assuming that this equation is appropriate, if the values of α and β had been calculated, then given a value of x, it would be possible to determine with certainty what the value of y would be. Imagine – a model which says with complete certainty what the value of one variable will be given any value of the other!

Clearly this model is not realistic. Statistically, it would correspond to the case where the model fitted the data perfectly – that is, all of the data points lay exactly on a straight line. To make the model more realistic, a random disturbance term, denoted by u, is added to the equation, thus

$$y_t = \alpha + \beta x_t + u_t \tag{3.2}$$

where the subscript t ($= 1, 2, 3, \ldots$) denotes the observation number. The disturbance term can capture a number of features (see box 3.2).

Box 3.2   Reasons for the inclusion of the disturbance term

- Even in the general case where there is more than one explanatory variable, some determinants of y_t will always in practice be omitted from the model. This might, for example, arise because the number of influences on y is too large to place in a single model, or because some determinants of y may be unobservable or not measurable.
- There may be errors in the way that y is measured which cannot be modelled.
- There are bound to be random outside influences on y that again cannot be modelled. For example, a terrorist attack, a hurricane or a computer failure could all affect financial asset returns in a way that cannot be captured in a model and cannot be forecast reliably. Similarly, many researchers would argue that human behaviour has an inherent randomness and unpredictability!

So how are the appropriate values of α and β determined? α and β are chosen so that the (vertical) distances from the data points to the fitted lines are minimised (so that the line fits the data as closely as possible). The parameters are thus chosen to minimise collectively the (vertical) distances from the data points to the fitted line. This could be done by 'eye-balling' the data and, for each set of variables y and x, one could form a scatter plot and draw on a line that looks as if it fits the data well by hand, as in figure 3.2.

Note that the *vertical distances* are usually minimised rather than the horizontal distances or those taken perpendicular to the line. This arises as a result of the assumption that x is fixed in repeated samples, so that the problem becomes one of determining the appropriate model for y given (or conditional upon) the observed values of x.

This 'eye-balling' procedure may be acceptable if only indicative results are required, but of course this method, as well as being tedious, is likely to be imprecise. The most common method used to fit a line to the data is known as ordinary least squares (OLS). This approach forms the workhorse of econometric model estimation, and will be discussed in detail in this and subsequent chapters.

Two alternative estimation methods (for determining the appropriate values of the coefficients α and β) are the method of moments and the method of maximum likelihood. A generalised version of the method of moments, due to Hansen (1982), is popular, but beyond the scope of this book. The method of maximum likelihood is also widely employed, and will be discussed in detail in chapter 9.

Suppose now, for ease of exposition, that the sample of data contains only five observations. The method of OLS entails taking each vertical distance from the point to the line, squaring it and then minimising the total sum of the areas

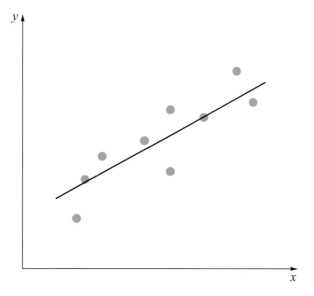

Figure 3.2   Scatter plot of two variables with a line of best fit chosen by eye

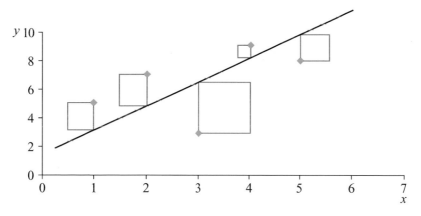

Figure 3.3   Method of OLS fitting a line to the data by minimising the sum of squared residuals

of squares (hence 'least squares'), as shown in figure 3.3. This can be viewed as equivalent to minimising the sum of the areas of the squares drawn from the points to the line.

Tightening up the notation, let y_t denote the actual data point for observation t and let $\hat{y}_t$ denote the fitted value from the regression line – in other words, for the given value of x of this observation t, $\hat{y}_t$ is the value for y which the model would have predicted. Note that a hat (ˆ) over a variable or parameter is used to denote a value estimated by a model. Finally, let $\hat{u}_t$ denote the residual, which is the difference between the actual value of y and the value fitted by the model for this data point – i.e. $(y_t - \hat{y}_t)$. This is shown for just one observation t in figure 3.4.

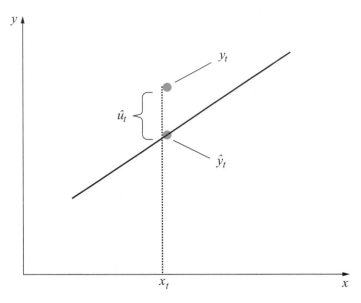

Figure 3.4   Plot of a single observation, together with the line of best fit, the residual and the fitted value

What is done is to minimise the sum of the $\hat{u}_t^2$. The reason that the sum of the squared distances is minimised rather than, for example, finding the sum of $\hat{u}_t$ that is as close to zero as possible, is that in the latter case some points will lie above the line while others lie below it. Then, when the sum to be made as close to zero as possible is formed, the points above the line would count as positive values, while those below would count as negatives. So these distances will in large part cancel each other out, which would mean that one could fit virtually any line to the data, so long as the sum of the distances of the points above the line and the sum of the distances of the points below the line were the same. In that case, there would not be a unique solution for the estimated coefficients. In fact, any fitted line that goes through the mean of the observations (i.e. $\bar{x}$, $\bar{y}$) would set the sum of the $\hat{u}_t$ to zero. However, taking the squared distances ensures that all deviations that enter the calculation are positive and therefore do not cancel out.

So minimising the sum of squared distances is given by minimising $(\hat{u}_1^2 + \hat{u}_2^2 + \hat{u}_3^2 + \hat{u}_4^2 + \hat{u}_5^2)$, or minimising

$$\left(\sum_{t=1}^{5} \hat{u}_t^2 \right)$$

This sum is known as the *residual sum of squares* (RSS) or the sum of squared residuals. But what is $\hat{u}_t$? Again, it is the difference between the actual point and the line, $y_t - \hat{y}_t$. So minimising $\sum_t \hat{u}_t^2$ is equivalent to minimising $\sum_t (y_t - \hat{y}_t)^2$.

Letting $\hat{\alpha}$ and $\hat{\beta}$ denote the values of α and β selected by minimising the RSS, respectively, the equation for the fitted line is given by $\hat{y}_t = \hat{\alpha} + \hat{\beta} x_t$. Now let L denote the RSS, which is also known as a loss function. Take the summation over all of the observations, i.e. from $t = 1$ to T, where T is the number of observations

$$L = \sum_{t=1}^{T} (y_t - \hat{y}_t)^2 = \sum_{t=1}^{T} (y_t - \hat{\alpha} - \hat{\beta} x_t)^2. \tag{3.3}$$

L is minimised with respect to (w.r.t.) $\hat{\alpha}$ and $\hat{\beta}$, to find the values of α and β which minimise the residual sum of squares to give the line that is closest to the data. So L is differentiated w.r.t. $\hat{\alpha}$ and $\hat{\beta}$, setting the first derivatives to zero. A derivation of the OLS estimator is given in the appendix to this chapter. The coefficient estimators for the slope and the intercept are given by

$$\hat{\beta} = \frac{\sum x_t y_t - T\bar{x}\bar{y}}{\sum x_t^2 - T\bar{x}^2} \tag{3.4} \qquad \hat{\alpha} = \bar{y} - \hat{\beta}\bar{x} \tag{3.5}$$

Equations (3.4) and (3.5) state that, given only the sets of observations x_t and y_t, it is always possible to calculate the values of the two parameters, $\hat{\alpha}$ and $\hat{\beta}$, that best fit the set of data. Equation (3.4) is the easiest formula to use to calculate the slope estimate, but the formula can also be written, more intuitively, as

$$\hat{\beta} = \frac{\sum (x_t - \bar{x})(y_t - \bar{y})}{\sum (x_t - \bar{x})^2} \tag{3.6}$$

which is equivalent to the sample covariance between x and y divided by the sample variance of x.

To reiterate, this method of finding the optimum is known as OLS. It is also worth noting that it is obvious from the equation for $\hat{\alpha}$ that the regression line will go through the mean of the observations – i.e. that the point $(\bar{x}, \bar{y})$ lies on the regression line.

Example 3.1 •

Suppose that some data have been collected on the excess returns on a fund manager's portfolio ('fund XXX') together with the excess returns on a market index as shown in table 3.1.

The fund manager has some intuition that the beta (in the CAPM framework) on this fund is positive, and she therefore wants to find whether there appears to be a relationship between x and y given the data. Again, the first stage could be to form a scatter plot of the two variables (figure 3.5).

Clearly, there appears to be a positive, approximately linear relationship between x and y, although there is not much data on which to base this conclusion! Plugging the five observations in to make up the formulae given in (3.4) and (3.5) would lead to the

Table 3.1   Sample data on fund XXX to motivate OLS estimation

Year, t	Excess return on fund XXX $= r_{XXX,t} - r f_t$	Excess return on market index $= rm_t - r f_t$
1	17.8	13.7
2	39.0	23.2
3	12.8	6.9
4	24.2	16.8
5	17.2	12.3

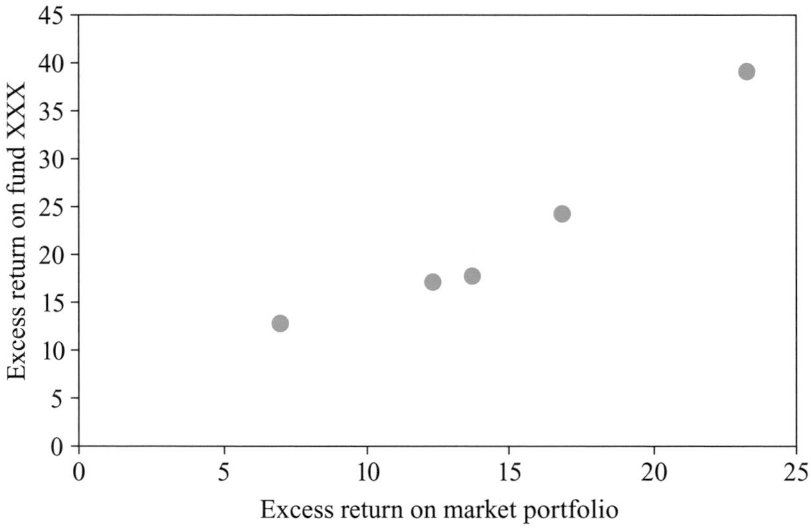

Figure 3.5   Scatter plot of excess returns on fund XXX versus excess returns on the market portfolio

estimates $\hat{\alpha} = -1.74$ and $\hat{\beta} = 1.64$. The fitted line would be written as

$$\hat{y}_t = -1.74 + 1.64x_t \tag{3.7}$$

where x_t is the excess return of the market portfolio over the risk free rate (i.e. $rm - rf$), also known as the *market risk premium*.

3.3.1   What are $\hat{\alpha}$ and $\hat{\beta}$ used for?

This question is probably best answered by posing another question. If an analyst tells you that she expects the market to yield a return 20% higher than the risk-free rate next year, what would you expect the return on fund XXX to be?

The expected value of $y =$ '$-1.74 + 1.64 \times$ value of x', so plug $x = 20$ into (3.7)

$$\hat{y}_t = -1.74 + 1.64 \times 20 = 31.06 \qquad (3.8)$$

Thus, for a given expected market risk premium of 20%, and given its riskiness, fund XXX would be expected to earn an excess over the risk-free rate of approximately 31%. In this setup, the regression beta is also the CAPM beta, so that fund XXX has an estimated beta of 1.64, suggesting that the fund is rather risky. In this case, the residual sum of squares reaches its minimum value of 30.33 with these OLS coefficient values.

Although it may be obvious, it is worth stating that it is not advisable to conduct a regression analysis using only five observations! Thus the results presented here can be considered indicative and for illustration of the technique only. Some further discussions on appropriate sample sizes for regression analysis are given in chapter 5.

The coefficient estimate of 1.64 for β is interpreted as saying that, 'if x increases by 1 unit, y will be expected, everything else being equal, to increase by 1.64 units'. Of course, if $\hat{\beta}$ had been negative, a rise in x would on average cause a fall in y. $\hat{\alpha}$, the intercept coefficient estimate, is interpreted as the value that would be taken by the dependent variable y if the independent variable x took a value of zero. 'Units' here refer to the units of measurement of x_t and y_t. So, for example, suppose that $\hat{\beta} = 1.64$, x is measured in per cent and y is measured in thousands of US dollars. Then it would be said that if x rises by 1%, y will be expected to rise on average by $1.64 thousand (or $1,640). Note that changing the scale of y or x will make no difference to the overall results since the coefficient estimates will change by an off-setting factor to leave the overall relationship between y and x unchanged (see Gujarati, 2003, pp. 169–73 for a proof). Thus, if the units of measurement of y were hundreds of dollars instead of thousands, and everything else remains unchanged, the slope coefficient estimate would be 16.4, so that a 1% increase in x would lead to an increase in y of $16.4 hundreds (or $1,640) as before. All other properties of the OLS estimator discussed below are also invariant to changes in the scaling of the data.

A word of caution is, however, in order concerning the reliability of estimates of the constant term. Although the strict interpretation of the intercept is indeed as stated above, in practice, it is often the case that there are no values of x close to zero in the sample. In such instances, estimates of the value of the intercept will be unreliable. For example, consider figure 3.6, which demonstrates a situation where no points are close to the y-axis.

In such cases, one could not expect to obtain robust estimates of the value of y when x is zero as all of the information in the sample pertains to the case where x is considerably larger than zero.

A similar caution should be exercised when producing predictions for y using values of x that are a long way outside the range of values in the sample. In example 3.1, x takes values between 7% and 23% in the available data. So, it would not be advisable to use this model to determine the expected excess return on the fund if

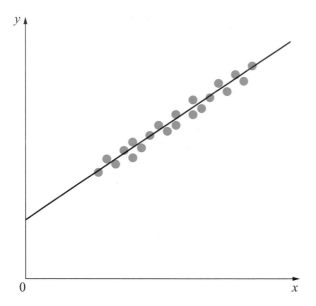

Figure 3.6   No observations close to the y-axis

the expected excess return on the market were, say 1% or 30%, or -5% (i.e. the market was expected to fall).

3.4   Some further terminology

3.4.1   The data generating process, the population regression function and the sample regression function

The population regression function (PRF) is a description of the model that is thought to be generating the actual data and it represents the *true relationship between the variables*. The population regression function is also known as the data generating process (DGP). The PRF embodies the true values of α and β, and is expressed as

$$y_t = \alpha + \beta x_t + u_t \tag{3.9}$$

Note that there is a disturbance term in this equation, so that even if one had at one's disposal the entire population of observations on x and y, it would still in general not be possible to obtain a perfect fit of the line to the data. In some textbooks, a distinction is drawn between the PRF (the underlying true relationship between y and x) and the DGP (the process describing the way that the actual observations on y come about), although in this book, the two terms will be used synonymously.

The sample regression function (SRF) is the relationship that has been estimated using the sample observations, and is often written as

$$\hat{y}_t = \hat{\alpha} + \hat{\beta} x_t \tag{3.10}$$

Notice that there is no error or residual term in (3.10); all this equation states is that given a particular value of x, multiplying it by $\hat{\beta}$ and adding $\hat{\alpha}$ will give the model fitted or expected value for y, denoted $\hat{y}$. It is also possible to write

$$y_t = \hat{\alpha} + \hat{\beta}x_t + \hat{u}_t \tag{3.11}$$

Equation (3.11) splits the observed value of y into two components: the fitted value from the model, and a residual term.

The SRF is used to infer likely values of the PRF. That is, the estimates $\hat{\alpha}$ and $\hat{\beta}$ are constructed, for the sample of data at hand, but what is really of interest is the true relationship between x and y – in other words, the PRF is what is really wanted, but all that is ever available is the SRF. However, what can be said is how likely it is, given the figures calculated for $\hat{\alpha}$ and $\hat{\beta}$, that the corresponding population parameters take on certain values.

3.4.2 Linearity and possible forms for the regression function

In order to use OLS, a model that is *linear* is required. This means that, in the simple bivariate case, the relationship between x and y must be capable of being expressed diagramatically using a straight line. More specifically, the model must be linear in the parameters (α and β), but it does not necessarily have to be linear in the variables (y and x). By 'linear in the parameters', it is meant that the parameters are not multiplied together, divided, squared or cubed, etc.

Models that are not linear in the variables can often be made to take a linear form by applying a suitable transformation or manipulation. For example, consider the following exponential regression model

$$Y_t = A X_t^{\beta} e^{u_t} \tag{3.12}$$

Taking logarithms of both sides, applying the laws of logs and rearranging the right-hand side (RHS)

$$\ln Y_t = \ln(A) + \beta \ln X_t + u_t \tag{3.13}$$

where A and β are parameters to be estimated. Now let $\alpha = \ln(A)$, $y_t = \ln Y_t$ and $x_t = \ln X_t$

$$y_t = \alpha + \beta x_t + u_t \tag{3.14}$$

This is known as an *exponential regression model* since Y varies according to some exponent (power) function of X. In fact, when a regression equation is expressed in 'double logarithmic form', which means that both the dependent and the independent variables are natural logarithms, the coefficient estimates are interpreted as elasticities (strictly, they are unit changes on a logarithmic scale). Thus a coefficient estimate of 1.2 for $\hat{\beta}$ in (3.13) or (3.14) is interpreted as stating that 'a rise in X of 1% will lead on average, everything else being equal, to a rise in Y of 1.2%'. Conversely, for y and x in levels (e.g. (3.9)) rather than logarithmic form, the coefficients denote unit changes as described above.

Similarly, if theory suggests that x should be inversely related to y according to a model of the form

$$y_t = \alpha + \frac{\beta}{x_t} + u_t \tag{3.15}$$

the regression can be estimated using OLS by setting

$$z_t = \frac{1}{x_t}$$

and regressing y on a constant and z. Clearly, then, a surprisingly varied array of models can be estimated using OLS by making suitable transformations to the variables. On the other hand, some models are *intrinsically non-linear*, e.g.

$$y_t = \alpha + \beta x_t^{\gamma} + u_t \tag{3.16}$$

Such models cannot be estimated using OLS, but might be estimable using a non-linear estimation method (see chapter 9).

3.4.3 Estimator or estimate?

Estimators are the formulae used to *calculate the coefficients* – for example, the expressions given in (3.4) and (3.5) above, while the estimates, on the other hand, are the *actual numerical values for the coefficients* that are obtained from the sample.

3.5 Simple linear regression in EViews – estimation of an optimal hedge ratio

This section shows how to run a bivariate regression using EViews. The example considers the situation where an investor wishes to hedge a long position in the S&P500 (or its constituent stocks) using a short position in futures contracts. Many academic studies assume that the objective of hedging is to minimise the variance of the hedged portfolio returns. If this is the case, then the appropriate hedge ratio (the number of units of the futures asset to sell per unit of the spot asset held) will be the slope estimate (i.e. $\hat{\beta}$) in a regression where the dependent variable is a time series of spot returns and the independent variable is a time series of futures returns.[2]

This regression will be run using the file 'SandPhedge.xls', which contains monthly returns for the S&P500 index (in column 2) and S&P500 futures (in column 3). As described in chapter 1, the first step is to open an appropriately dimensioned workfile. **Open EViews** and click on **File/New/Workfile**; choose **Dated – regular frequency** and **Monthly** frequency data. The start date is **2002:02** and the end date is **2013:04**. Then import the Excel file by clicking **File/Import** and **Import from file**. As for the previous example in chapter 1, the first column contains only dates which we do not need to read in so click **Next** twice. You will then be prompted with another screen as shown in screenshot 3.1

---

[2] See chapter 9 for a detailed discussion of why this is the appropriate hedge ratio.

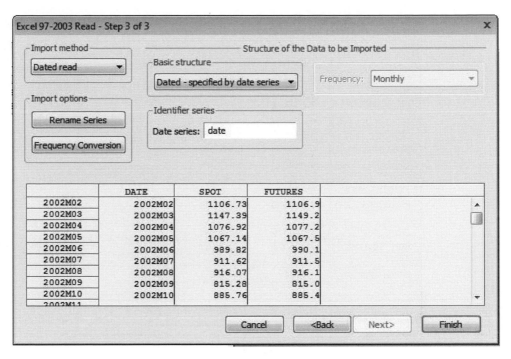

Screenshot 3.1   **How to deal with dated observations in EViews**

that invites you to decide how to deal with the dates – it is possible either to read the dates from the file or to use the date range specified when the workfile was set up. Since there are no missing data points in this case the two would give the same outcome so just click on **Finish**. The two imported series will now appear as objects in the workfile (the column of dates has not been imported) and can be verified by checking a couple of entries at random against the original Excel file.

The first step in the analysis is to transform the levels of the two series into percentage returns. It is common in academic research to use continuously compounded returns rather than simple returns. To achieve this (i.e. to produce continuously compounded returns), click on **Genr** and in the 'Enter Equation' dialog box, enter **rfutures=100*dlog(futures)**. Then click **Genr** again and do the same for the spot series: **rspot=100*dlog(spot)**. Do not forget to **Save the workfile** – call it 'hedge' and EViews will add the suffix '.wf1' to denote that it is an EViews workfile. Continue to re-save it at regular intervals to ensure that no work is lost.

Before proceeding to estimate the regression, now that we have imported more than one series, we can examine a number of descriptive statistics together and measures of association between the series. For example, click **Quick** and **Group Statistics**. From there you will see that it is possible to calculate the covariances or correlations between series and a number of other measures that will be discussed later in the book. For now, click on **Descriptive Statistics** and

Screenshot 3.2   Summary statistics for spot and futures

Common Sample.[3] In the dialog box that appears, type **rspot rfutures** and click **OK**. Some summary statistics for the spot and futures are presented, as displayed in screenshot 3.2, and these are quite similar across the two series, as one would expect.

Note that the number of observations has reduced from 135 for the levels of the series to 134 when we computed the returns (as one observation is 'lost' in constructing the $t - 1$ value of the prices in the returns formula). If you want to save the summary statistics, you must name them by clicking **Name** and then choose a name, e.g. **Descstats**. The default name is 'group01', which could have also been used. Click **OK**.

We can now proceed to estimate the regression. There are several ways to do this, but the easiest is to select **Quick** and then **Estimate Equation**. You will be presented with a dialog box, which, when it has been completed, will look like screenshot 3.3.

In the 'Equation Specification' window, you insert the list of variables to be used, with the dependent variable (y) first, and including a constant (c), so type

---

[3] 'Common sample' will use only the part of the sample that is available for all the series selected, whereas 'Individual sample' will use all available observations for each individual series. In this case, the number of observations is the same for both series and so identical results would be observed for both options.

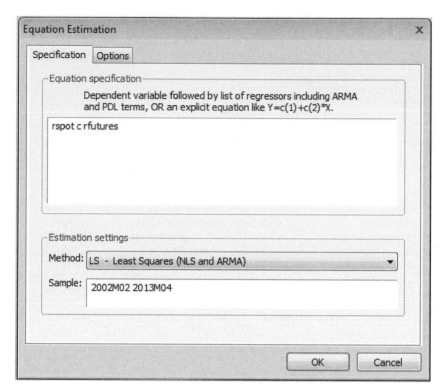

Screenshot 3.3   **Equation estimation window**

rspot c rfutures. Note that it would have been possible to write this in an equation format as rspot = c(1) + c(2)*rfutures, but this is more cumbersome.

In the 'Estimation settings' box, the default estimation method is OLS and the default sample is the whole sample, and these need not be modified. Click **OK** and the regression results will appear, as in screenshot 3.4.

The parameter estimates for the intercept $(\hat{\alpha})$ and slope $(\hat{\beta})$ are 0.00064 and 1.007 respectively. Name the regression results **returnreg**, and it will now appear as a new object in the list. A large number of other statistics are also presented in the regression output – the purpose and interpretation of these will be discussed later in this and subsequent chapters.

Now estimate a regression for the levels of the series rather than the returns (i.e. run a regression of spot on a constant and futures) and examine the parameter estimates. The return regression slope parameter estimated above measures the optimal hedge ratio and also measures the short run relationship between the two series. By contrast, the slope parameter in a regression using the raw spot and futures indices (or the log of the spot series and the log of the futures series) can be interpreted as measuring the long run relationship between them. This issue of the long and short runs will be discussed in detail in chapter 5. For now, click **Quick/Estimate Equation** and enter the variables **spot c futures** in the Equation Specification dialog box, click **OK**, then **name the regression results 'levelreg'**. The intercept estimate $(\hat{\alpha})$ in this regression is 5.4943 and

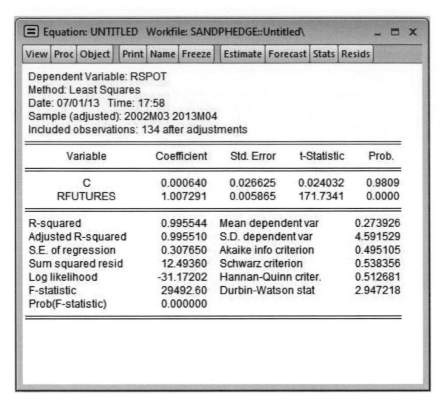

Screenshot 3.4   **Estimation results**

the slope estimate $(\hat{\beta})$ is 0.9956. The intercept can be considered to approximate the cost of carry, while as expected, the long-term relationship between spot and futures prices is almost 1:1 – see chapter 9 for further discussion of the estimation and interpretation of this equilibrium. Finally, click the **Save** button to save the whole workfile.

3.6 The assumptions underlying the classical linear regression model

The model $y_t = \alpha + \beta x_t + u_t$ that has been derived above, together with the assumptions listed below, is known as the *classical linear regression model* (CLRM). Data for x_t is observable, but since y_t also depends on u_t, it is necessary to be specific about how the u_t are generated. The set of assumptions shown in box 3.3 are usually made concerning the u_ts, the unobservable error or disturbance terms. Note that no assumptions are made concerning their observable counterparts, the estimated model's residuals.

As long as assumption 1 holds, assumption 4 can be equivalently written $E(x_t u_t) = 0$. Both formulations imply that the regressor is *orthogonal* to (i.e. unrelated to) the error term. An alternative assumption to 4, which is slightly stronger, is that the x_t are *non-stochastic* or fixed in repeated samples. This means that there is no sampling variation in x_t, and that its value is determined outside the model.

> ## Box 3.3 Assumptions concerning disturbance terms and their interpretation
>
> | *Technical notation* | *Interpretation* |
> |---|---|
> | (1) $E(u_t) = 0$ | The errors have zero mean |
> | (2) $var(u_t) = \sigma^2 < \infty$ | The variance of the errors is constant and finite over all values of x_t |
> | (3) $cov(u_i, u_j) = 0$ | The errors are linearly independent of one another |
> | (4) $cov(u_t, x_t) = 0$ | There is no relationship between the error and corresponding x variate |
> | (5) $u_t \sim N(0, \sigma^2)$ | – i.e. that u_t is normally distributed. |

A fifth assumption is required to make valid inferences about the population parameters (the actual α and β) from the sample parameters ($\hat{\alpha}$ and $\hat{\beta}$) estimated using a finite amount of data, namely that the disturbances follow a normal distribution.

3.7 Properties of the OLS estimator

If assumptions 1–4 hold, then the estimators $\hat{\alpha}$ and $\hat{\beta}$ determined by OLS will have a number of desirable properties, and are known as best linear unbiased estimators (BLUE). What does this acronym stand for?

- 'Estimator' – $\hat{\alpha}$ and $\hat{\beta}$ are estimators of the true value of α and β
- 'Linear' – $\hat{\alpha}$ and $\hat{\beta}$ are linear estimators – that means that the formulae for $\hat{\alpha}$ and $\hat{\beta}$ are linear combinations of the random variables (in this case, y)
- 'Unbiased' – on average, the actual values of $\hat{\alpha}$ and $\hat{\beta}$ will be equal to their true values
- 'Best' – means that the OLS estimator $\hat{\beta}$ has minimum variance among the class of linear unbiased estimators; the Gauss–Markov theorem proves that the OLS estimator is best by examining an arbitrary alternative linear unbiased estimator and showing in all cases that it must have a variance no smaller than the OLS estimator.

Under assumptions 1–4 listed above, the OLS estimator can be shown to have the desirable properties that it is consistent, unbiased and efficient. Unbiasedness and efficiency have already been discussed above, and consistency is an additional desirable property. These three characteristics will now be discussed in turn.

3.7.1　Consistency

The least squares estimators $\hat{\alpha}$ and $\hat{\beta}$ are consistent. One way to state this algebraically for $\hat{\beta}$ (with the obvious modifications made for $\hat{\alpha}$) is

$$\lim_{T \to \infty} \Pr \left[|\hat{\beta} - \beta| > \delta \right] = 0 \quad \forall \, \delta > 0 \tag{3.17}$$

This is a technical way of stating that the probability (Pr) that $\hat{\beta}$ is more than some arbitrary fixed distance δ away from its true value tends to zero as the sample size tends to infinity, for all positive values of δ. Thus β is the probability limit of $\hat{\beta}$. In the limit (i.e. for an infinite number of observations), the probability of the estimator being different from the true value is zero. That is, the estimates will converge to their true values as the sample size increases to infinity. Consistency is thus a large sample, or asymptotic property. If an estimator is inconsistent, then even if we had an infinite amount of data, we could not be sure that the estimated value of a parameter will be close to its true value. So consistency is sometimes argued to be the most important property of an estimator. The assumptions that $E(x_t u_t) = 0$ and $E(u_t) = 0$ are sufficient to derive the consistency of the OLS estimator.

3.7.2　Unbiasedness

The least squares estimates of $\hat{\alpha}$ and $\hat{\beta}$ are unbiased. That is

$$E(\hat{\alpha}) = \alpha \tag{3.18}$$

and

$$E(\hat{\beta}) = \beta \tag{3.19}$$

Thus, on average, the estimated values for the coefficients will be equal to their true values. That is, there is no systematic overestimation or underestimation of the true coefficients. To prove this also requires the assumption that $\text{cov}(u_t, x_t) = 0$. Clearly, unbiasedness is a stronger condition than consistency, since it holds for small as well as large samples (i.e. for all sample sizes). An estimator that is consistent may still be biased for small samples, but are all unbiased estimators also consistent? The answer is in fact no. An unbiased estimator will also be consistent if its variance falls as the sample size increases.

3.7.3　Efficiency

An estimator $\hat{\beta}$ of a parameter β is said to be efficient if no other estimator has a smaller variance. Broadly, if the estimator is efficient, it will be minimising the probability that it is a long way off from the true value of β. In other words, if the estimator is 'best', the uncertainty associated with estimation will be minimised for the class of linear unbiased estimators. A technical way to state this would be to say that an efficient estimator would have a probability distribution that is narrowly dispersed around the true value.

3.8 Precision and standard errors

Any set of regression estimates $\hat{\alpha}$ and $\hat{\beta}$ are specific to the sample used in their estimation. In other words, if a different sample of data was selected from within the population, the data points (the x_t and y_t) will be different, leading to different values of the OLS estimates.

Recall that the OLS estimators ($\hat{\alpha}$ and $\hat{\beta}$) are given by (3.4) and (3.5). It would be desirable to have an idea of how 'good' these estimates of α and β are in the sense of having some measure of the reliability or precision of the estimators ($\hat{\alpha}$ and $\hat{\beta}$). It is thus useful to know whether one can have confidence in the estimates, and whether they are likely to vary much from one sample to another sample within the given population. An idea of the sampling variability and hence of the precision of the estimates can be calculated using only the sample of data available. This estimate is given by its standard error. Given assumptions 1–4 above, valid estimators of the standard errors can be shown to be given by

$$SE(\hat{\alpha}) = s\sqrt{\frac{\sum x_t^2}{T\sum(x_t - \bar{x})^2}} = s\sqrt{\frac{\sum x_t^2}{T\left(\left(\sum x_t^2\right) - T\bar{x}^2\right)}} \tag{3.20}$$

$$SE(\hat{\beta}) = s\sqrt{\frac{1}{\sum(x_t - \bar{x})^2}} = s\sqrt{\frac{1}{\sum x_t^2 - T\bar{x}^2}} \tag{3.21}$$

where s is the estimated standard deviation of the residuals (see below). These formulae are derived in the appendix to this chapter.

It is worth noting that the standard errors give only a general indication of the likely accuracy of the regression parameters. They do not show how accurate a particular set of coefficient estimates is. If the standard errors are small, it shows that the coefficients are likely to be precise on average, not how precise they are for this particular sample. Thus standard errors give a measure of the *degree of uncertainty* in the estimated values for the coefficients. It can be seen that they are a function of the actual observations on the explanatory variable, x, the sample size, T, and another term, s. The last of these is an estimate of the variance of the disturbance term. The actual variance of the disturbance term is usually denoted by σ^2. How can an estimate of σ^2 be obtained?

3.8.1 Estimating the variance of the error term (σ^2)

From elementary statistics, the variance of a random variable u_t is given by

$$\text{var}(u_t) = E[(u_t) - E(u_t)]^2 \tag{3.22}$$

Assumption 1 of the CLRM was that the expected or average value of the errors is zero. Under this assumption, (3.22) above reduces to

$$\text{var}(u_t) = E\left[u_t^2\right] \tag{3.23}$$

So what is required is an estimate of the average value of u_t^2, which could be calculated as

$$s^2 = \frac{1}{T}\sum u_t^2 \tag{3.24}$$

Unfortunately (3.24) is not workable since u_t is a series of population disturbances, which is not observable. Thus the sample counterpart to u_t, which is $\hat{u}_t$, is used

$$s^2 = \frac{1}{T}\sum \hat{u}_t^2 \tag{3.25}$$

But this estimator is a biased estimator of σ^2. An unbiased estimator, s^2, would be given by the following equation instead of the previous one

$$s^2 = \frac{\sum \hat{u}_t^2}{T-2} \tag{3.26}$$

where $\sum \hat{u}_t^2$ is the residual sum of squares, so that the quantity of relevance for the standard error formulae is the square root of (3.26)

$$s = \sqrt{\frac{\sum \hat{u}_t^2}{T-2}} \tag{3.27}$$

s is also known as the *standard error of the regression* or the standard error of the estimate. It is sometimes used as a broad measure of the fit of the regression equation. Everything else being equal, the smaller this quantity is, the closer is the fit of the line to the actual data.

3.8.2   Some comments on the standard error estimators

It is possible, of course, to derive the formulae for the standard errors of the coefficient estimates from first principles using some algebra, and this is left to the appendix to this chapter. Some general intuition is now given as to why the formulae for the standard errors given by (3.20) and (3.21) contain the terms that they do and in the form that they do. The presentation offered in box 3.4 loosely follows that of Hill, Griffiths and Judge (1997), which is the clearest that this author has seen.

Box 3.4   Standard error estimators

(1) The larger the sample size, T, the smaller will be the coefficient standard errors. T appears explicitly in $SE(\hat{\alpha})$ and implicitly in $SE(\hat{\beta})$. T appears implicitly since the sum $\sum (x_t - \bar{x})^2$ is from $t = 1$ to T. The reason for this is simply that, at least for now, it is assumed that every observation on a series represents a piece of useful information which can be used to help determine the coefficient estimates. So the larger the size of the sample, the more information will have been used in estimation of the parameters, and hence the more confidence will be placed in those estimates.

(2) Both $SE(\hat{\alpha})$ and $SE(\hat{\beta})$ depend on s^2 (or s). Recall from above that s^2 is the estimate of the error variance. The larger this quantity is, the more dispersed are the residuals, and so the greater is the uncertainty in the model. If s^2 is large, the data points are collectively a long way away from the line.

(3) The sum of the squares of the x_t about their mean appears in both formulae – since $\sum (x_t - \bar{x})^2$ appears in the denominators. The larger the sum of squares, the smaller the coefficient variances. Consider what happens if $\sum (x_t - \bar{x})^2$ is small or large, as shown in figures 3.7 and 3.8, respectively.

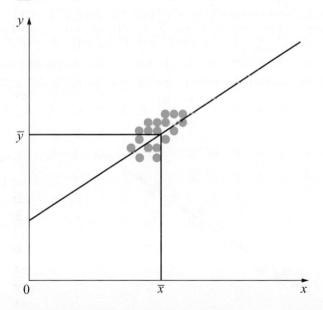

Figure 3.7   Effect on the standard errors of the coefficient estimates when $(x_t - \bar{x})$ are narrowly dispersed

In figure 3.7, the data are close together so that $\sum (x_t - \bar{x})^2$ is small. In this first case, it is more difficult to determine with any degree of certainty exactly where the line should be. On the other hand, in figure 3.8, the points are widely dispersed across a long section of the line, so that one could hold more confidence in the estimates in this case.

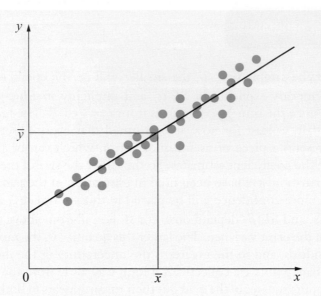

Figure 3.8 Effect on the standard errors of the coefficient estimates when $(x_t - \bar{x})$ are widely dispersed

(4) The term $\sum x_t^2$ affects only the intercept standard error and not the slope standard error. The reason is that $\sum x_t^2$ measures how far the points are away from the y-axis. Consider figures 3.9 and 3.10.

In figure 3.9, all of the points are bunched a long way from the y-axis, which makes it more difficult to accurately estimate the point at which the estimated line crosses the y-axis (the intercept). In figure 3.10, the points

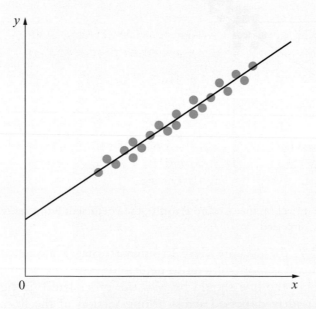

Figure 3.9 Effect on the standard errors of x_t^2 large

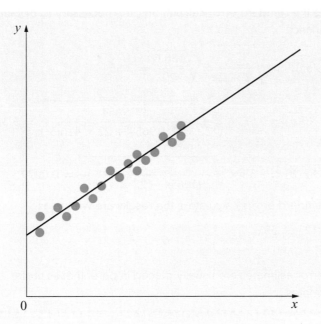

Figure 3.10 Effect on the standard errors of x_t^2 small

collectively are closer to the y-axis and hence it will be easier to determine where the line actually crosses the axis. Note that this intuition will work only in the case where all of the x_t are positive!

Example 3.2

Assume that the following data have been calculated from a regression of y on a single variable x and a constant over twenty-two observations

$$\sum x_t y_t = 830102, \quad T = 22, \quad \bar{x} = 416.5, \quad \bar{y} = 86.65,$$

$$\sum x_t^2 = 3919654, \quad RSS = 130.6$$

Determine the appropriate values of the coefficient estimates and their standard errors.

This question can simply be answered by plugging the appropriate numbers into the formulae given above. The calculations are

$$\hat{\beta} = \frac{830102 - (22 \times 416.5 \times 86.65)}{3919654 - 22 \times (416.5)^2} = 0.35$$

$$\hat{\alpha} = 86.65 - 0.35 \times 416.5 = -59.12$$

The sample regression function would be written as

$$\hat{y}_t = \hat{\alpha} + \hat{\beta} x_t$$

$$\hat{y}_t = -59.12 + 0.35 x_t$$

Now, turning to the standard error calculations, it is necessary to obtain an estimate, s, of the error variance

$$SE(\text{regression}), s = \sqrt{\frac{\sum \hat{u}_t^2}{T-2}} = \sqrt{\frac{130.6}{20}} = 2.55$$

$$SE(\hat{\alpha}) = 2.55 \times \sqrt{\frac{3919654}{22 \times (3919654 - 22 \times 416.5^2)}} = 3.35$$

$$SE(\hat{\beta}) = 2.55 \times \sqrt{\frac{1}{3919654 - 22 \times 416.5^2}} = 0.0079$$

With the standard errors calculated, the results are written as

$$\hat{y}_t = -59.12 + 0.35x_t$$
$$\quad\;\; (3.35) \quad (0.0079)$$

(3.28)

The standard error estimates are usually placed in parentheses under the relevant coefficient estimates.

3.9 An introduction to statistical inference

Often, financial theory will suggest that certain coefficients should take on particular values, or values within a given range. It is thus of interest to determine whether the relationships expected from financial theory are upheld by the data to hand or not. Estimates of α and β have been obtained from the sample, but these values are not of any particular interest; the population values that describe the true relationship between the variables would be of more interest, but are never available. Instead, inferences are made concerning the likely population values from the regression parameters that have been estimated from the sample of data to hand. In doing this, the aim is to determine whether the differences between the coefficient estimates that are actually obtained, and expectations arising from financial theory, are a long way from one another in a statistical sense.

Example 3.3

Suppose the following regression results have been calculated:

$$\hat{y}_t = 20.3 + 0.5091x_t$$
$$\quad (14.38) \quad (0.2561)$$

(3.29)

$\hat{\beta} = 0.5091$ is a single (point) estimate of the unknown population parameter, β. As stated above, the reliability of the point estimate is measured by the coefficient's standard error. The information from one or more of the sample coefficients and their standard errors can be used to make inferences about the population parameters. So the estimate of the slope coefficient is $\hat{\beta} = 0.5091$, but it is obvious that this number is likely to vary to some degree from one sample to the next. It might be of interest to answer the question, 'Is it plausible, given this estimate, that the true population parameter, β, could be 0.5? Is it plausible that β could be 1?', etc. Answers to these questions can be obtained through *hypothesis testing*.

3.9.1 Hypothesis testing: some concepts

In the hypothesis testing framework, there are always two hypotheses that go together, known as the *null hypothesis* (denoted H_0 or occasionally H_N) and the *alternative hypothesis* (denoted H_1 or occasionally H_A). The null hypothesis is the statement or the statistical hypothesis that is actually being tested. The alternative hypothesis represents the remaining outcomes of interest.

For example, suppose that given the regression results above, it is of interest to test the hypothesis that the true value of β is in fact 0.5. The following notation would be used.

$$H_0 : \beta = 0.5$$
$$H_1 : \beta \neq 0.5$$

This states that the hypothesis that the true but unknown value of β could be 0.5 is being tested against an alternative hypothesis where β is not 0.5. This would be known as a two-sided test, since the outcomes of both $\beta < 0.5$ and $\beta > 0.5$ are subsumed under the alternative hypothesis.

Sometimes, some prior information may be available, suggesting for example that $\beta > 0.5$ would be expected rather than $\beta < 0.5$. In this case, $\beta < 0.5$ is no longer of interest to us, and hence a one-sided test would be conducted:

$$H_0 : \beta = 0.5$$
$$H_1 : \beta > 0.5$$

Here the null hypothesis that the true value of β is 0.5 is being tested against a one-sided alternative that β is more than 0.5.

On the other hand, one could envisage a situation where there is prior information that $\beta < 0.5$ is expected. For example, suppose that an investment bank bought a piece of new risk management software that is intended to better track the riskiness inherent in its traders' books and that β is some measure of the risk that previously took the value 0.5. Clearly, it would not make sense to expect the risk to have risen, and so $\beta > 0.5$, corresponding to an increase in risk, is not of interest. In this case, the null and alternative hypotheses would be specified as

$$H_0 : \beta = 0.5$$
$$H_1 : \beta < 0.5$$

This prior information should come from the financial theory of the problem under consideration, and not from an examination of the estimated value of the coefficient. Note that there is always an equality under the null hypothesis. So, for example, $\beta < 0.5$ would not be specified under the null hypothesis.

There are two ways to conduct a hypothesis test: via the *test of significance* approach or via the *confidence interval* approach. Both methods centre on a statistical comparison of the estimated value of the coefficient, and its value under the null hypothesis. In very general terms, if the estimated value is a long way away from the hypothesised value, the null hypothesis is likely to be rejected; if the value under the null hypothesis and the estimated value are close to one another, the null hypothesis is less likely to be rejected. For example, consider $\hat{\beta} = 0.5091$ as above. A hypothesis that the true value of β is 5 is more likely to be rejected than a null hypothesis that the true value of β is 0.5. What is required now is a *statistical decision rule* that will permit the formal testing of such hypotheses.

3.9.2 The probability distribution of the least squares estimators

In order to test hypotheses, assumption 5 of the CLRM must be used, namely that $u_t \sim N(0, \sigma^2)$ – i.e. that the error term is normally distributed. The normal distribution is a convenient one to use for it involves only two parameters (its mean and variance). This makes the algebra involved in statistical inference considerably simpler than it otherwise would have been. Since y_t depends partially on u_t, it can be stated that if u_t is normally distributed, y_t will also be normally distributed.

Further, since the least squares estimators are linear combinations of the random variables, i.e. $\hat{\beta} = \sum w_t y_t$, where w_t are effectively weights, and since the weighted sum of normal random variables is also normally distributed, it can be said that the coefficient estimates will also be normally distributed. Thus

$$\hat{\alpha} \sim N(\alpha, \text{var}(\hat{\alpha})) \qquad \text{and} \qquad \hat{\beta} \sim N(\beta, \text{var}(\hat{\beta}))$$

Will the coefficient estimates still follow a normal distribution if the errors do not follow a normal distribution? Well, briefly, the answer is usually 'yes' as a result of the central limit theorem, provided that the other assumptions of the CLRM hold, and the sample size is sufficiently large. The issue of non-normality, how to test for it, and its consequences, will be further discussed in chapter 5.

Standard normal variables can be constructed from $\hat{\alpha}$ and $\hat{\beta}$ by subtracting the mean and dividing by the square root of the variance

$$\frac{\hat{\alpha} - \alpha}{\sqrt{\text{var}(\hat{\alpha})}} \sim N(0, 1) \qquad \text{and} \qquad \frac{\hat{\beta} - \beta}{\sqrt{\text{var}(\hat{\beta})}} \sim N(0, 1)$$

The square roots of the coefficient variances are the standard errors. Unfortunately, the standard errors of the true coefficient values under the PRF are never known – all that is available are their sample counterparts, the calculated standard errors of the coefficient estimates, $SE(\hat{\alpha})$ and $SE(\hat{\beta})$.[4]

---

[4] Strictly, these are the estimated standard errors conditional on the parameter estimates, and so should be denoted $S\hat{E}(\hat{\alpha})$ and $S\hat{E}(\hat{\beta})$, but the additional layer of hats will be omitted here since the meaning should be obvious from the context.

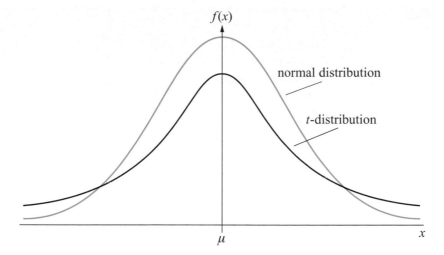

Figure 3.11 The *t*-distribution versus the normal

Replacing the true values of the standard errors with the sample estimated versions induces another source of uncertainty, and also means that the standardised statistics follow a *t*-distribution with $T - 2$ degrees of freedom (defined below) rather than a normal distribution, so

$$\frac{\hat{\alpha} - \alpha}{SE(\hat{\alpha})} \sim t_{T-2} \qquad \text{and} \qquad \frac{\hat{\beta} - \beta}{SE(\hat{\beta})} \sim t_{T-2}$$

This result is not formally proved here. For a formal proof, see Hill, Griffiths and Judge (1997, pp. 88–90).

3.9.3 A note on the *t* and the normal distributions

The normal distribution pdf was shown in shown in figure 2.8 with its characteristic 'bell' shape and its symmetry around the mean (of zero for a standard normal distribution). Any normal variate can be scaled to have zero mean and unit variance by subtracting its mean and dividing by its standard deviation. There is a specific relationship between the *t*- and the standard normal distribution, and the *t*-distribution has another parameter, its degrees of freedom.

What does the *t*-distribution look like? It looks similar to a normal distribution, but with fatter tails, and a smaller peak at the mean, as shown in figure 3.11.

Some examples of the percentiles from the normal and *t*-distributions taken from the statistical tables are given in table 3.2. When used in the context of a hypothesis test, these percentiles become critical values. The values presented in table 3.2 would be those critical values appropriate for a one-sided test of the given significance level.

Table 3.2 Critical values from the standard normal versus
t-distribution

Significance level (%)	$N(0,1)$	t_{40}	t_4
50	0	0	0
5	1.64	1.68	2.13
2.5	1.96	2.02	2.78
0.5	2.57	2.70	4.60

It can be seen that as the number of degrees of freedom for the *t*-distribution increases from 4 to 40, the critical values fall substantially. In figure 3.11, this is represented by a gradual increase in the height of the distribution at the centre and a reduction in the fatness of the tails as the number of degrees of freedom increases. In the limit, a *t*-distribution with an infinite number of degrees of freedom is a standard normal, i.e. $t_\infty = N(0, 1)$, so the normal distribution can be viewed as a special case of the *t*.

Putting the limit case, t_∞, aside, the critical values for the *t*-distribution are larger in absolute value than those from the standard normal. This arises from the increased uncertainty associated with the situation where the error variance must be estimated. So now the *t*-distribution is used, and for a given statistic to constitute the same amount of reliable evidence against the null, it has to be bigger in absolute value than in circumstances where the normal is applicable.

As stated above, there are broadly two approaches to testing hypotheses under regression analysis: the test of significance approach and the confidence interval approach. Each of these will now be considered in turn.

3.9.4 The test of significance approach

Assume the regression equation is given by $y_t = \alpha + \beta x_t + u_t, t = 1, 2, \ldots, T$. The steps involved in doing a test of significance are shown in box 3.5.

Steps 2–7 require further comment. In step 2, the estimated value of β is compared with the value that is subject to test under the null hypothesis, but this difference is 'normalised' or scaled by the standard error of the coefficient estimate. The standard error is a measure of how confident one is in the coefficient estimate obtained in the first stage. If a standard error is small, the value of the test statistic will be large relative to the case where the standard error is large. For a small standard error, it would not require the estimated and hypothesised values to be far away from one another for the null hypothesis to be rejected. Dividing by

Box 3.5   Conducting a test of significance

(1) Estimate $\hat{\alpha}$, $\hat{\beta}$ and $SE(\hat{\alpha})$, $SE(\hat{\beta})$ in the usual way.

(2) Calculate the test statistic. This is given by the formula

$$test\ statistic = \frac{\hat{\beta} - \beta^*}{SE(\hat{\beta})}$$

(3.30)

where β^* is the value of β under the null hypothesis. The null hypothesis is $H_0 : \beta = \beta^*$ and the alternative hypothesis is $H_1 : \beta \neq \beta^*$ (for a two-sided test).

(3) A tabulated distribution with which to compare the estimated test statistics is required. Test statistics derived in this way can be shown to follow a t-distribution with $T - 2$ degrees of freedom.

(4) Choose a 'significance level', often denoted α (*not* the same as the regression intercept coefficient). It is conventional to use a significance level of 5%.

(5) Given a significance level, a *rejection region* and *non-rejection region* can be determined. If a 5% significance level is employed, this means that 5% of the total distribution (5% of the area under the curve) will be in the rejection region. That rejection region can either be split in half (for a two-sided test) or it can all fall on one side of the y-axis, as is the case for a one-sided test.

For a two-sided test, the 5% rejection region is split equally between the two tails, as shown in figure 3.12.

For a one-sided test, the 5% rejection region is located solely in one tail of the distribution, as shown in figures 3.13 and 3.14, for a test where the alternative is of the 'less than' form, and where the alternative is of the 'greater than' form, respectively.

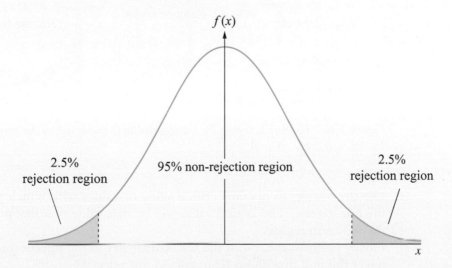

Figure 3.12   Rejection regions for a two-sided 5% hypothesis test

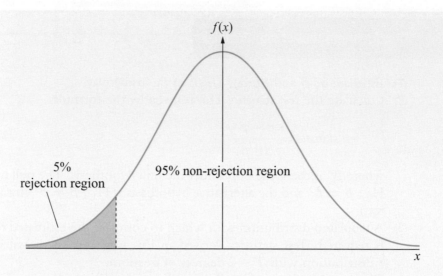

Figure 3.13   Rejection region for a one-sided hypothesis test of the form $H_0 : \beta = \beta^*$, $H_1 : \beta < \beta^*$

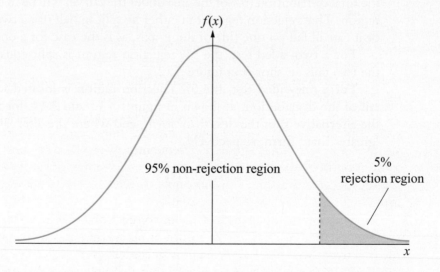

Figure 3.14   Rejection region for a one-sided hypothesis test of the form $H_0 : \beta = \beta^*$, $H_1 : \beta > \beta^*$

(6) Use the t-tables to obtain a critical value or values with which to compare the test statistic. The critical value will be that value of x that puts 5% into the rejection region.

(7) Finally perform the test. If the test statistic lies in the rejection region then reject the null hypothesis (H_0), else do not reject H_0.

the standard error also ensures that, under the five CLRM assumptions, the test statistic follows a tabulated distribution.

In this context, the number of degrees of freedom can be interpreted as the number of pieces of additional information beyond the minimum requirement. If two parameters are estimated (α and β – the intercept and the slope of the line, respectively), a minimum of two observations is required to fit this line to the data. As the number of degrees of freedom increases, the critical values in the tables decrease in absolute terms, since less caution is required and one can be more confident that the results are appropriate.

The significance level is also sometimes called the *size of the test* (note that this is completely different from the size of the sample) and it determines the region where the null hypothesis under test will be rejected or not rejected. Remember that the distributions in figures 3.13–3.15 are for a random variable. Purely by chance, a random variable will take on extreme values (either large and positive values or large and negative values) occasionally. More specifically, a significance level of 5% means that a result as extreme as this or more extreme would be expected only 5% of the time as a consequence of chance alone. To give one illustration, if the 5% critical value for a one-sided test is 1.68, this implies that the test statistic would be expected to be greater than this only 5% of the time by chance alone. There is nothing magical about the test – all that is done is to specify an arbitrary cutoff value for the test statistic that determines whether the null hypothesis would be rejected or not. It is conventional to use a 5% size of test, but 10% and 1% are also commonly used.

However, one potential problem with the use of a fixed (e.g. 5%) size of test is that if the sample size is sufficiently large, any null hypothesis can be rejected. This is particularly worrisome in finance, where tens of thousands of observations or more are often available. What happens is that the standard errors reduce as the sample size increases, thus leading to an increase in the value of all t-test statistics. This problem is frequently overlooked in empirical work, but some econometricians have suggested that a lower size of test (e.g. 1%) should be used for large samples (see, for example, Leamer, 1978, for a discussion of these issues).

Note also the use of terminology in connection with hypothesis tests: it is said that the null hypothesis is either *rejected* or *not rejected*. It is incorrect to state that if the null hypothesis is not rejected, it is 'accepted' (although this error is frequently made in practice), and it is never said that the alternative hypothesis is accepted or rejected. One reason why it is not sensible to say that the null hypothesis is 'accepted' is that it is impossible to know whether the null is actually true or not! In any given situation, many null hypotheses will not be rejected. For example, suppose that $H_0 : \beta = 0.5$ and $H_0 : \beta = 1$ are separately tested against the relevant two-sided alternatives and neither null is rejected. Clearly then it would not make sense to say that '$H_0 : \beta = 0.5$ is accepted' and '$H_0 : \beta = 1$ is accepted', since the true (but unknown) value of β cannot be both 0.5 and 1. So, to summarise, the null hypothesis is either rejected or not rejected on the basis of the available evidence.

Box 3.6   Carrying out a hypothesis test using confidence intervals

(1) Calculate $\hat{\alpha}$, $\hat{\beta}$ and $SE(\hat{\alpha})$, $SE(\hat{\beta})$ as before.

(2) Choose a significance level, α (again the convention is 5%). This is equivalent to choosing a $(1-\alpha)^*100\%$ confidence interval

i.e. 5% significance level = 95% confidence interval.

(3) Use the t-tables to find the appropriate critical value, which will again have $T-2$ degrees of freedom.

(4) The confidence interval for β is given by

$$(\hat{\beta} - t_{crit} \cdot SE(\hat{\beta}), \hat{\beta} + t_{crit} \cdot SE(\hat{\beta}))$$

Note that a centre dot ($\cdot$) is sometimes used instead of a cross ($\times$) to denote when two quantities are multiplied together.

(5) Perform the test: if the hypothesised value of β (i.e. β^*) lies outside the confidence interval, then reject the null hypothesis that $\beta = \beta^*$, otherwise do not reject the null.

3.9.5   The confidence interval approach to hypothesis testing (box 3.6)

To give an example of its usage, one might estimate a parameter, say $\hat{\beta}$, to be 0.93, and a '95% confidence interval' to be (0.77, 1.09). This means that in many repeated samples, 95% of the time, the true value of β will be contained within this interval. Confidence intervals are almost invariably estimated in a two-sided form, although in theory a one-sided interval can be constructed. Constructing a 95% confidence interval is equivalent to using the 5% level in a test of significance.

3.9.6   The test of significance and confidence interval approaches always give the same conclusion

Under the test of significance approach, the null hypothesis that $\beta = \beta^*$ will not be rejected if the test statistic lies within the non-rejection region, i.e. if the following condition holds

$$-t_{crit} \leq \frac{\hat{\beta} - \beta^*}{SE(\hat{\beta})} \leq + t_{crit}$$

Rearranging, the null hypothesis would not be rejected if

$$-t_{crit} \cdot SE(\hat{\beta}) \leq \hat{\beta} - \beta^* \leq + t_{crit} \cdot SE(\hat{\beta})$$

> **Box 3.7**   **The test of significance and confidence interval approaches compared**
>
> | Test of significance approach | Confidence interval approach |
> |---|---|
> | $\text{test stat} = \dfrac{\hat{\beta} - \beta^*}{SE(\hat{\beta})}$ | |
> | $\qquad = \dfrac{0.5091 - 1}{0.2561} = -1.917$ | Find $t_{crit} = t_{20;5\%} = \pm 2.086$ |
> | Find $t_{crit} = t_{20;5\%} = \pm 2.086$ | $\hat{\beta} \pm t_{crit} \cdot SE(\hat{\beta})$
 $\quad = 0.5091 \pm 2.086 \cdot 0.2561$
 $\quad = (-0.0251, 1.0433)$ |
> | Do not reject H_0 since test statistic lies within non-rejection region | Do not reject H_0 since 1 lies within the confidence interval |

i.e. one would not reject if

$$\hat{\beta} - t_{crit} \cdot SE(\hat{\beta}) \le \beta^* \le \hat{\beta} + t_{crit} \cdot SE(\hat{\beta})$$

But this is just the rule for non-rejection under the confidence interval approach. So it will always be the case that, for a given significance level, the test of significance and confidence interval approaches will provide the same conclusion by construction. One testing approach is simply an algebraic rearrangement of the other.

Example 3.4

Given the regression results above

$$\hat{y}_t = 20.3 + 0.5091 x_t \atop (14.38) \; (0.2561) \qquad , \qquad T = 22 \tag{3.31}$$

Using both the test of significance and confidence interval approaches, test the hypothesis that $\beta = 1$ against a two-sided alternative. This hypothesis might be of interest, for a unit coefficient on the explanatory variable implies a 1:1 relationship between movements in x and movements in y.

The null and alternative hypotheses are respectively:

$H_0 : \beta = 1$

$H_1 : \beta \neq 1$

The results of the test according to each approach are shown in box 3.7. A couple of comments are in order. First, the critical value from the t-distribution that is required is for twenty degrees of freedom and at the 5% level. This means

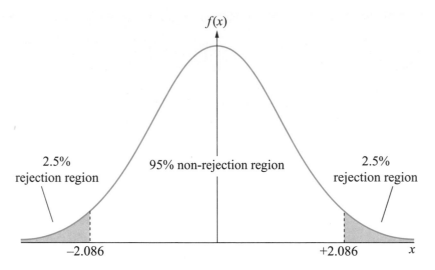

Figure 3.15   Critical values and rejection regions for a $t_{20;5\%}$

that 5% of the total distribution will be in the rejection region, and since this is a two–sided test, 2.5% of the distribution is required to be contained in each tail. From the symmetry of the t-distribution around zero, the critical values in the upper and lower tail will be equal in magnitude, but opposite in sign, as shown in figure 3.15.

What if instead the researcher wanted to test $H_0 : \beta = 0$ or $H_0 : \beta = 2$? In order to test these hypotheses using the test of significance approach, the test statistic would have to be reconstructed in each case, although the critical value would be the same. On the other hand, no additional work would be required if the confidence interval approach had been adopted, since it effectively permits the testing of an infinite number of hypotheses. So for example, suppose that the researcher wanted to test

$$H_0 : \beta = 0$$

versus

$$H_1 : \beta \neq 0$$

and

$$H_0 : \beta = 2$$

versus

$$H_1 : \beta \neq 2$$

In the first case, the null hypothesis (that $\beta = 0$) would not be rejected since 0 lies within the 95% confidence interval. By the same argument, the second null hypothesis (that $\beta = 2$) would be rejected since 2 lies outside the estimated confidence interval.

On the other hand, note that this book has so far considered only the results under a 5% size of test. In marginal cases (e.g. $H_0 : \beta = 1$, where the test statistic and critical value are close together), a completely different answer may arise if a different size of test was used. This is where the test of significance approach is preferable to the construction of a confidence interval.

For example, suppose that now a 10% size of test is used for the null hypothesis given in example 3.4. Using the test of significance approach,

$$test\ statistic = \frac{\hat{\beta} - \beta^*}{SE(\hat{\beta})}$$

$$= \frac{0.5091 - 1}{0.2561} = -1.917$$

as above. The only thing that changes is the critical t-value. At the 10% level (so that 5% of the total distribution is placed in each of the tails for this two-sided test), the required critical value is $t_{20;10\%} = \pm1.725$. So now, as the test statistic lies in the rejection region, H_0 would be rejected. In order to use a 10% test under the confidence interval approach, the interval itself would have to have been re-estimated since the critical value is embedded in the calculation of the confidence interval.

So the test of significance and confidence interval approaches both have their relative merits. The testing of a number of different hypotheses is easier under the confidence interval approach, while a consideration of the effect of the size of the test on the conclusion is easier to address under the test of significance approach.

Caution should therefore be used when placing emphasis on or making decisions in the context of marginal cases (i.e. in cases where the null is only just rejected or not rejected). In this situation, the appropriate conclusion to draw is that the results are marginal and that no strong inference can be made one way or the other. A thorough empirical analysis should involve conducting a sensitivity analysis on the results to determine whether using a different size of test alters the conclusions. It is worth stating again that it is conventional to consider sizes of test of 10%, 5% and 1%. If the conclusion (i.e. 'reject' or 'do not reject') is robust to changes in the size of the test, then one can be more confident that the conclusions are appropriate. If the outcome of the test is qualitatively altered when the size of the test is modified, the conclusion must be that there is no conclusion one way or the other!

It is also worth noting that if a given null hypothesis is rejected using a 1% significance level, it will also automatically be rejected at the 5% level, so that there is no need to actually state the latter. Dougherty (1992, p. 100), gives the analogy of a high jumper. If the high jumper can clear 2 metres, it is obvious that the jumper could also clear 1.5 metres. The 1% significance level is a higher hurdle than the 5% significance level. Similarly, if the null is not rejected at the 5% level of significance, it will automatically not be rejected at any stronger level of significance (e.g. 1%). In this case, if the jumper cannot clear 1.5 metres, there is no way s/he will be able to clear 2 metres.

		Reality	
		H_0 is true	H_0 is false
	Significant	Type I error $= \alpha$	✓
Result of test	(reject H_0)		
	Insignificant	✓	Type II error $= \beta$
	(do not reject H_0)		

Table 3.3   Classifying hypothesis testing errors and correct conclusions

3.9.7   Some more terminology

If the null hypothesis is rejected at the 5% level, it would be said that the result of the test is 'statistically significant'. If the null hypothesis is not rejected, it would be said that the result of the test is 'not significant', or that it is 'insignificant'. Finally, if the null hypothesis is rejected at the 1% level, the result is termed 'highly statistically significant'.

Note that a statistically significant result may be of no practical significance. For example, if the estimated beta for a stock under a CAPM regression is 1.05, and a null hypothesis that $\beta = 1$ is rejected, the result will be statistically significant. But it may be the case that a slightly higher beta will make no difference to an investor's choice as to whether to buy the stock or not. In that case, one would say that the result of the test was statistically significant but financially or practically insignificant.

3.9.8   Classifying the errors that can be made using hypothesis tests

H_0 is usually rejected if the test statistic is statistically significant at a chosen significance level. There are two possible errors that could be made:

(1) Rejecting H_0 when it was really true; this is called a *type I error*.
(2) Not rejecting H_0 when it was in fact false; this is called a *type II error*.

The possible scenarios can be summarised in table 3.3. The probability of a type I error is just α, the significance level or size of test chosen. To see this, recall what is meant by 'significance' at the 5% level: it is only 5% likely that a result as or more extreme as this could have occurred purely by chance. Or, to put this another way, it is only 5% likely that this null would be rejected when it was in fact true.

Note that there is no chance for a free lunch (i.e. a cost–less gain) here! What happens if the size of the test is reduced (e.g. from a 5% test to a 1% test)? The chances of making a type I error would be reduced . . . but so would the probability

Box 3.8 Type I and type II errors

			Less likely to falsely → reject ↗	Lower → chance of type I error
Reduce size of test (e.g. 5% to 1%)	→ More strict criterion for rejection	→ Reject null hypothesis less often ↘	More likely to incorrectly not reject	Higher → chance of type II error

that the null hypothesis would be rejected at all, so increasing the probability of a type II error. The two competing effects of reducing the size of the test are shown in box 3.8.

So there always exists, therefore, a direct trade-off between type I and type II errors when choosing a significance level. The only way to reduce the chances of both is to increase the sample size or to select a sample with more variation, thus increasing the amount of information upon which the results of the hypothesis test are based. In practice, up to a certain level, type I errors are usually considered more serious and hence a small size of test is usually chosen (5% or 1% are the most common).

The probability of a type I error is the probability of incorrectly rejecting a correct null hypothesis, which is also the size of the test. Another important piece of terminology in this area is the *power of a test*. The power of a test is defined as the probability of (appropriately) rejecting an incorrect null hypothesis. The power of the test is also equal to one minus the probability of a type II error.

An optimal test would be one with an actual test size that matched the nominal size and which had as high a power as possible. Such a test would imply, for example, that using a 5% significance level would result in the null being rejected exactly 5% of the time by chance alone, and that an incorrect null hypothesis would be rejected close to 100% of the time.

3.10 A special type of hypothesis test: the t-ratio

Recall that the formula under a test of significance approach to hypothesis testing using a t-test for the slope parameter was

$$test\ statistic = \frac{\hat{\beta} - \beta^*}{SE(\hat{\beta})} \qquad (3.32)$$

with the obvious adjustments to test a hypothesis about the intercept. If the test is

$$H_0 : \beta = 0$$
$$H_1 : \beta \neq 0$$

i.e. a test that the population parameter is zero against a two-sided alternative, this is known as a t-ratio test. Since $\beta^* = 0$, the expression in (3.32) collapses to

$$test\ statistic = \frac{\hat{\beta}}{SE(\hat{\beta})} \tag{3.33}$$

Thus the ratio of the coefficient to its standard error, given by this expression, is known as the t-ratio or t-statistic.

Example 3.5

Suppose that we have calculated the estimates for the intercept and the slope (1.10 and -19.88 respectively) and their corresponding standard errors (1.35 and 1.98 respectively). The t-ratios associated with each of the intercept and slope coefficients would be given by

	$\hat{\alpha}$	$\hat{\beta}$
Coefficient	1.10	-19.88
SE	1.35	1.98
t-ratio	0.81	-10.04

Note that if a coefficient is negative, its t-ratio will also be negative. In order to test (separately) the null hypotheses that $\alpha = 0$ and $\beta = 0$, the test statistics would be compared with the appropriate critical value from a t-distribution. In this case, the number of degrees of freedom, given by $T - k$, is equal to $15 - 2 = 13$. The 5% critical value for this two-sided test (remember, 2.5% in each tail for a 5% test) is 2.16, while the 1% two-sided critical value (0.5% in each tail) is 3.01. Given these t-ratios and critical values, would the following null hypotheses be rejected?

$H_0 : \alpha = 0$?　　　　(*No*)

$H_0 : \beta = 0$?　　　　(*Yes*)

If H_0 is rejected, it would be said that the test statistic is *significant*. If the variable is not 'significant', it means that while the estimated value of the coefficient is not exactly zero (e.g. 1.10 in the example above), the coefficient is indistinguishable statistically from zero. If a zero were placed in the fitted equation instead of the estimated value, this would mean that whatever happened to the value of that explanatory variable, the dependent variable would be unaffected. This would then be taken to mean that the variable is not helping to explain variations in y, and that it could therefore be removed from the regression equation. For example, if the t-ratio associated with x had been -1.04 rather than -10.04 (assuming that the standard error stayed the same), the variable would be classed as insignificant (i.e. not statistically different from zero). The only insignificant term in the above regression is the intercept. There are good statistical reasons for always retaining the constant, even if it is not significant; see chapter 5.

It is worth noting that, for degrees of freedom greater than around 25, the 5% two-sided critical value is approximately ± 2. So, as a rule of thumb (i.e. a rough guide), the null hypothesis would be rejected if the t-statistic exceeds 2 in absolute value.

Table 3.4 Summary statistics for the estimated regression results for (3.34)

Item	Mean value	Median value	Extremal values Minimum	Extremal values Maximum
$\hat{\alpha}$	−0.011	−0.009	−0.080	0.058
$\hat{\beta}$	0.840	0.848	0.219	1.405
Sample size	17	19	10	20

Source: Jensen (1968). Reprinted with the permission of Blackwell Publishers.

Some authors place the *t*-ratios in parentheses below the corresponding coefficient estimates rather than the standard errors. One thus needs to check which convention is being used in each particular application, and also to state this clearly when presenting estimation results.

There will now follow two finance case studies that involve only the estimation of bivariate linear regression models and the construction and interpretation of *t*-ratios.

3.11 An example of a simple *t*-test of a theory in finance: can US mutual funds beat the market?

Jensen (1968) was the first to systematically test the performance of mutual funds, and in particular examine whether any 'beat the market'. He used a sample of annual returns on the portfolios of 115 mutual funds from 1945–64. Each of the 115 funds was subjected to a separate OLS time series regression of the form

$$R_{jt} - R_{ft} = \alpha_j + \beta_j(R_{mt} - R_{ft}) + u_{jt} \tag{3.34}$$

where R_{jt} is the return on portfolio j at time t, R_{ft} is the return on a risk-free proxy (a one-year government bond), R_{mt} is the return on a market portfolio proxy, u_{jt} is an error term, and α_j, β_j are parameters to be estimated. The quantity of interest is the significance of α_j, since this parameter defines whether the fund outperforms or underperforms the market index. Thus the null hypothesis is given by: $H_0 : \alpha_j = 0$. A positive and significant α_j for a given fund would suggest that the fund is able to earn significant abnormal returns in excess of the market-required return for a fund of this given riskiness. This coefficient has become known as 'Jensen's alpha'. Some summary statistics across the 115 funds for the estimated regression results for (3.34) are given in table 3.4.

As table 3.4 shows, the average (defined as either the mean or the median) fund was unable to 'beat the market', recording a negative alpha in both cases. There were, however, some funds that did manage to perform significantly better than expected given their level of risk, with the best fund of all yielding an alpha of

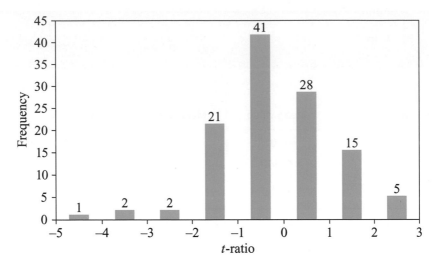

Figure 3.16   Frequency distribution of t-ratios of mutual fund alphas (gross of transactions costs). *Source:* Jensen (1968). Reprinted with the permission of Blackwell Publishers

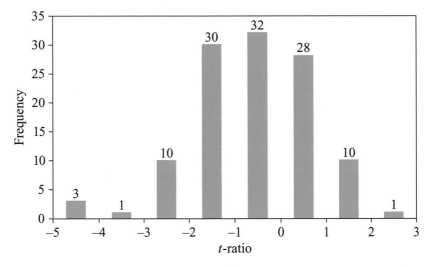

Figure 3.17   Frequency distribution of t-ratios of mutual fund alphas (net of transactions costs). *Source:* Jensen (1968). Reprinted with the permission of Blackwell Publishers

0.058. Interestingly, the average fund had a beta estimate of around 0.85, indicating that, in the CAPM context, most funds were less risky than the market index. This result may be attributable to the funds investing predominantly in (mature) blue chip stocks rather than small caps.

The most visual method of presenting the results was obtained by plotting the number of mutual funds in each t-ratio category for the alpha coefficient, first gross and then net of transactions costs, as in figure 3.16 and figure 3.17, respectively.

The appropriate critical value for a two-sided test of $\alpha_j = 0$ is approximately 2.10 (assuming twenty years of annual data leading to eighteen degrees of

Table 3.5   Summary statistics for unit trust returns, January 1979–May 2000

	Mean (%)	Minimum (%)	Maximum (%)	Median (%)
Average monthly return, 1979–2000	1.0	0.6	1.4	1.0
Standard deviation of returns over time	5.1	4.3	6.9	5.0

freedom). As can be seen, only five funds have estimated t-ratios greater than 2 and are therefore implied to have been able to outperform the market before transactions costs are taken into account. Interestingly, five firms have also significantly underperformed the market, with t-ratios of −2 or less.

When transactions costs are taken into account (figure 3.17), only one fund out of 115 is able to significantly outperform the market, while 14 significantly underperform it. Given that a nominal 5% two-sided size of test is being used, one would expect two or three funds to 'significantly beat the market' by chance alone. It would thus be concluded that, during the sample period studied, US fund managers appeared unable to systematically generate positive abnormal returns.

3.12 Can UK unit trust managers beat the market?

Jensen's study has proved pivotal in suggesting a method for conducting empirical tests of the performance of fund managers. However, it has been criticised on several grounds. One of the most important of these in the context of this book is that only between ten and twenty annual observations were used for each regression. Such a small number of observations is really insufficient for the asymptotic theory underlying the testing procedure to be validly invoked.

A variant on Jensen's test is now estimated in the context of the UK market, by considering monthly returns on seventy-six equity unit trusts. The data cover the period January 1979–May 2000 (257 observations for each fund). Some summary statistics for the funds are presented in table 3.5.

From these summary statistics, the average continuously compounded return is 1% per month, although the most interesting feature is the wide variation in the performances of the funds. The worst-performing fund yields an average return of 0.6% per month over the twenty-year period, while the best would give 1.4% per month. This variability is further demonstrated in figure 3.18, which plots over time the value of £100 invested in each of the funds in January 1979.

A regression of the form (3.34) is applied to the UK data, and the summary results presented in table 3.6. A number of features of the regression results are

Table 3.6   CAPM regression results for unit trust returns, January 1979–May 2000

Estimates of	Mean	Minimum	Maximum	Median
α(%)	−0.02	−0.54	0.33	−0.03
β	0.91	0.56	1.09	0.91
t-ratio on α	−0.07	−2.44	3.11	−0.25

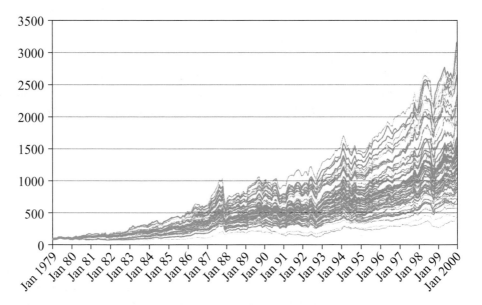

Figure 3.18   Performance of UK unit trusts, 1979–2000

worthy of further comment. First, most of the funds have estimated betas less than one again, perhaps suggesting that the fund managers have historically been risk-averse or investing disproportionately in blue chip companies in mature sectors. Second, gross of transactions costs, nine funds of the sample of seventy-six were able to significantly outperform the market by providing a significant positive alpha, while seven funds yielded significant negative alphas. The average fund (where 'average' is measured using either the mean or the median) is not able to earn any excess return over the required rate given its level of risk.

3.13   The overreaction hypothesis and the UK stock market

3.13.1   Motivation

Two studies by DeBondt and Thaler (1985, 1987) showed that stocks experiencing a poor performance over a three–five-year period subsequently tend to outperform

> **Box 3.9   Reasons for stock market overreactions**
>
> (1) *That the 'overreaction effect' is just another manifestation of the 'size effect'.*
> The size effect is the tendency of small firms to generate on average,
> superior returns to large firms. The argument would follow that the
> losers were small firms and that these small firms would subsequently
> outperform the large firms. DeBondt and Thaler did not believe this a
> sufficient explanation, but Zarowin (1990) found that allowing for firm
> size did reduce the subsequent return on the losers.
>
> (2) *That the reversals of fortune reflect changes in equilibrium required returns.* The
> losers are argued to be likely to have considerably higher CAPM betas,
> reflecting investors' perceptions that they are more risky. Of course,
> betas can change over time, and a substantial fall in the firms' share
> prices (for the losers) would lead to a rise in their leverage ratios,
> leading in all likelihood to an increase in their perceived riskiness.
> Therefore, the required rate of return on the losers will be larger, and
> their *ex post* performance better. Ball and Kothari (1989) find the
> CAPM betas of losers to be considerably higher than those of winners.

stocks that had previously performed relatively well. This implies that, on average, stocks which are 'losers' in terms of their returns subsequently become 'winners', and vice versa. This chapter now examines a paper by Clare and Thomas (1995) that conducts a similar study using monthly UK stock returns from January 1955 to 1990 (thirty-six years) on all firms traded on the London Stock exchange.

This phenomenon seems at first blush to be inconsistent with the efficient markets hypothesis, and Clare and Thomas propose two explanations (see box 3.9). Zarowin (1990) also finds that 80% of the extra return available from holding the losers accrues to investors in January, so that almost all of the 'overreaction effect' seems to occur at the start of the calendar year.

3.13.2   Methodology

Clare and Thomas take a random sample of 1,000 firms and, for each, they calculate the monthly excess return of the stock for the market over a twelve-, twenty-four- or thirty-six-month period for each stock i

$$U_{it} = R_{it} - R_{mt}\ t = 1, \ldots, n; \quad i = 1, \ldots, 1000;$$

$$n = 12, 24 \text{ or } 36 \tag{3.35}$$

Box 3.10   Ranking stocks and forming portfolios

Portfolio	Ranking
Portfolio 1	Best performing 20% of firms
Portfolio 2	Next 20%
Portfolio 3	Next 20%
Portfolio 4	Next 20%
Portfolio 5	Worst performing 20% of firms

Box 3.11   Portfolio monitoring

Estimate $\bar{R}_i$ for year 1
Monitor portfolios for year 2
Estimate $\bar{R}_i$ for year 3
$\vdots$

Monitor portfolios for year 36

Then the average monthly return over each stock i for the first twelve-, twenty-four-, or thirty-six-month period is calculated:

$$\bar{R}_i = \frac{1}{n} \sum_{t=1}^{n} U_{it} \tag{3.36}$$

The stocks are then ranked from highest average return to lowest and from these five portfolios are formed and returns are calculated assuming an equal weighting of stocks in each portfolio (box 3.10).

The same sample length n is used to monitor the performance of each portfolio. Thus, for example, if the portfolio formation period is one, two or three years, the subsequent portfolio tracking period will also be one, two or three years, respectively. Then another portfolio formation period follows and so on until the sample period has been exhausted. How many samples of length n will there be? $n = 1$, 2 or 3 years. First, suppose $n = 1$ year. The procedure adopted would be as shown in box 3.11.

So if $n = 1$, there are eighteen independent (non–overlapping) observation periods and eighteen independent tracking periods. By similar arguments, $n = 2$ gives nine independent periods and $n = 3$ gives six independent periods. The mean return for each month over the 18, 9, or 6 periods for the winner and loser portfolios (the top 20% and bottom 20% of firms in the portfolio formation

Table 3.7   Is there an overreaction effect in the UK stock market?

Panel A: all months

	$n = 12$	$n = 24$	$n = 36$
Return on loser	0.0033	0.0011	0.0129
Return on winner	0.0036	−0.0003	0.0115
Implied annualised return difference	−0.37%	1.68%	1.56%
Coefficient for (3.37): $\hat{\alpha}_1$	−0.00031	0.0014**	0.0013
	(0.29)	(2.01)	(1.55)
Coefficients for (3.38): $\hat{\alpha}_2$	−0.00034	0.00147**	0.0013*
	(−0.30)	(2.01)	(1.41)
Coefficients for (3.38): $\hat{\beta}$	−0.022	0.010	−0.0025
	(−0.25)	(0.21)	(−0.06)

Panel B: all months except January

Coefficient for (3.37): $\hat{\alpha}_1$	−0.0007	0.0012*	0.0009
	(−0.72)	(1.63)	(1.05)

Notes: t-ratios in parentheses; * and ** denote significance at the 10% and 5% levels, respectively.
Source: Clare and Thomas (1995). Reprinted with the permission of Blackwell Publishers.

period) are denoted by $\bar{R}_{pt}^{W}$ and $\bar{R}_{pt}^{L}$, respectively. Define the difference between these as $\bar{R}_{Dt} = \bar{R}_{pt}^{L} - \bar{R}_{pt}^{W}$.

The first regression to be performed is of the excess return of the losers over the winners on a constant only

$$\bar{R}_{Dt} = \alpha_1 + \eta_t \tag{3.37}$$

where η_t is an error term. The test is of whether α_1 is significant and positive. However, a significant and positive α_1 is not a sufficient condition for the overreaction effect to be confirmed because it could be owing to higher returns being required on loser stocks owing to loser stocks being more risky. The solution, Clare and Thomas (1995) argue, is to allow for risk differences by regressing against the market risk premium

$$\bar{R}_{Dt} = \alpha_2 + \beta(R_{mt} - R_{ft}) + \eta_t \tag{3.38}$$

where R_{mt} is the return on the FTA All-share, and R_{ft} is the return on a UK government three-month Treasury Bill. The results for each of these two regressions are presented in table 3.7.

As can be seen by comparing the returns on the winners and losers in the first two rows of table 3.7, twelve months is not a sufficiently long time for losers to become winners. By the two-year tracking horizon, however, the losers have become winners, and similarly for the three-year samples. This translates into an average 1.68% higher return on the losers than the winners at the two-year horizon, and 1.56% higher return at the three-year horizon. Recall that the estimated value of the coefficient in a regression of a variable on a constant only is equal to the average value of that variable. It can also be seen that the estimated coefficients on the constant terms for each horizon are exactly equal to the differences between the returns of the losers and the winners. This coefficient is statistically significant at the two-year horizon, and marginally significant at the three-year horizon.

In the second test regression, $\hat{\beta}$ represents the difference between the market betas of the winner and loser portfolios. None of the beta coefficient estimates are even close to being significant, and the inclusion of the risk term makes virtually no difference to the coefficient values or significances of the intercept terms.

Removal of the January returns from the samples reduces the subsequent degree of overperformance of the loser portfolios, and the significances of the $\hat{\alpha}_1$ terms is somewhat reduced. It is concluded, therefore, that only a part of the overreaction phenomenon occurs in January. Clare and Thomas then proceed to examine whether the overreaction effect is related to firm size, although the results are not presented here.

3.13.3   Conclusions

The main conclusions from Clare and Thomas' study are:

(1) There appears to be evidence of overreactions in UK stock returns, as found in previous US studies.
(2) These overreactions are unrelated to the CAPM beta.
(3) Losers that subsequently become winners tend to be small, so that most of the overreaction in the UK can be attributed to the size effect.

3.14   The exact significance level

The exact significance level is also commonly known as the *p*-value. It gives the *marginal significance level* where one would be indifferent between rejecting and not rejecting the null hypothesis. If the test statistic is 'large' in absolute value, the *p*-value will be small, and vice versa. For example, consider a test statistic that is distributed as a t_{62} and takes a value of 1.47. Would the null hypothesis be rejected? It would depend on the size of the test. Now, suppose that the *p*-value for this test is calculated to be 0.12:

- Is the null rejected at the 5% level?   *No*
- Is the null rejected at the 10% level?   *No*
- Is the null rejected at the 20% level?   *Yes*

	Coefficient	Std. Error	t-Statistic	Prob.
C	0.000640	0.026625	0.024032	0.9809
RFUTURES	1.007291	0.005865	171.7341	0.0000

Table 3.8   Part of the EViews regression output revisited

In fact, the null would have been rejected at the 12% level or higher. To see this, consider conducting a series of tests with size 0.1%, 0.2%, 0.3%, 0.4%, . . . 1%, . . . , 5%, . . . 10%, . . . Eventually, the critical value and test statistic will meet and this will be the p-value. p-values are almost always provided automatically by software packages. Note how useful they are! They provide all of the information required to conduct a hypothesis test without requiring of the researcher the need to calculate a test statistic or to find a critical value from a table – both of these steps have already been taken by the package in producing the p-value. The p-value is also useful since it avoids the requirement of specifying an arbitrary significance level (α). Sensitivity analysis of the effect of the significance level on the conclusion occurs automatically.

Informally, the p-value is also often referred to as the probability of being wrong when the null hypothesis is rejected. Thus, for example, if a p-value of 0.05 or less leads the researcher to reject the null (equivalent to a 5% significance level), this is equivalent to saying that if the probability of incorrectly rejecting the null is more than 5%, do not reject it. The p-value has also been termed the 'plausibility' of the null hypothesis; so, the smaller is the p-value, the less plausible is the null hypothesis.

3.15   Hypothesis testing in EViews – example 1: hedging revisited

Reload the 'hedge.wf1' EViews work file that was created above. If we re-examine the results table from the returns regression (screenshot 3.4), it can be seen that as well as the parameter estimates, EViews automatically calculates the standard errors, the t-ratios and the p-values associated with a two-sided test of the null hypothesis that the true value of a parameter is zero. Part of the results table for the returns regression is replicated again here (table 3.8) for ease of interpretation.

The third column presents the t-ratios, which are the test statistics for testing the null hypothesis that the true values of these parameters are zero against a two sided alternative – i.e. these statistics test $H_0 : \alpha = 0$ versus $H_1 : \alpha \neq 0$ in the first row of numbers and $H_0 : \beta = 0$ versus $H_1 : \beta \neq 0$ in the second. The fact that the first of these test statistics is very small is indicative that the corresponding null hypotheses is likely not to be rejected but it probably will be rejected for the slope. This suggestion is confirmed by the p-values given in the final column. The

Wald Test:
Equation: RETURNREG

Test Statistic	Value	df	Probability
t-statistic	1.243066	132	0.2160
F-statistic	1.545212	(1, 132)	0.2160
Chi-square	1.545212	1	0.2138

Null Hypothesis: C(2) = 1

Null Hypothesis Summary:

Normalised Restriction (= 0)	Value	Std. Err.
$-1 + C(2)$	0.007291	0.005865

Restrictions are linear in coefficients.

intercept p-value is considerably larger than 0.1, indicating that the corresponding test statistic is not even significant at the 10% level; for the slope coefficient, however, it is zero to four decimal places so the null hypothesis is decisively rejected.

Suppose now that we wanted to test the null hypothesis that $H_0 : \beta = 1$ rather than $H_0 : \beta = 0$. We could test this, or any other hypothesis about the coefficients, by hand, using the information we already have. But it is easier to let EViews do the work by typing **View** and then **Coefficient Diagnostics/Wald Test – Coefficient Restrictions . . . .** EViews defines all of the parameters in a vector C, so that C(1) will be the intercept and C(2) will be the slope. Type **C(2)=1** and click **OK**. Note that using this software, it is possible to test multiple hypotheses, which will be discussed in chapter 4, and also non-linear restrictions, which cannot be tested using the standard procedure for inference described above.

The test is performed in three different ways, but results suggest that the null hypothesis should clearly not be rejected as the p-value for the test is considerably greater than 0.05 in each case. Note that, since we are testing a single restriction, the t and F and Chi-squared versions of the test will give the same conclusions – more on this in the next chapter. EViews also reports the 'normalised restriction', although this can be ignored for the time being since it merely reports the regression slope parameter (in a different form) and its standard error.

Now go back to the regression in levels (i.e. with the raw prices rather than the returns) and test the null hypothesis that $\beta = 1$ in this regression. You should find in this case that the null hypothesis is strongly rejected (table below).

Wald Test: Equation: LEVELREG			
Test Statistic	Value	df	Probability
t-statistic	−2.329050	133	0.0214
F-statistic	5.424474	(1, 133)	0.0214
Chi-square	5.424474	1	0.0199
Null Hypothesis: C(2)=1			
Null Hypothesis Summary:			
Normalised Restriction (= 0)		Value	Std. Err.
−1 + C(2)		−0.004368	0.001876
Restrictions are linear in coefficients.			

3.16 Hypothesis testing in EViews – example 2: the CAPM

This exercise will estimate and test some hypotheses about the CAPM beta for several US stocks. First, **Open a new workfile** to accommodate monthly data commencing in January 2002 and ending in April 2013. Note that it is standard to employ five years of monthly data for estimating betas but let us use all of the observations (over ten years) for now. Then **import the Excel file 'capm.xls'.** The file is organised by observation and contains six columns of numbers plus the dates in the first column – you should be able to just click through with the default options. The monthly stock prices of four companies (Ford, General Electric, Microsoft and Oracle) will appear as objects, along with index values for the S&P500 ('sandp') and three-month US-Treasury bills ('ustb3m'). **Save the EViews workfile as 'capm.wk1'.**

In order to estimate a CAPM equation for the Ford stock, for example, we need to first transform the price series into returns and then the excess returns over the risk free rate. To transform the series, click on the Generate button (**Genr**) in the workfile window. In the new window, type

RSANDP=100*LOG(SANDP/SANDP(−1))

This will create a new series named RSANDP that will contain the returns of the S&P500. The operator (−1) is used to instruct EViews to use the one–period lagged observation of the series. To estimate percentage returns on the Ford stock, press the **Genr** button again and type

RFORD=100*LOG(FORD/FORD(−1))

This will yield a new series named RFORD that will contain the returns of the Ford stock. EViews allows various kinds of transformations to the series. For example

X2=X/2	creates a new variable called X2 that is half of X
XSQ=X^2	creates a new variable XSQ that is X squared
LX=LOG(X)	creates a new variable LX that is the log of X
LAGX=X(−1)	creates a new variable LAGX containing X lagged by one period
LAGX2=X(−2)	creates a new variable LAGX2 containing X lagged by two periods

Other functions include:

d(X)	first difference of X
d(X,n)	nth order difference of X
dlog(X)	first difference of the logarithm of X
dlog(X,n)	nth order difference of the logarithm of X
abs(X)	absolute value of X

If, in the transformation, the new series is given the same name as the old series, then the old series will be overwritten. Note that the returns for the S&P index could have been constructed using a simpler command in the 'Genr' window such as

RSANDP=100*DLOG(SANDP)

as we used previously but it is instructive to see how the 'dlog' formula is working. Before we can transform the returns into excess returns, we need to be slightly careful because the stock returns are monthly but the Treasury bill yields are annualised. We could run the whole analysis using monthly data or using annualised data and it should not matter which we use, but the two series must be measured consistently. So, to turn the T-bill yields into monthly figures and to write over the original series, press the **Genr** button again and type

USTB3M=USTB3M/12

Now, to compute the excess returns, click **Genr** again and type

ERSANDP=RSANDP-USTB3M

where 'ERSANDP' will be used to denote the excess returns, so that the original raw returns series will remain in the workfile. The Ford returns can similarly be transformed into a set of excess returns.

Now that the excess returns have been obtained for the two series, before running the regression, plot the data to examine visually whether the series appear to move together. To do this, create a new object by clicking on the **Object/New Object** menu on the menu bar. Select **Graph**, provide a name (call the graph **Graph1**) and then in the new window provide the names of the series to plot. In this new window, type

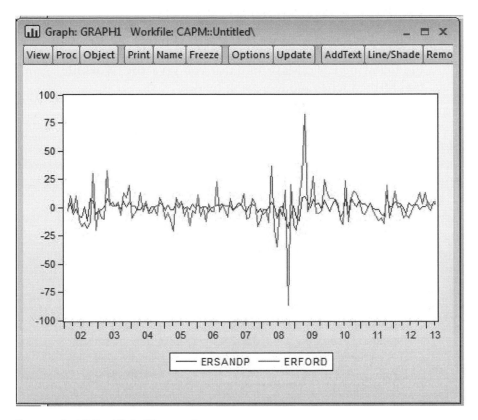

Screenshot 3.5   **Plot of two series**

ERSANDP ERFORD

Then press **OK** and screenshot 3.5 will appear. It is evident that the Ford series is far more volatile than the index as a whole, especially during the 2008–9 period, although on average the two series seem to move in the same direction at most points in time.

This is a time series plot of the two variables, but a scatter plot may be more informative. To examine a scatter plot, Click **Options**, choose the **Graph Type** tab, then select **Scatter** from the list and click **OK**. There appears to be a weak positive association between ERFTAS and ERFORD. Close the window of the graph and return to the workfile window.

To estimate the CAPM equation, click on **Object/New Object ....** In the new window, select **Equation** (the first option in the list) and name the object **CAPM**. Click on **OK**. In the window, specify the regression equation. The regression equation takes the form

$$(R_{Ford} - r_f)_t = \alpha + \beta(R_M - r_f)_t + u_t$$

Since the data have already been transformed to obtain the excess returns, in order to specify this regression equation, in the equation window type

ERFORD C ERSANDP

To use all the observations in the sample and to estimate the regression using LS – Least Squares (NLS and ARMA), click on **OK**. The results screen appears as in the following table. Make sure that you **save the Workfile** again to include the transformed series and regression results.

Dependent Variable: ERFORD
Method: Least Squares
Date: 07/02/13   Time: 10:55
Sample (adjusted): 2002M02 2013M04
Included observations: 135 after adjustments

	Coefficient	Std. Error	t-Statistic	Prob.
C	−0.319863	1.086409	−0.294423	0.7689
ERSANDP	2.026213	0.237743	8.522711	0.0000
R-squared	0.353228	Mean dependent var		−0.078204
Adjusted R-squared	0.348365	S.D. dependent var		15.63184
S.E. of regression	12.61863	Akaike info criterion		7.922930
Sum squared resid	21177.56	Schwarz criterion		7.965971
Log likelihood	−532.7977	Hannan-Quinn criter.		7.940420
F-statistic	72.63660	Durbin-Watson stat		2.588482
Prob(F-statistic)	0.000000			

Take a couple of minutes to examine the results of the regression. What is the slope coefficient estimate and what does it signify? Is this coefficient statistically significant? The beta coefficient (the slope coefficient) estimate is 2.026. The p-value of the t-ratio is 0.0000, signifying that the excess return on the market proxy has highly significant explanatory power for the variability of the excess returns of Ford stock. What is the interpretation of the intercept estimate? Is it statistically significant?

In fact, there is a considerably quicker method for using transformed variables in regression equations, and that is to write the transformation directly into the equation window. In the CAPM example above, this could be done by typing

(100*DLOG(FORD))–(USTB3M/12) C (100*DLOG(SANDP))–(USTB3M/12)

into the equation window. As well as being quicker, an advantage of this approach is that the output will show more clearly the regression that has actually been conducted, so that any errors in making the transformations can be seen more clearly.

How could the hypothesis that the value of the population coefficient is equal to 1 be tested? The answer is to click on **View/Coefficient Diagnostics/ Wald Test – Coefficient Restrictions...** and then in the box that appears,

3A.2 Derivation of the OLS standard error estimators for the intercept and slope in the bivariate case

Recall that the variance of the random variable $\hat{\alpha}$ can be written as

$$\text{var}(\hat{\alpha}) = E(\hat{\alpha} - E(\hat{\alpha}))^2 \tag{3A.15}$$

and since the OLS estimator is unbiased

$$\text{var}(\hat{\alpha}) = E(\hat{\alpha} - \alpha)^2 \tag{3A.16}$$

By similar arguments, the variance of the slope estimator can be written as

$$\text{var}(\hat{\beta}) = E(\hat{\beta} - \beta)^2 \tag{3A.17}$$

Working first with (3A.17), replacing $\hat{\beta}$ with the formula for it given by the OLS estimator

$$\text{var}(\hat{\beta}) = E\left(\frac{\sum (x_t - \bar{x})(y_t - \bar{y})}{\sum (x_t - \bar{x})^2} - \beta\right)^2 \tag{3A.18}$$

Replacing y_t with $\alpha + \beta x_t + u_t$, and replacing $\bar{y}$ with $\alpha + \beta \bar{x}$ in (3A.18)

$$\text{var}(\hat{\beta}) = E\left(\frac{\sum (x_t - \bar{x})(\alpha + \beta x_t + u_t - \alpha - \beta \bar{x})}{\sum (x_t - \bar{x})^2} - \beta\right)^2 \tag{3A.19}$$

Cancelling α and multiplying the last β term in (3A.19) by $\dfrac{\sum (x_t - \bar{x})^2}{\sum (x_t - \bar{x})^2}$

$$\text{var}(\hat{\beta}) = E\left(\frac{\sum (x_t - \bar{x})(\beta x_t + u_t - \beta \bar{x}) - \beta \sum (x_t - \bar{x})^2}{\sum (x_t - \bar{x})^2}\right)^2 \tag{3A.20}$$

Rearranging

$$\text{var}(\hat{\beta}) = E\left(\frac{\sum (x_t - \bar{x})\beta(x_t - \bar{x}) + \sum u_t(x_t - \bar{x}) - \beta \sum (x_t - \bar{x})^2}{\sum (x_t - \bar{x})^2}\right)^2 \tag{3A.21}$$

$$\text{var}(\hat{\beta}) = E\left(\frac{\beta \sum (x_t - \bar{x})^2 + \sum u_t(x_t - \bar{x}) - \beta \sum (x_t - \bar{x})^2}{\sum (x_t - \bar{x})^2}\right)^2 \tag{3A.22}$$

Now the β terms in (3A.22) will cancel to give

$$\text{var}(\hat{\beta}) = E\left(\frac{\sum u_t(x_t - \bar{x})}{\sum (x_t - \bar{x})^2}\right)^2 \tag{3A.23}$$

Now let x_t^* denote the mean-adjusted observation for x_t, i.e. $(x_t - \bar{x})$. Equation (3A.23) can be written

$$\text{var}(\hat{\beta}) = E\left(\frac{\sum u_t x_t^*}{\sum x_t^{*2}}\right)^2 \qquad (3A.24)$$

The denominator of (3A.24) can be taken through the expectations operator under the assumption that x is fixed or non-stochastic

$$\text{var}(\hat{\beta}) = \frac{1}{\left(\sum x_t^{*2}\right)^2} E\left(\sum u_t x_t^*\right)^2 \qquad (3A.25)$$

Writing the terms out in the last summation of (3A.25)

$$\text{var}(\hat{\beta}) = \frac{1}{\left(\sum x_t^{*2}\right)^2} E\left(u_1 x_1^* + u_2 x_2^* + \cdots + u_T x_T^*\right)^2 \qquad (3A.26)$$

Now expanding the brackets of the squared term in the expectations operator of (3A.26)

$$\text{var}(\hat{\beta}) = \frac{1}{\left(\sum x_t^{*2}\right)^2} E\left(u_1^2 x_1^{*2} + u_2^2 x_2^{*2} + \cdots + u_T^2 x_T^{*2} + \textit{cross-products}\right)$$

$$(3A.27)$$

where 'cross-products' in (3A.27) denotes all of the terms $u_i x_i^* u_j x_j^*$ $(i \neq j)$. These cross-products can be written as $u_i u_j x_i^* x_j^*$ $(i \neq j)$ and their expectation will be zero under the assumption that the error terms are uncorrelated with one another. Thus, the 'cross-products' term in (3A.27) will drop out. Recall also from the chapter text that $E(u_t^2)$ is the error variance, which is estimated using s^2

$$\text{var}(\hat{\beta}) = \frac{1}{\left(\sum x_t^{*2}\right)^2} \left(s^2 x_1^{*2} + s^2 x_2^{*2} + \cdots + s^2 x_T^{*2}\right) \qquad (3A.28)$$

which can also be written

$$\text{var}(\hat{\beta}) = \frac{s^2}{\left(\sum x_t^{*2}\right)^2} \left(x_1^{*2} + x_2^{*2} + \cdots + x_T^{*2}\right) = \frac{s^2 \sum x_t^{*2}}{\left(\sum x_t^{*2}\right)^2} \qquad (3A.29)$$

A term in $\sum x_t^{*2}$ can be cancelled from the numerator and denominator of (3A.29), and recalling that $x_t^* = (x_t - \bar{x})$, this gives the variance of the slope coefficient as

$$\text{var}(\hat{\beta}) = \frac{s^2}{\sum (x_t - \bar{x})^2} \qquad (3A.30)$$

so that the standard error can be obtained by taking the square root of (3A.30)

$$SE(\hat{\beta}) = s\sqrt{\frac{1}{\sum (x_t - \bar{x})^2}} \tag{3A.31}$$

Turning now to the derivation of the intercept standard error, this is much more difficult than that of the slope standard error. In fact, both are very much easier using matrix algebra as shown below. Therefore, this derivation will be offered in summary form. It is possible to express $\hat{\alpha}$ as a function of the true α and of the disturbances, u_t

$$\hat{\alpha} = \alpha + \frac{\sum u_t \left[\sum x_t^2 - x_t \sum x_t \right]}{\left[T \sum x_t^2 - \left(\sum x_t \right)^2 \right]} \tag{3A.32}$$

Denoting all of the elements in square brackets as g_t, (3A.32) can be written

$$\hat{\alpha} - \alpha = \sum u_t g_t \tag{3A.33}$$

From (3A.15), the intercept variance would be written

$$\text{var}(\hat{\alpha}) = E\left(\sum u_t g_t \right)^2 = \sum g_t^2 E\left(u_t^2 \right) = s^2 \sum g_t^2 \tag{3A.34}$$

Writing (3A.34) out in full for g_t^2 and expanding the brackets

$$\text{var}(\hat{\alpha}) = \frac{s^2 \left[T \left(\sum x_t^2 \right)^2 - 2 \sum x_t \left(\sum x_t^2 \right) \sum x_t + \left(\sum x_t^2 \right) \left(\sum x_t \right)^2 \right]}{\left[T \sum x_t^2 - \left(\sum x_t \right)^2 \right]^2} \tag{3A.35}$$

This looks rather complex, but fortunately, if we take $\sum x_t^2$ outside the square brackets in the numerator, the remaining numerator cancels with a term in the denominator to leave the required result

$$SE(\hat{\alpha}) = s\sqrt{\frac{\sum x_t^2}{T \sum (x_t - \bar{x})^2}} \tag{3A.36}$$

Self-study questions

1. (a) Why does OLS estimation involve taking vertical deviations of the points to the line rather than horizontal distances?
   (b) Why are the vertical distances squared before being added together?
   (c) Why are the squares of the vertical distances taken rather than the absolute values?

2. Explain, with the use of equations, the difference between the sample regression function and the population regression function.

3. What is an estimator? Is the OLS estimator superior to all other estimators? Why or why not?

4. What five assumptions are usually made about the unobservable error terms in the classical linear regression model (CLRM)? Briefly explain the meaning of each. Why are these assumptions made?

5. Which of the following models can be estimated (following a suitable rearrangement if necessary) using ordinary least squares (OLS), where X, y, Z are variables and α, β, γ are parameters to be estimated? (*Hint*: the models need to be linear in the parameters.)

$$y_t = \alpha + \beta x_t + u_t \tag{3.39}$$

$$y_t = e^{\alpha} x_t^{\beta} e^{u_t} \tag{3.40}$$

$$y_t = \alpha + \beta \gamma x_t + u_t \tag{3.41}$$

$$\ln(y_t) = \alpha + \beta \ln(x_t) + u_t \tag{3.42}$$

$$y_t = \alpha + \beta x_t z_t + u_t \tag{3.43}$$

6. The capital asset pricing model (CAPM) can be written as

$$E(R_i) = R_f + \beta_i[E(R_m) - R_f] \tag{3.44}$$

using the standard notation.

The first step in using the CAPM is to estimate the stock's beta using the market model. The market model can be written as

$$R_{it} = \alpha_i + \beta_i R_{mt} + u_{it} \tag{3.45}$$

where R_{it} is the excess return for security i at time t, R_{mt} is the excess return on a proxy for the market portfolio at time t, and u_t is an iid random disturbance term. The cofficient beta in this case is also the CAPM beta for security i.

Suppose that you had estimated (3.45) and found that the estimated value of beta for a stock, $\hat{\beta}$ was 1.147. The standard error associated with this coefficient $SE(\hat{\beta})$ is estimated to be 0.0548.

A city analyst has told you that this security closely follows the market, but that it is no more risky, on average, than the market. This can be tested by the null hypotheses that the value of beta is one. The model is estimated over sixty–two daily observations. Test this hypothesis against a one–sided alternative that the security is more risky than the market, at the 5% level. Write down the null and alternative hypothesis. What do you conclude? Are the analyst's claims empirically verified?

7. The analyst also tells you that shares in Chris Mining plc have no systematic risk, in other words that the returns on its shares are completely unrelated to movements in the market. The value of beta and its standard error are calculated to be 0.214 and 0.186, respectively. The model is estimated over

thirty-eight quarterly observations. Write down the null and alternative hypotheses. Test this null hypothesis against a two-sided alternative.

8. Form and interpret a 95% and a 99% confidence interval for beta using the figures given in question 7.

9. Are hypotheses tested concerning the actual values of the coefficients (i.e. β) or their estimated values (i.e. $\hat{\beta}$) and why?

10. Using EViews, select one of the other stock series from the 'capm.wk1' file and estimate a CAPM beta for that stock. Test the null hypothesis that the true beta is one and also test the null hypothesis that the true alpha (intercept) is zero. What are your conclusions?

4 Further development and analysis of the classical linear regression model

Learning outcomes

In this chapter, you will learn how to
- Construct models with more than one explanatory variable
- Test multiple hypotheses using an F-test
- Determine how well a model fits the data
- Form a restricted regression
- Derive the OLS parameter and standard error estimators using matrix algebra
- Estimate multiple regression models and test multiple hypotheses in EViews
- Construct and interpret quantile regression models

4.1 Generalising the simple model to multiple linear regression

Previously, a model of the following form has been used

$$y_t = \alpha + \beta x_t + u_t \quad t = 1, 2, \ldots, T \tag{4.1}$$

Equation (4.1) is a simple bivariate regression model. That is, changes in the dependent variable are explained by reference to changes in one single explanatory variable x. But what if the financial theory or idea that is sought to be tested suggests that the dependent variable is influenced by more than one independent variable? For example, simple estimation and tests of the capital asset pricing model (CAPM) can be conducted using an equation of the form of (4.1), but arbitrage pricing theory does not pre-suppose that there is only a single factor affecting stock returns. So, to give one illustration, stock returns might be purported to depend on their sensitivity to unexpected changes in:

(1) inflation
(2) the differences in returns on short- and long-dated bonds

(3) industrial production

(4) default risks.

Having just one independent variable would be no good in this case. It would of course be possible to use each of the four proposed explanatory factors in separate regressions. But it is of greater interest and it is more valid to have more than one explanatory variable in the regression equation at the same time, and therefore to examine the effect of all of the explanatory variables together on the explained variable.

It is very easy to generalise the simple model to one with k regressors (independent variables). Equation (4.1) becomes

$$y_t = \beta_1 + \beta_2 x_{2t} + \beta_3 x_{3t} + \cdots + \beta_k x_{kt} + u_t, \quad t = 1, 2, \ldots, T \tag{4.2}$$

So the variables $x_{2t}, x_{3t}, \ldots, x_{kt}$ are a set of $k - 1$ explanatory variables which are thought to influence y, and the coefficient estimates $\beta_1, \beta_2, \ldots, \beta_k$ are the parameters which quantify the effect of each of these explanatory variables on y. The coefficient interpretations are slightly altered in the multiple regression context. Each coefficient is now known as a partial regression coefficient, interpreted as representing the partial effect of the given explanatory variable on the explained variable, after holding constant, or eliminating the effect of, all other explanatory variables. For example, $\hat{\beta}_2$ measures the effect of x_2 on y after eliminating the effects of $x_3, x_4, \ldots, x_k$. Stating this in other words, each coefficient measures the average change in the dependent variable per unit change in a given independent variable, holding all other independent variables constant at their average values.

4.2 The constant term

In (4.2) above, astute readers will have noticed that the explanatory variables are numbered $x_2, x_3, \ldots$ i.e. the list starts with x_2 and not x_1. So, where is x_1? In fact, it is the constant term, usually represented by a column of ones of length T:

$$x_1 = \begin{bmatrix} 1 \\ 1 \\ \vdots \\ \vdots \\ 1 \end{bmatrix} \tag{4.3}$$

Thus there is a variable implicitly hiding next to β_1, which is a column vector of ones, the length of which is the number of observations in the sample. The x_1 in the regression equation is not usually written, in the same way that one unit of p and two units of q would be written as '$p + 2q$' and not '$1p + 2q$'. β_1 is the coefficient attached to the constant term (which was called α in the previous chapter). This coefficient can still be referred to as the *intercept*, which can be interpreted as the average value which y would take if all of the explanatory variables took a value of zero.

A tighter definition of k, the number of explanatory variables, is probably now necessary. Throughout this book, k is defined as the number of 'explanatory variables' or 'regressors' including the constant term. This is equivalent to the number of parameters that are estimated in the regression equation. Strictly speaking, it is not sensible to call the constant an explanatory variable, since it does not explain anything and it always takes the same values. However, this definition of k will be employed for notational convenience.

Equation (4.2) can be expressed even more compactly by writing it in matrix form

$$y = X\beta + u \tag{4.4}$$

where: y is of dimension $T \times 1$

X is of dimension $T \times k$

β is of dimension $k \times 1$

u is of dimension $T \times 1$

The difference between (4.2) and (4.4) is that all of the time observations have been stacked up in a vector, and also that all of the different explanatory variables have been squashed together so that there is a column for each in the X matrix. Such a notation may seem unnecessarily complex, but in fact, the matrix notation is usually more compact and convenient. So, for example, if k is 2, i.e. there are two regressors, one of which is the constant term (equivalent to a simple bivariate regression $y_t = \alpha + \beta x_t + u_t$), it is possible to write

$$\begin{bmatrix} y_1 \\ y_2 \\ \vdots \\ y_T \end{bmatrix} = \begin{bmatrix} 1 & x_{21} \\ 1 & x_{22} \\ \vdots & \vdots \\ 1 & x_{2T} \end{bmatrix} \begin{bmatrix} \beta_1 \\ \beta_2 \end{bmatrix} + \begin{bmatrix} u_1 \\ u_2 \\ \vdots \\ u_T \end{bmatrix} \tag{4.5}$$

$$T \times 1 \qquad T \times 2 \quad 2 \times 1 \quad T \times 1$$

so that the x_{ij} element of the matrix X represents the jth time observation on the ith variable. Notice that the matrices written in this way are *conformable* – in other words, there is a valid matrix multiplication and addition on the right hand side (RHS).

The above presentation is the standard way to express matrices in the time series econometrics literature, although the ordering of the indices is different to that used in the mathematics of matrix algebra (as presented in chapter 2 of this book). In the latter case, x_{ij} would represent the element in row i and column j, although in the notation used in the body of this book it is the other way around.

How are the parameters (the elements of the β vector) calculated in the generalised case?

Previously, the residual sum of squares, $\sum \hat{u}_i^2$ was minimised with respect to α and β. In the multiple regression context, in order to obtain estimates of the parameters, $\beta_1, \beta_2, \ldots, \beta_k$, the RSS would be minimised with respect to all the elements of β. Now, the residuals can be stacked in a vector:

$$\hat{u} = \begin{bmatrix} \hat{u}_1 \\ \hat{u}_2 \\ \vdots \\ \hat{u}_T \end{bmatrix} \tag{4.6}$$

The RSS is still the relevant loss function, and would be given in a matrix notation by

$$L = \hat{u}'\hat{u} = [\hat{u}_1 \hat{u}_2 \cdots \hat{u}_T] \begin{bmatrix} \hat{u}_1 \\ \hat{u}_2 \\ \vdots \\ \hat{u}_T \end{bmatrix} = \hat{u}_1^2 + \hat{u}_2^2 + \cdots + \hat{u}_T^2 = \sum \hat{u}_t^2 \tag{4.7}$$

Using a similar procedure to that employed in the bivariate regression case, i.e. substituting into (4.7), and denoting the vector of estimated parameters as $\hat{\beta}$, it can be shown (see the appendix to this chapter) that the coefficient estimates will be given by the elements of the expression

$$\hat{\beta} = \begin{bmatrix} \hat{\beta}_1 \\ \hat{\beta}_2 \\ \vdots \\ \hat{\beta}_k \end{bmatrix} = (X'X)^{-1}X'y \tag{4.8}$$

If one were to check the dimensions of the RHS of (4.8), it would be observed to be $k \times 1$. This is as required since there are k parameters to be estimated by the formula for $\hat{\beta}$.

But how are the standard errors of the coefficient estimates calculated? Previously, to estimate the variance of the errors, σ^2, an estimator denoted by s^2 was used

$$s^2 = \frac{\sum \hat{u}_t^2}{T - 2} \tag{4.9}$$

The denominator of (4.9) is given by $T - 2$, which is the number of degrees of freedom for the bivariate regression model (i.e. the number of observations minus two). This essentially applies since two observations are effectively 'lost' in estimating the two model parameters (i.e. in deriving estimates for α and β). In the case where there is more than one explanatory variable plus a constant, and using the matrix notation, (4.9) would be modified to

$$s^2 = \frac{\hat{u}'\hat{u}}{T - k} \tag{4.10}$$

where k = number of regressors including a constant. In this case, k observations are 'lost' as k parameters are estimated, leaving $T - k$ degrees of freedom. It can also be shown (see the appendix to this chapter) that the parameter variance–covariance matrix is given by

$$\text{var}(\hat{\beta}) = s^2 (X'X)^{-1} \tag{4.11}$$

The leading diagonal terms give the coefficient variances while the off-diagonal terms give the covariances between the parameter estimates, so that the variance of $\hat{\beta}_1$ is the first diagonal element, the variance of $\hat{\beta}_2$ is the second element on the leading diagonal, and the variance of $\hat{\beta}_k$ is the kth diagonal element. The coefficient standard errors are thus simply given by taking the square roots of each of the terms on the leading diagonal.

Example 4.1

The following model with three regressors (including the constant) is estimated over fifteen observations

$$y = \beta_1 + \beta_2 x_2 + \beta_3 x_3 + u \tag{4.12}$$

and the following data have been calculated from the original xs

$$(X'X)^{-1} = \begin{bmatrix} 2.0 & 3.5 & -1.0 \\ 3.5 & 1.0 & 6.5 \\ -1.0 & 6.5 & 4.3 \end{bmatrix}, \quad (X'y) = \begin{bmatrix} -3.0 \\ 2.2 \\ 0.6 \end{bmatrix}, \quad \hat{u}'\hat{u} = 10.96$$

Calculate the coefficient estimates and their standard errors.

$$\hat{\beta} = \begin{bmatrix} \hat{\beta}_1 \\ \hat{\beta}_2 \\ \vdots \\ \hat{\beta}_k \end{bmatrix} = (X'X)^{-1}X'y = \begin{bmatrix} 2.0 & 3.5 & -1.0 \\ 3.5 & 1.0 & 6.5 \\ -1.0 & 6.5 & 4.3 \end{bmatrix}$$

$$\times \begin{bmatrix} -3.0 \\ 2.2 \\ 0.6 \end{bmatrix} = \begin{bmatrix} 1.10 \\ -4.40 \\ 19.88 \end{bmatrix} \tag{4.13}$$

To calculate the standard errors, an estimate of σ^2 is required

$$s^2 = \frac{RSS}{T - k} = \frac{10.96}{15 - 3} = 0.91 \tag{4.14}$$

The variance–covariance matrix of $\hat{\beta}$ is given by

$$s^2(X'X)^{-1} = 0.91(X'X)^{-1} = \begin{bmatrix} 1.82 & 3.19 & -0.91 \\ 3.19 & 0.91 & 5.92 \\ -0.91 & 5.92 & 3.91 \end{bmatrix} \tag{4.15}$$

The coefficient variances are on the diagonals, and the standard errors are found by taking the square roots of each of the coefficient variances

$$\text{var}(\hat{\beta}_1) = 1.82 \quad SE(\hat{\beta}_1) = 1.35 \tag{4.16}$$

$$\text{var}(\hat{\beta}_2) = 0.91 \Leftrightarrow SE(\hat{\beta}_2) = 0.95 \tag{4.17}$$

$$\text{var}(\hat{\beta}_3) = 3.91 \quad SE(\hat{\beta}_3) = 1.98 \tag{4.18}$$

The estimated equation would be written

$$\hat{y} = 1.10 - 4.40x_2 + 19.88x_3$$
$$\quad (1.35) \ (0.95) \qquad (1.98) \tag{4.19}$$

Fortunately, in practice all econometrics software packages will estimate the coefficient values and their standard errors. Clearly, though, it is still useful to understand where these estimates came from.

4.4 Testing multiple hypotheses: the F-test

The t-test was used to test single hypotheses, i.e. hypotheses involving only one coefficient. But what if it is of interest to test more than one coefficient simultaneously? For example, what if a researcher wanted to determine whether a restriction that the coefficient values for β_2 and β_3 are both unity could be imposed, so that an increase in either one of the two variables x_2 or x_3 would cause y to rise by one unit? The t-testing framework is not sufficiently general to cope with this sort of hypothesis test. Instead, a more general framework is employed, centring on an F-test. Under the F-test framework, two regressions are required, known as the unrestricted and the restricted regressions. The unrestricted regression is the one in which the coefficients are freely determined by the data, as has been constructed previously. The restricted regression is the one in which the coefficients are restricted, i.e. the restrictions are imposed on some βs. Thus the F test approach to hypothesis testing is also termed restricted least squares, for obvious reasons.

The residual sums of squares from each regression are determined, and the two residual sums of squares are 'compared' in the test statistic. The F-test statistic for testing multiple hypotheses about the coefficient estimates is given by

$$\text{test statistic} = \frac{RRSS - URSS}{URSS} \times \frac{T - k}{m} \tag{4.20}$$

where the following notation applies:

$URSS$ = residual sum of squares from unrestricted regression

$RRSS$ = residual sum of squares from restricted regression

m = number of restrictions

T = number of observations

k = number of regressors in unrestricted regression including the constant

The most important part of the test statistic to understand is the numerator expression $RRSS - URSS$. To see why the test centres around a comparison of the residual sums of squares from the restricted and unrestricted regressions, recall that OLS estimation involved choosing the model that minimised the residual sum of squares, with no constraints imposed. Now if, after imposing constraints on the model, a residual sum of squares results that is not much higher than the unconstrained model's residual sum of squares, it would be concluded that the restrictions were supported by the data. On the other hand, if the residual sum of squares increased considerably after the restrictions were imposed, it would be concluded that the restrictions were not supported by the data and therefore that the hypothesis should be rejected.

It can be further stated that $RRSS \geq URSS$. Only under a particular set of very extreme circumstances will the residual sums of squares for the restricted and unrestricted models be exactly equal. This would be the case when the restriction was already present in the data, so that it is not really a restriction at all (it would be said that the restriction is 'not binding', i.e. it does not make any difference to the parameter estimates). So, for example, if the null hypothesis is H_0: $\beta_2 = 1$ and $\beta_3 = 1$, then $RRSS = URSS$ only in the case where the coefficient estimates for the unrestricted regression had been $\hat{\beta}_2 = 1$ and $\hat{\beta}_3 = 1$. Of course, such an event is extremely unlikely to occur in practice.

Example 4.2 •

Dropping the time subscripts for simplicity, suppose that the general regression is

$$y = \beta_1 + \beta_2 x_2 + \beta_3 x_3 + \beta_4 x_4 + u \tag{4.21}$$

and that the restriction $\beta_3 + \beta_4 = 1$ is under test (there exists some hypothesis from theory which suggests that this would be an interesting hypothesis to study). The unrestricted regression is (4.21) above, but what is the restricted regression? It could be expressed as

$$y = \beta_1 + \beta_2 x_2 + \beta_3 x_3 + \beta_4 x_4 + u \text{ s.t. (subject to) } \beta_3 + \beta_4 = 1 \tag{4.22}$$

The restriction ($\beta_3 + \beta_4 = 1$) is substituted into the regression so that it is automatically imposed on the data. The way that this would be achieved would be to make either β_3 or β_4 the subject of (4.22), e.g.

$$\beta_3 + \beta_4 = 1 \Rightarrow \beta_4 = 1 - \beta_3 \tag{4.23}$$

and then substitute into (4.21) for β_4

$$y = \beta_1 + \beta_2 x_2 + \beta_3 x_3 + (1 - \beta_3)x_4 + u \qquad (4.24)$$

Equation (4.24) is already a restricted form of the regression, but it is not yet in the form that is required to estimate it using a computer package. In order to be able to estimate a model using OLS, software packages usually require each RHS variable to be multiplied by one coefficient only. Therefore, a little more algebraic manipulation is required. First, expanding the brackets around $(1 - \beta_3)$

$$y = \beta_1 + \beta_2 x_2 + \beta_3 x_3 + x_4 - \beta_3 x_4 + u \qquad (4.25)$$

Then, gathering all of the terms in each β_i together and rearranging

$$(y - x_4) = \beta_1 + \beta_2 x_2 + \beta_3(x_3 - x_4) + u \qquad (4.26)$$

Note that any variables without coefficients attached (e.g. x_4 in (4.25)) are taken over to the LHS and are then combined with y. Equation (4.26) is the restricted regression. It is actually estimated by creating two new variables – call them, say, P and Q, where $P = y - x_4$ and $Q = x_3 - x_4$ – so the regression that is actually estimated is

$$P = \beta_1 + \beta_2 x_2 + \beta_3 Q + u \qquad (4.27)$$

What would have happened if instead β_3 had been made the subject of (4.23) and β_3 had therefore been removed from the equation? Although the equation that would have been estimated would have been different from (4.27), the value of the residual sum of squares for these two models (both of which have imposed upon them the same restriction) would be the same.

The test statistic follows the *F*-distribution under the null hypothesis. The *F*-distribution has two degrees of freedom parameters (recall that the *t*-distribution had only one degree of freedom parameter, equal to $T - k$). The value of the degrees of freedom parameters for the *F*-test are m, the number of restrictions imposed on the model, and $(T - k)$, the number of observations less the number of regressors for the unrestricted regression, respectively. Note that the order of the degree of freedom parameters is important. The appropriate critical value will be in column m, row $(T - k)$ of the *F*-distribution tables.

4.4.1 The relationship between the *t*- and the *F*-distributions

Any hypothesis that could be tested with a *t*-test could also have been tested using an *F*-test, but not the other way around. So, single hypotheses involving one coefficient can be tested using a *t*- or an *F*-test, but multiple hypotheses can be tested only using an *F*-test. For example, consider the hypothesis

$$H_0 : \beta_2 = 0.5$$

$$H_1 : \beta_2 \neq 0.5$$

This hypothesis could have been tested using the usual t-test

$$test\ stat = \frac{\hat{\beta}_2 - 0.5}{SE(\hat{\beta}_2)} \tag{4.28}$$

or it could be tested in the framework above for the F-test. Note that the two tests always give the same conclusion since the t-distribution is just a special case of the F-distribution. For example, consider any random variable Z that follows a t-distribution with $T - k$ degrees of freedom, and square it. The square of the t is equivalent to a particular form of the F-distribution

$$Z^2 \sim t^2\ (T - k) \text{ then also } Z^2 \sim F(1, T - k)$$

Thus the square of a t-distributed random variable with $T - k$ degrees of freedom also follows an F-distribution with 1 and $T - k$ degrees of freedom. This relationship between the t and the F-distributions will always hold – take some examples from the statistical tables and try it!

The F-distribution has only positive values and is not symmetrical. Therefore, the null is rejected only if the test statistic exceeds the critical F-value, although the test is a two-sided one in the sense that rejection will occur if $\hat{\beta}_2$ is significantly bigger or significantly smaller than 0.5.

4.4.2   Determining the number of restrictions, m

How is the appropriate value of m decided in each case? Informally, the number of restrictions can be seen as 'the number of equality signs under the null hypothesis'. To give some examples

H_0 : hypothesis	No. of restrictions, m
$\beta_1 + \beta_2 = 2$	1
$\beta_2 = 1$ and $\beta_3 = -1$	2
$\beta_2 = 0$, $\beta_3 = 0$ and $\beta_4 = 0$	3

At first glance, you may have thought that in the first of these cases, the number of restrictions was two. In fact, there is only one restriction that involves two coefficients. The number of restrictions in the second two examples is obvious, as they involve two and three separate component restrictions, respectively.

The last of these three examples is particularly important. If the model is

$$y = \beta_1 + \beta_2 x_2 + \beta_3 x_3 + \beta_4 x_4 + u \tag{4.29}$$

then the null hypothesis of

$$H_0 : \beta_2 = 0 \quad \text{and} \quad \beta_3 = 0 \quad \text{and} \quad \beta_4 = 0$$

is tested by 'THE' regression F-statistic. It tests the null hypothesis that all of the coefficients except the intercept coefficient are zero. This test is sometimes called a test for 'junk regressions', since if this null hypothesis cannot be rejected, it would imply that none of the independent variables in the model was able to explain variations in y.

Note the form of the alternative hypothesis for all tests when more than one restriction is involved

$$H_1 : \beta_2 \neq 0 \quad \text{or} \quad \beta_3 \neq 0 \quad \text{or} \quad \beta_4 \neq 0$$

In other words, 'and' occurs under the null hypothesis and 'or' under the alternative, so that it takes only one part of a joint null hypothesis to be wrong for the null hypothesis as a whole to be rejected.

4.4.3 Hypotheses that cannot be tested with either an F- or a t-test

It is not possible to test hypotheses that are not linear or that are multiplicative using this framework – for example, $H_0 : \beta_2 \beta_3 = 2$, or $H_0 : \beta_2^2 = 1$ cannot be tested.

Example 4.3

Suppose that a researcher wants to test whether the returns on a company stock (y) show unit sensitivity to two factors (factor x_2 and factor x_3) among three considered. The regression is carried out on 144 monthly observations. The regression is

$$y = \beta_1 + \beta_2 x_2 + \beta_3 x_3 + \beta_4 x_4 + u \tag{4.30}$$

(1) What are the restricted and unrestricted regressions?
(2) If the two RSS are 436.1 and 397.2, respectively, perform the test.

Unit sensitivity to factors x_2 and x_3 implies the restriction that the coefficients on these two variables should be unity, so H_0: $\beta_2 = 1$ and $\beta_3 = 1$. The unrestricted regression will be the one given by (4.30) above. To derive the restricted regression, first impose the restriction:

$$y = \beta_1 + \beta_2 x_2 + \beta_3 x_3 + \beta_4 x_4 + u \quad \text{s.t.} \quad \beta_2 = 1 \quad \text{and} \quad \beta_3 = 1 \tag{4.31}$$

Replacing β_2 and β_3 by their values under the null hypothesis

$$y = \beta_1 + x_2 + x_3 + \beta_4 x_4 + u \tag{4.32}$$

Rearranging

$$y - x_2 - x_3 = \beta_1 + \beta_4 x_4 + u \tag{4.33}$$

Defining $z = y - x_2 - x_3$, the restricted regression is one of z on a constant and x_4

$$z = \beta_1 + \beta_4 x_4 + u \tag{4.34}$$

The formula for the F-test statistic is given in (4.20) above. For this application, the following inputs to the formula are available: $T = 144$, $k = 4$, $m = 2$, $RRSS = 436.1$, $URSS = 397.2$. Plugging these into the formula gives an F-test statistic value of 6.86. This statistic should be compared with an $F(m, T - k)$, which in this case is an $F(2, 140)$. The critical values are 4.07 at the 5% level and 4.79 at the 1% level. The test statistic clearly exceeds the critical values at both the 5% and 1% levels, and hence the null hypothesis is rejected. It would thus be concluded that the restriction is not supported by the data.

The following sections will now re-examine the CAPM model as an illustration of how to conduct multiple hypothesis tests using EViews.

4.5 Sample EViews output for multiple hypothesis tests

Reload the 'capm.wk1' workfile constructed in the previous chapter. As a reminder, the results are included again below.

Dependent Variable: ERFORD
Method: Least Squares
Date: 07/02/13 Time: 10:55
Sample (adjusted): 2002M02 2013M04
Included observations: 135 after adjustments

	Coefficient	Std. Error	t-Statistic	Prob.
C	−0.319863	1.086409	−0.294423	0.7689
ERSANDP	2.026213	0.237743	8.522711	0.0000

R-squared	0.353228	Mean dependent var	−0.078204
Adjusted R-squared	0.348365	S.D. dependent var	15.63184
S.E. of regression	12.61863	Akaike info criterion	7.922930
Sum squared resid	21177.56	Schwarz criterion	7.965971
Log likelihood	−532.7977	Hannan-Quinn criter.	7.940420
F-statistic	72.63660	Durbin-Watson stat	2.588482
Prob(F-statistic)	0.000000		

If we examine the regression F-test, this also shows that the regression slope coefficient is very significantly different from zero, which in this case is exactly the same result as the t-test for the beta coefficient (since there is only one slope coefficient). Thus, in this instance, the F-test statistic is equal to the square of the slope t-ratio.

Now suppose that we wish to conduct a joint test that both the intercept and slope parameters are 1. We would perform this test exactly as for a test involving only one coefficient. Select **View/Coefficient Diagnostics/Wald Test – Coefficient Restrictions...** and then in the box that appears, type **C(1)=1, C(2)=1**. There are two versions of the test given: an F-version and a χ^2-version. The F-version is adjusted for small sample bias and should be used when the regression is estimated using a small sample (see chapter 5). Both statistics asymptotically yield the same result, and in this case the p-values are very similar. The conclusion is that the joint null hypothesis, $H_0 : \beta_1 = 1$ and $\beta_2 = 1$, is strongly rejected.

4.6 Multiple regression in EViews using an APT-style model

In the spirit of arbitrage pricing theory (APT), the following example will examine regressions that seek to determine whether the monthly returns on Microsoft stock can be explained by reference to unexpected changes in a set of macroeconomic and financial variables. **Open a new EViews workfile** to store the data. There are 326 monthly observations in the file 'macro.xls', starting in March 1986 and ending in April 2013. There are thirteen series in total plus a column of dates. The series in the Excel file are the Microsoft stock price, the S&P500 index value, the consumer price index, an industrial production index, Treasury bill yields for the following maturities: three months, six months, one year, three years, five years and ten years, a measure of 'narrow' money supply, a consumer credit series, and a 'credit spread' series. The latter is defined as the difference in annualised average yields between a portfolio of bonds rated AAA and a portfolio of bonds rated BAA.

> **Import the data** from the Excel file and save the resulting workfile as 'macro.wf1'.

The first stage is to generate a set of changes or *differences* for each of the variables, since the APT posits that the stock returns can be explained by reference to the *unexpected changes* in the macroeconomic variables rather than their levels. The unexpected value of a variable can be defined as the difference between the actual (realised) value of the variable and its expected value. The question then arises about how we believe that investors might have formed their expectations, and while there are many ways to construct measures of expectations, the easiest is to assume that investors have naive expectations that the next period value of the variable is equal to the current value. This being the case, the entire change in the variable from one period to the next is the unexpected change (because investors are assumed to expect no change).[1]

Transforming the variables can be done as described above. Press **Genr** and then enter the following in the 'Enter equation' box:

> **dspread = baa_aaa_spread − baa_aaa_spread(-1)**

Repeat these steps to conduct all of the following transformations:

> **dcredit = consumer_credit − consumer_credit(-1)**
> **dprod = industrial_production − industrial_production(-1)**
> **rmsoft = 100*dlog(microsoft)**
> **rsandp = 100*dlog(sandp)**
> **dmoney = m1money_supply − m1money_supply(-1)**

---

[1] It is an interesting question as to whether the differences should be taken on the levels of the variables or their logarithms. If the former, we have absolute changes in the variables, whereas the latter would lead to proportionate changes. The choice between the two is essentially an empirical one, and this example assumes that the former is chosen, apart from for the stock price series themselves and the consumer price series.

$$\text{inflation} = 100*\text{dlog(cpi)}$$
$$\text{term} = \text{ustb10y} - \text{ustb3m}$$

and then click **OK**. Next, we need to apply further transformations to some of the transformed series, so **repeat the above steps** to generate

$$\text{dinflation} = \text{inflation} - \text{inflation}(-1)$$
$$\text{mustb3m} = \text{ustb3m}/12$$
$$\text{rterm} = \text{term} - \text{term}(-1)$$
$$\text{ermsoft} = \text{rmsoft} - \text{mustb3m}$$
$$\text{ersandp} = \text{rsandp} - \text{mustb3m}$$

The final two of these calculate excess returns for the stock and for the index.

We can now run the regression. So click **Object/New Object/Equation** and name the object **'msoftreg'**. **Type the following variables** in the Equation specification window

ERMSOFT C ERSANDP DPROD DCREDIT DINFLATION DMONEY DSPREAD RTERM

and use **Least Squares** over the whole sample period. The table of results will appear as follows.

Dependent Variable: ERMSOFT
Method: Least Squares
Date: 07/02/13   Time: 12:23
Sample (adjusted): 1986M05 2013M04
Included observations: 324 after adjustments

	Coefficient	Std. Error	t-Statistic	Prob.
C	−0.151409	0.904787	−0.167342	0.8672
ERSANDP	1.360448	0.156615	8.686592	0.0000
DPROD	−1.425779	1.324467	−1.076493	0.2825
DCREDIT	−4.05E−05	7.64E−05	−0.530496	0.5961
DINFLATION	2.959910	2.166209	1.366401	0.1728
DMONEY	−0.011087	0.035175	−0.315184	0.7528
DSPREAD	5.366629	6.913915	0.776207	0.4382
RTERM	4.315813	2.515179	1.715907	0.0872

R-squared	0.206805	Mean dependent var	−0.311466
Adjusted R-squared	0.189234	S.D. dependent var	14.05871
S.E. of regression	12.65882	Akaike info criterion	7.938967
Sum squared resid	50637.65	Schwarz criterion	8.032319
Log likelihood	−1278.113	Hannan-Quinn criter.	7.976228
F-statistic	11.76981	Durbin-Watson stat	2.165384
Prob(F-statistic)	0.000000		

Take a few minutes to examine the main regression results. Which of the variables has a statistically significant impact on the Microsoft excess returns? Using your knowledge of the effects of the financial and macro-economic environment on stock returns, examine whether the coefficients have their expected signs and whether the sizes of the parameters are plausible.

The regression F-statistic takes a value 11.77. Remember that this tests the null hypothesis that all of the slope parameters are jointly zero. The p-value of zero attached to the test statistic shows that this null hypothesis should be rejected. However, there are a number of parameter estimates that are not significantly different from zero − specifically those on the DPROD, DCREDIT, DINFLA-TION, DMONEY and DSPREAD variables. Let us test the null hypothesis that the parameters on these three variables are jointly zero using an F-test. To test this, Click on **View/Coefficient Diagnostics/Wald Test − Coefficient Restrictions**... and in the box that appears type **C(3)=0, C(4)=0, C(5)=0, C(6)=0, C(7)=0 and click OK.** The resulting F-test statistic follows an $F(5, 316)$ distribution as there are five restrictions, 324 usable observations and eight parameters to estimate in the unrestricted regression. The F-statistic value is 0.853 with p-value 0.51, suggesting that the null hypothesis cannot be rejected. The parameter on RTERM is significant at the 10% level and so the parameter is not included in this F-test and the variable is retained.

Stepwise regression

There is a procedure known as a *stepwise regression* that is available in EViews. Stepwise regression is an automatic variable selection procedure which chooses the jointly most 'important' (variously defined) explanatory variables from a set of candidate variables. There are a number of different stepwise regression procedures, but the simplest is the uni-directional forwards method. This starts with no variables in the regression (or only those variables that are always required by the researcher to be in the regression) and then it selects first the variable with the lowest p-value (largest t-ratio) if it were included, then the variable with the second lowest p-value conditional upon the first variable already being included, and so on. The procedure continues until the next lowest p-value relative to those already included variables is larger than some specified threshold value, then the selection stops, with no more variables being incorporated into the model.

To conduct a stepwise regression which will automatically select from among these variables the most important ones for explaining the variations in Microsoft stock returns, click **Object/New Object** and then keep the default option **Equation**. Name the equation **Msoftstepwise** and then in the 'Estimation set-tings/Method' box, change *LS − Least Squares (NLS and ARMA)* to **STEPLS − Stepwise Least Squares** and then in the top box that appears, 'Dependent variable followed by list of always included regressors', enter

ERMSOFT C

This shows that the dependent variable will be the excess returns on Microsoft stock and that an intercept will always be included in the regression. If the researcher had

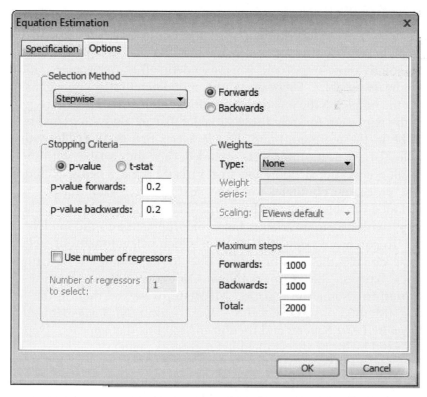

Screenshot 4.1   **Stepwise procedure equation estimation window**

Screenshot 4.2   **Stepwise procedure estimation options window**

a strong prior view that a particular explanatory variable must always be included in the regression, it should be listed in this first box. In the second box, 'List of search regressors', type the list of all of the explanatory variables used above: **ERSANDP DPROD DCREDIT DINFLATION DMONEY DSPREAD RTERM**. The window will appear as in screenshot 4.1.

Clicking on the 'Options' tab gives a number of ways to conduct the regression as shown in screenshot 4.2. For example, 'Forwards' will start with the list of required regressors (the intercept only in this case) and will sequentially add to them, while 'Backwards' will start by including all of the variables and will sequentially delete variables from the regression. The default criterion is to include variables if the p-value is less than 0.5, but this seems high and could potentially result in the inclusion of some very insignificant variables, so **modify this to 0.2** and then click **OK** to see the results.

Dependent Variable: ERMSOFT
Method: Stepwise Regression
Date: 08/27/07 Time: 10:21
Sample (adjusted): 1986M05 2007M04
Included observations: 252 after adjustments
Number of always included regressors: 1
Number of search regressors: 7
Selection method: Stepwise forwards
Stopping criterion: p-value forwards/backwards = 0.2/0.2

	Coefficient	Std. Error	t-Statistic	Prob.*
C	−0.687341	0.702716	−0.978120	0.3288
ERSANDP	1.338211	0.153056	8.743299	0.0000
RTERM	4.369891	2.497110	1.749979	0.0811
DINFLATION	2.876958	2.069933	1.389880	0.1655

R-squared	0.200924	Mean dependent var	−0.311466
Adjusted R-squared	0.193432	S.D. dependent var	14.05871
S.E. of regression	12.62600	Akaike info criterion	7.921663
Sum squared resid	51013.10	Schwarz criterion	7.968338
Log likelihood	−1379.309	Hannan-Quinn criter.	7.940293
F-statistic	26.82081	Durbin-Watson stat	2.144133
Prob(F-statistic)	0.000000		

Selection Summary

Added ERSANDP
Added RTERM
Added DINFLATION

*Note: p-values and subsequent tests do not account for stepwise selection.

As can be seen, the excess market return, the term structure, and unexpected inflation variables have been included, while the money supply, default spread and credit variables have been omitted.

Stepwise procedures have been strongly criticised by statistical purists. At the most basic level, they are sometimes argued to be no better than automated procedures for data mining, in particular if the list of potential candidate variables is long and results from a 'fishing trip' rather than a strong prior financial theory. More subtly, the iterative nature of the variable selection process implies that the size of the tests on parameters attached to variables in the final model will not be the nominal values (e.g. 5%) that would have applied had this model been the only one estimated. Thus the p-values for tests involving parameters in the final regression should really be modified to take into account that the model results from a sequential procedure, although they are usually not in statistical packages such as EViews.

4.6.1   A note on sample sizes and asymptotic theory

A question that is often asked by those new to econometrics is 'what is an appropriate sample size for model estimation?' While there is no definitive answer to this question, it should be noted that most testing procedures in econometrics rely on asymptotic theory. That is, the results in theory hold only if there is an *infinite number of observations*. In practice, an infinite number of observations will never be available and fortunately, an infinite number of observations are not usually required to invoke the asymptotic theory. An approximation to the asymptotic behaviour of the test statistics can be obtained using finite samples, provided that they are large enough. In general, as many observations as possible should be used (although there are important caveats to this statement relating to 'structural stability', discussed in chapter 5). The reason is that all the researcher has at his disposal is a sample of data from which to estimate parameter values and to infer their likely population counterparts. A sample may fail to deliver something close to the exact population values owing to sampling error. Even if the sample is randomly drawn from the population, some samples will be more representative of the behaviour of the population than others, purely owing to 'luck of the draw'. Sampling error is minimised by increasing the size of the sample, since the larger the sample, the less likely it is that all of the data drawn will be unrepresentative of the population.

4.7   Data mining and the true size of the test

Recall that the probability of rejecting a correct null hypothesis is equal to the size of the test, denoted α. The possibility of rejecting a correct null hypothesis arises from the fact that test statistics are assumed to follow a random distribution and hence they will take on extreme values that fall in the rejection region some of the time by chance alone. A consequence of this is that it will almost always be possible to find significant relationships between variables if enough variables are examined. For example, suppose that a dependent variable y_t and twenty explanatory variables $x_{2t}, \ldots, x_{21t}$ (excluding a constant term) are generated separately as independent normally distributed random variables. Then y is regressed separately on each of the twenty explanatory variables plus a constant, and the significance of each explanatory variable in the regressions is examined. If this experiment is repeated many times, on average one of the twenty regressions will have a slope coefficient that is significant at the 5% level for each experiment. The implication is that for any regression, if enough explanatory variables are employed in a regression, often one or more will be significant by chance alone. More concretely, it could be stated that if an α% size of test is used, on average one in every $(100/\alpha)$ regressions will have a significant slope coefficient by chance alone.

Trying many variables in a regression without basing the selection of the candidate variables on a financial or economic theory is known as 'data mining' or 'data snooping'. The result in such cases is that the true significance level will be considerably greater than the nominal significance level assumed. For example, suppose that twenty separate regressions are conducted, of which three contain a significant regressor, and a 5% nominal significance level is assumed, then the true significance level would be much higher (e.g. 25%). Therefore, if the researcher then shows only the results for the regression containing the final three equations and states that they are significant at the 5% level, inappropriate conclusions concerning the significance of the variables would result.

As well as ensuring that the selection of candidate regressors for inclusion in a model is made on the basis of financial or economic theory, another way to avoid data mining is by examining the forecast performance of the model in an 'out-of-sample' data set (see chapter 6). The idea is essentially that a proportion of the data is not used in model estimation, but is retained for model testing. A relationship observed in the estimation period that is purely the result of data mining, and is therefore spurious, is very unlikely to be repeated for the out-of-sample period. Therefore, models that are the product of data mining are likely to fit very poorly and to give very inaccurate forecasts for the out-of-sample period.

4.8 Goodness of fit statistics

4.8.1 R^2

It is desirable to have some measure of how well the regression model actually fits the data. In other words, it is desirable to have an answer to the question, 'how well does the model containing the explanatory variables that was proposed actually explain variations in the dependent variable?' Quantities known as *goodness of fit statistics* are available to test how well the sample regression function (SRF) fits the data – that is, how 'close' the fitted regression line is to all of the data points taken together. Note that it is not possible to say how well the sample regression function fits the population regression function – i.e. how the estimated model compares with the true relationship between the variables, since the latter is never known.

But what measures might make plausible candidates to be goodness of fit statistics? A first response to this might be to look at the residual sum of squares (*RSS*). Recall that OLS selected the coefficient estimates that minimised this quantity, so the lower was the minimised value of the RSS, the better the model fitted the data. Consideration of the RSS is certainly one possibility, but RSS is unbounded from above (strictly, RSS is bounded from above by the total sum of squares – see below) – i.e. it can take any (non-negative) value. So, for example, if the value of the RSS under OLS estimation was 136.4, what does this actually mean? It would therefore be very difficult, by looking at this number alone, to tell whether the regression line fitted the data closely or not. The value of RSS depends to a great extent on the scale of the dependent variable. Thus, one way to pointlessly reduce the RSS would be to divide all of the observations on y by 10!

In fact, a *scaled version* of the residual sum of squares is usually employed. The most common goodness of fit statistic is known as R^2. One way to define R^2 is to say that it is the square of the correlation coefficient between y and $\hat{y}$ – that is, the square of the correlation between the values of the dependent variable and the corresponding fitted values from the model. A correlation coefficient must lie between -1 and $+1$ by definition. Since R^2 defined in this way is the square of a correlation coefficient, it must lie between 0 and 1. If this correlation is high, the model fits the data well, while if the correlation is low (close to zero), the model is not providing a good fit to the data.

Another definition of R^2 requires a consideration of what the model is attempting to explain. What the model is trying to do in effect is to explain variability of y about its mean value, $\bar{y}$. This quantity, $\bar{y}$, which is more specifically known as the unconditional mean of y, acts like a benchmark since, if the researcher had no model for y, he could do no worse than to regress y on a constant only. In fact, the coefficient estimate for this regression would be the mean of y. So, from the regression

$$y_t = \beta_1 + u_t \tag{4.35}$$

the coefficient estimate $\hat{\beta}_1$, will be the mean of y, i.e. $\bar{y}$. The total variation across all observations of the dependent variable about its mean value is known as the total sum of squares, TSS, which is given by:

$$TSS = \sum_t (y_t - \bar{y})^2 \tag{4.36}$$

The TSS can be split into two parts: the part that has been explained by the model (known as the explained sum of squares, ESS) and the part that the model was not able to explain (the RSS). That is

$$TSS = ESS + RSS \tag{4.37}$$

$$\sum_t (y_t - \bar{y})^2 = \sum_t (\hat{y}_t - \bar{y})^2 + \sum_t \hat{u}_t^2 \tag{4.38}$$

Recall also that the residual sum of squares can also be expressed as

$$\sum_t (y_t - \hat{y}_t)^2$$

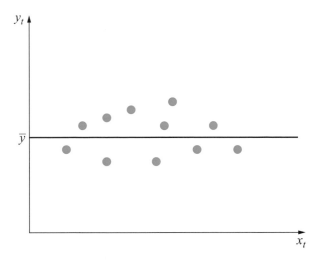

Figure 4.1 $R^2 = 0$ demonstrated by a flat estimated line, i.e. a zero slope coefficient

since a residual for observation t is defined as the difference between the actual and fitted values for that observation. The goodness of fit statistic is given by the ratio of the explained sum of squares to the total sum of squares:

$$R^2 = \frac{ESS}{TSS} \tag{4.39}$$

but since $TSS = ESS + RSS$, it is also possible to write

$$R^2 = \frac{ESS}{TSS} = \frac{TSS - RSS}{TSS} = 1 - \frac{RSS}{TSS} \tag{4.40}$$

R^2 must always lie between zero and one (provided that there is a constant term in the regression). This is intuitive from the correlation interpretation of R^2 given above, but for another explanation, consider two extreme cases

$$RSS = TSS \quad \text{i.e.} \quad ESS = 0 \quad \text{so} \quad R^2 = ESS/TSS = 0$$
$$ESS = TSS \quad \text{i.e.} \quad RSS = 0 \quad \text{so} \quad R^2 = ESS/TSS = 1$$

In the first case, the model has not succeeded in explaining any of the variability of y about its mean value, and hence the residual and total sums of squares are equal. This would happen only where the estimated values of all of the coefficients were exactly zero. In the second case, the model has explained all of the variability of y about its mean value, which implies that the residual sum of squares will be zero. This would happen only in the case where all of the observation points lie exactly on the fitted line. Neither of these two extremes is likely in practice, of course, but they do show that R^2 is bounded to lie between zero and one, with a higher R^2 implying, everything else being equal, that the model fits the data better.

To sum up, a simple way (but crude, as explained next) to tell whether the regression line fits the data well is to look at the value of R^2. A value of R^2 close to 1 indicates that the model explains nearly all of the variability of the dependent variable about its mean value, while a value close to zero indicates that

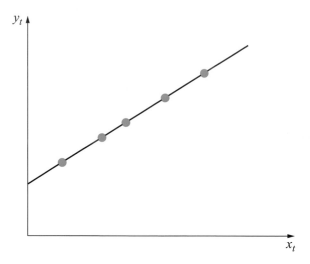

Figure 4.2 $R^2 = 1$ when all data points lie exactly on the estimated line

the model fits the data poorly. The two extreme cases, where $R^2 = 0$ and $R^2 = 1$, are indicated in figures 4.1 and 4.2 in the context of a simple bivariate regression.

4.8.2   Problems with R^2 as a goodness of fit measure

R^2 is simple to calculate, intuitive to understand, and provides a broad indication of the fit of the model to the data. However, there are a number of problems with R^2 as a goodness of fit measure:

(1) R^2 is defined in terms of variation about the mean of y so that if a model is reparameterised (rearranged) and the dependent variable changes, R^2 will change, even if the second model was a simple rearrangement of the first, with identical RSS. Thus it is not sensible to compare the value of R^2 across models with different dependent variables.

(2) R^2 never falls if more regressors are added to the regression. For example, consider the following two models:

$$\text{Regression 1: } y = \beta_1 + \beta_2 x_2 + \beta_3 x_3 + u \tag{4.41}$$

$$\text{Regression 2: } y = \beta_1 + \beta_2 x_2 + \beta_3 x_3 + \beta_4 x_4 + u \tag{4.42}$$

R^2 will always be at least as high for regression 2 relative to regression 1. The R^2 from regression 2 would be exactly the same as that for regression 1 only if the estimated value of the coefficient on the new variable were exactly zero, i.e. $\hat{\beta}_4 = 0$. In practice, $\hat{\beta}_4$ will always be non-zero, even if not significantly so, and thus in practice R^2 always rises as more variables are added to a model. This feature of R^2 essentially makes it impossible to use as a determinant of whether a given variable should be present in the model or not.

(3) R^2 can take values of 0.9 or higher for time series regressions, and hence it is not good at discriminating between models, since a wide array of models will frequently have broadly similar (and high) values of R^2.

4.8.3 Adjusted R^2

In order to get around the second of these three problems, a modification to R^2 is often made which takes into account the loss of degrees of freedom associated with adding extra variables. This is known as $\bar{R}^2$, or adjusted R^2, which is defined as

$$\bar{R}^2 = 1 - \left[\frac{T-1}{T-k}(1 - R^2) \right]$$

(4.43)

So if an extra regressor (variable) is added to the model, k increases and unless R^2 increases by a more than off-setting amount, $\bar{R}^2$ will actually fall. Hence $\bar{R}^2$ can be used as a decision-making tool for determining whether a given variable should be included in a regression model or not, with the rule being: include the variable if $\bar{R}^2$ rises and do not include it if $\bar{R}^2$ falls.

However, there are still problems with the maximisation of $\bar{R}^2$ as criterion for model selection, and principal among these is that it is a 'soft' rule, implying that by following it, the researcher will typically end up with a large model, containing a lot of marginally significant or insignificant variables. Also, while R^2 must be at least zero if an intercept is included in the regression, its adjusted counterpart may take negative values, even with an intercept in the regression, if the model fits the data very poorly.

Now reconsider the results from the previous exercises using EViews in the previous chapter and earlier in this chapter. If we first consider the hedging model from chapter 3, the R^2 value for the returns regression was 0.9955, indicating that almost all of the variation in spot returns is explained by the futures returns.

The fit is not so good for the Ford stock CAPM regression described in chapter 3, where the R^2 is around 35%. The conclusion here would be that for this stock and this sample period, around a third of the monthly movement in the excess returns can be attributed to movements in the market as a whole, as measured by the S&P500.

Finally, if we look at the results from the recently conducted regressions for Microsoft, we again find a reasonable fit. It is of interest to compare the model fit for the original regression that included all of the variables with the results of the stepwise procedure. We can see that the raw R^2 is slightly higher for the original regression containing all of the possible explanatory variables (0.207 versus 0.201 for the stepwise regression, to three decimal places), exactly as we would expect. Since the original regression contains more variables, the R^2-value must be at least as high. But comparing the $\bar{R}^2$s, the stepwise regression value (0.193) is slightly higher than for the full regression (0.189), indicating that the additional regressors in the full regression do not justify their presence, at least according to this criterion.

There now follows another case study of the application of the OLS method of regression estimation, including interpretation of t-ratios and R^2.

4.9 Hedonic pricing models

An application of econometric techniques where the coefficients have a particularly intuitively appealing interpretation is in the area of hedonic pricing models. *Hedonic models* are used to value real assets, especially housing, and view the asset as representing a bundle of characteristics, each of which gives either utility or disutility to its consumer. Hedonic models are often used to produce appraisals or valuations of properties, given their characteristics (e.g. size of dwelling, number of bedrooms, location, number of bathrooms, etc). In these models, the coefficient estimates represent 'prices of the characteristics'.

One such application of a hedonic pricing model is given by Des Rosiers and Thériault (1996), who consider the effect of various amenities on rental values for buildings and apartments in five sub-markets in the Quebec area of Canada. After accounting for the effect of 'contract-specific' features which will affect rental values (such as whether furnishings, lighting, or hot water are included in the rental price), they arrive at a model where the rental value in Canadian dollars per month (the dependent variable) is a function of nine–fourteen variables (depending on the area under consideration). The paper employs 1990 data for the Quebec City region, and there are 13,378 observations. The twelve explanatory variables are:

LnAGE	log of the apparent age of the property
NBROOMS	number of bedrooms
AREABYRM	area per room (in square metres)
ELEVATOR	a dummy variable = 1 if the building has an elevator; 0 otherwise
BASEMENT	a dummy variable = 1 if the unit is located in a basement; 0 otherwise
OUTPARK	number of outdoor parking spaces
INDPARK	number of indoor parking spaces
NOLEASE	a dummy variable = 1 if the unit has no lease attached to it; 0 otherwise
LnDISTCBD	log of the distance in kilometres to the central business district (CBD)
SINGLPAR	percentage of single parent families in the area where the building stands
DSHOPCNTR	distance in kilometres to the nearest shopping centre
VACDIFF1	vacancy difference between the building and the census figure

Table 4.1   Hedonic model of rental values in Quebec City, 1990. Dependent variable: Canadian dollars per month

Variable	Coefficient	t-ratio	sign expected a priori
Intercept	282.21	56.09	+
LnAGE	−53.10	−59.71	−
NBROOMS	48.47	104.81	+
AREABYRM	3.97	29.99	+
ELEVATOR	88.51	45.04	+
BASEMENT	−15.90	−11.32	−
OUTPARK	7.17	7.07	+
INDPARK	73.76	31.25	+
NOLEASE	−16.99	−7.62	−
LnDISTCBD	5.84	4.60	−
SINGLPAR	−4.27	−38.88	−
DSHOPCNTR	−10.04	−5.97	−
VACDIFF1	0.29	5.98	−

Notes: Adjusted $R^2 = 0.651$; regression F-statistic $= 2082.27$.
Source: Des Rosiers and Thériault (1996). Reprinted with the permission of the American Real Estate Society.

This list includes several variables that are dummy variables. Dummy variables are also known as *qualitative variables* because they are often used to numerically represent a qualitative entity. Dummy variables are usually specified to take on one of a narrow range of integer values, and in most instances only zero and one are used.

Dummy variables can be used in the context of cross-sectional or time series regressions. The latter case will be discussed extensively below. Examples of the use of dummy variables as cross-sectional regressors would be for sex in the context of starting salaries for new traders (e.g. male = 0, female = 1) or in the context of sovereign credit ratings (e.g. developing country = 0, developed country = 1), and so on. In each case, the dummy variables are used in the same way as other explanatory variables and the coefficients on the dummy variables can be interpreted as the average differences in the values of the dependent variable for each category, given all of the other factors in the model.

Des Rosiers and Thériault (1996) report several specifications for five different regions, and they present results for the model with variables as discussed here in their exhibit 4, which is adapted and reported here as table 4.1.

The adjusted R^2 value indicates that 65% of the total variability of rental prices about their mean value is explained by the model. For a cross-sectional regression,

Box 4.1   The relationship between the regression F-statistic and R^2

There is a particular relationship between a regression's R^2 value and the regression F-statistic. Recall that the regression F-statistic tests the null hypothesis that all of the regression slope parameters are simultaneously zero. Let us call the residual sum of squares for the unrestricted regression including all of the explanatory variables RSS, while the restricted regression will simply be one of y_t on a constant

$$y_t = \beta_1 + u_t \tag{4.44}$$

Since there are no slope parameters in this model, none of the variability of y_t about its mean value would have been explained. Thus the residual sum of squares for equation (4.44) will actually be the total sum of squares of y_t, TSS. We could write the usual F-statistic formula for testing this null that all of the slope parameters are jointly zero as

$$F\text{-}stat = \frac{TSS - RSS}{RSS} \times \frac{T - k}{k - 1} \tag{4.45}$$

In this case, the number of restrictions ('m') is equal to the number of slope parameters, $k - 1$. Recall that $TSS - RSS = ESS$ and dividing the numerator and denominator of equation (4.45) by TSS, we obtain

$$F\text{-}stat = \frac{ESS/TSS}{RSS/TSS} \times \frac{T - k}{k - 1} \tag{4.46}$$

Now the numerator of equation (4.46) is R^2, while the denominator is $1 - R^2$, so that the F-statistic can be written

$$F\text{-}stat = \frac{R^2(T - k)}{(1 - R^2)(k - 1)} \tag{4.47}$$

This relationship between the F-statistic and R^2 holds only for a test of this null hypothesis and not for any others.

this is quite high. Also, all variables are significant at the 0.01% level or lower and consequently, the regression F-statistic rejects very strongly the null hypothesis that all coefficient values on explanatory variables are zero. Note that there is a relationship between the regression F-statistic and R^2, as shown in box 4.1.

As stated above, one way to evaluate an econometric model is to determine whether it is consistent with theory. In this instance, no real theory is available, but instead there is a notion that each variable will affect rental values in a given direction. The actual signs of the coefficients can be compared with their expected values, given in the last column of table 4.1 (as determined by this author). It can be seen that all coefficients except two (the log of the distance to the CBD and the vacancy differential) have their predicted signs. It is argued by Des Rosiers and Thériault that the 'distance to the CBD' coefficient may be expected to have a positive sign since, while it is usually viewed as desirable to live close to a town centre, everything else being equal, in this instance most of the least desirable neighbourhoods are located towards the centre.

The coefficient estimates themselves show the Canadian dollar rental price per month of each feature of the dwelling. To offer a few illustrations, the NBROOMS value of 48 (rounded) shows that, everything else being equal, one additional bedroom will lead to an average increase in the rental price of the property by $48 per month at 1990 prices. A basement coefficient of -16 suggests that an apartment located in a basement commands a rental $16 less than an identical apartment above ground. Finally the coefficients for parking suggest that on average each outdoor parking space adds $7 to the rent while each indoor parking space adds $74, and so on. The intercept shows, in theory, the rental that would be required of a property that had zero values on all the attributes. This case demonstrates, as stated previously, that the coefficient on the constant term often has little useful interpretation, as it would refer to a dwelling that has just been built, has no bedrooms each of zero size, no parking spaces, no lease, right in the CBD and shopping centre, etc.

One limitation of such studies that is worth mentioning at this stage is their assumption that the implicit price of each characteristic is identical across types of property, and that these characteristics do not become saturated. In other words, it is implicitly assumed that if more and more bedrooms or allocated parking spaces are added to a dwelling indefinitely, the monthly rental price will rise each time by $48 and $7, respectively. This assumption is very unlikely to be upheld in practice, and will result in the estimated model being appropriate for only an 'average' dwelling. For example, an additional indoor parking space is likely to add far more value to a luxury apartment than a basic one. Similarly, the marginal value of an additional bedroom is likely to be bigger if the dwelling currently has one bedroom than if it already has ten. One potential remedy for this would be to use dummy variables with fixed effects in the regressions; see, for example, chapter 10 for an explanation of these.

4.10 Tests of non-nested hypotheses

All of the hypothesis tests conducted thus far in this book have been in the context of 'nested' models. This means that, in each case, the test involved imposing restrictions on the original model to arrive at a restricted formulation that would be a sub-set of, or nested within, the original specification.

However, it is sometimes of interest to compare between non-nested models. For example, suppose that there are two researchers working independently, each with a separate financial theory for explaining the variation in some variable, y_t. The models selected by the researchers respectively could be

$$y_t = \alpha_1 + \alpha_2 x_{2t} + u_t \tag{4.48}$$
$$y_t = \beta_1 + \beta_2 x_{3t} + v_t \tag{4.49}$$

where u_t and v_t are iid error terms. Model (4.48) includes variable x_2 but not x_3, while model (4.49) includes x_3 but not x_2. In this case, neither model can be viewed as a restriction of the other, so how then can the two models be compared

> ### Box 4.2 Selecting between models
>
> (1) γ_2 is statistically significant but γ_3 is not. In this case, (4.50) collapses to (4.48), and the latter is the preferred model.
> (2) γ_3 is statistically significant but γ_2 is not. In this case, (4.50) collapses to (4.49), and the latter is the preferred model.
> (3) γ_2 and γ_3 are both statistically significant. This would imply that both x_2 and x_3 have incremental explanatory power for y, in which case both variables should be retained. Models (4.48) and (4.49) are both ditched and (4.50) is the preferred model.
> (4) Neither γ_2 nor γ_3 are statistically significant. In this case, none of the models can be dropped, and some other method for choosing between them must be employed.

as to which better represents the data, y_t? Given the discussion in section 4.8, an obvious answer would be to compare the values of R^2 or adjusted R^2 between the models. Either would be equally applicable in this case since the two specifications have the same number of RHS variables. Adjusted R^2 could be used even in cases where the number of variables was different across the two models, since it employs a penalty term that makes an allowance for the number of explanatory variables. However, adjusted R^2 is based upon a particular penalty function (that is, $T - k$ appears in a specific way in the formula). This form of penalty term may not necessarily be optimal. Also, given the statement above that adjusted R^2 is a soft rule, it is likely on balance that use of it to choose between models will imply that models with more explanatory variables are favoured. Several other similar rules are available, each having more or less strict penalty terms; these are collectively known as 'information criteria'. These are explained in some detail in chapter 6, but suffice to say for now that a different strictness of the penalty term will in many cases lead to a different preferred model.

An alternative approach to comparing between non-nested models would be to estimate an encompassing or hybrid model. In the case of (4.48) and (4.49), the relevant encompassing model would be

$$y_t = \gamma_1 + \gamma_2 x_{2t} + \gamma_3 x_{3t} + w_t \tag{4.50}$$

where w_t is an error term. Formulation (4.50) contains both (4.48) and (4.49) as special cases when γ_3 and γ_2 are zero, respectively. Therefore, a test for the best model would be conducted via an examination of the significances of γ_2 and γ_3 in model (4.50). There will be four possible outcomes (box 4.2).

However, there are several limitations to the use of encompassing regressions to select between non-nested models. Most importantly, even if models (4.48) and (4.49) have a strong theoretical basis for including the RHS variables that they do, the hybrid model may be meaningless. For example, it could be the case that financial theory suggests that y could either follow model (4.48) or model (4.49), but model (4.50) is implausible.

Also, if the competing explanatory variables x_2 and x_3 are highly related (i.e. they are near collinear), it could be the case that if they are both included, neither γ_2 nor γ_3 are statistically significant, while each is significant in their separate regressions (4.48) and (4.49); see the section on multicollinearity in chapter 5.

An alternative approach is via the J-encompassing test due to Davidson and MacKinnon (1981). Interested readers are referred to their work or to Gujarati (2003, pp. 533–6) for further details.

4.11 Quantile regression

4.11.1 Background and motivation

Standard regression approaches effectively model the (conditional) mean of the dependent variable – that is, they capture the average value of y given the average values of all of the explanatory variables. We could of course calculate from the fitted regression line the value that y would take for any values of the explanatory variables, but this would essentially be an extrapolation of the behaviour of the relationship between y and x at the mean to the remainder of the data.

As a motivational example of why this approach will often be sub-optimal, suppose that it is of interest to capture the cross-sectional relationship across countries between the degree of regulation of banks and gross domestic product (GDP). Starting from a very low level of regulation (or no regulation), an increase in regulation is likely to encourage a rise in economic activity as the banking system functions better as a result of more trust and stability in the financial environment. However, there is likely to come a point where further increasing the amount of regulation may impede economic growth by stifling innovation and the responsiveness of the banking sector to the needs of the industries it serves. Thus we may think of there being a non-linear (∩-shaped) relationship between regulation and GDP growth, and estimating a standard linear regression model may lead to seriously misleading estimates of this relationship as it will 'average' the positive and negative effects from very low and very high regulation.

Of course, in this situation it would be possible to include non-linear (i.e. polynomial) terms in the regression model (for example, squared, cubic, . . . terms of regulation in the equation). But *quantile regressions*, developed by Koenker and Bassett (1978), represent a more natural and flexible way to capture the complexities inherent in the relationship by estimating models for the conditional quantile functions. Quantile regressions can be conducted in both time series and cross-sectional contexts, although the latter are more common. It is usually assumed that the dependent variable, often called the *response variable* in the literature on quantile regressions, is independently distributed and homoscedastic; these assumptions can of course be relaxed but at the cost of additional complexity. Quantile regressions represent a comprehensive way to analyse the relationships between a set of variables, and are far more robust to outliers and non-normality than OLS regressions, in the same fashion that the median is often a better measure of average or 'typical' behaviour than the mean when the distribution is considerably skewed by a few large outliers. Quantile regression is a non-parametric technique since no distributional assumptions are required to optimally estimate the parameters.

The notation and approaches commonly used in quantile regression modelling are different to those that we are familiar with in financial econometrics, and this probably limited the early take up of the technique, which was historically more widely used in other disciplines. Numerous applications in labour economics were developed, for example. However, the more recent availability of the techniques in econometric software packages and increased interest in modelling the 'tail behaviour' of series have spurred applications of quantile regression in finance. The most common use of the technique here is to value at risk modelling. This seems natural given that the models are based on estimating the quantile of a distribution of possible losses – see, for example, the study by Chernozhukov and Umanstev (2001) and the development of the CaViaR model by Engle and Manganelli (2004).[2]

Quantiles, denoted τ, refer to the position where an observation falls within an ordered series for y – for example, the median is the observation in the very middle; the (lower) tenth percentile is the value that places 10% of observations below it (and therefore 90% of observations above), and so on. More precisely, we can define the τ-th quantile, $Q(\tau)$, of a random variable y having cumulative distribution $F(y)$ as

$$Q(\tau) = \inf y : F(y) \geq \tau \tag{4.51}$$

where inf refers to the infimum, or the 'greatest lower bound' which is the smallest value of y satisfying the inequality. By definition, quantiles must lie between zero and one.

Quantile regressions take the concept of quantiles a stage further and effectively model the entire conditional distribution of y given the explanatory variables (rather than only the mean as is the case for OLS) – thus they examine their impact on not only the location and scale of the distribution of y, but also on the shape of the distribution as well. So we can determine how the explanatory variables affect the fifth or ninetieth percentiles of the distribution of y or its median and so on.

4.11.2   Estimation of quantile functions

In the same fashion as the ordinary least squares estimator finds the mean value that minimises the sum of the squared residuals, minimising the sum of the absolute values of the residuals will yield the median value. By definition, the absolute

---

[2] For further reading on quantile regression, Koenker and Hallock (2001) represents a very accessible, albeit brief, introduction to quantile regressions and their applications. A more thorough treatment is given in the book by Koenker (2005).

value function is symmetrical so that the median always has the same number of data points above it as below it. But if instead the absolute residuals are weighted differently depending on whether they are positive or negative, we can calculate the quantiles of the distribution. To estimate the τ-th quantile, we would set the weight on positive observations to τ, which is the quantile of interest, and that on negative observations to $1 - \tau$. We can select the quantiles of interest (or the software might do this for us), but common choices would be 0.05, 0.1, 0.25, 0.5, 0.75, 0.9, 0.95. The fit is not always good for values of τ too close to its limits of 0 and 1, so it is advisable to avoid such values.

We could write the minimisation problem for a set of quantile regression parameters $\hat{\beta}_\tau$, each element of which is a $k \times 1$ vector, as

$$\hat{\beta}_\tau = \mathrm{argmin}_\beta \left(\sum_{i:y_i > \beta x_i} \tau |y_i - \beta x_i| + \sum_{i:y_i < \beta x_i} (1 - \tau)|y_i - \beta x_i| \right) \tag{4.52}$$

This equation makes it clear where the weighting enters into the optimisation. As above, for the median, $\tau = 0.5$ and the weights are symmetric, but for all other quantiles they will be asymmetric. This optimisation problem can be solved using a linear programming representation via the simplex algorithm or it can be cast within the generalised method of moments framework.

As an alternative to quantile regression, it would be tempting to think of partitioning the data and running separate regressions on each of them – for example, dropping the top 90% of the observations on y and the corresponding data points for the xs, and running a regression on the remainder. However, this process, tantamount to truncating the dependent variable, would be wholly inappropriate and could lead to potentially severe sample selection biases of the sort discussed in chapter 12 below and highlighted by Heckman (1979). In fact, quantile regression does not partition the data – all observations are used in the estimation of the parameters for every quantile.

It is quite useful to plot each of the estimated parameters, $\hat{\beta}_{i,\tau}$ (for $i = 1, \ldots, k$), against the quantile, τ (from 0 to 1) so that we can see whether the estimates vary across the quantiles or are roughly constant. Sometimes ± 2 standard error bars are also included on the plot, and these tend to widen as the limits of τ are approached. Producing these standard errors for the quantile regression parameters is unfortunately more complex conceptually than estimating the parameters themselves and thus a discussion of these is beyond the scope of this book. Under some assumptions, Koenker (2005) demonstrates that the quantile regression parameters are asymptotically normally distributed. A number of approaches have been proposed for estimating the variance-covariance matrix of the parameters, including one based on a bootstrap – see chapter 13 for a discussion of this.

4.11.3　An application of quantile regression: evaluating fund performance

A study by Bassett and Chen (2001) performs a style attribution analysis for a mutual fund and, for comparison, the S&P500 index. In order to examine how a portfolio's exposure to various styles varies with performance, they use a quantile regression approach.

Effectively evaluating the performance of mutual fund managers is made difficult by the observation that certain investment styles – notably, value and small cap – yield higher returns on average than the equity market as a whole. In response to this, factor models such as those of Fama and French (1993) have been employed to remove the impact of these characteristics – see chapter 14 for a detailed presentation of these models. The use of such models also ensures that fund manager skill in picking highly performing stocks is not confused with randomly investing within value and small cap styles that will outperform the market in the long run. For example, if a manager invests a relatively high proportion of his portfolio in small firms, we would expect to observe higher returns than average from this manager because of the firm size effect alone.

Bassett and Chen (2001) conduct a style analysis in this spirit by regressing the returns of a fund on the returns of a large growth portfolio, the returns of a large value portfolio, the returns of a small growth portfolio, and the returns of a small value portfolio. These style portfolio returns are based on the Russell style indices. In this way, the parameter estimates on each of these style-mimicking portfolio returns will measure the extent to which the fund is exposed to that style. Thus we can determine the actual investment style of a fund without knowing anything about its holdings purely based on an analysis of its returns *ex post* and their relationships with the returns of style indices. Table 4.2 presents the results from a standard OLS regression and quintile regressions for $\tau = 0.1, 0.3, 0.5$ (i.e. the median), 0.7 and 0.9. The data are observed over the five years to December 1997 and the standard errors are based on a bootstrapping procedure.

Notice that the sum of the style parameters for a given regression is always one (except for rounding errors). To conserve space, I only present the results for the Magellan active fund and not those for the S&P – the latter exhibit very little variation in the estimates across the quantiles. The OLS results (column 2) show that the mean return has by far its biggest exposure to large value stocks (and this parameter estimate is also statistically significant), but it also exposed to small growth and, to a lesser extent, large growth stocks. It is of interest to compare the mean (OLS) results with those for the median, $Q(0.5)$. The latter show much higher exposure to large value, less to small growth and none at all to large growth.

It is also of interest to examine the factor tilts as we move through the quantiles from left ($Q(0.1)$) to right ($Q(0.9)$). We can see that the loading on large growth monotonically falls from 0.31 at $Q(0.1)$ to 0.01 at $Q(0.9)$ while the loadings on large value and small growth substantially increase. The loading on small value falls from 0.31 at $Q(0.1)$ to -0.51 at $Q(0.9)$. A way to interpret (mine, not the authors') these results is to say that when the fund has historically performed poorly, this has resulted in equal amounts from its overweight exposure to large value and growth, and small growth. On the other hand, when it has historically performed well, this is a result of its exposure to large value and small growth but it was underweight small value stocks. Finally, it is obvious that the intercept (coefficient on the constant) estimates should be monotonically increasing from

Table 4.2 OLS and quantile regression results for the Magellan fund

	OLS	$Q(0.1)$	$Q(0.3)$	$Q(0.5)$	$Q(0.7)$	$Q(0.9)$
Large growth	0.14	0.35	0.19	0.01	0.12	0.01
	(0.15)	(0.31)	(0.22)	(0.16)	(0.20)	(0.22)
Large value	0.69	0.31	0.75	0.83	0.85	0.82
	(0.20)	(0.38)	(0.30)	(0.25)	(0.30)	(0.36)
Small growth	0.21	−0.01	0.10	0.14	0.27	0.53
	(0.11)	(0.15)	(0.16)	(0.17)	(0.17)	(0.15)
Small value	−0.03	0.31	0.08	0.07	−0.31	−0.51
	(0.20)	(0.31)	(0.27)	(0.29)	(0.32)	(0.35)
Constant	−0.05	−1.90	−1.11	−0.30	0.89	2.31
	(0.25)	(0.39)	(0.27)	(0.38)	(0.40)	(0.57)

Notes: Standard errors in parentheses.
Source: Bassett and Chen (2001). Reprinted with the permission of Springer-Verlag.

left to right since the quantile regression effectively sorts on average performance and the intercept can be interpreted as the performance expected if the fund had zero exposure to all of the styles.

4.11.4 Quantile regression in EViews

To illustrate how to run quantile regressions using EViews, we will now employ the simple CAPM beta estimation conducted above. So **Re-open the 'CAPM.wf1' workfile** constructed previously. Click on **Quick/Estimate Equation...**, change Method in Estimation settings to **QREG – Quantile regression (including LAD)** and screenshot 4.3 will appear. Write '**erford c ersandp**' in the Equation specification window. As usual, there is an Options tab that allows the user to control various aspects of the estimation technique, but these can be left at the default so just click **OK** and the quantile regression results for the median will appear. EViews will estimate the median (0.5 quantile) by default, but any value of τ between 0 and 1 can be chosen. Rather than estimate each quantile separately and obtain a full statistical output in each case, after estimating a single quantile, click **View/Quantile Process/Process Coefficients**. EViews will then open a window that permits the simultaneous estimation of a number of quantiles. The default here is to estimate quantiles for the data split into ten segments ($\tau = 0.1, 0.2, \ldots, 0.9$). The quantile estimates can be displayed in a table or in a graph for all of the coefficients (the default) or for specific coefficients. Just click **OK** and the following table will appear.

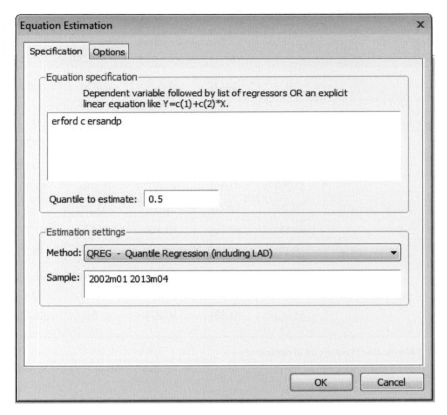

Screenshot 4.3   **Quantile regression estimation window**

As for the Magellan example, the monotonic fall in the intercept coefficients as the quantiles increase is to be expected since the data on y have been arranged that way. But the slope estimates are very revealing – they show that the beta estimate is much higher in the lower tail than in the rest of the distribution of ordered data. Thus the relationship between the excess returns on Ford stock and those of the S&P500 is much stronger when Ford share prices are falling most sharply. This is worrying, for it shows that the 'tail systematic risk' of the stock is greater than for the distribution as a whole. This is related to the observation that when stock prices fall, they tend to all fall at the same time, and thus the benefits of diversification that would be expected from examining only a standard regression of y on x could be much overstated.

Several diagnostic and specification tests for quantile regressions may be computed, and one of particular interest is whether the coefficients for each quantile can be restricted to be the same. To compute this test following estimation of a quantile regression, click **View/Quantile Process/Slope Equality Test. . . .** Again, several options are possible. Run the test for **10 quantiles** and click **OK**. Output is then shown first as a test of whether the corresponding slope coefficients are identical, followed by a pairwise comparison of one quantile with the next one (e.g. 0.1 with 0.2). The results in this case show that none of the statistics are significant, indicating that, despite the beta estimates differing across the quantiles by an economically large magnitude, they are not statistically significantly different.

Quantile Process Estimates
Equation: UNTITLED
Specification: ERFORD C ERSANDP
Estimated equation quantile tau = 0.5
Number of process quantiles
Display all coefficients

	Quantile	Coefficient	Std. Error	t-Statistic
C	0.100	−12.42521	1.550047	−8.016025
	0.200	−8.294803	1.088524	−7.620228
	0.300	−5.592712	0.964050	−5.801266
	0.400	−4.294994	0.994117	−4.320411
	0.500	−1.626581	1.006131	−1.616669
	0.600	1.039469	1.104484	0.941135
	0.700	2.739059	1.143703	2.394904
	0.800	7.115613	1.503729	4.731978
	0.900	14.43761	2.947024	4.899046
ERSANDP	0.100	2.399342	0.514023	4.667776
	0.200	1.845833	0.461919	3.996006
	0.300	1.599782	0.341128	4.689681
	0.400	1.670868	0.341534	4.892246
	0.500	1.659274	0.303687	5.463766
	0.600	1.767672	0.314817	5.614920
	0.700	1.652457	0.311495	5.304915
	0.800	1.970517	0.310818	6.339783
	0.900	1.615321	0.614305	2.629509

A further test can be conducted for whether the quantiles are symmetric – that is, the estimates for $\tau = 0.1$ and $\tau = 0.9$ are identical for instance. Again, if we run this test for the CAPM example here we would find that the null hypothesis is not rejected.

Key concepts

The key terms to be able to define and explain from this chapter are

- multiple regression model
- restricted regression
- residual sum of squares
- multiple hypothesis test
- R^2
- hedonic model
- data mining

- variance-covariance matrix
- F-distribution
- total sum of squares
- non-nested hypotheses
- $\bar{R}^2$
- encompassing regression
- quantile regression

Appendix 4.1   Mathematical derivations of CLRM results

Derivation of the OLS coefficient estimator in the multiple regression context

In the multiple regression context, in order to obtain the parameter estimates for $\beta_1, \beta_2, \ldots, \beta_k$, the RSS would be minimised with respect to all the elements of β. Now the residuals are expressed in a vector:

$$\hat{u} = \begin{bmatrix} \hat{u}_1 \\ \hat{u}_2 \\ \vdots \\ \hat{u}_T \end{bmatrix} \tag{4A.1}$$

The RSS is still the relevant loss function, and would be given in a matrix notation by expression (4A.2)

$$L = \hat{u}'\hat{u} = [\hat{u}_1 \hat{u}_2 \ldots \hat{u}_T] \begin{bmatrix} \hat{u}_1 \\ \hat{u}_2 \\ \vdots \\ \hat{u}_T \end{bmatrix} = \hat{u}_1^2 + \hat{u}_2^2 + \cdots + \hat{u}_T^2 = \sum \hat{u}_t^2 \tag{4A.2}$$

Denoting the vector of estimated parameters as $\hat{\beta}$, it is also possible to write

$$L = \hat{u}'\hat{u} = (y - X\hat{\beta})'(y - X\hat{\beta}) = y'y - \hat{\beta}'X'y - y'X\hat{\beta} + \hat{\beta}'X'X\hat{\beta} \tag{4A.3}$$

It turns out that $\hat{\beta}'X'y$ is $(1 \times k) \times (k \times T) \times (T \times 1) = 1 \times 1$, and also that $y'X\hat{\beta}$ is $(1 \times T) \times (T \times k) \times (k \times 1) = 1 \times 1$, so in fact $\hat{\beta}'X'y = y'X\hat{\beta}$. Thus (4A.3) can be written

$$L = \hat{u}'\hat{u} = (y - X\hat{\beta})'(y - X\hat{\beta}) = y'y - 2\hat{\beta}'X'y + \hat{\beta}'X'X\hat{\beta} \tag{4A.4}$$

Differentiating this expression with respect to $\hat{\beta}$ and setting it to zero in order to find the parameter values that minimise the residual sum of squares would yield

$$\frac{\partial L}{\partial \hat{\beta}} = -2X'y + 2X'X\hat{\beta} = 0 \tag{4A.5}$$

This expression arises since the derivative of $y'y$ is zero with respect to $\hat{\beta}$, and $\hat{\beta}'X'X\hat{\beta}$ acts like a square of $X\hat{\beta}$, which is differentiated to $2X'X\hat{\beta}$. Rearranging (4A.5)

$$2X'y = 2X'X\hat{\beta} \tag{4A.6}$$

$$X'y = X'X\hat{\beta} \tag{4A.7}$$

Pre-multiplying both sides of (4A.7) by the inverse of $X'X$

$$\hat{\beta} = (X'X)^{-1}X'y \tag{4A.8}$$

Thus, the vector of OLS coefficient estimates for a set of k parameters is given by

$$\hat{\beta} = \begin{bmatrix} \hat{\beta}_1 \\ \hat{\beta}_2 \\ \vdots \\ \hat{\beta}_k \end{bmatrix} = (X'X)^{-1}X'y \tag{4A.9}$$

Derivation of the OLS standard error estimator in the multiple regression context

The variance of a vector of random variables $\hat{\beta}$ is given by the formula $E[(\hat{\beta} - \beta)(\hat{\beta} - \beta)']$. Since $y = X\beta + u$, it can also be stated, given (4A.9), that

$$\hat{\beta} = (X'X)^{-1}X'(X\beta + u) \tag{4A.10}$$

Expanding the parentheses

$$\hat{\beta} = (X'X)^{-1}X'X\beta + (X'X)^{-1}X'u \tag{4A.11}$$

$$\hat{\beta} = \beta + (X'X)^{-1}X'u \tag{4A.12}$$

Thus, it is possible to express the variance of $\hat{\beta}$ as

$$E[(\hat{\beta} - \beta)(\hat{\beta} - \beta)'] = E[(\beta + (X'X)^{-1}X'u - \beta)(\beta + (X'X)^{-1}X'u - \beta)'] \tag{4A.13}$$

Cancelling the β terms in each set of parentheses

$$E[(\hat{\beta} - \beta)(\hat{\beta} - \beta)'] = E[((X'X)^{-1}X'u)((X'X)^{-1}X'u)'] \tag{4A.14}$$

Expanding the parentheses on the RHS of (4A.14) gives

$$E[(\hat{\beta} - \beta)(\hat{\beta} - \beta)'] = E[(X'X)^{-1}X'uu'X(X'X)^{-1}] \tag{4A.15}$$

$$E[(\hat{\beta} - \beta)(\hat{\beta} - \beta)'] = (X'X)^{-1}X'E[uu']X(X'X)^{-1} \tag{4A.16}$$

Now $E[uu']$ is estimated by $s^2 I$, so that

$$E[(\hat{\beta} - \beta)(\hat{\beta} - \beta)'] = (X'X)^{-1}X's^2 IX(X'X)^{-1} \tag{4A.17}$$

where I is a $k \times k$ identity matrix. Rearranging further,

$$E[(\hat{\beta} - \beta)(\hat{\beta} - \beta)'] = s^2(X'X)^{-1}X'X(X'X)^{-1} \tag{4A.18}$$

The $X'X$ and the last $(X'X)^{-1}$ term cancel out to leave

$$\text{var}(\hat{\beta}) = s^2(X'X)^{-1} \tag{4A.19}$$

as the expression for the parameter variance–covariance matrix. This quantity, $s^2(X'X)^{-1}$, is known as the estimated variance–covariance matrix of the coefficients. The leading diagonal terms give the estimated coefficient variances while the off-diagonal terms give the estimated covariances between the parameter estimates. The variance of $\hat{\beta}_1$ is the first diagonal element, the variance of $\hat{\beta}_2$ is the second element on the leading diagonal, ..., and the variance of $\hat{\beta}_k$ is the kth diagonal element, etc. as discussed in the body of the chapter.

Appendix 4.2 A brief introduction to factor models and principal components analysis

Factor models are employed primarily as dimensionality reduction techniques in situations where we have a large number of closely related variables and where we wish to allow for the most important influences from all of these variables at the same time. Factor models decompose the structure of a set of series into factors that are common to all series and a proportion that is specific to each series (idiosyncratic variation). There are broadly two types of such models, which can be loosely characterised as either macroeconomic or mathematical factor models. The key distinction between the two is that the factors are observable for the former but are latent (unobservable) for the latter. Observable factor models include the APT model of Ross (1976). The most common mathematical factor model is principal components analysis (PCA). PCA is a technique that may be useful where explanatory variables are closely related – for example, in the context of near multicollinearity. Specifically, if there are k explanatory variables in the regression model, PCA will transform them into k uncorrelated new variables. To elucidate, suppose that the original explanatory variables are denoted $x_1, x_2, \ldots, x_k$, and denote the principal components by $p_1, p_2, \ldots, p_k$. These principal components are independent linear combinations of the original data

$$
\begin{aligned}
p_1 &= \alpha_{11} x_1 + \alpha_{12} x_2 + \cdots + \alpha_{1k} x_k \\
p_2 &= \alpha_{21} x_1 + \alpha_{22} x_2 + \cdots + \alpha_{2k} x_k \\
\cdots \quad &\cdots \quad \cdots \qquad \cdots \\
p_k &= \alpha_{k1} x_1 + \alpha_{k2} x_2 + \cdots + \alpha_{kk} x_k
\end{aligned}
\tag{4A.20}
$$

where α_{ij} are coefficients to be calculated, representing the coefficient on the jth explanatory variable in the ith principal component. These coefficients are also known as factor loadings. Note that there will be T observations on each principal component if there were T observations on each explanatory variable.

It is also required that the sum of the squares of the coefficients for each component is one, i.e.

$$
\alpha_{11}^2 + \alpha_{12}^2 + \cdots + \alpha_{1k}^2 = 1
$$
$$
\vdots \qquad \vdots
$$
$$
\alpha_{k1}^2 + \alpha_{k2}^2 + \cdots + \alpha_{kk}^2 = 1
\tag{4A.21}
$$

This requirement could also be expressed using sigma notation

$$\sum_{j=1}^{k} \alpha_{ij}^2 = 1 \quad \forall \quad i = 1, \ldots, k \tag{4A.22}$$

Constructing the components is a purely mathematical exercise in constrained optimisation, and thus no assumption is made concerning the structure, distribution, or other properties of the variables.

The principal components are derived in such a way that they are in descending order of importance. Although there are k principal components, the same as the number of explanatory variables, if there is some collinearity between these original explanatory variables, it is likely that some of the (last few) principal components will account for so little of the variation that they can be discarded. However, if all of the original explanatory variables were already essentially uncorrelated, all of the components would be required, although in such a case there would have been little motivation for using PCA in the first place.

The principal components can also be understood as the eigenvalues of $(X'X)$, where X is the matrix of observations on the original variables. Thus the number of eigenvalues will be equal to the number of variables, k. If the ordered eigenvalues are denoted λ_i ($i = 1, \ldots, k$), the ratio

$$\phi_i = \frac{\lambda_i}{\displaystyle\sum_{i=1}^{k} \lambda_i}$$

gives the proportion of the total variation in the original data explained by the principal component i. Suppose that only the first r $(0 < r < k)$ principal components are deemed sufficiently useful in explaining the variation of $(X'X)$, and that they are to be retained, with the remaining $k - r$ components being discarded. The regression finally estimated, after the principal components have been formed, would be one of y on the r principal components

$$y_t = \gamma_0 + \gamma_1 p_{1t} + \cdots + \gamma_r p_{rt} + u_t \tag{4A.23}$$

In this way, the principal components are argued to keep most of the important information contained in the original explanatory variables, but are orthogonal. This may be particularly useful for independent variables that are very closely related. The principal component estimates ($\hat{\gamma}_i$, $i = 1, \ldots, r$) will be biased estimates, although they will be more efficient than the OLS estimators since redundant information has been removed. In fact, if the OLS estimator for the original regression of y on x is denoted $\hat{\beta}$, it can be shown that

$$\hat{\gamma}_r = P_r' \hat{\beta} \tag{4A.24}$$

where $\hat{\gamma}_r$ are the coefficient estimates for the principal components, and P_r is a matrix of the first r principal components. The principal component coefficient estimates are thus simply linear combinations of the original OLS estimates.

An application of principal components to interest rates

Many economic and financial models make use of interest rates in some form or another as independent variables. Researchers may wish to include interest rates on a large number of different assets in order to reflect the variety of investment opportunities open to investors. However, market interest rates could be argued to be not sufficiently independent of one another to make the inclusion of several interest rate series in an econometric model statistically sensible. One approach to examining this issue would be to use PCA on several related interest rate series to determine whether they did move independently of one another over some historical time period or not.

Fase (1973) conducted such a study in the context of monthly Dutch market interest rates from January 1962 until December 1970 (108 months). Fase examined both 'money market' and 'capital market' rates, although only the money market results will be discussed here in the interests of brevity. The money market instruments investigated were:

- Call money
- Three-month Treasury paper
- One-year Treasury paper
- Two-year Treasury paper
- Three-year Treasury paper
- Five-year Treasury paper
- Loans to local authorities: three-month
- Loans to local authorities: one-year
- Eurodollar deposits
- Netherlands Bank official discount rate.

Prior to analysis, each series was standardised to have zero mean and unit variance by subtracting the mean and dividing by the standard deviation in each case. The three largest of the ten eigenvalues are given in table 4A.1.

The results in table 4A.1 are presented for the whole period using the monthly data, for two monthly sub-samples, and for the whole period using data sampled quarterly instead of monthly. The results show clearly that the first principal component is sufficient to describe the common variation in these Dutch interest rate series. The first component is able to explain over 90% of the variation in all four cases, as given in the last row of table 4A.1. Clearly, the estimated eigenvalues are fairly stable across the sample periods and are relatively invariant to the frequency of sampling of the data. The factor loadings (coefficient estimates) for the first two ordered components are given in table 4A.2.

As table 4A.2 shows, the loadings on each factor making up the first principal component are all positive. Since each series has been standardised to have zero mean and unit variance, the coefficients α_{j1} and α_{j2} can be interpreted as the

Table 4A.1   Principal component ordered eigenvalues for Dutch interest rates, 1962–70

	Monthly data			Quarterly data
	Jan 62–Dec 70	Jan 62–Jun 66	Jul 66–Dec 70	Jan 62–Dec 70
λ_1	9.57	9.31	9.32	9.67
λ_2	0.20	0.31	0.40	0.16
λ_3	0.09	0.20	0.17	0.07
ϕ_1	95.7%	93.1%	93.2%	96.7%

Source: Fase (1973). Reprinted with the permission of Elsevier.

correlations between the interest rate j and the first and second principal components, respectively. The factor loadings for each interest rate series on the first component are all very close to one. Fase (1973) therefore argues that the first component can be interpreted simply as an equally weighted combination of all of the market interest rates. The second component, which explains much less of the variability of the rates, shows a factor loading pattern of positive coefficients for the Treasury paper series and negative or almost zero values for the other series. Fase (1973) argues that this is owing to the characteristics of the Dutch Treasury instruments that they rarely change hands and have low transactions costs, and therefore have less sensitivity to general interest rate movements. Also, they are not subject to default risks in the same way as, for example Eurodollar deposits. Therefore, the second principal component is broadly interpreted as relating to default risk and transactions costs.

Principal components can be useful in some circumstances, although the technique has limited applicability for the following reasons:

- A change in the units of measurement of x will change the principal components. It is thus usual to transform all of the variables to have zero mean and unit variance prior to applying PCA.
- The principal components usually have no theoretical motivation or interpretation whatsoever.
- The r principal components retained from the original k are the ones that explain most of the variation in x, but these components might not be the most useful as explanations for y.

Calculating principal components in EViews

In order to calculate the principal components of a set of series with EViews, the first stage is to compile the series concerned into a group. **Re-open the**

Table 4A.2   Factor loadings of the first and second principal components for Dutch interest rates, 1962–70

j	Debt instrument	α_{j1}	α_{j2}
1	Call money	0.95	−0.22
2	3-month Treasury paper	0.98	0.12
3	1-year Treasury paper	0.99	0.15
4	2-year Treasury paper	0.99	0.13
5	3-year Treasury paper	0.99	0.11
6	5-year Treasury paper	0.99	0.09
7	Loans to local authorities: 3-month	0.99	−0.08
8	Loans to local authorities: 1-year	0.99	−0.04
9	Eurodollar deposits	0.96	−0.26
10	Netherlands Bank official discount rate	0.96	−0.03
	Eigenvalue, λ_i	9.57	0.20
	Proportion of variability explained by eigenvalue i, $\phi_i(\%)$	95.7	2.0

Source: Fase (1973). Reprinted with the permission of Elsevier.

'macro.wf1' file which contains US Treasury bill and bond series of various maturities. Select **Object/New Object** and change 'Equation' to 'Group' but do not name the object and click **OK**. When EViews prompts you to give a 'List of series, groups and/or series expressions', enter

USTB3M USTB6M USTB1Y USTB3Y USTB5Y USTB10Y

and click **OK**. You will then see a spreadsheet containing all six of the series. Name the group **Interest** by clicking the **Name** tab. From within this window, click **View/Principal Components. . . .** Screenshot 4.4 will appear.

There are many features of principal components that can be examined, but for now keep the defaults and click **OK**. The results will appear as in the following table.

It is evident that there is a great deal of common variation in the series, since the first principal component captures over 96% of the variation in the series and the first two components capture 99.8%. Consequently, if we wished, we could reduce the dimensionality of the system by using two components rather than the entire six interest rate series. Interestingly, the first component comprises almost

Principal Components Analysis
Date: 07/04/13 Time: 10:27
Sample: 1986M03 2013M04
Included observations: 326
Computed using: Ordinary correlations
Extracting 6 of 6 possible components

Eigenvalues: (Sum = 6, Average = 1)

Number	Value	Difference	Proportion	Cumulative Value	Cumulative Proportion
1	5.791739	5.594419	0.9653	5.791739	0.9653
2	0.197320	0.189221	0.0329	5.989059	0.9982
3	0.008100	0.005865	0.0013	5.997159	0.9995
4	0.002235	0.001831	0.0004	5.999394	0.9999
5	0.000404	0.000203	0.0001	5.999798	1.0000
6	0.000202	–	0.0000	6.000000	1.0000

Eigenvectors (loadings):

Variable	PC 1	PC 2	PC 3	PC 4	PC 5	PC 6
USTB3M	0.406637	−0.44824	0.514612	−0.46067	0.313742	−0.24136
USTB6M	0.408960	−0.39631	0.101355	0.198316	−0.498750	0.61427
USTB1Y	0.412145	−0.27130	−0.31644	0.598774	0.059054	−0.54257
USTB3Y	0.414372	0.117583	−0.56123	−0.21834	0.539421	0.40105
USTB5Y	0.409819	0.364608	−0.22123	−0.46562	−0.576110	−0.31854
USTB10Y	0.397340	0.649350	0.510727	0.35419	0.162654	0.08785

Ordinary correlations:

	USTB3M	USTB6M	USTB1Y	USTB3Y	USTB5Y	USTB10Y
USTB3M	1.000000					
USTB6M	0.998334	1.000000				
USTB1Y	0.99275	0.997345	1.000000			
USTB3Y	0.963436	0.971666	0.98394	1.000000		
USTB5Y	0.932431	0.941871	0.958699	0.993079	1.000000	
USTB10Y	0.880137	0.890911	0.912862	0.966203	0.988502	1.000000

exactly equal weights in all six series while the second component puts a large
negative weight on the shortest yield and gradually increasing weights thereafter.
This ties in with the common belief that the first component captures the level of
interest rates, the second component captures the slope of the term structure (and
the third component captures curvature in the yield curve).

Screenshot 4.4　**Conducting PCA in EViews**

Then **Minimise this group** and you will see that the 'Interest' group has been added to the list of objects.

Self-study questions

1. By using examples from the relevant statistical tables, explain the relationship between the t- and the F-distributions.

   For questions 2–5, assume that the econometric model is of the form

$$y_t = \beta_1 + \beta_2 x_{2t} + \beta_3 x_{3t} + \beta_4 x_{4t} + \beta_5 x_{5t} + u_t \qquad (4.53)$$

2. Which of the following hypotheses about the coefficients can be tested using a t-test? Which of them can be tested using an F-test? In each case, state the number of restrictions.
   (a) $H_0 : \beta_3 = 2$
   (b) $H_0 : \beta_3 + \beta_4 = 1$
   (c) $H_0 : \beta_3 + \beta_4 = 1$ and $\beta_5 = 1$
   (d) $H_0 : \beta_2 = 0$ and $\beta_3 = 0$ and $\beta_4 = 0$ and $\beta_5 = 0$
   (e) $H_0 : \beta_2\beta_3 = 1$
3. Which of the above null hypotheses constitutes 'THE' regression F-statistic in the context of (4.53)? Why is this null hypothesis always of interest

whatever the regression relationship under study? What exactly would constitute the alternative hypothesis in this case?

4. Which would you expect to be bigger – the unrestricted residual sum of squares or the restricted residual sum of squares, and why?

5. You decide to investigate the relationship given in the null hypothesis of question 2, part (c). What would constitute the restricted regression? The regressions are carried out on a sample of 96 quarterly observations, and the residual sums of squares for the restricted and unrestricted regressions are 102.87 and 91.41, respectively. Perform the test. What is your conclusion?

6. You estimate a regression of the form given by (4.54) below in order to evaluate the effect of various firm-specific factors on the returns of a sample of firms. You run a cross-sectional regression with 200 firms

$$r_i = \beta_0 + \beta_1 S_i + \beta_2 MB_i + \beta_3 PE_i + \beta_4 BETA_i + u_i \qquad (4.54)$$

where: r_i is the percentage annual return for the stock
S_i is the size of firm i measured in terms of sales revenue
MB_i is the market to book ratio of the firm
PE_i is the price/earnings (P/E) ratio of the firm
$BETA_i$ is the stock's CAPM beta coefficient

You obtain the following results (with standard errors in parentheses)

$$\hat{r}_i = 0.080 + 0.801 S_i + 0.321 MB_i + 0.164 PE_i - 0.084 BETA_i$$

$$(0.064) \quad (0.147) \quad (0.136) \quad (0.420) \quad (0.120) \qquad (4.55)$$

Calculate the t-ratios. What do you conclude about the effect of each variable on the returns of the security? On the basis of your results, what variables would you consider deleting from the regression? If a stock's beta increased from 1 to 1.2, what would be the expected effect on the stock's return? Is the sign on beta as you would have expected? Explain your answers in each case.

7. A researcher estimates the following econometric models including a lagged dependent variable

$$y_t = \beta_1 + \beta_2 x_{2t} + \beta_3 x_{3t} + \beta_4 y_{t-1} + u_t \qquad (4.56)$$

$$\Delta y_t = \gamma_1 + \gamma_2 x_{2t} + \gamma_3 x_{3t} + \gamma_4 y_{t-1} + v_t \qquad (4.57)$$

where u_t and v_t are iid disturbances.

Will these models have the same value of (a) The residual sum of squares (RSS), (b) R^2, (c) Adjusted R^2? Explain your answers in each case.

8. A researcher estimates the following two econometric models

$$y_t = \beta_1 + \beta_2 x_{2t} + \beta_3 x_{3t} + u_t \qquad (4.58)$$

$$y_t = \beta_1 + \beta_2 x_{2t} + \beta_3 x_{3t} + \beta_4 x_{4t} - v_t \qquad (4.59)$$

where u_t and v_t are iid disturbances and x_{3t} is an irrelevant variable which does not enter into the data generating process for y_t. Will the value of (a)

R^2, (b) Adjusted R^2, be higher for the second model than the first? Explain your answers.

9. Re-open the CAPM Eviews file and estimate CAPM betas for each of the other stocks in the file.

   (a) Which of the stocks, on the basis of the parameter estimates you obtain, would you class as defensive stocks and which as aggressive stocks? Explain your answer.

   (b) Is the CAPM able to provide any reasonable explanation of the overall variability of the returns to each of the stocks over the sample period? Why or why not?

10. Re-open the Macro file and apply the same APT-type model to some of the other time series of stock returns contained in the CAPM-file.

   (a) Run the stepwise procedure in each case. Is the same sub-set of variables selected for each stock? Can you rationalise the differences between the series chosen?

   (b) Examine the sizes and signs of the parameters in the regressions in each case – do these make sense?

11. What are the units of R^2?

12. What are quantile regressions and why are they useful?

13. A researcher wishes to examine the link between the returns on two assets A and B in situations where the price of B is falling rapidly. To do this, he orders the data according to changes in the price of B and drops the top 80% of ordered observations. He then runs a regression of the returns of A on the returns of B for the remaining lowest 20% of observations. Would this be a good way to proceed? Explain your answer.

5 Classical linear regression model assumptions and diagnostic tests

Learning outcomes

In this chapter, you will learn how to

- Describe the steps involved in testing regression residuals for heteroscedasticity and autocorrelation
- Explain the impact of heteroscedasticity or autocorrelation on the optimality of OLS parameter and standard error estimation
- Distinguish between the Durbin–Watson and Breusch–Godfrey tests for autocorrelation
- Highlight the advantages and disadvantages of dynamic models
- Test for whether the functional form of the model employed is appropriate
- Determine whether the residual distribution from a regression differs significantly from normality
- Investigate whether the model parameters are stable
- Appraise different philosophies of how to build an econometric model
- Conduct diagnostic tests in EViews

5.1 Introduction

Recall that five assumptions were made relating to the classical linear regression model (CLRM). These were required to show that the estimation technique, ordinary least squares (OLS), had a number of desirable properties, and also so that hypothesis tests regarding the coefficient estimates could validly be conducted. Specifically, it was assumed that:

(1) $E(u_t) = 0$
(2) $\text{var}(u_t) = \sigma^2 < \infty$
(3) $\text{cov}(u_i, u_j) = 0$
(4) $\text{cov}(u_t, x_t) = 0$
(5) $u_t \sim N(0, \sigma^2)$

These assumptions will now be studied further, in particular looking at the following:

● How can violations of the assumptions be detected?
● What are the most likely causes of the violations in practice?
● What are the consequences for the model if an assumption is violated but this fact is ignored and the researcher proceeds regardless?

The answer to the last of these questions is that, in general, the model could encounter any combination of three problems:

● the coefficient estimates ($\hat{\beta}$s) are wrong
● the associated standard errors are wrong
● the distributions that were assumed for the test statistics are inappropriate.

A pragmatic approach to 'solving' problems associated with the use of models where one or more of the assumptions is not supported by the data will then be adopted. Such solutions usually operate such that:

● the assumptions are no longer violated, or
● the problems are side-stepped, so that alternative techniques are used which are still valid.

5.2 Statistical distributions for diagnostic tests

The text below discusses various regression diagnostic (misspecification) tests that are based on the calculation of a test statistic. These tests can be constructed in several ways, and the precise approach to constructing the test statistic will determine the distribution that the test statistic is assumed to follow. Two particular approaches are in common usage and their results are given by the statistical packages: the Lagrange Multiplier (LM) test and the Wald test. Further details concerning these procedures are given in chapter 9. For now, all that readers require to know is that LM test statistics in the context of the diagnostic tests presented here follow a χ^2 distribution with degrees of freedom equal to the number of restrictions placed on the model, and denoted m. The Wald version of the test follows an F-distribution with $(m, T - k)$ degrees of freedom. Asymptotically, these two tests are equivalent, although their results will differ somewhat in small samples. They are equivalent as the sample size increases towards infinity since there is a direct relationship between the χ^2- and F-distributions. Asymptotically, an F-variate will tend towards a χ^2 variate divided by its degrees of freedom

$$F(m, T - k) \to \frac{\chi^2(m)}{m} \quad \text{as} \quad T \to \infty$$

Computer packages typically present results using both approaches, although only one of the two will be illustrated for each test below. They will usually give the same conclusion, although if they do not, the F-version is usually considered preferable for finite samples, since it is sensitive to sample size (one of its degrees of freedom parameters depends on sample size) in a way that the χ^2-version is not.

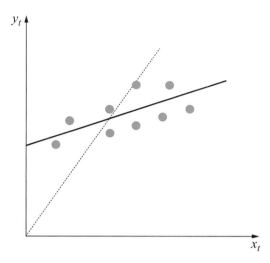

Figure 5.1   Effect of no intercept on a regression line

5.3   Assumption 1: $E(u_t) = 0$

The first assumption required is that the average value of the errors is zero. In fact, if a constant term is included in the regression equation, this assumption will never be violated. But what if financial theory suggests that, for a particular application, there should be no intercept so that the regression line is forced through the origin? If the regression did not include an intercept, and the average value of the errors was non-zero, several undesirable consequences could arise. First, R^2, defined as ESS/TSS can be negative, implying that the sample average, $\bar{y}$, 'explains' more of the variation in y than the explanatory variables. Second, and more fundamentally, a regression with no intercept parameter could lead to potentially severe biases in the slope coefficient estimates. To see this, consider figure 5.1.

The solid line shows the regression estimated including a constant term, while the dotted line shows the effect of suppressing (i.e. setting to zero) the constant term. The effect is that the estimated line in this case is forced through the origin, so that the estimate of the slope coefficient ($\hat{\beta}$) is biased. Additionally, R^2 and $\bar{R}^2$ are usually meaningless in such a context. This arises since the mean value of the dependent variable, $\bar{y}$, will not be equal to the mean of the fitted values from the model, i.e. the mean of $\hat{y}$ if there is no constant in the regression.

5.4   Assumption 2: $\mathrm{var}(u_t) = \sigma^2 < \infty$

It has been assumed thus far that the variance of the errors is constant, σ^2 – this is known as the *assumption of homoscedasticity*. If the errors do not have a constant variance, they are said to be *heteroscedastic*. To consider one illustration of heteroscedasticity, suppose that a regression had been estimated and the residuals, $\hat{u}_t$, have been calculated and then plotted against one of the explanatory variables, x_{2t}, as shown in figure 5.2.

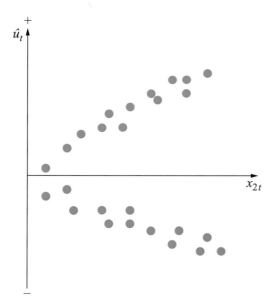

Figure 5.2   Graphical illustration of heteroscedasticity

It is clearly evident that the errors in figure 5.2 are heteroscedastic — that is, although their mean value is roughly constant, their variance is increasing systematically with x_{2t}.

5.4.1   Detection of heteroscedasticity

How can one tell whether the errors are heteroscedastic or not? It is possible to use a graphical method as above, but unfortunately one rarely knows the cause or the form of the heteroscedasticity, so that a plot is likely to reveal nothing. For example, if the variance of the errors was an increasing function of x_{3t}, and the researcher had plotted the residuals against x_{2t}, he would be unlikely to see any pattern and would thus wrongly conclude that the errors had constant variance. It is also possible that the variance of the errors changes over time rather than systematically with one of the explanatory variables; this phenomenon is known as 'ARCH' and is described in chapter 9.

Fortunately, there are a number of formal statistical tests for heteroscedasticity, and one of the simplest such methods is the Goldfeld–Quandt (1965) test. Their approach is based on splitting the total sample of length T into two sub-samples of length T_1 and T_2. The regression model is estimated on each sub-sample and the two residual variances are calculated as $s_1^2 = \hat{u}_1'\hat{u}_1/(T_1 - k)$ and $s_2^2 = \hat{u}_2'\hat{u}_2/(T_2 - k)$ respectively. The null hypothesis is that the variances of the disturbances are equal, which can be written $H_0 : \sigma_1^2 = \sigma_2^2$, against a two-sided alternative. The test statistic, denoted GQ, is simply the ratio of the two residual variances where the larger of the two variances must be placed in the numerator (i.e. s_1^2 is the higher sample variance for the sample with length T_1, even if it comes from the second sub-sample):

$$GQ = \frac{s_1^2}{s_2^2} \tag{5.1}$$

The test statistic is distributed as an $F(T_1 - k, T_2 - k)$ under the null hypothesis, and the null of a constant variance is rejected if the test statistic exceeds the critical value.

The GQ test is simple to construct but its conclusions may be contingent upon a particular, and probably arbitrary, choice of where to split the sample. Clearly, the test is likely to be more powerful when this choice is made on theoretical grounds – for example, before and after a major structural event. Suppose that it is thought that the variance of the disturbances is related to some observable variable z_t (which may or may not be one of the regressors). A better way to perform the test would be to order the sample according to values of z_t (rather than through time) and then to split the re-ordered sample into T_1 and T_2.

An alternative method that is sometimes used to sharpen the inferences from the test and to increase its power is to omit some of the observations from the centre of the sample so as to introduce a degree of separation between the two sub-samples.

A further popular test is White's (1980) general test for heteroscedasticity. The test is particularly useful because it makes few assumptions about the likely form of the heteroscedasticity. The test is carried out as in box 5.1.

5.4.2 Consequences of using OLS in the presence of heteroscedasticity

What happens if the errors are heteroscedastic, but this fact is ignored and the researcher proceeds with estimation and inference? In this case, OLS estimators will still give unbiased (and also consistent) coefficient estimates, but they are no longer best linear unbiased estimators (BLUE) – that is, they no longer have the minimum variance among the class of unbiased estimators. The reason is that the error variance, σ^2, plays no part in the proof that the OLS estimator is consistent and unbiased, but σ^2 does appear in the formulae for the coefficient variances. If the errors are heteroscedastic, the formulae presented for the coefficient standard errors no longer hold. For a very accessible algebraic treatment of the consequences of heteroscedasticity, see Hill, Griffiths and Judge (1997, pp. 217–18).

Box 5.1   Conducting White's test

(1) Assume that the regression model estimated is of the standard linear form, e.g.

$$y_t = \beta_1 + \beta_2 x_{2t} + \beta_3 x_{3t} + u_t \tag{5.2}$$

To test var(u_t) = σ^2, estimate the model above, obtaining the residuals, $\hat{u}_t$

(2) Then run the auxiliary regression

$$\hat{u}_t^2 = \alpha_1 + \alpha_2 x_{2t} + \alpha_3 x_{3t} + \alpha_4 x_{2t}^2 + \alpha_5 x_{3t}^2 + \alpha_6 x_{2t} x_{3t} + v_t \qquad (5.3)$$

where v_t is a normally distributed disturbance term independent of u_t. This regression is of the squared residuals on a constant, the original explanatory variables, the squares of the explanatory variables and their cross-products. To see why the squared residuals are the quantity of interest, recall that for a random variable u_t, the variance can be written

$$\text{var}(u_t) = \text{E}[(u_t - \text{E}(u_t))^2] \qquad (5.4)$$

Under the assumption that $\text{E}(u_t) = 0$, the second part of the RHS of this expression disappears:

$$\text{var}(u_t) = \text{E}[u_t^2] \qquad (5.5)$$

Once again, it is not possible to know the squares of the population disturbances, u_t^2, so their sample counterparts, the squared residuals, are used instead.

The reason that the auxiliary regression takes this form is that it is desirable to investigate whether the variance of the residuals (embodied in $\hat{u}_t^2$) varies systematically with any known variables relevant to the model. Relevant variables will include the original explanatory variables, their squared values and their cross-products. Note also that this regression should include a constant term, even if the original regression did not. This is as a result of the fact that $\hat{u}_t^2$ will always have a non-zero mean, even if $\hat{u}_t$ has a zero mean.

(3) Given the auxiliary regression, as stated above, the test can be conducted using two different approaches. First, it is possible to use the F-test framework described in chapter 4. This would involve estimating (5.3) as the unrestricted regression and then running a restricted regression of $\hat{u}_t^2$ on a constant only. The RSS from each specification would then be used as inputs to the standard F-test formula.

With many diagnostic tests, an alternative approach can be adopted that does not require the estimation of a second (restricted) regression. This approach is known as a Lagrange Multiplier (LM) test, which centres around the value of R^2 for the auxiliary regression. If one or more coefficients in (5.3) is statistically significant, the value of R^2 for that equation will be relatively high, while if none of the variables is significant, R^2 will be relatively low. The LM test would thus operate by obtaining R^2 from the auxiliary regression and multiplying it by the number of observations, T. It can be shown that

$$TR^2 \sim \chi^2(m)$$

where m is the number of regressors in the auxiliary regression (excluding the constant term), equivalent to the number of restrictions that would have to be placed under the F-test approach.

(4) The test is one of the joint null hypothesis that $\alpha_2 = 0$, and $\alpha_3 = 0$, and $\alpha_4 = 0$, and $\alpha_5 = 0$, and $\alpha_6 = 0$. For the LM test, if the χ^2-test statistic from step 3 is greater than the corresponding value from the statistical table then reject the null hypothesis that the errors are homoscedastic.

Example 5.1

Suppose that the model (5.2) above has been estimated using 120 observations, and the R^2 from the auxiliary regression (5.3) is 0.234. The test statistic will be given by $TR^2 = 120 \times 0.234 = 28.8$, which will follow a $\chi^2(5)$ under the null hypothesis. The 5% critical value from the χ^2 table is 11.07. The test statistic is therefore more than the critical value and hence the null hypothesis is rejected. It would be concluded that there is significant evidence of heteroscedasticity, so that it would not be plausible to assume that the variance of the errors is constant in this case.

So, the upshot is that if OLS is still used in the presence of heteroscedasticity, the standard errors could be wrong and hence any inferences made could be misleading. In general, the OLS standard errors will be too large for the intercept when the errors are heteroscedastic. The effect of heteroscedasticity on the slope standard errors will depend on its form. For example, if the variance of the errors is positively related to the square of an explanatory variable (which is often the case in practice), the OLS standard error for the slope will be too low. On the other hand, the OLS slope standard errors will be too big when the variance of the errors is inversely related to an explanatory variable.

5.4.3 Dealing with heteroscedasticity

If the form (i.e. the cause) of the heteroscedasticity is known, then an alternative estimation method which takes this into account can be used. One possibility is called generalised least squares (GLS). For example, suppose that the error variance was related to z_t by the expression

$$\mathrm{var}(u_t) = \sigma^2 z_t^2 \tag{5.6}$$

All that would be required to remove the heteroscedasticity would be to divide the regression equation through by z_t

$$\frac{y_t}{z_t} = \beta_1 \frac{1}{z_t} + \beta_2 \frac{x_{2t}}{z_t} + \beta_3 \frac{x_{3t}}{z_t} + v_t \tag{5.7}$$

where $v_t = \dfrac{u_t}{z_t}$ is an error term.

Now, if $\mathrm{var}(u_t) = \sigma^2 z_t^2$, $\mathrm{var}(v_t) = \mathrm{var}\left(\dfrac{u_t}{z_t}\right) = \dfrac{\mathrm{var}(u_t)}{z_t^2} = \dfrac{\sigma^2 z_t^2}{z_t^2} = \sigma^2$ for known z.

> ### Box 5.2 'Solutions' for heteroscedasticity
>
> (1) *Transforming the variables into logs or reducing by some other measure of 'size'.* This has the effect of rescaling the data to 'pull in' extreme observations. The regression would then be conducted upon the natural logarithms or the transformed data. Taking logarithms also has the effect of making a multiplicative model, such as the exponential regression model discussed previously (with a multiplicative error term), into an additive one. However, logarithms of a variable cannot be taken in situations where the variable can take on zero or negative values, for the log will not be defined in such cases.
>
> (2) *Using heteroscedasticity-consistent standard error estimates.* Most standard econometrics software packages have an option (usually called something like 'robust') that allows the user to employ standard error estimates that have been modified to account for the heteroscedasticity following White (1980). The effect of using the correction is that, if the variance of the errors is positively related to the square of an explanatory variable, the standard errors for the slope coefficients are increased relative to the usual OLS standard errors, which would make hypothesis testing more 'conservative', so that more evidence would be required against the null hypothesis before it would be rejected.

Therefore, the disturbances from (5.7) will be homoscedastic. Note that this latter regression does not include a constant since β_1 is multiplied by $(1/z_t)$. GLS can be viewed as OLS applied to transformed data that satisfy the OLS assumptions. GLS is also known as weighted least squares (WLS), since under GLS a weighted sum of the squared residuals is minimised, whereas under OLS it is an unweighted sum.

However, researchers are typically unsure of the exact cause of the heteroscedasticity, and hence this technique is usually infeasible in practice. Two other possible 'solutions' for heteroscedasticity are shown in box 5.2.

Examples of tests for heteroscedasticity in the context of the single index market model are given in Fabozzi and Francis (1980). Their results are strongly suggestive of the presence of heteroscedasticity, and they examine various factors that may constitute the form of the heteroscedasticity.

5.4.4 Testing for heteroscedasticity using EViews

Re-open the Microsoft ('Macro') Workfile that was examined in the previous chapter and the regression that included all the macroeconomic explanatory variables and make sure that the regression output window is open (showing the table of parameter estimates). First, plot the residuals by selecting **View/Actual, Fitted, Residuals/Residual Graph.** If the residuals of the regression have systematically changing variability over the sample, that is a sign of heteroscedasticity. In this case, it is hard to see any clear pattern (although it is interesting to note the considerable reduction in volatility post-2003), so we need to run the formal statistical test. To test for heteroscedasticity using White's test, click on the **View** button in the regression window and select **Residual Diagnostics/Heteroscedasticity Tests. . . .** You will see a large number of different tests available, including the autoregressive conditional heteroscedasticity (ARCH) test that will be discussed in chapter 9. For now, select the **White** specification. You can also select whether to include the cross-product terms or not (i.e. each variable multiplied by each other variable) or include only the squares of the variables in the auxiliary regression. Uncheck the '**Include White cross terms**' given the relatively large number of variables in this regression and then click **OK**. The results of the test will appear as follows.

Heteroscedasticity Test: White

F-statistic	0.285965	Prob. F(7,316)	0.9592
Obs*R-squared	2.039511	Prob. Chi-Square(7)	0.9576
Scaled explained SS	12.15911	Prob. Chi-Square(7)	0.0954

Test Equation:
Dependent Variable: RESID^2
Method: Least Squares
Date: 07/04/13   Time: 13:42
Sample: 1986M05 20013M04
Included observations: 324

	Coefficient	Std. Error	t-Statistic	Prob.
C	193.5672	42.83306	4.519108	0.0000
ERSAND^2	−0.16274	0.698446	−0.23300	0.8159
DPROD^2	−11.3366	31.19290	−0.36344	0.7165
DCREDIT^2	−1.01E−08	3.98E−08	−0.25438	0.7994
DINFLATION^2	−65.7807	150.0464	−0.43840	0.6614
DMONEY^2	−0.01229	0.027218	−0.45135	0.6520
DSPREAD^2	−2.02297	638.3524	−0.00317	0.9975
RTERM^2	−196.336	294.3750	−0.66696	0.5053

R-squared	0.006295	Mean dependent var	156.2891
Adjusted R-squared	−0.015718	S.D. dependent var	554.1926
S.E. of regression	558.5309	Akaike info criterion	15.51288
Sum squared resid	98578340	Schwarz criterion	15.60623
Log likelihood	−2505.086	Hannan-Quinn criter.	15.55014
F-statistic	0.285965	Durbin-Watson stat	2.028098
Prob(F-statistic)	0.959219		

EViews presents three different types of tests for heteroscedasticity and then the auxiliary regression in the first results table displayed. The test statistics give us the information we need to determine whether the assumption of homoscedasticity is valid or not, but seeing the actual auxiliary regression in the second table can provide useful additional information on the source of the heteroscedasticity if any is found. In this case, both the F- and χ^2 ('LM') versions of the test statistic give the same conclusion that there is no evidence for the presence of heteroscedasticity, since the p-values are considerably in excess of 0.05. The third version of the test statistic, 'Scaled explained SS', which as the name suggests is based on a normalised version of the explained sum of squares from the auxiliary regression, suggests in this case that there is some limited evidence of heteroscedasticity (with the test result significant at the 10% level but not lower). Thus the conclusion of the test is slightly ambiguous but overall we would probably be satisfied that there is not a serious problem here.

5.4.5   Using White's modified standard error estimates in EViews

In order to estimate the regression with heteroscedasticity-robust standard errors in EViews, select this from the option button in the regression entry window. In other words, **close** the heteroscedasticity test window and **click** on the original 'Msoftreg' regression results, then click on the **Estimate** button and in the Equation Estimation window, choose the **Options** tab and screenshot 5.1 will appear.

In the 'Coefficient covariance matrix' box at the top left of the tab, change the option to **White** and click **OK**. Comparing the results of the regression using heteroscedasticity-robust standard errors with those using the ordinary standard errors, the changes in the significances of the parameters are only marginal. Of course, only the standard errors have changed and the parameter estimates have remained identical to those from before. The heteroscedasticity-consistent standard errors are smaller for all variables, resulting in the t-ratios growing in absolute value and the p-values being smaller. The main changes in the conclusions reached are that the term structure variable, which was previously significant only at the 10% level, is now significant at 5%, and the unexpected inflation and change in industrial production variables are now significant at the 10% level.

5.5   **Assumption 3**: $\mathrm{cov}(u_i, u_j) = 0$ for $i \neq j$

Assumption 3 that is made of the CLRM's disturbance terms is that the covariance between the error terms over time (or cross-sectionally, for that type of data) is zero. In other words, it is assumed that the errors are uncorrelated with one another. If the errors are not uncorrelated with one another, it would be stated that they are 'autocorrelated' or that they are 'serially correlated'. A test of this assumption is therefore required.

Again, the population disturbances cannot be observed, so tests for autocorrelation are conducted on the residuals, $\hat{u}$. Before one can proceed to see how

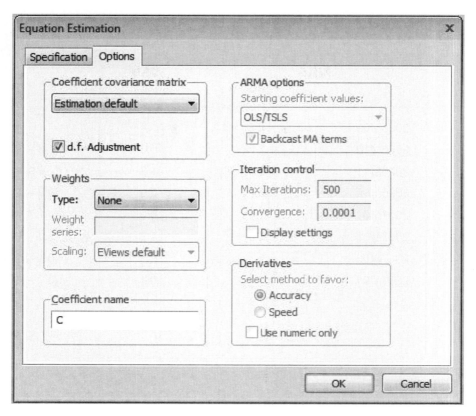

Screenshot 5.1   **Regression options window**

formal tests for autocorrelation are formulated, the concept of the lagged value of a variable needs to be defined.

5.5.1 The concept of a lagged value

The lagged value of a variable (which may be y_t, x_t, or u_t) is simply the value that the variable took during a previous period. So for example, the value of y_t lagged one period, written y_{t-1}, can be constructed by shifting all of the observations forward one period in a spreadsheet, as illustrated in table 5.1.

So, the value in the $2006M10$ row and the y_{t-1} column shows the value that y_t took in the previous period, $2006M09$, which was 0.8. The last column in table 5.1 shows another quantity relating to y, namely the 'first difference'. The first difference of y, also known as the change in y, and denoted Δy_t, is calculated as the difference between the values of y in this period and in the previous period. This is calculated as

$$\Delta y_t = y_t - y_{t-1} \tag{5.8}$$

Note that when one-period lags or first differences of a variable are constructed, the first observation is lost. Thus a regression of Δy_t using the above data would begin with the October 2006 data point. It is also possible to produce two-period

Table 5.1   Constructing a series of lagged values and first differences

t	y_t	y_{t-1}	Δy_t
2006M09	0.8	–	–
2006M10	1.3	0.8	$(1.3 - 0.8) = 0.5$
2006M11	−0.9	1.3	$(-0.9 - 1.3) = -2.2$
2006M12	0.2	−0.9	$(0.2 - -0.9) = 1.1$
2007M01	−1.7	0.2	$(-1.7 - 0.2) = -1.9$
2007M02	2.3	−1.7	$(2.3 - -1.7) = 4.0$
2007M03	0.1	2.3	$(0.1 - 2.3) = -2.2$
2007M04	0.0	0.1	$(0.0 - 0.1) = -0.1$
.	.	.	.
.	.	.	.
.	.	.	.

lags, three-period lags and so on. These would be accomplished in the obvious way.

5.5.2 Graphical tests for autocorrelation

In order to test for autocorrelation, it is necessary to investigate whether any relationships exist between the current value of $\hat{u}$, $\hat{u}_t$, and any of its previous values, $\hat{u}_{t-1}, \hat{u}_{t-2}, \ldots$. The first step is to consider possible relationships between the current residual and the immediately previous one, $\hat{u}_{t-1}$, via a graphical exploration. Thus $\hat{u}_t$ is plotted against $\hat{u}_{t-1}$, and $\hat{u}_t$ is plotted over time. Some stereotypical patterns that may be found in the residuals are discussed below.

Figures 5.3 and 5.4 show positive autocorrelation in the residuals, which is indicated by a cyclical residual plot over time. This case is known as *positive autocorrelation* since on average if the residual at time $t - 1$ is positive, the residual at time t is likely to be also positive; similarly, if the residual at $t - 1$ is negative, the residual at t is also likely to be negative. Figure 5.3 shows that most of the dots representing observations are in the first and third quadrants, while figure 5.4 shows that a positively autocorrelated series of residuals will not cross the time-axis very frequently.

Figures 5.5 and 5.6 show negative autocorrelation, indicated by an alternating pattern in the residuals. This case is known as negative autocorrelation since on average if the residual at time $t - 1$ is positive, the residual at time t is likely to be negative; similarly, if the residual at $t - 1$ is negative, the residual at t is likely to be positive. Figure 5.5 shows that most of the dots are in the second and fourth

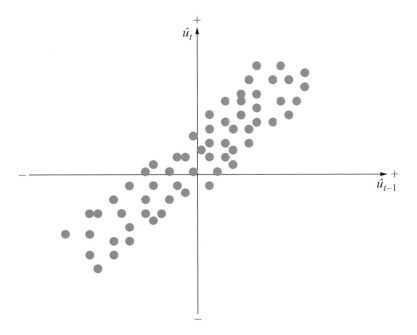

Figure 5.3   Plot of $\hat{u}_t$ against $\hat{u}_{t-1}$, showing positive autocorrelation

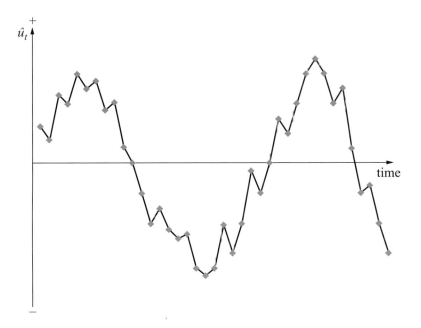

Figure 5.4   Plot of $\hat{u}_t$ over time, showing positive autocorrelation

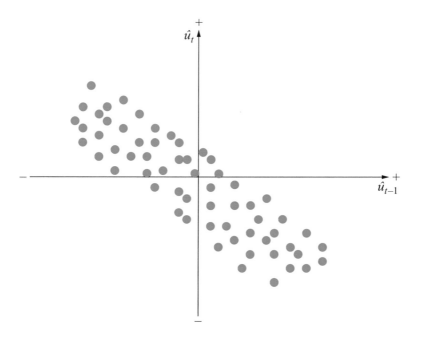

Figure 5.5   Plot of $\hat{u}_t$ against $\hat{u}_{t-1}$, showing negative autocorrelation

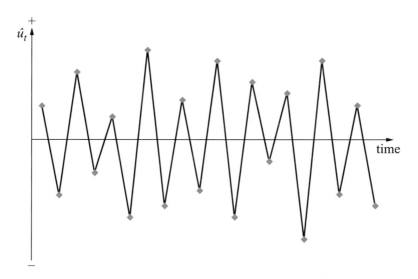

Figure 5.6   Plot of $\hat{u}_t$ over time, showing negative autocorrelation

quadrants, while figure 5.6 shows that a negatively autocorrelated series of residuals will cross the time-axis more frequently than if they were distributed randomly.

Finally, figures 5.7 and 5.8 show no pattern in residuals at all: this is what is desirable to see. In the plot of $\hat{u}_t$ against $\hat{u}_{t-1}$ (figure 5.7), the points are randomly spread across all four quadrants, and the time series plot of the residuals (figure 5.8) does not cross the x-axis either too frequently or too little.

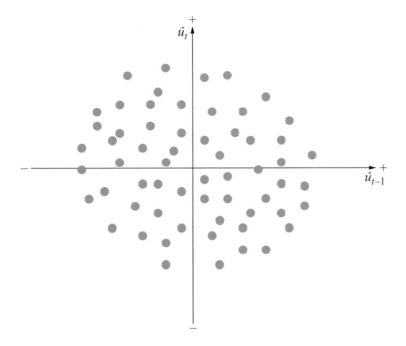

Figure 5.7   Plot of $\hat{u}_t$ against $\hat{u}_{t-1}$, showing no autocorrelation

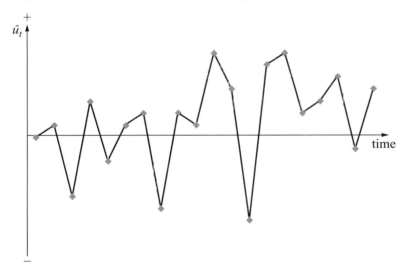

Figure 5.8   Plot of $\hat{u}_t$ over time, showing no autocorrelation

5.5.3   Detecting autocorrelation: the Durbin–Watson test

Of course, a first step in testing whether the residual series from an estimated model are autocorrelated would be to plot the residuals as above, looking for any patterns. Graphical methods may be difficult to interpret in practice, however, and hence a formal statistical test should also be applied. The simplest test is due to Durbin and Watson (1951).

Durbin–Watson (DW) is a test for first order autocorrelation – i.e. it tests only for a relationship between an error and its immediately previous value. One way to motivate the test and to interpret the test statistic would be in the context of a regression of the time t error on its previous value

$$u_t = \rho u_{t-1} + v_t \tag{5.9}$$

where $v_t \sim N(0, \sigma_v^2)$. The DW test statistic has as its null and alternative hypotheses

$$H_0 : \rho = 0 \quad \text{and} \quad H_1 : \rho \neq 0$$

Thus, under the null hypothesis, the errors at time $t - 1$ and t are independent of one another, and if this null were rejected, it would be concluded that there was evidence of a relationship between successive residuals. In fact, it is not necessary to run the regression given by (5.9) since the test statistic can be calculated using quantities that are already available after the first regression has been run

$$DW = \frac{\sum\limits_{t=2}^{T} (\hat{u}_t - \hat{u}_{t-1})^2}{\sum\limits_{t=2}^{T} \hat{u}_t^2} \tag{5.10}$$

The denominator of the test statistic is simply (the number of observations -1) $\times$ the variance of the residuals. This arises since if the average of the residuals is zero

$$\text{var}(\hat{u}_t) = E(\hat{u}_t^2) = \frac{1}{T-1} \sum\limits_{t=2}^{T} \hat{u}_t^2$$

so that

$$\sum\limits_{t=2}^{T} \hat{u}_t^2 = \text{var}(\hat{u}_t) \times (T - 1)$$

The numerator 'compares' the values of the error at times $t - 1$ and t. If there is positive autocorrelation in the errors, this difference in the numerator will be relatively small, while if there is negative autocorrelation, with the sign of the error changing very frequently, the numerator will be relatively large. No autocorrelation would result in a value for the numerator between small and large.

It is also possible to express the DW statistic as an approximate function of the estimated value of ρ

$$DW \approx 2(1 - \hat{\rho}) \tag{5.11}$$

where $\hat{\rho}$ is the estimated correlation coefficient that would have been obtained from an estimation of (5.9). To see why this is the case, consider that the numerator of (5.10) can be written as the parts of a quadratic

$$\sum\limits_{t=2}^{T} (\hat{u}_t - \hat{u}_{t-1})^2 = \sum\limits_{t=2}^{T} \hat{u}_t^2 + \sum\limits_{t=2}^{T} \hat{u}_{t-1}^2 - 2\sum\limits_{t=2}^{T} \hat{u}_t \hat{u}_{t-1} \tag{5.12}$$

Consider now the composition of the first two summations on the RHS of (5.12). The first of these is

$$\sum_{t=2}^{T} \hat{u}_t^2 = \hat{u}_2^2 + \hat{u}_3^2 + \hat{u}_4^2 + \cdots + \hat{u}_T^2$$

while the second is

$$\sum_{t=2}^{T} \hat{u}_{t-1}^2 = \hat{u}_1^2 + \hat{u}_2^2 + \hat{u}_3^2 + \cdots + \hat{u}_{T-1}^2$$

Thus, the only difference between them is that they differ in the first and last terms in the summation, so

$$\sum_{t=2}^{T} \hat{u}_t^2$$

contains $\hat{u}_T^2$ but not $\hat{u}_1^2$, while

$$\sum_{t=2}^{T} \hat{u}_{t-1}^2$$

contains $\hat{u}_1^2$ but not $\hat{u}_T^2$. As the sample size, T, increases towards infinity, the difference between these two will become negligible. Hence, the expression in (5.12), the numerator of (5.10), is approximately

$$2\sum_{t=2}^{T} \hat{u}_t^2 - 2\sum_{t=2}^{T} \hat{u}_t \hat{u}_{t-1}$$

Replacing the numerator of (5.10) with this expression leads to

$$DW \approx \frac{2\sum_{t=2}^{T} \hat{u}_t^2 - 2\sum_{t=2}^{T} \hat{u}_t \hat{u}_{t-1}}{\sum_{t=2}^{T} \hat{u}_t^2} = 2\left(1 - \frac{\sum_{t=2}^{T} \hat{u}_t \hat{u}_{t-1}}{\sum_{t=2}^{T} \hat{u}_t^2}\right) \tag{5.13}$$

The covariance between u_t and u_{t-1} can be written as $E[(u_t - E(u_t))(u_{t-1} - E(u_{t-1}))]$. Under the assumption that $E(u_t) = 0$ (and therefore that $E(u_{t-1}) = 0$), the covariance will be $E[u_t u_{t-1}]$. For the sample residuals, this covariance will be evaluated as

$$\frac{1}{T-1} \sum_{t=2}^{T} \hat{u}_t \hat{u}_{t-1}$$

Thus, the sum in the numerator of the expression on the right of (5.13) can be seen as $T - 1$ times the covariance between $\hat{u}_t$ and $\hat{u}_{t-1}$, while the sum in the

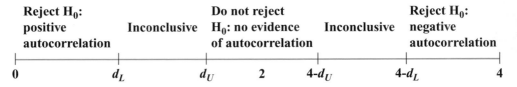

Figure 5.9   Rejection and non-rejection regions for DW test

denominator of the expression on the right of (5.13) can be seen from the previous exposition as $T - 1$ times the variance of $\hat{u}_t$. Thus, it is possible to write

$$DW \approx 2 \left(1 - \frac{(T-1)\,\text{cov}(\hat{u}_t, \hat{u}_{t-1})}{(T-1)\,\text{var}(\hat{u}_t)} \right) = 2 \left(1 - \frac{\text{cov}(\hat{u}_t, \hat{u}_{t-1})}{\text{var}(\hat{u}_t)} \right)$$

$$= 2\,(1 - \text{corr}(\hat{u}_t, \hat{u}_{t-1})) \tag{5.14}$$

so that the DW test statistic is approximately equal to $2(1 - \hat{\rho})$. Since $\hat{\rho}$ is a correlation, it implies that $-1 \le \hat{\rho} \le 1$. That is, $\hat{\rho}$ is bounded to lie between -1 and $+1$. Substituting in these limits for $\hat{\rho}$ to calculate DW from (5.11) would give the corresponding limits for DW as $0 \le DW \le 4$. Consider now the implication of DW taking one of three important values (0, 2, and 4):

- $\hat{\rho} = 0, DW = 2$ This is the case where there is no autocorrelation in the residuals. So roughly speaking, the null hypothesis would not be rejected if DW is near $2 \to$ i.e. there is little evidence of autocorrelation.
- $\hat{\rho} = 1, DW = 0$ This corresponds to the case where there is perfect positive autocorrelation in the residuals.
- $\hat{\rho} = -1, DW = 4$ This corresponds to the case where there is perfect negative autocorrelation in the residuals.

The DW test does not follow a standard statistical distribution such as a t, F, or χ^2. DW has 2 critical values: an upper critical value (d_U) and a lower critical value (d_L), and there is also an intermediate region where the null hypothesis of no autocorrelation can neither be rejected nor not rejected! The rejection, non-rejection and inconclusive regions are shown on the number line in figure 5.9.

So, to reiterate, the null hypothesis is rejected and the existence of positive autocorrelation presumed if DW is less than the lower critical value; the null hypothesis is rejected and the existence of negative autocorrelation presumed if DW is greater than 4 minus the lower critical value; the null hypothesis is not rejected and no significant residual autocorrelation is presumed if DW is between the upper and 4 minus the upper limits.

Example 5.2 •

A researcher wishes to test for first order serial correlation in the residuals from a linear regression. The DW test statistic value is 0.86. There are eighty quarterly observations in the regression, which is of the form

$$y_t = \beta_1 + \beta_2 x_{2t} + \beta_3 x_{3t} + \beta_4 x_{4t} + u_t \tag{5.15}$$

> **Box 5.3 Conditions for *DW* to be a valid test**
>
> (1) There must be a constant term in the regression
> (2) The regressors must be non-stochastic – as assumption 4 of the CLRM (see chapter 7)
> (3) There must be no lags of dependent variable (see section 5.5.8) in the regression.

The relevant critical values for the test (see table A2.6 in the appendix of statistical distributions at the end of this book), are $d_L = 1.42$, $d_U = 1.57$, so $4 - d_U = 2.43$ and $4 - d_L = 2.58$. The test statistic is clearly lower than the lower critical value and hence the null hypothesis of no autocorrelation is rejected and it would be concluded that the residuals from the model appear to be positively autocorrelated.

5.5.4 Conditions which must be fulfilled for *DW* to be a valid test

In order for the *DW* test to be valid for application, three conditions must be fulfilled (box 5.3).

If the test were used in the presence of lags of the dependent variable or otherwise stochastic regressors, the test statistic would be biased towards 2, suggesting that in some instances the null hypothesis of no autocorrelation would not be rejected when it should be.

5.5.5 Another test for autocorrelation: the Breusch–Godfrey test

Recall that *DW* is a test only of whether consecutive errors are related to one another. So, not only can the *DW* test not be applied if a certain set of circumstances are not fulfilled, there will also be many forms of residual autocorrelation that *DW* cannot detect. For example, if $\text{corr}(\hat{u}_t, \hat{u}_{t-1}) = 0$, but $\text{corr}(\hat{u}_t, \hat{u}_{t-2}) \neq 0$, *DW* as defined above will not find any autocorrelation. One possible solution would be to replace $\hat{u}_{t-1}$ in (5.10) with $\hat{u}_{t-2}$. However, pairwise examinations of the correlations $(\hat{u}_t, \hat{u}_{t-1})$, $(\hat{u}_t, \hat{u}_{t-2})$, $(\hat{u}_t, \hat{u}_{t-3})$, ... will be tedious in practice and is not coded in econometrics software packages, which have been programmed to construct *DW* using only a one-period lag. In addition, the approximation in (5.11) will deteriorate as the difference between the two time indices increases. Consequently, the critical values should also be modified somewhat in these cases.

Therefore, it is desirable to examine a joint test for autocorrelation that will allow examination of the relationship between $\hat{u}_t$ and several of its lagged values at the same time. The Breusch–Godfrey test is a more general test for autocorrelation up to the rth order. The model for the errors under this test is

$$u_t = \rho_1 u_{t-1} + \rho_2 u_{t-2} + \rho_3 u_{t-3} + \cdots + \rho_r u_{t-r} + v_t, \qquad v_t \sim N\left(0, \sigma_v^2\right)$$

(5.16)

The null and alternative hypotheses are:

$H_0 : \rho_1 = 0$ and $\rho_2 = 0$ and $\ldots$ and $\rho_r = 0$

$H_1 : \rho_1 \neq 0$ or $\rho_2 \neq 0$ or $\ldots$ or $\rho_r \neq 0$

So, under the null hypothesis, the current error is not related to any of its r previous values. The test is carried out as in box 5.4.

Box 5.4 Conducting a Breusch–Godfrey test

(1) Estimate the linear regression using OLS and obtain the residuals, $\hat{u}_t$
(2) Regress $\hat{u}_t$ on all of the regressors from stage 1 (the xs) plus $\hat{u}_{t-1}$, $\hat{u}_{t-2}, \ldots, \hat{u}_{t-r}$; the regression will thus be

$$\hat{u}_t = \gamma_1 + \gamma_2 x_{2t} + \gamma_3 x_{3t} + \gamma_4 x_{4t} + \rho_1 \hat{u}_{t-1} + \rho_2 \hat{u}_{t-2} + \rho_3 \hat{u}_{t-3}$$

$$+ \cdots + \rho_r \hat{u}_{t-r} + v_t, v_t \sim N\left(0, \sigma_v^2\right) \qquad (5.17)$$

Obtain R^2 from this auxiliary regression
(3) Letting T denote the number of observations, the test statistic is given by

$$(T - r)R^2 \sim \chi_r^2$$

Note that $(T - r)$ pre-multiplies R^2 in the test for autocorrelation rather than T (as was the case for the heteroscedasticity test). This arises because the first r observations will effectively have been lost from the sample in order to obtain the r lags used in the test regression, leaving $(T - r)$ observations from which to estimate the auxiliary regression. If the test statistic exceeds the critical value from the chi–squared statistical tables, reject the null hypothesis of no autocorrelation. As with any joint test, only one part of the null hypothesis has to be rejected to lead to rejection of the hypothesis as a whole. So the error at time t has to be significantly related only to one of its previous r values in the sample for the null of no autocorrelation to be rejected. The test is more general than the DW test, and can be applied in a wider variety of circumstances since it does not impose the DW restrictions on the format of the first stage regression.

One potential difficulty with Breusch–Godfrey, however, is in determining an appropriate value of r, the number of lags of the residuals, to use in computing the test. There is no obvious answer to this, so it is typical to experiment with a range of values, and also to use the frequency of the data to decide. So, for example, if the data is monthly or quarterly, set r equal to 12 or 4, respectively. The argument would then be that errors at any given time would be expected to be related only to those errors in the previous year. Obviously, if the model is statistically adequate, no evidence of autocorrelation should be found in the residuals whatever value of r is chosen.

5.5.6 Consequences of ignoring autocorrelation if it is present

In fact, the consequences of ignoring autocorrelation when it is present are similar to those of ignoring heteroscedasticity. The coefficient estimates derived using OLS are still unbiased, but they are inefficient, i.e. they are not BLUE, even at large sample sizes, so that the standard error estimates could be wrong. There thus exists the possibility that the wrong inferences could be made about whether a variable is or is not an important determinant of variations in y. In the case of positive serial correlation in the residuals, the OLS standard error estimates will be biased downwards relative to the true standard errors. That is, OLS will understate their true variability. This would lead to an increase in the probability of type I error – that is, a tendency to reject the null hypothesis sometimes when it is correct. Furthermore, R^2 is likely to be inflated relative to its 'correct' value if autocorrelation is present but ignored, since residual autocorrelation will lead to an underestimate of the true error variance (for positive autocorrelation).

5.5.7 Dealing with autocorrelation

If the form of the autocorrelation is known, it would be possible to use a GLS procedure. One approach, which was once fairly popular, is known as the Cochrane–Orcutt procedure (see box 5.5). Such methods work by assuming a particular form for the structure of the autocorrelation (usually a first order autoregressive process – see chapter 6 for a general description of these models). The model would thus be specified as follows:

$$y_t = \beta_1 + \beta_2 x_{2t} + \beta_3 x_{3t} + u_t, \qquad u_t = \rho u_{t-1} + v_t \tag{5.18}$$

Note that a constant is not required in the specification for the errors since $E(u_t) = 0$. If this model holds at time t, it is assumed to also hold for time $t-1$, so that the model in (5.18) is lagged one period

$$y_{t-1} = \beta_1 + \beta_2 x_{2t-1} + \beta_3 x_{3t-1} + u_{t-1} \tag{5.19}$$

Multiplying (5.19) by ρ

$$\rho y_{t-1} = \rho \beta_1 + \rho \beta_2 x_{2t-1} + \rho \beta_3 x_{3t-1} + \rho u_{t-1} \tag{5.20}$$

Subtracting (5.20) from (5.18) would give

$$y_t - \rho y_{t-1} = \beta_1 - \rho \beta_1 + \beta_2 x_{2t} - \rho \beta_2 x_{2t-1} + \beta_3 x_{3t} - \rho \beta_3 x_{3t-1} + u_t - \rho u_{t-1} \tag{5.21}$$

Factorising, and noting that $v_t = u_t - \rho u_{t-1}$

$$(y_t - \rho y_{t-1}) = (1 - \rho)\beta_1 + \beta_2(x_{2t} - \rho x_{2t-1}) + \beta_3(x_{3t} - \rho x_{3t-1}) + v_t \quad (5.22)$$

Setting $\qquad y_t^* = y_t - \rho y_{t-1}, \beta_1^* = (1 - \rho)\beta_1, x_{2t}^* = (x_{2t} - \rho x_{2t-1}),$ and $x_{3t}^* = (x_{3t} - \rho x_{3t-1}),$ the model in (5.22) can be written

$$y_t^* = \beta_1^* + \beta_2 x_{2t}^* + \beta_3 x_{3t}^* + v_t \quad (5.23)$$

Since the final specification (5.23) contains an error term that is free from auto-correlation, OLS can be directly applied to it. This procedure is effectively an application of GLS. Of course, the construction of y_t^* etc. requires ρ to be known. In practice, this will never be the case so that ρ has to be estimated before (5.23) can be used.

A simple method would be to use the ρ obtained from rearranging the equation for the DW statistic given in (5.11). However, this is only an approximation as the related algebra showed. This approximation may be poor in the context of small samples.

The Cochrane–Orcutt procedure is an alternative, which operates as in box 5.5. This could be the end of the process. However, Cochrane and Orcutt (1949) argue that better estimates can be obtained by going through steps 2–4 again. That is, given the new coefficient estimates, $\beta_1^*, \beta_2, \beta_3$, etc. construct again the residual and regress it on its previous value to obtain a new estimate for $\hat{\rho}$. This would then be used to construct new values of the variables $y_t^*, x_{2t}^*, x_{3t}^*$ and a new (5.23) is estimated. This procedure would be repeated until the change in $\hat{\rho}$ between one iteration and the next is less than some fixed amount (e.g. 0.01). In practice, a small number of iterations (no more than five) will usually suffice.

However, the Cochrane–Orcutt procedure and similar approaches require a specific assumption to be made concerning the form of the model for the auto-correlation. Consider again (5.22). This can be rewritten taking ρy_{t-1} over to the RHS

$$y_t = (1 - \rho)\beta_1 + \beta_2(x_{2t} - \rho x_{2t-1}) + \beta_3(x_{3t} - \rho x_{3t-1}) + \rho y_{t-1} + v_t \quad (5.24)$$

Expanding the brackets around the explanatory variable terms would give

$$y_t = (1 - \rho)\beta_1 + \beta_2 x_{2t} - \rho\beta_2 x_{2t-1} + \beta_3 x_{3t} - \rho\beta_3 x_{3t-1} + \rho y_{t-1} + v_t \quad (5.25)$$

Now, suppose that an equation containing the same variables as (5.26) were estimated using OLS

$$y_t = \gamma_1 + \gamma_2 x_{2t} + \gamma_3 x_{2t-1} + \gamma_4 x_{3t} + \gamma_5 x_{3t-1} + \gamma_6 y_{t-1} + v_t \quad (5.26)$$

It can be seen that (5.25) is a restricted version of (5.26), with the restrictions imposed that the coefficient on x_{2t} in (5.25) multiplied by the negative of the coefficient on y_{t-1} gives the coefficient on x_{2t-1}, and that the coefficient on x_{3t} multiplied by the negative of the coefficient on y_{t-1} gives the coefficient on x_{3t-1}. Thus, the restrictions implied for (5.26) to get (5.25) are

$$\gamma_2\gamma_6 = -\gamma_3 \quad \text{and} \quad \gamma_4\gamma_6 = -\gamma_5$$

Box 5.5   The Cochrane–Orcutt procedure

(1) Assume that the general model is of the form (5.18) above. Estimate the equation in (5.18) using OLS, ignoring the residual autocorrelation.
(2) Obtain the residuals, and run the regression

$$\hat{u}_t = \rho \hat{u}_{t-1} + v_t \tag{5.27}$$

(3) Obtain $\hat{\rho}$ and construct y_t^* etc. using this estimate of $\hat{\rho}$.
(4) Run the GLS regression (5.23).

These are known as the *common factor restrictions*, and they should be tested before the Cochrane–Orcutt or similar procedure is implemented. If the restrictions hold, Cochrane–Orcutt can be validly applied. If not, however, Cochrane–Orcutt and similar techniques would be inappropriate, and the appropriate step would be to estimate an equation such as (5.26) directly using OLS. Note that in general there will be a common factor restriction for every explanatory variable (excluding a constant) $x_{2t}, x_{3t}, \ldots, x_{kt}$ in the regression. Hendry and Mizon (1978) argued that the restrictions are likely to be invalid in practice and therefore a dynamic model that allows for the structure of y should be used rather than a residual correction on a static model – see also Hendry (1980).

The White variance–covariance matrix of the coefficients (that is, calculation of the standard errors using the White correction for heteroscedasticity) is appropriate when the residuals of the estimated equation are heteroscedastic but serially uncorrelated. Newey and West (1987) develop a variance–covariance estimator that is consistent in the presence of both heteroscedasticity and autocorrelation. So an alternative approach to dealing with residual autocorrelation would be to use appropriately modified standard error estimates.

While White's correction to standard errors for heteroscedasticity as discussed above does not require any user input, the Newey–West procedure requires the specification of a truncation lag length to determine the number of lagged residuals used to evaluate the autocorrelation. EViews uses INTEGER$[4(T/100)^{2/9}]$. In EViews, the Newey–West procedure for estimating the standard errors is employed by invoking it from the same place as the White heteroscedasticity correction. That is, click the **Estimate** button and in the Equation Estimation window, choose the **Options** tab and then instead of checking the 'White' box, check **Newey-West**. While this option is listed under 'Heteroskedasticity consistent coefficient variance', the Newey-West procedure in fact produces 'HAC' (Heteroscedasticity and Autocorrelation Consistent) standard errors that correct for both autocorrelation and heteroscedasticity that may be present.

A more 'modern' view concerning autocorrelation is that it presents an opportunity rather than a problem. This view, associated with Sargan, Hendry and Mizon, suggests that serial correlation in the errors arises as a consequence of 'misspecified dynamics'. For another explanation of the reason why this stance is taken, recall that it is possible to express the dependent variable as the sum of the parts that can be explained using the model, and a part which cannot (the residuals)

$$y_t = \hat{y}_t + \hat{u}_t \tag{5.28}$$

where $\hat{y}_t$ are the fitted values from the model $(= \hat{\beta}_1 + \hat{\beta}_2 x_{2t} + \hat{\beta}_3 x_{3t} + \cdots + \hat{\beta}_k x_{kt})$. Autocorrelation in the residuals is often caused by a dynamic structure in y that has not been modelled and so has not been captured in the fitted values. In other words, there exists a richer structure in the dependent variable y and more information in the sample about that structure than has been captured by the models previously estimated. What is required is a dynamic model that allows for this extra structure in y.

5.5.8 Dynamic models

All of the models considered so far have been static in nature, e.g.

$$y_t = \beta_1 + \beta_2 x_{2t} + \beta_3 x_{3t} + \beta_4 x_{4t} + \beta_5 x_{5t} + u_t \tag{5.29}$$

In other words, these models have allowed for only a *contemporaneous relationship* between the variables, so that a change in one or more of the explanatory variables at time t causes an instant change in the dependent variable at time t. But this analysis can easily be extended to the case where the current value of y_t depends on previous values of y or on previous values of one or more of the variables, e.g.

$$y_t = \beta_1 + \beta_2 x_{2t} + \beta_3 x_{3t} + \beta_4 x_{4t} + \beta_5 x_{5t} + \gamma_1 y_{t-1} + \gamma_2 x_{2t-1}$$
$$+ \cdots + \gamma_k x_{kt-1} + u_t \tag{5.30}$$

It is of course possible to extend the model even more by adding further lags, e.g. x_{2t-2}, y_{t-3}. Models containing lags of the explanatory variables (but no lags of the explained variable) are known as *distributed lag models*. Specifications with lags of both explanatory and explained variables are known as *autoregressive distributed lag* (ADL) models.

How many lags and of which variables should be included in a dynamic regression model? This is a tricky question to answer, but hopefully recourse to financial theory will help to provide an answer; for another response, see section 5.14.

Another potential 'remedy' for autocorrelated residuals would be to switch to a model in first differences rather than in levels. As explained previously, the first difference of y_t, i.e. $y_t - y_{t-1}$ is denoted Δy_t; similarly, one can construct a series of first differences for each of the explanatory variables, e.g. $\Delta x_{2t} = x_{2t} - x_{2t-1}$, etc. Such a model has a number of other useful features (see chapter 8 for more details) and could be expressed as

$$\Delta y_t = \beta_1 + \beta_2 \Delta x_{2t} + \beta_3 \Delta x_{3t} + u_t \tag{5.31}$$

Sometimes the change in y is purported to depend on previous values of the level of y or $x_i(i = 2, \ldots, k)$ as well as changes in the explanatory variables

$$\Delta y_t = \beta_1 + \beta_2 \Delta x_{2t} + \beta_3 \Delta x_{3t} + \beta_4 x_{2t-1} + \beta_5 y_{t-1} + u_t \tag{5.32}$$

5.5.9   Why might lags be required in a regression?

Lagged values of the explanatory variables or of the dependent variable (or both) may capture important dynamic structure in the dependent variable that might be caused by a number of factors. Two possibilities that are relevant in finance are as follows:

- **Inertia of the dependent variable**   Often a change in the value of one of the explanatory variables will not affect the dependent variable immediately during one time period, but rather with a lag over several time periods. For example, the effect of a change in market microstructure or government policy may take a few months or longer to work through since agents may be initially unsure of what the implications for asset pricing are, and so on. More generally, many variables in economics and finance will change only slowly. This phenomenon arises partly as a result of pure psychological factors – for example, in financial markets, agents may not fully comprehend the effects of a particular news announcement immediately, or they may not even believe the news. The speed and extent of reaction will also depend on whether the change in the variable is expected to be permanent or transitory. Delays in response may also arise as a result of technological or institutional factors. For example, the speed of technology will limit how quickly investors' buy or sell orders can be executed. Similarly, many investors have savings plans or other financial products where they are 'locked in' and therefore unable to act for a fixed period. It is also worth noting that dynamic structure is likely to be stronger and more prevalent the higher is the frequency of observation of the data.
- **Overreactions**   It is sometimes argued that financial markets overreact to good and to bad news. So, for example, if a firm makes a profit warning, implying that its profits are likely to be down when formally reported later in the year, the markets might be anticipated to perceive this as implying that the value of the firm is less than was previously thought, and hence that the price of its shares will fall. If there is an overreaction, the price will initially fall below that which is appropriate for the firm given this bad news, before subsequently bouncing back up to a new level (albeit lower than the initial level before the announcement).

Moving from a purely static model to one which allows for lagged effects is likely to reduce, and possibly remove, serial correlation which was present in the static model's residuals. However, other problems with the regression could cause the null hypothesis of no autocorrelation to be rejected, and these would not be remedied by adding lagged variables to the model.

- **Omission of relevant variables, which are themselves autocorrelated** In other words, if there is a variable that is an important determinant of movements in y, but which has not been included in the model, and which itself is autocorrelated, this will induce the residuals from the estimated model to be serially correlated. To give a financial context in which this may arise, it is often assumed that investors assess one-step-ahead expected returns on a stock using a linear relationship

$$r_t = \alpha_0 + \alpha_1 \Omega_{t-1} + u_t \tag{5.33}$$

  where Ω_{t-1} is a set of lagged information variables (i.e. Ω_{t-1} is a vector of observations on a set of variables at time $t-1$). However, (5.33) cannot be estimated since the actual information set used by investors to form their expectations of returns is not known. Ω_{t-1} is therefore proxied with an assumed sub-set of that information, Z_{t-1}. For example, in many popular arbitrage pricing specifications, the information set used in the estimated model includes unexpected changes in industrial production, the term structure of interest rates, inflation and default risk premia. Such a model is bound to omit some informational variables used by actual investors in forming expectations of returns, and if these are autocorrelated, it will induce the residuals of the estimated model to be also autocorrelated.

- **Autocorrelation owing to unparameterised seasonality** Suppose that the dependent variable contains a seasonal or cyclical pattern, where certain features periodically occur. This may arise, for example, in the context of sales of gloves, where sales will be higher in the autumn and winter than in the spring or summer. Such phenomena are likely to lead to a positively autocorrelated residual structure that is cyclical in shape, such as that of figure 5.4, unless the seasonal patterns are captured by the model. See chapter 10 for a discussion of seasonality and how to deal with it.

- **If 'misspecification' error has been committed by using an inappropriate functional form** For example, if the relationship between y and the explanatory variables was a non-linear one, but the researcher had specified a linear regression model, this may again induce the residuals from the estimated model to be serially correlated.

5.5.10 The long-run static equilibrium solution

Once a general model of the form given in (5.32) has been found, it may contain many differenced and lagged terms that make it difficult to interpret from a theoretical perspective. For example, if the value of x_2 were to increase in period t, what would be the effect on y in periods, $t, t+1, t+2$, and so on? One interesting property of a dynamic model that can be calculated is its long-run or static equilibrium solution.

The relevant definition of 'equilibrium' in this context is that a system has reached equilibrium if the variables have attained some steady state values and are no longer changing, i.e. if y and x are in equilibrium, it is possible to write

$$y_t = y_{t+1} = \ldots = y \text{ and } x_{2t} = x_{2t+1} = \ldots = x_2, \text{ and so on.}$$

Consequently, $\Delta y_t = y_t - y_{t-1} = y - y = 0$, $\Delta x_{2t} = x_{2t} - x_{2t-1} = x_2 - x_2 = 0$, etc. since the values of the variables are no longer changing. So the way to obtain a long-run static solution from a given empirical model such as (5.32) is:

(1) Remove all time subscripts from the variables
(2) Set error terms equal to their expected values of zero, i.e $E(u_t) = 0$
(3) Remove differenced terms (e.g. Δy_t) altogether
(4) Gather terms in x together and gather terms in y together
(5) Rearrange the resulting equation if necessary so that the dependent variable y is on the left-hand side (LHS) and is expressed as a function of the independent variables.

Example 5.3

Calculate the long-run equilibrium solution for the following model

$$\Delta y_t = \beta_1 + \beta_2 \Delta x_{2t} + \beta_3 \Delta x_{3t} + \beta_4 x_{2t-1} + \beta_5 y_{t-1} + u_t \tag{5.34}$$

Applying first steps 1–3 above, the static solution would be given by

$$0 = \beta_1 + \beta_4 x_2 + \beta_5 y \tag{5.35}$$

Rearranging (5.35) to bring y to the LHS

$$\beta_5 y = -\beta_1 - \beta_4 x_2 \tag{5.36}$$

and finally, dividing through by β_5

$$y = -\frac{\beta_1}{\beta_5} - \frac{\beta_4}{\beta_5} x_2 \tag{5.37}$$

Equation (5.37) is the long-run static solution to (5.34). Note that this equation does not feature x_3, since the only term which contained x_3 was in first differenced form, so that x_3 does not influence the long-run equilibrium value of y.

5.5.11 Problems with adding lagged regressors to 'cure' autocorrelation

In many instances, a move from a static model to a dynamic one will result in a removal of residual autocorrelation. The use of lagged variables in a regression model does, however, bring with it additional problems:

● **Inclusion of lagged values of the dependent variable violates the assumption that the explanatory variables are non–stochastic** (assumption 4 of the CLRM), since by definition the value of y is determined partly by a random error term, and so its lagged values cannot be non–stochastic. In small samples, inclusion of lags of the dependent variable can lead to biased coefficient estimates, although they are still consistent, implying that the bias will disappear asymptotically (that is, as the sample size increases towards infinity).

- **What does an equation with a large number of lags actually mean?**
  A model with many lags may have solved a statistical problem (autocorrelated residuals) at the expense of creating an interpretational one (the empirical model containing many lags or differenced terms is difficult to interpret and may not test the original financial theory that motivated the use of regression analysis in the first place).

Note that if there is still autocorrelation in the residuals of a model including lags, then the OLS estimators will not even be consistent. To see why this occurs, consider the following regression model

$$y_t = \beta_1 + \beta_2 x_{2t} + \beta_3 x_{3t} + \beta_4 y_{t-1} + u_t \tag{5.38}$$

where the errors, u_t, follow a first order autoregressive process

$$u_t = \rho u_{t-1} + v_t \tag{5.39}$$

Substituting into (5.38) for u_t from (5.39)

$$y_t = \beta_1 + \beta_2 x_{2t} + \beta_3 x_{3t} + \beta_4 y_{t-1} + \rho u_{t-1} + v_t \tag{5.40}$$

Now, clearly y_t depends upon y_{t-1}. Taking (5.38) and lagging it one period (i.e. subtracting one from each time index)

$$y_{t-1} = \beta_1 + \beta_2 x_{2t-1} + \beta_3 x_{3t-1} + \beta_4 y_{t-2} + u_{t-1} \tag{5.41}$$

It is clear from (5.41) that y_{t-1} is related to u_{t-1} since they both appear in that equation. Thus, the assumption that $E(X'u) = 0$ is not satisfied for (5.41) and therefore for (5.38). Thus the OLS estimator will not be consistent, so that even with an infinite quantity of data, the coefficient estimates would be biased.

5.5.12   Autocorrelation and dynamic models in EViews

In EViews, the lagged values of variables can be used as regressors or for other purposes by using the notation $x(-1)$ for a one-period lag, $x(-5)$ for a five-period lag, and so on, where x is the variable name. EViews will automatically adjust the sample period used for estimation to take into account the observations that are lost in constructing the lags. For example, if the regression contains five lags of the dependent variable, five observations will be lost and estimation will commence with observation six.

In EViews, the DW statistic is calculated automatically, and was given in the general estimation output screens that result from estimating any regression model. To view the results screen again, click on the **View** button in the regression window and select **Estimation output**. For the Microsoft macroeconomic regression that included all of the explanatory variables, the value of the DW statistic was 2.165. What is the appropriate conclusion regarding the presence or otherwise of first order autocorrelation in this case?

The Breusch–Godfrey test can be conducted by selecting **View/Residual Diagnostics/Serial Correlation LM Test . . .** In the new window, type again the number of lagged residuals you want to include in the test and click on **OK**. Assuming that you selected to employ ten lags in the test, the results would be as given in the following table.

Breusch-Godfrey Serial Correlation LM Test:			
F-statistic	2.296984	Prob. F(10,306)	0.0130
Obs*R-squared	22.62283	Prob. Chi-Square(10)	0.0122

Test Equation:
Dependent Variable: RESID
Method: Least Squares
Date: 07/04/13 Time: 14:11
Sample: 1986M05 2013M04
Included observations: 324
Presample missing value lagged residuals set to zero.

	Coefficient	Std. Error	t-Statistic	Prob.
C	0.055522	0.887748	0.062542	0.9502
ERSANDP	−0.00123	0.155137	−0.00792	0.9937
DPROD	0.217579	1.308076	0.166335	0.8680
DCREDIT	−1.19E-05	7.55E-05	−0.15797	0.8746
DINFLATION	−0.52145	2.170113	−2.40E-01	8.10E-01
DMONEY	−0.00521	0.034704	−0.15008	0.8808
DSPREAD	0.108645	6.816919	0.015938	0.9873
RTERM	0.377417	2.502172	0.150836	0.8802
RESID(-1)	−0.13700	0.057579	−2.37928	0.0180
RESID(-2)	−0.05756	0.057540	−1.00042	0.3179
RESID(-3)	−0.03018	0.057403	−0.52574	0.5994
RESID(-4)	−0.13534	0.057235	−2.36454	0.0187
RESID(-5)	−0.13527	0.056885	−2.37803	0.0180
RESID(-6)	−0.11296	0.057015	−1.98118	0.0485
RESID(-7)	−0.07431	0.057277	−1.29740	0.1955
RESID(-8)	−0.10770	0.057247	−1.88125	0.0609
RESID(-9)	−0.15779	0.057370	−2.75032	0.0063
RESID(-10)	−0.05742	0.057536	−0.99800	0.3191

R-squared	0.069824	Mean dependent var	−4.93E-16
Adjusted R-squared	0.018147	S.D. dependent var	12.52090
S.E. of regression	12.40677	Akaike info criterion	7.928310
Sum squared resid	47101.95	Schwarz criterion	8.138356
Log likelihood	−1266.387	Hannan-Quinn criter.	8.012151
F-statistic	1.351167	Durbin-Watson stat	2.008661
Prob(F-statistic)	0.159775		

In the first table of output, EViews offers two versions of the test – an F-version and a χ^2 version, while the second table presents the estimates from the auxiliary regression. The conclusion from both versions of the test in this case is that the null hypothesis of no autocorrelation should be rejected since the p-values are below 0.05. Does this agree with the DW test result? We might thus wish to consider taking remedial action along the lines described above so think about the possibilities.

5.5.13　Autocorrelation in cross-sectional data

The possibility that autocorrelation may occur in the context of a time-series regression is quite intuitive. However, it is also plausible that autocorrelation could be present in certain types of cross-sectional data. For example, if the cross-sectional data comprise the profitability of banks in different regions of the US, autocorrelation may arise in a spatial sense, if there is a regional dimension to bank profitability that is not captured by the model. Thus the residuals from banks of the same region or in neighbouring regions may be correlated. Testing for autocorrelation in this case would be rather more complex than in the time series context, and would involve the construction of a square, symmetric 'spatial contiguity matrix' or a 'distance matrix'. Both of these matrices would be $N \times N$, where N is the sample size. The former would be a matrix of zeros and ones, with one for element i, j when observation i occurred for a bank in the same region to, or sufficiently close to, region j and zero otherwise $(i, j = 1, \ldots, N)$. The distance matrix would comprise elements that measured the distance (or the inverse of the distance) between bank i and bank j. A potential solution to a finding of autocorrelated residuals in such a model would be again to use a model containing a lag structure, in this case known as a 'spatial lag'. Further details are contained in Anselin (1988).

5.6　Assumption 4: the x_t are non-stochastic

Fortunately, it turns out that the OLS estimator is consistent and unbiased in the presence of stochastic regressors, provided that the regressors are not correlated with the error term of the estimated equation. To see this, recall that

$$\hat{\beta} = (X'X)^{-1}X'y \quad \text{and} \quad y = X\beta + u \tag{5.42}$$

Thus

$$\hat{\beta} = (X'X)^{-1}X'(X\beta + u) \tag{5.43}$$

$$\hat{\beta} = (X'X)^{-1}X'X\beta + (X'X)^{-1}X'u \tag{5.44}$$

$$\hat{\beta} = \beta + (X'X)^{-1}X'u \tag{5.45}$$

Taking expectations, and provided that X and u are independent,[1]

$$E(\hat{\beta}) = E(\beta) + E((X'X)^{-1}X'u) \tag{5.46}$$

$$E(\hat{\beta}) = \beta + E[(X'X)^{-1}X']E(u) \tag{5.47}$$

Since $E(u) = 0$, this expression will be zero and therefore the estimator is still unbiased, even if the regressors are stochastic.

However, if one or more of the explanatory variables is contemporaneously correlated with the disturbance term, the OLS estimator will not even be consistent. This results from the estimator assigning explanatory power to the variables where in reality it is arising from the correlation between the error term and y_t. Suppose for illustration that x_{2t} and u_t are positively correlated. When the disturbance term happens to take a high value, y_t will also be high (because $y_t = \beta_1 + \beta_2 x_{2t} + \cdots + u_t$). But if x_{2t} is positively correlated with u_t, then x_{2t} is also likely to be high. Thus the OLS estimator will incorrectly attribute the high value of y_t to a high value of x_{2t}, where in reality y_t is high simply because u_t is high, which will result in biased and inconsistent parameter estimates and a fitted line that appears to capture the features of the data much better than it does in reality.

5.7 Assumption 5: the disturbances are normally distributed

Recall that the normality assumption ($u_t \sim N(0, \sigma^2)$) is required in order to conduct single or joint hypothesis tests about the model parameters.

5.7.1 Testing for departures from normality

One of the most commonly applied tests for normality is the Bera–Jarque (hereafter BJ) test. BJ uses the property of a normally distributed random variable that the entire distribution is characterised by the first two moments – the mean and the variance. Recall from chapter 2 that standardised third and fourth moments of a distribution are known as its *skewness* and *kurtosis*. A normal distribution is not skewed and is defined to have a coefficient of kurtosis of 3. It is possible to define a coefficient of excess kurtosis, equal to the coefficient of kurtosis minus 3; a normal distribution will thus have a coefficient of excess kurtosis of zero. Bera and Jarque (1981) formalise these ideas by testing whether the coefficient of skewness and the coefficient of excess kurtosis are jointly zero. Denoting the errors by u and their variance by σ^2, it can be proved that the coefficients of skewness and kurtosis can be expressed respectively as

$$b_1 = \frac{E[u^3]}{(\sigma^2)^{3/2}} \quad \text{and} \quad b_2 = \frac{E[u^4]}{(\sigma^2)^2} \tag{5.48}$$

The kurtosis of the normal distribution is 3 so its excess kurtosis ($b_2 - 3$) is zero.

---

[1] A situation where X and u are not independent is discussed at length in chapter 7.

The Bera–Jarque test statistic is given by

$$W = T \left[\frac{b_1^2}{6} + \frac{(b_2 - 3)^2}{24} \right] \tag{5.49}$$

where T is the sample size. The test statistic asymptotically follows a $\chi^2(2)$ under the null hypothesis that the distribution of the series is symmetric and mesokurtic.

b_1 and b_2 can be estimated using the residuals from the OLS regression, $\hat{u}$. The null hypothesis is of normality, and this would be rejected if the residuals from the model were either significantly skewed or leptokurtic/platykurtic (or both).

5.7.2 Testing for non-normality using EViews

The Bera–Jarque normality tests results can be viewed by selecting **View/Residual Diagnostics/Histogram – Normality Test**. The statistic has a χ^2 distribution with two degrees of freedom under the null hypothesis of normally distributed errors. If the residuals are normally distributed, the histogram should be bell-shaped and the Bera–Jarque statistic would not be significant. This means that the p-value given at the bottom of the normality test screen should be bigger than 0.05 to not reject the null of normality at the 5% level. In the example of the Microsoft regression, the screen would appear as in screenshot 5.2.

In this case, the residuals are very negatively skewed and are leptokurtic. Hence the null hypothesis for residual normality is rejected very strongly (the p-value for the BJ test is zero to six decimal places), implying that the inferences we make about the coefficient estimates could be wrong, although the sample is probably large enough that we need be less concerned than we would be with a small sample. The non-normality in this case appears to have been caused by a small number of very large negative residuals representing monthly stock price falls of more than 25%.

5.7.3 What should be done if evidence of non-normality is found?

It is not obvious what should be done! It is, of course, possible to employ an estimation method that does not assume normality, but such a method may be difficult to implement, and one can be less sure of its properties. It is thus desirable to stick with OLS if possible, since its behaviour in a variety of circumstances has been well researched. For sample sizes that are sufficiently large, violation of the normality assumption is virtually inconsequential. Appealing to a central limit theorem, the test statistics will asymptotically follow the appropriate distributions even in the absence of error normality.[2]

---

[2] The law of large numbers states that the average of a sample (which is a random variable) will converge to the population mean (which is fixed), and the central limit theorem states that the sample mean converges to a normal distribution.

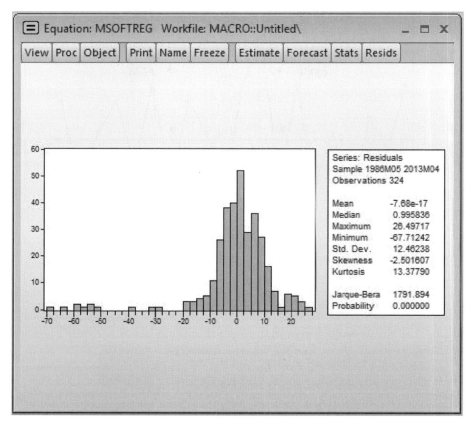

Screenshot 5.2   **Non-normality test results**

In economic or financial modelling, it is quite often the case that one or two very extreme residuals cause a rejection of the normality assumption. Such observations would appear in the tails of the distribution, and would therefore lead u^4, which enters into the definition of kurtosis, to be very large. Such observations that do not fit in with the pattern of the remainder of the data are known as *outliers*. If this is the case, one way to improve the chances of error normality is to use dummy variables or some other method to effectively remove those observations.

In the time series context, suppose that a monthly model of asset returns from 1980–90 had been estimated, and the residuals plotted, and that a particularly large outlier has been observed for October 1987, shown in figure 5.10.

A new variable called $D87M10_t$ could be defined as $D87M10_t = 1$ during October 1987 and zero otherwise. The observations for the dummy variable would appear as in box 5.6. The dummy variable would then be used just like any other variable in the regression model, e.g.

$$y_t = \beta_1 + \beta_2 x_{2t} + \beta_3 x_{3t} + \beta_4 D87M10_t + u_t \tag{5.50}$$

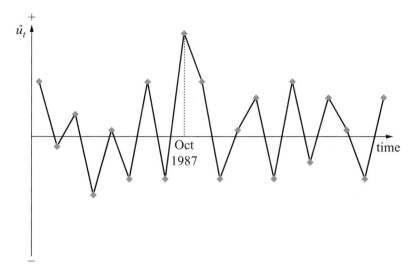

Figure 5.10   Regression residuals from stock return data, showing large outlier for October 1987

Box 5.6   Observations for the dummy variable

Time	Value of dummy variable $D87M10_t$
1986$M$12	0
1987M01	0
⋮	⋮
1987M09	0
1987$M$10	1
1987$M$11	0
⋮	⋮

This type of dummy variable that takes the value one for only a single observation has an effect exactly equivalent to knocking out that observation from the sample altogether, by forcing the residual for that observation to zero. The estimated coefficient on the dummy variable will be equal to the residual that the dummied observation would have taken if the dummy variable had not been included.

However, many econometricians would argue that dummy variables to remove outlying residuals can be used to artificially improve the characteristics of the

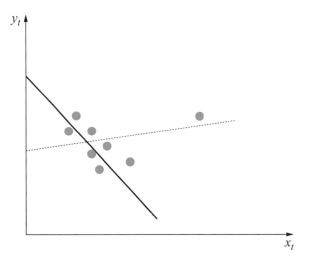

Figure 5.11   Possible effect of an outlier on OLS estimation

model – in essence fudging the results. Removing outlying observations will reduce standard errors, reduce the RSS, and therefore increase R^2, thus improving the apparent fit of the model to the data. The removal of observations is also hard to reconcile with the notion in statistics that each data point represents a useful piece of information.

The other side of this argument is that observations that are 'a long way away' from the rest, and seem not to fit in with the general pattern of the rest of the data are known as *outliers*. Outliers can have a serious effect on coefficient estimates, since by definition, OLS will receive a big penalty, in the form of an increased RSS, for points that are a long way from the fitted line. Consequently, OLS will try extra hard to minimise the distances of points that would have otherwise been a long way from the line. A graphical depiction of the possible effect of an outlier on OLS estimation, is given in figure 5.11.

In figure 5.11, one point is a long way away from the rest. If this point is included in the estimation sample, the fitted line will be the dotted one, which has a slight positive slope. If this observation were removed, the full line would be the one fitted. Clearly, the slope is now large and negative. OLS would not select this line if the outlier is included since the observation is a long way from the others and hence when the residual (the distance from the point to the fitted line) is squared, it would lead to a big increase in the RSS. Note that outliers could be detected by plotting y against x only in the context of a bivariate regression. In the case where there are more explanatory variables, outliers are easiest identified by plotting the residuals over time, as in figure 5.10, etc.

So, it can be seen that a trade-off potentially exists between the need to remove outlying observations that could have an undue impact on the OLS estimates and cause residual non-normality on the one hand, and the notion that each data point represents a useful piece of information on the other. The latter is coupled with the fact that removing observations at will could artificially improve the fit of the model. A sensible way to proceed is by introducing dummy variables to the model only if there is both a statistical need to do so and a theoretical justification for their inclusion. This justification would normally come from the researcher's knowledge of the historical events that relate to the dependent variable and the model over the relevant sample period. Dummy variables may be justifiably used to remove observations corresponding to 'one-off' or extreme events that are considered highly unlikely to be repeated, and the information content of which is deemed of no relevance for the data as a whole. Examples may include stock market crashes, financial panics, government crises, and so on.

Non-normality in financial data could also arise from certain types of heteroscedasticity, known as ARCH – see chapter 9. In this case, the non-normality is intrinsic to all of the data and therefore outlier removal would not make the residuals of such a model normal.

Another important use of dummy variables is in the modelling of seasonality in financial data, and accounting for so-called 'calendar anomalies', such as day-of-the-week effects and weekend effects. These are discussed in chapter 10.

5.7.4   Dummy variable construction and use in EViews

As we saw from the plot of the distribution above, the non-normality in the residuals from the Microsoft regression appears to have been caused by a small number of outliers in the sample. Such events can be identified if they are present by plotting the actual values, the fitted values and the residuals of the regression. This can be achieved in EViews by selecting **View/Actual, Fitted, Residual/Actual, Fitted, Residual Graph**. The plot should look as in screenshot 5.3.

From the graph, it can be seen that there are several large (negative) outliers, but the largest of all occur in early 1998 and early 2003. All of the large outliers correspond to months where the actual return was much smaller (i.e. more negative) than the model would have predicted. Interestingly, the residual in October 1987 is not quite so prominent because even though the stock price fell, the market index value fell as well, so that the stock price fall was at least in part predicted (this can be seen by comparing the actual and fitted values during that month).

In order to identify the exact dates that the biggest outliers were realised, we could use the shading option by right clicking on the graph and selecting the 'add lines & shading' option. But it is probably easier to just examine a table of values for the residuals, which can be achieved by selecting **View/Actual, Fitted, Residual/Actual, Fitted, Residual Table**. If we do this, it is evident that the two most extreme residuals (with values to the nearest integer) were in February 1998 (−64.3) and February 2003 (−67.7).

As stated above, one way to remove big outliers in the data is by using dummy variables. It would be tempting, but incorrect, to construct one dummy variable that takes the value 1 for both Feb 1998 and Feb 2003, but this would not have the desired effect of setting both residuals to zero. Instead, to remove two outliers

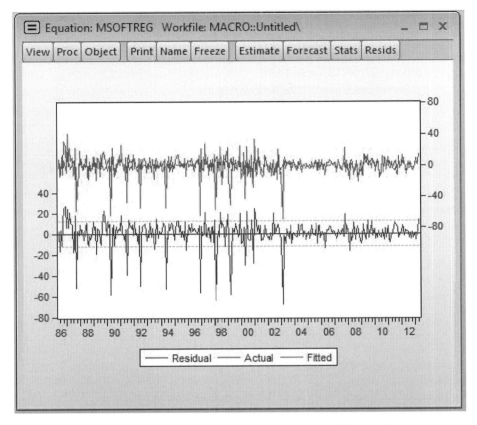

Screenshot 5.3   Regression residuals, actual values and fitted series

requires us to construct two separate dummy variables. In order to create the Feb 1998 dummy first, we generate a series called 'FEB98DUM' that will initially contain only zeros. **Generate this series** (hint: you can use 'Quick/Generate Series' and then type in the box 'FEB98DUM = 0'. **Double click on the new object** to open the spreadsheet and **turn on the editing mode** by clicking 'Edit +/−' and input a single **1** in the cell that corresponds to February 1998. Leave all other cell entries as zeros).

Once this dummy variable has been created, repeat the process above to **create another dummy variable** called 'FEB03DUM' that takes the value 1 in February 2003 and zero elsewhere and then **rerun the regression** including all the previous variables plus these two dummy variables. This can most easily be achieved by clicking on the **'Msoftreg' results object**, then the **Estimate** button and **adding the dummy variables** to the end of the variable list. The full list of variables is

ermsoft c ersandp dprod dcredit dinflation dmoney dspread rterm feb98dum feb03dum

and the results of this regression are as in the following table.

	Coefficient	Std. Error	t-Statistic	Prob.
C	0.294125	0.826235	0.355982	0.7221
ERSANDP	1.401288	0.143171	9.787491	0.0000
DPROD	−1.33384	1.206715	−1.10535	0.2699
DCREDIT	−3.95E-05	6.96E-05	−0.56709	0.5711
DINFLATION	3.517510	1.975394	1.78E+00	7.59E-02
DMONEY	−0.02196	0.032097	−0.68416	0.4944
DSPREAD	5.351376	6.302128	0.849138	0.3965
RTERM	4.650169	2.291471	2.029337	0.0433
FEB98DUM	−66.4813	11.60474	−5.72881	0.0000
FEB03DUM	−67.6132	11.58117	−5.83821	0.0000

Dependent Variable: ERMSOFT
Method: Least Squares
Date: 07/04/13 Time: 14:45
Sample (adjusted): 1986M05 2013M04
Included observations: 324 after adjustments

R-squared	0.346058	Mean dependent var	−0.311466
Adjusted R-squared	0.327315	S.D. dependent var	14.05871
S.E. of regression	11.53059	Akaike info criterion	7.758261
Sum squared resid	41747.69	Schwarz criterion	7.874951
Log likelihood	−1246.838	Hannan-Quinn criter.	7.804837
F-statistic	18.46280	Durbin-Watson stat	2.156576
Prob(F-statistic)	0.000000		

Note that the dummy variable parameters are both highly significant and take approximately the values that the corresponding residuals would have taken if the dummy variables had not been included in the model.[3] By comparing the results with those of the regression above that excluded the dummy variables, it can be seen that the coefficient estimates on the remaining variables change quite a bit in this instance and the significances improve considerably. The term structure parameter is now significant at the 5% level and the unexpected inflation parameter is now significant at the 10% level. The R^2 value has risen from 0.21 to 0.35 because of the perfect fit of the dummy variables to those two extreme outlying observations.

Finally, if we re-examine the normality test results by clicking **View/Residual Tests/Histogram − Normality Test**, we will see that while the skewness and

---

[3] Note the inexact correspondence between the values of the residuals and the values of the dummy variable parameters because two dummies are being used together; had we included only one dummy, the value of the dummy variable coefficient and that which the residual would have taken would be identical.

kurtosis are both slightly closer to the values that they would take under normality, the Bera–Jarque test statistic still takes a value of 1601 (compared with 1845 previously). We would thus conclude that the residuals are still a long way from following a normal distribution, and the distribution plot shows that there are still several more very large negative residuals. While it would be possible to continue to generate dummy variables, there is a limit to the extent to which it would be desirable to do so. With this particular regression, we are unlikely to be able to achieve a residual distribution that is close to normality without using an excessive number of dummy variables. As a rule of thumb, in a monthly sample with 324 observations, it is reasonable to include, perhaps, two or three dummy variables for outliers, but more would probably be excessive.

5.8   Multicollinearity

An implicit assumption that is made when using the OLS estimation method is that the explanatory variables are not correlated with one another. If there is no relationship between the explanatory variables, they would be said to be *orthogonal* to one another. If the explanatory variables were orthogonal to one another, adding or removing a variable from a regression equation would not cause the values of the coefficients on the other variables to change.

In any practical context, the correlation between explanatory variables will be non-zero, although this will generally be relatively benign in the sense that a small degree of association between explanatory variables will almost always occur but will not cause too much loss of precision. However, a problem occurs when the explanatory variables are very highly correlated with each other, and this problem is known as *multicollinearity*. It is possible to distinguish between two classes of multicollinearity: perfect multicollinearity and near multicollinearity.

Perfect multicollinearity occurs when there is an exact relationship between two or more variables. In this case, it is not possible to estimate all of the coefficients in the model. Perfect multicollinearity will usually be observed only when the same explanatory variable is inadvertently used twice in a regression. For illustration, suppose that two variables were employed in a regression function such that the value of one variable was always twice that of the other (e.g. suppose $x_3 = 2x_2$). If both x_3 and x_2 were used as explanatory variables in the same regression, then the model parameters cannot be estimated. Since the two variables are perfectly related to one another, together they contain only enough information to estimate one parameter, not two. Technically, the difficulty would occur in trying to invert the $(X'X)$ matrix since it would not be of full rank (two of the columns would be linearly dependent on one another), so that the inverse of $(X'X)$ would not exist and hence the OLS estimates $\hat{\beta} = (X'X)^{-1}X'y$ could not be calculated.

Near multicollinearity is much more likely to occur in practice, and would arise when there was a non-negligible, but not perfect, relationship between two or more of the explanatory variables. Note that a high correlation between the dependent variable and one of the independent variables is not multicollinearity.

Visually, we could think of the difference between near and perfect multi-collinearity as follows. Suppose that the variables x_{2t} and x_{3t} were highly correlated. If we produced a scatter plot of x_{2t} against x_{3t}, then perfect multicollinearity would correspond to all of the points lying exactly on a straight line, while near multi-collinearity would correspond to the points lying close to the line, and the closer they were to the line (taken altogether), the stronger would be the relationship between the two variables.

5.8.1 Measuring near multicollinearity

Testing for multicollinearity is surprisingly difficult, and hence all that is presented here is a simple method to investigate the presence or otherwise of the most easily detected forms of near multicollinearity. This method simply involves looking at the matrix of correlations between the individual variables. Suppose that a regression equation has three explanatory variables (plus a constant term), and that the pair-wise correlations between these explanatory variables are:

corr	x_2	x_3	x_4
x_2	–	0.2	0.8
x_3	0.2	–	0.3
x_4	0.8	0.3	–

Clearly, if multicollinearity was suspected, the most likely culprit would be a high correlation between x_2 and x_4. Of course, if the relationship involves three or more variables that are collinear – e.g. $x_2 + x_3 \approx x_4$ – then multicollinearity would be very difficult to detect.

5.8.2 Problems if near multicollinearity is present but ignored

First, R^2 will be high but the individual coefficients will have high standard errors, so that the regression 'looks good' as a whole, but the individual variables are not significant.[4] This arises in the context of very closely related explanatory variables as a consequence of the difficulty in observing the individual contribution of each variable to the overall fit of the regression. Second, the regression becomes very sensitive to small changes in the specification, so that adding or removing an explanatory variable leads to large changes in the coefficient values or significances of the other variables. Finally, near multicollinearity will thus make confidence intervals for the parameters very wide, and significance tests might therefore give inappropriate conclusions, and so make it difficult to draw sharp inferences.

5.8.3 Solutions to the problem of multicollinearity

A number of alternative estimation techniques have been proposed that are valid in the presence of multicollinearity – for example, ridge regression, or principal components. Principal components analysis was discussed briefly in an appendix

---

[4] Note that multicollinearity does not affect the value of R^2 in a regression.

to the previous chapter. Many researchers do not use these techniques, however, as they can be complex, their properties are less well understood than those of the OLS estimator and, above all, many econometricians would argue that multicollinearity is more a problem with the data than with the model or estimation method.

Other, more ad hoc methods for dealing with the possible existence of near multicollinearity include:

- **Ignore it,** if the model is otherwise adequate, i.e. statistically and in terms of each coefficient being of a plausible magnitude and having an appropriate sign. Sometimes, the existence of multicolinearity does not reduce the t-ratios on variables that would have been significant without the multicollinearity sufficiently to make them insignificant. It is worth stating that the presence of near multicollinearity does not affect the BLUE properties of the OLS estimator – i.e. it will still be consistent, unbiased and efficient since the presence of near multicollinearity does not violate any of the CLRM assumptions 1–4. However, in the presence of near multicolinearity, it will be hard to obtain small standard errors. This will not matter if the aim of the model-building exercise is to produce forecasts from the estimated model, since the forecasts will be unaffected by the presence of near multicollinearity so long as this relationship between the explanatory variables continues to hold over the forecasted sample.

- **Drop one of the collinear variables,** so that the problem disappears. However, this may be unacceptable to the researcher if there were strong *a priori* theoretical reasons for including both variables in the model. Also, if the removed variable was relevant in the data generating process for y, an omitted variable bias would result (see section 5.10).

- **Transform the highly correlated variables into a ratio** and include only the ratio and not the individual variables in the regression. Again, this may be unacceptable if financial theory suggests that changes in the dependent variable should occur following changes in the individual explanatory variables, and not a ratio of them.

- Finally, as stated above, it is also often said that near multicollinearity is *more a problem with the data than with the model*, so that there is insufficient information in the sample to obtain estimates for all of the coefficients. This is why near multicollinearity leads coefficient estimates to have wide standard errors, which is exactly what would happen if the sample size were small. An increase in the sample size will usually lead to an increase in the accuracy of coefficient estimation and consequently a reduction in the coefficient standard errors, thus enabling the model to better dissect the effects of the various explanatory variables on the explained variable. A further possibility, therefore, is for the researcher to **go out and collect more data** – for example, by taking a longer run of data, or switching to a higher frequency of sampling. Of course, it may be infeasible to increase the sample size if all available data is being utilised already. A further method of increasing the available quantity of data as a potential remedy for near multicollinearity would be to **use a pooled sample**. This would involve the use of data with both cross-sectional and time series dimensions (see chapter 11).

5.8.4   Multicollinearity in EViews

For the Microsoft stock return example given above previously, a correlation matrix for the macroeconomic independent variables can be constructed in EViews by clicking **Quick/Group Statistics/Correlations** and then entering the list of regressors (not including the regressand or the S&P returns) in the dialog box that appears:

dprod dcredit dinflation dmoney dspread rterm

A new window will be displayed that contains the correlation matrix of the series in a spreadsheet format:

	DPROD	DCREDIT	DINFLATION	DMONEY	DSPREAD	RTERM
DPROD	1.000000	0.141066	−0.124269	−0.130060	−0.055573	−0.002375
DCREDIT	0.141066	1.000000	0.045164	−0.011724	0.015264	0.009675
DINFLATION	−0.124269	0.045164	1.000000	−0.097972	−0.224838	−0.054192
DMONEY	−0.130060	−0.011724	−0.097972	1.000000	0.213576	−0.086218
DSPREAD	−0.055573	0.015264	−0.224838	0.213576	1.000000	0.001571
RTERM	−0.002375	0.009675	−0.054192	−0.086218	0.001571	1.000000

Do the results indicate any significant correlations between the independent variables? In this particular case, the largest observed correlations (in absolute value) are is 0.21 between the money supply and term structure variables, and −0.22 between the term structure and unexpected inflation. This is probably sufficiently small that it can reasonably be ignored.

5.9   Adopting the wrong functional form

A further implicit assumption of the classical linear regression model is that the appropriate 'functional form' is linear. This means that the appropriate model is assumed to be linear in the parameters, and that in the bivariate case, the relationship between y and x can be represented by a straight line. However, this assumption may not always be upheld. Whether the model should be linear can be formally tested using Ramsey's (1969) RESET test, which is a general test for misspecification of functional form. Essentially, the method works by using higher order terms of the fitted values (e.g. $\hat{y}_t^2$, $\hat{y}_t^3$, etc.) in an auxiliary regression. The auxiliary regression is thus one where y_t, the dependent variable from the original regression, is regressed on powers of the fitted values together with the original explanatory variables

$$y_t = \alpha_1 + \alpha_2 \hat{y}_t^2 + \alpha_3 \hat{y}_t^3 + \cdots + \alpha_p \hat{y}_t^p + \sum \beta_i x_{it} + v_t \tag{5.51}$$

Higher order powers of the fitted values of y can capture a variety of non-linear relationships, since they embody higher order powers and cross-products of the original explanatory variables, e.g.

$$\hat{y}_t^2 = (\hat{\beta}_1 + \hat{\beta}_2 x_{2t} + \hat{\beta}_3 x_{3t} + \cdots + \hat{\beta}_k x_{kt})^2 \tag{5.52}$$

The value of R^2 is obtained from the regression (5.51), and the test statistic, given by TR^2, is distributed asymptotically as a $\chi^2(p-1)$. Note that the degrees of freedom for this test will be $(p-1)$ and not p. This arises because p is the highest order term in the fitted values used in the auxiliary regression and thus the test will involve $p-1$ terms, one for the square of the fitted value, one for the cube, . . . , one for the pth power. If the value of the test statistic is greater than the χ^2 critical value, reject the null hypothesis that the functional form was correct.

5.9.1 What if the functional form is found to be inappropriate?

One possibility would be to switch to a non-linear model, but the RESET test presents the user with no guide as to what a better specification might be! Also, non-linear models in the parameters typically preclude the use of OLS, and require the use of a non-linear estimation technique. Some non-linear models can still be estimated using OLS, provided that they are linear in the parameters. For example, if the true model is of the form

$$y_t = \beta_1 + \beta_2 x_{2t} + \beta_3 x_{2t}^2 + \beta_4 x_{2t}^3 + u_t \tag{5.53}$$

– that is, a third order polynomial in x – and the researcher assumes that the relationship between y_t and x_t is linear (i.e. x_{2t}^2 and x_{2t}^3 are missing from the specification), this is simply a special case of omitted variables, with the usual problems (see section 5.10) and obvious remedy.

However, the model may be multiplicatively non-linear. A second possibility that is sensible in this case would be to transform the data into logarithms. This will linearise many previously multiplicative models into additive ones. For example, consider again the exponential growth model

$$y_t = \beta_1 x_t^{\beta_2} u_t \tag{5.54}$$

Taking logs, this becomes

$$\ln(y_t) = \ln(\beta_1) + \beta_2 \ln(x_t) + \ln(u_t) \tag{5.55}$$

or

$$Y_t = \alpha + \beta_2 X_t + v_t \tag{5.56}$$

where $Y_t = \ln(y_t)$, $\alpha = \ln(\beta_1)$, $X_t = \ln(x_t)$, $v_t = \ln(u_t)$. Thus a simple logarithmic transformation makes this model a standard linear bivariate regression equation that can be estimated using OLS.

Loosely following the treatment given in Stock and Watson (2011), the following list shows four different functional forms for models that are either linear or can be made linear following a logarithmic transformation to one or more of the dependent or independent variables, examining only a bivariate specification for simplicity. Care is needed when interpreting the coefficient values in each case.

(1) Linear model: $y_t = \beta_1 + \beta_2 x_{2t} + u_t$; a 1-unit increase in x_{2t} causes a β_2-unit increase in y_t.

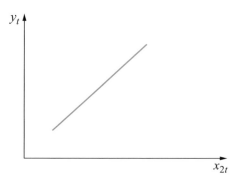

(2) Log-linear: $ln(y_t) = \beta_1 + \beta_2 x_{2t} + u_t$; a 1-unit increase in x_{2t} causes a $100 \times \beta_2\%$ increase in y_t.

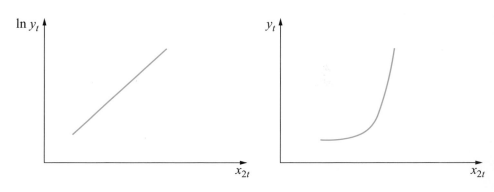

(3) Linear-log: $y_t = \beta_1 + \beta_2 ln(x_{2t}) + u_t$; a 1% increase in x_{2t} causes a $0.01 \times \beta_2$-unit increase in y_t.

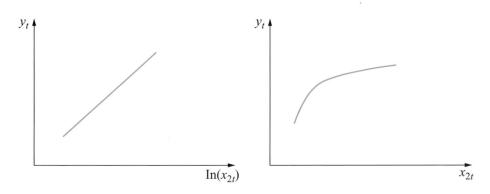

(4) Double log: $ln(y_t) = \beta_1 + \beta_2 ln(x_{2t}) + u_t$; a 1% increase in x_{2t} causes a $\beta_2\%$ increase in y_t. Note that to plot y against x_2 would be more complex since the shape would depend on the size of β_2.

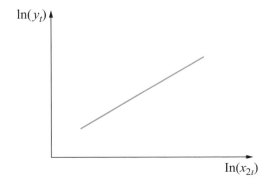

Note also that we cannot use R^2 or adjusted R^2 to determine which of these four types of model is most appropriate since the dependent variables are different across some of the models.

5.9.2   RESET tests using EViews

Using EViews, the Ramsey RESET test is found in the **View** menu of the regression window (for 'Msoftreg') under **Stability diagnostics/Ramsey RESET test. ...**. EViews will prompt you for the 'number of fitted terms', equivalent to the number of powers of the fitted value to be used in the regression; leave the default of **1** to consider only the square of the fitted values. The Ramsey RESET test for this regression is in effect testing whether the relationship between the Microsoft stock excess returns and the explanatory variables is linear or not. The results of this test for one fitted term are shown in the following table.

Ramsey RESET Test:

Equation: MSOFTREG
Specification: ERMSOFT C ERSANDP DPROD DCREDIT DINFLATION
   DMONEY DSPREAD RTERM FEB98DUM FEB03DUM
Omitted Variables: Squares of fitted values

	Value	df	Probability
t-statistic	1.672232	313	0.0955
F-statistic	2.796359	(1,313)	0.0955
Likelihood ratio	2.881779	1	0.0860

F-test summary:

	Sum of Sq.	df	Mean Squares
Test SSR	369.6734	1	369.6734
Restricted SSR	41747.69	314	132.9544
Unrestricted SSR	41378.02	313	132.1981

LR-test summary:

	Value	df
Restricted LogL	−1246.838	314
Unrestricted LogL	−1245.397	313

Test Equation:
Dependent Variable: ERMSOFT
Method: Least Squares
Date: 07/04/13 Time: 15:24
Sample: 1986M05 2013M04
Included observations: 324

	Coefficient	Std. Error	t-Statistic	Prob.
C	−0.283755	0.893422	−0.317605	0.7510
ERSANDP	1.500030	0.154493	9.709365	0.0000
DPROD	−1.447299	1.205189	−1.200890	0.2307
DCREDIT	−0.000031	0.000070	−0.442150	0.6587
DINFLATION	3.586413	1.970198	1.820331	0.0697
DMONEY	−0.022506	0.032008	−0.703158	0.4825
DSPREAD	4.487382	6.305382	0.711675	0.4772
RTERM	4.517819	2.286315	1.976026	0.0490
FEB98DUM	−104.6090	25.56902	−4.091250	0.0001
FEB03DUM	−123.6420	35.43968	−3.488800	0.0006
FITTED^2	0.011717	0.007007	1.672232	0.0955

R-squared	0.351849	Mean dependent var	−0.311466
Adjusted R-squared	0.331141	S.D. dependent var	14.05871
S.E. of regression	11.49774	Akaike info criterion	7.755540
Sum squared resid	41378.02	Schwarz criterion	7.883898
Log likelihood	−1245.397	Hannan-Quinn criter.	7.806774
F-statistic	16.99122	Durbin-Watson stat	2.109156
Prob(F-statistic)	0.000000		

t, $F-$ and χ^2 versions of the test are presented in the first three rows respectively, and it can be seen that there is limited evidence for non–linearity in the regression equation (the p-values indicate that the test statistics are significant at the 10% level but not at 5%). So it would be concluded that there is some support for the notion that the linear model for the Microsoft returns is appropriate.

5.10 Omission of an important variable

What would be the effects of excluding from the estimated regression a variable that is a determinant of the dependent variable? For example, suppose that the true, but unknown, data generating process is represented by

$$y_t = \beta_1 + \beta_2 x_{2t} + \beta_3 x_{3t} + \beta_4 x_{4t} + \beta_5 x_{5t} + u_t \tag{5.57}$$

but the researcher estimated a model of the form

$$y_t = \beta_1 + \beta_2 x_{2t} + \beta_3 x_{3t} + \beta_4 x_{4t} + u_t \tag{5.58}$$

so that the variable x_{5t} is omitted from the model. The consequence would be that the estimated coefficients on all the other variables will be biased and inconsistent unless the excluded variable is uncorrelated with all the included variables. Even if this condition is satisfied, the estimate of the coefficient on the constant term will be biased, which would imply that any forecasts made from the model would be biased. The standard errors will also be biased (upwards), and hence hypothesis tests could yield inappropriate inferences. Further intuition is offered in Dougherty (1992, pp. 168–73).

5.11 Inclusion of an irrelevant variable

Suppose now that the researcher makes the opposite error to section 5.10, i.e. that the true data generating process (DGP) was represented by

$$y_t = \beta_1 + \beta_2 x_{2t} + \beta_3 x_{3t} + \beta_4 x_{4t} + u_t \tag{5.59}$$

but the researcher estimates a model of the form

$$y_t = \beta_1 + \beta_2 x_{2t} + \beta_3 x_{3t} + \beta_4 x_{4t} + \beta_5 x_{5t} + u_t \tag{5.60}$$

thus incorporating the superfluous or irrelevant variable x_{5t}. As x_{5t} is irrelevant, the expected value of β_5 is zero, although in any practical application, its estimated value is very unlikely to be exactly zero. The consequence of including an irrelevant variable would be that the coefficient estimators would still be consistent and unbiased, but the estimators would be inefficient. This would imply that the standard errors for the coefficients are likely to be inflated relative to the values which they would have taken if the irrelevant variable had not been included. Variables which would otherwise have been marginally significant may no longer be so in the presence of irrelevant variables. In general, it can also be stated that the extent of the loss of efficiency will depend positively on the absolute value of the correlation between the included irrelevant variable and the other explanatory variables.

Summarising the last two sections it is evident that when trying to determine whether to err on the side of including too many or too few variables in a regression model, there is an implicit trade-off between inconsistency and efficiency; many researchers would argue that while in an ideal world, the model will incorporate precisely the correct variables – no more and no less – the former problem is more serious than the latter and therefore in the real world, one should err on the side of incorporating marginally significant variables.

5.12 Parameter stability tests

So far, regressions of a form such as

$$y_t = \beta_1 + \beta_2 x_{2t} + \beta_3 x_{3t} + u_t \tag{5.61}$$

have been estimated. These regressions embody the implicit assumption that the parameters (β_1, β_2 and β_3) are constant for the entire sample, both for the data period used to estimate the model, and for any subsequent period used in the construction of forecasts.

This implicit assumption can be tested using parameter stability tests. The idea is essentially to split the data into sub-periods and then to estimate up to three models, for each of the sub-parts and for all the data and then to 'compare' the RSS of each of the models. There are two types of test that will be considered, namely the Chow (analysis of variance) test and predictive failure tests.

Box 5.7   Conducting a Chow test

(1) *Split the data into two sub-periods.* Estimate the regression over the whole period and then for the two sub-periods separately (three regressions). Obtain the RSS for each regression.

(2) *The restricted regression is now the regression for the whole period* while the 'unrestricted regression' comes in two parts: one for each of the sub-samples. It is thus possible to form an F-test, which is based on the difference between the RSSs. The statistic is

$$\textit{test statistic} = \frac{RSS - (RSS_1 + RSS_2)}{RSS_1 + RSS_2} \times \frac{T - 2k}{k} \tag{5.62}$$

where RSS = residual sum of squares for whole sample
RSS_1 = residual sum of squares for sub-sample 1
RSS_2 = residual sum of squares for sub-sample 2
T = number of observations
$2k$ = number of regressors in the 'unrestricted' regression (since it comes in two parts)
k = number of regressors in (each) 'unrestricted' regression

The unrestricted regression is the one where the restriction has not been imposed on the model. Since the restriction is that the coefficients are equal across the sub-samples, the restricted regression will be the single regression for the whole sample. Thus, the test is one of how much the residual sum of squares for the whole sample (RSS) is bigger than the sum of the residual sums of squares for the two sub-samples ($RSS_1 + RSS_2$). If the coefficients do not change much between the samples, the residual sum of squares will not rise much upon imposing the restriction. Thus the

test statistic in (5.62) can be considered a straightforward application of the standard F-test formula discussed in chapter 4. The restricted residual sum of squares in (5.62) is RSS,
while the unrestricted residual sum of squares is $(RSS_1 + RSS_2)$. The number of restrictions is equal to the number of coefficients that are estimated for each of the regressions, i.e. k. The number of regressors in the unrestricted regression (including the constants) is $2k$, since the unrestricted regression comes in two parts, each with k regressors.

(3) *Perform the test.* If the value of the test statistic is greater than the critical value from the F-distribution, which is an $F(k,\ T-2k)$, then reject the null hypothesis that the parameters are stable over time.

5.12.1　The Chow test

The steps involved are shown in box 5.7. Note that it is also possible to use a dummy variables approach to calculating both Chow and predictive failure tests. In the case of the Chow test, the unrestricted regression would contain dummy variables for the intercept and for all of the slope coefficients (see also chapter 10). For example, suppose that the regression is of the form

$$y_t = \beta_1 + \beta_2 x_{2t} + \beta_3 x_{3t} + u_t \tag{5.63}$$

If the split of the total of T observations is made so that the sub-samples contain T_1 and T_2 observations (where $T_1 + T_2 = T$), the unrestricted regression would be given by

$$y_t = \beta_1 + \beta_2 x_{2t} + \beta_3 x_{3t} + \beta_4 D_t + \beta_5 D_t x_{2t} + \beta_6 D_t x_{3t} + v_t \tag{5.64}$$

where $D_t = 1$ for $t \in T_1$ and zero otherwise. In other words, D_t takes the value one for observations in the first sub-sample and zero for observations in the second sub-sample. The Chow test viewed in this way would then be a standard F-test of the joint restriction H$_0$: $\beta_4 = 0$ and $\beta_5 = 0$ and $\beta_6 = 0$, with (5.64) and (5.63) being the unrestricted and restricted regressions, respectively.

Example 5.4 ●

Suppose that it is now January 1993. Consider the following regression for the standard CAPM β for the returns on a stock

$$r_{gt} = \alpha + \beta r_{Mt} + u_t \tag{5.65}$$

where r_{gt} and r_{Mt} are excess returns on Glaxo shares and on a market portfolio, respectively. Suppose that you are interested in estimating beta using monthly data from 1981 to 1992, to aid a stock selection decision. Another researcher expresses concern that the October 1987 stock market crash fundamentally altered the risk–return relationship. Test this conjecture using a Chow test. The model for each sub-period is

1981M1–1987M10

$$\hat{r}_{gt} = 0.24 + 1.2 r_{Mt} \quad T = 82 \quad RSS_1 = 0.03555 \tag{5.66}$$

1987M11–1992M12

$$\hat{r}_{gt} = 0.68 + 1.53 r_{Mt} \quad T = 62 \quad RSS_2 = 0.00336 \tag{5.67}$$

1981M1–1992M12

$$\hat{r}_{gt} = 0.39 + 1.37 r_{Mt} \quad T = 144 \quad RSS = 0.0434 \tag{5.68}$$

The null hypothesis is

$$H_0 : \alpha_1 = \alpha_2 \ \text{ and } \ \beta_1 = \beta_2$$

where the subscripts 1 and 2 denote the parameters for the first and second sub-samples, respectively. The test statistic will be given by

$$test \ statistic = \frac{0.0434 - (0.0355 + 0.00336)}{0.0355 + 0.00336} \times \frac{144 - 4}{2} \tag{5.69}$$

$$= 7.698$$

The test statistic should be compared with a 5%, $F(2, 140) = 3.06$. H_0 is rejected at the 5% level and hence it is concluded that the restriction that the coefficients are the same in the two periods cannot be employed. The appropriate modelling response would probably be to employ only the second part of the data in estimating the CAPM beta relevant for investment decisions made in early 1993.

5.12.2 The predictive failure test

A problem with the Chow test is that it is necessary to have enough data to do the regression on both sub-samples, i.e. $T_1 \gg k$, $T_2 \gg k$. This may not hold in the situation where the total number of observations available is small. Even more likely is the situation where the researcher would like to examine the effect of splitting the sample at some point very close to the start or very close to the end of the sample. An alternative formulation of a test for the stability of the model is the predictive failure test, which requires estimation for the full sample and one of the sub-samples only. The predictive failure test works by estimating the regression over a 'long' sub-period (i.e. most of the data) and then using those coefficient estimates for predicting values of y for the other period. These predictions for y are then implicitly compared with the actual values. Although it can be expressed in several different ways, the null hypothesis for this test is that the prediction errors for all of the forecasted observations are zero.

To calculate the test:

- **Run the regression for the whole period** (the restricted regression) and obtain the RSS.

- **Run the regression for the 'large' sub-period** and obtain the RSS (called RSS_1). Note that in this book, the number of observations for the long estimation sub-period will be denoted by T_1 (even though it may come second). The test statistic is given by

$$test\ statistic = \frac{RSS - RSS_1}{RSS_1} \times \frac{T_1 - k}{T_2} \tag{5.70}$$

where $T_2 =$ number of observations that the model is attempting to 'predict'. The test statistic will follow an $F(T_2, T_1 - k)$.

For an intuitive interpretation of the predictive failure test statistic formulation, consider an alternative way to test for predictive failure using a regression containing dummy variables. A separate dummy variable would be used for each observation that was in the prediction sample. The unrestricted regression would then be the one that includes the dummy variables, which will be estimated using all T observations, and will have $(k + T_2)$ regressors (the k original explanatory variables, and a dummy variable for each prediction observation, i.e. a total of T_2 dummy variables). Thus the numerator of the last part of (5.70) would be the total number of observations (T) minus the number of regressors in the unrestricted regression $(k + T_2)$. Noting also that $T - (k + T_2) = (T_1 - k)$, since $T_1 + T_2 = T$, this gives the numerator of the last term in (5.70). The restricted regression would then be the original regression containing the explanatory variables but none of the dummy variables. Thus the number of restrictions would be the number of observations in the prediction period, which would be equivalent to the number of dummy variables included in the unrestricted regression, T_2.

To offer an illustration, suppose that the regression is again of the form of (5.63), and that the last three observations in the sample are used for a predictive failure test. The unrestricted regression would include three dummy variables, one for each of the observations in T_2

$$r_{gt} = \alpha + \beta r_{Mt} + \gamma_1 D1_t + \gamma_2 D2_t + \gamma_3 D3_t + u_t \tag{5.71}$$

where $D1_t = 1$ for observation $T - 2$ and zero otherwise, $D2_t = 1$ for observation $T - 1$ and zero otherwise, $D3_t = 1$ for observation T and zero otherwise. In this case, $k = 2$, and $T_2 = 3$. The null hypothesis for the predictive failure test in this regression is that the coefficients on all of the dummy variables are zero (i.e. $H_0 : \gamma_1 = 0$ and $\gamma_2 = 0$ and $\gamma_3 = 0$). Both approaches to conducting the predictive failure test described above are equivalent, although the dummy variable regression is likely to take more time to set up.

However, for both the Chow and the predictive failure tests, the dummy variables approach has the one major advantage that it provides the user with more information. This additional information comes from the fact that one can examine the significances of the coefficients on the individual dummy variables to see which part of the joint null hypothesis is causing a rejection. For example, in the context of the Chow regression, is it the intercept or the slope coefficients that are significantly different across the two sub-samples? In the context of the predictive failure test, use of the dummy variables approach would show for which period(s) the prediction errors are significantly different from zero.

5.12.3　Backward versus forward predictive failure tests

There are two types of predictive failure tests – forward tests and backwards tests. Forward predictive failure tests are where the last few observations are kept back for forecast testing. For example, suppose that observations for 1980Q1–2013Q4 are available. A forward predictive failure test could involve estimating the model over 1980Q1–2012Q4 and forecasting 2013Q1–2013Q4. Backward predictive failure tests attempt to 'back-cast' the first few observations, e.g. if data for 1980Q1–2013Q4 are available, and the model is estimated over 1981Q1–2013Q4 and back-cast 1980Q1–1980Q4. Both types of test offer further evidence on the stability of the regression relationship over the whole sample period.

Example 5.5

Suppose that the researcher decided to determine the stability of the estimated model for stock returns over the whole sample in example 5.4 by using a predictive failure test of the last two years of observations. The following models would be estimated:

1981M1–1992M12 (whole sample)

$$\hat{r}_{gt} = 0.39 + 1.37 r_{Mt} \qquad T = 144 \qquad RSS = 0.0434 \tag{5.72}$$

1981M1–1990M12 ('long sub-sample')

$$\hat{r}_{gt} = 0.32 + 1.31 r_{Mt} \qquad T = 120 \qquad RSS_1 = 0.0420 \tag{5.73}$$

Can this regression adequately 'forecast' the values for the last two years? The test statistic would be given by

$$test\ statistic = \frac{0.0434 - 0.0420}{0.0420} \times \frac{120 - 2}{24} \tag{5.74}$$

$$= 0.164$$

Compare the test statistic with an $F(24, 118) = 1.66$ at the 5% level. So the null hypothesis that the model can adequately predict the last few observations would not be rejected. It would thus be concluded that the model did not suffer from predictive failure during the 1991M1–1992M12 period.

5.12.4　How can the appropriate sub-parts to use be decided?

As a rule of thumb, some or all of the following methods for selecting where the overall sample split occurs could be used:

- Plot the dependent variable over time and split the data accordingly to *any obvious structural changes in the series*, as illustrated in figure 5.12.

  It is clear that y in figure 5.12 underwent a large fall in its value around observation 175, and it is possible that this may have caused a change in its behaviour. A Chow test could be conducted with the sample split at this observation.

- Split the data according to *any known important historical events* (e.g. a stock market crash, change in market microstructure, new government elected). The argument is that a major change in the underlying environment in which *y* is measured is more likely to cause a structural change in the model's parameters than a relatively trivial change.
- Use all but the last few observations and do a *forward predictive failure test* on those.
- Use all but the first few observations and do a *backward predictive failure test* on those.

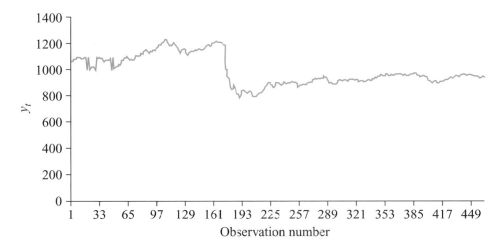

Figure 5.12   Plot of a variable showing suggestion for break date

If a model is good, it will survive a Chow or predictive failure test with any break date. If the Chow or predictive failure tests are failed, two approaches could be adopted. Either the model is respecified, for example, by including additional variables, or separate estimations are conducted for each of the sub-samples. On the other hand, if the Chow and predictive failure tests show no rejections, it is empirically valid to pool all of the data together in a single regression. This will increase the sample size and therefore the number of degrees of freedom relative to the case where the sub-samples are used in isolation.

5.12.5   The QLR test

The Chow and predictive failure tests will work satisfactorily if the date of a structural break in a financial time series can be specified. But more often, a researcher will not know the break date in advance, or may know only that it lies within a given range (sub-set) of the sample period. In such circumstances, a modified version of the Chow test, known as the *Quandt likelihood ratio (QLR) test*, named after Quandt (1960), can be used instead. The test works by automatically computing the usual Chow *F*-test statistic repeatedly with different break dates, then the break date giving the largest *F*-statistic value is chosen. While the test statistic is of the F-variety, it will follow a non-standard distribution rather than an F-distribution since we are selecting the largest from a number of F-statistics rather than examining a single one.

The test is well behaved only when the range of possible break dates is sufficiently far from the end points of the whole sample, so it is usual to 'trim' the sample by (typically) 5% at each end. To illustrate, suppose that the full sample comprises 200 observations; then we would test for a structural break between observations 31 and 170 inclusive. The critical values will depend on how much of the sample is trimmed away, the number of restrictions under the null hypothesis (the number of regressors in the original regression as this is effectively a Chow test) and the significance level.

5.12.6　Stability tests based on recursive estimation

An alternative to the QLR test for use in the situation where a researcher believes that a series may contain a structural break but is unsure of the date is to perform a recursive estimation. This is sometimes known as *recursive least squares* (RLS). The procedure is appropriate only for time-series data or cross-sectional data that have been ordered in some sensible way (for example, a sample of annual stock returns, ordered by market capitalisation). Recursive estimation simply involves starting with a sub-sample of the data, estimating the regression, then sequentially adding one observation at a time and re-running the regression until the end of the sample is reached. It is common to begin the initial estimation with the very minimum number of observations possible, which will be $k + 1$. So at the first step, the model is estimated using observations 1 to $k + 1$; at the second step, observations 1 to $k + 2$ are used and so on; at the final step, observations 1 to T are used. The final result will be the production of $T - k$ separate estimates of every parameter in the regression model.

It is to be expected that the parameter estimates produced near the start of the recursive procedure will appear rather unstable since these estimates are being produced using so few observations, but the key question is whether they then gradually settle down or whether the volatility continues through the whole sample. Seeing the latter would be an indication of parameter instability.

It should be evident that RLS in itself is not a statistical test for parameter stability as such, but rather it provides qualitative information which can be plotted and thus gives a very visual impression of how stable the parameters appear to be. But two important stability tests, known as the *CUSUM* and *CUSUMSQ* tests, are derived from the residuals of the recursive estimation (known as the recursive residuals).[5] The CUSUM statistic is based on a normalised (i.e. scaled) version of the cumulative sums of the residuals. Under the null hypothesis of perfect parameter stability, the CUSUM statistic is zero however many residuals are included in the sum (because the expected value of a disturbance is always zero). A set of ± 2

---

[5] Strictly, the CUSUM and CUSUMSQ statistics are based on the one-step ahead prediction errors – i.e. the differences between y_t and its predicted value based on the parameters estimated at time $t - 1$. See Greene (2002, chapter 7) for full technical details.

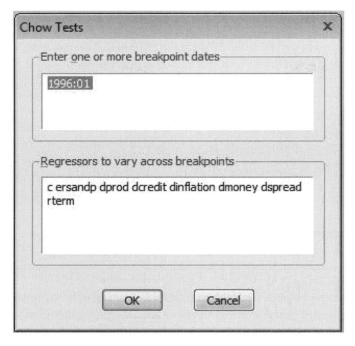

Screenshot 5.4   **Chow test for parameter stability**

standard error bands is usually plotted around zero and any statistic lying outside the bands is taken as evidence of parameter instability.

The CUSUMSQ test is based on a normalised version of the cumulative sums of squared residuals. The scaling is such that under the null hypothesis of parameter stability, the CUSUMSQ statistic will start at zero and end the sample with a value of 1. Again, a set of ± 2 standard error bands is usually plotted around zero and any statistic lying outside these is taken as evidence of parameter instability.

5.12.7 Stability tests in EViews

In EViews, to access the Chow test, click on **View/Stability Diagnostics/Chow Breakpoint Test . . .** in the 'Msoftreg' regression window. In the new window that appears, enter the date at which it is believed that a breakpoint occurred. Input **1996:01** in the dialog box in screenshot 5.4 to split the sample roughly in half. Note that it is not possible to conduct a Chow test or a parameter stability test when there are outlier dummy variables in the regression, so make sure that FEB98DUM and FEB03DUM are omitted from the variable list. This occurs because when the sample is split into two parts, the dummy variable for one of the parts will have values of zero for all observations, which would thus cause perfect multicollinearity with the column of ones that is used for the constant term. So ensure that the Chow test is performed using the regression containing all of the explanatory variables except the dummies. By default, EViews allows the values of all the parameters to vary across the two sub-samples in the unrestricted regressions, although if we wanted, we could force some of the parameters to be fixed across the two sub-samples.

EViews gives three versions of the test statistics, as shown in the following table.

Chow Breakpoint Test: 1996M01
Null Hypothesis: No breaks at specified breakpoints
Varying regressors: C ERSANDP DPROD DCREDIT
DINFLATION DMONEY DSPREAD RTERM
Equation Sample: 1986M05 2013M04

F-statistic	0.756884	Prob. F(8,306)	0.6411
Log likelihood ratio	6.348645	Prob. Chi-Square(8)	0.6082
Wald Statistic	6.055072	Prob. Chi-Square(8)	0.6411

The first version of the test is the familiar F-test, which computes a restricted version and an unrestricted version of the auxiliary regression and 'compares' the residual sums of squares, while the second and third versions are based on χ^2 formulations. In this case, all three test statistics are smaller than their critical values and so the null hypothesis that the parameters are constant across the two sub-samples is not rejected. Note that the Chow forecast (i.e. the predictive failure) test could also be employed by clicking on the **View/Stability Diagnostics/Chow Forecast Test...** in the regression window. **Determine whether the model can predict the last four observations** by entering 2013:01 in the dialog box. The results of this test are given in the following table (note that only the first two lines of results are presented since the remainder are not needed for interpretation).

Chow Forecast Test
Equation: MSOFTREG
C ERSANDP DPROD DCREDIT DINFLATION DMONEY DSPREAD RTERM
Test predictions for observations from 2013M01 to 2013M04

	Value	df	Probability
F-statistic	0.518180	(4,310)	0.7224
Likelihood ratio	2.159117	4	0.7065

The table indicates that the model can indeed adequately predict the 2007 observations. Thus the conclusions from both forms of the test are that there is no evidence of parameter instability. However, the conclusion should really be that the parameters are stable *with respect to these particular break dates*. It is important to note that for the model to be deemed adequate, it needs to be stable with respect to any break dates that we may choose. A good way to test this is to use one of the tests based on recursive estimation.

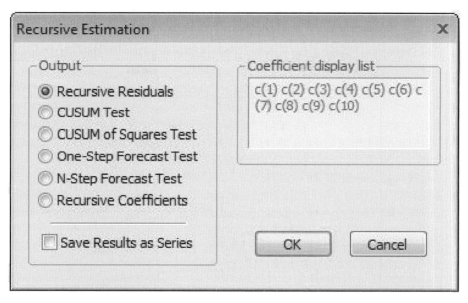

Screenshot 5.5   **Plotting recursive coefficient estimates**

Click on **View/Stability Diagnostics/Recursive Estimates (OLS Only)** .... You will be presented with a menu as shown in screenshot 5.5 containing a number of options including the CUSUM and CUSUMSQ tests described above and also the opportunity to plot the recursively estimated coefficients.

First, check the box next to **Recursive coefficients** and then recursive estimates will be given for all those parameters listed in the 'Coefficient display list' box, which by default is all of them. Click **OK** and you will be presented with eight small figures, one for each parameter, showing the recursive estimates and ±2 standard error bands around them. As discussed above, it is bound to take some time for the coefficients to stabilise since the first few sets are estimated using such small samples. Given this, the parameter estimates in all cases are remarkably stable over time. Now go back to **View/Stability Diagnostics/Recursive Estimates (OLS Only)...** and choose **CUSUM Test**. The resulting graph is in screenshot 5.6.

Since the line is well within the confidence bands, the conclusion would be again that the null hypothesis of stability is not rejected. **Now repeat the above but using the CUSUMSQ test rather than CUSUM**. Do we retain the same conclusion? (Yes) Why?

5.13   Measurement errors

As stated above, one of the of the assumptions of the classical linear regression model is that the explanatory variables are non-stochastic. One way in which this assumption can be violated is when there is a two-way causal relationship between the explanatory and explained variable, and this situation (*simultaneous equations bias*) is discussed in detail in chapter 7. A further situation where the assumption will not

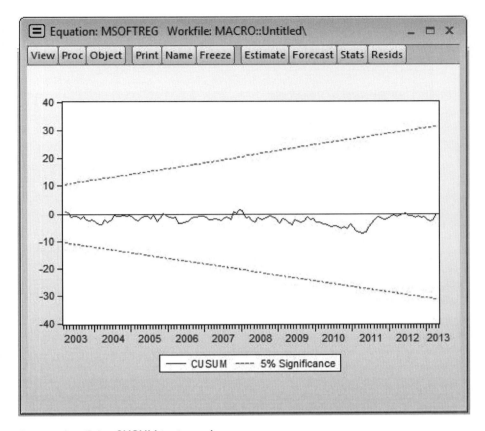

Screenshot 5.6   **CUSUM test graph**

apply is when there is *measurement error* in one or more of the explanatory variables. Sometimes this is also known as the *errors-in-variables* problem. Measurement errors can occur in a variety of circumstances – for example, macroeconomic variables are almost always estimated quantities (GDP, inflation and so on), as is most information contained in company accounts. Similarly, it is sometimes the case that we cannot observe or obtain data on a variable we require and so we need to use a *proxy variable* – for instance, many models include expected quantities (e.g. expected inflation) but since we cannot typically measure expectations, we need to use a proxy. More generally, measurement error could be present in the dependent or independent variables, and each of these cases is considered in the following sub-sections.

5.13.1 Measurement error in the explanatory variable(s)

For simplicity, suppose that we wish to estimate a model containing just one explanatory variable, x_t

$$y_t = \beta_1 + \beta_2 x_t + u_t \tag{5.75}$$

where u_t is a disturbance term. Suppose further that x_t is measured with error so that instead of observing its true value, we observe a noisy version, $\tilde{x}_t$ that comprises the actual x_t plus some additional noise, v_t that is independent of x_t and u_t

$$\tilde{x}_t = x_t + v_t \tag{5.76}$$

Taking equation (5.75) and substituting in for x_t from (5.76), we get

$$y_t = \beta_1 + \beta_2(\tilde{x}_t - v_t) + u_t \tag{5.77}$$

We can rewrite this equation by separately expressing the composite error term, $(u_t - \beta_2 v_t)$

$$y_t = \beta_1 + \beta_2 \tilde{x}_t + (u_t - \beta_2 v_t) \tag{5.78}$$

It should be clear from (5.76) and (5.78) that the explanatory variable measured with error, $(\tilde{x})$, and the composite error term $(u_t - \beta_2 v_t)$ are correlated since both depend on v_t. Thus the requirement that the explanatory variables are non-stochastic does not hold. This causes the parameters to be estimated inconsistently. It can be shown that the size of the bias in the estimates will be a function of the variance of the noise in x_t as a proportion of the overall disturbance variance. It can be further shown that if β_2 is positive, the bias will be negative but if β_2 is negative, the bias will be positive − in other words, the parameter estimate will always be biased towards zero as a result of the measurement noise.

The impact of this estimation bias when the explanatory variables are measured with error can be quite important and is a serious issue in particular when testing asset pricing models. The standard approach to testing the CAPM pioneered by Fama and MacBeth (1973) comprises two stages (discussed more fully in chapter 14). Stage one is to run separate time series regressions for each firm to estimate the betas and the second stage involves running a cross-sectional regression of the stock returns on the betas. Since the betas are estimated at the first stage rather than being directly observable, they will surely contain measurement error. In the finance literature, the effect of this has sometimes been termed *attenuation bias*. Early tests of the CAPM showed that the relationship between beta and returns was positive but smaller than expected, and this is precisely what would happen as a result of measurement error in the betas. Various approaches to solving this issue have been proposed, the most common of which is to use portfolio betas in place of individual stock betas in the second stage. The hope is that this will smooth out the estimation error in the betas. An alternative approach attributed to Shanken (1992) is to modify the standard errors in the second stage regression to adjust directly for the measurement errors in the betas. More discussion of this issue will be presented in chapter 14.

5.13.2 Measurement error in the explained variable

Measurement error in the explained variable is much less serious than in the explanatory variable(s); recall that one of the motivations for the inclusion of the disturbance term in a regression model is that it can capture measurement errors in

y. Thus, when the explained variable is measured with error, the disturbance term will in effect be a composite of the usual disturbance term and another source of noise from the measurement error. In such circumstances, the parameter estimates will still be consistent and unbiased and the usual formulae for calculating standard errors will still be appropriate. The only consequence is that the additional noise means the standard errors will be enlarged relative to the situation where there was no measurement error in y.

5.14 A strategy for constructing econometric models and a discussion of model-building philosophies

The objective of many econometric model-building exercises is to build a statistically adequate empirical model which satisfies the assumptions of the CLRM, is parsimonious, has the appropriate theoretical interpretation, and has the right 'shape' (i.e. all signs on coefficients are 'correct' and all sizes of coefficients are 'correct').

But how might a researcher go about achieving this objective? A common approach to model building is the 'LSE' or general-to-specific methodology associated with Sargan and Hendry. This approach essentially involves starting with a large model which is statistically adequate and restricting and rearranging the model to arrive at a parsimonious final formulation. Hendry's approach (see Gilbert, 1986) argues that a good model is consistent with the data and with theory. A good model will also encompass rival models, which means that it can explain all that rival models can and more. The Hendry methodology suggests the extensive use of diagnostic tests to ensure the statistical adequacy of the model.

An alternative philosophy of econometric model-building, which pre-dates Hendry's research, is that of starting with the simplest model and adding to it sequentially so that it gradually becomes more complex and a better description of reality. This approach, associated principally with Koopmans (1937), is sometimes known as a 'specific-to-general' or 'bottoms-up' modelling approach. Gilbert (1986) termed this the 'Average Economic Regression' since most applied econometric work had been tackled in that way. This term was also having a joke at the expense of a top economics journal that published many papers using such a methodology.

Hendry and his co-workers have severely criticised this approach, mainly on the grounds that diagnostic testing is undertaken, if at all, almost as an after-thought and in a very limited fashion. However, if diagnostic tests are not performed, or are performed only at the end of the model-building process, all earlier inferences are potentially invalidated. Moreover, if the specific initial model is generally misspecified, the diagnostic tests themselves are not necessarily reliable in indicating the source of the problem. For example, if the initially specified model omits relevant variables which are themselves autocorrelated, introducing lags of the included variables would not be an appropriate remedy for a significant DW test statistic. Thus the eventually selected model under a specific-to-general approach could be sub-optimal in the sense that the model selected using a general-to-specific approach might represent the data better. Under the Hendry approach, diagnostic tests of the statistical adequacy of the model come first, with an examination of inferences for financial theory drawn from the model left until after a statistically adequate model has been found.

According to Hendry and Richard (1982), a final acceptable model should satisfy several criteria (adapted slightly here). The model should:

- be logically plausible
- be consistent with underlying financial theory, including satisfying any relevant parameter restrictions
- have regressors that are uncorrelated with the error term
- have parameter estimates that are stable over the entire sample
- have residuals that are white noise (i.e. completely random and exhibiting no patterns)
- be capable of explaining the results of all competing models and more.

The last of these is known as the *encompassing principle*. A model that nests within it a smaller model always trivially encompasses it. But a small model is particularly favoured if it can explain all of the results of a larger model; this is known as *parsimonious encompassing*.

The advantages of the general-to-specific approach are that it is statistically sensible and also that the theory on which the models are based usually has nothing to say about the lag structure of a model. Therefore, the lag structure incorporated in the final model is largely determined by the data themselves. Furthermore, the statistical consequences from excluding relevant variables are usually considered more serious than those from including irrelevant variables.

The general-to-specific methodology is conducted as follows. The first step is to form a 'large' model with lots of variables on the RHS. This is known as a generalised unrestricted model (GUM), which should originate from financial theory, and which should contain all variables thought to influence the dependent variable. At this stage, the researcher is required to ensure that the model satisfies all of the assumptions of the CLRM. If the assumptions are violated, appropriate actions should be taken to address or allow for this, e.g. taking logs, adding lags, adding dummy variables.

It is important that the steps above are conducted prior to any hypothesis testing. It should also be noted that the diagnostic tests presented above should be cautiously interpreted as general rather than specific tests. In other words, rejection of a particular diagnostic test null hypothesis should be interpreted as showing that there is something wrong with the model. So, for example, if the RESET test or White's test show a rejection of the null, such results should not be immediately interpreted as implying that the appropriate response is to find a solution for inappropriate functional form or heteroscedastic residuals, respectively. It is quite often the case that one problem with the model could cause several assumptions to be violated simultaneously. For example, an omitted variable could cause failures of the RESET, heteroscedasticity and autocorrelation tests. Equally, a small number of large outliers could cause non-normality and residual autocorrelation (if they occur close together in the sample) and heteroscedasticity (if the outliers occur for a narrow range of the explanatory variables). Moreover, the diagnostic tests themselves do not operate optimally in the presence of other types of misspecification since they essentially assume that the model is correctly specified in all other respects. For example, it is not clear that tests for heteroscedasticity will behave well if the residuals are autocorrelated.

Once a model that satisfies the assumptions of the CLRM has been obtained, it could be very big, with large numbers of lags and independent variables. The next stage is therefore to reparameterise the model by knocking out very insignificant regressors. Also, some coefficients may be insignificantly different from each other, so that they can be combined. At each stage, it should be checked whether the assumptions of the CLRM are still upheld. If this is the case, the researcher should have arrived at a statistically adequate empirical model that can be used for testing underlying financial theories, forecasting future values of the dependent variable, or for formulating policies.

However, needless to say, the general-to-specific approach also has its critics. For small or moderate sample sizes, it may be impractical. In such instances, the large number of explanatory variables will imply a small number of degrees of freedom. This could mean that none of the variables is significant, especially if they are highly correlated. This being the case, it would not be clear which of the original long list of candidate regressors should subsequently be dropped. Moreover, in any case the decision on which variables to drop may have profound implications for the final specification of the model. A variable whose coefficient was not significant might have become significant at a later stage if other variables had been dropped instead.

In theory, sensitivity of the final specification to the various possible paths of variable deletion should be carefully checked. However, this could imply checking many (perhaps even hundreds) of possible specifications. It could also lead to several final models, none of which appears noticeably better than the others.

The general-to-specific approach, if followed faithfully to the end, will hopefully lead to a statistically valid model that passes all of the usual model diagnostic tests and contains only statistically significant regressors. However, the final model could also be a bizarre creature that is devoid of any theoretical interpretation. There would also be more than just a passing chance that such a model could be the product of a statistically vindicated data mining exercise. Such a model would closely fit the sample of data at hand, but could fail miserably when applied to other samples if it is not based soundly on theory.

There now follows another example of the use of the classical linear regression model in finance, based on an examination of the determinants of sovereign credit ratings by Cantor and Packer (1996).

5.15 Determinants of sovereign credit ratings

5.15.1 Background

Sovereign credit ratings are an assessment of the riskiness of debt issued by governments. They embody an estimate of the probability that the borrower will default on her obligation. Two famous US ratings agencies, Moody's and Standard and

Poor's (S&P), provide ratings for many governments. Although the two agencies use different symbols to denote the given riskiness of a particular borrower, the ratings of the two agencies are comparable. Gradings are split into two broad categories: investment grade and speculative grade. Investment grade issuers have good or adequate payment capacity, while speculative grade issuers either have a high degree of uncertainty about whether they will make their payments, or are already in default. The highest grade offered by the agencies, for the highest quality of payment capacity, is 'triple A', which Moody's denotes 'Aaa' and S&P denotes 'AAA'. The lowest grade issued to a sovereign in the Cantor and Packer sample was B3 (Moody's) or B− (S&P). Thus the number of grades of debt quality from the highest to the lowest given to governments in their sample is 16.

The central aim of Cantor and Packer's paper is an attempt to explain and model how the agencies arrived at their ratings. Although the ratings themselves are publicly available, the models or methods used to arrive at them are shrouded in secrecy. The agencies also provide virtually no explanation as to what the relative weights of the factors that make up the rating are. Thus, a model of the determinants of sovereign credit ratings could be useful in assessing whether the ratings agencies appear to have acted rationally. Such a model could also be employed to try to predict the rating that would be awarded to a sovereign that has not previously been rated and when a re-rating is likely to occur. The paper continues, among other things, to consider whether ratings add to publicly available information, and whether it is possible to determine what factors affect how the sovereign yields react to ratings announcements.

5.15.2 Data

Cantor and Packer (1996) obtain a sample of government debt ratings for forty-nine countries as of September 1995 that range between the above gradings. The ratings variable is quantified, so that the highest credit quality (Aaa/AAA) in the sample is given a score of 16, while the lowest rated sovereign in the sample is given a score of 1 (B3/B−). This score forms the dependent variable. The factors that are used to explain the variability in the ratings scores are macroeconomic variables. All of these variables embody factors that are likely to influence a government's ability and willingness to service its debt costs. Ideally, the model would also include proxies for socio-political factors, but these are difficult to measure objectively and so are not included. It is not clear in the paper from where the list of factors was drawn. The included variables (with their units of measurement) are:

- *Per capita income* (in 1994 US dollars, thousands).   Cantor and Packer argue that *per capita* income determines the tax base, which in turn influences the government's ability to raise revenue.
- *GDP growth* (annual 1991–4 average, %).   The growth rate of increase in GDP is argued to measure how much easier it will become to service debt costs in the future.
- *Inflation* (annual 1992–4 average, %).   Cantor and Packer argue that high inflation suggests that inflationary money financing will be used to service

debt when the government is unwilling or unable to raise the required revenue through the tax system.

- *Fiscal balance* (average annual government budget surplus as a proportion of GDP 1992–4, %). Again, a large fiscal deficit shows that the government has a relatively weak capacity to raise additional revenue and to service debt costs.
- *External balance* (average annual current account surplus as a proportion of GDP 1992–4, %). Cantor and Packer argue that a persistent current account deficit leads to increasing foreign indebtedness, which may be unsustainable in the long run.
- *External debt* (foreign currency debt as a proportion of exports in 1994, %). Reasoning as for external balance (which is the change in external debt over time).
- *Dummy for economic development* (=1 for a country classified by the International Monetary Fund (IMF) as developed, 0 otherwise). Cantor and Packer argue that credit ratings agencies perceive developing countries as relatively more risky beyond that suggested by the values of the other factors listed above.
- *Dummy for default history* (=1 if a country has defaulted, 0 otherwise). It is argued that countries that have previously defaulted experience a large fall in their credit rating.

The income and inflation variables are transformed to their logarithms. The model is linear and estimated using OLS. Some readers of this book who have a background in econometrics will note that strictly, OLS is not an appropriate technique when the dependent variable can take on only one of a certain limited set of values (in this case, 1, 2, 3, . . . 16). In such applications, a technique such as ordered probit (not covered in this text) would usually be more appropriate. Cantor and Packer argue that any approach other than OLS is infeasible given the relatively small sample size (forty-nine), and the large number (sixteen) of ratings categories.

The results from regressing the rating value on the variables listed above are presented in their exhibit 5, adapted and presented here as table 5.2. Four regressions are conducted, each with identical independent variables but a different dependent variable. Regressions are conducted for the rating score given by each agency separately, with results presented in columns (4) and (5) of table 5.2. Occasionally, the ratings agencies give different scores to a country – for example, in the case of Italy, Moody's gives a rating of 'A1', which would generate a score of 12 on a 16-scale. S&P, on the other hand, gives a rating of 'AA', which would score 14 on the 16-scale, two gradings higher. Thus a regression with the average score across the two agencies, and with the difference between the two scores as dependent variables, is also conducted, and presented in columns (3) and (6), respectively of table 5.2.

5.15.3   Interpreting the models

The models are difficult to interpret in terms of their statistical adequacy, since virtually no diagnostic tests have been undertaken. The values of the adjusted R^2, at over 90% for each of the three ratings regressions, are high for cross-sectional

Table 5.2   Determinants and impacts of sovereign credit ratings

Explanatory variable (1)	Expected sign (2)	Dependent variable			
		Average rating (3)	Moody's rating (4)	S&P rating (5)	Difference Moody's/S&P (6)
Intercept	?	1.442	3.408	−0.524	3.932**
		(0.663)	(1.379)	(−0.223)	(2.521)
Per capita income	+	1.242***	1.027***	1.458***	−0.431***
		(5.302)	(4.041)	(6.048)	(−2.688)
GDP growth	+	0.151	0.130	0.171**	−0.040
		(1.935)	(1.545)	(2.132)	(0.756)
Inflation	−	−0.611***	−0.630***	−0.591***	−0.039
		(−2.839)	(−2.701)	(−2.671)	(−0.265)
Fiscal balance	+	0.073	0.049	0.097*	−0.048
		(1.324)	(0.818)	(1.71)	(−1.274)
External balance	+	0.003	0.006	0.001	0.006
		(0.314)	(0.535)	(0.046)	(0.779)
External debt	−	−0.013***	−0.015***	−0.011***	−0.004***
		(−5.088)	(−5.365)	(−4.236)	(−2.133)
Development dummy	+	2.776***	2.957***	2.595***	0.362
		(4.25)	(4.175)	(3.861)	(0.81)
Default dummy	−	−2.042***	−1.63**	−2.622***	1.159***
		(−3.175)	(−2.097)	(−3.962)	(2.632)
Adjusted R^2		0.924	0.905	0.926	0.836

Notes: *t*-ratios in parentheses; *, ** and *** indicate significance at the 10%, 5% and 1% levels, respectively.
Source: Cantor and Packer (1996). Reprinted with permission from *Institutional Investor*.

regressions, indicating that the model seems able to capture almost all of the variability of the ratings about their mean values across the sample. There does not appear to be any attempt at reparameterisation presented in the paper, so it is assumed that the authors reached this set of models after some searching.

In this particular application, the residuals have an interesting interpretation as the difference between the actual and fitted ratings. The actual ratings will be integers from 1 to 16, although the fitted values from the regression and therefore the residuals can take on any real value. Cantor and Packer argue that the model is working well as no residual is bigger than 3, so that no fitted rating is more than three categories out from the actual rating, and only four countries have residuals bigger than two categories. Furthermore, 70% of the countries have ratings predicted exactly (i.e. the residuals are less than 0.5 in absolute value).

Now, turning to interpret the models from a financial perspective, it is of interest to investigate whether the coefficients have their expected signs and sizes. The expected signs for the regression results of columns (3)–(5) are displayed in column (2) of table 5.2 (as determined by this author). As can be seen, all of the coefficients have their expected signs, although the fiscal balance and external balance variables are not significant or are only very marginally significant in all three cases. The coefficients can be interpreted as the average change in the rating score that would result from a unit change in the variable. So, for example, a rise in *per capita* income of $1,000 will on average increase the rating by 1.0 units according to Moody's and 1.5 units according to S&P. The development dummy suggests that, on average, a developed country will have a rating three notches higher than an otherwise identical developing country. And everything else equal, a country that has defaulted in the past will have a rating two notches lower than one that has always kept its obligation.

By and large, the ratings agencies appear to place similar weights on each of the variables, as evidenced by the similar coefficients and significances across columns (4) and (5) of table 5.2. This is formally tested in column (6) of the table, where the dependent variable is the difference between Moody's and S&P ratings. Only three variables are statistically significantly differently weighted by the two agencies. S&P places higher weights on income and default history, while Moody's places more emphasis on external debt.

5.15.4   The relationship between ratings and yields

In this section of the paper, Cantor and Packer try to determine whether ratings have any additional information useful for modelling the cross-sectional variability of sovereign yield spreads over and above that contained in publicly available macroeconomic data. The dependent variable is now the log of the yield spread, i.e.

ln(Yield on the sovereign bond − Yield on a US Treasury Bond)

One may argue that such a measure of the spread is imprecise, for the true credit spread should be defined by the entire credit quality curve rather than by just two points on it. However, leaving this issue aside, the results are presented in table 5.3.

Three regressions are presented in table 5.3, denoted specifications (1), (2) and (3). The first of these is a regression of the ln(spread) on only a constant and the average rating (column (1)), and this shows that ratings have a highly significant inverse impact on the spread. Specification (2) is a regression of the ln(spread) on the macroeconomic variables used in the previous analysis. The expected signs are given (as determined by this author) in column (2). As can be seen, all coefficients have their expected signs, although now only the coefficients belonging to the

		Dependent variable: ln (yield spread)		
Variable	Expected sign	(1)	(2)	(3)
Intercept	?	2.105***	0.466	0.074
		(16.148)	(0.345)	(0.071)
Average rating	–	−0.221***		−0.218***
		(−19.175)		(−4.276)
Per capita income	–		−0.144	0.226
			(−0.927)	(1.523)
GDP growth	–		−0.004	0.029
			(−0.142)	(1.227)
Inflation	+		0.108	−0.004
			(1.393)	(−0.068)
Fiscal balance	–		−0.037	−0.02
			(−1.557)	(−1.045)
External balance	–		−0.038	−0.023
			(−1.29)	(−1.008)
External debt	+		0.003***	0.000
			(2.651)	(0.095)
Development dummy	–		−0.723***	−0.38
			(−2.059)	(−1.341)
Default dummy	+		0.612***	0.085
			(2.577)	(0.385)
Adjusted R^2		0.919	0.857	0.914

Table 5.3   Do ratings add to public information?

Notes: *t*-ratios in parentheses; *, **and *** indicate significance at the 10%, 5% and 1% levels, respectively.
Source: Cantor and Packer (1996). Reprinted with permission from *Institutional Investor*.

external debt and the two dummy variables are statistically significant. Specification (3) is a regression on both the average rating and the macroeconomic variables. When the rating is included with the macroeconomic factors, none of the latter is any longer significant – only the rating coefficient is statistically significantly different from zero. This message is also portrayed by the adjusted R^2 values, which are highest for the regression containing only the rating, and slightly lower for the regression containing the macroeconomic variables and the rating. One may also observe that, under specification (3), the coefficients on the *per capita* income, GDP growth and inflation variables now have the wrong sign. This is, in fact, never really an issue, for if a coefficient is not statistically significant, it is indistinguishable from zero in the context of hypothesis testing, and therefore it does not matter whether it is actually insignificant and positive or insignificant and negative. Only coefficients that are both of the wrong sign and statistically significant imply that there is a problem with the regression.

It would thus be concluded from this part of the paper that there is no more incremental information in the publicly available macroeconomic variables that is useful for predicting the yield spread than that embodied in the rating. The information contained in the ratings encompasses that contained in the macroeconomic variables.

5.15.5 What determines how the market reacts to ratings announcements?

Cantor and Packer also consider whether it is possible to build a model to predict how the market will react to ratings announcements, in terms of the resulting change in the yield spread. The dependent variable for this set of regressions is now the change in the log of the relative spread, i.e. log[(yield − treasury yield)/treasury yield], over a two-day period at the time of the announcement. The sample employed for estimation comprises every announcement of a ratings change that occurred between 1987 and 1994; seventy-nine such announcements were made, spread over eighteen countries. Of these, thirty nine were actual ratings changes by one or more of the agencies, and forty were listed as likely in the near future to experience a regrading. Moody's calls this a 'watchlist', while S&P term it their 'outlook' list. The explanatory variables are mainly dummy variables for:

- whether the announcement was positive − i.e. an upgrade
- whether there was an actual ratings change or just listing for probable regrading
- whether the bond was speculative grade or investment grade
- whether there had been another ratings announcement in the previous sixty days
- the ratings gap between the announcing and the other agency.

The following cardinal variable was also employed:

- the change in the spread over the previous sixty days.

The results are presented in table 5.4, but in this text, only the final specification (numbered 5 in Cantor and Packer's exhibit 11) containing all of the variables described above is included.

As can be seen from table 5.4, the models appear to do a relatively poor job of explaining how the market will react to ratings announcements. The adjusted R^2 value is only 12%, and this is the highest of the five specifications tested by the authors. Further, only two variables are significant and one marginally

Table 5.4 What determines reactions to ratings announcements?	
Dependent variable: log relative spread	
Independent variable	**Coefficient (*t*-ratio)**
Intercept	−0.02
	(−1.4)
Positive announcements	0.01
	(0.34)
Ratings changes	−0.01
	(−0.37)
Moody's announcements	0.02
	(1.51)
Speculative grade	0.03**
	(2.33)
Change in relative spreads from day −60 to day −1	−0.06
	(−1.1)
Rating gap	0.03*
	(1.7)
Other rating announcements from day −60 to day −1	0.05**
	(2.15)
Adjusted R^2	0.12

Note: * and ** denote significance at the 10% and 5% levels, respectively.
Source: Cantor and Packer (1996). Reprinted with permission from *Institutional Investor*.

significant of the seven employed in the model. It can therefore be stated that yield changes are significantly higher following a ratings announcement for speculative than investment grade bonds, and that ratings changes have a bigger impact on yield spreads if there is an agreement between the ratings agencies at the time the announcement is made. Further, yields change significantly more if there has been a previous announcement in the past sixty days than if not. On the other hand, neither whether the announcement is an upgrade or a downgrade, nor whether it is an actual ratings change or a name on the watchlist, nor whether the announcement is made by Moody's or S&P, nor the amount by which the relative spread has already changed over the past sixty days, has any significant impact on how the market reacts to ratings announcements.

5.15.6 Conclusions

- To summarise, six factors appear to play a big role in determining sovereign credit ratings – incomes, GDP growth, inflation, external debt, industrialised or not and default history
- The ratings provide more information on yields than all of the macro-economic factors put together
- One cannot determine with any degree of confidence what factors determine how the markets will react to ratings announcements.

Key concepts

The key terms to be able to define and explain from this chapter are

• homoscedasticity	• heteroscedasticity
• autocorrelation	• dynamic model
• equilibrium solution	• robust standard errors
• skewness	• kurtosis
• outlier	• functional form
• multicollinearity	• omitted variable
• irrelevant variable	• parameter stability
• recursive least squares	• general-to-specific approach
• measurement error	

Self-study questions

1. Are assumptions made concerning the unobservable error terms (u_t) or about their sample counterparts, the estimated residuals ($\hat{u}_t$)? Explain your answer.

2. What pattern(s) would one like to see in a residual plot and why?

3. A researcher estimates the following model for stock market returns, but thinks that there may be a problem with it. By calculating the t-ratios and considering their significance and by examining the value of R^2 or otherwise, suggest what the problem might be.

$$\hat{y}_t = 0.638 + 0.402x_{2t} - 0.891x_{3t} \quad R^2 = 0.96, \quad \bar{R}^2 = 0.89$$
$$\phantom{\hat{y}_t = } (0.436) \quad (0.291) \quad\quad (0.763)$$

(5.79)

How might you go about solving the perceived problem?

4. (a) State in algebraic notation and explain the assumption about the CLRM's disturbances that is referred to by the term 'homoscedasticity'.

(b) What would the consequence be for a regression model if the errors were not homoscedastic?

(c) How might you proceed if you found that (b) were actually the case?

5. (a) What do you understand by the term 'autocorrelation'?
   (b) An econometrician suspects that the residuals of her model might be autocorrelated. Explain the steps involved in testing this theory using the Durbin–Watson (DW) test.
   (c) The econometrician follows your guidance (!!!) in part (b) and calculates a value for the Durbin–Watson statistic of 0.95. The regression has sixty quarterly observations and three explanatory variables (plus a constant term). Perform the test. What is your conclusion?
   (d) In order to allow for autocorrelation, the econometrician decides to use a model in first differences with a constant

$$\Delta y_t = \beta_1 + \beta_2 \Delta x_{2t} + \beta_3 \Delta x_{3t} + \beta_4 \Delta x_{4t} + u_t \qquad (5.80)$$

By attempting to calculate the long-run solution to this model, explain what might be a problem with estimating models entirely in first differences.
   (e) The econometrician finally settles on a model with both first differences and lagged levels terms of the variables

$$\Delta y_t = \beta_1 + \beta_2 \Delta x_{2t} + \beta_3 \Delta x_{3t} + \beta_4 \Delta x_{4t} + \beta_5 x_{2t-1}$$
$$+ \beta_6 x_{3t-1} + \beta_7 x_{4t-1} + v_t \qquad (5.81)$$

Can the Durbin–Watson test still validly be used in this case?

6. Calculate the long-run static equilibrium solution to the following dynamic econometric model

$$\Delta y_t = \beta_1 + \beta_2 \Delta x_{2t} + \beta_3 \Delta x_{3t} + \beta_4 y_{t-1} + \beta_5 x_{2t-1}$$
$$+ \beta_6 x_{3t-1} + \beta_7 x_{3t-4} + u_t \qquad (5.82)$$

7. What might Ramsey's RESET test be used for? What could be done if it were found that the RESET test has been failed?

8. (a) Why is it necessary to assume that the disturbances of a regression model are normally distributed?
   (b) In a practical econometric modelling situation, how might the problem that the residuals are not normally distributed be addressed?

9. (a) Explain the term 'parameter structural stability'?
   (b) A financial econometrician thinks that the stock market crash of October 1987 fundamentally changed the risk–return relationship given by the CAPM equation. He decides to test this hypothesis using a Chow test. The model is estimated using monthly data from January 1981–December 1995, and then two separate regressions are run for the sub-periods corresponding to data before and after the crash. The model is

$$r_t = \alpha + \beta R_{mt} + u_t \qquad (5.83)$$

so that the excess return on a security at time t is regressed upon the excess return on a proxy for the market portfolio at time t. The results for the three models estimated for a given stock are as follows:

1981M1–1995M12

$$r_t = 0.0215 + 1.491\, r_{mt} \qquad RSS = 0.189 \ \ T = 180 \qquad\qquad (5.84)$$

1981M1–1987M10

$$r_t = 0.0163 + 1.308\, r_{mt} \qquad RSS = 0.079 \ \ T = 82 \qquad\qquad (5.85)$$

1987M11–1995M12

$$r_t = 0.0360 + 1.613\, r_{mt} \qquad RSS = 0.082 \ \ T = 98 \qquad\qquad (5.86)$$

    (c) What are the null and alternative hypotheses that are being tested here, in terms of α and β?

    (d) Perform the test. What is your conclusion?

10. For the same model as above, and given the following results, do a forward and backward predictive failure test:

1981M1–1995M12

$$r_t = 0.0215 + 1.491\, r_{mt} \qquad RSS = 0.189 \ \ T = 180 \qquad\qquad (5.87)$$

1981M1–1994M12

$$r_t = 0.0212 + 1.478\, r_{mt} \qquad RSS = 0.148 \ \ T = 168 \qquad\qquad (5.88)$$

1982M1–1995M12

$$r_t = 0.0217 + 1.523\, r_{mt} \qquad RSS = 0.182 \ \ T = 168 \qquad\qquad (5.89)$$

    What is your conclusion?

11. Why is it desirable to remove insignificant variables from a regression?

12. Explain why it is not possible to include an outlier dummy variable in a regression model when you are conducting a Chow test for parameter stability. Will the same problem arise if you were to conduct a predictive failure test? Why or why not?

13. Re-open the 'macro.wf1' and apply the stepwise procedure including all of the explanatory variables as listed above, i.e. ersandp dprod dcredit dinflation dmoney dspread rterm with a strict 5% threshold criterion for inclusion in the model. Then examine the resulting model both financially and statistically by investigating the signs, sizes and significances of the parameter estimates and by conducting all of the diagnostic tests for model adequacy.

14. (a) Explain the term 'measurement error'.

    (b) How does measurement error arise?

    (c) Is measurement error more serious if it is present in the dependent variable or the independent variable(s) of a regression? Explain your answer.

    (d) What is the likely impact of measurement error on tests of the CAPM and what are the possible solutions?

6
Univariate time series modelling and forecasting

Learning outcomes

In this chapter, you will learn how to
- Explain the defining characteristics of various types of stochastic processes
- Identify the appropriate time series model for a given data series
- Produce forecasts for autoregressive moving average (ARMA) and exponential smoothing models
- Evaluate the accuracy of predictions using various metrics
- Estimate time series models and produce forecasts from them in EViews

6.1 Introduction

Univariate time series models are a class of specifications where one attempts to model and to predict financial variables using only information contained in their own past values and possibly current and past values of an error term. This practice can be contrasted with *structural models*, which are multivariate in nature, and attempt to explain changes in a variable by reference to the movements in the current or past values of other (explanatory) variables. Time series models are usually a-theoretical, implying that their construction and use is not based upon any underlying theoretical model of the behaviour of a variable. Instead, time series models are an attempt to capture empirically relevant features of the observed data that may have arisen from a variety of different (but unspecified) structural models. An important class of time series models is the family of autoregressive integrated moving average (ARIMA) models, usually associated with Box and Jenkins (1976). Time series models may be useful when a structural model is inappropriate. For example, suppose that there is some variable y_t whose movements a researcher wishes to explain. It may be that the variables thought to drive movements of y_t are not observable or not measurable, or that these forcing variables are measured at a lower frequency of observation than y_t. For instance, y_t might be a series of daily stock returns, where possible explanatory variables could be macroeconomic indicators that are available monthly. Additionally, as will be examined later in this chapter, structural models are often not useful for out–of–sample forecasting. These observations motivate the consideration of pure time series models, which are the focus of this chapter.

The approach adopted for this topic is as follows. In order to define, estimate and use ARIMA models, one first needs to specify the notation and to define several important concepts. The chapter will then consider the properties and characteristics of a number of specific models from the ARIMA family. The book endeavours to answer the following question: 'For a specified time series model with given parameter values, what will be its defining characteristics?' Following this, the problem will be reversed, so that the reverse question is asked: 'Given a set of data, with characteristics that have been determined, what is a plausible model to describe that data?'

6.2 Some notation and concepts

The following sub–sections define and describe several important concepts in time series analysis. Each will be elucidated and drawn upon later in the chapter. The first of these concepts is the notion of whether a series is *stationary* or not. Determining whether a series is stationary or not is very important, for the stationarity or otherwise of a series can strongly influence its behaviour and properties. Further detailed discussion of stationarity, testing for it, and implications of it not being present, are covered in chapter 8.

6.2.1 A strictly stationary process

A strictly stationary process is one where, for any $t_1, t_2, \ldots, t_T \in Z$, any $k \in Z$ and $T = 1, 2, \ldots$

$$F_{y_{t_1}, y_{t_2}, \ldots, y_{t_T}}(y_1, \ldots, y_T) = F_{y_{t_1+k}, y_{t_2+k}, \ldots, y_{t_T+k}}(y_1, \ldots, y_T) \qquad (6.1)$$

where F denotes the joint distribution function of the set of random variables (Tong, 1990, p.3). It can also be stated that the probability measure for the sequence $\{y_t\}$ is the same as that for $\{y_{t+k}\} \forall k$ (where '$\forall k$' means 'for all values of k'). In other words, a series is strictly stationary if the distribution of its values remains the same as time progresses, implying that the probability that y falls within a particular interval is the same now as at any time in the past or the future.

6.2.2 A weakly stationary process

If a series satisfies (6.2)–(6.4) for $t = 1, 2, \ldots, \infty$, it is said to be weakly or covariance stationary

$$E(y_t) = \mu \qquad (6.2)$$

$$E(y_t - \mu)(y_t - \mu) = \sigma^2 < \infty \qquad (6.3)$$

$$E(y_{t_1} - \mu)(y_{t_2} - \mu) = \gamma_{t_2-t_1} \quad \forall t_1, t_2 \qquad (6.4)$$

These three equations state that a stationary process should have a constant mean, a constant variance and a constant autocovariance structure, respectively. Definitions of the mean and variance of a random variable are probably well known to readers, but the autocovariances may not be.

The autocovariances determine how y is related to its previous values, and for a stationary series they depend only on the difference between t_1 and t_2, so that the covariance between y_t and y_{t-1} is the same as the covariance between y_{t-10} and y_{t-11}, etc. The moment

$$E(y_t - E(y_t))(y_{t-s} - E(y_{t-s})) = \gamma_s, s = 0, 1, 2, \ldots \tag{6.5}$$

is known as the *autocovariance function*. When $s = 0$, the autocovariance at lag zero is obtained, which is the autocovariance of y_t with y_t, i.e. the variance of y. These covariances, γ_s, are also known as autocovariances since they are the covariances of y with its own previous values. The autocovariances are not a particularly useful measure of the relationship between y and its previous values, however, since the values of the autocovariances depend on the units of measurement of y_t, and hence the values that they take have no immediate interpretation.

It is thus more convenient to use the autocorrelations, which are the autocovariances normalised by dividing by the variance

$$\tau_s = \frac{\gamma_s}{\gamma_0}, \quad s = 0, 1, 2, \ldots \tag{6.6}$$

The series τ_s now has the standard property of correlation coefficients that the values are bounded to lie between ± 1. In the case that $s = 0$, the autocorrelation at lag zero is obtained, i.e. the correlation of y_t with y_t, which is of course 1. If τ_s is plotted against $s = 0, 1, 2, \ldots$, a graph known as the *autocorrelation function* (acf) or *correlogram* is obtained.

6.2.3 A white noise process

Roughly speaking, a white noise process is one with no discernible structure. A definition of a white noise process is

$$E(y_t) = \mu \tag{6.7}$$

$$\text{var}(y_t) = \sigma^2 \tag{6.8}$$

$$\gamma_{t-r} = \begin{cases} \sigma^2 & \text{if} \quad t = r \\ 0 & \text{otherwise} \end{cases} \tag{6.9}$$

Thus a white noise process has constant mean and variance, and zero autocovariances, except at lag zero. Another way to state this last condition would be to say that each observation is uncorrelated with all other values in the sequence. Hence the autocorrelation function for a white noise process will be zero apart from a single peak of 1 at $s = 0$. If $\mu = 0$, and the three conditions hold, the process is known as zero mean white noise.

If it is further assumed that y_t is distributed normally, then the sample auto-correlation coefficients are also approximately normally distributed

$$\hat{\tau}_s \sim approx.\ N(0, 1/T)$$

where T is the sample size, and $\hat{\tau}_s$ denotes the autocorrelation coefficient at lag s estimated from a sample. This result can be used to conduct significance tests for the autocorrelation coefficients by constructing a non-rejection region (like a confidence interval) for an estimated autocorrelation coefficient to determine whether it is significantly different from zero. For example, a 95% non-rejection region would be given by

$$\pm 1.96 \times \frac{1}{\sqrt{T}}$$

for $s \neq 0$. If the sample autocorrelation coefficient, $\hat{\tau}_s$, falls outside this region for a given value of s, then the null hypothesis that the true value of the coefficient at that lag s is zero is rejected.

It is also possible to test the joint hypothesis that all m of the τ_k correlation coefficients are simultaneously equal to zero using the Q-statistic developed by Box and Pierce (1970)

$$Q = T \sum_{k=1}^{m} \hat{\tau}_k^2 \tag{6.10}$$

where T = sample size, m = maximum lag length.

The correlation coefficients are squared so that the positive and negative coefficients do not cancel each other out. Since the sum of squares of independent standard normal variates is itself a χ^2 variate with degrees of freedom equal to the number of squares in the sum, it can be stated that the Q-statistic is asymptotically distributed as a χ_m^2 under the null hypothesis that all m autocorrelation coefficients are zero. As for any joint hypothesis test, only one autocorrelation coefficient needs to be statistically significant for the test to result in a rejection.

However, the Box–Pierce test has poor small sample properties, implying that it leads to the wrong decision too frequently for small samples. A variant of the Box–Pierce test, having better small sample properties, has been developed. The modified statistic is known as the Ljung–Box (1978) statistic

$$Q^* = T(T+2) \sum_{k=1}^{m} \frac{\hat{\tau}_k^2}{T-k} \sim \chi_m^2 \tag{6.11}$$

It should be clear from the form of the statistic that asymptotically (that is, as the sample size increases towards infinity), the $(T+2)$ and $(T-k)$ terms in the Ljung–Box formulation will cancel out, so that the statistic is equivalent to the Box–Pierce test. This statistic is very useful as a portmanteau (general) test of linear dependence in time series.

Example 6.1

Suppose that a researcher had estimated the first five autocorrelation coefficients using a series of length 100 observations, and found them to be

Lag	1	2	3	4	5
Autocorrelation coefficient	0.207	−0.013	0.086	0.005	−0.022

Test each of the individual correlation coefficients for significance, and test all five jointly using the Box–Pierce and Ljung–Box tests.

A 95% confidence interval can be constructed for each coefficient using

$$\pm 1.96 \times \frac{1}{\sqrt{T}}$$

where $T = 100$ in this case. The decision rule is thus to reject the null hypothesis that a given coefficient is zero in the cases where the coefficient lies outside the range $(-0.196, +0.196)$. For this example, it would be concluded that only the first autocorrelation coefficient is significantly different from zero at the 5% level.

Now, turning to the joint tests, the null hypothesis is that all of the first five autocorrelation coefficients are jointly zero, i.e.

$$H_0 : \tau_1 = 0, \tau_2 = 0, \tau_3 = 0, \tau_4 = 0, \tau_5 = 0$$

The test statistics for the Box–Pierce and Ljung–Box tests are given respectively as

$$Q = 100 \times (0.207^2 + -0.013^2 + 0.086^2 + 0.005^2 + -0.022^2)$$
$$= 5.09 \tag{6.12}$$

$$Q^* = 100 \times 102 \times \left(\frac{0.207^2}{100 - 1} + \frac{-0.013^2}{100 - 2} + \frac{0.086^2}{100 - 3} \right.$$

$$\left. + \frac{0.005^2}{100 - 4} + \frac{-0.022^2}{100 - 5} \right) = 5.26 \tag{6.13}$$

The relevant critical values are from a χ^2 distribution with five degrees of freedom, which are 11.1 at the 5% level, and 15.1 at the 1% level. Clearly, in both cases, the joint null hypothesis that all of the first five autocorrelation coefficients are zero cannot be rejected. Note that, in this instance, the individual test caused a rejection while the joint test did not. This is an unexpected result that may have arisen as a result of the low power of the joint test when four of the five individual autocorrelation coefficients are insignificant. Thus the effect of the significant autocorrelation coefficient is diluted in the joint test by the insignificant coefficients. The sample size used in this example is also modest relative to those commonly available in finance.

6.3   Moving average processes

The simplest class of time series model that one could entertain is that of the moving average process. Let u_t $(t = 1, 2, 3, \ldots)$ be a white noise process with $E(u_t) = 0$ and $var(u_t) = \sigma^2$. Then

$$y_t = \mu + u_t + \theta_1 u_{t-1} + \theta_2 u_{t-2} + \cdots + \theta_q u_{t-q} \tag{6.14}$$

is a qth order moving average model, denoted MA(q). This can be expressed using sigma notation as

$$y_t = \mu + \sum_{i=1}^{q} \theta_i u_{t-i} + u_t \tag{6.15}$$

A moving average model is simply a linear combination of white noise processes, so that y_t depends on the current and previous values of a white noise disturbance term. Equation (6.15) will later have to be manipulated, and such a process is most easily achieved by introducing the lag operator notation. This would be written $Ly_t = y_{t-1}$ to denote that y_t is lagged once. In order to show that the ith lag of y_t is being taken (that is, the value that y_t took i periods ago), the notation would be $L^i y_t = y_{t-i}$. Note that in some books and studies, the lag operator is referred to as the 'backshift operator', denoted by B. Using the lag operator notation, (6.15) would be written as

$$y_t = \mu + \sum_{i=1}^{q} \theta_i L^i u_t + u_t \tag{6.16}$$

or as

$$y_t = \mu + \theta(L) u_t \tag{6.17}$$

where: $\theta(L) = 1 + \theta_1 L + \theta_2 L^2 + \cdots + \theta_q L^q$.

In much of what follows, the constant (μ) is dropped from the equations. Removing μ considerably eases the complexity of algebra involved, and is inconsequential for it can be achieved without loss of generality. To see this, consider a sample of observations on a series, z_t that has a mean $\bar{z}$. A zero-mean series, y_t can be constructed by simply subtracting $\bar{z}$ from each observation z_t.

The distinguishing properties of the moving average process of order q given above are

(1) $E(y_t) = \mu$ \hfill (6.18)

(2) $var(y_t) = \gamma_0 = \left(1 + \theta_1^2 + \theta_2^2 + \cdots + \theta_q^2\right)\sigma^2$ \hfill (6.19)

(3) covariances γ_s

$$= \begin{cases} (\theta_s + \theta_{s+1}\theta_1 + \theta_{s+2}\theta_2 + \cdots + \theta_q \theta_{q-s})\,\sigma^2 & for \ s = 1, 2, \ldots, q \\ 0 & for \ s > q \end{cases} \tag{6.20}$$

So, a moving average process has constant mean, constant variance, and autocovariances which may be non-zero to lag q and will always be zero thereafter. Each of these results will be derived below.

Example 6.2

Consider the following MA(2) process

$$y_t = u_t + \theta_1 u_{t-1} + \theta_2 u_{t-2} \tag{6.21}$$

where u_t is a zero mean white noise process with variance σ^2.

(1) Calculate the mean and variance of y_t.
(2) Derive the autocorrelation function for this process (i.e. express the autocorrelations, $\tau_1, \tau_2, \ldots$ as functions of the parameters θ_1 and θ_2).
(3) If $\theta_1 = -0.5$ and $\theta_2 = 0.25$, sketch the acf of y_t.

Solution

(1) If $E(u_t) = 0$, then $E(u_{t-i}) = 0 \; \forall \; i$ (6.22)

So the expected value of the error term is zero for all time periods. Taking expectations of both sides of (6.21) gives

$$E(y_t) = E(u_t + \theta_1 u_{t-1} + \theta_2 u_{t-2})$$

$$= E(u_t) + \theta_1 E(u_{t-1}) + \theta_2 E(u_{t-2}) = 0 \tag{6.23}$$

$$\text{var}(y_t) = E[y_t - E(y_t)][y_t - E(y_t)] \tag{6.24}$$

but $E(y_t) = 0$, so that the last component in each set of square brackets in (6.24) is zero and this reduces to

$$\text{var}(y_t) = E[(y_t)(y_t)] \tag{6.25}$$

Replacing y_t in (6.25) with the RHS of (6.21)

$$\text{var}(y_t) = E[(u_t + \theta_1 u_{t-1} + \theta_2 u_{t-2})(u_t - \theta_1 u_{t-1} + \theta_2 u_{t-2})] \tag{6.26}$$

$$\text{var}(y_t) = E\left[u_t^2 + \theta_1^2 u_{t-1}^2 + \theta_2^2 u_{t-2}^2 + \textit{cross-products}\right] \tag{6.27}$$

But $E[\textit{cross-products}] = 0$ since $\text{cov}(u_t, u_{t-s}) = 0$ for $s \neq 0$. 'Cross-products' is thus a catchall expression for all of the terms in u which have different time subscripts, such as $u_{t-1}u_{t-2}$ or $u_{t-5}u_{t-20}$, etc. Again, one does not need to worry about these cross-product terms, since these are effectively the autocovariances of u_t, which will all be zero by definition since u_t is a random error process, which will have zero autocovariances (except at lag zero). So

$$\text{var}(y_t) = \gamma_0 = E\left[u_t^2 + \theta_1^2 u_{t-1}^2 + \theta_2^2 u_{t-2}^2\right] \tag{6.28}$$

$$\text{var}(y_t) = \gamma_0 = \sigma^2 + \theta_1^2 \sigma^2 + \theta_2^2 \sigma^2 \tag{6.29}$$

$$\text{var}(y_t) = \gamma_0 = \left(1 + \theta_1^2 + \theta_2^2\right)\sigma^2 \tag{6.30}$$

γ_0 can also be interpreted as the autocovariance at lag zero.

(2) Calculating now the acf of y_t, first determine the autocovariances and then the autocorrelations by dividing the autocovariances by the variance.

The autocovariance at lag 1 is given by

$$\gamma_1 = E[y_t - E(y_t)][y_{t-1} - E(y_{t-1})] \tag{6.31}$$

$$\gamma_1 = E[y_t][y_{t-1}] \tag{6.32}$$

$$\gamma_1 = E[(u_t + \theta_1 u_{t-1} + \theta_2 u_{t-2})(u_{t-1} + \theta_1 u_{t-2} + \theta_2 u_{t-3})] \tag{6.33}$$

Again, ignoring the cross-products, (6.33) can be written as

$$\gamma_1 = E\left[\left(\theta_1 u_{t-1}^2 + \theta_1 \theta_2 u_{t-2}^2\right)\right] \tag{6.34}$$

$$\gamma_1 = \theta_1 \sigma^2 + \theta_1 \theta_2 \sigma^2 \tag{6.35}$$

$$\gamma_1 = (\theta_1 + \theta_1 \theta_2)\sigma^2 \tag{6.36}$$

The autocovariance at lag 2 is given by

$$\gamma_2 = E[y_t - E(y_t)][y_{t-2} - E(y_{t-2})] \tag{6.37}$$

$$\gamma_2 = E[y_t][y_{t-2}] \tag{6.38}$$

$$\gamma_2 = E[(u_t + \theta_1 u_{t-1} + \theta_2 u_{t-2})(u_{t-2} + \theta_1 u_{t-3} + \theta_2 u_{t-4})] \tag{6.39}$$

$$\gamma_2 = E\left[\left(\theta_2 u_{t-2}^2\right)\right] \tag{6.40}$$

$$\gamma_2 = \theta_2 \sigma^2 \tag{6.41}$$

The autocovariance at lag 3 is given by

$$\gamma_3 = E[y_t - E(y_t)][y_{t-3} - E(y_{t-3})] \tag{6.42}$$

$$\gamma_3 = E[y_t][y_{t-3}] \tag{6.43}$$

$$\gamma_3 = E[(u_t + \theta_1 u_{t-1} + \theta_2 u_{t-2})(u_{t-3} + \theta_1 u_{t-4} + \theta_2 u_{t-5})] \tag{6.44}$$

$$\gamma_3 = 0 \tag{6.45}$$

So $\gamma_s = 0$ for $s > 2$. All autocovariances for the MA(2) process will be zero for any lag length, s, greater than 2.

The autocorrelation at lag 0 is given by

$$\tau_0 = \frac{\gamma_0}{\gamma_0} = 1 \tag{6.46}$$

The autocorrelation at lag 1 is given by

$$\tau_1 = \frac{\gamma_1}{\gamma_0} = \frac{(\theta_1 + \theta_1 \theta_2)\sigma^2}{\left(1 + \theta_1^2 + \theta_2^2\right)\sigma^2} = \frac{(\theta_1 + \theta_1 \theta_2)}{\left(1 + \theta_1^2 + \theta_2^2\right)} \tag{6.47}$$

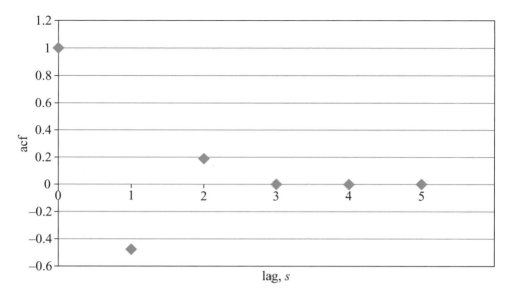

Figure 6.1   Autocorrelation function for sample MA(2) process

The autocorrelation at lag 2 is given by

$$\tau_2 = \frac{\gamma_2}{\gamma_0} = \frac{(\theta_2)\sigma^2}{\left(1 + \theta_1^2 + \theta_2^2\right)\sigma^2} = \frac{\theta_2}{\left(1 + \theta_1^2 + \theta_2^2\right)} \tag{6.48}$$

The autocorrelation at lag 3 is given by

$$\tau_3 = \frac{\gamma_3}{\gamma_0} = 0 \tag{6.49}$$

The autocorrelation at lag s is given by

$$\tau_s = \frac{\gamma_s}{\gamma_0} = 0 \ \forall \ s > 2 \tag{6.50}$$

(3) For $\theta_1 = -0.5$ and $\theta_2 = 0.25$, substituting these into the formulae above gives the first two autocorrelation coefficients as $\tau_1 = -0.476$, $\tau_2 = 0.190$. Autocorrelation coefficients for lags greater than 2 will all be zero for an MA(2) model. Thus the acf plot will appear as in figure 6.1.

6.4 Autoregressive processes

An autoregressive model is one where the current value of a variable, y, depends upon only the values that the variable took in previous periods plus an error term. An autoregressive model of order p, denoted as AR(p), can be expressed as

$$y_t = \mu + \phi_1 y_{t-1} + \phi_2 y_{t-2} + \cdots + \phi_p y_{t-p} + u_t \tag{6.51}$$

where u_t is a white noise disturbance term. A manipulation of expression (6.51) will be required to demonstrate the properties of an autoregressive model. This expression can be written more compactly using sigma notation

$$y_t = \mu + \sum_{i=1}^{p} \phi_i y_{t-i} + u_t \tag{6.52}$$

or using the lag operator, as

$$y_t = \mu + \sum_{i=1}^{p} \phi_i L^i y_t + u_t \tag{6.53}$$

or

$$\phi(L) y_t = \mu + u_t \tag{6.54}$$

where $\phi(L) = (1 - \phi_1 L - \phi_2 L^2 - \cdots - \phi_p L^p)$.

Box 6.1   The stationarity condition for an AR(p) model

Setting μ to zero in (6.54), for a zero mean AR(p) process, y_t, given by

$$\phi(L) y_t = u_t \tag{6.55}$$

it would be stated that the process is stationary if it is possible to write

$$y_t = \phi(L)^{-1} u_t \tag{6.56}$$

with $\phi(L)^{-1}$ converging to zero. This means that the autocorrelations will decline eventually as the lag length is increased. When the expansion $\phi(L)^{-1}$ is calculated, it will contain an infinite number of terms, and can be written as an MA(∞), e.g. $a_1 u_{t-1} + a_2 u_{t-2} + a_3 u_{t-3} + \cdots + u_t$. If the process given by (6.54) is stationary, the coefficients in the MA(∞) representation will decline eventually with lag length. On the other hand, if the process is non-stationary, the coefficients in the MA(∞) representation would not converge to zero as the lag length increases.

The condition for testing for the stationarity of a general AR(p) model is that the roots of the 'characteristic equation'

$$1 - \phi_1 z - \phi_2 z^2 - \cdots - \phi_p z^p = 0 \tag{6.57}$$

all lie outside the unit circle. The notion of a characteristic equation is so-called because its roots determine the characteristics of the process y_t — for example, the acf for an AR process will depend on the roots of this characteristic equation, which is a polynomial in z.

6.4.1 The stationarity condition

Stationarity is a desirable property of an estimated AR model, for several reasons. One important reason is that a model whose coefficients are non-stationary will exhibit the unfortunate property that previous values of the error term will have a non-declining effect on the current value of y_t as time progresses. This is arguably counter-intuitive and empirically implausible in many cases. More discussion on this issue will be presented in chapter 8. Box 6.1 defines the stationarity condition algebraically.

Example 6.3

Is the following model stationary?

$$y_t = y_{t-1} + u_t \tag{6.58}$$

In order to test this, first write y_{t-1} in lag operator notation (i.e. as Ly_t), and take this term over to the LHS of (6.58), and factorise

$$y_t = Ly_t + u_t \tag{6.59}$$

$$y_t - Ly_t = u_t \tag{6.60}$$

$$y_t(1 - L) = u_t \tag{6.61}$$

Then the characteristic equation is

$$1 - z = 0, \tag{6.62}$$

having the root $z = 1$, which lies on, not outside, the unit circle. In fact, the particular AR(p) model given by (6.58) is a non-stationary process known as a random walk (see chapter 8).

This procedure can also be adopted for autoregressive models with longer lag lengths and where the stationarity or otherwise of the process is less obvious. For example, is the following process for y_t stationary?

$$y_t = 3y_{t-1} - 2.75y_{t-2} + 0.75y_{t-3} + u_t \tag{6.63}$$

Again, the first stage is to express this equation using the lag operator notation, and then taking all the terms in y over to the left hand side (LHS)

$$y_t = 3Ly_t - 2.75L^2y_t + 0.75L^3y_t + u_t \tag{6.64}$$

$$(1 - 3L + 2.75L^2 - 0.75L^3)y_t = u_t \tag{6.65}$$

The characteristic equation is

$$1 - 3z + 2.75z^2 - 0.75z^3 = 0 \tag{6.66}$$

which fortunately factorises to

$$(1 - z)(1 - 1.5z)(1 - 0.5z) = 0 \tag{6.67}$$

so that the roots are $z = 1$, $z = 2/3$, and $z = 2$. Only one of these lies outside the unit circle and hence the process for y_t described by (6.63) is not stationary.

6.4.2 Wold's decomposition theorem

Wold's decomposition theorem states that any stationary series can be decomposed into the sum of two unrelated processes, a purely deterministic part and a purely stochastic part, which will be an MA(∞). A simpler way of stating this in the context of AR modelling is that any stationary autoregressive process of order p with no constant and no other terms can be expressed as an infinite order moving average model. This result is important for deriving the autocorrelation function for an autoregressive process.

For the AR(p) model, given in, for example, (6.51) (with μ set to zero for simplicity) and expressed using the lag polynomial notation, $\phi(L)y_t = u_t$, the Wold decomposition is

$$y_t = \psi(L)u_t \tag{6.68}$$

where $\psi(L) = \phi(L)^{-1} = (1 - \phi_1 L - \phi_2 L^2 - \cdots - \phi_p L^p)^{-1}$

The characteristics of an autoregressive process are as follows. The (unconditional) mean of y is given by

$$E(y_t) = \frac{\mu}{1 - \phi_1 - \phi_2 - \cdots - \phi_p} \tag{6.69}$$

The autocovariances and autocorrelation functions can be obtained by solving a set of simultaneous equations known as the Yule–Walker equations. The Yule–Walker equations express the correlogram (the τs) as a function of the autoregressive coefficients (the ϕs)

$$\tau_1 = \phi_1 + \tau_1 \phi_2 + \cdots + \tau_{p-1} \phi_p$$
$$\tau_2 = \tau_1 \phi_1 + \phi_2 + \cdots + \tau_{p-2} \phi_p$$

$$\vdots \quad \vdots \quad \vdots \tag{6.70}$$

$$\tau_p = \tau_{p-1} \phi_1 + \tau_{p-2} \phi_2 + \cdots + \phi_p$$

For any AR model that is stationary, the autocorrelation function will decay geometrically to zero.[1] These characteristics of an autoregressive process will be derived from first principles below using an illustrative example.

Example 6.4

Consider the following simple AR(1) model

$$y_t = \mu + \phi_1 y_{t-1} + u_t \tag{6.71}$$

---

[1] Note that the τ_s will not follow an exact geometric sequence, but rather the absolute value of the τ_s is bounded by a geometric series. This means that the autocorrelation function does not have to be monotonically decreasing and may change sign.

(1) Calculate the (unconditional) mean of y_t.
    For the remainder of the question, set the constant to zero ($\mu = 0$) for simplicity.
(2) Calculate the (unconditional) variance of y_t.
(3) Derive the autocorrelation function for this process.

Solution

(i) The unconditional mean will be given by the expected value of expression (6.71)

$$E(y_t) = E(\mu + \phi_1 y_{t-1}) \tag{6.72}$$

$$E(y_t) = \mu + \phi_1 E(y_{t-1}) \tag{6.73}$$

But also

$$y_{t-1} = \mu + \phi_1 y_{t-2} + u_{t-1} \tag{6.74}$$

So, replacing y_{t-1} in (6.73) with the RHS of (6.74)

$$E(y_t) = \mu + \phi_1(\mu + \phi_1 E(y_{t-2})) \tag{6.75}$$

$$E(y_t) = \mu + \phi_1\mu + \phi_1^2 E(y_{t-2}) \tag{6.76}$$

Lagging (6.74) by a further one period

$$y_{t-2} = \mu + \phi_1 y_{t-3} + u_{t-2} \tag{6.77}$$

Repeating the steps given above one more time

$$E(y_t) = \mu + \phi_1\mu + \phi_1^2(\mu + \phi_1 E(y_{t-3})) \tag{6.78}$$

$$E(y_t) = \mu + \phi_1\mu + \phi_1^2\mu + \phi_1^3 E(y_{t-3}) \tag{6.79}$$

Hopefully, readers will by now be able to see a pattern emerging. Making n such substitutions would give

$$E(y_t) = \mu(1 + \phi_1 + \phi_1^2 + \cdots + \phi_1^{n-1}) + \phi_1^n E(y_{t-n}) \tag{6.80}$$

So long as the model is stationary, i.e. $|\phi_1| < 1$, then $\phi_1^\infty = 0$. Therefore, taking limits as $n \to \infty$, then $lim_{n\to\infty}\phi_1^t E(y_{t-n}) = 0$, and so

$$E(y_t) = \mu(1 + \phi_1 + \phi_1^2 + \cdots) \tag{6.81}$$

Recall the rule of algebra that the finite sum of an infinite number of geometrically declining terms in a series is given by 'first term in series divided by (1 minus common difference)', where the common difference is the quantity that each term in the series is multiplied by to arrive at the next term. It can thus be stated from (6.81) that

$$E(y_t) = \frac{\mu}{1 - \phi_1} \tag{6.82}$$

Thus the expected or mean value of an autoregressive process of order one is given by the intercept parameter divided by one minus the autoregressive coefficient.

(ii) Calculating now the variance of y_t, with μ set to zero

$$y_t = \phi_1 y_{t-1} + u_t \tag{6.83}$$

This can be written equivalently as

$$y_t(1 - \phi_1 L) = u_t \tag{6.84}$$

From Wold's decomposition theorem, the AR(p) can be expressed as an MA(∞)

$$y_t = (1 - \phi_1 L)^{-1} u_t \tag{6.85}$$

$$y_t = \left(1 + \phi_1 L + \phi_1^2 L^2 + \cdots\right) u_t \tag{6.86}$$

or

$$y_t = u_t + \phi_1 u_{t-1} + \phi_1^2 u_{t-2} + \phi_1^3 u_{t-3} + \cdots \tag{6.87}$$

So long as $|\phi_1| < 1$, i.e. so long as the process for y_t is stationary, this sum will converge.

From the definition of the variance of any random variable y, it is possible to write

$$\text{var}(y_t) = \text{E}[y_t - \text{E}(y_t)][y_t - \text{E}(y_t)] \tag{6.88}$$

but $\text{E}(y_t) = 0$, since μ is set to zero to obtain (6.83) above. Thus

$$\text{var}(y_t) = \text{E}[(y_t)(y_t)] \tag{6.89}$$

$$\text{var}(y_t) = \text{E}\left[\left(u_t + \phi_1 u_{t-1} + \phi_1^2 u_{t-2} + \cdots\right)\left(u_t + \phi_1 u_{t-1} + \phi_1^2 u_{t-2} + \cdots\right)\right] \tag{6.90}$$

$$\text{var}(y_t) = \text{E}\left[u_t^2 + \phi_1^2 u_{t-1}^2 + \phi_1^4 u_{t-2}^2 + \cdots + \textit{cross-products}\right] \tag{6.91}$$

As discussed above, the 'cross-products' can be set to zero.

$$\text{var}(y_t) = \gamma_0 = \text{E}\left[u_t^2 + \phi_1^2 u_{t-1}^2 + \phi_1^4 u_{t-2}^2 + \cdots\right] \tag{6.92}$$

$$\text{var}(y_t) = \sigma^2 + \phi_1^2 \sigma^2 + \phi_1^4 \sigma^2 + \cdots \tag{6.93}$$

$$\text{var}(y_t) = \sigma^2 \left(1 + \phi_1^2 + \phi_1^4 + \cdots\right) \tag{6.94}$$

Provided that $|\phi_1| < 1$, the infinite sum in (6.94) can be written as

$$\text{var}(y_t) = \frac{\sigma^2}{\left(1 - \phi_1^2\right)} \tag{6.95}$$

(iii) Turning now to the calculation of the autocorrelation function, the auto-covariances must first be calculated. This is achieved by following similar algebraic manipulations as for the variance above, starting with the definition of the autocovariances for a random variable. The autocovariances for lags 1, 2, 3, ... , s, will be denoted by $\gamma_1, \gamma_2, \gamma_3, \ldots, \gamma_s$, as previously.

$$\gamma_1 = \text{cov}\,(y_t, y_{t-1}) = E[y_t - E(y_t)][y_{t-1} - E(y_{t-1})] \tag{6.96}$$

Since μ has been set to zero, $E(y_t) = 0$ and $E(y_{t-1}) = 0$, so

$$\gamma_1 = E[y_t y_{t-1}] \tag{6.97}$$

under the result above that $E(y_t) = E(y_{t-1}) = 0$. Thus

$$\gamma_1 = E\left[\left(u_t + \phi_1 u_{t-1} + \phi_1^2 u_{t-2} + \cdots\right)\left(u_{t-1} + \phi_1 u_{t-2} + \phi_1^2 u_{t-3} + \cdots\right)\right] \tag{6.98}$$

$$\gamma_1 = E\left[\phi_1 u_{t-1}^2 + \phi_1^3 u_{t-2}^2 + \cdots + cross\text{-}products\right] \tag{6.99}$$

Again, the cross-products can be ignored so that

$$\gamma_1 = \phi_1 \sigma^2 + \phi_1^3 \sigma^2 + \phi_1^5 \sigma^2 + \cdots \tag{6.100}$$

$$\gamma_1 = \phi_1 \sigma^2 \left(1 + \phi_1^2 + \phi_1^4 + \cdots\right) \tag{6.101}$$

$$\gamma_1 = \frac{\phi_1 \sigma^2}{\left(1 - \phi_1^2\right)} \tag{6.102}$$

For the second autocovariance,

$$\gamma_2 = \text{cov}(y_t, y_{t-2}) = E[y_t - E(y_t)][y_{t-2} - E(y_{t-2})] \tag{6.103}$$

Using the same rules as applied above for the lag 1 covariance

$$\gamma_2 = E[y_t y_{t-2}] \tag{6.104}$$

$$\gamma_2 = E\left[\left(u_t + \phi_1 u_{t-1} + \phi_1^2 u_{t-2} + \cdots\right)\left(u_{t-2} + \phi_1 u_{t-3} + \phi_1^2 u_{t-4} + \cdots\right)\right] \tag{6.105}$$

$$\gamma_2 = E\left[\phi_1^2 u_{t-2}^2 + \phi_1^4 u_{t-3}^2 + \cdots + cross\text{-}products\right] \tag{6.106}$$

$$\gamma_2 = \phi_1^2 \sigma^2 + \phi_1^4 \sigma^2 + \cdots \tag{6.107}$$

$$\gamma_2 = \phi_1^2 \sigma^2 \left(1 + \phi_1^2 + \phi_1^4 + \cdots\right) \tag{6.108}$$

$$\gamma_2 = \frac{\phi_1^2 \sigma^2}{\left(1 - \phi_1^2\right)} \tag{6.109}$$

By now it should be possible to see a pattern emerging. If these steps were repeated for γ_3, the following expression would be obtained

$$\gamma_3 = \frac{\phi_1^3 \sigma^2}{\left(1 - \phi_1^2\right)} \tag{6.110}$$

and for any lag s, the autocovariance would be given by

$$\gamma_s = \frac{\phi_1^s \sigma^2}{\left(1 - \phi_1^2\right)} \qquad (6.111)$$

The acf can now be obtained by dividing the covariances by the variance, so that

$$\tau_0 = \frac{\gamma_0}{\gamma_0} = 1 \qquad (6.112)$$

$$\tau_1 = \frac{\gamma_1}{\gamma_0} = \frac{\left(\dfrac{\phi_1 \sigma^2}{\left(1 - \phi_1^2\right)}\right)}{\left(\dfrac{\sigma^2}{\left(1 - \phi_1^2\right)}\right)} = \phi_1 \qquad (6.113)$$

$$\tau_2 = \frac{\gamma_2}{\gamma_0} = \frac{\left(\dfrac{\phi_1^2 \sigma^2}{\left(1 - \phi_1^2\right)}\right)}{\left(\dfrac{\sigma^2}{\left(1 - \phi_1^2\right)}\right)} = \phi_1^2 \qquad (6.114)$$

$$\tau_3 = \phi_1^3 \qquad (6.115)$$

The autocorrelation at lag s is given by

$$\tau_s = \phi_1^s \qquad (6.116)$$

which means that $\text{corr}(y_t, y_{t-s}) = \phi_1^s$. Note that use of the Yule–Walker equations would have given the same answer.

6.5 The partial autocorrelation function

The partial autocorrelation function, or pacf (denoted τ_{kk}), measures the correlation between an observation k periods ago and the current observation, after controlling for observations at intermediate lags (i.e. all lags $< k$) – i.e. the correlation between y_t and y_{t-k}, after removing the effects of $y_{t-k+1}, y_{t-k+2}, \ldots, y_{t-1}$. For example, the pacf for lag 3 would measure the correlation between y_t and y_{t-3} after controlling for the effects of y_{t-1} and y_{t-2}.

At lag 1, the autocorrelation and partial autocorrelation coefficients are equal, since there are no intermediate lag effects to eliminate. Thus, $\tau_{11} = \tau_1$, where τ_1 is the autocorrelation coefficient at lag 1.

At lag 2

$$\tau_{22} = \left(\tau_2 - \tau_1^2\right) / \left(1 - \tau_1^2\right) \qquad (6.117)$$

where τ_1 and τ_2 are the autocorrelation coefficients at lags 1 and 2, respectively. For lags greater than two, the formulae are more complex and hence a presentation of these is beyond the scope of this book. There now proceeds, however, an intuitive explanation of the characteristic shape of the pacf for a moving average and for an autoregressive process.

In the case of an autoregressive process of order p, there will be direct connections between y_t and y_{t-s} for $s \leq p$, but no direct connections for $s > p$. For example, consider the following AR(3) model

$$y_t = \phi_0 + \phi_1 y_{t-1} + \phi_2 y_{t-2} + \phi_3 y_{t-3} + u_t \tag{6.118}$$

There is a direct connection through the model between y_t and y_{t-1}, and between y_t and y_{t-2}, and between y_t and y_{t-3}, but not between y_t and y_{t-s}, for $s > 3$. Hence the pacf will usually have non-zero partial autocorrelation coefficients for lags up to the order of the model, but will have zero partial autocorrelation coefficients thereafter. In the case of the AR(3), only the first three partial autocorrelation coefficients will be non-zero.

What shape would the partial autocorrelation function take for a moving average process? One would need to think about the MA model as being transformed into an AR in order to consider whether y_t and y_{t-k}, $k = 1, 2, \ldots$, are directly connected. In fact, so long as the MA(q) process is invertible, it can be expressed as an AR(∞). Thus a definition of invertibility is now required.

6.5.1 The invertibility condition

An MA(q) model is typically required to have roots of the characteristic equation $\theta(z) = 0$ greater than one in absolute value. The invertibility condition is mathematically the same as the stationarity condition, but is different in the sense that the former refers to MA rather than AR processes. This condition prevents the model from exploding under an AR(∞) representation, so that $\theta^{-1}(L)$ converges to zero. Box 6.2 shows the invertibility condition for an MA(2) model.

Box 6.2   The invertibility condition for an MA(2) model

In order to examine the shape of the pacf for moving average processes, consider the following MA(2) process for y_t

$$y_t = u_t + \theta_1 u_{t-1} + \theta_2 u_{t-2} = \theta(L) u_t \tag{6.119}$$

Provided that this process is invertible, this MA(2) can be expressed as an AR(∞)

$$y_t = \sum_{i=1}^{\infty} c_i L^i y_{t-i} + u_t \tag{6.120}$$

$$y_t = c_1 y_{t-1} + c_2 y_{t-2} + c_3 y_{t-3} + \cdots + u_t \tag{6.121}$$

It is now evident when expressed in this way that for a moving average model, there are direct connections between the current value of y and all of its previous values. Thus, the partial autocorrelation function for an MA(q) model will decline geometrically, rather than dropping off to zero after q lags, as is the case for its autocorrelation function. It could thus be stated that the acf for an AR has the same basic shape as the pacf for an MA, and the acf for an MA has the same shape as the pacf for an AR.

6.6 ARMA processes

By combining the AR(p) and MA(q) models, an ARMA(p, q) model is obtained. Such a model states that the current value of some series y depends linearly on its own previous values plus a combination of current and previous values of a white noise error term. The model could be written

$$\phi(L)y_t = \mu + \theta(L)u_t \tag{6.122}$$

where

$$\phi(L) = 1 - \phi_1 L - \phi_2 L^2 - \cdots - \phi_p L^p \quad \text{and}$$

$$\theta(L) = 1 + \theta_1 L + \theta_2 L^2 + \cdots + \theta_q L^q$$

or

$$y_t = \mu + \phi_1 y_{t-1} + \phi_2 y_{t-2} + \cdots + \phi_p y_{t-p} + \theta_1 u_{t-1}$$

$$+ \theta_2 u_{t-2} + \cdots + \theta_q u_{t-q} + u_t \tag{6.123}$$

with

$$E(u_t) = 0; E\left(u_t^2\right) = \sigma^2; E(u_t u_s) = 0, t \neq s$$

The characteristics of an ARMA process will be a combination of those from the autoregressive (AR) and moving average (MA) parts. Note that the pacf is particularly useful in this context. The acf alone can distinguish between a pure autoregressive and a pure moving average process. However, an ARMA process will have a geometrically declining acf, as will a pure AR process. So, the pacf is useful for distinguishing between an AR(p) process and an ARMA(p, q) process – the former will have a geometrically declining autocorrelation function, but a partial autocorrelation function which cuts off to zero after p lags, while the latter will have both autocorrelation and partial autocorrelation functions which decline geometrically.

We can now summarise the defining characteristics of AR, MA and ARMA processes.

An autoregressive process has:

- a geometrically decaying acf
- a number of non-zero points of pacf = AR order.

A moving average process has:

- number of non-zero points of acf = MA order
- a geometrically decaying pacf.

A combination autoregressive moving average process has:

- a geometrically decaying acf
- a geometrically decaying pacf.

In fact, the mean of an ARMA series is given by

$$E(y_t) = \frac{\mu}{1 - \phi_1 - \phi_2 - \cdots - \phi_p} \qquad (6.124)$$

The autocorrelation function will display combinations of behaviour derived from the AR and MA parts, but for lags beyond q, the acf will simply be identical to the individual AR(p) model, so that the AR part will dominate in the long term. Deriving the acf and pacf for an ARMA process requires no new algebra, but is tedious and hence is left as an exercise for interested readers.

6.6.1 Sample acf and pacf plots for standard processes

Figures 6.2–6.8 give some examples of typical processes from the ARMA family with their characteristic autocorrelation and partial autocorrelation functions. The acf and pacf are not produced analytically from the relevant formulae for a model of that type, but rather are estimated using 100,000 simulated observations with disturbances drawn from a normal distribution. Each figure also has 5% (two-sided) rejection bands represented by dotted lines. These are based on $(\pm 1.96/\sqrt{100000}) = \pm 0.0062$, calculated in the same way as given above. Notice how, in each case, the acf and pacf are identical for the first lag.

In figure 6.2, the MA(1) has an acf that is significant for only lag 1, while the pacf declines geometrically, and is significant until lag 7. The acf at lag 1 and all of the pacfs are negative as a result of the negative coefficient in the MA generating process.

Again, the structures of the acf and pacf in figure 6.3 are as anticipated. The first two autocorrelation coefficients only are significant, while the partial autocorrelation coefficients are geometrically declining. Note also that, since the second coefficient on the lagged error term in the MA is negative, the acf and pacf alternate between positive and negative. In the case of the pacf, we term this alternating and declining function a 'damped sine wave' or 'damped sinusoid'.

For the autoregressive model of order 1 with a fairly high coefficient – i.e. relatively close to 1 – the autocorrelation function would be expected to die away relatively slowly, and this is exactly what is observed here in figure 6.4. Again, as expected for an AR(1), only the first pacf coefficient is significant, while all others are virtually zero and are not significant.

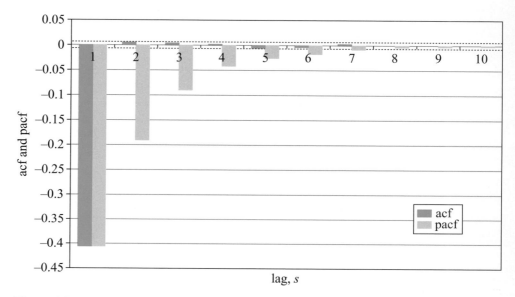

Figure 6.2   Sample autocorrelation and partial autocorrelation functions for an MA(1) model: $y_t = -0.5u_{t-1} + u_t$

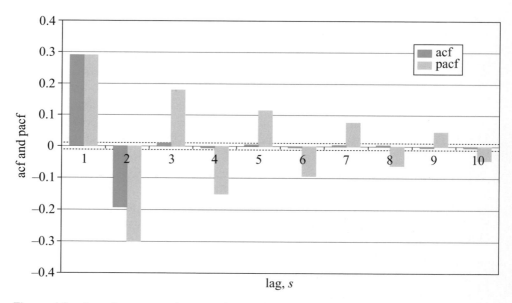

Figure 6.3   Sample autocorrelation and partial autocorrelation functions for an MA(2) model: $y_t = 0.5u_{t-1} - 0.25u_{t-2} + u_t$

Figure 6.5 plots an AR(1), which was generated using identical error terms, but a much smaller autoregressive coefficient. In this case, the autocorrelation function dies away much more quickly than in the previous example, and in fact becomes insignificant after around five lags.

Figure 6.6 shows the acf and pacf for an identical AR(1) process to that used for figure 6.5, except that the autoregressive coefficient is now negative. This results

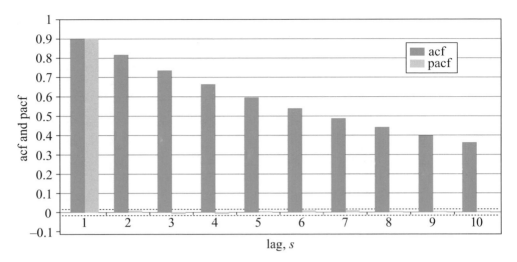

Figure 6.4   Sample autocorrelation and partial autocorrelation functions for a slowly decaying AR(1) model: $y_t = 0.9y_{t-1} + u_t$

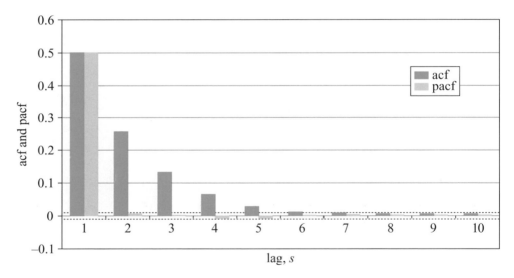

Figure 6.5   Sample autocorrelation and partial autocorrelation functions for a more rapidly decaying AR(1) model: $y_t = 0.5y_{t-1} + u_t$

in a damped sinusoidal pattern for the acf, which again becomes insignificant after around lag 5. Recalling that the autocorrelation coefficient for this AR(1) at lag s is equal to $(-0.5)^s$, this will be positive for even s, and negative for odd s. Only the first pacf coefficient is significant (and negative).

Figure 6.7 plots the acf and pacf for a non-stationary series (see chapter 8 for an extensive discussion) that has a unit coefficient on the lagged dependent variable. The result is that shocks to y never die away, and persist indefinitely in the system. Consequently, the acf function remains relatively flat at unity, even up to lag 10. In fact, even by lag 10, the autocorrelation coefficient has fallen only to 0.9989.

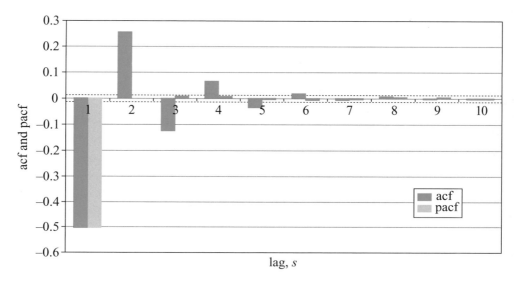

Figure 6.6   Sample autocorrelation and partial autocorrelation functions for a more rapidly decaying AR(1) model with negative coefficient: $y_t = -0.5y_{t-1} + u_t$

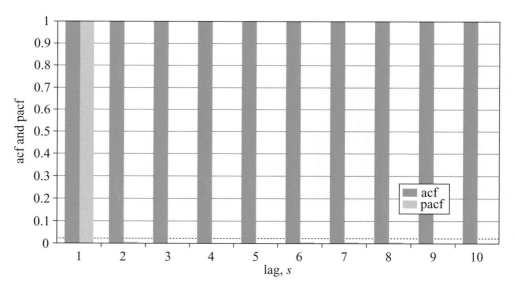

Figure 6.7   Sample autocorrelation and partial autocorrelation functions for a non-stationary model (i.e. a unit coefficient): $y_t = y_{t-1} + u_t$

Note also that on some occasions, the acf does die away, rather than looking like figure 6.7, even for such a non-stationary process, owing to its inherent instability combined with finite computer precision. The pacf, however, is significant only for lag 1, correctly suggesting that an autoregressive model with no moving average term is most appropriate.

Finally, figure 6.8 plots the acf and pacf for a mixed ARMA process. As one would expect of such a process, both the acf and the pacf decline geometrically – the acf as a result of the AR part and the pacf as a result of the MA part. The

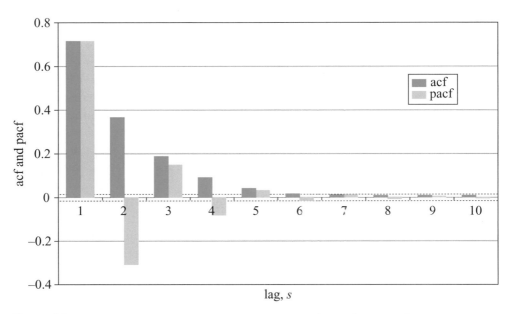

Figure 6.8   Sample autocorrelation and partial autocorrelation functions for an ARMA(1, 1) model: $y_t = 0.5y_{t-1} + 0.5u_{t-1} + u_t$

coefficients on the AR and MA are, however, sufficiently small that both acf and pacf coefficients have become insignificant by lag 6.

6.7 Building ARMA models: the Box–Jenkins approach

Although the existence of ARMA models predates them, Box and Jenkins (1976) were the first to approach the task of estimating an ARMA model in a systematic manner. Their approach was a practical and pragmatic one, involving three steps:

(1) Identification
(2) Estimation
(3) Diagnostic checking.

These steps are now explained in greater detail.

Step 1

This involves *determining the order of the model required* to capture the dynamic features of the data. Graphical procedures are used (plotting the data over time and plotting the acf and pacf) to determine the most appropriate specification.

Step 2

This involves *estimation of the parameters of the model* specified in step 1. This can be done using least squares or another technique, known as maximum likelihood, depending on the model.

Step 3

This involves *model checking* – i.e. determining whether the model specified and estimated is adequate. Box and Jenkins suggest two methods: overfitting and residual diagnostics. *Overfitting* involves deliberately fitting a larger model than that required to capture the dynamics of the data as identified in stage 1. If the model specified at step 1 is adequate, any extra terms added to the ARMA model would be insignificant. *Residual diagnostics* imply checking the residuals for evidence of linear dependence which, if present, would suggest that the model originally specified was inadequate to capture the features of the data. The acf, pacf or Ljung–Box tests could be used.

It is worth noting that 'diagnostic testing' in the Box–Jenkins world essentially involves only autocorrelation tests rather than the whole barrage of tests outlined in chapter 5. Also, such approaches to determining the adequacy of the model could only reveal a model that is underparameterised ('too small') and would not reveal a model that is overparameterised ('too big').

Examining whether the residuals are free from autocorrelation is much more commonly used than overfitting, and this may partly have arisen since for ARMA models, it can give rise to common factors in the overfitted model that make estimation of this model difficult and the statistical tests ill behaved. For example, if the true model is an ARMA(1,1) and we deliberately then fit an ARMA(2,2) there will be a common factor so that not all of the parameters in the latter model can be identified. This problem does not arise with pure AR or MA models, only with mixed processes.

It is usually the objective to form a *parsimonious model*, which is one that describes all of the features of data of interest using as few parameters (i.e. as simple a model) as possible. A parsimonious model is desirable because:

- The residual sum of squares is *inversely proportional* to the number of degrees of freedom. A model which contains irrelevant lags of the variable or of the error term (and therefore unnecessary parameters) will usually lead to increased coefficient standard errors, implying that it will be more difficult to find significant relationships in the data. Whether an increase in the number of variables (i.e. a reduction in the number of degrees of freedom) will actually cause the estimated parameter standard errors to rise or fall will obviously depend on how much the RSS falls, and on the relative sizes of T and k. If T is very large relative to k, then the decrease in RSS is likely to outweigh the reduction in $T - k$ so that the standard errors fall. Hence 'large' models with many parameters are more often chosen when the sample size is large.

- Models that are profligate might be inclined to fit to data specific features, which would not be replicated out-of-sample. This means that the models may appear to fit the data very well, with perhaps a high value of R^2, but would give very inaccurate forecasts. Another interpretation of this concept, borrowed from physics, is that of the distinction between 'signal' and 'noise'. The idea is to fit a model which *captures the signal* (the important features of the data, or the underlying trends or patterns), but which does not try to fit a spurious model to the noise (the completely random aspect of the series).

6.7.1 Information criteria for ARMA model selection

The identification stage would now typically not be done using graphical plots of the acf and pacf. The reason is that when 'messy' real data is used, it unfortunately rarely exhibits the simple patterns of figures 6.2–6.8. This makes the acf and pacf very hard to interpret, and thus it is difficult to specify a model for the data. Another technique, which removes some of the subjectivity involved in interpreting the acf and pacf, is to use what are known as *information criteria*. Information criteria embody two factors: a term which is a function of the residual sum of squares (*RSS*), and some penalty for the loss of degrees of freedom from adding extra parameters. So, adding a new variable or an additional lag to a model will have two competing effects on the information criteria: the residual sum of squares will fall but the value of the penalty term will increase.

The object is to choose the number of parameters which minimises the value of the information criteria. So, adding an extra term will reduce the value of the criteria only if the fall in the residual sum of squares is sufficient to more than outweigh the increased value of the penalty term. There are several different criteria, which vary according to how stiff the penalty term is. The three most popular information criteria are Akaike's (1974) information criterion (*AIC*), Schwarz's (1978) Bayesian information criterion (*SBIC*) and the Hannan–Quinn criterion (*HQIC*). Algebraically, these are expressed, respectively, as

$$AIC = \ln(\hat{\sigma}^2) + \frac{2k}{T} \tag{6.125}$$

$$SBIC = \ln(\hat{\sigma}^2) + \frac{k}{T} \ln T \tag{6.126}$$

$$HQIC = \ln(\hat{\sigma}^2) + \frac{2k}{T} \ln(\ln(T)) \tag{6.127}$$

where $\hat{\sigma}^2$ is the residual variance (also equivalent to the residual sum of squares divided by the number of observations, T), $k = p + q + 1$ is the total number of parameters estimated and T is the sample size. The information criteria are actually minimised subject to $p \leq \bar{p}, q \leq \bar{q}$, i.e. an upper limit is specified on the number of moving average ($\bar{q}$) and/or autoregressive ($\bar{p}$) terms that will be considered.

It is worth noting that *SBIC* embodies a much stiffer penalty term than *AIC*, while *HQIC* is somewhere in between. The adjusted R^2 measure can also be viewed as an information criterion, although it is a very soft one, which would typically select the largest models of all.

6.7.2 Which criterion should be preferred if they suggest different model orders?

SBIC is strongly consistent (but inefficient) and *AIC* is not consistent, but is generally more efficient. In other words, *SBIC* will asymptotically deliver the correct model order, while *AIC* will deliver on average too large a model, even with an infinite amount of data. On the other hand, the average variation in selected model orders from different samples within a given population will be greater in the context of *SBIC* than *AIC*. Overall, then, no criterion is definitely superior to others.

6.7.3   ARIMA modelling

ARIMA modelling, as distinct from ARMA modelling, has the additional letter 'I' in the acronym, standing for 'integrated'. An *integrated autoregressive process* is one whose characteristic equation has a root on the unit circle. Typically researchers difference the variable as necessary and then build an ARMA model on those differenced variables. An ARMA(p, q) model in the variable differenced d times is equivalent to an ARIMA(p, d, q) model on the original data – see chapter 8 for further details. For the remainder of this chapter, it is assumed that the data used in model construction are stationary, or have been suitably transformed to make them stationary. Thus only ARMA models will be considered further.

6.8   Constructing ARMA models in EViews

6.8.1   Getting started

This example uses the monthly UK house price series which was already incorporated in an EViews workfile in chapter 1. There were a total of 268 monthly observations running from February 1991 (recall that the January observation was 'lost' in constructing the lagged value) to May 2013 for the percentage change in house price series.

    The objective of this exercise is to build an ARMA model for the house price changes. Recall that there are three stages involved: identification, estimation and diagnostic checking. The first stage is carried out by looking at the autocorrelation and partial autocorrelation coefficients to identify any structure in the data.

6.8.2   Estimating the autocorrelation coefficients for up to twelve lags

Double click on the **DHP series** and then click **View** and choose **Correlogram . . . .** In the 'Correlogram Specification' window, choose **Level** (since the series we are investigating has already been transformed into percentage returns or percentage changes) and in the 'Lags to include' box, type **12**. Click on **OK**. The output, including relevant test statistics, is given in screenshot 6.1.

    It is clearly evident from the first columns that the series is quite persistent given that it is already in percentage change form. The autocorrelation function dies away quite slowly. Only the first two partial autocorrelation coefficients appear strongly significant while the autocorrelation coefficients are significant until lag six

Series: DHP Workfile: UKHP::Untitled\												

View | Proc | Object | Properties | | Print | Name | Freeze | | Sample | Genr | Sheet | Graph | Stats | I

Correlogram of DHP

Date: 07/06/13   Time: 10:10
Sample: 1991M01 2013M05
Included observations: 268

Autocorrelation	Partial Correlation		AC	PAC	Q-Stat	Prob
		1	0.356	0.356	34.360	0.000
		2	0.432	0.350	85.175	0.000
		3	0.240	0.021	100.96	0.000
		4	0.200	-0.013	111.96	0.000
		5	0.139	0.006	117.26	0.000
		6	0.138	0.047	122.55	0.000
		7	0.074	-0.022	124.07	0.000
		8	0.117	0.052	127.87	0.000
		9	0.176	0.147	136.49	0.000
		10	0.141	0.024	142.09	0.000
		11	0.247	0.127	159.32	0.000
		12	0.295	0.181	183.90	0.000

Screenshot 6.1   **Estimating the correlogram**

(they are all outside the dotted lines in the picture), the coefficient is insignificant at lag seven but then they become significant again from lag eight. The numerical values of the autocorrelation and partial autocorrelation coefficients at lags 1–12 are given in the fourth and fifth columns of the output, with the lag length given in the third column.

The penultimate column of output gives the statistic resulting from a Ljung–Box test with number of lags in the sum equal to the row number (i.e. the number in the third column). The test statistics will follow a $\chi^2(1)$ for the first row, a $\chi^2(2)$ for the second row, and so on. p-values associated with these test statistics are given in the last column.

Remember that as a rule of thumb, a given autocorrelation coefficient is classed as significant if it is outside a $\pm 1.96 \times 1/(T)^{\frac{1}{2}}$ band, where T is the number of observations. In this case, it would imply that a correlation coefficient is classed as significant if it is bigger than approximately 0.11 or smaller than -0.11. The band is of course wider when the sampling frequency is monthly, as it is here, rather than daily where there would be more observations. It can be deduced that the first six autocorrelation coefficients (then eight through twelve) and the first two partial autocorrelation coefficients (then nine, eleven and twelve) are significant under this rule. Since the first acf coefficient is highly significant, the Ljung–Box joint test statistic rejects the null hypothesis of no autocorrelation at the 1% level for all numbers of lags considered. It could be concluded that a mixed ARMA process could be appropriate, although it is hard to precisely determine the appropriate order given these results. In order to investigate this issue further, the information criteria are now employed.

6.8.3 Using information criteria to decide on model orders

As demonstrated above, deciding on the appropriate model orders from autocorrelation functions could be very difficult in practice. An easier way is to choose the model order that minimises the value of an information criterion.

An important point to note is that books and statistical packages often differ in their construction of the test statistic. For example, the formulae given earlier in this chapter for Akaike's and Schwarz's Information Criteria were

$$AIC = \ln(\hat{\sigma}^2) + \frac{2k}{T} \tag{6.128}$$

$$SBIC = \ln(\hat{\sigma}^2) + \frac{k}{T}(\ln T) \tag{6.129}$$

where $\hat{\sigma}^2$ is the estimator of the variance of regressions disturbances u_t, k is the number of parameters and T is the sample size. When using the criterion based on the estimated standard errors, the model with the lowest value of AIC and $SBIC$ should be chosen. However, EViews uses a formulation of the test statistic derived from the log-likelihood function value based on a maximum likelihood estimation (see chapter 9). The corresponding EViews formulae are

$$AIC_\ell = -2\ell/T + \frac{2k}{T} \tag{6.130}$$

$$SBIC_\ell = -2\ell/T + \frac{k}{T}(\ln T) \tag{6.131}$$

where $l = -\frac{T}{2}(1 + \ln(2\pi) + \ln(\hat{u}'\hat{u}/T))$

Unfortunately, this modification is not benign, since it affects the relative strength of the penalty term compared with the error variance, sometimes leading different packages to select different model orders for the same data and criterion.

Suppose that it is thought that ARMA models from order (0,0) to (5,5) are plausible for the house price changes. This would entail considering thirty-six models (ARMA(0,0), ARMA(1,0), ARMA(2,0), ... ARMA(5,5)), i.e. from zero up to five lags in both the autoregressive and moving average terms.

In EViews, this can be done by separately estimating each of the models and noting down the value of the information criteria in each case.[2] This would be

---

[2] Alternatively, any reader who knows how to write programs in EViews could set up a structure to loop over the model orders and calculate all the values of the information criteria together – see chapter 13.

done in the following way. From the EViews main menu, click on **Quick** and choose **Estimate Equation** .... EViews will open an Equation Specification window. In the Equation Specification editor, type, for example

dhp c ar(1) ma(1)

For the estimation settings, select **LS – Least Squares (NLS and ARMA)**, select the whole sample, and click **OK** – this will specify an ARMA(1,1). The output is given in the table below.

Dependent Variable: DHP
Method: Least Squares
Date: 07/06/13 Time: 10:20
Sample (adjusted): 1991M03 2013M05
Included observations: 267 after adjustments
Convergence achieved after 8 iterations
MA Backcast: 1991M02

	Coefficient	Std. Error	t-Statistic	Prob.
C	0.448704	0.180581	2.484784	0.0136
AR(1)	0.840140	0.063711	13.18666	0.0000
MA(1)	−0.56410	0.097038	−5.81321	0.0000

R-squared	0.205312	Mean dependent var	0.436493
Adjusted R-squared	0.199292	S.D. dependent var	1.202504
S.E. of regression	1.076028	Akaike info criterion	2.995603
Sum squared resid	305.5590	Schwarz criterion	3.035909
Log likelihood	−396.9130	Hannan-Quinn criter.	3.011794
F-statistic	34.10301	Durbin-Watson stat	2.114776
Prob(F-statistic)	0.000000		

Inverted AR Roots	.84
Inverted MA Roots	.56

In theory, the output would then be interpreted in a similar way to that discussed in chapter 3. However, in reality it is very difficult to interpret the parameter estimates in the sense of, for example, saying, 'a one unit increase in x leads to a β unit increase in y'. In part because the construction of ARMA models is not based on any economic or financial theory, it is often best not to even try to interpret the individual parameter estimates, but rather to examine the plausibility of the model as a whole and to determine whether it describes the data well and produces accurate forecasts (if this is the objective of the exercise, which it often is).

The inverses of the AR and MA roots of the characteristic equation are also shown. These can be used to check whether the process implied by the model is stationary and invertible. For the AR and MA parts of the process to be stationary and invertible, respectively, the inverted roots in each case must be smaller than one in absolute value, which they are in this case. Note also that the roots are identical to (absolute values of) the values of the parameter estimates in this case (since there is only one AR term and one MA term) – in general this will not be the case when there are more lags. The header for the EViews output for ARMA models states the number of iterations that have been used in the model estimation process. This shows that, in fact, an iterative numerical optimisation procedure has been employed to estimate the coefficients (see chapter 9 for further details).

Repeating these steps for the other ARMA models would give all of the required values for the information criteria. To give just one more example, in the case of an ARMA(5,5), the following would be typed in the Equation Specification editor box:

dhp c ar(1) ar(2) ar(3) ar(4) ar(5) ma(1) ma(2) ma(3) ma(4) ma(5)

Note that, in order to estimate an ARMA(5,5) model, it is necessary to write out the whole list of terms as above rather than to simply write, for example, 'dhp c ar(5) ma(5)', which would give a model with a fifth lag of the dependent variable and a fifth lag of the error term but no other variables. The values of all of the Akaike and Schwarz information criteria calculated using EViews are as follows.

Information criteria for ARMA models of the percentage changes in UK house prices

AIC

p/q	0	1	2	3	4	5
0	3.207	3.137	2.999	2.989	2.983	2.981
1	3.082	2.995	2.968	2.959	2.990	2.982
2	2.953	2.960	2.968	2.952	2.952	2.941
3	2.958	2.964	2.969	2.960	2.949	2.953
4	2.965	2.972	2.925	2.932	2.940	**2.903**
5	2.976	2.957	2.955	2.919	2.945	2.918

SBIC

p/q	0	1	2	3	4	5
0	3.220	3.164	3.039	3.043	3.050	3.061
1	3.109	3.036	3.021	3.026	3.071	3.076
2	**2.993**	3.014	3.036	3.033	3.046	3.049
3	3.012	3.031	3.050	3.054	3.057	3.075
4	3.033	3.054	3.019	3.041	3.062	3.038
5	3.058	3.052	3.063	3.041	3.080	3.067

So which model actually minimises the two information criteria? In this case, the criteria choose different models: *AIC* selects an ARMA(4,5), while *SBIC* selects the smaller ARMA(2,0) model – i.e. an AR(2). These chosen models are highlighted in bold in the table. It will always be the case that *SBIC* selects a model that is at least as small (i.e. with fewer or the same number of parameters) as *AIC*, because the former criterion has a stricter penalty term. This means that *SBIC* penalises the incorporation of additional terms more heavily. Many different models provide almost identical values of the information criteria, suggesting that the chosen models do not provide particularly sharp characterisations of the data and that a number of other specifications would fit the data almost as well. Note that we could also have employed the Hannan-Quinn criterion and as an exercise, you might determine the appropriate model order using that approach too.

6.9 Examples of time series modelling in finance

6.9.1 Covered and uncovered interest parity

The determination of the price of one currency in terms of another (i.e. the exchange rate) has received a great deal of empirical examination in the international finance literature. Of these, three hypotheses in particular are studied – covered interest parity (CIP), uncovered interest parity (UIP) and purchasing power parity (PPP). The first two of these will be considered as illustrative examples in this chapter, while PPP will be discussed in chapter 8. All three relations are relevant for students of finance, for violation of one or more of the parities may offer the potential for arbitrage, or at least will offer further insights into how financial markets operate. All are discussed briefly here; for a more comprehensive treatment, see Cuthbertson and Nitzsche (2004) or the many references therein.

6.9.2 Covered interest parity

Stated in its simplest terms, CIP implies that, if financial markets are efficient, it should not be possible to make a riskless profit by borrowing at a risk-free rate of interest in a domestic currency, switching the funds borrowed into another (foreign) currency, investing them there at a risk-free rate and locking in a forward sale to guarantee the rate of exchange back to the domestic currency. Thus, if CIP holds, it is possible to write

$$f_t - s_t = (r - r^*)_t \tag{6.132}$$

where f_t and s_t are the log of the forward and spot prices of the domestic in terms of the foreign currency at time t, r is the domestic interest rate and r^* is the foreign interest rate. This is an equilibrium condition which must hold otherwise there would exist riskless arbitrage opportunities, and the existence of such arbitrage would ensure that any deviation from the condition cannot hold indefinitely. It is worth noting that, underlying CIP are the assumptions that the risk-free rates are truly risk-free – that is, there is no possibility for default risk. It is also assumed that there are no transactions costs, such as broker's fees, bid–ask spreads, stamp duty, etc., and that there are no capital controls, so that funds can be moved without restriction from one currency to another.

6.9.3   Uncovered interest parity

UIP takes CIP and adds to it a further condition known as 'forward rate unbiasedness' (FRU). Forward rate unbiasedness states that the forward rate of foreign exchange should be an unbiased predictor of the future value of the spot rate. If this condition does not hold, again in theory riskless arbitrage opportunities could exist. UIP, in essence, states that the expected change in the exchange rate should be equal to the interest rate differential between that available risk-free in each of the currencies. Algebraically, this may be stated as

$$s^e_{t+1} - s_t = (r - r^*)_t \tag{6.133}$$

where the notation is as above and s^e_{t+1} is the expectation, made at time t of the spot exchange rate that will prevail at time $t+1$.

The literature testing CIP and UIP is huge with literally hundreds of published papers. Tests of CIP unsurprisingly (for it is a pure arbitrage condition) tend not to reject the hypothesis that the condition holds. Taylor (1987, 1989) has conducted extensive examinations of CIP, and concluded that there were historical periods when arbitrage was profitable, particularly during periods where the exchange rates were under management.

Relatively simple tests of UIP and FRU take equations of the form (6.133) and add intuitively relevant additional terms. If UIP holds, these additional terms should be insignificant. Ito (1988) tests UIP for the yen/dollar exchange rate with the three-month forward rate for January 1973 until February 1985. The sample period is split into three as a consequence of perceived structural breaks in the series. Strict controls on capital movements were in force in Japan until 1977, when some were relaxed and finally removed in 1980. A Chow test confirms Ito's intuition and suggests that the three sample periods should be analysed separately. Two separate regressions are estimated for each of the three sample sub-periods

$$s_{t+3} - f_{t,3} = a + b_1(s_t - f_{t-3,3}) + b_2(s_{t-1} - f_{t-4,3}) + u_t \tag{6.134}$$

where s_{t+3} is the spot interest rate prevailing at time $t+3$, $f_{t,3}$ is the forward rate for three periods ahead available at time t, and so on, and u_t is an error term. A natural joint hypothesis to test is H_0: $a = 0$ and $b_1 = 0$ and $b_2 = 0$. This hypothesis represents the restriction that the deviation of the forward rate from the realised rate should have a mean value insignificantly different from zero ($a = 0$) and it should be independent of any information available at time t ($b_1 = 0$ and $b_2 = 0$). All three of these conditions must be fulfilled for UIP to hold. The second equation that Ito tests is

$$s_{t+3} - f_{t,3} = a + b(s_t - f_{t,3}) + v_t \tag{6.135}$$

where v_t is an error term and the hypothesis of interest in this case is H_0: $a = 0$ and $b = 0$.

Equation (6.134) tests whether past forecast errors have information useful for predicting the difference between the actual exchange rate at time $t+3$, and the value of it that was predicted by the forward rate. Equation (6.135) tests whether the forward premium has any predictive power for the difference between the

Sample period	1973M1–1977M3	1977M4–1980M12	1981M1–1985M2
Panel A: Estimates and hypothesis tests for $S_{t+3} - f_{t,3} = a + b_1(s_t - f_{t-3\,3}) + b_2(s_{t-1} - f_{t-4,3}) + u_t$			
Estimate of a	0.0099	0.0031	0.027
Estimate of b_1	0.0200	0.240	0.077
Estimate of b_2	−0.370	0.160	−0.210
Joint test $\chi^2(3)$	23.388	5.248	6.022
P-value for joint test	0.000	0.155	0.111
Panel B: Estimates and hypothesis tests for $S_{t+3} - f_{t,3} = a + b(s_t - f_{t,3}) + v_t$			
Estimate of a	0.00	−0.05	−0.89
Estimate of b	0.09	4.18	2.93
Joint test $\chi^2(2)$	31.92	22.06	5.39
p-value for joint test	0.00	0.00	0.07

Source: Ito (1988). Reprinted with permission from MIT Press Journals.

actual exchange rate at time $t + 3$, and the value of it that was predicted by the forward rate. The results for the three sample periods are presented in Ito's table 3, and are adapted and reported here in table 6.1.

The main conclusion is that UIP clearly failed to hold throughout the period of strictest controls, but there is less and less evidence against UIP as controls were relaxed.

6.10   Exponential smoothing

Exponential smoothing is another modelling technique (not based on the ARIMA approach) that uses only a linear combination of the previous values of a series for modelling it and for generating forecasts of its future values. Given that only previous values of the series of interest are used, the only question remaining is how much weight should be attached to each of the previous observations. Recent observations would be expected to have the most power in helping to forecast future values of a series. If this is accepted, a model that places more weight on recent observations than those further in the past would be desirable. On the other hand, observations a long way in the past may still contain some information useful for forecasting future values of a series, which would not be the case under a centred moving average. An exponential smoothing model will achieve this, by imposing a geometrically declining weighting scheme on the lagged values of a series. The equation for the model is

$$S_t = \alpha y_t + (1 - \alpha) S_{t-1} \tag{6.136}$$

where α is the smoothing constant, with $0 < \alpha < 1$, y_t is the current realised value, S_t is the current smoothed value.

Since $\alpha + (1 - \alpha) = 1$, S_t is modelled as a weighted average of the current observation y_t and the previous smoothed value. The model above can be rewritten to express the exponential weighting scheme more clearly. By lagging (6.136) by one period, the following expression is obtained

$$S_{t-1} = \alpha y_{t-1} + (1 - \alpha)S_{t-2} \tag{6.137}$$

and lagging again

$$S_{t-2} = \alpha y_{t-2} + (1 - \alpha)S_{t-3} \tag{6.138}$$

Substituting into (6.136) for S_{t-1} from (6.137)

$$S_t = \alpha y_t + (1 - \alpha)(\alpha y_{t-1} + (1 - \alpha)S_{t-2}) \tag{6.139}$$

$$S_t = \alpha y_t + (1 - \alpha)\alpha y_{t-1} + (1 - \alpha)^2 S_{t-2} \tag{6.140}$$

Substituting into (6.140) for S_{t-2} from (6.138)

$$S_t = \alpha y_t + (1 - \alpha)\alpha y_{t-1} + (1 - \alpha)^2(\alpha y_{t-2} + (1 - \alpha)S_{t-3}) \tag{6.141}$$

$$S_t = \alpha y_t + (1 - \alpha)\alpha y_{t-1} + (1 - \alpha)^2\alpha y_{t-2} + (1 - \alpha)^3 S_{t-3} \tag{6.142}$$

T successive substitutions of this kind would lead to

$$S_t = \left(\sum_{i=0}^{T} \alpha(1 - \alpha)^i y_{t-i}\right) + (1 - \alpha)^{T+1} S_{t-1-T} \tag{6.143}$$

Since $\alpha > 0$, the effect of each observation declines geometrically as the variable moves another observation forward in time. In the limit as $T \to \infty$, $(1-\alpha)^T S_0 \to 0$, so that the current smoothed value is a geometrically weighted infinite sum of the previous realisations.

The forecasts from an exponential smoothing model are simply set to the current smoothed value, for any number of steps ahead, s

$$f_{t,s} = S_t, s = 1, 2, 3, \ldots \tag{6.144}$$

The exponential smoothing model can be seen as a special case of a Box–Jenkins model, an ARIMA(0,1,1), with MA coefficient $(1 - \alpha)$ – see Granger and Newbold (1986, p. 174).

The technique above is known as single or simple exponential smoothing, and it can be modified to allow for trends (Holt's method) or to allow for seasonality (Winter's method) in the underlying variable. These augmented models are not pursued further in this text since there is a much better way to model the trends (using a unit root process – see chapter 8) and the seasonalities (see chapter 10) of the form that are typically present in financial data.

Exponential smoothing has several advantages over the slightly more complex ARMA class of models discussed above. First, exponential smoothing is obviously very simple to use. There is no decision to be made on how many parameters to estimate (assuming only single exponential smoothing is considered). Thus it is easy to update the model if a new realisation becomes available.

Among the disadvantages of exponential smoothing is the fact that it is overly simplistic and inflexible. Exponential smoothing models can be viewed as but one model from the ARIMA family, which may not necessarily be optimal for capturing any linear dependence in the data. Also, the forecasts from an exponential smoothing model do not converge on the long-term mean of the variable as the horizon increases. The upshot is that long-term forecasts are overly affected by recent events in the history of the series under investigation and will therefore be sub-optimal.

A discussion of how exponential smoothing models can be estimated using EViews will be given after the following section on forecasting in econometrics.

6.11 Forecasting in econometrics

Although the words 'forecasting' and 'prediction' are sometimes given different meanings in some studies, in this text the words will be used synonymously. In this context, prediction or forecasting simply means an attempt to *determine the values that a series is likely to take*. Of course, forecasts might also usefully be made in a cross-sectional environment. Although the discussion below refers to time series data, some of the arguments will carry over to the cross-sectional context.

Determining the forecasting accuracy of a model is an important test of its adequacy. Some econometricians would go as far as to suggest that the statistical adequacy of a model in terms of whether it violates the CLRM assumptions or whether it contains insignificant parameters, is largely irrelevant if the model produces accurate forecasts. The following sub-sections of the book discuss why forecasts are made, how they are made from several important classes of models, how to evaluate the forecasts, and so on.

6.11.1 Why forecast?

Forecasts are made essentially because they are useful! Financial decisions often involve a long-term commitment of resources, the returns to which will depend upon what happens in the future. In this context, the decisions made today will reflect forecasts of the future state of the world, and the more accurate those forecasts are, the more utility (or money!) is likely to be gained from acting on them.

Some examples in finance of where forecasts from econometric models might be useful include:

- Forecasting tomorrow's return on a particular *share*
- Forecasting the *price of a house* given its characteristics
- Forecasting the *riskiness of a portfolio* over the next year
- Forecasting the *volatility of bond returns*
- Forecasting the *correlation between US and UK stock market movements* tomorrow
- Forecasting the likely number of *defaults* on a portfolio of home loans.

Again, it is evident that forecasting can apply either in a cross-sectional or a time series context. It is useful to distinguish between two approaches to forecasting:

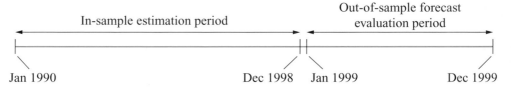

Figure 6.9   Use of in-sample and out-of-sample periods for analysis

- *Econometric (structural) forecasting* – relates a dependent variable to one or more independent variables. Such models often work well in the long run, since a long-run relationship between variables often arises from no–arbitrage or market efficiency conditions. Examples of such forecasts would include return predictions derived from arbitrage pricing models, or long-term exchange rate prediction based on purchasing power parity or uncovered interest parity theory.
- *Time series forecasting* – involves trying to forecast the future values of a series given its previous values and/or previous values of an error term.

The distinction between the two types is somewhat blurred – for example, it is not clear where vector autoregressive models (see chapter 7 for an extensive overview) fit into this classification.

It is also worth distinguishing between point and interval forecasts. *Point* forecasts predict a single value for the variable of interest, while *interval* forecasts provide a range of values in which the future value of the variable is expected to lie with a given level of confidence.

6.11.2   The difference between in-sample and out-of-sample forecasts

In-sample forecasts are those generated for the same set of data that was used to estimate the model's parameters. One would expect the 'forecasts' of a model to be relatively good in-sample, for this reason. Therefore, a sensible approach to model evaluation through an examination of forecast accuracy is not to use all of the observations in estimating the model parameters, but rather to hold some observations back. The latter sample, sometimes known as a *holdout sample*, would be used to construct out-of-sample forecasts.

To give an illustration of this distinction, suppose that some monthly FTSE returns for 120 months (January 1990–December 1999) are available. It would be possible to use all of them to build the model (and generate only in–sample forecasts), or some observations could be kept back, as shown in figure 6.9.

What would be done in this case would be to use data from $1990M1$ until $1998M12$ to estimate the model parameters, and then the observations for 1999 would be forecasted from the estimated parameters. Of course, where each of the in-sample and out-of-sample periods should start and finish is somewhat arbitrary and at the discretion of the researcher. One could then compare how close the forecasts for the 1999 months were relative to their actual values that are in the holdout sample. This procedure would represent a better test of the model than an examination of the in-sample fit of the model since the information from 1999*M*1 onwards has not been used when estimating the model parameters.

6.11.3 Some more terminology: one-step-ahead versus multi-step-ahead forecasts and rolling versus recursive samples

A *one-step-ahead forecast* is a forecast generated for the next observation only, whereas *multi-step-ahead forecasts* are those generated for 1, 2, 3, . . . , *s* steps ahead, so that the forecasting horizon is for the next *s* periods. Whether one-step- or multi-step-ahead forecasts are of interest will be determined by the forecasting horizon of interest to the researcher.

Suppose that the monthly FTSE data are used as described in the example above. If the in-sample estimation period stops in December 1998, then up to twelve-step-ahead forecasts could be produced, giving twelve predictions that can be compared with the actual values of the series. Comparing the actual and forecast values in this way is not ideal, for the forecasting horizon is varying from one to twelve steps ahead. It might be the case, for example, that the model produces very good forecasts for short horizons (say, one or two steps), but that it produces inaccurate forecasts further ahead. It would not be possible to evaluate whether this was in fact the case or not since only a single one-step-ahead forecast, a single two-step-ahead forecast, and so on, are available. An evaluation of the forecasts would require a considerably larger holdout sample.

A useful way around this problem is to use a *recursive or rolling window*, which generates a series of forecasts for a given number of steps ahead. A recursive forecasting model would be one where the initial estimation date is fixed, but additional observations are added one at a time to the estimation period. A rolling window, on the other hand, is one where the length of the in-sample period used to estimate the model is fixed, so that the start date and end date successively increase by one observation. Suppose now that only one-, two-, and three-step-ahead forecasts are of interest. They could be produced using the following recursive and rolling window approaches:

Objective: to produce	Data used to estimate model parameters	
1-, 2-, 3-step-ahead forecasts for:	Rolling window	Recursive window
1999*M*1, *M*2, *M*3	1990*M*1–1998*M*12	1990*M*1–1998*M*12
1999*M*2, *M*3, *M*4	1990*M*2–1999*M*1	1990*M*1–1999*M*1
1999*M*3, *M*4, *M*5	1990*M*3–1999*M*2	1990*M*1–1999*M*2
1999*M*4, *M*5, *M*6	1990*M*4–1999*M*3	1990*M*1–1999*M*3
1999*M*5, *M*6, *M*7	1990*M*5–1999*M*4	1990*M*1–1999*M*4
1999*M*6, *M*7, *M*8	1990*M*6–1999*M*5	1990*M*1–1999*M*5
1999*M*7, *M*8, *M*9	1990*M*7–1999*M*6	1990*M*1–1999*M*6
1999*M*8, *M*9, *M*10	1990*M*8–1999*M*7	1990*M*1–1999*M*7
1999*M*9, *M*10, *M*11	1990*M*9–1999*M*8	1990*M*1–1999*M*8
1999*M*10, *M*11, *M*12	1990*M*10–1999*M*9	1990*M*1–1999*M*9

The sample length for the rolling windows above is always set at 108 observations, while the number of observations used to estimate the parameters in the recursive case increases as we move down the table and through the sample.

6.11.4 Forecasting with time series versus structural models

To understand how to construct forecasts, the idea of *conditional expectations* is required. A conditional expectation would be expressed as

$$E(y_{t+1}|\Omega_t)$$

This expression states that the expected value of y is taken for time $t+1$, conditional upon, or given, ($|$) all information available up to and including time t (Ω_t). Contrast this with the unconditional expectation of y, which is the expected value of y without any reference to time, i.e. the unconditional mean of y. The conditional expectations operator is used to generate forecasts of the series.

How this conditional expectation is evaluated will of course depend on the model under consideration. Several families of models for forecasting will be developed in this and subsequent chapters.

A first point to note is that by definition the optimal forecast for a zero mean white noise process is zero

$$E(u_{t+s}|\Omega_t) = 0 \, \forall \, s > 0 \tag{6.145}$$

The two simplest forecasting 'methods' that can be employed in almost every situation are shown in box 6.3.

Box 6.3 Naive forecasting methods

(1) Assume no change so that the forecast, f, of the value of y, s steps into the future is the current value of y

$$E(y_{t+s}|\Omega_t) = y_t \tag{6.146}$$

Such a forecast would be optimal if y_t followed a random walk process.
(2) In the absence of a full model, forecasts can be generated using the long-term average of the series. Forecasts using the unconditional mean would be more useful than 'no change' forecasts for any series that is 'mean-reverting' (i.e. stationary).

Time series models are generally better suited to the production of time series forecasts than structural models. For an illustration of this, consider the following linear regression model

$$y_t = \beta_1 + \beta_2 x_{2t} + \beta_3 x_{3t} + \cdots + \beta_k x_{kt} + u_t \tag{6.147}$$

To forecast y, the conditional expectation of its future value is required. Taking expectations of both sides of (6.147) yields

$$E(y_t \mid \Omega_{t-1}) = E(\beta_1 + \beta_2 x_{2t} + \beta_3 x_{3t} + \cdots + \beta_k x_{kt} + u_t) \qquad (6.148)$$

The parameters can be taken through the expectations operator, since this is a population regression function and therefore they are assumed known. The following expression would be obtained

$$E(y_t \mid \Omega_{t-1}) = \beta_1 + \beta_2 E(x_{2t}) + \beta_3 E(x_{3t}) + \cdots + \beta_k E(x_{kt}) \qquad (6.149)$$

But there is a problem: what are $E(x_{2t})$, etc.? Remembering that information is available only until time $t - 1$, the values of these variables are unknown. It may be possible to forecast them, but this would require another set of forecasting models for every explanatory variable. To the extent that forecasting the explanatory variables may be as difficult, or even more difficult, than forecasting the explained variable, this equation has achieved nothing! In the absence of a set of forecasts for the explanatory variables, one might think of using $\bar{x}_2$, etc., i.e. the mean values of the explanatory variables, giving

$$E(y_t) = \beta_1 + \beta_2 \bar{x}_2 + \beta_3 \bar{x}_3 + \cdots + \beta_k \bar{x}_k = \bar{y}! \qquad (6.150)$$

Thus, if the mean values of the explanatory variables are used as inputs to the model, all that will be obtained as a forecast is the average value of y. Forecasting using pure time series models is relatively common, since it avoids this problem.

6.11.5 Forecasting with ARMA models

Forecasting using ARMA models is a fairly simple exercise in calculating conditional expectations. Although any consistent and logical notation could be used, the following conventions will be adopted in this book. Let $f_{t,s}$ denote a forecast made using an ARMA(p,q) model at time t for s steps into the future for some series y. The forecasts are generated by what is known as a forecast function, typically of the form

$$f_{t,s} = \sum_{i=1}^{p} a_i f_{t,s-i} + \sum_{j=1}^{q} b_j u_{t+s-j} \qquad (6.151)$$

where $f_{t,s} = y_{t+s},\ s \le 0;\quad u_{t+s} = 0,\ s > 0 = u_{t+s},\ s \le 0$

and a_i and b_i are the autoregressive and moving average coefficients, respectively.

A demonstration of how one generates forecasts for separate AR and MA processes, leading to the general equation (6.151) above, will now be given.

6.11.6 Forecasting the future value of an MA(q) process

A moving average process has a memory only of length q, and this limits the sensible forecasting horizon. For example, suppose that an MA(3) model has been estimated

$$y_t = \mu + \theta_1 u_{t-1} + \theta_2 u_{t-2} + \theta_3 u_{t-3} + u_t \tag{6.152}$$

Since parameter constancy over time is assumed, if this relationship holds for the series y at time t, it is also assumed to hold for y at time $t+1, t+2, \ldots$, so 1 can be added to each of the time subscripts in (6.152), and 2 added to each of the time subscripts, and then 3, and so on, to arrive at the following

$$y_{t+1} = \mu + \theta_1 u_t + \theta_2 u_{t-1} + \theta_3 u_{t-2} + u_{t+1} \tag{6.153}$$

$$y_{t+2} = \mu + \theta_1 u_{t+1} + \theta_2 u_t + \theta_3 u_{t-1} + u_{t+2} \tag{6.154}$$

$$y_{t+3} = \mu + \theta_1 u_{t+2} + \theta_2 u_{t+1} + \theta_3 u_t + u_{t+3} \tag{6.155}$$

Suppose that all information up to and including that at time t is available and that forecasts for $1, 2, \ldots, s$ steps ahead – i.e. forecasts for y at times $t+1, t+2, \ldots, t+s$ are wanted. $y_t, y_{t-1}, \ldots$, and u_t, u_{t-1}, are known, so producing the forecasts is just a matter of taking the conditional expectation of (6.153)

$$f_{t,1} = E(y_{t+1|t}) = E(\mu + \theta_1 u_t + \theta_2 u_{t-1} + \theta_3 u_{t-2} + u_{t+1} | \Omega_t) \tag{6.156}$$

where $E(y_{t+1|t})$ is a short-hand notation for $E(y_{t+1}|\Omega_t)$

$$f_{t,1} = E(y_{t+1|t}) = \mu + \theta_1 u_t + \theta_2 u_{t-1} + \theta_3 u_{t-2} \tag{6.157}$$

Thus the forecast for y, one step ahead, made at time t, is given by this linear combination of the disturbance terms. Note that it would not be appropriate to set the values of these disturbance terms to their unconditional mean of zero. This arises because it is the *conditional expectation* of their values that is of interest. Given that all information is known up to and including that at time t is available, the values of the error terms up to time t are known. But u_{t+1} is not known at time t and therefore $E(u_{t+1|t}) = 0$, and so on.

The forecast for two steps ahead is formed by taking the conditional expectation of (6.154)

$$f_{t,2} = E(y_{t+2|t}) = E(\mu + \theta_1 u_{t+1} + \theta_2 u_t + \theta_3 u_{t-1} + u_{t+2} | \Omega_t) \tag{6.158}$$

$$f_{t,2} = E(y_{t+2|t}) = \mu + \theta_2 u_t + \theta_3 u_{t-1} \tag{6.159}$$

In the case above, u_{t+2} is not known since information is available only to time t, so $E(u_{t+2})$ is set to zero. Continuing and applying the same rules to generate 3-, 4-, $\ldots$, s-step-ahead forecasts

$$f_{t,3} = E(y_{t+3|t}) = E(\mu + \theta_1 u_{t+2} + \theta_2 u_{t+1} + \theta_3 u_t + u_{t+3} | \Omega_t) \tag{6.160}$$

$$f_{t,3} = E(y_{t+3|t}) = \mu + \theta_3 u_t \tag{6.161}$$

$$f_{t,4} = E(y_{t+4|t}) = \mu \tag{6.162}$$

$$f_{t,s} = E(y_{t+s|t}) = \mu \; \forall \; s \geq 4 \tag{6.163}$$

As the MA(3) process has a memory of only three periods, all forecasts four or more steps ahead collapse to the intercept. Obviously, if there had been no constant term in the model, the forecasts four or more steps ahead for an MA(3) would be zero.

6.11.7 Forecasting the future value of an AR(p) process

Unlike a moving average process, an autoregressive process has infinite memory. To illustrate, suppose that an AR(2) model has been estimated

$$y_t = \mu + \phi_1 y_{t-1} + \phi_2 y_{t-2} + u_t \tag{6.164}$$

Again, by appealing to the assumption of parameter stability, this equation will hold for times $t+1$, $t+2$, and so on

$$y_{t+1} = \mu + \phi_1 y_t + \phi_2 y_{t-1} + u_{t+1} \tag{6.165}$$

$$y_{t+2} = \mu + \phi_1 y_{t+1} + \phi_2 y_t + u_{t+2} \tag{6.166}$$

$$y_{t+3} = \mu + \phi_1 y_{t+2} + \phi_2 y_{t+1} + u_{t+3} \tag{6.167}$$

Producing the one-step-ahead forecast is easy, since all of the information required is known at time t. Applying the expectations operator to (6.165), and setting $E(u_{t+1})$ to zero would lead to

$$f_{t,1} = E(y_{t+1|t}) = E(\mu + \phi_1 y_t + \phi_2 y_{t-1} + u_{t+1} \mid \Omega_t) \tag{6.168}$$

$$f_{t,1} = E(y_{t+1|t}) = \mu + \phi_1 E(y_t \mid t) + \phi_2 E(y_{t-1} \mid t) \tag{6.169}$$

$$f_{t,1} = E(y_{t+1|t}) = \mu + \phi_1 y_t + \phi_2 y_{t-1} \tag{6.170}$$

Applying the same procedure in order to generate a two-step-ahead forecast

$$f_{t,2} = E(y_{t+2|t}) = E(\mu + \phi_1 y_{t+1} + \phi_2 y_t + u_{t+2} \mid \Omega_t) \tag{6.171}$$

$$f_{t,2} = E(y_{t+2|t}) = \mu + \phi_1 E(y_{t+1} \mid t) + \phi_2 E(y_t \mid t) \tag{6.172}$$

The case above is now slightly more tricky, since $E(y_{t+1})$ is not known, although this in fact is the one-step-ahead forecast, so that (6.172) becomes

$$f_{t,2} = E(y_{t+2|t}) = \mu + \phi_1 f_{t,1} + \phi_2 y_t \tag{6.173}$$

Similarly, for three, four, ... and s steps ahead, the forecasts will be, respectively, given by

$$f_{t,3} = E(y_{t+3|t}) = E(\mu + \phi_1 y_{t+2} + \phi_2 y_{t+1} + u_{t+3} \mid \Omega_t) \tag{6.174}$$

$$f_{t,3} = E(y_{t+3|t}) = \mu + \phi_1 E(y_{t+2} \mid t) + \phi_2 E(y_{t+1} \mid t) \tag{6.175}$$

$$f_{t,3} = E(y_{t+3|t}) = \mu + \phi_1 f_{t,2} + \phi_2 f_{t,1} \tag{6.176}$$

$$f_{t,4} = \mu + \phi_1 f_{t,3} + \phi_2 f_{t,2} \tag{6.177}$$

etc. so

$$f_{t,s} = \mu + \phi_1 f_{t,s-1} + \phi_2 f_{t,s-2} \tag{6.178}$$

Table 6.2	Forecast error aggregation			
Steps ahead	Forecast	Actual	Squared error	Absolute error
1	0.20	−0.40	$(0.20 - -0.40)^2 = 0.360$	$\|0.20 - -0.40\| = 0.600$
2	0.15	0.20	$(0.15 - 0.20)^2 = 0.002$	$\|0.15 - 0.20\| = 0.050$
3	0.10	0.10	$(0.10 - 0.10)^2 = 0.000$	$\|0.10 - 0.10\| = 0.000$
4	0.06	−0.10	$(0.06 - -0.10)^2 = 0.026$	$\|0.06 - -0.10\| = 0.160$
5	0.04	−0.05	$(0.04 - -0.05)^2 = 0.008$	$\|0.04 - -0.05\| = 0.090$

Thus the s-step-ahead forecast for an AR(2) process is given by the intercept + the coefficient on the one-period lag multiplied by the time $s - 1$ forecast + the coefficient on the two-period lag multiplied by the $s - 2$ forecast.

ARMA(p,q) forecasts can easily be generated in the same way by applying the rules for their component parts, and using the general formula given by (6.151).

6.11.8 Determining whether a forecast is accurate or not

For example, suppose that tomorrow's return on the FTSE is predicted to be 0.2, and that the outcome is actually −0.4. Is this an accurate forecast? Clearly, one cannot determine whether a forecasting model is good or not based upon only one forecast and one realisation. Thus in practice, forecasts would usually be produced for the whole of the out-of-sample period, which would then be compared with the actual values, and the difference between them aggregated in some way. The forecast error for observation i is defined as the difference between the actual value for observation i and the forecast made for it. The forecast error, defined in this way, will be positive (negative) if the forecast was too low (high). Therefore, it is not possible simply to sum the forecast errors, since the positive and negative errors will cancel one another out. Thus, before the forecast errors are aggregated, they are usually squared or the absolute value taken, which renders them all positive. To see how the aggregation works, consider the example in table 6.2, where forecasts are made for a series up to five steps ahead, and are then compared with the actual realisations (with all calculations rounded to three decimal places).

The mean squared error (MSE) and mean absolute error (MAE) are now calculated by taking the average of the fourth and fifth columns, respectively

$$MSE = (0.360 + 0.002 + 0.000 + 0.026 + 0.008)/5 = 0.079 \tag{6.179}$$

$$MAE = (0.600 + 0.050 + 0.000 + 0.160 + 0.090)/5 = 0.180 \tag{6.180}$$

Taken individually, little can be gleaned from considering the size of the MSE or MAE, for the statistic is unbounded from above (like the residual sum of squares or RSS). Instead, the MSE or MAE from one model would be compared with those of other models for the same data and forecast period, and the model(s) with the lowest value of the error measure would be argued to be the most accurate.

MSE provides a quadratic loss function, and so may be particularly useful in situations where large forecast errors are disproportionately more serious than smaller errors. This may, however, also be viewed as a disadvantage if large errors are not disproportionately more serious, although the same critique could also, of course, be applied to the whole least squares methodology. Indeed Dielman (1986) goes as far as to say that when there are outliers present, least absolute values should be used to determine model parameters rather than least squares. Makridakis (1993, p. 528) argues that mean absolute percentage error (*MAPE*) is 'a relative measure that incorporates the best characteristics among the various accuracy criteria'. Once again, denoting s-step-ahead forecasts of a variable made at time t as $f_{t,s}$ and the actual value of the variable at time t as y_t, then the MSE can be defined as

$$\text{MSE} = \frac{1}{T - (T_1 - 1)} \sum_{t=T_1}^{T} (y_{t+s} - f_{t,s})^2 \tag{6.181}$$

where T is the total sample size (in-sample + out-of-sample), and T_1 is the first out-of-sample forecast observation. Thus in-sample model estimation initially runs from observation 1 to $(T_1 - 1)$, and observations T_1 to T are available for out-of-sample estimation, i.e. a total holdout sample of $T - (T_1 - 1)$.

MAE measures the average absolute forecast error, and is given by

$$\text{MAE} = \frac{1}{T - (T_1 - 1)} \sum_{t=T_1}^{T} |y_{t+s} - f_{t,s}| \tag{6.182}$$

Adjusted *MAPE* (*AMAPE*) or symmetric *MAPE* corrects for the problem of asymmetry between the actual and forecast values

$$\text{AMAPE} = \frac{100}{T - (T_1 - 1)} \sum_{t=T_1}^{T} \left| \frac{y_{t+s} - f_{t,s}}{y_{t+s} + f_{t,s}} \right| \tag{6.183}$$

The symmetry in (6.183) arises since the forecast error is divided by twice the average of the actual and forecast values. So, for example, *AMAPE* will be the same whether the forecast is 0.5 and the actual value is 0.3, or the actual value is 0.5 and the forecast is 0.3. The same is not true of the standard *MAPE* formula, where the denominator is simply y_{t+s}, so that whether y_t or $f_{t,s}$ is larger will affect the result

$$\text{MAPE} = \frac{100}{T - (T_1 - 1)} \sum_{t=T_1}^{T} \left| \frac{y_{t+s} - f_{t,s}}{y_{t+s}} \right| \tag{6.184}$$

MAPE also has the attractive additional property compared to *MSE* that it can be interpreted as a percentage error, and furthermore, its value is bounded from below by 0.

Unfortunately, it is not possible to use the adjustment if the series and the forecasts can take on opposite signs (as they could in the context of returns forecasts, for example). This is due to the fact that the prediction and the actual value may, purely by coincidence, take on values that are almost equal and opposite, thus almost cancelling each other out in the denominator. This leads to extremely large and erratic values of $AMAPE$. In such an instance, it is not possible to use $MAPE$ as a criterion either. Consider the following example: say we forecast a value of $f_{t,s} = 3$, but the out-turn is that $y_{t+s} = 0.0001$. The addition to total MSE from this one observation is given by

$$\frac{1}{391} \times (0.0001 - 3)^2 = 0.0230 \tag{6.185}$$

This value for the forecast is large, but perfectly feasible since in many cases it will be well within the range of the data. But the addition to total $MAPE$ from just this single observation is given by

$$\frac{100}{391} \left| \frac{0.0001 - 3}{0.0001} \right| = 7670 \tag{6.186}$$

$MAPE$ has the advantage that for a random walk in the log levels (i.e. a zero forecast), the criterion will take the value one (or 100 if we multiply the formula by 100 to get a percentage, as was the case for the equation above). So if a forecasting model gives a $MAPE$ smaller than one (or 100), it is superior to the random walk model. In fact the criterion is also not reliable if the series can take on absolute values less than one. This point may seem somewhat obvious, but it is clearly important for the choice of forecast evaluation criteria.

Another criterion which is popular is Theil's U-statistic (1966). The metric is defined as follows

$$U = \frac{\sqrt{\displaystyle\sum_{t=T_1}^{T} \left(\frac{y_{t+s} - f_{t,s}}{y_{t+s}} \right)^2}}{\sqrt{\displaystyle\sum_{t=T_1}^{T} \left(\frac{y_{t+s} - fb_{t,s}}{y_{t+s}} \right)^2}} \tag{6.187}$$

where $fb_{t,s}$ is the forecast obtained from a benchmark model (typically a simple model such as a naive or random walk). A U-statistic of one implies that the model under consideration and the benchmark model are equally (in)accurate, while a value of less than one implies that the model is superior to the benchmark, and vice versa for $U > 1$. Although the measure is clearly useful, as Makridakis and Hibon (1995) argue, it is not without problems since if $fb_{t,s}$ is the same as y_{t+s}, U will be infinite since the denominator will be zero. The value of U will also be influenced by outliers in a similar vein to MSE and has little intuitive meaning.[3]

---

[3] Note that the Theil's U-formula reported by EViews is slightly different.

6.11.9   Statistical versus financial or economic loss functions

Many econometric forecasting studies evaluate the models' success using statistical loss functions such as those described above. However, it is not necessarily the case that models classed as accurate because they have small mean squared forecast errors are useful in practical situations. To give one specific illustration, it has been shown (Gerlow, Irwin and Liu, 1993) that the accuracy of forecasts according to traditional statistical criteria may give little guide to the potential profitability of employing those forecasts in a market trading strategy. So models that perform poorly on statistical grounds may still yield a profit if used for trading, and vice versa.

On the other hand, models that can accurately forecast the sign of future returns, or can predict turning points in a series have been found to be more profitable (Leitch and Tanner, 1991). Two possible indicators of the ability of a model to predict direction changes irrespective of their magnitude are those suggested by Pesaran and Timmerman (1992) and by Refenes (1995). The relevant formulae to compute these measures are, respectively

$$\% \text{ correct sign predictions} = \frac{1}{T - (T_1 - 1)} \sum_{t=T_1}^{T} z_{t+s} \tag{6.188}$$

where $z_{t+s} = 1$ if $(y_{t+s} f_{t,s}) > 0$

$z_{t+s} = 0$ *otherwise*

and

$$\% \text{ correct direction change predictions} = \frac{1}{T - (T_1 - 1)} \sum_{t=T_1}^{T} z_{t+s} \tag{6.189}$$

where $z_{t+s} = 1$ if $(y_{t+s} - y_t)(f_{t,s} - y_t) > 0$

$z_{t+s} = 0$ *otherwise*

Thus, in each case, the criteria give the proportion of correctly predicted signs and directional changes for some given lead time s, respectively.

Considering how strongly each of the three criteria outlined above (*MSE*, *MAE* and proportion of correct sign predictions) penalises large errors relative to small ones, the criteria can be ordered as follows:

Penalises large errors least $\rightarrow$ penalises large errors most heavily

Sign prediction $\rightarrow$ *MAE* $\rightarrow$ *MSE*

MSE penalises large errors disproportionately more heavily than small errors, *MAE* penalises large errors proportionately equally as heavily as small errors, while the sign prediction criterion does not penalise large errors any more than small errors.

6.11.10 Finance theory and time series analysis

An example of ARIMA model identification, estimation and forecasting in the context of commodity prices is given by Chu (1978). He finds ARIMA models useful compared with structural models for short-term forecasting, but also finds that they are less accurate over longer horizons. It also observed that ARIMA models have limited capacity to forecast unusual movements in prices.

Chu (1978) argues that, although ARIMA models may appear to be completely lacking in theoretical motivation, and interpretation, this may not necessarily be the case. He cites several papers and offers an additional example to suggest that ARIMA specifications quite often arise naturally as reduced form equations (see chapter 7) corresponding to some underlying structural relationships. In such a case, not only would ARIMA models be convenient and easy to estimate, they could also be well grounded in financial or economic theory after all.

6.12 Forecasting using ARMA models in EViews

Once a specific model order has been chosen and the model estimated for a particular set of data, it may be of interest to use the model to forecast future values of the series. Suppose that the AR(2) model selected for the house price percentage changes series were estimated using observations February 1991–December 2010, leaving twenty-nine remaining observations to construct forecasts for and to test forecast accuracy (for the period January 2011–May 2013).

Once the required model has been estimated and EViews has opened a window displaying the output, click on the **Forecast** icon. In this instance, the sample range to forecast would be entered as 2011M01–2013M05. There are two methods available in EViews for constructing forecasts: dynamic and static. Select the option **Dynamic** to calculate multi-step forecasts starting from the first period in the forecast sample or **Static** to calculate a sequence of one-step-ahead forecasts, rolling the sample forwards one observation after each forecast. There is also a box that allows you to choose to use actual rather than forecasted values for lagged dependent variables for the out-of-sample observations. Screenshot 6.2 shows the window to enter these options while the outputs for the dynamic and static forecasts are given in screenshots 6.3 and 6.4. By default, EViews will store the forecasts in a new series DHPF. If you examine this series you will see that all of the observations up to and including December 2010 are the same as the original series (since we did not forecast those data points) but the data points from January 2011 onwards represent the forecasts from the AR(2).

The forecasts are plotted using the continuous line, while a confidence interval is given by the two dotted lines in each case. For the dynamic forecasts, it is clearly evident that the forecasts quickly converge upon the long-term unconditional mean value as the horizon increases. Of course, this does not occur with the series of one-step-ahead forecasts produced by the 'static' command. Several other useful measures concerning the forecast errors are displayed in the plot box, including the

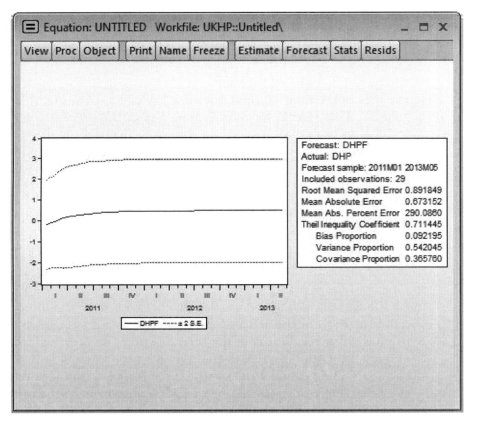

Screenshot 6.2   **The options available when producing forecasts**

Screenshot 6.3   **Dynamic forecasts for the percentage changes in house prices**

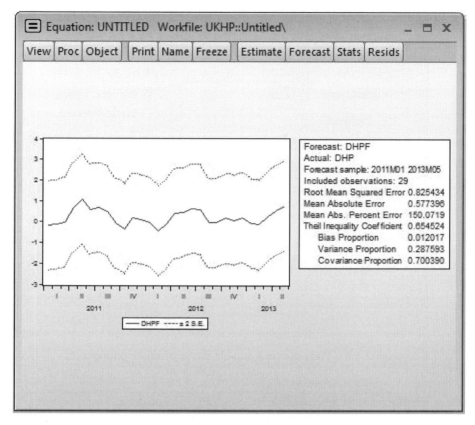

Screenshot 6.4   **Static forecasts for the percentage changes in house prices**

square root of the mean squared error (RMSE), the MAE, the MAPE and Theil's U-statistic. The MAPE for the dynamic and static forecasts for DHP are well over 100% in both cases, which can sometimes happen for the reasons outlined above. This indicates that the model forecasts are unable to account for much of the variability of the out-of-sample part of the data. This is to be expected as forecasting changes in house prices, along with the changes in the prices of any other assets, is difficult!

EViews provides another piece of useful information – a decomposition of the forecast errors. The mean squared forecast error can be decomposed into a bias proportion, a variance proportion and a covariance proportion. The *bias component* measures the extent to which the mean of the forecasts is different to the mean of the actual data (i.e. whether the forecasts are biased). Similarly, the *variance component* measures the difference between the variation of the forecasts and the variation of the actual data, while the *covariance component* captures any remaining unsystematic part of the forecast errors. As one might have expected, the forecasts are not biased. Accurate forecasts would be unbiased and also have a small variance proportion, so that most of the forecast error should be attributable to the covariance (unsystematic or residual) component. For further details, see Granger and Newbold (1986).

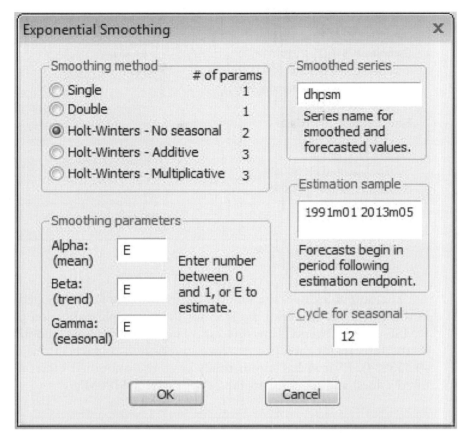

Screenshot 6.5   **Estimating exponential smoothing models**

A robust forecasting exercise would of course employ a longer out-of-sample period than the two years or so used here, would perhaps employ several competing models in parallel, and would also compare the accuracy of the predictions by examining the error measures given in the box after the forecast plots.

6.13 Exponential smoothing models in EViews

This class of models can be easily estimated in EViews by double clicking on the desired variable in the workfile, so that the spreadsheet for that variable appears, and selecting **Proc** on the button bar for that variable and then **Exponential Smoothing/Simple Exponential Smoothing. . . .** The screen with options will appear as in screenshot 6.5.

There is a variety of smoothing methods available, including single and double, or various methods to allow for seasonality and trends in the data. Select **Single** (exponential smoothing), which is the only smoothing method that has been discussed in this book, and specify the estimation sample period as **1991M1 − 2010M12** to leave twenty-nine observations for out-of-sample forecasting. Clicking **OK** will give the results in the following table.

Date: 07/06/13 Time: 14:31
Sample: 1991M02 2010M12
Included observations: 239
Method: Single Exponential
Original Series: DHP
Forecast Series: DHPSM

Parameters: Alpha	0.2400
Sum of Squared Residuals	299.3045
Root Mean Squared Error	1.119071

End of Period Levels:	Mean	−0.458934

The output includes the value of the estimated smoothing coefficient ($= 0.24$ in this case), together with the RSS for the in-sample estimation period and the RMSE for the twenty-nine forecasts. The final in-sample smoothed value will be the forecast for those twenty-nine observations (which in this case would be –0.458934). EViews has automatically saved the smoothed values (i.e. the model fitted values) and the forecasts in a series called 'DHPSM'.

Key concepts

The key terms to be able to define and explain from this chapter are

- ARIMA models
- invertible MA
- autocorrelation function
- Box–Jenkins methodology
- exponential smoothing
- rolling window
- multi-step forecast
- mean absolute percentage error

- Ljung–Box test
- Wold's decomposition theorem
- partial autocorrelation function
- information criteria
- recursive window
- out-of-sample
- mean squared error

Self-study questions

1. What are the differences between autoregressive and moving average models?
2. Why might ARMA models be considered particularly useful for financial time series? Explain, without using any equations or mathematical notation, the difference between AR, MA and ARMA processes.

3. Consider the following three models that a researcher suggests might be a reasonable model of stock market prices

$$y_t = y_{t-1} + u_t \tag{6.190}$$
$$y_t = 0.5y_{t-1} + u_t \tag{6.191}$$
$$y_t = 0.8u_{t-1} + u_t \tag{6.192}$$

(a) What classes of models are these examples of?

(b) What would the autocorrelation function for each of these processes look like? (You do not need to calculate the acf, simply consider what shape it might have given the class of model from which it is drawn.)

(c) Which model is more likely to represent stock market prices from a theoretical perspective, and why? If any of the three models truly represented the way stock market prices move, which could potentially be used to make money by forecasting future values of the series?

(d) By making a series of successive substitutions or from your knowledge of the behaviour of these types of processes, consider the extent of persistence of shocks in the series in each case.

4. (a) Describe the steps that Box and Jenkins (1976) suggested should be involved in constructing an ARMA model.

(b) What particular aspect of this methodology has been the subject of criticism and why?

(c) Describe an alternative procedure that could be used for this aspect.

5. You obtain the following estimates for an AR(2) model of some returns data

$$y_t = 0.803y_{t-1} + 0.682y_{t-2} + u_t$$

where u_t is a white noise error process. By examining the characteristic equation, check the estimated model for stationarity.

6. A researcher is trying to determine the appropriate order of an ARMA model to describe some actual data, with 200 observations available. She has the following figures for the log of the estimated residual variance (i.e. log $(\hat{\sigma}^2)$) for various candidate models. She has assumed that an order greater than (3,3) should not be necessary to model the dynamics of the data. What is the 'optimal' model order?

ARMA(p,q) model order	$\log(\hat{\sigma}^2)$
(0,0)	0.932
(1,0)	0.864
(0,1)	0.902
(1,1)	0.836
(2,1)	0.801
(1,2)	0.821
(2,2)	0.789
(3,2)	0.773
(2,3)	0.782
(3,3)	0.764

7. How could you determine whether the order you suggested for question 6 was in fact appropriate?

8. 'Given that the objective of any econometric modelling exercise is to find the model that most closely 'fits' the data, then adding more lags to an ARMA model will almost invariably lead to a better fit. Therefore a large model is best because it will fit the data more closely.'

   Comment on the validity (or otherwise) of this statement.

9. (a) You obtain the following sample autocorrelations and partial autocorrelations for a sample of 100 observations from actual data:

Lag	1	2	3	4	5	6	7	8
acf	0.420	0.104	0.032	−0.206	−0.138	0.042	−0.018	0.074
pacf	0.632	0.381	0.268	0.199	0.205	0.101	0.096	0.082

   Can you identify the most appropriate time series process for this data?

   (b) Use the Ljung–Box Q^* test to determine whether the first three autocorrelation coefficients taken together are jointly significantly different from zero.

10. You have estimated the following ARMA(1,1) model for some time series data

    $$y_t = 0.036 + 0.69y_{t-1} + 0.42u_{t-1} + u_t$$

    Suppose that you have data for time to $t-1$, i.e. you know that $y_{t-1} = 3.4$, and $\hat{u}_{t-1} = -1.3$

    (a) Obtain forecasts for the series y for times t, $t+1$, and $t+2$ using the estimated ARMA model.

    (b) If the actual values for the series turned out to be -0.032, 0.961, 0.203 for t, $t+1$, $t+2$, calculate the (out-of-sample) mean squared error.

    (c) A colleague suggests that a simple exponential smoothing model might be more useful for forecasting the series. The estimated value of the smoothing constant is 0.15, with the most recently available smoothed value, S_{t-1} being 0.0305. Obtain forecasts for the series y for times t, $t+1$, and $t+2$ using this model.

    (d) Given your answers to parts (a) to (c) of the question, determine whether Box–Jenkins or exponential smoothing models give the most accurate forecasts in this application.

11. (a) Explain what stylised shapes would be expected for the autocorrelation and partial autocorrelation functions for the following stochastic processes:
    - white noise
    - an AR(2)
    - an MA(1)
    - an ARMA (2,1).

    (b) Consider the following ARMA process.

    $$y_t = 0.21 + 1.32y_{t-1} + 0.58u_{t-1} + u_t$$

Determine whether the MA part of the process is invertible.

(c) Produce one-, two-, three- and four-step-ahead forecasts for the process given in part (b).

(d) Outline two criteria that are available for evaluating the forecasts produced in part (c), highlighting the differing characteristics of each.

(e) What procedure might be used to estimate the parameters of an ARMA model? Explain, briefly, how such a procedure operates, and why OLS is not appropriate.

12. (a) Briefly explain any difference you perceive between the characteristics of macroeconomic and financial data. Which of these features suggest the use of different econometric tools for each class of data?

(b) Consider the following autocorrelation and partial autocorrelation coefficients estimated using 500 observations for a weakly stationary series, y_t:

Lag	acf	pacf
1	0.307	0.307
2	−0.013	0.264
3	0.086	0.147
4	0.031	0.086
5	−0.197	0.049

Using a simple 'rule of thumb', determine which, if any, of the acf and pacf coefficients are significant at the 5% level. Use both the Box–Pierce and Ljung–Box statistics to test the joint null hypothesis that the first five autocorrelation coefficients are jointly zero.

(c) What process would you tentatively suggest could represent the most appropriate model for the series in part (b)? Explain your answer.

(d) Two researchers are asked to estimate an ARMA model for a daily USD/GBP exchange rate return series, denoted x_t. Researcher A uses Schwarz's criterion for determining the appropriate model order and arrives at an ARMA(0,1). Researcher B uses Akaike's information criterion which deems an ARMA(2,0) to be optimal. The estimated models are

$$A : \hat{x}_t = 0.38 + 0.10u_{t-1}$$
$$B : \hat{x}_t = 0.63 + 0.17x_{t-1} - 0.09x_{t-2}$$

where u_t is an error term.
You are given the following data for time until day z (i.e. $t = z$)

$$x_z = 0.31, \ x_{z-1} = 0.02, \ x_{z-2} = -0.16$$
$$u_z = -0.02, \ u_{z-1} = 0.13, \ u_{z-2} = 0.19$$

Produce forecasts for the next four days (i.e. for times $z+1$, $z+2$, $z+3$, $z+4$) from both models.

(e) Outline two methods proposed by Box and Jenkins (1970) for determining the adequacy of the models proposed in part (d).

(f) Suppose that the actual values of the series x on days $z+1$, $z+2$, $z+3$, $z+4$ turned out to be 0.62, 0.19, -0.32, 0.72, respectively. Determine which researcher's model produced the most accurate forecasts.

13. Select two of the stock series from the 'CAPM.XLS' Excel file, construct a set of continuously compounded returns, and then perform a time series analysis of these returns. The analysis should include

(a) An examination of the autocorrelation and partial autocorrelation functions.

(b) An estimation of the information criteria for each ARMA model order from (0,0) to (5,5).

(c) An estimation of the model that you feel most appropriate given the results that you found from the previous two parts of the question.

(d) The construction of a forecasting framework to compare the forecasting accuracy of

   i. Your chosen ARMA model

   ii. An arbitrary ARMA(1,1)

   iii. An single exponential smoothing model

   iv. A random walk with drift in the log price levels (hint: this is easiest achieved by treating the returns as an ARMA(0,0) – i.e. simply estimating a model including only a constant).

(e) Then compare the fitted ARMA model with the models that were estimated in chapter 4 based on exogenous variables. Which type of model do you prefer and why?

7 Multivariate models

Learning outcomes

In this chapter, you will learn how to
- Compare and contrast single equation and systems-based approaches to building models
- Discuss the cause, consequence and solution to simultaneous equations bias
- Derive the reduced form equations from a structural model
- Describe several methods for estimating simultaneous equations models
- Explain the relative advantages and disadvantages of VAR modelling
- Determine whether an equation from a system is identified
- Estimate optimal lag lengths, impulse responses and variance decompositions
- Conduct Granger causality tests
- Construct simultaneous equations models and VARs in EViews

7.1 Motivations

All of the structural models that have been considered thus far have been single equations models of the form

$$y = X\beta + u \tag{7.1}$$

One of the assumptions of the classical linear regression model (CLRM) is that the explanatory variables are *non-stochastic*, or fixed in repeated samples. There are various ways of stating this condition, some of which are slightly more or less strict, but all of which have the same broad implication. It could also be stated that all of the variables contained in the X matrix are assumed to be *exogenous* – that is, their values are determined outside that equation. This is a rather simplistic working definition of exogeneity, although several alternatives are possible; this issue will be revisited later in the chapter. Another way to state this is that the model is 'conditioned on' the variables in X.

As stated in chapter 3, the X matrix is assumed not to have a probability distribution. Note also that causality in this model runs from X to y, and not vice versa, i.e. that changes in the values of the explanatory variables cause changes in the values of y, but that changes in the value of y will not impact upon the explanatory variables. On the other hand, y is an *endogenous* variable – that is, its value is determined by (7.1).

The purpose of the first part of this chapter is to investigate one of the important circumstances under which the assumption presented above will be violated. The impact on the OLS estimator of such a violation will then be considered.

To illustrate a situation in which such a phenomenon may arise, consider the following two equations that describe a possible model for the total aggregate (country-wide) supply of new houses (or any other physical asset).

$$Q_{dt} = \alpha + \beta P_t + \gamma S_t + u_t \tag{7.2}$$

$$Q_{st} = \lambda + \mu P_t + \kappa T_t + v_t \tag{7.3}$$

$$Q_{dt} = Q_{st} \tag{7.4}$$

where

$Q_{dt} =$ quantity of new houses demanded at time t
$Q_{st} =$ quantity of new houses supplied (built) at time t
$P_t =$ (average) price of new houses prevailing at time t
$S_t =$ price of a substitute (e.g. older houses)
$T_t =$ some variable embodying the state of housebuilding technology, u_t and v_t are error terms.

Equation (7.2) is an equation for modelling the demand for new houses, and (7.3) models the supply of new houses. (7.4) is an equilibrium condition for there to be no excess demand (people willing and able to buy new houses but cannot) and no excess supply (constructed houses that remain empty owing to lack of demand).

Assuming that the market always clears, that is, that the market is always in equilibrium, and dropping the time subscripts for simplicity, (7.2)–(7.4) can be written

$$Q = \alpha + \beta P + \gamma S + u \tag{7.5}$$

$$Q = \lambda + \mu P + \kappa T + v \tag{7.6}$$

Equations (7.5) and (7.6) together comprise a simultaneous structural form of the model, or a set of structural equations. These are the equations incorporating the variables that economic or financial theory suggests should be related to one another in a relationship of this form. The point is that price and quantity are determined simultaneously (price affects quantity and quantity affects price). Thus, in order to sell more houses, everything else equal, the builder will have to lower the price. Equally, in order to obtain a higher price for each house, the builder should construct and expect to sell fewer houses. P and Q are endogenous variables, while S and T are exogenous.

A set of reduced form equations corresponding to (7.5) and (7.6) can be obtained by solving (7.5) and (7.6) for P and for Q (separately). There will be a reduced form equation for each endogenous variable in the system.

Solving for Q

$$\alpha + \beta P + \gamma S + u = \lambda + \mu P + \kappa T + v \tag{7.7}$$

Solving for P

$$\frac{Q}{\beta} - \frac{\alpha}{\beta} - \frac{\gamma S}{\beta} - \frac{u}{\beta} = \frac{Q}{\mu} - \frac{\lambda}{\mu} - \frac{\kappa T}{\mu} - \frac{v}{\mu} \tag{7.8}$$

Rearranging (7.7)

$$\beta P - \mu P = \lambda - \alpha + \kappa T - \gamma S + v - u \tag{7.9}$$

$$(\beta - \mu)P = (\lambda - \alpha) + \kappa T - \gamma S + (v - u) \tag{7.10}$$

$$P = \frac{\lambda - \alpha}{\beta - \mu} + \frac{\kappa}{\beta - \mu}T - \frac{\gamma}{\beta - \mu}S + \frac{v - u}{\beta - \mu} \tag{7.11}$$

Multiplying (7.8) through by $\beta\mu$ and rearranging

$$\mu Q - \mu\alpha - \mu\gamma S - \mu u = \beta Q - \beta\lambda - \beta\kappa T - \beta v \tag{7.12}$$

$$\mu Q - \beta Q = \mu\alpha - \beta\lambda - \beta\kappa T + \mu\gamma S + \mu u - \beta v \tag{7.13}$$

$$(\mu - \beta)Q = (\mu\alpha - \beta\lambda) - \beta\kappa T + \mu\gamma S + (\mu u - \beta v) \tag{7.14}$$

$$Q = \frac{\mu\alpha - \beta\lambda}{\mu - \beta} - \frac{\beta\kappa}{\mu - \beta}T + \frac{\mu\gamma}{\mu - \beta}S + \frac{\mu u - \beta v}{\mu - \beta} \tag{7.15}$$

(7.11) and (7.15) are the reduced form equations for P and Q. They are the equations that result from solving the simultaneous structural equations given by (7.5) and (7.6). Notice that these reduced form equations have only exogenous variables on the right hand side (RHS).

7.2 Simultaneous equations bias

It would not be possible to estimate (7.5) and (7.6) validly using OLS, as they are clearly related to one another since they both contain P and Q, and OLS would require them to be estimated separately. But what would have happened if a researcher had estimated them separately using OLS? Both equations depend on P. One of the CLRM assumptions was that X and u are independent (where X is a matrix containing all the variables on the RHS of the equation), and given also the assumption that $E(u) = 0$, then $E(X'u) = 0$, i.e. the errors are uncorrelated with the explanatory variables. But it is clear from (7.11) that P is related to the errors in (7.5) and (7.6) – i.e. it is *stochastic*. So this assumption has been violated.

What would be the consequences for the OLS estimator, $\hat{\beta}$ if the simultaneity were ignored? Recall that

$$\hat{\beta} = (X'X)^{-1}X'y \tag{7.16}$$

and that

$$y = X\beta + u \tag{7.17}$$

Replacing y in (7.16) with the RHS of (7.17)

$$\hat{\beta} = (X'X)^{-1}X'(X\beta + u) \tag{7.18}$$

so that

$$\hat{\beta} = (X'X)^{-1}X'X\beta + (X'X)^{-1}X'u \tag{7.19}$$

$$\hat{\beta} = \beta + (X'X)^{-1}X'u \tag{7.20}$$

Taking expectations,

$$E(\hat{\beta}) = E(\beta) + E((X'X)^{-1}X'u) \tag{7.21}$$

$$E(\hat{\beta}) = \beta + E((X'X)^{-1}X'u) \tag{7.22}$$

If the Xs are non-stochastic (i.e. if the assumption had not been violated), $E[(X'X)^{-1}X'u] = (X'X)^{-1}X'E[u] = 0$, which would be the case in a single equation system, so that $E(\hat{\beta}) = \beta$ in (7.22). The implication is that the OLS estimator, $\hat{\beta}$, would be unbiased.

But, if the equation is part of a system, then $E[(X'X)^{-1}X'u] \neq 0$, in general, so that the last term in (7.22) will not drop out, and so it can be concluded that application of OLS to structural equations which are part of a simultaneous system will lead to biased coefficient estimates. This is known as *simultaneity bias* or *simultaneous equations bias*.

Is the OLS estimator still consistent, even though it is biased? No, in fact, the estimator is inconsistent as well, so that the coefficient estimates would still be biased even if an infinite amount of data were available, although proving this would require a level of algebra beyond the scope of this book.

7.3 So how can simultaneous equations models be validly estimated?

Taking (7.11) and (7.15), i.e. the reduced form equations, they can be rewritten as

$$P = \pi_{10} + \pi_{11}T + \pi_{12}S + \varepsilon_1 \tag{7.23}$$

$$Q = \pi_{20} + \pi_{21}T + \pi_{22}S + \varepsilon_2 \tag{7.24}$$

where the π coefficients in the reduced form are simply combinations of the original coefficients, so that

$$\pi_{10} = \frac{\lambda - \alpha}{\beta - \mu}, \quad \pi_{11} = \frac{\kappa}{\beta - \mu}, \quad \pi_{12} = \frac{-\gamma}{\beta - \mu}, \quad \varepsilon_1 = \frac{v - u}{\beta - \mu},$$

$$\pi_{20} = \frac{\mu\alpha - \beta\lambda}{\mu - \beta}, \quad \pi_{21} = \frac{-\beta\kappa}{\mu - \beta}, \quad \pi_{22} = \frac{\mu\gamma}{\mu - \beta}, \quad \varepsilon_2 = \frac{\mu u - \beta v}{\mu - \beta}$$

Equations (7.23) and (7.24) can be estimated using OLS since all the RHS variables are exogenous, so the usual requirements for consistency and unbiasedness of the OLS estimator will hold (provided that there are no other misspecifications). Estimates of the π_{ij} coefficients would thus be obtained. But, the values of the π coefficients are probably not of much interest; what was wanted were the original parameters in the structural equations – α, β, γ, λ, μ, κ. The latter are the parameters whose values determine how the variables are related to one another according to financial or economic theory.

7.4 Can the original coefficients be retrieved from the πs?

The short answer to this question is 'sometimes', depending upon whether the equations are identified. *Identification* is the issue of whether there is enough information in the reduced form equations to enable the structural form coefficients to be calculated. Consider the following demand and supply equations

$$Q = \alpha + \beta P \quad \text{Supply equation} \tag{7.25}$$

$$Q = \lambda + \mu P \quad \text{Demand equation} \tag{7.26}$$

It is impossible to tell which equation is which, so that if one simply observed some quantities of a good sold and the price at which they were sold, it would not be possible to obtain the estimates of α, β, λ and μ. This arises since there is insufficient information from the equations to estimate four parameters. Only two parameters could be estimated here, although each would be some combination of demand and supply parameters, and so neither would be of any use. In this case, it would be stated that both equations are *unidentified* (or not identified or underidentified). Notice that this problem would not have arisen with (7.5) and (7.6) since they have different exogenous variables.

7.4.1 What determines whether an equation is identified or not?

Any one of three possible situations could arise, as shown in box 7.1.

How can it be determined whether an equation is identified or not? Broadly, the answer to this question depends upon how many and which variables are present in each structural equation. There are two conditions that could be examined to determine whether a given equation from a system is identified – the *order condition* and the *rank condition*:

- The *order condition* – is a necessary but not sufficient condition for an equation to be identified. That is, even if the order condition is satisfied, the equation might not be identified.
- The *rank condition* – is a necessary and sufficient condition for identification. The structural equations are specified in a matrix form and the rank of a coefficient matrix of all of the variables excluded from a particular equation is examined. An examination of the rank condition requires some technical algebra beyond the scope of this text.

> ### Box 7.1   Determining whether an equation is identified
>
> (1) An equation is *unidentified*, such as (7.25) or (7.26). In the case of an unidentified equation, structural coefficients cannot be obtained from the reduced form estimates by any means.
> (2) An equation is *exactly identified* (*just identified*), such as (7.5) or (7.6). In the case of a just identified equation, unique structural form coefficient estimates can be obtained by substitution from the reduced form equations.
> (3) If an equation is *overidentified*, more than one set of structural coefficients can be obtained from the reduced form. An example of this will be presented later in this chapter.

Even though the order condition is not sufficient to ensure identification of an equation from a system, the rank condition will not be considered further here. For relatively simple systems of equations, the two rules would lead to the same conclusions. Also, in fact, most systems of equations in economics and finance are overidentified, so that underidentification is not a big issue in practice.

7.4.2   Statement of the order condition

There are a number of different ways of stating the order condition; that employed here is an intuitive one (taken from Ramanathan, 1995, p. 666, and slightly modified):

Let G denote the number of structural equations. An equation is just identified if the number of variables excluded from an equation is $G-1$, where 'excluded' means the number of all endogenous and exogenous variables that are not present in this particular equation. If more than $G-1$ are absent, it is over-identified. If less than $G-1$ are absent, it is not identified.

One obvious implication of this rule is that equations in a system can have differing degrees of identification, as illustrated by the following example.

Example 7.1 •••

In the following system of equations, the Ys are endogenous, while the Xs are exogenous (with time subscripts suppressed). Determine whether each equation is overidentified, underidentified, or just identified.

$$Y_1 = \alpha_0 + \alpha_1 Y_2 + \alpha_3 Y_3 + \alpha_4 X_1 + \alpha_5 X_2 + u_1 \tag{7.27}$$

$$Y_2 = \beta_0 + \beta_1 Y_3 + \beta_2 X_1 + u_2 \tag{7.28}$$

$$Y_3 = \gamma_0 + \gamma_1 Y_2 + u_3 \tag{7.29}$$

In this case, there are $G = 3$ equations and 3 endogenous variables. Thus, if the number of excluded variables is exactly 2, the equation is just identified. If the number of excluded variables is more than 2, the equation is overidentified. If the number of excluded variables is less than 2, the equation is not identified.

The variables that appear in one or more of the three equations are Y_1, Y_2, Y_3, X_1, X_2. Applying the order condition to (7.27)–(7.29):

- Equation (7.27): contains all variables, with none excluded, so that it is not identified
- Equation (7.28): has variables Y_1 and X_2 excluded, and so is just identified
- Equation (7.29): has variables Y_1, X_1, X_2 excluded, and so is overidentified

7.5 Simultaneous equations in finance

There are of course numerous situations in finance where a simultaneous equations framework is more relevant than a single equation model. Two illustrations from the market microstructure literature are presented later in this chapter, while another, drawn from the banking literature, will be discussed now.

There has recently been much debate internationally, but especially in the UK, concerning the effectiveness of competitive forces in the banking industry. Governments and regulators express concern at the increasing concentration in the industry, as evidenced by successive waves of merger activity, and at the enormous profits that many banks made in the late 1990s and early twenty-first century. They argue that such profits result from a lack of effective competition. However, many (most notably, of course, the banks themselves!) suggest that such profits are not the result of excessive concentration or anti-competitive practices, but rather partly arise owing to recent world prosperity at that phase of the business cycle (the 'profits won't last' argument) and partly owing to massive cost-cutting by the banks, given recent technological improvements. These debates have fuelled a resurgent interest in models of banking profitability and banking competition. One such model is employed by Shaffer and DiSalvo (1994) in the context of two banks operating in south central Pennsylvania. The model is given by

$$\ln q_{it} = a_0 + a_1 \ln P_{it} + a_2 \ln P_{jt} + a_3 \ln Y_t + a_4 \ln Z_t + a_5 t + u_{i1t} \tag{7.30}$$

$$\ln TR_{it} = b_0 + b_1 \ln q_{it} + \sum_{k=1}^{3} b_{k+1} \ln w_{ikt} + u_{i2t} \tag{7.31}$$

where $i = 1, 2$ are the two banks, q is bank output, P_t is the price of the output at time t, Y_t is a measure of aggregate income at time t, Z_t is the price of a substitute for bank activity at time t, the variable t represents a time trend, TR_{it} is the total revenue of bank i at time t, w_{ikt} are the prices of input k ($k = 1, 2, 3$ for labour, bank deposits and physical capital) for bank i at time t and the u are unobservable error terms. The coefficient estimates are not presented here, but suffice to say that a simultaneous framework, with the resulting model estimated separately using annual time series data for each bank, is necessary. Output is a function of price on the RHS of (7.30), while in (7.31), total revenue, which is a function of output on the RHS, is obviously related to price. Therefore, OLS is again an inappropriate estimation technique. Both of the equations in this system are overidentified, since there are only two equations, and the income, the substitute for banking activity and the trend terms are missing from (7.31), whereas the three input prices are missing from (7.30).

7.6　A definition of exogeneity

Leamer (1985) defines a variable x as exogenous if the conditional distribution of y given x does not change with modifications of the process generating x. Although several slightly different definitions exist, it is possible to classify two forms of exogeneity – predeterminedness and strict exogeneity:

- A *predetermined* variable is one that is independent of the contemporaneous and future errors in that equation
- A *strictly exogenous* variable is one that is independent of all contemporaneous, future and past errors in that equation.

7.6.1　Tests for exogeneity

How can a researcher tell whether variables really need to be treated as endogenous or not? In other words, financial theory might suggest that there should be a two-way relationship between two or more variables, but how can it be tested whether a simultaneous equations model is necessary in practice?

Example 7.2

Consider again (7.27)–(7.29). Equation (7.27) contains Y_2 and Y_3 – but are separate equations required for them, or could the variables Y_2 and Y_3 be treated as exogenous variables (in which case, they would be called X_3 and X_4!)? This can be formally investigated using a Hausman test, which is calculated as shown in box 7.2.

Box 7.2　Conducting a Hausman test for exogeneity

(1) Obtain the reduced form equations corresponding to (7.27)–(7.29). The reduced form equations are obtained as follows.

Substituting in (7.28) for Y_3 from (7.29):

$$Y_2 = \beta_0 + \beta_1(\gamma_0 + \gamma_1 Y_2 + u_3) + \beta_2 X_1 + u_2 \tag{7.32}$$

$$Y_2 = \beta_0 + \beta_1\gamma_0 + \beta_1\gamma_1 Y_2 + \beta_1 u_3 + \beta_2 X_1 + u_2 \tag{7.33}$$

$$Y_2(1 - \beta_1\gamma_1) = (\beta_0 + \beta_1\gamma_0) + \beta_2 X_1 + (u_2 + \beta_1 u_3) \tag{7.34}$$

$$Y_2 = \frac{(\beta_0 + \beta_1\gamma_0)}{(1 - \beta_1\gamma_1)} + \frac{\beta_2 X_1}{(1 - \beta_1\gamma_1)} + \frac{(u_2 + \beta_1 u_3)}{(1 - \beta_1\gamma_1)} \tag{7.35}$$

(7.35) is the reduced form equation for Y_2, since there are no endogenous variables on the RHS. Substituting in (7.27) for Y_3 from (7.29):

$$Y_1 = \alpha_0 + \alpha_1 Y_2 + \alpha_3(\gamma_0 + \gamma_1 Y_2 + u_3) + \alpha_4 X_1 + \alpha_5 X_2 + u_1 \quad (7.36)$$

$$Y_1 = \alpha_0 + \alpha_1 Y_2 + \alpha_3\gamma_0 + \alpha_3\gamma_1 Y_2 + \alpha_3 u_3 + \alpha_4 X_1 + \alpha_5 X_2 + u_1$$

$$(7.37)$$

$$Y_1 = (\alpha_0 + \alpha_3\gamma_0) + (\alpha_1 + \alpha_3\gamma_1)Y_2 + \alpha_4 X_1 + \alpha_5 X_2 + (u_1 + \alpha_3 u_3)$$

$$(7.38)$$

Substituting in (7.38) for Y_2 from (7.35):

$$Y_1 = (\alpha_0 + \alpha_3\gamma_0) + (\alpha_1 + \alpha_3\gamma_1)\left(\frac{(\beta_0 + \beta_1\gamma_0)}{(1 - \beta_1\gamma_1)} + \frac{\beta_2 X_1}{(1 - \beta_1\gamma_1)}\right.$$

$$\left. + \frac{(u_2 + \beta_1 u_3)}{(1 - \beta_1\gamma_1)}\right) + \alpha_4 X_1 + \alpha_5 X_2 + (u_1 + \alpha_3 u_3) \quad (7.39)$$

$$Y_1 = \left(\alpha_0 + \alpha_3\gamma_0 + (\alpha_1 + \alpha_3\gamma_1)\frac{(\beta_0 + \beta_1\gamma_0)}{(1 - \beta_1\gamma_1)}\right) + \frac{(\alpha_1 + \alpha_3\gamma_1)\beta_2 X_1}{(1 - \beta_1\gamma_1)}$$

$$+ \frac{(\alpha_1 + \alpha_3\gamma_1)(u_2 + \beta_1 u_3)}{(1 - \beta_1\gamma_1)} + \alpha_4 X_1 + \alpha_5 X_2 + (u_1 + \alpha_3 u_3)$$

$$(7.40)$$

$$Y_1 = \left(\alpha_0 + \alpha_3\gamma_0 + (\alpha_1 + \alpha_3\gamma_1)\frac{(\beta_0 + \beta_1\gamma_0)}{(1 - \beta_1\gamma_1)}\right)$$

$$+ \left(\frac{(\alpha_1 + \alpha_3\gamma_1)\beta_2}{(1 - \beta_1\gamma_1)} + \alpha_4\right) X_1 + \alpha_5 X_2$$

$$+ \left(\frac{(\alpha_1 + \alpha_3\gamma_1)(u_2 + \beta_1 u_3)}{(1 - \beta_1\gamma_1)} + (u_1 + \alpha_3 u_3)\right) \quad (7.41)$$

(7.41) is the reduced form equation for Y_1. Finally, to obtain the reduced form equation for Y_3, substitute in (7.29) for Y_2 from (7.35):

$$Y_3 = \left(\gamma_0 + \frac{\gamma_1(\beta_0 + \beta_1\gamma_0)}{(1 - \beta_1\gamma_1)}\right) + \frac{\gamma_1\beta_2 X_1}{(1 - \beta_1\gamma_1)} + \left(\frac{\gamma_1(u_2 + \beta_1 u_3)}{(1 - \beta_1\gamma_1)} + u_3\right)$$

$$(7.42)$$

So, the reduced form equations corresponding to (7.27)–(7.29) are, respectively, given by (7.41), (7.35) and (7.42). These three equations can also be expressed using π_{ij} for the coefficients, as discussed above:

$$Y_1 = \pi_{10} + \pi_{11} X_1 + \pi_{12} X_2 + v_1 \quad (7.43)$$

$$Y_2 = \pi_{20} + \pi_{21} X_1 + v_2 \quad (7.44)$$

$$Y_3 = \pi_{30} + \pi_{31} X_1 + v_3 \quad (7.45)$$

Estimate the reduced form equations (7.43)–(7.45) using OLS, and obtain the fitted values, $\hat{Y}_1^1$, $\hat{Y}_2^1$, $\hat{Y}_3^1$, where the superfluous superscript ^{1} denotes the fitted values from the reduced form estimation.

(2) Run the regression corresponding to (7.27) – i.e. the structural form equation, at this stage ignoring any possible simultaneity.

(3) Run the regression (7.27) again, but now also including the fitted values from the reduced form equations, $\hat{Y}_2^1$, $\hat{Y}_3^1$, as additional regressors

$$Y_1 = \alpha_0 + \alpha_1 Y_2 + \alpha_3 Y_3 + \alpha_4 X_1 + \alpha_5 X_2 + \lambda_2 \hat{Y}_2^1 + \lambda_3 \hat{Y}_3^1 + \varepsilon_1 \quad (7.46)$$

(4) Use an F-test to test the joint restriction that $\lambda_2 = 0$, and $\lambda_3 = 0$. If the null hypothesis is rejected, Y_2 and Y_3 should be treated as endogenous. If λ_2 and λ_3 are significantly different from zero, there is extra important information for modelling Y_1 from the reduced form equations. On the other hand, if the null is not rejected, Y_2 and Y_3 can be treated as exogenous for Y_1, and there is no useful additional information available for Y_1 from modelling Y_2 and Y_3 as endogenous variables.

Steps 2–4 would then be repeated for (7.28) and (7.29).

7.7 Triangular systems

Consider the following system of equations, with time subscripts omitted for simplicity

$$Y_1 = \beta_{10} + \gamma_{11} X_1 + \gamma_{12} X_2 + u_1 \tag{7.47}$$

$$Y_2 = \beta_{20} + \beta_{21} Y_1 + \gamma_{21} X_1 + \gamma_{22} X_2 + u_2 \tag{7.48}$$

$$Y_3 = \beta_{30} + \beta_{31} Y_1 + \beta_{32} Y_2 + \gamma_{31} X_1 + \gamma_{32} X_2 + u_3 \tag{7.49}$$

Assume that the error terms from each of the three equations are not correlated with each other. Can the equations be estimated individually using OLS? At first blush, an appropriate answer to this question might appear to be, 'No, because this is a simultaneous equations system'. But consider the following:

- Equation (7.47): contains no endogenous variables, so X_1 and X_2 are not correlated with u_1. So OLS can be used on (7.47).
- Equation (7.48): contains endogenous Y_1 together with exogenous X_1 and X_2. OLS can be used on (7.48) if all the RHS variables in (7.48) are uncorrelated with that equation's error term. In fact, Y_1 is not correlated with u_2 because there is no Y_2 term in (7.47). So OLS can be used on (7.48).
- Equation (7.49): contains both Y_1 and Y_2; these are required to be uncorrelated with u_3. By similar arguments to the above, (7.47) and (7.48) do not contain Y_3. So OLS can be used on (7.49).

This is known as a *recursive or triangular system*, which is really a special case – a set of equations that looks like a simultaneous equations system, but isn't. In fact, there is not a simultaneity problem here, since the dependence is not bi-directional, for each equation it all goes one way.

7.8 Estimation procedures for simultaneous equations systems

Each equation that is part of a recursive system can be estimated separately using OLS. But in practice, not many systems of equations will be recursive, so a direct way to address the estimation of equations that are from a true simultaneous system must be sought. In fact, there are potentially many methods that can be used, three of which – indirect least squares, two-stage least squares and instrumental variables – will be detailed here. Each of these will be discussed below.

7.8.1 Indirect least squares (ILS)

Although it is not possible to use OLS directly on the structural equations, it is possible to validly apply OLS to the reduced form equations. If the system is just identified, ILS involves estimating the reduced form equations using OLS, and then using them to substitute back to obtain the structural parameters. ILS is intuitive to understand in principle; however, it is not widely applied because:

(1) *Solving back to get the structural parameters can be tedious.* For a large system, the equations may be set up in a matrix form, and to solve them may therefore require the inversion of a large matrix.
(2) *Most simultaneous equations systems are overidentified*, and ILS can be used to obtain coefficients only for just identified equations. For overidentified systems, ILS would not yield unique structural form estimates.

ILS estimators are consistent and asymptotically efficient, but in general they are biased, so that in finite samples ILS will deliver biased structural form estimates. In a nutshell, the bias arises from the fact that the structural form coefficients under ILS estimation are transformations of the reduced form coefficients. When expectations are taken to test for unbiasedness, it is in general not the case that the expected value of a (non-linear) combination of reduced form coefficients will be equal to the combination of their expected values (see Gujarati, 2003 for a proof).

7.8.2 Estimation of just identified and overidentified systems using 2SLS

This technique is applicable for the estimation of overidentified systems, where ILS cannot be used. In fact, it can also be employed for estimating the coefficients of just identified systems, in which case the method would yield asymptotically equivalent estimates to those obtained from ILS.

Two-stage least squares (2SLS or TSLS) is done in two stages:
- *Stage 1* Obtain and estimate the reduced form equations using OLS. Save the fitted values for the dependent variables.

- *Stage 2* Estimate the structural equations using OLS, but replace any RHS endogenous variables with their stage 1 fitted values.

Example 7.3 •

Suppose that (7.27)–(7.29) are required. 2SLS would involve the following two steps:

- *Stage 1* Estimate the reduced form equations (7.43)–(7.45) individually by OLS and obtain the fitted values, and denote them $\hat{Y}_1^1$, $\hat{Y}_2^1$, $\hat{Y}_3^1$, where the superfluous superscript [1] indicates that these are the fitted values from the first stage.
- *Stage 2* Replace the RHS endogenous variables with their stage 1 estimated values

$$Y_1 = \alpha_0 + \alpha_1 \hat{Y}_2^1 + \alpha_3 \hat{Y}_3^1 + \alpha_4 X_1 + \alpha_5 X_2 + u_1 \tag{7.50}$$

$$Y_2 = \beta_0 + \beta_1 \hat{Y}_3^1 + \beta_2 X_1 + u_2 \tag{7.51}$$

$$Y_3 = \gamma_0 + \gamma_1 \hat{Y}_2^1 + u_3 \tag{7.52}$$

where $\hat{Y}_2^1$ and $\hat{Y}_3^1$ are the fitted values from the reduced form estimation. Now $\hat{Y}_2^1$ and $\hat{Y}_3^1$ will not be correlated with u_1, $\hat{Y}_3^1$ will not be correlated with u_2, and $\hat{Y}_2^1$ will not be correlated with u_3. The simultaneity problem has therefore been removed. It is worth noting that the 2SLS estimator is consistent, but not unbiased.

In a simultaneous equations framework, it is still of concern whether the usual assumptions of the CLRM are valid or not, although some of the test statistics require modifications to be applicable in the systems context. Most econometrics packages will automatically make any required changes. To illustrate one potential consequence of the violation of the CLRM assumptions, if the disturbances in the structural equations are autocorrelated, the 2SLS estimator is not even consistent.

The standard error estimates also need to be modified compared with their OLS counterparts (again, econometrics software will usually do this automatically), but once this has been done, the usual t-tests can be used to test hypotheses about the structural form coefficients. This modification arises as a result of the use of the reduced form fitted values on the RHS rather than actual variables, which implies that a modification to the error variance is required.

• •

7.8.3 Instrumental variables

Broadly, the method of instrumental variables (IV) is another technique for parameter estimation that can be validly used in the context of a simultaneous equations system. Recall that the reason that OLS cannot be used directly on the structural equations is that the endogenous variables are correlated with the errors.

One solution to this would be not to use Y_2 or Y_3, but rather to use some other variables instead. These other variables should be (highly) correlated with Y_2 and Y_3, but not correlated with the errors – such variables would be known as *instruments*. Suppose that suitable instruments for Y_2 and Y_3, were found and denoted z_2 and z_3, respectively. The instruments are not used in the structural equations directly, but rather, regressions of the following form are run

$$Y_2 = \lambda_1 + \lambda_2 z_2 + \varepsilon_1 \tag{7.53}$$

$$Y_3 = \lambda_3 + \lambda_4 z_3 + \varepsilon_2 \tag{7.54}$$

Obtain the fitted values from (7.53) and (7.54), $\hat{Y}_2^1$ and $\hat{Y}_3^1$, and replace Y_2 and Y_3 with these in the structural equation. It is typical to use more than one instrument per endogenous variable. If the instruments are the variables in the reduced form equations, then IV is equivalent to 2SLS, so that the latter can be viewed as a special case of the former.

7.8.4 What happens if IV or 2SLS are used unnecessarily?

In other words, suppose that one attempted to estimate a simultaneous system when the variables specified as endogenous were in fact independent of one another. The consequences are similar to those of including irrelevant variables in a single equation OLS model. That is, the coefficient estimates will still be consistent, but will be inefficient compared to those that just used OLS directly.

7.8.5 Other estimation techniques

There are, of course, many other estimation techniques available for systems of equations, including three-stage least squares (3SLS), full information maximum likelihood (FIML) and limited information maximum likelihood (LIML). Three-stage least squares provides a third step in the estimation process that allows for non-zero covariances between the error terms in the structural equations. It is asymptotically more efficient than 2SLS since the latter ignores any information that may be available concerning the error covariances (and also any additional information that may be contained in the endogenous variables of other equations). Full information maximum likelihood involves estimating all of the equations in the system simultaneously using maximum likelihood (see chapter 8 for a discussion of the principles of maximum likelihood estimation). Thus under FIML, all of the parameters in all equations are treated jointly, and an appropriate likelihood function is formed and maximised. Finally, limited information maximum likelihood involves estimating each equation separately by maximum likelihood. LIML and 2SLS are asymptotically equivalent. For further technical details on each of these procedures, see Greene (2002, chapter 15).

The following section presents an application of the simultaneous equations approach in finance to the joint modelling of bid–ask spreads and trading activity in the S&P100 index options market. Two related applications of this technique that are also worth examining are by Wang, Yau and Baptiste (1997) and by Wang and Yau (2000). The former employs a bivariate system to model trading volume and bid–ask spreads and they show using a Hausman test that the two are indeed simultaneously related and so must both be treated as endogenous variables and are modelled using 2SLS. The latter paper employs a trivariate system to model trading volume, spreads and intra-day volatility.

7.9 An application of a simultaneous equations approach to modelling bid–ask spreads and trading activity

7.9.1 Introduction

One of the most rapidly growing areas of empirical research in finance is the study of market microstructure. This research is involved with issues such as price formation in financial markets, how the structure of the market may affect the way it operates, determinants of the bid–ask spread, and so on. One application of simultaneous equations methods in the market microstructure literature is a study by George and Longstaff (1993). Among other issues, this paper considers the questions:

- Is trading activity related to the size of the bid–ask spread?
- How do spreads vary across options, and how is this related to the volume of contracts traded? 'Across options' in this case means for different maturities and strike prices for an option on a given underlying asset.

This chapter will now examine the George and Longstaff models, results and conclusions.

7.9.2 The data

The data employed by George and Longstaff comprise options prices on the S&P100 index, observed on all trading days during 1989. The S&P100 index has been traded on the Chicago Board Options Exchange (CBOE) since 1983 on a continuous open-outcry auction basis. The option price as used in the paper is defined as the average of the bid and the ask. The average bid and ask prices are calculated for each option during the time 2.00p.m.–2.15p.m. (US Central Standard Time) to avoid time-of-day effects, such as differences in behaviour at the open and the close of the market. The following are then dropped from the sample for that day to avoid any effects resulting from stale prices:

- Any options that do not have bid and ask quotes reported during the fifteen minutes
- Any options with fewer than ten trades during the day.

This procedure results in a total of 2,456 observations. A 'pooled' regression is conducted since the data have both time series and cross-sectional dimensions. That is, the data are measured every trading day and across options with different strikes and maturities, and the data is stacked in a single column for analysis.

7.9.3 How might the option price/trading volume and the bid–ask spread be related?

George and Longstaff argue that the bid–ask spread will be determined by the interaction of market forces. Since there are many market makers trading the S&P100 contract on the CBOE, the bid–ask spread will be set to just cover marginal costs. There are three components of the costs associated with being a market maker. These are administrative costs, inventory holding costs and 'risk costs'. George and Longstaff consider three possibilities for how the bid–ask spread might be determined:

- *Market makers equalise spreads across options* This is likely to be the case if order-processing (administrative) costs make up the majority of costs associated with being a market maker. This could be the case since the CBOE charges market makers the same fee for each option traded. In fact, for every contract (100 options) traded, a CBOE fee of 9 cents and an Options Clearing Corporation (OCC) fee of 10 cents is levied on the firm that clears the trade.
- *The spread might be a constant proportion of the option value* This would be the case if the majority of the market maker's cost is in inventory holding costs, since the more expensive options will cost more to hold and hence the spread would be set wider.
- *Market makers might equalise marginal costs across options irrespective of trading volume* This would occur if the riskiness of an unwanted position were the most important cost facing market makers. Market makers typically do not hold a particular view on the direction of the market – they simply try to make money by buying and selling. Hence, they would like to be able to offload any unwanted (long or short) positions quickly. But trading is not continuous, and in fact the average time between trades in 1989 was approximately five minutes. The longer market makers hold an option, the higher the risk they face since the higher the probability that there will be a large adverse price movement. Thus options with low trading volumes would command higher spreads since it is more likely that the market maker would be holding these options for longer.

In a non-quantitative exploratory analysis, George and Longstaff find that, comparing across contracts with different maturities, the bid–ask spread does indeed increase with maturity (as the option with longer maturity is worth more) and with 'moneyness' (that is, an option that is deeper in the money has a higher spread than one which is less in the money). This is seen to be true for both call and put options.

7.9.4 The influence of tick-size rules on spreads

The CBOE limits the *tick size* (the minimum granularity of price quotes), which will of course place a lower limit on the size of the spread. The tick sizes are:

- $1/8 for options worth $3 or more
- $1/16 for options worth less than $3.

7.9.5 The models and results

The intuition that the bid–ask spread and trading volume may be simultaneously related arises since a wider spread implies that trading is relatively more expensive so that marginal investors would withdraw from the market. On the other hand, market makers face additional risk if the level of trading activity falls, and hence they may be expected to respond by increasing their fee (the spread). The models developed seek to simultaneously determine the size of the bid–ask spread and the time between trades.

For the calls, the model is:

$$CBA_i = \alpha_0 + \alpha_1 CDUM_i + \alpha_2 C_i + \alpha_3 CL_i + \alpha_4 T_i + \alpha_5 CR_i + e_i \tag{7.55}$$

$$CL_i = \gamma_0 + \gamma_1 CBA_i + \gamma_2 T_i + \gamma_3 T_i^2 + \gamma_4 M_i^2 + v_i \tag{7.56}$$

And symmetrically for the puts:

$$PBA_i = \beta_0 + \beta_1 PDUM_i + \beta_2 P_i + \beta_3 PL_i + \beta_4 T_i + \beta_5 PR_i + u_i \tag{7.57}$$

$$PL_i = \delta_0 + \delta_1 PBA_i + \delta_2 T_i + \delta_3 T_i^2 + \delta_4 M_i^2 + w_i \tag{7.58}$$

where CBA_i and PBA_i are the call bid–ask spread and the put bid–ask spread for option i, respectively

C_i and P_i are the call price and put price for option i, respectively
CL_i and PL_i are the times between trades for the call and put option i, respectively
CR_i and PR_i are the squared deltas of the options
$CDUM_i$ and $PDUM_i$ are dummy variables to allow for the minimum tick size

$$= 0 \quad \text{if } C_i \text{ or } P_i < \$3$$
$$= 1 \quad \text{if } C_i \text{ or } P_i \geq \$3$$

T is the time to maturity
T^2 allows for a non-linear relationship between time to maturity and the spread
M^2 is the square of moneyness, which is employed in quadratic form since at-the-money options have a higher trading volume, while out-of-the-money and in-the-money options both have lower trading activity
CR_i and PR_i are measures of risk for the call and put, respectively, given by the square of their deltas.

Equations (7.55) and (7.56), and then separately (7.57) and (7.58), are estimated using 2SLS. The results are given here in tables 7.1 and 7.2.

The adjusted $R^2 \approx 0.6$ for all four equations, indicating that the variables selected do a good job of explaining the spread and the time between trades. George and Longstaff argue that strategic market maker behaviour, which cannot

Table 7.1 Call bid–ask spread and trading volume regression

$$CBA_i = \alpha_0 + \alpha_1 CDUM_i + \alpha_2 C_i + \alpha_3 CL_i + \alpha_4 T_i + \alpha_5 CR_i + e_i \qquad (7.55)$$

$$CL_i = \gamma_0 + \gamma_1 CBA_i + \gamma_2 T_i + \gamma_3 T_i^2 + \gamma_4 M_i^2 + v_i \qquad (7.56)$$

α_0	α_1	α_2	α_3	α_4	α_5	Adj. R^2
0.08362	0.06114	0.01679	0.00902	−0.00228	−0.15378	0.688
(16.80)	(8.63)	(15.49)	(14.01)	(−12.31)	(−12.52)	
γ_0	γ_1	γ_2	γ_3	γ_4	Adj. R^2	
−3.8542	46.592	−0.12412	0.00406	0.00866	0.618	
(−10.50)	(30.49)	(−6.01)	(14.43)	(4.76)		

Note: t-ratios in parentheses.
Source: George and Longstaff (1993). Reprinted with the permission of School of Business Administration, University of Washington.

Table 7.2 Put bid–ask spread and trading volume regression

$$PBA_i = \beta_0 + \beta_1 PDUM_i + \beta_2 P_i + \beta_3 PL_i + \beta_4 T_i + \beta_5 PR_i + u_i \qquad (7.57)$$

$$PL_i = \delta_0 + \delta_1 PBA_i + \delta_2 T_i + \delta_3 T_i^2 + \delta_4 M_i^2 + w_i \qquad (7.58)$$

β_0	β_1	β_2	β_3	β_4	β_5	Adj.R^2
0.05707	0.03258	0.01726	0.00839	−0.00120	−0.08662	0.675
(15.19)	(5.35)	(15.90)	(12.56)	(−7.13)	(−7.15)	
δ_0	δ_1	δ_2	δ_3	δ_4	Adj. R^2	
−2.8932	46.460	−0.15151	0.00339	0.01347	0.517	
(−8.42)	(34.06)	(−7.74)	(12.90)	(10.86)		

Note: t-ratios in parentheses.
Source: George and Longstaff (1993). Reprinted with the permission of School of Business Administration, University of Washington.

be easily modelled, is important in influencing the spread and that this precludes a higher adjusted R^2.

A next step in examining the empirical plausibility of the estimates is to consider the sizes, signs and significances of the coefficients. In the call and put spread regressions, respectively, α_1 and β_1 measure the tick size constraint on the spread – both are statistically significant and positive. α_2 and β_2 measure the effect of the option price on the spread. As expected, both of these coefficients are again significant and positive since these are inventory or holding costs. The coefficient value of approximately 0.017 implies that a one dollar increase in the price of the option will on average lead to a 1.7 cent increase in the spread. α_3 and β_3 measure the effect of trading activity on the spread. Recalling that an inverse trading activity variable is used in the regressions, again, the coefficients have their correct sign. That is, as the time between trades increases (that is, as trading activity falls), the bid–ask spread widens. Furthermore, although the coefficient values are small, they are statistically significant. In the put spread regression, for example, the coefficient of approximately 0.009 implies that, even if the time between trades widened from one minute to one hour, the spread would increase by only 54 cents. α_4 and β_4 measure the effect of time to maturity on the spread; both are negative and statistically significant. The authors argue that this may arise as market making is a more risky activity for near-maturity options. A possible alternative explanation, which they dismiss after further investigation, is that the early exercise possibility becomes more likely for very short-dated options since the loss of time value would be negligible. Finally, α_5 and β_5 measure the effect of risk on the spread; in both the call and put spread regressions, these coefficients are negative and highly statistically significant. This seems an odd result, which the authors struggle to justify, for it seems to suggest that more risky options will command lower spreads.

Turning attention now to the trading activity regressions, γ_1 and δ_1 measure the effect of the spread size on call and put trading activity, respectively. Both are positive and statistically significant, indicating that a rise in the spread will increase the time between trades. The coefficients are such that a one *cent* increase in the spread would lead to an increase in the average time between call and put trades of nearly half a minute. γ_2 and δ_2 give the effect of an increase in time to maturity, while γ_3 and δ_3 are coefficients attached to the square of time to maturity. For both the call and put regressions, the coefficient on the level of time to maturity is negative and significant, while that on the square is positive and significant. As time to maturity increases, the squared term would dominate, and one could therefore conclude that the time between trades will show a U-shaped relationship with time to maturity. Finally, γ_4 and δ_4 give the effect of an increase in the square of moneyness (i.e. the effect of an option going deeper into the money or deeper out of the money) on the time between trades. For both the call and put regressions, the coefficients are statistically significant and positive, showing that as the option moves further from the money in either direction, the time between trades rises. This is consistent with the authors' supposition that trade is most active in at-the-money options, and less active in both out-of-the-money and in-the-money options.

7.9.6 Conclusions

The value of the bid–ask spread on S&P100 index options and the time between trades (a measure of market liquidity) can be usefully modelled in a simultaneous system with exogenous variables such as the options' deltas, time to maturity, moneyness, etc.

This study represents a nice example of the use of a simultaneous equations system, but, in this author's view, it can be criticised on several grounds. First, there are no diagnostic tests performed. Second, clearly the equations are all overidentified, but it is not obvious how the over-identifying restrictions have been generated. Did they arise from consideration of financial theory? For example, why do the *CL* and *PL* equations not contain the *CR* and *PR* variables? Why do the *CBA* and *PBA* equations not contain moneyness or squared maturity variables? The authors could also have tested for endogeneity of *CBA* and *CL*. Finally, the wrong sign on the highly statistically significant squared deltas is puzzling.

7.10 Simultaneous equations modelling using EViews

What is the relationship between inflation and stock returns? Holding stocks is often thought to provide a good hedge against inflation, since the payments to equity holders are not fixed in nominal terms and represent a claim on real assets (unlike the coupons on bonds, for example). However, the majority of empirical studies that have investigated the sign of this relationship have found it to be negative. Various explanations of this puzzling empirical phenomenon have been proposed, including a link through real activity, so that real activity is negatively related to inflation but positively related to stock returns and therefore stock returns and inflation vary positively. Clearly, inflation and stock returns ought to be simultaneously related given that the rate of inflation will affect the discount rate applied to cashflows and therefore the value of equities, but the performance of the stock market may also affect consumer demand and therefore inflation through its impact on householder wealth (perceived or actual).[1]

This simple example uses the same macroeconomic data as used previously to estimate this relationship simultaneously. Suppose (without justification) that we wish to estimate the following model, which does not allow for dynamic effects or partial adjustments and does not distinguish between expected and unexpected inflation

$$inflation_t = \alpha_0 + \alpha_1\ returns_t + \alpha_2\ dcredit_t + \alpha_3\ dprod_t + \alpha_4\ dmoney + u_{1t}$$

(7.59)

$$returns_t = \beta_0 + \beta_1\ dprod_t + \beta_2\ dspread_t + \beta_3\ inflation_t + \beta_4\ rterm_t + u_{2t}$$

(7.60)

where 'returns' are stock returns and all of the other variables are defined as in the previous example in chapter 5.

It is evident that there is feedback between the two equations since the *inflation* variable appears in the *stock returns* equation and vice versa. Are the equations identified? Since there are two equations, each will be identified if one variable is missing from that equation. Equation (7.59), the inflation equation, omits two variables. It does not contain the default spread or the term spread, and so is over-identified. Equation (7.60), the stock returns equation, omits two variables as well – the consumer credit and money supply variables – and so is over-identified too. Two-stage least squares (2SLS) is therefore the appropriate technique to use.

[1] Crucially, good econometric models are based on solid financial theory. This model is clearly not, but represents a simple way to illustrate the estimation and interpretation of simultaneous equations models using EViews with freely available data!

Screenshot 7.1   **Estimating the inflation equation**

In EViews, to do this we need to specify a list of instruments, which would be all of the variables from the reduced form equation. In this case, the reduced form equations would be

$$inflation = f(constant, \; dprod, \; dspread, \; rterm, \; dcredit, \; qrev, \; dmoney) \qquad (7.61)$$

$$returns = g(constant, \; dprod, \; dspread, \; rterm, \; dcredit, \; qrev, \; dmoney) \qquad (7.62)$$

We can perform both stages of 2SLS in one go, but by default, EViews estimates each of the two equations in the system separately. To do this, click **Quick, Estimate Equation** and then select **TSLS – Two Stage Least Squares (TSNLS and ARMA)** from the list of estimation methods. Then fill in the dialog box as in screenshot 7.1 to estimate the inflation equation.

Thus the format of writing out the variables in the first window is as usual, and the full structural equation for inflation as a dependent variable should be specified here. In the instrument list, include every variable from the reduced form equation, including the constant, and click **OK**. The results would then appear as in the following table.

Dependent Variable: INFLATION
Method: Two-Stage Least Squares
Date: 07/06/13 Time: 14:39
Sample (adjusted): 1986M04 2013M04
Included observations: 325 after adjustments
Instrument list: C DCREDIT DPROD RTERM DSPREAD DMONEY

	Coefficient	Std. Error	t-Statistic	Prob.
C	0.195313	0.048012	4.067988	0.0001
DPROD	0.013887	0.064302	0.215958	0.8292
DCREDIT	−7.46E-07	3.79E-06	−0.197000	0.8440
DMONEY	−0.004408	0.001662	−2.652566	0.0084
RSANDP	0.115471	0.041049	2.813014	0.0052

R-squared	−2.571046	Mean dependent var	0.233696
Adjusted R-squared	−2.615684	S.D. dependent var	0.324318
S.E. of regression	0.616689	Sum squared resid	121.6975
F-statistic	3.627476	Durbin-Watson stat	1.814403
Prob(F-statistic)	0.006583	Second-Stage SSR	28.56077
J-statistic	0.270084	Instrument Rank	6
Prob(J-statistic)	0.603275		

Similarly, the dialog box for the rsandp equation would be specified as in screenshot 7.2. The output for the returns equation is shown in the following table.

The results overall show the stock index returns are a positive and significant determinant of inflation (changes in the money supply negatively affect inflation), while inflation has a negative effect on the stock market, albeit not significantly so. The R^2 and $\bar{R}^2$ values from the inflation equation are also negative, so should be interpreted with caution. As the EViews *User's Guide* warns, this can sometimes happen even when there is an intercept in the regression. The *J*-statistic is essentially a transformed version of the residual sum of squares that evaluates the model fit.

It may also be of relevance to conduct a Hausman test for the endogeneity of the inflation and stock return variables. To do this, **estimate the reduced form equations** and **save the residuals**. Then **create series of fitted values** by constructing new variables which are equal to the actual values minus the residuals. Call the fitted value series **inflation_fit** and **rsandp_fit**. Then **estimate the structural equations** (separately), adding the fitted values from the relevant reduced form equations. The two sets of variables (in EViews format, with the dependent variables first followed by the lists of independent variables) are as follows.

```
Dependent Variable: RSANDP
Method: Two-Stage Least Squares
Date: 07/06/13   Time: 22:05
Sample (adjusted): 1986M04 2013M04
Included observations: 325 after adjustments
Instrument list: C DCREDIT DPROD RTERM DSPREAD DMONEY
```

	Coefficient	Std. Error	t-Statistic	Prob.
C	1.110730	0.927393	1.197691	0.2319
DPROD	−0.269418	0.461822	−0.583381	0.5600
DSPREAD	−9.615083	4.627064	−2.078009	0.0385
RTERM	−0.261785	0.918059	−0.285150	0.7757
INFLATION	−2.173678	3.846050	−0.565171	0.5724
R-squared	0.027482	Mean dependent var		0.584671
Adjusted R-squared	0.015325	S.D. dependent var		4.589186
S.E. of regression	4.553886	Sum squared resid		6636.120
F-statistic	2.665537	Durbin-Watson stat		1.935389
Prob(F-statistic)	0.032509	Second-Stage SSR		6602.534
J-statistic	0.929368	Instrument Rank		6
Prob(J-statistic)	0.335027			

For the stock returns equation:

> rsandp c dprod dspread rterm inflation inflation_fit

and for the inflation equation:

> inflation c dprod dcredit dmoney rsandp rsandp_fit

The conclusion is that the inflation fitted value term is not significant in the stock return equation and so inflation can be considered exogenous for stock returns. Thus it would be valid to simply estimate this equation (minus the fitted value term) on its own using OLS. But the fitted stock return term is significant in the inflation equation, suggesting that stock returns are endogenous.

7.11 Vector autoregressive models

Vector autoregressive models (VARs) were popularised in econometrics by Sims (1980) as a natural generalisation of univariate autoregressive models discussed in chapter 6. A VAR is a systems regression model (i.e. there is more than one dependent variable) that can be considered a kind of hybrid between the univariate time series models considered in chapter 6 and the simultaneous equations models developed previously in this chapter. VARs have often been advocated as an alternative to large-scale simultaneous equations structural models.

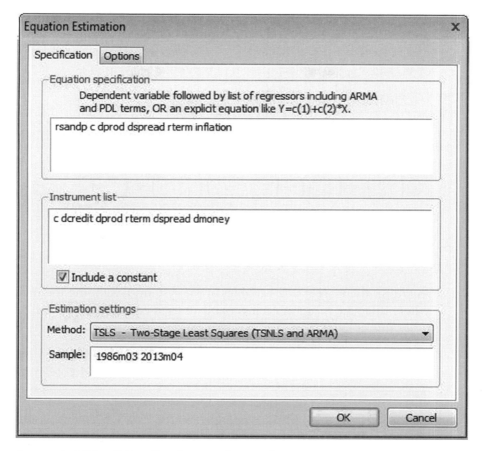

Screenshot 7.2 **Estimating the rsandp equation**

The simplest case that can be entertained is a bivariate VAR, where there are only two variables, y_{1t} and y_{2t}, each of whose current values depend on different combinations of the previous k values of both variables, and error terms

$$y_{1t} = \beta_{10} + \beta_{11}y_{1t-1} + \cdots + \beta_{1k}y_{1t-k} + \alpha_{11}y_{2t-1} + \cdots + \alpha_{1k}y_{2t-k} + u_{1t}$$

(7.63)

$$y_{2t} = \beta_{20} + \beta_{21}y_{2t-1} + \cdots + \beta_{2k}y_{2t-k} + \alpha_{21}y_{1t-1} + \cdots + \alpha_{2k}y_{1t-k} + u_{2t}$$

(7.64)

where u_{it} is a white noise disturbance term with $E(u_{it}) = 0$, $(i = 1, 2)$, $E(u_{1t}u_{2t}) = 0$.

As should already be evident, an important feature of the VAR model is its flexibility and the ease of generalisation. For example, the model could be extended to encompass moving average errors, which would be a multivariate version of an ARMA model, known as a VARMA. Instead of having only two variables, y_{1t} and y_{2t}, the system could also be expanded to include g variables, $y_{1t}, y_{2t}, y_{3t}, \ldots, y_{gt}$, each of which has an equation.

Another useful facet of VAR models is the compactness with which the notation can be expressed. For example, consider the case from above where $k = 1$, so that each variable depends only upon the immediately previous values of y_{1t} and y_{2t}, plus an error term. This could be written as

$$y_{1t} = \beta_{10} + \beta_{11}y_{1t-1} + \alpha_{11}y_{2t-1} + u_{1t} \tag{7.65}$$

$$y_{2t} = \beta_{20} + \beta_{21}y_{2t-1} + \alpha_{21}y_{1t-1} + u_{2t} \tag{7.66}$$

or

$$\begin{pmatrix} y_{1t} \\ y_{2t} \end{pmatrix} = \begin{pmatrix} \beta_{10} \\ \beta_{20} \end{pmatrix} + \begin{pmatrix} \beta_{11} & \alpha_{11} \\ \alpha_{21} & \beta_{21} \end{pmatrix} \begin{pmatrix} y_{1t-1} \\ y_{2t-1} \end{pmatrix} + \begin{pmatrix} u_{1t} \\ u_{2t} \end{pmatrix} \tag{7.67}$$

or even more compactly as

$$\begin{array}{ccccc} y_t & = & \beta_0 & + & \beta_1 y_{t-1} & + & u_t \\ g \times 1 & & g \times 1 & & g \times g \; g \times 1 & & g \times 1 \end{array} \tag{7.68}$$

In (7.68), there are $g = 2$ variables in the system. Extending the model to the case where there are k lags of each variable in each equation is also easily accomplished using this notation

$$\begin{array}{ccccccccccc} y_t & = & \beta_0 & + & \beta_1 y_{t-1} & + & \beta_2 y_{t-2} & + \cdots + & \beta_k y_{t-k} & + & u_t \\ g \times 1 & & g \times 1 & & g \times g \; g \times 1 & & g \times g \; g \times 1 & & g \times g \; g \times 1 & & g \times 1 \end{array}$$
$$\tag{7.69}$$

The model could be further extended to the case where the model includes first difference terms and cointegrating relationships (a vector error correction model (VECM) – see chapter 8).

7.11.1 Advantages of VAR modelling

VAR models have several advantages compared with univariate time series models or simultaneous equations structural models:

- The researcher does not need to specify which variables are endogenous or exogenous – *all are endogenous*. This is a very important point, since a requirement for simultaneous equations structural models to be estimable is that all equations in the system are identified. Essentially, this requirement boils down to a condition that some variables are treated as exogenous and that the equations contain different RHS variables. Ideally, this restriction should arise naturally from financial or economic theory. However, in practice theory will be at best vague in its suggestions of which variables should be treated as exogenous. This leaves the researcher with a great deal of discretion concerning how to classify the variables. Since Hausman-type tests are often not employed in practice when they should be, the specification of certain variables as exogenous, required to form identifying restrictions, is likely in many cases to be invalid. Sims termed these identifying restrictions 'incredible'. VAR estimation, on the other hand, requires no such restrictions to be imposed.

- VARs allow the value of a variable to depend on more than just its own lags or combinations of white noise terms, so VARs are more flexible than univariate AR models; the latter can be viewed as a restricted case of VAR models. VAR models can therefore offer a very *rich structure*, implying that they may be able to capture more features of the data.
- Provided that there are no contemporaneous terms on the RHS of the equations, it is possible to *simply use OLS separately on each equation*. This arises from the fact that all variables on the RHS are pre-determined – that is, at time t, they are known. This implies that there is no possibility for feedback from any of the LHS variables to any of the RHS variables. Pre-determined variables include all exogenous variables and lagged values of the endogenous variables.
- The forecasts generated by VARs are often *better than traditional structural' models*. It has been argued in a number of articles (see, for example, Sims, 1980) that large-scale structural models performed badly in terms of their out-of-sample forecast accuracy. This could perhaps arise as a result of the ad hoc nature of the restrictions placed on the structural models to ensure identification discussed above. McNees (1986) shows that forecasts for some variables (e.g. the US unemployment rate and real gross national product (GNP), etc.) are produced more accurately using VARs than from several different structural specifications.

7.11.2 Problems with VARs

VAR models of course also have drawbacks and limitations relative to other model classes:

- VARs are *a-theoretical* (as are ARMA models), since they use little theoretical information about the relationships between the variables to guide the specification of the model. On the other hand, valid exclusion restrictions that ensure identification of equations from a simultaneous structural system will inform on the structure of the model. An upshot of this is that VARs are less amenable to theoretical analysis and therefore to policy prescriptions. There also exists an increased possibility under the VAR approach that a hapless researcher could obtain an essentially spurious relationship by mining the data. It is also often not clear how the VAR coefficient estimates should be interpreted.
- How should the appropriate *lag lengths* for the VAR be determined? There are several approaches available for dealing with this issue, which will be discussed below.
- *So many parameters*! If there are g equations, one for each of g variables and with k lags of each of the variables in each equation, $(g + kg^2)$ parameters will have to be estimated. For example, if $g = 3$ and $k = 3$ there will be thirty parameters to estimate. For relatively small sample sizes, degrees of freedom will rapidly be used up, implying large standard errors and therefore wide confidence intervals for model coefficients.

- Should *all of the components of the VAR be stationary*? Obviously, if one wishes to use hypothesis tests, either singly or jointly, to examine the statistical significance of the coefficients, then it is essential that all of the components in the VAR are stationary. However, many proponents of the VAR approach recommend that differencing to induce stationarity should not be done. They would argue that the purpose of VAR estimation is purely to examine the relationships between the variables, and that differencing will throw information on any long-run relationships between the series away. It is also possible to combine levels and first differenced terms in a VECM – see chapter 8.

7.11.3   Choosing the optimal lag length for a VAR

Often, financial theory will have little to say on what is an appropriate lag length for a VAR and how long changes in the variables should take to work through the system. In such instances, there are broadly two methods that could be used to arrive at the optimal lag length: cross-equation restrictions and information criteria.

7.11.4   Cross-equation restrictions for VAR lag length selection

A first (but incorrect) response to the question of how to determine the appropriate lag length would be to use the block *F*-tests highlighted in section 7.13 below. These, however, are not appropriate in this case as the *F*-test would be used separately for the set of lags in each equation, and what is required here is a procedure to test the coefficients on a set of lags on all variables for all equations in the VAR at the same time.

It is worth noting here that in the spirit of VAR estimation (as Sims, for example, thought that model specification should be conducted), the models should be as unrestricted as possible. A VAR with different lag lengths for each equation could be viewed as a restricted VAR. For example, consider a VAR with three lags of both variables in one equation and four lags of each variable in the other equation. This could be viewed as a restricted model where the coefficient on the fourth lags of each variable in the first equation have been set to zero.

An alternative approach would be to specify the same number of lags in each equation and to determine the model order as follows. Suppose that a VAR estimated using quarterly data has eight lags of the two variables in each equation, and it is desired to examine a restriction that the coefficients on lags five–eight are jointly zero. This can be done using a likelihood ratio test (see chapter 9 for more general details concerning such tests). Denote the variance–covariance matrix of residuals (given by $\hat{u}\hat{u}'$), as $\hat{\Sigma}$. The likelihood ratio test for this joint hypothesis is given by

$$LR = T[\log|\hat{\Sigma}_r| - \log|\hat{\Sigma}_u|]$$

(7.70)

where $|\hat{\Sigma}_r|$ is the determinant of the variance–covariance matrix of the residuals for the restricted model (with four lags), $|\hat{\Sigma}_u|$ is the determinant of the variance–covariance matrix of residuals for the unrestricted VAR (with eight lags) and T is the sample size. The test statistic is asymptotically distributed as a χ^2 variate with degrees of freedom equal to the total number of restrictions. In the VAR case above, four lags of two variables are being restricted in each of the two equations = a total of $4 \times 2 \times 2 = 16$ restrictions. In the general case of a VAR with g equations, to impose the restriction that the last q lags have zero coefficients, there would be $g^2 q$ restrictions altogether. Intuitively, the test is a multivariate equivalent to examining the extent to which the RSS rises when a restriction is imposed. If $\hat{\Sigma}_r$ and $\hat{\Sigma}_u$ are 'close together', the restriction is supported by the data.

7.11.5 Information criteria for VAR lag length selection

The likelihood ratio (LR) test explained above is intuitive and fairly easy to estimate, but has its limitations. Principally, one of the two VARs must be a special case of the other and, more seriously, only pairwise comparisons can be made. In the above example, if the most appropriate lag length had been seven or even ten, there is no way that this information could be gleaned from the LR test conducted. One could achieve this only by starting with a VAR(10), and successively testing one set of lags at a time.

A further disadvantage of the LR test approach is that the χ^2 test will strictly be valid asymptotically only under the assumption that the errors from each equation are normally distributed. This assumption is unlikely to be upheld for financial data. An alternative approach to selecting the appropriate VAR lag length would be to use an information criterion, as defined in chapter 6 in the context of ARMA model selection. Information criteria require no such normality assumptions concerning the distributions of the errors. Instead, the criteria trade off a fall in the RSS of each equation as more lags are added, with an increase in the value of the penalty term. The univariate criteria could be applied separately to each equation but, again, it is usually deemed preferable to require the number of lags to be the same for each equation. This requires the use of multivariate versions of the information criteria, which can be defined as

$$MAIC = \log\left|\hat{\Sigma}\right| + 2k'/T \tag{7.71}$$

$$MSBIC = \log\left|\hat{\Sigma}\right| + \frac{k'}{T}\log(T) \tag{7.72}$$

$$MHQIC = \log\left|\hat{\Sigma}\right| + \frac{2k'}{T}\log(\log(T)) \tag{7.73}$$

where again $\hat{\Sigma}$ is the variance–covariance matrix of residuals, T is the number of observations and k' is the total number of regressors in all equations, which will be equal to $p^2 k + p$ for p equations in the VAR system, each with k lags of the p variables, plus a constant term in each equation. As previously, the values of the information criteria are constructed for $0, 1, \ldots, \bar{k}$ lags (up to some pre-specified maximum $\bar{k}$), and the chosen number of lags is that number minimising the value of the given information criterion.

7.12 Does the VAR include contemporaneous terms?

So far, it has been assumed that the VAR specified is of the form

$$y_{1t} = \beta_{10} + \beta_{11}y_{1t-1} + \alpha_{11}y_{2t-1} + u_{1t} \tag{7.74}$$

$$y_{2t} = \beta_{20} + \beta_{21}y_{2t-1} + \alpha_{21}y_{1t-1} + u_{2t} \tag{7.75}$$

so that there are no contemporaneous terms on the RHS of (7.74) or (7.75) – i.e. there is no term in y_{2t} on the RHS of the equation for y_{1t} and no term in y_{1t} on the RHS of the equation for y_{2t}. But what if the equations had a contemporaneous feedback term, as in the following case?

$$y_{1t} = \beta_{10} + \beta_{11}y_{1t-1} + \alpha_{11}y_{2t-1} + \alpha_{12}y_{2t} + u_{1t} \tag{7.76}$$

$$y_{2t} = \beta_{20} + \beta_{21}y_{2t-1} + \alpha_{21}y_{1t-1} + \alpha_{22}y_{1t} + u_{2t} \tag{7.77}$$

Equations (7.76) and (7.77) could also be written by stacking up the terms into matrices and vectors:

$$\begin{pmatrix} y_{1t} \\ y_{2t} \end{pmatrix} = \begin{pmatrix} \beta_{10} \\ \beta_{20} \end{pmatrix} + \begin{pmatrix} \beta_{11} & \alpha_{11} \\ \alpha_{21} & \beta_{21} \end{pmatrix}\begin{pmatrix} y_{1t-1} \\ y_{2t-1} \end{pmatrix} + \begin{pmatrix} \alpha_{12} & 0 \\ 0 & \alpha_{22} \end{pmatrix}\begin{pmatrix} y_{2t} \\ y_{1t} \end{pmatrix} + \begin{pmatrix} u_{1t} \\ u_{2t} \end{pmatrix} \tag{7.78}$$

This would be known as a *VAR in primitive form*, similar to the structural form for a simultaneous equations model. Some researchers have argued that the a-theoretical nature of reduced form VARs leaves them unstructured and their results difficult to interpret theoretically. They argue that the forms of VAR given previously are merely reduced forms of a more general structural VAR (such as (7.78)), with the latter being of more interest.

The contemporaneous terms from (7.78) can be taken over to the LHS and written as

$$\begin{pmatrix} 1 & -\alpha_{12} \\ -\alpha_{22} & 1 \end{pmatrix}\begin{pmatrix} y_{1t} \\ y_{2t} \end{pmatrix} = \begin{pmatrix} \beta_{10} \\ \beta_{20} \end{pmatrix} + \begin{pmatrix} \beta_{11} & \alpha_{11} \\ \alpha_{21} & \beta_{21} \end{pmatrix}\begin{pmatrix} y_{1t-1} \\ y_{2t-1} \end{pmatrix} + \begin{pmatrix} u_{1t} \\ u_{2t} \end{pmatrix} \tag{7.79}$$

or

$$Ay_t = \beta_0 + \beta_1 y_{t-1} + u_t \tag{7.80}$$

If both sides of (7.80) are pre-multiplied by A^{-1}

$$y_t = A^{-1}\beta_0 + A^{-1}\beta_1 y_{t-1} + A^{-1}u_t \tag{7.81}$$

or

$$y_t = A_0 + A_1 y_{t-1} + e_t \tag{7.82}$$

This is known as a *standard form VAR*, which is akin to the reduced form from a set of simultaneous equations. This VAR contains only pre-determined values on the RHS (i.e. variables whose values are known at time t), and so there is no contemporaneous feedback term. This VAR can therefore be estimated equation by equation using OLS.

Equation (7.78), the structural or primitive form VAR, is not identified, since identical pre-determined (lagged) variables appear on the RHS of both equations. In order to circumvent this problem, a restriction that one of the coefficients on the contemporaneous terms is zero must be imposed. In (7.78), either α_{12} or α_{22} must be set to zero to obtain a triangular set of VAR equations that can be validly estimated. The choice of which of these two restrictions to impose is ideally made on theoretical grounds. For example, if financial theory suggests that the current value of y_{1t} should affect the current value of y_{2t} but not the other way around, set $\alpha_{12} = 0$, and so on. Another possibility would be to run separate estimations, first imposing $\alpha_{12} = 0$ and then $\alpha_{22} = 0$, to determine whether the general features of the results are much changed. It is also very common to estimate only a reduced form VAR, which is of course perfectly valid provided that such a formulation is not at odds with the relationships between variables that financial theory says should hold.

One fundamental weakness of the VAR approach to modelling is that its a-theoretical nature and the large number of parameters involved make the estimated models difficult to interpret. In particular, some lagged variables may have coefficients which change sign across the lags, and this, together with the interconnectivity of the equations, could render it difficult to see what effect a given change in a variable would have upon the future values of the variables in the system. In order to partially alleviate this problem, three sets of statistics are usually constructed for an estimated VAR model: block significance tests, impulse responses and variance decompositions. How important an intuitively interpretable model is will of course depend on the purpose of constructing the model. Interpretability may not be an issue at all if the purpose of producing the VAR is to make forecasts – see box 7.3.

7.13 Block significance and causality tests

It is likely that, when a VAR includes many lags of variables, it will be difficult to see which sets of variables have significant effects on each dependent variable and which do not. In order to address this issue, tests are usually conducted that restrict all of the lags of a particular variable to zero. For illustration, consider the following bivariate VAR(3)

$$\begin{pmatrix} y_{1t} \\ y_{2t} \end{pmatrix} = \begin{pmatrix} \alpha_{10} \\ \alpha_{20} \end{pmatrix} + \begin{pmatrix} \beta_{11} & \beta_{12} \\ \beta_{21} & \beta_{22} \end{pmatrix} \begin{pmatrix} y_{1t-1} \\ y_{2t-1} \end{pmatrix} + \begin{pmatrix} \gamma_{11} & \gamma_{12} \\ \gamma_{21} & \gamma_{22} \end{pmatrix} \begin{pmatrix} y_{1t-2} \\ y_{2t-2} \end{pmatrix}$$

$$+ \begin{pmatrix} \delta_{11} & \delta_{12} \\ \delta_{21} & \delta_{22} \end{pmatrix} \begin{pmatrix} y_{1t-3} \\ y_{2t-3} \end{pmatrix} + \begin{pmatrix} u_{1t} \\ u_{2t} \end{pmatrix} \tag{7.83}$$

> ### Box 7.3   Forecasting with VARs
>
>   One of the main advantages of the VAR approach to modelling and
> forecasting is that since only lagged variables are used on the right hand
> side, forecasts of the future values of the dependent variables can be
> calculated using only information from within the system. We could term
> these *unconditional forecasts* since they are not constructed conditional on a
> particular set of assumed values. However, conversely it may be useful to
> produce forecasts of the future values of some variables *conditional upon*
> known values of other variables in the system. For example, it may be the
> case that the values of some variables become known before the values of
> the others. If the known values of the former are employed, we would
> anticipate that the forecasts should be more accurate than if estimated values
> were used unnecessarily, thus throwing known information away.
> Alternatively, conditional forecasts can be employed for counterfactual
> analysis based on examining the impact of certain scenarios. For example,
> in a trivariate VAR system incorporating monthly stock returns, inflation
> and gross domestic product (GDP), we could answer the question: 'What is
> the likely impact on the stock market over the next 1–6 months of a
> 2-percentage point increase in inflation and a 1% rise in GDP?'

This VAR could be written out to express the individual equations as

$$y_{1t} = \alpha_{10} + \beta_{11}y_{1t-1} + \beta_{12}y_{2t-1} + \gamma_{11}y_{1t-2} + \gamma_{12}y_{2t-2}$$

$$+ \delta_{11}y_{1t-3} + \delta_{12}y_{2t-3} + u_{1t}$$

$$y_{2t} = \alpha_{20} + \beta_{21}y_{1t-1} + \beta_{22}y_{2t-1} + \gamma_{21}y_{1t-2} + \gamma_{22}y_{2t-2}$$

$$+ \delta_{21}y_{1t-3} + \delta_{22}y_{2t-3} + u_{2t}$$

(7.84)

One might be interested in testing the hypotheses and their implied restrictions
on the parameter matrices given in table 7.3.

Assuming that all of the variables in the VAR are stationary, the joint hypotheses
can easily be tested within the *F*-test framework, since each individual set of
restrictions involves parameters drawn from only one equation. The equations
would be estimated separately using OLS to obtain the unrestricted *RSS*, then the
restrictions imposed and the models re-estimated to obtain the restricted *RSS*. The
F-statistic would then take the usual form described in chapter 4. Thus, evaluation
of the significance of variables in the context of a VAR almost invariably occurs
on the basis of joint tests on all of the lags of a particular variable in an equation,
rather than by examination of individual coefficient estimates.

In fact, the tests described above could also be referred to as causality tests. Tests
of this form were described by Granger (1969) and a slight variant due to Sims
(1972). Causality tests seek to answer simple questions of the type, 'Do changes

Table 7.3   Granger causality tests and implied restrictions on VAR models

	Hypothesis	Implied restriction
1	Lags of y_{1t} do not explain current y_{2t}	$\beta_{21} = 0$ and $\gamma_{21} = 0$ and $\delta_{21} = 0$
2	Lags of y_{1t} do not explain current y_{1t}	$\beta_{11} = 0$ and $\gamma_{11} = 0$ and $\delta_{11} = 0$
3	Lags of y_{2t} do not explain current y_{1t}	$\beta_{12} = 0$ and $\gamma_{12} = 0$ and $\delta_{12} = 0$
4	Lags of y_{2t} do not explain current y_{2t}	$\beta_{22} = 0$ and $\gamma_{22} = 0$ and $\delta_{22} = 0$

in y_1 cause changes in y_2?' The argument follows that if y_1 causes y_2, lags of y_1 should be significant in the equation for y_2. If this is the case and not vice versa, it would be said that y_1 'Granger-causes' y_2 or that there exists unidirectional causality from y_1 to y_2. On the other hand, if y_2 causes y_1, lags of y_2 should be significant in the equation for y_1. If both sets of lags were significant, it would be said that there was 'bi-directional causality' or 'bi-directional feedback'. If y_1 is found to Granger-cause y_2, but not vice versa, it would be said that variable y_1 is strongly exogenous (in the equation for y_2). If neither set of lags are statistically significant in the equation for the other variable, it would be said that y_1 and y_2 are independent. Finally, the word 'causality' is somewhat of a misnomer, for Granger-causality really means only a correlation between the *current* value of one variable and the *past* values of others; it does not mean that movements of one variable cause movements of another.

7.14 VARs with exogenous variables

Consider the following specification for a VAR(1) where X_t is a vector of exogenous variables and B is a matrix of coefficients

$$y_t = A_0 + A_1 y_{t-1} + B X_t + e_t \tag{7.85}$$

The components of the vector X_t are known as exogenous variables since their values are determined outside of the VAR system – in other words, there are no equations in the VAR with any of the components of X_t as dependent variables. Such a model is sometimes termed a VARX, although it could be viewed as simply a restricted VAR where there are equations for each of the exogenous variables, but with the coefficients on the RHS in those equations restricted to zero. Such a restriction may be considered desirable if theoretical considerations suggest it, although it is clearly not in the true spirit of VAR modelling, which is not to impose any restrictions on the model but rather to 'let the data decide'.

7.15 Impulse responses and variance decompositions

Block F-tests and an examination of causality in a VAR will suggest which of the variables in the model have statistically significant impacts on the future values of each of the variables in the system. But F-test results will not, by construction, be able to explain the sign of the relationship or how long these effects require to take place. That is, F-test results will not reveal whether changes in the value of a given variable have a positive or negative effect on other variables in the system, or how long it would take for the effect of that variable to work through the system. Such information will, however, be given by an examination of the VAR's impulse responses and variance decompositions.

Impulse responses trace out the responsiveness of the dependent variables in the VAR to shocks to each of the variables. So, for each variable from each equation separately, a unit shock is applied to the error, and the effects upon the VAR system over time are noted. Thus, if there are g variables in a system, a total of g^2 impulse responses could be generated. The way that this is achieved in practice is by expressing the VAR model as a VMA – that is, the vector autoregressive model is written as a vector moving average (in the same way as was done for univariate autoregressive models in chapter 5). Provided that the system is stable, the shock should gradually die away.

To illustrate how impulse responses operate, consider the following bivariate VAR(1)

$$y_t = A_1 y_{t-1} + u_t \tag{7.86}$$

where $A_1 = \begin{bmatrix} 0.5 & 0.3 \\ 0.0 & 0.2 \end{bmatrix}$

The VAR can also be written out using the elements of the matrices and vectors as

$$\begin{bmatrix} y_{1t} \\ y_{2t} \end{bmatrix} = \begin{bmatrix} 0.5 & 0.3 \\ 0.0 & 0.2 \end{bmatrix} \begin{bmatrix} y_{1t-1} \\ y_{2t-1} \end{bmatrix} + \begin{bmatrix} u_{1t} \\ u_{2t} \end{bmatrix} \tag{7.87}$$

Consider the effect at time $t = 0, 1, \ldots$, of a unit shock to y_{1t} at time $t = 0$

$$y_0 = \begin{bmatrix} u_{10} \\ u_{20} \end{bmatrix} = \begin{bmatrix} 1 \\ 0 \end{bmatrix} \tag{7.88}$$

$$y_1 = A_1 y_0 = \begin{bmatrix} 0.5 & 0.3 \\ 0.0 & 0.2 \end{bmatrix} \begin{bmatrix} 1 \\ 0 \end{bmatrix} = \begin{bmatrix} 0.5 \\ 0 \end{bmatrix} \tag{7.89}$$

$$y_2 = A_1 y_1 = \begin{bmatrix} 0.5 & 0.3 \\ 0.0 & 0.2 \end{bmatrix} \begin{bmatrix} 0.5 \\ 0 \end{bmatrix} = \begin{bmatrix} 0.25 \\ 0 \end{bmatrix} \tag{7.90}$$

and so on. It would thus be possible to plot the impulse response functions of y_{1t} and y_{2t} to a unit shock in y_{1t}. Notice that the effect on y_{2t} is always zero, since the variable y_{1t-1} has a zero coefficient attached to it in the equation for y_{2t}.

Now consider the effect of a unit shock to y_{2t} at time $t = 0$

$$y_0 = \begin{bmatrix} u_{10} \\ u_{20} \end{bmatrix} = \begin{bmatrix} 0 \\ 1 \end{bmatrix} \tag{7.91}$$

$$y_1 = A_1 y_0 = \begin{bmatrix} 0.5 & 0.3 \\ 0.0 & 0.2 \end{bmatrix} \begin{bmatrix} 0 \\ 1 \end{bmatrix} = \begin{bmatrix} 0.3 \\ 0.2 \end{bmatrix} \tag{7.92}$$

$$y_2 = A_1 y_1 = \begin{bmatrix} 0.5 & 0.3 \\ 0.0 & 0.2 \end{bmatrix} \begin{bmatrix} 0.3 \\ 0.2 \end{bmatrix} = \begin{bmatrix} 0.21 \\ 0.04 \end{bmatrix} \tag{7.93}$$

and so on. Although it is probably fairly easy to see what the effects of shocks to the variables will be in such a simple VAR, the same principles can be applied in the context of VARs containing more equations or more lags, where it is much more difficult to see by eye what are the interactions between the equations.

Variance decompositions offer a slightly different method for examining VAR system dynamics. They give the proportion of the movements in the dependent variables that are due to their 'own' shocks, versus shocks to the other variables. A shock to the ith variable will directly affect that variable of course, but it will also be transmitted to all of the other variables in the system through the dynamic structure of the VAR. Variance decompositions determine how much of the s-step-ahead forecast error variance of a given variable is explained by innovations to each explanatory variable for $s = 1, 2, \ldots$ In practice, it is usually observed that own series shocks explain most of the (forecast) error variance of the series in a VAR. To some extent, impulse responses and variance decompositions offer very similar information.

For calculating impulse responses and variance decompositions, the ordering of the variables is important. To see why this is the case, recall that the impulse responses refer to a unit shock to the errors of one VAR equation alone. This implies that the error terms of all other equations in the VAR system are held constant. However, this is not realistic since the error terms are likely to be correlated across equations to some extent. Thus, assuming that they are completely independent would lead to a misrepresentation of the system dynamics. In practice, the errors will have a common component that cannot be associated with a single variable alone.

The usual approach to this difficulty is to generate *orthogonalised impulse responses*. In the context of a bivariate VAR, the whole of the common component of the errors is attributed somewhat arbitrarily to the first variable in the VAR. In the general case where there are more than two variables in the VAR, the calculations are more complex but the interpretation is the same. Such a restriction in effect implies an 'ordering' of variables, so that the equation for y_{1t} would be estimated first and then that of y_{2t}, a bit like a recursive or triangular system.

Assuming a particular ordering is necessary to compute the impulse responses and variance decompositions, although the restriction underlying the ordering used may not be supported by the data. Again, ideally, financial theory should suggest an ordering (in other words, that movements in some variables are likely to follow, rather than precede, others). Failing this, the sensitivity of the results to changes in the ordering can be observed by assuming one ordering, and then exactly reversing it and re-computing the impulse responses and variance decompositions. It is also worth noting that the more highly correlated are the residuals from an estimated equation, the more the variable ordering will be important. But when the residuals are almost uncorrelated, the ordering of the variables will make little difference (see Lütkepohl, 1991, chapter 2 for further details).

Runkle (1987) argues that both impulse responses and variance decompositions are notoriously difficult to interpret accurately. He argues that confidence bands around the impulse responses and variance decompositions should always be constructed. However, he further states that, even then, the confidence intervals are typically so wide that sharp inferences are impossible.

7.16 VAR model example: the interaction between property returns and the macroeconomy

7.16.1 Background, data and variables

Brooks and Tsolacos (1999) employ a VAR methodology for investigating the interaction between the UK property market and various macroeconomic variables. Monthly data, in logarithmic form, are used for the period from December 1985 to January 1998. The selection of the variables for inclusion in the VAR model is governed by the time series that are commonly included in studies of stock return predictability. It is assumed that stock returns are related to macroeconomic and business conditions, and hence time series which may be able to capture both current and future directions in the broad economy and the business environment are used in the investigation.

Broadly, there are two ways to measure the value of property-based assets – *direct measures of property value* and *equity-based measures*. Direct property measures are based on periodic appraisals or valuations of the actual properties in a portfolio by surveyors, while equity-based measures evaluate the worth of properties indirectly by considering the values of stock market traded property companies. Both sources of data have their drawbacks. Appraisal-based value measures suffer from valuation biases and inaccuracies. Surveyors are typically prone to 'smooth' valuations over time, such that the measured returns are too low during property market booms and too high during periods of property price falls. Additionally, not every property in the portfolio that comprises the value measure is appraised during every period, resulting in some stale valuations entering the aggregate valuation, further increasing the degree of excess smoothness of the recorded property price series. Indirect property vehicles – property-related companies traded on stock exchanges – do not suffer from the above problems, but are excessively influenced by general stock market movements. It has been argued, for example, that over three-quarters of the variation over time in the value of stock exchange traded property companies can be attributed to general stock market-wide price movements. Therefore, the value of equity-based property series reflects much more the sentiment in the general stock market than the sentiment in the property market specifically.

Brooks and Tsolacos (1999) elect to use the equity-based FTSE Property Total Return Index to construct property returns. In order to purge the real estate return series of its general stock market influences, it is common to regress property returns on a general stock market index (in this case the FTA All-Share Index is used), saving the residuals. These residuals are expected to reflect only the variation in property returns, and thus become the property market return measure used in subsequent analysis, and are denoted PROPRES.

Hence, the variables included in the VAR are the property returns (with general stock market effects removed), the rate of unemployment, nominal interest rates, the spread between the long- and short-term interest rates, unanticipated inflation and the dividend yield. The motivations for including these particular variables in the VAR together with the property series, are as follows:

- *The rate of unemployment* (denoted UNEM) is included to indicate general economic conditions. In US research, authors tend to use aggregate consumption, a variable that has been built into asset pricing models and examined as a determinant of stock returns. Data for this variable and for alternative variables such as GDP are not available on a monthly basis in the UK. Monthly data are available for industrial production series but other studies have not shown any evidence that industrial production affects real estate returns. As a result, this series was not considered as a potential causal variable.
- *Short-term nominal interest rates* (denoted SIR) are assumed to contain information about future economic conditions and to capture the state of investment opportunities. It was found in previous studies that short-term interest rates have a very significant negative influence on property stock returns.
- *Interest rate spreads* (denoted SPREAD), i.e. the yield curve, are usually measured as the difference in the returns between long-term Treasury Bonds (of maturity, say, ten or twenty years), and the one-month or three-month Treasury Bill rate. It has been argued that the yield curve has extra predictive power, beyond that contained in the short-term interest rate, and can help predict GDP up to four years ahead. It has also been suggested that the term structure also affects real estate market returns.
- *Inflation rate* influences are also considered important in the pricing of stocks. For example, it has been argued that unanticipated inflation could be a source of economic risk and as a result, a risk premium will also be added if the stock of firms has exposure to unanticipated inflation. The unanticipated inflation variable (denoted UNINFL) is defined as the difference between the realised inflation rate, computed as the percentage change in the Retail Price Index (RPI), and an estimated series of expected inflation. The latter series was produced by fitting an ARMA model to the actual series and making a one-period(month)-ahead forecast, then rolling the sample forward one period, and re-estimating the parameters and making another one-step-ahead forecast, and so on.

- *Dividend yields* (denoted DIVY) have been widely used to model stock market returns, and also real estate property returns, based on the assumption that movements in the dividend yield series are related to long-term business conditions and that they capture some predictable components of returns.

All variables to be included in the VAR are required to be stationary in order to carry out joint significance tests on the lags of the variables. Hence, all variables are subjected to augmented Dickey–Fuller (ADF) tests (see chapter 8). Evidence that the log of the RPI and the log of the unemployment rate both contain a unit root is observed. Therefore, the first differences of these variables are used in subsequent analysis. The remaining four variables led to rejection of the null hypothesis of a unit root in the log-levels, and hence these variables were not first differenced.

7.16.2 Methodology

A reduced form VAR is employed and therefore each equation can effectively be estimated using OLS. For a VAR to be unrestricted, it is required that the same number of lags of all of the variables is used in all equations. Therefore, in order to determine the appropriate lag lengths, the multivariate generalisation of Akaike's information criterion (AIC) is used.

Within the framework of the VAR system of equations, the significance of all the lags of each of the individual variables is examined jointly with an F-test. Since several lags of the variables are included in each of the equations of the system, the coefficients on individual lags may not appear significant for all lags, and may have signs and degrees of significance that vary with the lag length. However, F-tests will be able to establish whether all of the lags of a particular variable are jointly significant. In order to consider further the effect of the macro-economy on the real estate returns index, the impact multipliers (orthogonalised impulse responses) are also calculated for the estimated VAR model. Two standard error bands are calculated using the Monte Carlo integration approach employed by McCue and Kling (1994), and based on Doan (1994). The forecast error variance is also decomposed to determine the proportion of the movements in the real estate series that are a consequence of its own shocks rather than shocks to other variables.

7.16.3 Results

The number of lags that minimises the value of Akaike's information criterion is fourteen, consistent with the fifteen lags used by McCue and Kling (1994). There are thus $(1 + 14 \times 6) = 85$ variables in each equation, implying fifty-nine degrees of freedom. F-tests for the null hypothesis that all of the lags of a given variable are jointly insignificant in a given equation are presented in table 7.4.

In contrast to a number of US studies which have used similar variables, it is found to be difficult to explain the variation in the UK real estate returns index using macroeconomic factors, as the last row of table 7.4 shows. Of all the

Dependent variable	Lags of variable					
	SIR	DIVY	SPREAD	UNEM	UNINFL	PROPRES
SIR	0.0000	0.0091	0.0242	0.0327	0.2126	0.0000
DIVY	0.5025	0.0000	0.6212	0.4217	0.5654	0.4033
SPREAD	0.2779	0.1328	0.0000	0.4372	0.6563	0.0007
UNEM	0.3410	0.3026	0.1151	0.0000	0.0758	0.2765
UNINFL	0.3057	0.5146	0.3420	0.4793	0.0004	0.3885
PROPRES	0.5537	0.1614	0.5537	0.8922	0.7222	0.0000

Table 7.4   Marginal significance levels associated with joint *F*-tests

The test is that all fourteen lags have no explanatory power for that particular equation in the VAR.
Source: Brooks and Tsolacos (1999).

lagged variables in the real estate equation, only the lags of the real estate returns themselves are highly significant, and the dividend yield variable is significant only at the 20% level. No other variables have any significant explanatory power for the real estate returns. Therefore, based on the *F*-tests, an initial conclusion is that the variation in property returns, net of stock market influences, cannot be explained by any of the main macroeconomic or financial variables used in existing research. One possible explanation for this might be that, in the UK, these variables do not convey the information about the macro–economy and business conditions assumed to determine the intertemporal behaviour of property returns. It is possible that property returns may reflect property market influences, such as rents, yields or capitalisation rates, rather than macroeconomic or financial variables. However, again the use of monthly data limits the set of both macroeconomic and property market variables that can be used in the quantitative analysis of real estate returns in the UK.

It appears, however, that lagged values of the real estate variable have explanatory power for some other variables in the system. These results are shown in the last column of table 7.4. The property sector appears to help in explaining variations in the term structure and short-term interest rates, and moreover since these variables are not significant in the property index equation, it is possible to state further that the property residual series Granger-causes the short-term interest rate and the term spread. This is a bizarre result. The fact that property returns are explained by own lagged values – i.e. that is there is interdependency between neighbouring data points (observations) – may reflect the way that property market information is produced and reflected in the property return indices.

Table 7.5 gives variance decompositions for the property returns index equation of the VAR for one, two, three, four, twelve and twenty-four steps ahead for the two variable orderings:

Table 7.5 Variance decompositions for the property sector index residuals

Months ahead	Explained by innovations in											
	SIR		DIVY		SPREAD		UNEM		UNINFL		PROPRES	
	I	II	I	II	I	II	I	II	I	II	I	II
1	0.0	0.8	0.0	38.2	0.0	9.1	0.0	0.7	0.0	0.2	100.0	51.0
2	0.2	0.8	0.2	35.1	0.2	12.3	0.4	1.4	1.6	2.9	97.5	47.5
3	3.8	2.5	0.4	29.4	0.2	17.8	1.0	1.5	2.3	3.0	92.3	45.8
4	3.7	2.1	5.3	22.3	1.4	18.5	1.6	1.1	4.8	4.4	83.3	51.5
12	2.8	3.1	15.5	8.7	15.3	19.5	3.3	5.1	17.0	13.5	46.1	50.0
24	8.2	6.3	6.8	3.9	38.0	36.2	5.5	14.7	18.1	16.9	23.4	22.0

Source: Brooks and Tsolacos (1999).

Order I: PROPRES, DIVY, UNINFL, UNEM, SPREAD, SIR
Order II: SIR, SPREAD, UNEM, UNINFL, DIVY, PROPRES.

Unfortunately, the ordering of the variables is important in the decomposition. Thus two orderings are applied, which are the exact opposite of one another, and the sensitivity of the result is considered. It is clear that by the two-year forecasting horizon, the variable ordering has become almost irrelevant in most cases. An interesting feature of the results is that shocks to the term spread and unexpected inflation together account for over 50% of the variation in the real estate series. The short-term interest rate and dividend yield shocks account for only 10–15% of the variance of the property index. One possible explanation for the difference in results between the F-tests and the variance decomposition is that the former is a causality test and the latter is effectively an exogeneity test. Hence the latter implies the stronger restriction that both current and lagged shocks to the explanatory variables do not influence the current value of the dependent variable of the property equation. Another way of stating this is that the term structure and unexpected inflation have a contemporaneous rather than a lagged effect on the property index, which implies insignificant F-test statistics but explanatory power in the variance decomposition. Therefore, although the F-tests did not establish any significant effects, the error variance decompositions show evidence of a contemporaneous relationship between PROPRES and both SPREAD and UNINFL. The lack of lagged effects could be taken to imply speedy adjustment of the market to changes in these variables.

Figures 7.1 and 7.2 give the impulse responses for PROPRES associated with separate unit shocks to unexpected inflation and the dividend yield, as examples (as stated above, a total of thirty-six impulse responses could be calculated since there are six variables in the system).

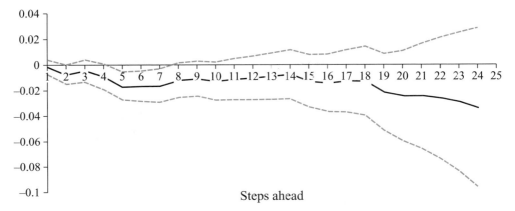

Figure 7.1   Impulse responses and standard error bands for innovations in unexpected inflation equation errors

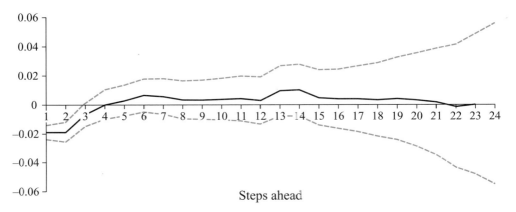

Figure 7.2   Impulse responses and standard error bands for innovations in the dividend yields

Considering the signs of the responses, innovations to unexpected inflation (figure 7.1) always have a negative impact on the real estate index, since the impulse response is negative, and the effect of the shock does not die down, even after twenty-four months. Increasing stock dividend yields (figure 7.2) have a negative impact for the first three periods, but beyond that, the shock appears to have worked its way out of the system.

7.16.4   Conclusions

The conclusion from the VAR methodology adopted in the Brooks and Tsolacos paper is that overall, UK real estate returns are difficult to explain on the basis of the information contained in the set of the variables used in existing studies based on non-UK data. The results are not strongly suggestive of any significant influences of these variables on the variation of the filtered property returns series. There is, however, some evidence that the interest rate term structure and unexpected

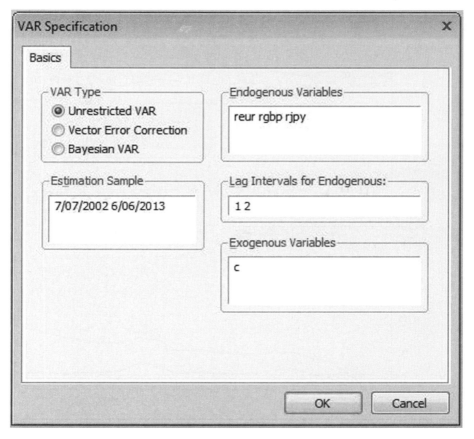

Screenshot 7.3   **VAR inputs screen**

inflation have a contemporaneous effect on property returns, in agreement with the results of a number of previous studies.

7.17   VAR estimation in EViews

By way of illustration, a VAR is estimated in order to examine whether there are lead–lag relationships for the returns to three exchange rates against the US dollar – the euro, the British pound and the Japanese yen. The data are daily and run from 7 July 2002 to 6 June 2013, giving a total of 3,986 observations. The data are contained in the Excel file 'currencies.xls'. First **Create a new workfile**, called 'currencies.wf1', and import the three currency series. Construct a set of continuously compounded percentage returns called **'reur', 'rgbp' and 'rjpy'**. VAR estimation in EViews can be accomplished by clicking on the **Quick** menu and then **Estimate VAR. . . .** The VAR inputs screen appears as in screenshot 7.3.

Vector Autoregression Estimates
Date: 07/07/13 Time: 12:01
Sample (adjusted): 7/10/2002 6/06/2013
Included observations: 3985 after adjustments
Standard errors in ( ) & t-statistics in [ ]

	REUR	RGBP	RJPY
REUR(-1)	0.200155	−0.042777	0.024186
	−0.022710	−0.020790	−0.022510
	[8.81447]	[−2.05766]	[1.07460]
REUR(-2)	−0.033413	0.056771	−0.031334
	−0.022620	−0.020710	−0.022420
	[−1.47722]	[2.74149]	[−1.39762]
RGBP(-1)	−0.061566	0.261643	−0.067979
	−0.024110	−0.022070	−0.023890
	[−2.55382]	[11.8548]	[−2.84494]
RGBP(-2)	0.024656	−0.092099	0.032403
	−0.024080	−0.022040	−0.023870
	[1.02395]	[−4.17778]	[1.35768]
RJPY(-1)	−0.020151	−0.056639	0.150845
	−0.016660	−0.015250	−0.016510
	[−1.20970]	[−3.71393]	[9.13617]
RJPY(-2)	0.002628	0.002964	0.000718
	−0.016680	−0.015270	−0.016530
	[0.15753]	[0.19409]	[0.04345]
C	−0.005836	0.000045	−0.003682
	−0.007450	−0.006820	−0.007390
	[−0.78299]	[0.00665]	[−0.49847]

	REUR	RGBP	RJPY
R-squared	0.025479	0.05224	0.024297
Adj. R-squared	0.024009	0.050815	0.022826
Sum sq. resids	879.8663	737.4698	864.4051
S.E. equation	0.470301	0.430566	0.466151
F-statistic	17.33423	36.54742	16.51038
Log likelihood	−2644.754	−2292.988	−2609.430
Akaike AIC	1.330868	1.154323	1.313139
Schwarz SC	1.341917	1.165372	1.324189
Mean dependent	−0.0006978	0.000162	−0.004320
S.D. dependent	0.476051	0.441941	0.471564

Determinant resid covariance (dof adj.)	0.004189
Determinant resid covariance	0.004167
Log likelihood	−6043.540
Akaike information criterion	3.043684
Schwarz criterion	3.076832

In the Endogenous variables box, type the three variable names, **reur rgbp rjpy**. In the Exogenous box, leave the default 'C' and in the Lag Interval box, enter **1 2** to estimate a VAR(2), just as an example. The output appears in a neatly organised table as shown on the previous page, with one column for each equation in the first and second panels, and a single column of statistics that describes the system as a whole in the third. So values of the information criteria are given separately for each equation in the second panel and jointly for the model as a whole in the third.

We will shortly discuss the interpretation of the output, but the example so far has assumed that we know *the appropriate lag length* for the VAR. However, in practice, the first step in the construction of any VAR model, once the variables that will enter the VAR have been decided, will be to determine the appropriate lag length. This can be achieved in a variety of ways, but one of the easiest is to employ a multivariate information criterion. In EViews, this can be done easily from the EViews VAR output we have by clicking **View/Lag Structure/Lag Length Criteria. . . .** You will be invited to specify the maximum number of lags to entertain including in the model, and for this example, arbitrarily select **10**. The output in the following table would be observed.

VAR Lag Order Selection Criteria
Endogenous variables: REUR RGBP RJPY
Exogenous variables: C
Date: 07/07/13   Time: 12:19
Sample: 7/07/2002 6/06/2013
Included observations: 3977

Lag	LogL	LR	FPE	AIC	SC	HQ
0	−6324.3310	NA	0.004836	3.181962	3.186705	3.183644
1	−6060.2640	527.6036	0.004254	3.053690	3.072664*	3.060418
2	−6034.8720	50.69431	0.004219*	3.045447*	3.078652	3.057221*
3	−6030.9570	7.808927	0.004230	3.048005	3.095440	3.064824
4	−6022.9370	15.98760	0.004232	3.048498	3.110163	3.070363
5	−6015.1100	15.59165	0.004234	3.049087	3.124983	3.075998
6	−6009.1700	11.82421	0.004241	3.050626	3.140752	3.082583
7	−6000.1710	17.89848*	0.004241	3.050626	3.154983	3.087629
8	−5992.9660	14.31748	0.004245	3.051530	3.170117	3.093578
9	−5988.1330	9.599241	0.004254	3.053625	3.186442	3.100719

* indicates lag order selected by the criterion
LR: sequential modified LR test statistic (each test at 5% level)
FPE: Final prediction error
AIC: Akaike information criterion
SC: Schwarz information criterion
HQ: Hannan-Quinn information criterion

EViews presents the values of various information criteria and other methods for determining the lag order. In this case, the Akaike and Hannan–Quinn criteria both select a lag length of two as optimal, while Schwarz's criterion chooses a VAR(1). **Estimate a VAR(1)** and examine the results. Does the model look as if it fits the data well? Why or why not?

Next, run a Granger causality test by clicking **View/Lag Structure/ Granger Causality/Block Exogeneity Tests**. The table of statistics will appear immediately as follows.

VAR Granger Causality/Block Exogeneity Wald Tests
Date: 07/07/13 Time: 14:36
Sample: 7/07/2002 6/06/13
Included observations: 3986

Dependent variable: REUR

Excluded	Chi-sq	df	Prob.
RGBP	5.736328	1	0.0166
RJPY	1.413860	1	0.2344
All	6.844297	2	0.0326

Dependent variable: RGBP

Excluded	Chi-sq	df	Prob.
REUR	1.508416	1	0.2194
RJPY	12.94274	1	0.0003
All	17.61849	2	0.0001

Dependent variable: RJPY

Excluded	Chi-sq	df	Prob.
REUR	0.568845	1	0.4507
RGBP	6.702967	1	0.0096
All	8.551943	2	0.0139

The results show only modest evidence of lead–lag interactions between the series. Since we have estimated a tri-variate VAR, three panels are displayed, with one for each dependent variable in the system. There is causality from the pound to the euro and from the pound to the yen that is significant at the 5% and 1% levels respectively but no causality between the euro–dollar and the yen–dollar in either direction. These results might be interpreted as suggesting that information is incorporated slightly more quickly in the pound–dollar rate than in the euro–dollar or yen–dollar rates.

It is worth also noting that the term 'Granger causality' is something of a misnomer since a finding of 'causality' does not mean that movements in one variable physically cause movements in another. For example, in the above analysis, if movements in the euro–dollar market were found to Granger-cause movements in the pound–dollar market, this would not have meant that the pound–dollar rate changed as a direct result of, or because of, movements in the euro–dollar market. Rather, causality simply implies a *chronological ordering of movements in the series*. It could validly be stated that movements in the pound–dollar rate appear to lead those of the euro–dollar rate, and so on.

The EViews manual suggests that block *F*-test restrictions can be performed by estimating the VAR equations individually using OLS and then by using the **View** then **Lag Structure** then **Lag Exclusion Tests**. EViews tests for whether the parameters for a given lag of all the variables in a particular equation can be restricted to zero.

To obtain the impulse responses for the estimated model, simply click the **Impulse** on the button bar above the VAR object and a new dialog box will appear as in screenshot 7.4.

By default, EViews will offer to estimate and plot all of the responses to separate shocks of all of the variables in the order that the variables were listed in the estimation window, using ten steps and confidence intervals generated using analytic formulae. If twenty steps ahead had been selected, with 'combined response graphs', you would see the graphs in the format in screenshot 7.5 (obviously they appear small on the page and the colour has been lost, but the originals are much clearer). As one would expect given the parameter estimates and the Granger causality test results, only a few linkages between the series are established here. The responses to the shocks are very small, except for the response of a variable to its own shock, and they die down to almost nothing after the first lag. The only exceptions are that the pound (second graph in the screenshot) and the yen (third graph) both respond to shocks to the euro rate against the dollar.

Plots of the variance decompositions can also be generated by clicking on **View** and then **Variance Decomposition. . . .** A similar plot for the variance decompositions would appear as in screenshot 7.6.

There is little again that can be seen from these variance decomposition graphs that appear small on a printed page apart from the fact that the behaviour is observed to settle down to a steady state very quickly. Interestingly, while the percentage of the errors that is attributable to own shocks is 100% in the case of the euro rate, for the pound, the euro series explains around 47% of the variation in returns, and for the yen, the euro series explains around 7% of the variation and the pound 37%.

We should remember that the ordering of the variables has an effect on the impulse responses and variance decompositions, and when, as in this case, theory does not suggest an obvious ordering of the series, some sensitivity analysis should

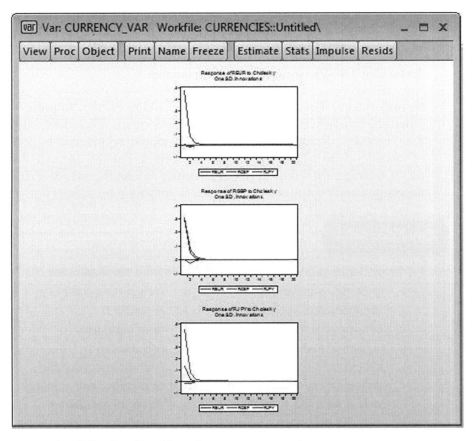

Screenshot 7.4   Constructing the VAR impulse responses

Screenshot 7.5   Combined impulse response graphs

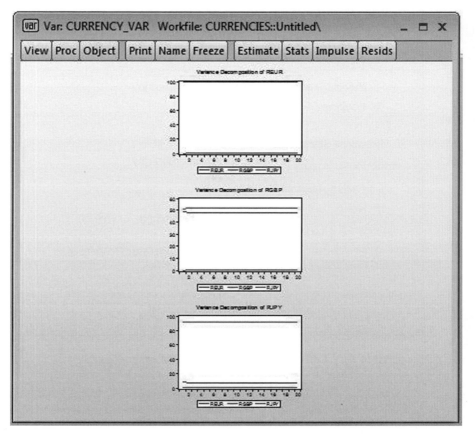

Screenshot 7.6   **Variance decomposition graphs**

be undertaken. This can be achieved by clicking on the 'Impulse Definition' tab when the window that creates the impulses is open. A window entitled 'Ordering for Cholesky' should be apparent, and it would be possible to reverse the order of variables or to select any other order desired. For the variance decompositions, the 'Ordering for Cholesky' box is observed in the window for creating the decompositions without having to select another tab.

Key concepts

The key terms to be able to define and explain from this chapter are

- endogenous variable
- simultaneous equations bias
- order condition
- Hausman test
- structural form
- indirect least squares
- vector autoregression
- impulse response

- exogenous variable
- identified
- rank condition
- reduced form
- instrumental variables
- two-stage least squares
- Granger causality
- variance decomposition

Self-study questions

1. Consider the following simultaneous equations system

$$y_{1t} = \alpha_0 + \alpha_1 y_{2t} + \alpha_2 y_{3t} + \alpha_3 X_{1t} - \alpha_4 X_{2t} + u_{1t} \tag{7.94}$$

$$y_{2t} = \beta_0 + \beta_1 y_{3t} + \beta_2 X_{1t} + \beta_3 X_{3t} + u_{2t} \tag{7.95}$$

$$y_{3t} = \gamma_0 + \gamma_1 y_{1t} + \gamma_2 X_{2t} + \gamma_3 X_{3t} + u_{3t} \tag{7.96}$$

(a) Derive the reduced form equations corresponding to (7.94)–(7.96).
(b) What do you understand by the term 'identification'? Describe a rule for determining whether a system of equations is identified. Apply this rule to (7.94)–(7.96). Does this rule guarantee that estimates of the structural parameters can be obtained?
(c) Which would you consider the more serious misspecification: treating exogenous variables as endogenous, or treating endogenous variables as exogenous? Explain your answer.
(d) Describe a method of obtaining the structural form coefficients corresponding to an overidentified system.
(e) Using EViews, estimate a VAR model for the interest rate series used in the principal components example of chapter 4. Use a method for selecting the lag length in the VAR optimally. Determine whether certain maturities lead or lag others, by conducting Granger causality tests and plotting impulse responses and variance decompositions. Is there any evidence that new information is reflected more quickly in some maturities than others?

2. Consider the following system of two equations

$$y_{1t} = \alpha_0 + \alpha_1 y_{2t} + \alpha_2 X_{1t} + \alpha_3 X_{2t} + u_{1t} \tag{7.97}$$

$$y_{2t} = \beta_0 + \beta_1 y_{1t} + \beta_2 X_{1t} + u_{2t} \tag{7.98}$$

(a) Explain, with reference to these equations, the undesirable consequences that would arise if (7.97) and (7.98) were estimated separately using OLS.
(b) What would be the effect upon your answer to (a) if the variable y_{1t} had not appeared in (7.98)?
(c) State the order condition for determining whether an equation which is part of a system is identified. Use this condition to determine whether (7.97) or (7.98) or both or neither are identified.
(d) Explain whether indirect least squares (ILS) or two-stage least squares (2SLS) could be used to obtain the parameters of (7.97) and (7.98). Describe how each of these two procedures (ILS and 2SLS) are used to calculate the parameters of an equation. Compare and evaluate the usefulness of ILS, 2SLS and IV.
(e) Explain briefly the Hausman procedure for testing for exogeneity.

3. Explain, using an example if you consider it appropriate, what you understand by the equivalent terms 'recursive equations' and 'triangular system'. Can a triangular system be validly estimated using OLS? Explain your answer.

4. Consider the following vector autoregressive model

$$y_t = \beta_0 + \sum_{i=1}^{k} \beta_i y_{t-i} + u_t \tag{7.99}$$

where y_t is a $p \times 1$ vector of variables determined by k lags of all p variables in the system, u_t is a $p \times 1$ vector of error terms, β_0 is a $p \times 1$ vector of constant term coefficients and β_i are $p \times p$ matrices of coefficients on the ith lag of y.

(a) If $p = 2$, and $k = 3$, write out all the equations of the VAR in full, carefully defining any new notation you use that is not given in the question.

(b) Why have VARs become popular for application in economics and finance, relative to structural models derived from some underlying theory?

(c) Discuss any weaknesses you perceive in the VAR approach to econometric modelling.

(d) Two researchers, using the same set of data but working independently, arrive at different lag lengths for the VAR equation (7.99). Describe and evaluate two methods for determining which of the lag lengths is more appropriate.

5. Define carefully the following terms
   - Simultaneous equations system
   - Exogenous variables
   - Endogenous variables
   - Structural form model
   - Reduced form model.

Modelling long-run relationships in finance

8.1 Stationarity and unit root testing

8.1.1 Why are tests for non-stationarity necessary?

There are several reasons why the concept of non-stationarity is important and why it is essential that variables that are non-stationary be treated differently from those that are stationary. Two definitions of non-stationarity were presented at the start of chapter 6. For the purpose of the analysis in this chapter, a stationary series can be defined as one with a *constant mean*, *constant variance* and *constant autocovariances* for each given lag. Therefore, the discussion in this chapter relates to the concept of weak stationarity. An examination of whether a series can be viewed as stationary or not is essential for the following reasons:

- The stationarity or otherwise of a series can *strongly influence its behaviour and properties*. To offer one illustration, the word 'shock' is usually used to denote a change or an unexpected change in a variable or perhaps simply the value of the error term during a particular time period. For a stationary series, 'shocks' to the system will gradually die away. That is, a shock during time t will have

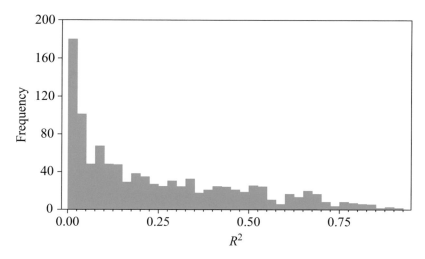

Figure 8.1   Value of R^2 for 1,000 sets of regressions of a non-stationary variable on another independent non-stationary variable

a smaller effect in time $t+1$, a smaller effect still in time $t+2$, and so on. This can be contrasted with the case of non-stationary data, where the persistence of shocks will always be infinite, so that for a non-stationary series, the effect of a shock during time t will not have a smaller effect in time $t+1$, and in time $t+2$, etc.

- The use of non-stationary data can lead to *spurious regressions*. If two stationary variables are generated as independent random series, when one of those variables is regressed on the other, the t-ratio on the slope coefficient would be expected not to be significantly different from zero, and the value of R^2 would be expected to be very low. This seems obvious, for the variables are not related to one another. However, if two variables are trending over time, a regression of one on the other could have a high R^2 even if the two are totally unrelated. So, if standard regression techniques are applied to non-stationary data, the end result could be a regression that 'looks' good under standard measures (significant coefficient estimates and a high R^2), but which is really valueless. Such a model would be termed a 'spurious regression'.

    To give an illustration of this, two independent sets of non-stationary variables, y and x, were generated with sample size 500, one regressed on the other and the R^2 noted. This was repeated 1,000 times to obtain 1,000 R^2 values. A histogram of these values is given in figure 8.1.

    As figure 8.1 shows, although one would have expected the R^2 values for each regression to be close to zero, since the explained and explanatory variables in each case are independent of one another, in fact R^2 takes on values across the whole range. For one set of data, R^2 is bigger than 0.9, while it is bigger than 0.5 over 16% of the time!

- If the variables employed in a regression model are *not stationary*, then it can be proved that the standard assumptions for asymptotic analysis will not be valid. In other words, the usual 't-ratios' will not follow a t-distribution, and

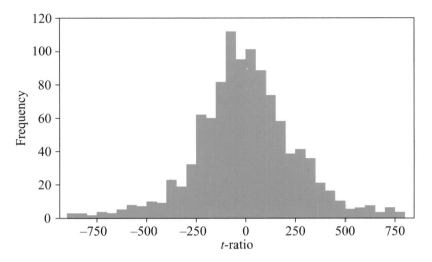

Figure 8.2   Value of t-ratio of slope coefficient for $1,000$ sets of regressions of a non-stationary variable on another independent non-stationary variable

the F-statistic will not follow an F-distribution, and so on. Using the same simulated data as used to produce figure 8.1, figure 8.2 plots a histogram of the estimated t-ratio on the slope coefficient for each set of data.

In general, if one variable is regressed on another unrelated variable, the t-ratio on the slope coefficient will follow a t-distribution. For a sample of size 500, this implies that 95% of the time, the t-ratio will lie between ± 2. As figure 8.2 shows quite dramatically, however, the standard t-ratio in a regression of non-stationary variables can take on enormously large values. In fact, in the above example, the t-ratio is bigger than 2 in absolute value over 98% of the time, when it should be bigger than 2 in absolute value only approximately 5% of the time! Clearly, it is therefore not possible to validly undertake hypothesis tests about the regression parameters if the data are non-stationary.

8.1.2 Two types of non-stationarity

There are two models that have been frequently used to characterise the non-stationarity, the *random walk model with drift*

$$y_t = \mu + y_{t-1} + u_t \tag{8.1}$$

and the *trend-stationary process* — so-called because it is stationary around a linear trend

$$y_t = \alpha + \beta t + u_t \tag{8.2}$$

where u_t is a white noise disturbance term in both cases.

Note that the model (8.1) could be generalised to the case where y_t is an explosive process

$$y_t = \mu + \phi y_{t-1} + u_t \tag{8.3}$$

where $\phi > 1$. Typically, this case is ignored and $\phi = 1$ is used to characterise the non-stationarity because $\phi > 1$ does not describe many data series in economics and finance, but $\phi = 1$ has been found to describe accurately many financial and economic time series. Moreover, $\phi > 1$ has an intuitively unappealing property: shocks to the system are not only persistent through time, they are propagated so that a given shock will have an increasingly large influence. In other words, the effect of a shock during time t will have a larger effect in time $t + 1$, a larger effect still in time $t + 2$, and so on. To see this, consider the general case of an AR(1) with no drift

$$y_t = \phi y_{t-1} + u_t \tag{8.4}$$

Let ϕ take any value for now. Lagging (8.4) one and then two periods

$$y_{t-1} = \phi y_{t-2} + u_{t-1} \tag{8.5}$$

$$y_{t-2} = \phi y_{t-3} + u_{t-2} \tag{8.6}$$

Substituting into (8.4) from (8.5) for y_{t-1} yields

$$y_t = \phi(\phi y_{t-2} + u_{t-1}) + u_t \tag{8.7}$$

$$y_t = \phi^2 y_{t-2} + \phi u_{t-1} + u_t \tag{8.8}$$

Substituting again for y_{t-2} from (8.6)

$$y_t = \phi^2(\phi y_{t-3} + u_{t-2}) + \phi u_{t-1} + u_t \tag{8.9}$$

$$y_t = \phi^3 y_{t-3} + \phi^2 u_{t-2} + \phi u_{t-1} + u_t \tag{8.10}$$

T successive substitutions of this type lead to

$$y_t = \phi^{T+1} y_{t-(T+1)} + \phi u_{t-1} + \phi^2 u_{t-2} + \phi^3 u_{t-3} + \cdots + \phi^T u_{t-T} + u_t \tag{8.11}$$

There are three possible cases:

(1) $\phi < 1 \Rightarrow \phi^T \to 0$ as $T \to \infty$
So the shocks to the system gradually die away – this is the *stationary case*.
(2) $\phi = 1 \Rightarrow \phi^T = 1 \; \forall \; T$
So shocks persist in the system and never die away. The following is obtained

$$y_t = y_0 + \sum_{t=0}^{\infty} u_t \text{ as } T \to \infty \tag{8.12}$$

So the current value of y is just an infinite sum of past shocks plus some starting value of y_0. This is known as the *unit root case*, for the root of the characteristic equation would be unity.
(3) $\phi > 1$. Now given shocks become more influential as time goes on, since if $\phi > 1$, $\phi^3 > \phi^2 > \phi$, etc. This is the *explosive case* which, for the reasons listed above, will not be considered as a plausible description of the data.

Going back to the two characterisations of non-stationarity, the random walk with drift

$$y_t = \mu + y_{t-1} + u_t \tag{8.13}$$

and the trend-stationary process

$$y_t = \alpha + \beta t + u_t \tag{8.14}$$

The two will require different treatments to induce stationarity. The second case is known as *deterministic non-stationarity* and de-trending is required. In other words, if it is believed that only this class of non-stationarity is present, a regression of the form given in (8.14) would be run, and any subsequent estimation would be done on the residuals from (8.14), which would have had the linear trend removed.

The first case is known as stochastic non-stationarity, where there is a stochastic trend in the data. Letting $\Delta y_t = y_t - y_{t-1}$ and $Ly_t = y_{t-1}$ so that $(1-L)y_t = y_t - Ly_t = y_t - y_{t-1}$. If (8.13) is taken and y_{t-1} subtracted from both sides

$$y_t - y_{t-1} = \mu + u_t \tag{8.15}$$

$$(1-L)y_t = \mu + u_t \tag{8.16}$$

$$\Delta y_t = \mu + u_t \tag{8.17}$$

There now exists a new variable Δy_t, which will be stationary. It would be said that stationarity has been induced by 'differencing once'. It should also be apparent from the representation given by (8.16) why y_t is also known as a *unit root process*: i.e. that the root of the characteristic equation $(1-z) = 0$, will be unity.

Although trend-stationary and difference-stationary series are both 'trending' over time, the correct approach needs to be used in each case. If first differences of a trend-stationary series were taken, it would 'remove' the non-stationarity, but at the expense of introducing an MA(1) structure into the errors. To see this, consider the trend-stationary model

$$y_t = \alpha + \beta t + u_t \tag{8.18}$$

This model can be expressed for time $t-1$, which would be obtained by removing 1 from all of the time subscripts in (8.18)

$$y_{t-1} = \alpha + \beta(t-1) + u_{t-1} \tag{8.19}$$

Subtracting (8.19) from (8.18) gives

$$\Delta y_t = \beta + u_t - u_{t-1} \tag{8.20}$$

Not only is this a moving average in the errors that has been created, it is a non-invertible MA (i.e. one that cannot be expressed as an autoregressive process). Thus the series, Δy_t would in this case have some very undesirable properties.

Conversely if one tried to de-trend a series which has stochastic trend, then the non-stationarity would not be removed. Clearly then, it is not always obvious which way to proceed. One possibility is to nest both cases in a more general model and to test that. For example, consider the model

$$\Delta y_t = \alpha_0 + \alpha_1 t + (\gamma - 1)y_{t-1} + u_t \tag{8.21}$$

Although again, of course the *t*-ratios in (8.21) will not follow a *t*-distribution. Such a model could allow for both deterministic and stochastic non-stationarity. However, this book will now concentrate on the stochastic stationarity model

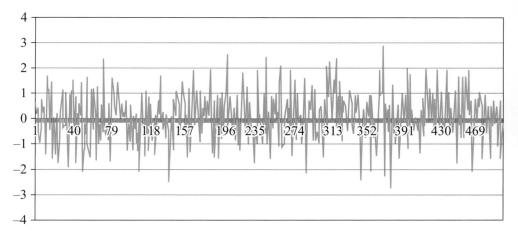

Figure 8.3   Example of a white noise process

since it is the model that has been found to best describe most non-stationary financial and economic time series. Consider again the simplest stochastic trend model

$$y_t = y_{t-1} + u_t \qquad\qquad (8.22)$$

or

$$\Delta y_t = u_t \qquad\qquad (8.23)$$

This concept can be generalised to consider the case where the series contains more than one 'unit root'. That is, the first difference operator, Δ, would need to be applied more than once to induce stationarity. This situation will be described later in this chapter.

Arguably the best way to understand the ideas discussed above is to consider some diagrams showing the typical properties of certain relevant types of processes. Figure 8.3 plots a white noise (pure random) process, while figures 8.4 and 8.5 plot a random walk versus a random walk with drift and a deterministic trend process, respectively.

Comparing these three figures gives a good idea of the differences between the properties of a stationary, a stochastic trend and a deterministic trend process. In figure 8.3, a white noise process visibly has no trending behaviour, and it frequently crosses its mean value of zero. The random walk (thick line) and random walk with drift (faint line) processes of figure 8.4 exhibit 'long swings' away from their mean value, which they cross very rarely. A comparison of the two lines in this graph reveals that the positive drift leads to a series that is more likely to rise over time than to fall; obviously, the effect of the drift on the series becomes greater and greater the further the two processes are tracked. Finally, the deterministic trend process of figure 8.5 clearly does not have a constant mean, and exhibits completely random fluctuations about its upward trend. If the trend were removed from the series, a plot similar to the white noise process of figure 8.3 would result. In this

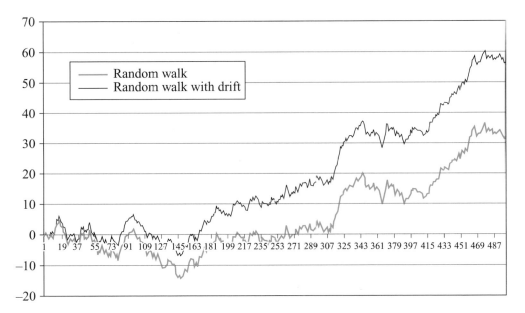

Figure 8.4   Time series plot of a random walk versus a random walk with drift

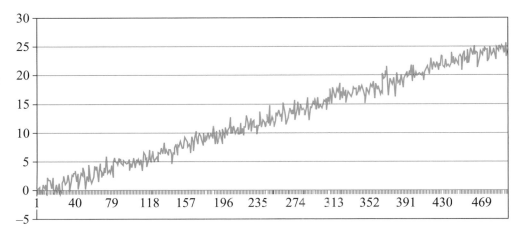

Figure 8.5   Time series plot of a deterministic trend process

author's opinion, more time series in finance and economics look like figure 8.4 than either figure 8.3 or 8.5. Consequently, as stated above, the stochastic trend model will be the focus of the remainder of this chapter.

Finally, figure 8.6 plots the value of an autoregressive process of order 1 with different values of the autoregressive coefficient as given by (8.4). Values of $\phi = 0$ (i.e. a white noise process), $\phi = 0.8$ (i.e. a stationary AR(1)) and $\phi = 1$ (i.e. a random walk) are plotted over time.

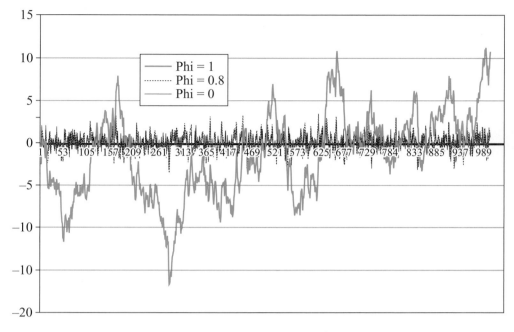

Figure 8.6 Autoregressive processes with differing values of ϕ (0, 0.8, 1)

8.1.3 Some more definitions and terminology

If a non-stationary series, y_t must be differenced d times before it becomes stationary, then it is said to be integrated of order d. This would be written $y_t \sim I(d)$. So if $y_t \sim I(d)$ then $\Delta^d y_t \sim I(0)$. This latter piece of terminology states that applying the difference operator, Δ, d times, leads to an I(0) process, i.e. a process with no unit roots. In fact, applying the difference operator more than d times to an I(d) process will still result in a stationary series (but with an MA error structure). An I(0) series is a stationary series, while an I(1) series contains one unit root. For example, consider the random walk

$$y_t = y_{t-1} + u_t \tag{8.24}$$

An I(2) series contains two unit roots and so would require differencing twice to induce stationarity. I(1) and I(2) series can wander a long way from their mean value and cross this mean value rarely, while I(0) series should cross the mean frequently. The majority of financial and economic time series contain a single unit root, although some are stationary and some have been argued to possibly contain two unit roots (series such as nominal consumer prices and nominal wages). The efficient markets hypothesis together with rational expectations suggest that asset prices (or the natural logarithms of asset prices) should follow a random walk or a random walk with drift, so that their differences are unpredictable (or only predictable to their long-term average value).

To see what types of data generating process could lead to an I(2) series, consider the equation

$$y_t = 2y_{t-1} - y_{t-2} + u_t \tag{8.25}$$

taking all of the terms in y over to the left hand side, and then applying the lag operator notation

$$y_t - 2y_{t-1} + y_{t-2} = u_t \tag{8.26}$$

$$(1 - 2L + L^2)y_t = u_t \tag{8.27}$$

$$(1 - L)(1 - L)y_t = u_t \tag{8.28}$$

It should be evident now that this process for y_t contains two unit roots, and would require differencing twice to induce stationarity.

What would happen if y_t in (8.25) were differenced only once? Taking first differences of (8.25), i.e. subtracting y_{t-1} from both sides

$$y_t - y_{t-1} = y_{t-1} - y_{t-2} + u_t \tag{8.29}$$

$$y_t - y_{t-1} = (y_t - y_{t-1})_{-1} + u_t \tag{8.30}$$

$$\Delta y_t = \Delta y_{t-1} + u_t \tag{8.31}$$

$$(1 - L)\Delta y_t = u_t \tag{8.32}$$

First differencing would therefore have removed one of the unit roots, but there is still a unit root remaining in the new variable, Δy_t.

8.1.4 Testing for a unit root

One immediately obvious (but inappropriate) method that readers may think of to test for a unit root would be to examine the autocorrelation function of the series of interest. However, although shocks to a unit root process will remain in the system indefinitely, the acf for a unit root process (a random walk) will often be seen to decay away very slowly to zero. Thus, such a process may be mistaken for a highly persistent but stationary process. Hence it is not possible to use the acf or pacf to determine whether a series is characterised by a unit root or not. Furthermore, even if the true data generating process for y_t contains a unit root, the results of the tests for a given sample could lead one to believe that the process is stationary. Therefore, what is required is some kind of formal hypothesis testing procedure that answers the question, 'given the sample of data to hand, is it plausible that the true data generating process for y contains one or more unit roots?'

The early and pioneering work on testing for a unit root in time series was done by Dickey and Fuller (Fuller, 1976; Dickey and Fuller, 1979). The basic objective of the test is to examine the null hypothesis that $\phi = 1$ in

$$y_t = \phi y_{t-1} + u_t \tag{8.33}$$

against the one-sided alternative $\phi < 1$. Thus the hypotheses of interest are H_0: series contains a unit root versus H_1: series is stationary.

In practice, the following regression is employed, rather than (8.33), for ease of computation and interpretation

$$\Delta y_t = \psi y_{t-1} + u_t \tag{8.34}$$

so that a test of $\phi = 1$ is equivalent to a test of $\psi = 0$ (since $\phi - 1 = \psi$).

Table 8.1   Critical values for DF tests (Fuller, 1976, p. 373)

Significance level	10%	5%	1%
CV for constant but no trend	−2.57	−2.86	−3.43
CV for constant and trend	−3.12	−3.41	−3.96

Dickey–Fuller (DF) tests are also known as τ-tests, and can be conducted allowing for an intercept, or an intercept and deterministic trend, or neither, in the test regression. The model for the unit root test in each case is

$$y_t = \phi y_{t-1} + \mu + \lambda t + u_t \tag{8.35}$$

The tests can also be written, by subtracting y_{t-1} from each side of the equation, as

$$\Delta y_t = \psi y_{t-1} + \mu + \lambda t + u_t \tag{8.36}$$

In another paper, Dickey and Fuller (1981) provide a set of additional test statistics and their critical values for joint tests of the significance of the lagged y, and the constant and trend terms. These are not examined further here. The test statistics for the original DF tests are defined as

$$test\ statistic = \frac{\hat{\psi}}{SE(\hat{\psi})} \tag{8.37}$$

The test statistics do not follow the usual t-distribution under the null hypothesis, since the null is one of non-stationarity, but rather they follow a non-standard distribution. Critical values are derived from simulations experiments in, for example, Fuller (1976); see also chapter 13 in this book. Relevant examples of the distribution are shown in table 8.1. A full set of DF critical values is given in the appendix of statistical tables at the end of this book. A discussion and example of how such critical values (CV) are derived using simulations methods are presented in chapter 13.

Comparing these with the standard normal critical values, it can be seen that the DF critical values are much bigger in absolute terms (i.e. more negative). Thus more evidence against the null hypothesis is required in the context of unit root tests than under standard t-tests. This arises partly from the inherent instability of the unit root process, the fatter distribution of the t-ratios in the context of non-stationary data (see figure 8.2), and the resulting uncertainty in inference. The null hypothesis of a unit root is rejected in favour of the stationary alternative in each case if the test statistic is more negative than the critical value.

The tests above are valid only if u_t is white noise. In particular, u_t is assumed not to be autocorrelated, but would be so if there was autocorrelation in the dependent variable of the regression (Δy_t) which has not been modelled. If this is the case, the test would be 'oversized', meaning that the true size of the test (the proportion of times a correct null hypothesis is incorrectly rejected) would be higher than the nominal size used (e.g. 5%). The solution is to 'augment' the test using p lags of the dependent variable. The alternative model in case (i) is now written

$$\Delta y_t = \psi y_{t-1} + \sum_{i=1}^{p} \alpha_i \Delta y_{t-i} + u_t \tag{8.38}$$

The lags of Δy_t now 'soak up' any dynamic structure present in the dependent variable, to ensure that u_t is not autocorrelated. The test is known as an augmented Dickey–Fuller (ADF) test and is still conducted on ψ, and the same critical values from the DF tables are used as before.

A problem now arises in determining the optimal number of lags of the dependent variable. Although several ways of choosing p have been proposed, they are all somewhat arbitrary, and are thus not presented here. Instead, the following two simple rules of thumb are suggested. First, the *frequency of the data* can be used to decide. So, for example, if the data are monthly, use twelve lags, if the data are quarterly, use four lags, and so on. Clearly, there would not be an obvious choice for the number of lags to use in a regression containing higher frequency financial data (e.g. hourly or daily)! Second, an *information criterion* can be used to decide. So choose the number of lags that minimises the value of an information criterion, as outlined in chapter 7.

It is quite important to attempt to use an optimal number of lags of the dependent variable in the test regression, and to examine the sensitivity of the outcome of the test to the lag length chosen. In most cases, hopefully the conclusion will not be qualitatively altered by small changes in p, but sometimes it will. Including too few lags will not remove all of the autocorrelation, thus biasing the results, while using too many will increase the coefficient standard errors. The latter effect arises since an increase in the number of parameters to estimate uses up degrees of freedom. Therefore, everything else being equal, the absolute values of the test statistics will be reduced. This will result in a reduction in the power of the test, implying that for a stationary process the null hypothesis of a unit root will be rejected less frequently than would otherwise have been the case.

8.1.5 Testing for higher orders of integration

Consider the simple regression

$$\Delta y_t = \psi y_{t-1} + u_t \tag{8.39}$$

H_0: $\psi = 0$ is tested against H_1: $\psi < 0$.

If H_0 is rejected, it would simply be concluded that y_t does not contain a unit root. But what should be the conclusion if H_0 is not rejected? The series contains a unit root, but is that it? No! What if $y_t \sim I(2)$? The null hypothesis would still not have been rejected. It is now necessary to perform a test of

$$H_0 : y_t \sim I(2) \text{ vs. } H_1 : y_t \sim I(1)$$

$\Delta^2 y_t (= \Delta y_t - \Delta y_{t-1})$ would now be regressed on Δy_{t-1} (plus lags of $\Delta^2 y_t$ to augment the test if necessary). Thus, testing H_0: $\Delta y_t \sim I(1)$ is equivalent to H_0: $y_t \sim I(2)$. So in this case, if H_0 is not rejected (very unlikely in practice), it would be concluded that y_t is at least I(2). If H_0 is rejected, it would be concluded that y_t contains a single unit root. The tests should continue for a further unit root until H_0 is rejected.

Dickey and Pantula (1987) have argued that an ordering of the tests as described above (i.e. testing for I(1), then I(2), and so on) is, strictly speaking, invalid. The theoretically correct approach would be to start by assuming some highest plausible order of integration (e.g. I(2)), and to test I(2) against I(1). If I(2) is rejected, then test I(1) against I(0). In practice, however, to the author's knowledge, no financial time series contain more than a single unit root, so that this matter is of less concern in finance.

8.1.6 Phillips–Perron (PP) tests

Phillips and Perron have developed a more comprehensive theory of unit root non-stationarity. The tests are similar to ADF tests, but they incorporate an automatic correction to the DF procedure to allow for autocorrelated residuals. The tests often give the same conclusions as, and suffer from most of the same important limitations as, the ADF tests.

8.1.7 Criticisms of Dickey–Fuller- and Phillips–Perron-type tests

The most important criticism that has been levelled at unit root tests is that their power is low if the process is stationary but with a root close to the non-stationary boundary. So, for example, consider an AR(1) data generating process with coefficient 0.95. If the true data generating process is

$$y_t = 0.95 y_{t-1} + u_t \tag{8.40}$$

the null hypothesis of a unit root should be rejected. It has been thus argued that the tests are poor at deciding, for example, whether $\phi = 1$ or $\phi = 0.95$, especially with small sample sizes. The source of this problem is that, under the classical hypothesis-testing framework, the null hypothesis is never accepted, it is simply stated that it is either rejected or not rejected. This means that a failure to reject the null hypothesis could occur either because the null was correct, or because there is insufficient information in the sample to enable rejection. One way to get around this problem is to use a stationarity test as well as a unit root test, as described in box 8.1.

Box 8.1 Stationarity tests

Stationarity tests have stationarity under the null hypothesis, thus reversing the null and alternatives under the Dickey–Fuller approach. Thus, under stationarity tests, the data will appear stationary by default if there is little information in the sample. One such stationarity test is the KPSS test (Kwaitkowski *et al.*, 1992). The computation of the test statistic is not discussed here but the test is available within the EViews software. The results of these tests can be compared with the ADF/PP procedure to see if the same conclusion is obtained. The null and alternative hypotheses under each testing approach are as follows:

$$ADF/PP \qquad KPSS$$
$$H_0 : y_t \sim I(1) \qquad H_0 : y_t \sim I(0)$$
$$H_1 : y_t \sim I(0) \qquad H_1 : y_t \sim I(1)$$

There are four possible outcomes:

(1) Reject H_0 and   Do not reject H_0
(2) Do not reject H_0 and   Reject H_0
(3) Reject H_0 and   Reject H_0
(4) Do not reject H_0 and   Do not reject H_0

For the conclusions to be robust, the results should fall under outcomes 1 or 2, which would be the case when both tests concluded that the series is stationary or non-stationary, respectively. Outcomes 3 or 4 imply conflicting results. The joint use of stationarity and unit root tests is known as *confirmatory data analysis*.

8.2 Tests for unit roots in the presence of structural breaks

8.2.1 Motivation

The standard Dickey-Fuller-type unit root tests presented above do not perform well if there are one or more structural breaks in the series under investigation, either in the intercept or the slope of the regression. More specifically, the tests have low power in such circumstances and they fail to reject the unit root null hypothesis when it is incorrect as the slope parameter in the regression of y_t on y_{t-1} is biased towards unity by an unparameterised structural break. In general, the larger the break and the smaller the sample, the lower the power of the test. As Leybourne *et al.* (1998) have shown, unit root tests are also oversized in the presence of structural breaks, so they reject the null hypothesis too frequently when it is correct.[1]

Perron's (1989) work is important since he was able to demonstrate that if we allow for structural breaks in the testing framework, a whole raft of macroeconomic series that Nelson and Plosser (1982) had identified as non-stationary may turn out to be stationary. He argues that most economic time series are best characterised by *broken trend stationary processes*, where the data generating process is a deterministic trend but with a structural break around 1929 that permanently changed the levels (i.e. the intercepts) of the series.

8.2.2   The Perron (1989) procedure

Recall from above that the flexible framework for unit root testing involves a regression of the form

$$\Delta y_t = \psi y_{t-1} + \mu + \lambda t + \sum_{i=1}^{p} \alpha_i \Delta y_{t-i} + u_t \tag{8.41}$$

where μ is an intercept and λt captures the time trend, one or both of which could be excluded from the regression if they were thought to be unnecessary.

Perron (1989) proposes three test equations differing dependent on the type of break that was thought to be present. The first he terms a 'crash' model that allows a break in the level (i.e. the intercept) of the series; the second is a 'changing growth' model that allows for a break in the growth rate (i.e. the slope) of the series; the final model allows for both types of break to occur at the same time, changing both the intercept and the slope of the trend. If we define the break point in the data as T_b, and D_t is a dummy variable defined as

$$D_t = \begin{cases} 0 & \text{if } t < T_b \\ 1 & \text{if } t \geq T_b \end{cases}$$

the general equation for the third type of test (i.e. the most general) is

$$\Delta y_t = \psi y_{t-1} + \mu + \alpha_1 D_t + \alpha_2 (t - T_b) D_t + \lambda t + \sum_{i=1}^{p} \alpha_i \Delta y_{t-i} + u_t \tag{8.42}$$

For the crash only model, set $\alpha_2 = 0$, while for the changing growth only model, set $\alpha_1 = 0$. In all three cases, there is a unit root with a structural break at T_b under the null hypothesis and a series that is a stationary process with a break under the alternative.

---

[1] This material is fairly specialised and thus is not well covered by most of the standard textbooks. But for any readers wishing to see more detail, there is a useful and accessible chapter by Perron in the book *Cointegration for the Applied Economist* edited by B. B. Rao (1994), Macmillan, Basingstoke, UK. There is also a chapter on structural change in the book *Unit Roots, Cointegration and Structural Change* by G. S. Maddala and I-M. Kim (1998), Cambridge University Press.

While Perron (1989) commences a new literature on testing for unit roots in the presence of structural breaks, an important limitation of this approach is that it assumes that the break date is known in advance and the test is constructed using this information. It is possible, and perhaps even likely, however, that the date will not be known and must be determined from the data. More seriously, Christiano (1992) has argued that the critical values employed with the test will presume the break date to be chosen exogenously, and yet most researchers will select a break point based on an examination of the data and thus the asymptotic theory assumed will no longer hold.

As a result, Banerjee et al. (1992) and Zivot and Andrews (1992) introduce an approach to testing for unit roots in the presence of structural change that allows the break date to be selected endogenously. Their methods are based on recursive, rolling and sequential tests. For the recursive and rolling tests, Banerjee et al. propose four specifications. First, the standard Dickey–Fuller test on the whole sample, which they term $\hat{t}_{DF}$; second, the ADF test is conducted repeatedly on the sub-samples and the minimal DF statistic, $\hat{t}_{DF}^{min}$, is obtained; third, the maximal DF statistic is obtained from the sub-samples, $\hat{t}_{DF}^{max}$; finally, the difference between the maximal and minimal statistics, $\hat{t}_{DF}^{diff} = \hat{t}_{DF}^{max} - \hat{t}_{DF}^{min}$, is taken. For the sequential test, the whole sample is used each time with the following regression being run

$$\Delta y_t = \psi y_{t-1} + \mu + \alpha \tau_t(t_{used}) + \lambda t + \sum_{i=1}^{p} \alpha_i \Delta y_{t-i} + u_t \tag{8.43}$$

where $t_{used} = T_b/T$. The test is run repeatedly for different values of T_b over as much of the data as possible (a 'trimmed sample') that excludes the first few and the last few observations (since it is not possible to reliably detect breaks there). Clearly it is $\tau_t(t_{used})$ that allows for the break, which can either be in the level (where $\tau_t(t_{used}) = 1$ if $t > t_{used}$ and 0 otherwise); or the break can be in the deterministic trend (where $\tau_t(t_{used}) = t - t_{used}$ if $t > t_{used}$ and 0 otherwise). For each specification, a different set of critical values is required, and these can be found in Banerjee et al. (1992).

Perron (1997) proposes an extension of the Perron (1989) technique but using a sequential procedure that estimates the test statistic allowing for a break at any point during the sample to be determined by the data. This technique is very similar to that of Zivot and Andrews, except that his is more flexible, and therefore arguably preferable, since it allows for a break under both the null and alternative hypotheses, whereas according to Zivot and Andrews' model it can only arise under the alternative.

A further extension would be to allow for more than one structural break in the series – for example, Lumsdaine and Papell (1997) enhance the Zivot and Andrews (1992) approach to allow for two structural breaks. It is also possible to allow for structural breaks in the cointegrating relationship between series (see section 8.4 below for a thorough discussion of cointegration) using an extension of the first step in the Engle-Granger approach – see Gregory and Hansen (1996).

Table 8.2 Recursive unit root tests for interest rates allowing for structural breaks

Maturity	t_{DF}	Recursive statistics			Sequential statistics	
		$\hat{t}_{DF}^{max}$	$\hat{t}_{DF}^{min}$	$\hat{t}_{DF}^{diff}$	$\hat{t}_{DF,trend}^{min}$	$\hat{t}_{DF,mean}^{min}$
Short rate	−2.44	−1.33	−3.29	1.96	−2.99	−4.79
7-days	−1.95	−1.33	−3.19	1.86	−2.44	−5.65
1-month	−1.82	−1.07	−2.90	1.83	−2.32	−4.78
3-months	−1.80	−1.02	−2.75	1.73	−2.28	−4.02
6-months	−1.86	−1.00	−2.85	1.85	−2.28	−4.10
1-year	−1.97	−0.74	−2.88	2.14	−2.35	−4.55
Critical values	−3.13	−1.66	−3.88	3.21	−4.11	−4.58

Notes: Source: Brooks and Rew (2002), taken from tables 1, 4 and 5. $\hat{t}_{DF,trend}^{min}$ denotes the sequential test statistic allowing for a break in the trend, while $\hat{t}_{DF,mean}^{min}$ is the test statistic allowing for a break in the level. The final row presents the 10% level critical values for each type of test obtained from Banerjee *et al.* (1992, p. 278, table 2).

8.2.3 An example: testing for unit roots in EuroSterling interest rates

Section 8.12 discusses the expectations hypothesis of the term structure of interest rates based on cointegration between the long and short rates. Clearly, key to this analysis is the question as to whether the interest rates themselves are I(1) or I(0) processes. Perhaps surprisingly, there is not a consensus in the empirical literature on whether this is the case. Brooks and Rew (2002) examine whether EuroSterling interest rates are best viewed as unit root process or not, allowing for the possibility of structural breaks in the series.[2] They argue that failure to account for structural breaks that may be present in the data (caused, for example, by changes in monetary policy or the removal of exchange rate controls) may lead to incorrect inferences regarding the validity or otherwise of the expectations hypothesis. Their sample covers the period 1 January 1981 to 1 September 1997 to total 4,348 data points.

Brooks and Rew use the standard Dickey–Fuller test, the recursive and sequential tests of Banerjee *et al.* (1992), and their results are presented in table 8.2. They also employ the rolling test, the Perron (1997) approach and several other techniques that are not shown here due to space limitations.

The findings for the recursive tests are the same as those for the standard DF test, and show that the unit root null should not be rejected at the 10% level for

---

[2] EuroSterling interest rates are those at which money is loaned/borrowed in British pounds but outside of the UK.

any of the maturities examined. For the sequential tests, the results are slightly more mixed with the break in trend model still showing no signs of rejecting the null hypothesis, while it is rejected for the short, seven-day and the one-month rates when a structural break is allowed for in the mean.

Brooks and Rew's overall conclusion is that the weight of evidence across all the tests they examine indicates that short term interest rates are best viewed as unit root processes that have a structural break in their level around the time of 'Black Wednesday' (16 September 1992) when the UK dropped out of the European Exchange Rate Mechanism. The longer term rates, on the other hand, are I(1) processes with no breaks.

8.2.4   Seasonal unit roots

As we will discuss in detail in chapter 10, many time series exhibit seasonal patterns. One approach to capturing such characteristics would be to use deterministic dummy variables at the frequency of the data (e.g., monthly dummy variables if the data are monthly). However, if the seasonal characteristics of the data are themselves changing over time so that their mean is not constant, then the use of dummy variables will be inadequate. Instead, we can entertain the possibility that a series may contain seasonal unit roots, so that it requires seasonal differencing to induce stationarity. We would use the notation $I(d, D)$ to denote a series that is integrated of order d, D and requires differencing d times and seasonal differencing D times to obtain a stationary process. Osborn (1990) develops a test for seasonal unit roots based on a natural extension of the Dickey–Fuller approach. Groups of series with seasonal unit roots may also be seasonally cointegrated. However, Osborn also shows that only a small proportion of macroeconomic series exhibit seasonal unit roots; the majority have seasonal patterns that can better be characterised using dummy variables, which may explain why the concept of seasonal unit roots has not been widely adopted.[3]

8.3   Testing for unit roots in EViews

This example uses the same data on UK house prices as employed in previous chapters. Assuming that the data have been loaded, and the variables are defined as before, double click on the icon next to the name of the series that you want to perform the unit root test on, so that a spreadsheet appears containing the observations on that series. Open the raw house price series, 'hp' by clicking on the **hp** icon. Next, click on the **View** button on the button bar above the spreadsheet and then **Unit Root Test. . .** . You will then be presented with a menu containing various options, as in screenshot 8.1.

---

[3] For further reading on this topic, the book by Harris (1995) provides an extremely clear introduction to unit roots and cointegration including a section on seasonal unit roots.

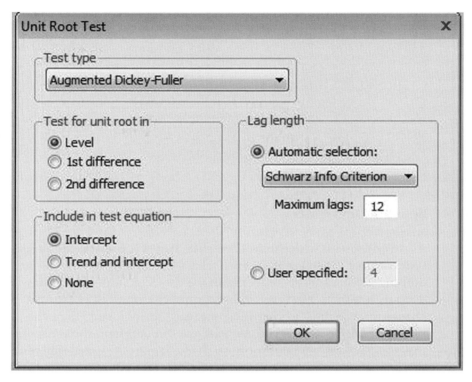

Screenshot 8.1   **Options menu for unit root tests**

From this, choose the following options:

(1) Test Type   Augmented Dickey–Fuller
(2) Test for Unit Root in   Levels
(3) Include in test equation   Intercept
(4) Maximum lags   12

and click **OK**.

This will obviously perform an ADF test with up to twelve lags of the dependent variable in a regression equation on the raw data series with a constant but no trend in the test equation. EViews presents a large number of options here – for example, instead of the Dickey–Fuller series, we could run the Phillips–Perron or KPSS tests as described above. Or, if we find that the levels of the series are non-stationary, we could repeat the analysis on the first differences directly from this menu rather than having to create the first differenced series separately. We can also choose between various methods for determining the optimum lag length in an augmented Dickey–Fuller test, with the Schwarz criterion being the default. The results for the raw house price series would appear as in the following table.

The value of the test statistic and the relevant critical values given the type of test equation (e.g. whether there is a constant and/or trend included) and sample size, are given in the first panel of the output above. Schwarz's criterion has in this case chosen to include two lags of the dependent variable in the

Null Hypothesis: HP has a unit root
Exogenous: Constant
Lag Length: 2 (Automatic based on SIC, MAXLAG=11)

	t-Statistic	Prob.*
Augmented Dickey-Fuller test statistic	−0.470202	0.8934

Test critical values:	1% level	−3.454812	
	5% level	−2.872203	
	10% level	−2.572525	

*MacKinnon (1996) one-sided p-values.

Augmented Dickey-Fuller Test Equation
Dependent Variable: D(HP)
Method: Least Squares
Date: 07/07/13 Time: 14:59
Sample (adjusted): 1991M04 2013M05
Included observations: 266 after adjustments

	Coefficient	Std. Error	t-Statistic	Prob.
HP(-1)	−0.000686	0.001459	−0.470202	0.6386
D(HP(-1))	0.316199	0.058368	5.417290	0.0000
D(HP(-2))	0.333239	0.058398	5.706296	0.0000
C	234.5155	176.8386	1.326156	0.1859

R-squared	0.308614	Mean dependent var		432.4012
Adjusted R-squared	0.300697	S.D. dependent var		1419.201
S.E. of regression	1186.798	Akaike info criterion		17.01083
Sum squared resid	3.69E+08	Schwarz criterion		17.06472
Log likelihood	−2258.440	Hannan-Quinn criter.		17.03248
F-statistic	38.98292	Durbin-Watson stat		2.006505
Prob(F-statistic)	0.000000			

test regression. Clearly, the test statistic is not more negative than the critical value, so the null hypothesis of a unit root in the house price series cannot be rejected. The remainder of the output presents the estimation results. Since one of the independent variables in this regression is non-stationary, it is not appropriate to examine the coefficient standard errors or their t-ratios in the test regression.

Now repeat all of the above steps for the **first difference of the house price series** (use the 'First Difference' option in the unit root testing window rather than using the level of the dhp series). The output would appear as in the following table.

Null Hypothesis: D(HP) has a unit root
Exogenous: Constant
Lag Length: 1 (Automatic based on SIC, MAXLAG=15)

		t-Statistic	Prob.*
Augmented Dickey-Fuller test statistic		−5.857817	0.0000
Test critical values:	1% level	−3.454812	
	5% level	−2.872203	
	10% level	−2.572525	

*MacKinnon (1996) one-sided p-values.

Augmented Dickey-Fuller Test Equation
Dependent Variable: D(HP,2)
Method: Least Squares
Date: 07/07/13 Time: 21:30
Sample (adjusted): 1991M04 2013M05
Included observations: 266 after adjustments

	Coefficient	Std. Error	t-Statistic	Prob.
D(HP(-1))	−0.351258	0.059964	−5.857817	0.0000
D(HP(-1),2)	−0.332625	0.058297	−5.705656	0.0000
C	159.6672	76.90883	2.076058	0.0389
R-squared	0.343699	Mean dependent var		11.01290
Adjusted R-squared	0.338708	S.D. dependent var		1457.257
S.E. of regression	1185.039	Akaike info criterion		17.00415
Sum squared resid	3.69E+08	Schwarz criterion		17.04457
Log likelihood	−2258.552	Hannan-Quinn criter.		17.02039
F-statistic	68.86536	Durbin-Watson stat		2.005980
Prob(F-statistic)	0.000000			

In this case, as one would expect, the test statistic is more negative than the critical value and hence the null hypothesis of a unit root in the first differences is convincingly rejected. For completeness, run a unit root test on the **levels of the dhp series**, which are the percentage changes rather than the absolute differences in prices. You should find that these are also stationary.

Finally, run the KPSS test on the hp levels series by selecting it from the **'Test Type'** box in the unit root testing window. You should observe now that the test statistic exceeds the critical value, even at the 1% level, so that the null hypothesis of a *stationary series* is strongly rejected, thus confirming the result of the unit root test previously conducted on the same series.

8.4 Cointegration

In most cases, if two variables that are I(1) are linearly combined, then the combination will also be I(1). More generally, if a set of variables $X_{i,t}$ with differing orders of integration are combined, the combination will have an order of integration equal to the largest. If $X_{i,t} \sim I(d_i)$ for $i = 1, 2, 3, \ldots, k$ so that there are k variables each integrated of order d_i, and letting

$$z_t = \sum_{i=1}^{k} \alpha_i X_{i,t} \tag{8.44}$$

Then $z_t \sim I(\max d_i)$. z_t in this context is simply a linear combination of the k variables X_i. Rearranging (8.44)

$$X_{1,t} = \sum_{i=2}^{k} \beta_i X_{i,t} + z'_t \tag{8.45}$$

where $\beta_i = -\frac{\alpha_i}{\alpha_1}, z'_t = \frac{z_t}{\alpha_1}, i = 2, \ldots, k$. All that has been done is to take one of the variables, $X_{1,t}$, and to rearrange (8.44) to make it the subject. It could also be said that the equation has been normalised on $X_{1,t}$. But viewed another way, (8.45) is just a regression equation where z'_t is a disturbance term. These disturbances would have some very undesirable properties: in general, z'_t will not be stationary and is autocorrelated if all of the X_i are I(1).

As a further illustration, consider the following regression model containing variables y_t, x_{2t}, x_{3t} which are all I(1)

$$y_t = \beta_1 + \beta_2 x_{2t} + \beta_3 x_{3t} + u_t \tag{8.46}$$

For the estimated model, the SRF would be written

$$y_t = \hat{\beta}_1 + \hat{\beta}_2 x_{2t} + \hat{\beta}_3 x_{3t} + \hat{u}_t \tag{8.47}$$

Taking everything except the residuals to the LHS

$$y_t - \hat{\beta}_1 - \hat{\beta}_2 x_{2t} - \hat{\beta}_3 x_{3t} = \hat{u}_t \tag{8.48}$$

Again, the residuals when expressed in this way can be considered a linear combination of the variables. Typically, this linear combination of I(1) variables will itself be I(1), but it would obviously be desirable to obtain residuals that are I(0). Under what circumstances will this be the case? The answer is that a linear combination of I(1) variables will be I(0), in other words stationary, if the variables are *cointegrated*.

8.4.1   Definition of cointegration (Engle and Granger, 1987)

Let w_t be a $k \times 1$ vector of variables, then the components of w_t are integrated of order (d, b) if:

(1) All components of w_t are I(d)
(2) There is at least one vector of coefficients α such that

$$\alpha' w_t \sim \text{I}(d - b)$$

In practice, many financial variables contain one unit root, and are thus I(1), so that the remainder of this chapter will restrict analysis to the case where $d = b = 1$. In this context, a set of variables is defined as cointegrated if a linear combination of them is stationary. Many time series are non-stationary but 'move together' over time – that is, there exist some influences on the series (for example, market forces), which imply that the two series are bound by some relationship in the long run. A cointegrating relationship may also be seen as a long-term or equilibrium phenomenon, since it is possible that cointegrating variables may deviate from their relationship in the short run, but their association would return in the long run.

8.4.2   Examples of possible cointegrating relationships in finance

Financial theory should suggest where two or more variables would be expected to hold some long-run relationship with one another. There are many examples in finance of areas where cointegration might be expected to hold, including:

- Spot and futures prices for a given commodity or asset
- Ratio of relative prices and an exchange rate
- Equity prices and dividends.

In all three cases, market forces arising from no-arbitrage conditions suggest that there should be an equilibrium relationship between the series concerned. The easiest way to understand this notion is perhaps to consider what would be the effect if the series were not cointegrated. If there were no cointegration, there would be no long-run relationship binding the series together, so that the series could wander apart without bound. Such an effect would arise since all linear combinations of the series would be non-stationary, and hence would not have a constant mean that would be returned to frequently.

Spot and futures prices may be expected to be cointegrated since they are obviously prices for the same asset at different points in time, and hence will be affected in very similar ways by given pieces of information. The long-run relationship between spot and futures prices would be given by the cost of carry.

Purchasing power parity (PPP) theory states that a given representative basket of goods and services should cost the same wherever it is bought when converted into a common currency. Further discussion of PPP occurs in section 8.10, but for now suffice it to say that PPP implies that the ratio of relative prices in two countries and the exchange rate between them should be cointegrated. If they did not cointegrate, assuming zero transactions costs, it would be profitable to buy goods in one country, sell them in another, and convert the money obtained back to the currency of the original country.

Finally, if it is assumed that some stock in a particular company is held to perpetuity (i.e. for ever), then the only return that would accrue to that investor would be in the form of an infinite stream of future dividend payments. Hence the discounted dividend model argues that the appropriate price to pay for a share today is the present value of all future dividends. Hence, it may be argued that one would not expect current prices to 'move out of line' with future anticipated dividends in the long run, thus implying that share prices and dividends should be cointegrated.

An interesting question to ask is whether a potentially cointegrating regression should be estimated using the levels of the variables or the logarithms of the levels of the variables. Financial theory may provide an answer as to the more appropriate functional form, but fortunately even if not, Hendry and Juselius (2000) note that if a set of series is cointegrated in levels, they will also be cointegrated in log levels.

8.5 Equilibrium correction or error correction models

When the concept of non-stationarity was first considered in the 1970s, a usual response was to independently take the first differences of each of the I(1) variables and then to use these first differences in any subsequent modelling process. In the context of univariate modelling (e.g. the construction of ARMA models), this is entirely the correct approach. However, when the relationship between variables is important, such a procedure is inadvisable. While this approach is statistically valid, it does have the problem that pure first difference models have no long-run solution. For example, consider two series, y_t and x_t, that are both I(1). The model that one may consider estimating is

$$\Delta y_t = \beta \Delta x_t + u_t \tag{8.49}$$

One definition of the long run that is employed in econometrics implies that the variables have converged upon some long-term values and are no longer changing, thus $y_t = y_{t-1} = y$; $x_t = x_{t-1} = x$. Hence all the difference terms will be zero in (8.49), i.e. $\Delta y_t = 0$; $\Delta x_t = 0$, and thus everything in the equation cancels. Model (8.49) has no long-run solution and it therefore has nothing to say about whether x and y have an equilibrium relationship (see chapter 5).

Fortunately, there is a class of models that can overcome this problem by using combinations of first differenced and lagged levels of cointegrated variables. For example, consider the following equation

$$\Delta y_t = \beta_1 \Delta x_t + \beta_2(y_{t-1} - \gamma x_{t-1}) + u_t \tag{8.50}$$

This model is known as an *error correction model* or an *equilibrium correction model*, and $y_{t-1} - \gamma x_{t-1}$ is known as the *error correction term*. Provided that y_t and x_t are cointegrated with cointegrating coefficient γ, then $(y_{t-1} - \gamma x_{t-1})$ will be I(0) even though the constituents are I(1). It is thus valid to use OLS and standard procedures for statistical inference on (8.50). It is of course possible to have an intercept in either the cointegrating term (e.g. $y_{t-1} - \alpha - \gamma x_{t-1}$) or in the model for Δy_t (e.g. $\Delta y_t = \beta_0 + \beta_1 \Delta x_t + \beta_2(y_{t-1} - \gamma x_{t-1}) + u_t$) or both. Whether a constant is included or not could be determined on the basis of financial theory, considering the arguments on the importance of a constant discussed in chapter 5.

The error correction model is sometimes termed an equilibrium correction model, and the two terms will be used synonymously for the purposes of this book. Error correction models are interpreted as follows. y is purported to change between $t-1$ and t as a result of changes in the values of the explanatory variable(s), x, between $t-1$ and t, and also in part to correct for any disequilibrium that existed during the previous period. Note that the error correction term $(y_{t-1} - \gamma x_{t-1})$ appears in (8.50) with a lag. It would be implausible for the term to appear without any lag (i.e. as $y_t - \gamma x_t$), for this would imply that y changes between $t-1$ and t in response to a disequilibrium at time t. γ defines the long-run relationship between x and y, while β_1 describes the short-run relationship between changes in x and changes in y. Broadly, β_2 describes the speed of adjustment back to equilibrium, and its strict definition is that it measures the proportion of last period's equilibrium error that is corrected for.

Of course, an error correction model can be estimated for more than two variables. For example, if there were three variables, x_t, w_t, y_t, that were cointegrated, a possible error correction model would be

$$\Delta y_t = \beta_1 \Delta x_t + \beta_2 \Delta w_t + \beta_3(y_{t-1} - \gamma_1 x_{t-1} - \gamma_2 w_{t-1}) + u_t \tag{8.51}$$

The *Granger representation theorem* states that if there exists a dynamic linear model with stationary disturbances and the data are I(1), then the variables must be cointegrated of order (1,1).

8.6 Testing for cointegration in regression: a residuals-based approach

The model for the equilibrium correction term can be generalised further to include k variables (y and the $k-1$ xs)

$$y_t = \beta_1 + \beta_2 x_{2t} + \beta_3 x_{3t} + \cdots + \beta_k x_{kt} + u_t \tag{8.52}$$

u_t should be I(0) if the variables y_t, x_{2t}, ... x_{kt} are cointegrated, but u_t will still be non-stationary if they are not.

Thus it is necessary to test the residuals of (8.52) to see whether they are non-stationary or stationary. The DF or ADF test can be used on $\hat{u}_t$, using a regression of the form

$$\Delta \hat{u}_t = \psi \hat{u}_{t-1} + v_t \tag{8.53}$$

with v_t an iid error term.

However, since this is a test on residuals of a model, $\hat{u}_t$, then the critical values are changed compared to a DF or an ADF test on a series of raw data. Engle and

Granger (1987) have tabulated a new set of critical values for this application and hence the test is known as the Engle–Granger (*EG*) test. The reason that modified critical values are required is that the test is now operating on the residuals of an estimated model rather than on raw data. The residuals have been constructed from a particular set of coefficient estimates, and the sampling estimation error in those coefficients will change the distribution of the test statistic. Engle and Yoo (1987) tabulate a new set of critical values that are larger in absolute value (i.e. more negative) than the DF critical values, also given at the end of this book. The critical values also become more negative as the number of variables in the potentially cointegrating regression increases.

It is also possible to use the Durbin–Watson (*DW*) test statistic or the Phillips–Perron (*PP*) approach to test for non-stationarity of $\hat{u}_t$. If the *DW* test is applied to the residuals of the potentially cointegrating regression, it is known as the Cointegrating Regression Durbin Watson (*CRDW*). Under the null hypothesis of a unit root in the errors, $CRDW \approx 0$, so the null of a unit root is rejected if the *CRDW* statistic is larger than the relevant critical value (which is approximately 0.5).

What are the null and alternative hypotheses for any unit root test applied to the residuals of a potentially cointegrating regression?

$$H_0 : \hat{u}_t \sim I(1)$$
$$H_1 : \hat{u}_t \sim I(0).$$

Thus, under the null hypothesis there is a unit root in the potentially cointegrating regression residuals, while under the alternative, the residuals are stationary. Under the null hypothesis, therefore, a stationary linear combination of the non-stationary variables has not been found. Hence, if this null hypothesis is not rejected, there is no cointegration. The appropriate strategy for econometric modelling in this case would be to employ specifications in first differences only. Such models would have no long-run equilibrium solution, but this would not matter since no cointegration implies that there is no long-run relationship anyway.

On the other hand, if the null of a unit root in the potentially cointegrating regression's residuals is rejected, it would be concluded that a stationary linear combination of the non-stationary variables had been found. Therefore, the variables would be classed as cointegrated. The appropriate strategy for econometric modelling in this case would be to form and estimate an error correction model, using a method described in the following section.

8.7 Methods of parameter estimation in cointegrated systems

What should be the modelling strategy if the data at hand are thought to be non-stationary and possibly cointegrated? There are (at least) three methods that could be used: Engle–Granger, Engle–Yoo and Johansen. The first and third of these will be considered in some detail below.

8.7.1 The Engle–Granger 2-step method

This is a single equation technique, which is conducted as follows:

Step 1

Make sure that all the individual variables are I(1). Then estimate the cointegrating regression using OLS. Note that it is not possible to perform any inferences on the coefficient estimates in this regression – all that can be done is to estimate the parameter values. Save the residuals of the cointegrating regression, $\hat{u}_t$. Test these residuals to ensure that they are I(0). If they are I(0), proceed to Step 2; if they are I(1), estimate a model containing only first differences.

Step 2

Use the step 1 residuals as one variable in the error correction model, e.g.

$$\Delta y_t = \beta_1 \Delta x_t + \beta_2(\hat{u}_{t-1}) + v_t \tag{8.54}$$

where $\hat{u}_{t-1} = y_{t-1} - \hat{\tau}x_{t-1}$. The stationary, linear combination of non-stationary variables is also known as the *cointegrating vector*. In this case, the cointegrating vector would be $[1 - \hat{\tau}]$. Additionally, any linear transformation of the cointegrating vector will also be a cointegrating vector. So, for example, $-10y_{t-1} + 10\hat{\tau}x_{t-1}$ will also be stationary. In (8.48) above, the cointegrating vector would be $[1 - \hat{\beta}_1 - \hat{\beta}_2 - \hat{\beta}_3]$. It is now valid to perform inferences in the second-stage regression, i.e. concerning the parameters β_1 and β_2 (provided that there are no other forms of misspecification, of course), since all variables in this regression are stationary.

The Engle–Granger 2-step method suffers from a number of problems:

(1) The usual finite sample problem of a *lack of power in unit root and cointegration tests* discussed above.
(2) There could be a *simultaneous equations bias* if the causality between y and x runs in both directions, but this single equation approach requires the researcher to normalise on one variable (i.e. to specify one variable as the dependent variable and the others as independent variables). The researcher is forced to treat y and x asymmetrically, even though there may have been no theoretical reason for doing so. A further issue is the following. Suppose that the following specification had been estimated as a potential cointegrating regression

$$y_t = \alpha_1 + \beta_1 x_t + u_{1t} \tag{8.55}$$

What if instead the following equation was estimated?

$$x_t = \alpha_2 + \beta_2 y_t + u_{2t} \tag{8.56}$$

If it is found that $u_{1t} \sim I(0)$, does this imply automatically that $u_{2t} \sim I(0)$? The answer in theory is 'yes', but in practice different conclusions may be reached in finite samples. Also, if there is an error in the model specification at stage 1, this will be carried through to the cointegration test at stage 2, as a

> ### Box 8.2 Multiple cointegrating relationships
>
> In the case where there are only two variables in an equation, y_t, and x_t, say, there can be at most only one linear combination of y_t, and x_t that is stationary – i.e. at most one cointegrating relationship. However, suppose that there are k variables in a system (ignoring any constant term), denoted $y_t, x_{2t}, \ldots x_{kt}$. In this case, there may be up to r linearly independent cointegrating relationships (where $r \leq k - 1$). This potentially presents a problem for the OLS regression approach described above, which is capable of finding at most one cointegrating relationship no matter how many variables there are in the system. And if there are multiple cointegrating relationships, how can one know if there are others, or whether the 'best' or strongest cointegrating relationship has been found? An OLS regression will find the minimum variance stationary linear combination of the variables, but there may be other linear combinations of the variables that have more intuitive appeal.[1] The answer to this problem is to use a systems approach to cointegration, which will allow determination of all r cointegrating relationships. One such approach is Johansen's method – see section 8.9.

consequence of the sequential nature of the computation of the cointegration test statistic.

(3) It is not possible to perform any *hypothesis tests* about the actual cointegrating relationship estimated at stage 1.

(4) There may be more than one cointegrating relationship – see box 8.2.

Problems 1 and 2 are small sample problems that should disappear asymptotically. Problem 3 is addressed by another method due to Engle and Yoo. There is also another alternative technique, which overcomes problems 2 and 3 by adopting a different approach based on estimation of a VAR system – see section 8.9.

8.7.2 The Engle and Yoo 3-step method

The Engle and Yoo (1987) 3-step procedure takes its first two steps from Engle–Granger (EG). Engle and Yoo then add a third step giving updated estimates of the cointegrating vector and its standard errors. The Engle and Yoo (EY) third step is algebraically technical and additionally, EY suffers from all of the remaining problems of the EG approach. There is arguably a far superior procedure available to remedy the lack of testability of hypotheses concerning the cointegrating relationship – namely, the Johansen (1988) procedure. For these reasons, the Engle–Yoo

---

[1] Readers who are familiar with the literature on hedging with futures will recognise that running an OLS regression will minimise the variance of the hedged portfolio, i.e. it will minimise the regression's residual variance, and the situation here is analogous.

procedure is rarely employed in empirical applications and is not considered further here.

There now follows an application of the Engle–Granger procedure in the context of spot and futures markets.

8.8 Lead–lag and long-term relationships between spot and futures markets

8.8.1 Background

If the markets are frictionless and functioning efficiently, changes in the (log of the) spot price of a financial asset and its corresponding changes in the (log of the) futures price would be expected to be perfectly contemporaneously correlated and not to be cross-autocorrelated. Mathematically, these notions would be represented as

$$\text{corr}(\Delta \log(f_t), \Delta \ln(s_t)) \approx 1 \tag{a}$$

$$\text{corr}(\Delta \log(f_t), \Delta \ln(s_{t-k})) \approx 0 \quad \forall \ k > 0 \tag{b}$$

$$\text{corr}(\Delta \log(f_{t-j}), \Delta \ln(s_t)) \approx 0 \quad \forall \ j > 0 \tag{c}$$

In other words, changes in spot prices and changes in futures prices are expected to occur at the same time (condition (a)). The current change in the futures price is also expected not to be related to previous changes in the spot price (condition (b)), and the current change in the spot price is expected not to be related to previous changes in the futures price (condition (c)). The changes in the log of the spot and futures prices are also of course known as the spot and futures returns.

For the case when the underlying asset is a stock index, the equilibrium relationship between the spot and futures prices is known as the *cost of carry model*, given by

$$F_t^* = S_t \, e^{(r-d)(T-t)} \tag{8.57}$$

where F_t^* is the fair futures price, S_t is the spot price, r is a continuously compounded risk-free rate of interest, d is the continuously compounded yield in terms of dividends derived from the stock index until the futures contract matures, and $(T - t)$ is the time to maturity of the futures contract. Taking logarithms of both sides of (8.57) gives

$$f_t^* = s_t + (r - d)(T - t) \tag{8.58}$$

where f_t^* is the log of the fair futures price and s_t is the log of the spot price. Equation (8.58) suggests that the long-term relationship between the logs of the spot and futures prices should be one to one. Thus the basis, defined as the difference between the futures and spot prices (and if necessary adjusted for the cost of carry) should be stationary, for if it could wander without bound, arbitrage opportunities would arise, which would be assumed to be quickly acted upon by traders such that the relationship between spot and futures prices will be brought back to equilibrium.

Table 8.3   DF tests on log-prices and returns for high frequency FTSE data

	Futures	Spot
Dickey–Fuller statistics for log-price data	−0.1329	−0.7335
Dickey–Fuller statistics for returns data	−84.9968	−114.1803

The notion that there should not be any lead–lag relationships between the spot and futures prices and that there should be a long-term one to one relationship between the logs of spot and futures prices can be tested using simple linear regressions and cointegration analysis. This book will now examine the results of two related papers – Tse (1995), who employs daily data on the Nikkei Stock Average (NSA) and its futures contract, and Brooks, Rew and Ritson (2001), who examine high-frequency data from the FTSE 100 stock index and index futures contract.

The data employed by Tse (1995) consists of 1,055 daily observations on NSA stock index and stock index futures values from December 1988 to April 1993. The data employed by Brooks *et al.* comprises 13,035 ten-minutely observations for all trading days in the period June 1996–May 1997, provided by FTSE International. In order to form a statistically adequate model, the variables should first be checked as to whether they can be considered stationary. The results of applying a DF test to the logs of the spot and futures prices of the ten-minutely FTSE data are shown in table 8.3.

As one might anticipate, both studies conclude that the two log-price series contain a unit root, while the returns are stationary. Of course, it may be necessary to augment the tests by adding lags of the dependent variable to allow for autocorrelation in the errors (i.e. an ADF test). Results for such tests are not presented, since the conclusions are not altered. A statistically valid model would therefore be one in the returns. However, a formulation containing only first differences has no long-run equilibrium solution. Additionally, theory suggests that the two series should have a long-run relationship. The solution is therefore to see whether there exists a cointegrating relationship between f_t and s_t which would mean that it is valid to include levels terms along with returns in this framework. This is tested by examining whether the residuals, $\hat{z}_t$, of a regression of the form

$$s_t = \gamma_0 + \gamma_1 f_t + z_t \tag{8.59}$$

are stationary, using a DF test, where z_t is the error term. The coefficient values for the estimated (8.59) and the DF test statistic are given in table 8.4.

Table 8.4 Estimated potentially cointegrating equation and test for cointegration for high frequency FTSE data

Coefficient	Estimated value
$\hat{\gamma}_0$	0.1345
$\hat{\gamma}_1$	0.9834
DF test on residuals	**Test statistic**
$\hat{z}_t$	−14.7303

Source: Brooks, Rew and Ritson (2001).

Table 8.5 Estimated error correction model for high frequency FTSE data

Coefficient	Estimated value	*t*-ratio
$\hat{\beta}_0$	9.6713E−06	1.6083
$\hat{\delta}$	−0.8388	−5.1298
$\hat{\beta}_1$	0.1799	19.2886
$\hat{\alpha}_1$	0.1312	20.4946

Source: Brooks, Rew and Ritson (2001).

Clearly, the residuals from the cointegrating regression can be considered stationary. Note also that the estimated slope coefficient in the cointegrating regression takes on a value close to unity, as predicted from the theory. It is not possible to formally test whether the true population coefficient could be one, however, since there is no way in this framework to test hypotheses about the cointegrating relationship.

The final stage in building an error correction model using the Engle–Granger two-step approach is to use a lag of the first-stage residuals, $\hat{z}_t$, as the equilibrium correction term in the general equation. The overall model is

$$\Delta \log s_t = \beta_0 + \delta \hat{z}_{t-1} + \beta_1 \Delta \ln s_{t-1} + \alpha_1 \Delta \ln f_{t-1} + v_t \tag{8.60}$$

where v_t is an error term. The coefficient estimates for this model are presented in table 8.5.

Table 8.6 Comparison of out-of-sample forecasting accuracy				
	ECM	ECM-COC	ARIMA	VAR
RMSE	0.0004382	0.0004350	0.0004531	0.0004510
MAE	0.4259	0.4255	0.4382	0.4378
% Correct direction	67.69%	68.75%	64.36%	66.80%

Source: Brooks, Rew and Ritson (2001).

Consider first the signs and significances of the coefficients (these can now be interpreted validly since all variables used in this model are stationary). $\hat{\alpha}_1$ is positive and highly significant, indicating that the futures market does indeed lead the spot market, since lagged changes in futures prices lead to a positive change in the subsequent spot price. $\hat{\beta}_1$ is positive and highly significant, indicating on average a positive autocorrelation in spot returns. $\hat{\delta}$, the coefficient on the error correction term, is negative and significant, indicating that if the difference between the logs of the spot and futures prices is positive in one period, the spot price will fall during the next period to restore equilibrium, and vice versa.

8.8.2 Forecasting spot returns

Both Brooks, Rew and Ritson (2001) and Tse (1995) show that it is possible to use an error correction formulation to model changes in the log of a stock index. An obvious related question to ask is whether such a model can be used to forecast the future value of the spot series for a holdout sample of data not used previously for model estimation. Both sets of researchers employ forecasts from three other models for comparison with the forecasts of the error correction model. These are an error correction model with an additional term that allows for the cost of carry, an ARMA model (with lag length chosen using an information criterion) and an unrestricted VAR model (with lag length chosen using a multivariate information criterion).

The results are evaluated by comparing their root-mean squared errors, mean absolute errors and percentage of correct direction predictions. The forecasting results from the Brooks, Rew and Ritson paper are given in table 8.6.

It can be seen from table 8.6 that the error correction models have both the lowest mean squared and mean absolute errors, and the highest proportion of correct direction predictions. There is, however, little to choose between the models, and all four have over 60% of the signs of the next returns predicted correctly.

It is clear that on statistical grounds the out-of-sample forecasting performances of the error correction models are better than those of their competitors, but this does not necessarily mean that such forecasts have any practical use. Many studies have questioned the usefulness of statistical measures of forecast accuracy as indicators of the profitability of using these forecasts in a practical trading setting (see, for example, Leitch and Tanner, 1991). Brooks, Rew and Ritson (2001) investigate this proposition directly by developing a set of trading rules based on the forecasts of the error correction model with the cost of carry term, the best statistical forecasting model. The trading period is an out-of-sample data series not used in model estimation, running from 1 May–30 May 1997. The error correction model with cost of carry (ECM-COC) model yields ten-minutely one-step-ahead forecasts. The trading strategy involves analysing the forecast for the spot return, and incorporating the decision dictated by the trading rules described below. It is assumed that the original investment is £1,000, and if the holding in the stock index is zero, the investment earns the risk-free rate. Five trading strategies are employed, and their profitabilities are compared with that obtained by passively buying and holding the index. There are of course an infinite number of strategies that could be adopted for a given set of spot return forecasts, but Brooks, Rew and Ritson use the following:

- *Liquid trading strategy*   This trading strategy involves making a round-trip trade (i.e. a purchase and sale of the FTSE 100 stocks) every ten minutes that the return is predicted to be positive by the model. If the return is predicted to be negative by the model, no trade is executed and the investment earns the risk-free rate.
- *Buy-and-hold while forecast positive strategy*   This strategy allows the trader to continue holding the index if the return at the next predicted investment period is positive, rather than making a round-trip transaction for each period.
- *Filter strategy: better predicted return than average*   This strategy involves purchasing the index only if the predicted returns are greater than the average positive return (there is no trade for negative returns therefore the average is only taken of the positive returns).
- *Filter strategy: better predicted return than first decile*   This strategy is similar to the previous one, but rather than utilising the average as previously, only the returns predicted to be in the top 10% of all returns are traded on.
- *Filter strategy: high arbitrary cutoff*   An arbitrary filter of 0.0075% is imposed, which will result in trades only for returns that are predicted to be extremely large for a ten-minute interval.

The results from employing each of the strategies using the forecasts for the spot returns obtained from the ECM-COC model are presented in table 8.7.

The test month of May 1997 was a particularly bullish one, with a pure buy-and-hold-the-index strategy netting a return of 4%, or almost 50% on an annualised basis. Ideally, the forecasting exercise would be conducted over a much longer period than one month, and preferably over different market conditions. However, this was simply impossible due to the lack of availability of very high frequency data over a long time period. Clearly, the forecasts have some market timing ability in the sense that they seem to ensure trades that, on average, would have invested in the index when it rose, but be out of the market when it fell. The most profitable trading strategies in gross terms are those that trade on the basis

Table 8.7 Trading profitability of the error correction model with cost of carry

Trading strategy	Terminal wealth (£)	Return(%) annualised	Terminal wealth (£) with slippage	Return(%) annualised with slippage	Number of trades
Passive investment	1040.92	4.09 {49.08}	1040.92	4.09 {49.08}	1
Liquid trading	1156.21	15.62 {187.44}	1056.38	5.64 {67.68}	583
Buy-and-hold while forecast positive	1156.21	15.62 {187.44}	1055.77	5.58 {66.96}	383
Filter I	1144.51	14.45 {173.40}	1123.57	12.36 {148.32}	135
Filter II	1100.01	10.00 {120.00}	1046.17	4.62 {55.44}	65
Filter III	1019.82	1.98 {23.76}	1003.23	0.32 {3.84}	8

Source: Brooks, Rew and Ritson (2001).

of every positive spot return forecast, and all rules except the strictest filter make more money than a passive investment. The strict filter appears not to work well since it is out of the index for too long during a period when the market is rising strongly.

However, the picture of immense profitability painted thus far is somewhat misleading for two reasons: slippage time and transactions costs. First, it is unreasonable to assume that trades can be executed in the market the minute they are requested, since it may take some time to find counterparties for all the trades required to 'buy the index'. (Note, of course, that in practice, a similar returns profile to the index can be achieved with a very much smaller number of stocks.) Brooks, Rew and Ritson therefore allow for ten minutes of 'slippage time', which assumes that it takes ten minutes from when the trade order is placed to when it is executed. Second, it is unrealistic to consider gross profitability, since transactions costs in the spot market are non-negligible and the strategies examined suggested a lot of trades. Sutcliffe (1997, p. 47) suggests that total round-trip transactions costs for FTSE stocks are of the order of 1.7% of the investment.

The effect of slippage time is to make the forecasts less useful than they would otherwise have been. For example, if the spot price is forecast to rise, and it does, it may have already risen and then stopped rising by the time that the order is executed, so that the forecasts lose their market timing ability. Terminal wealth appears to fall substantially when slippage time is allowed for, with the monthly return falling by between 1.5% and 10%, depending on the trading rule.

Finally, if transactions costs are allowed for, none of the trading rules can outperform the passive investment strategy, and all in fact make substantial losses.

8.8.3 Conclusions

If the markets are frictionless and functioning efficiently, changes in the spot price of a financial asset and its corresponding futures price would be expected to be perfectly contemporaneously correlated and not to be cross-autocorrelated. Many academic studies, however, have documented that the futures market systematically 'leads' the spot market, reflecting news more quickly as a result of the fact that the stock index is not a single entity. The latter implies that:

- Some components of the index are infrequently traded, implying that the observed index value contains 'stale' component prices
- It is more expensive to transact in the spot market and hence the spot market reacts more slowly to news
- Stock market indices are recalculated only every minute so that new information takes longer to be reflected in the index.

Clearly, such spot market impediments cannot explain the inter-daily lead–lag relationships documented by Tse (1995). In any case, however, since it appears impossible to profit from these relationships, their existence is entirely consistent with the absence of arbitrage opportunities and is in accordance with modern definitions of the efficient markets hypothesis.

8.9 Testing for and estimating cointegrating systems using the Johansen technique based on VARs

Suppose that a set of g variables ($g \geq 2$) are under consideration that are I(1) and which are thought may be cointegrated. A VAR with k lags containing these variables could be set up:

$$y_t = \beta_1 y_{t-1} + \beta_2 y_{t-2} + \cdots + \beta_k y_{t-k} + u_t$$
$$g \times 1 \quad g \times g \; g \times 1 \quad g \times g \; g \times 1 \qquad g \times g \; g \times 1 \quad g \times 1 \tag{8.61}$$

In order to use the Johansen test, the VAR (8.58) above needs to be turned into a vector error correction model (VECM) of the form

$$\Delta y_t = \Pi y_{t-k} + \Gamma_1 \Delta y_{t-1} + \Gamma_2 \Delta y_{t-2} + \cdots + \Gamma_{k-1} \Delta y_{t-(k-1)} + u_t \tag{8.62}$$

where $\Pi = \left(\sum_{i=1}^{k} \beta_i\right) - I_g$ and $\Gamma_i = \left(\sum_{j=1}^{i} \beta_j\right) - I_g$

This VAR contains g variables in first differenced form on the LHS, and $k-1$ lags of the dependent variables (differences) on the RHS, each with a Γ coefficient matrix attached to it. In fact, the Johansen test can be affected by the lag length employed in the VECM, and so it is useful to attempt to select the lag length optimally, as outlined in chapter 7. The Johansen test centres around an examination of the Π matrix. Π can be interpreted as a long-run coefficient matrix, since in equilibrium, all the Δy_{t-i} will be zero, and setting the error terms, u_t, to their expected value of zero will leave $\Pi y_{t-k} = 0$. Notice the comparability between this set of equations and the testing equation for an ADF test, which has a first differenced term as the dependent variable, together with a lagged levels term and lagged differences on the RHS.

The test for cointegration between the ys is calculated by looking at the rank of the Π matrix via its eigenvalues.[2] The rank of a matrix is equal to the number of its characteristic roots (eigenvalues) that are different from zero (see the appendix at the end of this book for some algebra and examples). The eigenvalues, denoted λ_i are put in ascending order $\lambda_1 \geq \lambda_2 \geq \ldots \geq \lambda_g$. If the λs are roots, in this context they must be less than one in absolute value and positive, and λ_1 will be the largest (i.e. the closest to one), while λ_g will be the smallest (i.e. the closest to zero). If the variables are not cointegrated, the rank of Π will not be significantly different from zero, so $\lambda_i \approx 0 \, \forall \, i$. The test statistics actually incorporate $\ln(1 - \lambda_i)$, rather than the λ_i themselves, but still, when $\lambda_i = 0$, $\ln(1 - \lambda_i) = 0$.

Suppose now that rank $(\Pi) = 1$, then $\ln(1 - \lambda_1)$ will be negative and $\ln(1 - \lambda_i) = 0 \, \forall \, i > 1$. If the eigenvalue i is non-zero, then $\ln(1 - \lambda_i) < 0 \, \forall \, i > 1$. That is, for Π to have a rank of 1, the largest eigenvalue must be significantly non-zero, while others will not be significantly different from zero.

There are two test statistics for cointegration under the Johansen approach, which are formulated as

$$\lambda_{trace}(r) = -T \sum_{i=r+1}^{g} \ln(1 - \hat{\lambda}_i) \tag{8.63}$$

and

$$\lambda_{max}(r, r + 1) = -T \ln(1 - \hat{\lambda}_{r+1}) \tag{8.64}$$

where r is the number of cointegrating vectors under the null hypothesis and $\hat{\lambda}_i$ is the estimated value for the ith ordered eigenvalue from the Π matrix. Intuitively, the larger is $\hat{\lambda}_i$, the more large and negative will be $\ln(1 - \hat{\lambda}_i)$ and hence the larger will be the test statistic. Each eigenvalue will have associated with it a different cointegrating vector, which will be an eigenvector. A significantly non-zero eigenvalue indicates a significant cointegrating vector.

λ_{trace} is a joint test where the null is that the number of cointegrating vectors is less than or equal to r against an unspecified or general alternative that there are more than r. It starts with p eigenvalues, and then successively the largest is removed. $\lambda_{trace} = 0$ when all the $\lambda_i = 0$, for $i = 1, \ldots, g$.

λ_{max} conducts separate tests on each eigenvalue, and has as its null hypothesis that the number of cointegrating vectors is r against an alternative of $r + 1$.

---

[2] Strictly, the eigenvalues used in the test statistics are taken from rank-restricted product moment matrices and not of Π itself.

Johansen and Juselius (1990) provide critical values for the two statistics. The distribution of the test statistics is non-standard, and the critical values depend on the value of $g - r$, the number of non-stationary components and whether constants are included in each of the equations. Intercepts can be included either in the cointegrating vectors themselves or as additional terms in the VAR. The latter is equivalent to including a trend in the data generating processes for the levels of the series. Osterwald-Lenum (1992) provides a more complete set of critical values for the Johansen test, some of which are also given in the appendix of statistical tables at the end of this book.

If the test statistic is greater than the critical value from Johansen's tables, reject the null hypothesis that there are r cointegrating vectors in favour of the alternative that there are $r + 1$ (for λ_{max}) or more than r (for λ_{trace}). The testing is conducted in a sequence and under the null, $r = 0, 1, \ldots, g - 1$ so that the hypotheses for λ_{trace} are

$$
\begin{array}{lll}
H_0 : r = 0 & \text{versus} & H_1 : 0 < r \leq g \\
H_0 : r = 1 & \text{versus} & H_1 : 1 < r \leq g \\
H_0 : r = 2 & \text{versus} & H_1 : 2 < r \leq g \\
\quad \vdots & \quad \vdots & \quad \vdots \\
H_0 : r = g - 1 & \text{versus} & H_1 : r = g
\end{array}
$$

The first test involves a null hypothesis of no cointegrating vectors (corresponding to Π having zero rank). If this null is not rejected, it would be concluded that there are no cointegrating vectors and the testing would be completed. However, if $H_0 : r = 0$ is rejected, the null that there is one cointegrating vector (i.e. $H_0 : r = 1$) would be tested and so on. Thus the value of r is continually increased until the null is no longer rejected.

But how does this correspond to a test of the rank of the Π matrix? r is the rank of Π. Π cannot be of full rank (g) since this would correspond to the original y_t being stationary. If Π has zero rank, then by analogy to the univariate case, Δy_t depends only on Δy_{t-j} and not on y_{t-1}, so that there is no long-run relationship between the elements of y_{t-1}. Hence there is no cointegration. For $1 < \text{rank}(\Pi) < g$, there are r cointegrating vectors. Π is then defined as the product of two matrices, α and β', of dimension $(g \times r)$ and $(r \times g)$, respectively, i.e.

$$\Pi = \alpha\beta' \tag{8.65}$$

The matrix β gives the cointegrating vectors, while α gives the amount of each cointegrating vector entering each equation of the VECM, also known as the 'adjustment parameters'.

For example, suppose that $g = 4$, so that the system contains four variables. The elements of the Π matrix would be written

$$\Pi = \begin{pmatrix} \pi_{11} & \pi_{12} & \pi_{13} & \pi_{14} \\ \pi_{21} & \pi_{22} & \pi_{23} & \pi_{24} \\ \pi_{31} & \pi_{32} & \pi_{33} & \pi_{34} \\ \pi_{41} & \pi_{42} & \pi_{43} & \pi_{44} \end{pmatrix} \tag{8.66}$$

If $r = 1$, so that there is one cointegrating vector, then α and β will be (4×1)

$$\Pi = \alpha\beta' = \begin{pmatrix} \alpha_{11} \\ \alpha_{12} \\ \alpha_{13} \\ \alpha_{14} \end{pmatrix} (\beta_{11} \quad \beta_{12} \quad \beta_{13} \quad \beta_{14}) \tag{8.67}$$

If $r = 2$, so that there are two cointegrating vectors, then α and β will be (4×2)

$$\Pi = \alpha\beta' = \begin{pmatrix} \alpha_{11} & \alpha_{21} \\ \alpha_{12} & \alpha_{22} \\ \alpha_{13} & \alpha_{23} \\ \alpha_{14} & \alpha_{24} \end{pmatrix} \begin{pmatrix} \beta_{11} & \beta_{12} & \beta_{13} & \beta_{14} \\ \beta_{21} & \beta_{22} & \beta_{23} & \beta_{24} \end{pmatrix} \tag{8.68}$$

and so on for $r = 3, \ldots$

Suppose now that $g = 4$, and $r = 1$, as in (8.67) above, so that there are four variables in the system, y_1, y_2, y_3, and y_4, that exhibit one cointegrating vector. Then Πy_{t-k} will be given by

$$\Pi = \begin{pmatrix} \alpha_{11} \\ \alpha_{12} \\ \alpha_{13} \\ \alpha_{14} \end{pmatrix} (\beta_{11} \quad \beta_{12} \quad \beta_{13} \quad \beta_{14}) \begin{pmatrix} y_1 \\ y_2 \\ y_3 \\ y_4 \end{pmatrix}_{t-k} \tag{8.69}$$

Equation (8.69) can also be written

$$\Pi = \begin{pmatrix} \alpha_{11} \\ \alpha_{12} \\ \alpha_{13} \\ \alpha_{14} \end{pmatrix} (\beta_{11}y_1 + \beta_{12}y_2 + \beta_{13}y_3 + \beta_{14}y_4)_{t-k} \tag{8.70}$$

Given (8.70), it is possible to write out the separate equations for each variable Δy_t. It is also common to 'normalise' on a particular variable, so that the coefficient on that variable in the cointegrating vector is one. For example, normalising on y_1 would make the cointegrating term in the equation for Δy_1

$$\alpha_{11} \left(y_1 + \frac{\beta_{12}}{\beta_{11}} y_2 + \frac{\beta_{13}}{\beta_{11}} y_3 + \frac{\beta_{14}}{\beta_{11}} y_4 \right)_{t-k}, \text{etc.}$$

Finally, it must be noted that the above description is not exactly how the Johansen procedure works, but is an intuitive approximation to it.

8.9.1 Hypothesis testing using Johansen

Engle–Granger did not permit the testing of hypotheses on the cointegrating relationships themselves, but the Johansen setup does permit the testing of hypotheses about the equilibrium relationships between the variables. Johansen allows a researcher to test a hypothesis about one or more coefficients in the cointegrating relationship by viewing the hypothesis as a restriction on the Π matrix. If there exist r cointegrating vectors, only these linear combinations or linear transformations of them, or combinations of the cointegrating vectors, will be stationary. In fact, the matrix of cointegrating vectors β can be multiplied by any non-singular conformable matrix to obtain a new set of cointegrating vectors.

A set of required long-run coefficient values or relationships between the coefficients does not necessarily imply that the cointegrating vectors have to be restricted. This is because any combination of cointegrating vectors is also a cointegrating vector. So it may be possible to combine the cointegrating vectors thus far obtained to provide a new one or, in general, a new set, having the required properties. The simpler and fewer are the required properties, the more likely that this recombination process (called *renormalisation*) will automatically yield cointegrating vectors with the required properties. However, as the restrictions become more numerous or involve more of the coefficients of the vectors, it will eventually become impossible to satisfy all of them by renormalisation. After this point, all other linear combinations of the variables will be non-stationary. If the restriction does not affect the model much, i.e. if the restriction is not binding, then the eigenvectors should not change much following imposition of the restriction. A test statistic to test this hypothesis is given by

$$test\ statistic = -T \sum_{i=1}^{r} [\ln(1 - \lambda_i) - \ln(1 - \lambda_i^*)] \sim \chi^2(m) \tag{8.71}$$

where λ_i^* are the characteristic roots of the restricted model, λ_i are the characteristic roots of the unrestricted model, r is the number of non-zero characteristic roots in the unrestricted model and m is the number of restrictions.

Restrictions are actually imposed by substituting them into the relevant α or β matrices as appropriate, so that tests can be conducted on either the cointegrating vectors or their loadings in each equation in the system (or both). For example, considering (8.66)–(8.68) above, it may be that theory suggests that the coefficients on the loadings of the cointegrating vector(s) in each equation should take on certain values, in which case it would be relevant to test restrictions on the elements of α (e.g. $\alpha_{11} = 1$, $\alpha_{23} = -1$, etc.). Equally, it may be of interest to examine whether only a sub-set of the variables in y_t is actually required to obtain a stationary linear combination. In that case, it would be appropriate to test restrictions of elements of β. For example, to test the hypothesis that y_4 is not necessary to form a long-run relationship, set $\beta_{14} = 0$, $\beta_{24} = 0$, etc.

For an excellent detailed treatment of cointegration in the context of both single equation and multiple equation models, see Harris (1995). Several applications of tests for cointegration and modelling cointegrated systems in finance will now be given.

8.10 Purchasing power parity

Purchasing power parity (PPP) states that the equilibrium or long-run exchange rate between two countries is equal to the ratio of their relative price levels. Purchasing power parity implies that the real exchange rate, Q_t, is stationary. The real exchange rate can be defined as

$$Q_t = \frac{E_t P_t^*}{P_t} \tag{8.72}$$

where E_t is the nominal exchange rate in domestic currency per unit of foreign currency, P_t is the domestic price level and P_t^* is the foreign price level. Taking logarithms of (8.72) and rearranging, another way of stating the PPP relation is obtained

$$e_t - p_t + p_t^* = q_t \tag{8.73}$$

where the lower case letters in (8.73) denote logarithmic transforms of the corresponding upper case letters used in (8.72). A necessary and sufficient condition for PPP to hold is that the variables on the LHS of (8.73) – that is the log of the exchange rate between countries A and B, and the logs of the price levels in countries A and B be cointegrated with cointegrating vector $[1 - 1\ 1]$.

A test of this form is conducted by Chen (1995) using monthly data from Belgium, France, Germany, Italy and the Netherlands over the period April 1973 to December 1990. Pair-wise evaluations of the existence or otherwise of cointegration are examined for all combinations of these countries (ten country pairs). Since there are three variables in the system (the log exchange rate and the two log nominal price series) in each case, and that the variables in their log-levels forms are non-stationary, there can be at most two linearly independent cointegrating relationships for each country pair. The results of applying Johansen's trace test are presented in Chen's table 1, adapted and presented here as table 8.8.

As can be seen from the results, the null hypothesis of no cointegrating vectors is rejected for all country pairs, and the null of one or fewer cointegrating vectors is rejected for France–Belgium, Germany–Italy, Germany–Belgium, Italy–Belgium, Netherlands–Belgium. In no cases is the null of two or less cointegrating vectors rejected. It is therefore concluded that the PPP hypothesis is upheld and that there are either one or two cointegrating relationships between the series depending on the country pair. Estimates of α_1 and α_2 are given in the last two columns of table 8.8. PPP suggests that the estimated values of these coefficients should be 1 and -1, respectively. In most cases, the coefficient estimates are a long way from these expected values. Of course, it would be possible to impose this restriction and to test it in the Johansen framework as discussed above, but Chen does not conduct this analysis.

8.11 Cointegration between international bond markets

Often, investors will hold bonds from more than one national market in the expectation of achieving a reduction in risk via the resulting diversification. If international bond markets are very strongly correlated in the long run, diversification will be less effective than if the bond markets operated independently of one another. An important indication of the degree to which long-run diversification is available to international bond market investors is given by determining whether the markets are cointegrated. This book will now study two examples from the

Table 8.8   Cointegration tests of PPP with European data

Tests for cointegration between	$r = 0$	$r \leq 1$	$r \leq 2$	α_1	α_2
FRF–DEM	34.63*	17.10	6.26	1.33	−2.50
FRF–ITL	52.69*	15.81	5.43	2.65	−2.52
FRF–NLG	68.10*	16.37	6.42	0.58	−0.80
FRF–BEF	52.54*	26.09*	3.63	0.78	−1.15
DEM–ITL	42.59*	20.76*	4.79	5.80	−2.25
DEM–NLG	50.25*	17.79	3.28	0.12	−0.25
DEM–BEF	69.13*	27.13*	4.52	0.87	−0.52
ITL–NLG	37.51*	14.22	5.05	0.55	−0.71
ITL–BEF	69.24*	32.16*	7.15	0.73	−1.28
NLG–BEF	64.52*	21.97*	3.88	1.69	−2.17
Critical values	31.52	17.95	8.18	–	–

Notes: FRF – French franc; DEM – German mark; NLG – Dutch guilder; ITL – Italian lira; BEF – Belgian franc.
Source: Chen (1995). Reprinted with the permission of Taylor and Francis Ltd (www.tandf.co.uk).

academic literature that consider this issue: Clare, Maras and Thomas (1995), and Mills and Mills (1991).

8.11.1   Cointegration between international bond markets: a univariate approach

Clare, Maras and Thomas (1995) use the Dickey–Fuller and Engle–Granger single-equation method to test for cointegration using a pair-wise analysis of four countries' bond market indices: US, UK, Germany and Japan. Monthly Salomon Brothers' total return government bond index data from January 1978 to April 1990 are employed. An application of the Dickey–Fuller test to the log of the indices reveals the following results (adapted from their table 1), given in table 8.9.

Neither the critical values, nor a statement of whether a constant or trend are included in the test regressions, are offered in the paper. Nevertheless, the results are clear. Recall that the null hypothesis of a unit root is rejected if the test statistic is smaller (more negative) than the critical value. For samples of the size given here, the 5% critical value would be somewhere between −1.95 and −3.50. It is thus demonstrated quite conclusively that the logarithms of the indices are non-stationary, while taking the first difference of the logs (that is, constructing the returns) induces stationarity.

Table 8.9 DF tests for international bond indices	
Panel A: test on log-index for country	**DF Statistic**
Germany	−0.395
Japan	−0.799
UK	−0.884
US	0.174
Panel B: test on log-returns for country	
Germany	−10.37
Japan	−10.11
UK	−10.56
US	−10.64

Source: Clare, Maras and Thomas (1995). Reprinted with the permission of Blackwell Publishers.

Given that all logs of the indices in all four cases are shown to be I(1), the next stage in the analysis is to test for cointegration by forming a potentially cointegrating regression and testing its residuals for non-stationarity. Clare, Maras and Thomas use regressions of the form

$$B_i = \alpha_0 + \alpha_1 B_j + u \tag{8.74}$$

with time subscripts suppressed and where B_i and B_j represent the log-bond indices for any two countries i and j. The results are presented in their tables 3 and 4, which are combined into table 8.10 here. They offer findings from applying seven different tests, while we present the results for only the Cointegrating Regression Durbin Watson (CRDW), Dickey–Fuller and Augmented Dickey–Fuller tests (although the lag lengths for the latter are not given in their paper).

In this case, the null hypothesis of a unit root in the residuals from regression (8.74) cannot be rejected. The conclusion is therefore that there is no cointegration between any pair of bond indices in this sample.

8.11.2 Cointegration between international bond markets: a multivariate approach

Mills and Mills (1991) also consider the issue of cointegration or non-cointegration between the same four international bond markets. However, unlike Clare *et al.* (1995), who use bond price indices, Mills and Mills employ daily closing observations on the redemption yields. The latter's sample period runs from 1 April 1986 to 29 December 1989, giving 960 observations. They employ a

Table 8.10   Cointegration tests for pairs of international bond indices

Test	UK–Germany	UK–Japan	UK–US	Germany–Japan	Germany–US	Japan–US	5% Critical value
CRDW	0.189	0.197	0.097	0.230	0.169	0.139	0.386
DF	2.970	2.770	2.020	3.180	2.160	2.160	3.370
ADF	3.160	2.900	1.800	3.360	1.640	1.890	3.170

Source: Clare, Maras and Thomas (1995). Reprinted with the permission of Blackwell Publishers.

Table 8.11   Johansen tests for cointegration between international bond yields

r (number of cointegrating vectors under the null hypothesis)	Test statistic	Critical values 10%	5%
0	22.06	35.6	38.6
1	10.58	21.2	23.8
2	2.52	10.3	12.0
3	0.12	2.9	4.2

Source: Mills and Mills (1991). Reprinted with the permission of Blackwell Publishers.

Dickey–Fuller-type regression procedure to test the individual series for non-stationarity and conclude that all four yields series are I(1).

The Johansen systems procedure is then used to test for cointegration between the series. Unlike Clare *et al.*, Mills and Mills consider all four indices together rather than investigating them in a pair-wise fashion. Therefore, since there are four variables in the system (the redemption yield for each country), i.e. $g = 4$, there can be at most three linearly independent cointegrating vectors, i.e., $r \leq 3$. The trace statistic is employed, and it takes the form

$$\lambda_{trace}(r) = -T \sum_{i=r+1}^{g} \ln(1 - \hat{\lambda}_i) \qquad (8.75)$$

where λ_i are the ordered eigenvalues. The results are presented in their table 2, which is modified slightly here, and presented in table 8.11.

Looking at the first row under the heading, it can be seen that the test statistic is smaller than the critical value, so the null hypothesis that $r = 0$ cannot be rejected, even at the 10% level. It is thus not necessary to look at the remaining rows of the table. Hence, reassuringly, the conclusion from this analysis is the same as that of Clare *et al.* − i.e. that there are no cointegrating vectors.

Given that there are no linear combinations of the yields that are stationary, and therefore that there is no error correction representation, Mills and Mills then continue to estimate a VAR for the first differences of the yields. The VAR is of the form

$$\Delta X_t = \sum_{i=1}^{k} \Gamma_i \Delta X_{t-i} + v_t \qquad (8.76)$$

where:

$$X_t = \begin{bmatrix} X(US)_t \\ X(UK)_t \\ X(WG)_t \\ X(JAP)_t \end{bmatrix}, \Gamma_i = \begin{bmatrix} \Gamma_{11i} & \Gamma_{12i} & \Gamma_{13i} & \Gamma_{14i} \\ \Gamma_{21i} & \Gamma_{22i} & \Gamma_{23i} & \Gamma_{24i} \\ \Gamma_{31i} & \Gamma_{32i} & \Gamma_{33i} & \Gamma_{34i} \\ \Gamma_{41i} & \Gamma_{42i} & \Gamma_{43i} & \Gamma_{44i} \end{bmatrix}, v_t = \begin{bmatrix} v_{1t} \\ v_{2t} \\ v_{3t} \\ v_{4t} \end{bmatrix}$$

They set k, the number of lags of each change in the yield in each regression, to 8, arguing that likelihood ratio tests rejected the possibility of smaller numbers of lags. Unfortunately, and as one may anticipate for a regression of daily yield changes, the R^2 values for the VAR equations are low, ranging from 0.04 for the US to 0.17 for Germany. Variance decompositions and impulse responses are calculated for the estimated VAR. Two orderings of the variables are employed: one based on a previous study and one based on the chronology of the opening (and closing) of the financial markets considered: Japan → Germany → UK → US. Only results for the latter, adapted from tables 4 and 5 of Mills and Mills (1991), are presented here. The variance decompositions and impulse responses for the VARs are given in tables 8.12 and 8.13, respectively.

As one may expect from the low R^2 of the VAR equations, and the lack of cointegration, the bond markets seem very independent of one another. The variance decompositions, which show the proportion of the movements in the dependent variables that are due to their 'own' shocks, versus shocks to the other variables, seem to suggest that the US, UK and Japanese markets are to a certain extent exogenous in this system. That is, little of the movement of the US, UK or Japanese series can be explained by movements other than their own bond yields. In the German case, however, after twenty days, only 83% of movements in the German yield are explained by German shocks. The German yield seems particularly influenced by US (8.4% after twenty days) and UK (6.5% after twenty days) shocks. It also seems that Japanese shocks have the least influence on the bond yields of other markets.

A similar pattern emerges from the impulse response functions, which show the effect of a unit shock applied separately to the error of each equation of the VAR. The markets appear relatively independent of one another, and also informationally efficient in the sense that shocks work through the system very

Table 8.12	Variance decompositions for VAR of international bond yields				
Explaining movements in	Days ahead	Explained by movements in			
		US	UK	Germany	Japan
US	1	95.6	2.4	1.7	0.3
	5	94.2	2.8	2.3	0.7
	10	92.9	3.1	2.9	1.1
	20	92.8	3.2	2.9	1.1
UK	1	0.0	98.3	0.0	1.7
	5	1.7	96.2	0.2	1.9
	10	2.2	94.6	0.9	2.3
	20	2.2	94.6	0.9	2.3
Germany	1	0.0	3.4	94.6	2.0
	5	6.6	6.6	84.8	3.0
	10	8.3	6.5	82.9	3.6
	20	8.4	6.5	82.7	3.7
Japan	1	0.0	0.0	1.4	100.0
	5	1.3	1.4	1.1	96.2
	10	1.5	2.1	1.8	94.6
	20	1.6	2.2	1.9	94.2

Source: Mills and Mills (1991). Reprinted with the permission of Blackwell Publishers.

quickly. There is never a response of more than 10% to shocks in any series three days after they have happened; in most cases, the shocks have worked through the system in two days. Such a result implies that the possibility of making excess returns by trading in one market on the basis of 'old news' from another appears very unlikely.

8.11.3 Cointegration in international bond markets: conclusions

A single set of conclusions can be drawn from both of these papers. Both approaches have suggested that international bond markets are not cointegrated. This implies that investors can gain substantial diversification benefits. This is in contrast to results reported for other markets, such as foreign exchange (Baillie and Boller-slev, 1989), commodities (Baillie, 1989) and equities (Taylor and Tonks, 1989). Clare, Maras and Thomas (1995) suggest that the lack of long-term integration

Table 8.13   Impulse responses for VAR of international bond yields

	Response of US to innovations in			
Days after shock	US	UK	Germany	Japan
0	0.98	0.00	0.00	0.00
1	0.06	0.01	−0.10	0.05
2	−0.02	0.02	−0.14	0.07
3	0.09	−0.04	0.09	0.08
4	−0.02	−0.03	0.02	0.09
10	−0.03	−0.01	−0.02	−0.01
20	0.00	0.00	−0.10	−0.01

	Response of UK to innovations in			
Days after shock	US	UK	Germany	Japan
0	0.19	0.97	0.00	0.00
1	0.16	0.07	0.01	−0.06
2	−0.01	−0.01	−0.05	0.09
3	0.06	0.04	0.06	0.05
4	0.05	−0.01	0.02	0.07
10	0.01	0.01	−0.04	−0.01
20	0.00	0.00	−0.01	0.00

	Response of Germany to innovations in			
Days after shock	US	UK	Germany	Japan
0	0.07	0.06	0.95	0.00
1	0.13	0.05	0.11	0.02
2	0.04	0.03	0.00	0.00
3	0.02	0.00	0.00	0.01
4	0.01	0.00	0.00	0.09
10	0.01	0.01	−0.01	0.02
20	0.00	0.00	0.00	0.00

(cont.)

Table 8.13   *(cont.)*

| Days after shock | Response of Japan to innovations in | | | |
	US	UK	Germany	Japan
0	0.03	0.05	0.12	0.97
1	0.06	0.02	0.07	0.04
2	0.02	0.02	0.00	0.21
3	0.01	0.02	0.06	0.07
4	0.02	0.03	0.07	0.06
10	0.01	0.01	0.01	0.04
20	0.00	0.00	0.00	0.01

Source: Mills and Mills (1991). Reprinted with the permission of Blackwell Publishers.

between the markets may be due to 'institutional idiosyncrasies', such as heterogeneous maturity and taxation structures, and differing investment cultures, issuance patterns and macroeconomic policies between countries, which imply that the markets operate largely independently of one another.

8.12 Testing the expectations hypothesis of the term structure of interest rates

The following notation replicates that employed by Campbell and Shiller (1991) in their seminal paper. The single, linear expectations theory of the term structure used to represent the expectations hypothesis (hereafter EH), defines a relationship between an n-period interest rate or yield, denoted $R_t^{(n)}$, and an m-period interest rate, denoted $R_t^{(m)}$, where $n > m$. Hence $R_t^{(n)}$ is the interest rate or yield on a longer-term instrument relative to a shorter-term interest rate or yield, $R_t^{(m)}$. More precisely, the EH states that the expected return from investing in an n-period rate will equal the expected return from investing in m-period rates up to $n - m$ periods in the future plus a constant risk-premium, c, which can be expressed as

$$R_t^{(n)} = \frac{1}{q}\sum_{i=0}^{q-1} E_t R_{t+mi}^{(m)} + c \tag{8.77}$$

where $q = n/m$. Consequently, the longer-term interest rate, $R_t^{(n)}$, can be expressed as a weighted-average of current and expected shorter-term interest rates, $R_t^{(m)}$, plus a constant risk premium, c. If (8.77) is considered, it can be seen that by subtracting $R_t^{(m)}$ from both sides of the relationship we have

$$R_t^{(n)} - R_t^{(m)} = \frac{1}{q}\sum_{i=0}^{q-1}\sum_{j=1}^{j=i}E_t\big[\Delta^{(m)}R_{t+jm}^{(m)}\big] + c \tag{8.78}$$

Examination of (8.78) generates some interesting restrictions. If the interest rates under analysis, say $R_t^{(n)}$ and $R_t^{(m)}$, are I(1) series, then, by definition, $\Delta R_t^{(n)}$ and $\Delta R_t^{(m)}$ will be stationary series. There is a general acceptance that interest rates, Treasury Bill yields, etc. are well described as I(1) processes and this can be seen in Campbell and Shiller (1988) and Stock and Watson (1988). Further, since c is a constant then it is by definition a stationary series. Consequently, if the EH is to hold, given that c and $\Delta R_t^{(m)}$ are I(0) implying that the RHS of (8.78) is stationary, then $R_t^{(n)} - R_t^{(m)}$ must by definition be stationary, otherwise we will have an inconsistency in the order of integration between the RHS and LHS of the relationship. $R_t^{(n)} - R_t^{(m)}$ is commonly known as the *spread* between the n-period and m-period rates, denoted $S_t^{(n,m)}$, which in turn gives an indication of the slope of the term structure. Consequently, it follows that if the EH is to hold, then the spread will be found to be stationary and therefore $R_t^{(n)}$ and $R_t^{(m)}$ will cointegrate with a cointegrating vector $(1, -1)$ for $[R_t^{(n)}, R_t^{(m)}]$. Therefore, the integrated process driving each of the two rates is common to both and hence it can be said that the rates have a common stochastic trend. As a result, since the EH predicts that each interest rate series will cointegrate with the one-period interest rate, it must be true that the stochastic process driving all the rates is the same as that driving the one-period rate, i.e. any combination of rates formed to create a spread should be found to cointegrate with a cointegrating vector $(1, -1)$.

Many examinations of the expectations hypothesis of the term structure have been conducted in the literature, and still no overall consensus appears to have emerged concerning its validity. One such study that tested the expectations hypothesis using a standard data-set due to McCulloch (1987) was conducted by Shea (1992). The data comprises a zero coupon term structure for various maturities from one month to twenty-five years, covering the period January 1952–February 1987. Various techniques are employed in Shea's paper, while only his application of the Johansen technique is discussed here. A vector X_t containing the interest rate at each of the maturities is constructed

$$X_t = \big[R_t\, R_t^{(2)}\, \ldots\, R_t^{(n)}\big]' \tag{8.79}$$

where R_t denotes the spot interest rate. It is argued that each of the elements of this vector is non-stationary, and hence the Johansen approach is used to model the system of interest rates and to test for cointegration between the rates. Both the λ_{max} and λ_{trace} statistics are employed, corresponding to the use of the maximum eigenvalue and the cumulated eigenvalues, respectively. Shea tests for cointegration between various combinations of the interest rates, measured as returns to maturity. A selection of Shea's results is presented in table 8.14.

Table 8.14 Tests of the expectations hypothesis using the US zero coupon yield curve with monthly data

Sample period	Interest rates included	Lag length of VAR	Hypothesis is	λ_{max}	λ_{trace}
1952M1–1978M12	$X_t = [R_t \, R_t^{(6)}]'$	2	$r = 0$	47.54***	49.82***
			$r \leq 1$	2.28	2.28
1952M1–1987M2	$X_t = [R_t \, R_t^{(120)}]'$	2	$r = 0$	40.66***	43.73***
			$r \leq 1$	3.07	3.07
1952M1–1987M2	$X_t = [R_t \, R_t^{(60)} \, R_t^{(120)}]'$	2	$r = 0$	40.13***	42.63***
			$r \leq 1$	2.50	2.50
1973M5–1987M2	$X_t = [R_t \, R_t^{(60)} \, R_t^{(120)} \, R_t^{(180)} \, R_t^{(240)}]'$	7	$r = 0$	34.78***	75.50***
			$r \leq 1$	23.31*	40.72
			$r \leq 2$	11.94	17.41
			$r \leq 3$	3.80	5.47
			$r \leq 4$	1.66	1.66

Notes: *,** and *** denote significance at the 20%, 10% and 5% levels, respectively; r is the number of cointegrating vectors under the null hypothesis.
Source: Shea (1992). Reprinted with the permission of American Statistical Association. All rights reserved.

The results below, together with the other results presented by Shea, seem to suggest that the interest rates at different maturities are typically cointegrated, usually with one cointegrating vector. As one may have expected, the cointegration becomes weaker in the cases where the analysis involves rates a long way apart on the maturity spectrum. However, cointegration between the rates is a necessary but not sufficient condition for the expectations hypothesis of the term structure to be vindicated by the data. Validity of the expectations hypothesis also requires that any combination of rates formed to create a spread should be found to cointegrate with a cointegrating vector $(1, -1)$. When comparable restrictions are placed on the β estimates associated with the cointegrating vectors, they are typically rejected, suggesting only limited support for the expectations hypothesis.

8.13 Testing for cointegration and modelling cointegrated systems using EViews

The S&P500 spot and futures series that were discussed in chapters 3 and 4 will now be examined for cointegration using EViews. If the two series are cointegrated, this means that the spot and futures prices have a long-term relationship, which prevents them from wandering apart without bound. To test for cointegration

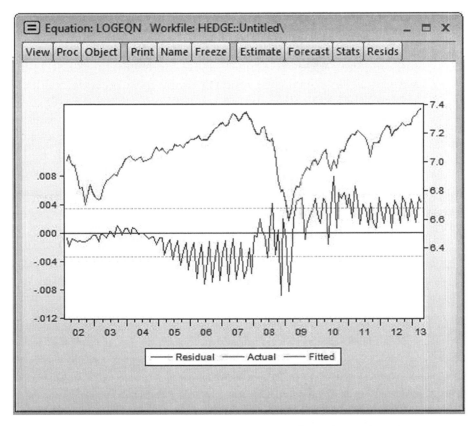

Screenshot 8.2   **Actual, fitted and residual plot to check for stationarity**

using the Engle–Granger approach, the residuals of a regression of the spot price on the futures price are examined.[3] **Create two new variables**, for the log of the spot series and the log of the futures series, and call them '**lspot**' and '**lfutures**' respectively. Then generate a new equation object and run the regression:

LSPOT C LFUTURES

Note again that it is not valid to examine anything other than the coefficient values in this regression. The residuals of this regression are found in the object called RESID. From viewing the regression results, **click View/Actual,Fitted,Residual and then Actual,Fitted,Residual Graph**. You will see a plot of the levels of the residuals (blue line), which looks much more like a stationary series than the original spot series (the red line corresponding to the actual values of y) does. Note how close together the actual and fitted lines are – the two are virtually indistinguishable and hence the very small left-hand scale for the residuals. The plot should appear as in screenshot 8.2.

[3] Note that it is common to run a regression of the log of the spot price on the log of the futures rather than a regression in levels; the main reason for using logarithms is that the differences of the logs are returns, whereas this is not true for the levels.

Generate a new series that will keep these residuals in an object for later use:

STATRESIDS = RESID

This is required since every time a regression is run, the RESID object is updated (overwritten) to contain the residuals of the most recently conducted regression. **Perform the ADF Test** on the residual series STATRESIDS. Assuming again that up to twelve lags are permitted, that Schwarz's criterion is used to select the optimal lag length, and that a constant but not a trend are employed in a regression on the levels of the series, the results are:

Null Hypothesis: STATRESIDS has a unit root
Exogenous: Constant
Lag Length: 2 (Automatic based on SIC, MAXLAG=12)

	t-Statistic	Prob.*
Augmented Dickey-Fuller test statistic	−1.738437	0.4096

Test critical values:	1% level	−3.480425
	5% level	−2.883408
	10% level	−2.578510

*MacKinnon (1996) one-sided p-values.

Augmented Dickey-Fuller Test Equation
Dependent Variable: D(STATRESIDS)
Method: Least Squares
Date: 08/05/13 Time: 16:36
Sample (adjusted): 2002M03 2013M04
Included observations: 132 after adjustments

	Coefficient	Std. Error	t-Statistic	Prob.
STATRESIDS(-1)	−0.120172	0.069127	−1.738437	0.0845
D(STATRESIDS(-1))	−0.658848	0.083894	−7.853369	0.0000
D(STATRESIDS(-2))	−0.558155	0.074282	−7.513974	0.0000
C	7.97E-05	0.000193	0.412030	0.6810

R-squared	0.506131	Mean dependent var	3.78E-05
Adjusted R-squared	0.494556	S.D. dependent var	0.003124
S.E. of regression	0.002221	Akaike info criterion	−9.351697
Sum squared resid	0.000632	Schwarz criterion	−9.264340
Log likelihood	621.2120	Hannan-Quinn criter.	−9.316199
F-statistic	43.72608	Durbin-Watson stat	2.010767
Prob(F-statistic)	0.000000		

Since the test statistic (-1.74) is not more negative than the critical values, even at the 10% level, the null hypothesis of a unit root in the test regression residuals cannot be rejected. We would thus conclude that the two series are not cointegrated. This means that the most appropriate form of model to estimate would be one containing only first differences of the variables as they have no long-run relationship.

If instead we had found the two series to be cointegrated, an error correction model (ECM) could have been estimated, as there would be a linear combination of the spot and futures prices that would be stationary. The ECM would be the appropriate model in that case rather than a model in pure first difference form because it would enable us to capture the long-run relationship between the series as well as the short-run one. We could estimate an error correction model by running the regression

rspot c rfutures statresids(-1)

However, if you estimate the model, the estimate on the error correction term is not really plausible and given that the two series are not cointegrated, a model of the form

rspot c rfutures rspot(-1) rfutures(-1)

would be more appropriate. Note that we can either include or exclude the lagged terms and either form would be valid from the perspective that all of the elements in the equation are stationary.

Before moving on, we should note that this result is not an entirely stable one − for instance, if we run the regression containing no lags (i.e. the pure Dickey–Fuller test) or on a sub-sample of the data, we would find that the unit root null hypothesis should be rejected, indicating that the series are cointegrated. We thus need to be careful about drawing a firm conclusion in this case.

Although the Engle–Granger approach is evidently very easy to use, as outlined above, one of its major drawbacks is that it can estimate only up to one cointegrating relationship between the variables. In the spot-futures example, there can be at most one cointegrating relationship since there are only two variables in the system. But in other situations, if there are more variables, there could potentially be more than one linearly independent cointegrating relationship. Thus, it is appropriate instead to examine the issue of cointegration within the Johansen VAR framework.

The application we will now examine centres on whether the yields on treasury bills of different maturities are cointegrated. **Re–open the 'macro.wf1' workfile** that was used in chapter 4. There are six interest rate series corresponding to three and six months, and one, three, five and ten years. Each series has a name in the file starting with the letters 'ustb'. The first step in any cointegration analysis is to ensure that the variables are all non-stationary in their levels form, so **confirm that this is the case** for each of the six series, by running a unit root test on each one.

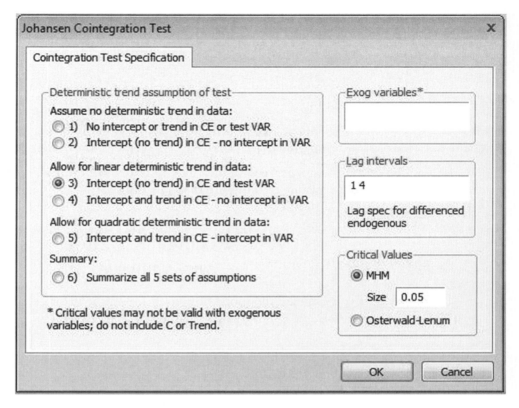

Screenshot 8.3 **Johansen cointegration test**

Next, to run the cointegration test, **highlight the six series** and then click **Quick/Group Statistics/Johansen Cointegration Test**. A box should then appear with the names of the six series in it. Click **OK**, and then the list of options will be seen (screenshot 8.3).

The differences between models 1 to 6 centre on whether an intercept or a trend or both are included in the potentially cointegrating relationship and/or the VAR. It is usually a good idea to examine the sensitivity of the result to the type of specification used, so select **Option 6** which will do this and click **OK**. The results appear as in the following table.

The findings across the six types of model and the type of test (the 'trace' or 'max' statistics) are a little mixed concerning the number of cointegrating vectors (the top panel), with the trace statistic always suggesting at least one cointegrating vector but the max approach selecting between zero and two cointegrating vectors dependent on the specification of the VAR model. We thus have an inconclusive result regarding whether the six interest rate series are in fact cointegrated or not, but the weight of evidence is slightly in favour that they are.

The following three panels all provide information that could be used to determine the appropriate lag length for the VAR. The values of the log-likelihood function could be used to run tests of whether a VAR of a given order could be restricted to a VAR of lower order; AIC and SBIC values are provided in the final

Date: 08/05/13 Time: 17:03
Sample: 1986M03 2013M04
Included observations: 321
Series: USTB10Y USTB1Y USTB3M USTB3Y USTB5Y USTB6M
Lags interval: 1 to 4
Selected (0.05 level*) Number of Cointegrating Relations by Model

Data Trend:	None	None	Linear	Linear	Quadratic
Test Type	No Intercept No Trend	Intercept No Trend	Intercept No Trend	Intercept Trend	Intercept Trend
Trace	2	2	2	3	4
Max-Eig	2	0	0	1	1

*Critical values based on MacKinnon-Haug-Michelis (1999)

Information Criteria by Rank and Model

Data Trend:	None	None	Linear	Linear	Quadratic
Rank or No. of CEs	No Intercept No Trend	Intercept No Trend	Intercept No Trend	Intercept Trend	Intercept Trend

Log Likelihood by Rank (rows) and Model (columns)

0	1967.692	1967.692	1968.534	1968.534	1969.015
1	1986.205	1987.518	1988.320	1990.809	1991.289
2	2002.157	2003.584	2004.375	2009.071	2009.549
3	2012.684	2015.717	2016.425	2024.588	2025.059
4	2019.151	2022.448	2022.786	2035.103	2035.291
5	2021.371	2025.817	2026.083	2041.377	2041.461
6	2021.729	2026.855	2026.855	2044.069	2044.069

Akaike Information Criteria by Rank (rows) and Model (columns)

0	−11.36257	−11.36257	−11.33043	−11.33043	−11.29604
1	−11.40315	−11.40509	−11.37894	−11.38822	−11.36005
2	−11.42777	−11.42420	−11.40383	−11.42100	−11.39906
3	−11.41859	−11.41879	−11.40452	−11.43669*	−11.42093
4	−11.38412	−11.37974	−11.36938	−11.42121	−11.40991
5	−11.32318	−11.31973	−11.31516	−11.37930	−11.37359
6	−11.25065	−11.24520	−11.24520	−11.31507	−11.31507

Schwarz Criteria by Rank (rows) and Model (columns)

0	−9.67070*	−9.67070*	−9.56807	−9.56807	−9.46319
1	−9.57030	−9.56050	−9.47559	−9.47313	−9.38622
2	−9.45393	−9.42686	−9.35950	−9.35317	−9.28423
3	−9.30376	−9.26872	−9.21920	−9.21612	−9.16511
4	−9.12830	−9.07693	−9.04308	−9.04790	−9.01311
5	−8.92638	−8.86418	−8.84786	−8.85325	−8.83580
6	−8.71286	−8.63691	−8.63691	−8.63629	−8.63629

two panels. AIC selects a VAR with either three or four lags depending on whether intercepts and/or trends are incorporated, while SBIC always selects a VAR with no lags. Note that the difference in optimal model order could be attributed to the relatively small sample size available with this monthly sample compared with the number of observations that would have been available were daily data used, implying that the penalty term in SBIC is more severe on extra parameters in this case.

So, in order to see the estimated models, click **View/Cointegration Test/ Johansen System Cointegration Test...** and select **Option 3** (Intercept (no trend) in CE and test VAR), changing the 'Lag Intervals' to **1 3**, and clicking **OK**. EViews produces a very large quantity of output, as shown in the following table.[4]

The first two panels of the table show the results for the λ_{trace} and λ_{max} statistics respectively. The second column in each case presents the ordered eigenvalues, the third column the test statistics, the fourth column the critical values and the final column the p-values. Examining the trace test, if we look at the first row after the headers, the statistic of 142.4602 considerably exceeds the critical value (of 95.75) and so the null of no cointegrating vectors is rejected. If we then move to the next row, the test statistic (95.03525) again exceeds the critical value so that the null of at most one cointegrating vector is also rejected. This continues, and we also

---

Date: 08/05/13 Time: 18:30
Sample (adjusted): 1986M07 2013M04
Included observations: 322 after adjustments
Trend assumption: Linear deterministic trend
Series: USTB10Y USTB1Y USTB3M USTB3Y USTB5Y USTB6M
Lags interval (in first differences): 1 to 3

Unrestricted Cointegration Rank Test (Trace)

| Hypothesized No. of CE(s) | Eigenvalue | Trace 0.05 | | Prob.** |
		Statistic	Critical Value	
None*	0.136950	142.4602	95.75366	0.0000
At most 1*	0.118267	95.03524	69.81889	0.0001
At most 2*	0.089649	54.50629	47.85613	0.0105
At most 3*	0.043899	24.26233	29.79707	0.1896
At most 4	0.024827	9.807123	15.49471	0.2959
At most 5	0.005303	1.712066	3.841466	0.1907

Trace test indicates 3 cointegrating eqn(s) at the 0.05 level
*denotes rejection of the hypothesis at the 0.05 level
**MacKinnon-Haug-Michelis (1999) p-values

---

[4] Estimated cointegrating vectors and loadings are provided by EViews for 2–5 cointegrating vectors as well, but these are not shown to preserve space.

Unrestricted Cointegration Rank Test (Maximum Eigenvalue)

Hypothesized No. of CE(s)	Eigenvalue	Max-Eigen Statistic	0.05 Critical Value	Prob.**
None*	0.136950	47.42496	40.07757	0.0063
At most 1*	0.118267	40.52895	33.87687	0.0070
At most 2*	0.089649	30.24396	27.58434	0.0222
At most 3*	0.043899	14.45521	21.13162	0.3289
At most 4	0.024827	8.095058	14.26460	0.3691
At most 5	0.005303	1.712066	3.841466	0.1907

Max-eigenvalue test indicates 3 cointegrating eqn(s) at the 0.05 level
*denotes rejection of the hypothesis at the 0.05 level
**MacKinnon-Haug-Michelis (1999) p-values

Unrestricted Cointegrating Coefficients (normalized by $b'{}^*S11{}^*b = I$):

USTB10Y	USTB1Y	USTB3M	USTB3Y	USTB5Y	USTB6M
2.684473	−18.296340	−12.359460	10.792730	−8.712903	25.780170
−0.449156	2.335248	−0.630527	8.305166	−5.503590	−4.615958
−2.721505	8.091580	−6.936259	−14.941690	12.300630	4.363734
5.106830	4.395845	1.184519	5.364618	−11.363300	−4.452396
4.873386	−0.273274	−0.306956	2.703060	−6.990166	0.301395
0.745641	−0.345006	0.062957	−0.855164	0.641708	0.342586

Unrestricted Adjustment Coefficients (alpha):

D(USTB10Y)	0.019584	0.011721	−0.029932	0.022940	0.004912	−0.015252
D(USTB1Y)	0.021022	0.027672	−0.013588	0.006678	0.026106	−0.009241
D(USTB3M)	0.030206	0.045208	0.010914	0.007775	0.016975	−0.004310
D(USTB3Y)	0.014473	0.010067	−0.014191	0.023590	0.024070	−0.014902
D(USTB5Y)	0.019761	0.008199	−0.026057	0.030408	0.016818	−0.014461
D(USTB6M)	0.013243	0.043250	−0.006139	0.007435	0.021381	−0.006117

1 Cointegrating Equation(s): Log likelihood 1948.484

Normalized cointegrating coefficients (standard error in parentheses)

USTB10Y	USTB1Y	USTB3M	USTB3Y	USTB5Y	USTB6M
1.000000	−6.815619	−4.604054	4.020428	−3.245667	9.603439
	(1.05558)	(0.76368)	(0.89029)	(0.53162)	(1.42615)

Adjustment coefficients (standard error in parentheses)

D(USTB10Y)	0.052573
	(0.040990)
D(USTB1Y)	0.056434
	(0.036520)
D(USTB3M)	0.081088
	(0.031220)
D(USTB3Y)	0.038852
	(0.044320)
D(USTB5Y)	0.053047
	(0.044370)
D(USTB6M)	0.035550
	(0.032430)

2 Cointegrating Equation(s): Log likelihood 1968.748

Normalized cointegrating coefficients (standard error in parentheses)

USTB10Y	USTB1Y	USTB3M	USTB3Y	USTB5Y	USTB6M
1.000000	0.000000	20.727950	-90.896910	62.104930	12.443350
		(16.897300)	(19.780600)	(14.172400)	(21.355500)
0.000000	1.000000	3.716758	-13.926450	9.588359	0.416677
		(2.491280)	(2.916370)	(2.089530)	(3.148560)

Adjustment coefficients (standard error in parentheses)

D(USTB10Y)	0.047309	-0.330950
	(0.041510)	(0.281330)
D(USTB1Y)	0.044005	-0.320010
	(0.036770)	(0.249190)
D(USTB3M)	0.060783	-0.447095
	(0.030850)	(0.209070)
D(USTB3Y)	0.034330	-0.241293
	(0.044910)	(0.304330)
D(USTB5Y)	0.049364	-0.342399
	(0.044970)	(0.304730)
D(USTB6M)	0.016124	-0.141293
	(0.032170)	(0.218030)

Note: Table truncated.

reject the null of at most two cointegrating vectors, but we stop at the next row, where we do not reject the null hypothesis of at most three cointegrating vectors at the 5% level, and this is the conclusion. The *max* test, shown in the second panel, confirms this result.

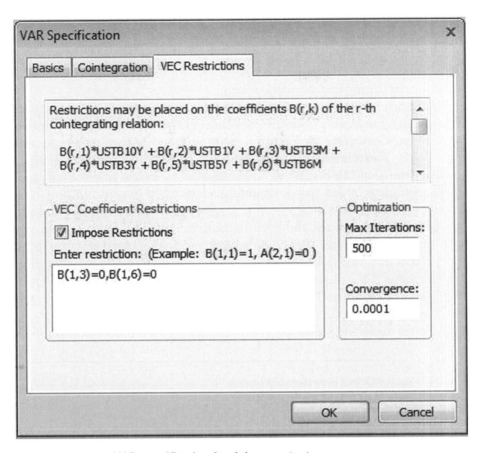

Screenshot 8.4   VAR specification for Johansen tests

The unrestricted coefficient values are the estimated values of coefficients in the cointegrating vector, and these are presented in the third panel. However, it is sometimes useful to normalise the coefficient values to set the coefficient value on one of them to unity, as would be the case in the cointegrating regression under the Engle–Granger approach. The normalisation will be done by EViews with respect to the first variable given in the variable list (i.e. whichever variable you listed first in the system will by default be given a coefficient of 1 in the normalised cointegrating vector). Panel 6 of the table presents the estimates if there were only one cointegrating vector, which has been normalised so that the coefficient on the ten-year bond yield is unity. The adjustment coefficients, or loadings in each regression (the 'amount of the cointegrating vector' in each equation), are also given in this panel. In the next panel, the same format is used (i.e. the normalised cointegrating vectors are presented and then the adjustment parameters) but under the assumption that there are two cointegrating vectors, and this proceeds until the situation where there are five cointegrating vectors, the maximum number possible for a system containing six variables.

In order to see the whole VECM model, select **Proc/Make Vector Autoregression. . . .** Starting on the default 'Basics' tab, in 'VAR type', select **Vector**

Error Correction, and in the 'Lag Intervals for D(Endogenous):' box, type **1 3**. Then click on the **cointegration tab** and leave the default as 1 cointegrating vector for simplicity in the 'Rank' box and option 3 to have an intercept but no trend in the cointegrating equation and the VAR. When **OK** is clicked, the output for the entire VECM will be seen.

It is sometimes of interest to test hypotheses about either the parameters in the cointegrating vector or their loadings in the VECM. To do this from the 'Vector Error Correction Estimates' screen, click the **Estimate** button and click on the **VEC Restrictions** tab. In EViews, restrictions concerning the cointegrating relationships embodied in β are denoted by $B(i,j)$, where $B(i,j)$ represents the jth coefficient in the ith cointegrating relationship (screenshot 8.4).

In this case, we are allowing for only one cointegrating relationship, so suppose that we want to test the hypothesis that the three-month and six-month yields do not appear in the cointegrating equation. We could test this by specifying the restriction that their parameters are zero, which in EViews terminology would be achieved by writing **B(1,3) = 0, B(1,6) = 0** in the 'VEC Coefficient Restrictions' box and clicking **OK**. EViews will then show the value of the test statistic, followed by the restricted cointegrating vector and the VECM. To preseve space, only the test statistic and restricted cointegrating vector are shown in the following table.

Vector Error Correction Estimates
Date: 08/06/13 Time: 07:25
Sample (adjusted): 1986M07 2013M04
Included observations: 322 after adjustments
Standard errors in ( ) & t-statistics in [ ]

Cointegration Restrictions:
  B(1,3) = 0, B(1,6) = 0
Convergence achieved after 12 iterations.
Not all cointegrating vectors are identified
LR test for binding restrictions (rank = 1):

Chi-square(2)	9.042452
Probability	0.010876

Cointegrating Eq:	CointEq1
USTB10Y(-1)	0.459023
USTB1Y(-1)	−1.950770
USTB3M(-1)	0.000000
USTB3Y(-1)	5.177136
USTB5Y(-1)	−3.863573
USTB6M(-1)	0.000000
C	0.799548

Note: Table truncated

There are two restrictions, so that the test statistic follows a χ^2 distribution with two degrees of freedom. Here, the p-value for the test is 0.010876, and so the restrictions are not supported by the data at the 5% level and we would conclude that the cointegrating relationship must also include the short end of the yield curve.

When performing hypothesis tests concerning the adjustment coefficients (i.e. the loadings in each equation), the restrictions are denoted by $A(i, j)$, which is the coefficient on the cointegrating vector for the ith variable in the jth cointegrating relation. For example, $A(2, 1) = 0$ would test the null that the equation for the second variable in the order that they were listed in the original specification (USTB1Y in this case) does not include the first cointegrating vector, and so on. Examining some restrictions of this type is left as an exercise.

A note on long-memory models

It is widely believed that (the logs of) asset prices contain a unit root. However, asset return series evidently do not possess a further unit root, although this does not imply that the returns are independent. In particular, it is possible (and indeed, it has been found to be the case with some financial and economic data) that observations from a given series taken some distance apart, show signs of dependence. Such series are argued to possess *long memory*. One way to represent this phenomenon is using a 'fractionally integrated' model. In simple terms, a series is integrated of a given order d if it becomes stationary on differencing a minimum of d times. In the fractionally integrated framework, d is allowed to take on non-integer values. This framework has been applied to the estimation of ARMA models (see, for example, Mills and Markellos, 2008). Under fractionally integrated models, the corresponding autocorrelation function (ACF) will decline hyperbolically, rather than exponentially to zero. Thus, the ACF for a fractionally integrated model dies away considerably more slowly than that of an ARMA model with $d = 0$. The notion of long memory has also been applied to GARCH models (discussed in chapter 9), where volatility has been found to exhibit long-range dependence. A new class of models known as fractionally integrated GARCH (FIGARCH) have been proposed to allow for this phenomenon (see Ding, Granger and Engle, 1993 or Bollerslev and Mikkelsen, 1996).

Key concepts

The key terms to be able to define and explain from this chapter are

- non-stationary
- unit root
- augmented Dickey–Fuller test
- error correction model
- Johansen technique
- eigenvalues

- explosive process
- spurious regression
- cointegration
- Engle–Granger 2-step approach
- vector error correction model

Self-study questions

1. (a) What kinds of variables are likely to be non-stationary? How can such variables be made stationary?
   (b) Why is it in general important to test for non-stationarity in time series data before attempting to build an empirical model?
   (c) Define the following terms and describe the processes that they represent
      (i)   Weak stationarity
      (ii) Strict stationarity
      (iii) Deterministic trend
      (iv) Stochastic trend.

2. A researcher wants to test the order of integration of some time series data. He decides to use the DF test. He estimates a regression of the form

   $$\Delta y_t = \mu + \psi y_{t-1} + u_t$$

   and obtains the estimate $\hat{\psi} = -0.02$ with standard error $= 0.31$.
   (a) What are the null and alternative hypotheses for this test?
   (b) Given the data, and a critical value of -2.88, perform the test.
   (c) What is the conclusion from this test and what should be the next step?
   (d) Why is it not valid to compare the estimated test statistic with the corresponding critical value from a t-distribution, even though the test statistic takes the form of the usual t-ratio?

3. Using the same regression as for question 2, but on a different set of data, the researcher now obtains the estimate $\hat{\psi} = -0.52$ with standard error $= 0.16$.
   (a) Perform the test.
   (b) What is the conclusion, and what should be the next step?
   (c) Another researcher suggests that there may be a problem with this methodology since it assumes that the disturbances (u_t) are white noise. Suggest a possible source of difficulty and how the researcher might in practice get around it.

4. (a) Consider a series of values for the spot and futures prices of a given commodity. In the context of these series, explain the concept of cointegration. Discuss how a researcher might test for cointegration between the variables using the Engle–Granger approach. Explain also the steps involved in the formulation of an error correction model.
   (b) Give a further example from finance where cointegration between a set of variables may be expected. Explain, by reference to the implication of non-cointegration, why cointegration between the series might be expected.

5. (a) Briefly outline Johansen's methodology for testing for cointegration between a set of variables in the context of a VAR.

(b) A researcher uses the Johansen procedure and obtains the following test statistics (and critical values):

r	λ_{max}	95% critical value
0	38.962	33.178
1	29.148	27.169
2	16.304	20.278
3	8.861	14.036
4	1.994	3.962

Determine the number of cointegrating vectors.

(c) 'If two series are cointegrated, it is not possible to make inferences regarding the cointegrating relationship using the Engle–Granger technique since the residuals from the cointegrating regression are likely to be autocorrelated.' How does Johansen circumvent this problem to test hypotheses about the cointegrating relationship?

(d) Give one or more examples from the academic finance literature of where the Johansen systems technique has been employed. What were the main results and conclusions of this research?

(e) Compare the Johansen maximal eigenvalue test with the test based on the trace statistic. State clearly the null and alternative hypotheses in each case.

6. (a) Suppose that a researcher has a set of three variables, $y_t(t = 1, \ldots, T)$, i.e. y_t denotes a p-variate, or $p \times 1$ vector, that she wishes to test for the existence of cointegrating relationships using the Johansen procedure.

What is the implication of finding that the rank of the appropriate matrix takes on a value of

(i) 0   (ii) 1   (iii) 2   (iv) 3?

(b) The researcher obtains results for the Johansen test using the variables outlined in part (a) as follows:

r	λ_{max}	5% critical value
0	38.65	30.26
1	26.91	23.84
2	10.67	17.72
3	8.55	10.71

Determine the number of cointegrating vectors, explaining your answer.

7. Compare and contrast the Engle–Granger and Johansen methodologies for testing for cointegration and modelling cointegrated systems. Which, in your view, represents the superior approach and why?

8. In EViews, open the 'currencies.wf1' file that will be discussed in detail in the following chapter. Determine whether the exchange rate series (in their raw levels forms) are non-stationary. If that is the case, test for cointegration between them using both the Engle–Granger and Johansen approaches. Would you have expected the series to cointegrate? Why or why not?

9. (a) What issues arise when testing for a unit root if there is a structural break in the series under investigation?

   (b) What are the limitations of the Perron (1989) approach for dealing with structural breaks in testing for a unit root?

9 Modelling volatility and correlation

9.1 Motivations: an excursion into non-linearity land

All of the models that have been discussed in chapters 3–8 of this book have been linear in nature – that is, the model is linear in the parameters, so that there is one parameter multiplied by each variable in the model. For example, a structural model could be something like

$$y = \beta_1 + \beta_2 x_2 + \beta_3 x_3 + \beta_4 x_4 + u \tag{9.1}$$

or more compactly $y = X\beta + u$. It was additionally assumed that $u_t \sim N(0, \sigma^2)$.

The linear paradigm as described above is a useful one. The properties of linear estimators are very well researched and very well understood. Many models that appear, *prima facie*, to be non-linear, can be made linear by taking logarithms or some other suitable transformation. However, it is likely that many relationships in finance are intrinsically non-linear. As Campbell, Lo and MacKinlay (1997) state, the payoffs to options are non-linear in some of the input variables, and investors' willingness to trade off returns and risks are also non-linear. These observations provide clear motivations for consideration of non-linear models in a variety of circumstances in order to capture better the relevant features of the data.

Linear structural (and time series) models such as (9.1) are also unable to explain a number of important features common to much financial data, including:

- *Leptokurtosis* – that is, the tendency for financial asset returns to have distributions that exhibit fat tails and excess peakedness at the mean.
- *Volatility clustering or volatility pooling* – the tendency for volatility in financial markets to appear in bunches. Thus large returns (of either sign) are expected to follow large returns, and small returns (of either sign) to follow small returns. A plausible explanation for this phenomenon, which seems to be an almost universal feature of asset return series in finance, is that the information arrivals which drive price changes themselves occur in bunches rather than being evenly spaced over time.
- *Leverage effects* – the tendency for volatility to rise more following a large price fall than following a price rise of the same magnitude.

Campbell *et al.* (1997) broadly define a non-linear data generating process as one where the current value of the series is related non-linearly to current and previous values of the error term

$$y_t = f(u_t, u_{t-1}, u_{t-2}, \ldots) \tag{9.2}$$

where u_t is an iid error term and f is a non-linear function. According to Campbell *et al.*, a more workable and slightly more specific definition of a non-linear model is given by the equation

$$y_t = g(u_{t-1}, u_{t-2}, \ldots) + u_t \, \sigma^2(u_{t-1}, u_{t-2}, \ldots) \tag{9.3}$$

where g is a function of past error terms only, and σ^2 can be interpreted as a variance term, since it is multiplied by the current value of the error. Campbell *et al.* usefully characterise models with non-linear $g(\bullet)$ as being non-linear in mean, while those with non-linear $\sigma(\bullet)^2$ are characterised as being non-linear in variance.

Models can be linear in mean and variance (e.g. the CLRM, ARMA models) or linear in mean, but non-linear in variance (e.g. GARCH models). Models could also be classified as non-linear in mean but linear in variance (e.g. bicorrelations models, a simple example of which is of the following form (see Brooks and Hinich, 1999))

$$y_t = \alpha_0 + \alpha_1 y_{t-1} y_{t-2} + u_t \tag{9.4}$$

Finally, models can be non-linear in both mean and variance (e.g. the hybrid threshold model with GARCH errors employed by Brooks, 2001).

9.1.1 Types of non-linear models

There are an infinite number of different types of non-linear model. However, only a small number of non-linear models have been found to be useful for modelling financial data. The most popular non-linear financial models are the ARCH or GARCH models used for modelling and forecasting volatility, and switching models, which allow the behaviour of a series to follow different processes at different points in time. Models for volatility and correlation will be discussed in this chapter, with switching models being covered in chapter 10.

9.1.2 Testing for non-linearity

How can it be determined whether a non-linear model may potentially be appropriate for the data? The answer to this question should come at least in part from financial theory: a non-linear model should be used where financial theory suggests that the relationship between variables should be such as to require a non-linear model. But the linear versus non-linear choice may also be made partly on statistical grounds – deciding whether a linear specification is sufficient to describe all of the most important features of the data at hand.

So what tools are available to detect non-linear behaviour in financial time series? Unfortunately, 'traditional' tools of time series analysis (such as estimates of the autocorrelation or partial autocorrelation function, or 'spectral analysis', which involves looking at the data in the frequency domain) are likely to be of little use. Such tools may find no evidence of linear structure in the data, but this would not necessarily imply that the same observations are independent of one another.

However, there are a number of tests for non-linear patterns in time series that are available to the researcher. These tests can broadly be split into two types: general tests and specific tests. General tests, also sometimes called 'portmanteau' tests, are usually designed to detect many departures from randomness in data. The implication is that such tests will detect a variety of non-linear structures in data, although these tests are unlikely to tell the researcher which type of non-linearity is present! Perhaps the simplest general test for non-linearity is Ramsey's RESET test discussed in chapter 4, although there are many other popular tests available. One of the most widely used tests is known as the BDS test (see Brock *et al.*, 1996) named after the three authors who first developed it. BDS is a pure hypothesis test. That is, it has as its null hypothesis that the data are pure noise (completely random), and it has been argued to have power to detect a variety of departures from randomness – linear or non-linear stochastic processes, deterministic chaos, etc. (see Brock *et al.*, 1991). The BDS test follows a standard normal distribution under the null hypothesis. The details of this test, and others, are technical and beyond the scope of this book, although computer code for BDS estimation is now widely available free of charge on the internet.

As well as applying the BDS test to raw data in an attempt to 'see if there is anything there', another suggested use of the test is as a model diagnostic. The idea is that a proposed model (e.g. a linear model, GARCH, or some other non-linear model) is estimated, and the test applied to the (standardised) residuals in order to 'see what is left'. If the proposed model is adequate, the standardised residuals should be white noise, while if the postulated model is insufficient to capture all of the relevant features of the data, the BDS test statistic for the standardised residuals will be statistically significant. This is an excellent idea in theory, but has difficulties in practice. First, if the postulated model is a non-linear one (such as GARCH), the asymptotic distribution of the test statistic will be altered, so that it will no longer follow a normal distribution. This requires new critical values to be constructed via simulation for every type of non-linear model whose residuals are to be tested. More seriously, if a non-linear model is fitted to the data, any remaining structure is typically garbled, resulting in the test either being unable to detect additional structure present in the data (see Brooks and Henry, 2000) or selecting as adequate a model which is not even in the correct class for that data generating process (see Brooks and Heravi, 1999).

The BDS test is available in EViews. To run it on a given series, simply open the series to be tested (which may be a set of raw data or residuals from an estimated model) so that it appears as a spreadsheet. Then select the **View** menu and **BDS Independence Test . . . .** You will then be offered various options. Further details are given in the EViews *User's Guide.*

Other popular tests for non-linear structure in time series data include the bispectrum test due to Hinich (1982), the bicorrelation test (see Hsieh, 1993; Hinich, 1996; or Brooks and Hinich, 1999 for its multivariate generalisation).

Most applications of the above tests conclude that there is non-linear dependence in financial asset returns series, but that the dependence is best characterised by a GARCH-type process (see Hinich and Patterson, 1985; Baillie and Bollerslev, 1989; Brooks, 1996; and the references therein for applications of non-linearity tests to financial data).

Specific tests, on the other hand, are usually designed to have power to find specific types of non-linear structure. Specific tests are unlikely to detect other forms of non-linearities in the data, but their results will by definition offer a class of models that should be relevant for the data at hand. Examples of specific tests will be offered later in this and subsequent chapters.

9.1.3 Chaos in financial markets

Econometricians have searched long and hard for chaos in financial, macroeconomic and microeconomic data, with very limited success to date. *Chaos theory* is a notion taken from the physical sciences that suggests that there could be a deterministic, non-linear set of equations underlying the behaviour of financial series or markets. Such behaviour will appear completely random to the standard statistical tests developed for application to linear models. The motivation behind this endeavour is clear: a positive sighting of chaos implies that while, by definition, long-term forecasting would be futile, short-term forecastability and controllability are possible, at least in theory, since there is some deterministic structure underlying the data. Varying definitions of what actually constitutes chaos can be found in the literature, but a robust definition is that a system is chaotic if it exhibits sensitive dependence on initial conditions (SDIC). The concept of SDIC embodies the fundamental characteristic of chaotic systems that if an infinitesimal change is made to the initial conditions (the initial state of the system), then the corresponding change iterated through the system for some arbitrary length of time will grow exponentially. Although several statistics are commonly used to test for the presence of chaos, only one is arguably a true test for chaos, namely estimation of the largest Lyapunov exponent. The largest Lyapunov exponent measures the rate at which information is lost from a system. A positive largest Lyapunov exponent implies sensitive dependence, and therefore that evidence of chaos has been obtained. This has important implications for the predictability of the underlying system, since the fact that all initial conditions are in practice estimated with some error (owing either to measurement error or exogenous noise), will imply that long-term forecasting of the system is impossible as all useful information is likely to be lost in just a few time steps.

Chaos theory was hyped and embraced by both the academic literature and in financial markets worldwide in the 1980s. However, almost without exception, applications of chaos theory to financial markets have been unsuccessful. Consequently, although the ideas generate continued interest owing to the interesting mathematical properties and the possibility of finding a prediction holy grail, academic and practitioner interest in chaotic models for financial markets has arguably almost disappeared. The primary reason for the failure of the chaos theory approach appears to be the fact that financial markets are extremely complex, involving a very large number of different participants, each with different objectives and different sets of information – and, above all, each of whom are human with human emotions and irrationalities. The consequence of this is that financial and economic data are usually far noisier and 'more random' than data from other disciplines, making the specification of a deterministic model very much harder and possibly even futile.

9.1.4 Neural network models

Artificial neural networks (ANNs) are a class of models whose structure is broadly motivated by the way that *the brain performs computation*. ANNs have been widely employed in finance for tackling time series and classification problems. Recent applications have included forecasting financial asset returns, volatility, bankruptcy and takeover prediction. Applications are contained in the books by Trippi and Turban (1993), Van Eyden (1996) and Refenes (1995). A technical collection of papers on the econometric aspects of neural networks is given by White (1992), while an excellent general introduction and a description of the issues surrounding neural network model estimation and analysis is contained in Franses and van Dijk (2000).

Neural networks have virtually no theoretical motivation in finance (they are often termed a 'black box' technology), but owe their popularity to their ability to fit any functional relationship in the data to an arbitrary degree of accuracy. The most common class of ANN models in finance are known as *feedforward network models*. These have a set of inputs (akin to regressors) linked to one or more outputs (akin to the regressand) via one or more 'hidden' or intermediate layers. The size and number of hidden layers can be modified to give a closer or less close fit to the data sample, while a feedforward network with no hidden layers is simply a standard linear regression model.

Neural network models are likely to work best in situations where financial theory has virtually nothing to say about the likely functional form for the relationship between a set of variables. However, their popularity has arguably waned over the past five years or so as a consequence of several perceived problems with their employment. First, the coefficient estimates from neural networks do not have any real theoretical interpretation. Second, virtually no diagnostic or specification tests are available for estimated models to determine whether the model under consideration is adequate. Third, ANN models can provide excellent fits in-sample to a given set of 'training' data, but typically provide poor out-of-sample forecast accuracy. The latter result usually arises from the tendency of neural networks to fit closely to sample-specific data features and 'noise', and therefore their inability to generalise. Various methods of resolving this problem exist, including 'pruning' (removing some parts of the network) or the use of information criteria to guide the network size. Finally, the non-linear estimation of neural network models can be cumbersome and computationally time-intensive, particularly, for example, if the model must be estimated rolling through a sample to produce a series of one-step-ahead forecasts.

9.2 Models for volatility

Modelling and forecasting stock market volatility has been the subject of vast empirical and theoretical investigation over the past decade or so by academics and practitioners alike. There are a number of motivations for this line of inquiry. Arguably, volatility is one of the most important concepts in the whole of finance. Volatility, as measured by the standard deviation or variance of returns, is often used as a crude measure of the total risk of financial assets. Many value-at-risk models for measuring market risk require the estimation or forecast of a volatility parameter. The volatility of stock market prices also enters directly into the Black–Scholes formula for deriving the prices of traded options.

The next few sections will discuss various models that are appropriate to capture the stylised features of volatility, discussed below, that have been observed in the literature.

9.3 Historical volatility

The simplest model for volatility is the historical estimate. Historical volatility simply involves calculating the variance (or standard deviation) of returns in the usual way over some historical period, and this then becomes the volatility forecast for all future periods. The historical average variance (or standard deviation) was traditionally used as the volatility input to options pricing models, although there is a growing body of evidence suggesting that the use of volatility predicted from more sophisticated time series models will lead to more accurate option valuations (see, for example, Akgiray, 1989; or Chu and Freund, 1996). Historical volatility is still useful as a benchmark for comparing the forecasting ability of more complex time models.

9.4 Implied volatility models

All pricing models for financial options require a volatility estimate or forecast as an input. Given the price of a traded option obtained from transactions data, it is possible to determine the volatility forecast over the lifetime of the option implied by the option's valuation. For example, if the standard Black–Scholes model is used, the option price, the time to maturity, a risk-free rate of interest, the strike price and the current value of the underlying asset, are all either specified in the details of the options contracts or are available from market data. Therefore, given all of these quantities, it is possible to use a numerical procedure, such as the method of bisections or Newton–Raphson to derive the volatility implied by the option (see Watsham and Parramore, 2004). This implied volatility is the market's forecast of the volatility of underlying asset returns over the lifetime of the option.

9.5 Exponentially weighted moving average models

The exponentially weighted moving average (EWMA) is essentially a simple extension of the historical average volatility measure, which allows more recent observations to have a stronger impact on the forecast of volatility than older data points. Under an EWMA specification, the latest observation carries the largest weight, and weights associated with previous observations decline exponentially over time. This approach has two advantages over the simple historical model. First, volatility is in practice likely to be affected more by recent events, which carry more weight, than events further in the past. Second, the effect on volatility of a single given observation declines at an exponential rate as weights attached to recent events fall. On the other hand, the simple historical approach could lead to an abrupt change in volatility once the shock falls out of the measurement sample. And if the shock is still included in a relatively long measurement sample period, then an abnormally large observation will imply that the forecast will remain at an artificially high level even if the market is subsequently tranquil. The exponentially weighted moving average model can be expressed in several ways, e.g.

$$\sigma_t^2 = (1 - \lambda) \sum_{j=0}^{\infty} \lambda^j (r_{t-j} - \bar{r})^2 \tag{9.5}$$

where σ_t^2 is the estimate of the variance for period t, which also becomes the forecast of future volatility for all periods, $\bar{r}$ is the average return estimated over the observations and λ is the 'decay factor', which determines how much weight is given to recent versus older observations. The decay factor could be estimated, but in many studies is set at 0.94 as recommended by RiskMetrics, producers of popular risk measurement software. Note also that RiskMetrics and many academic papers assume that the average return, $\bar{r}$, is zero. For data that is of daily frequency or higher, this is not an unreasonable assumption, and is likely to lead to negligible loss of accuracy since it will typically be very small. Obviously, in practice, an infinite number of observations will not be available on the series, so that the sum in (9.5) must be truncated at some fixed lag. As with exponential smoothing models, the forecast from an EWMA model for all prediction horizons is the most recent weighted average estimate.

It is worth noting two important limitations of EWMA models. First, while there are several methods that could be used to compute the EWMA, the crucial element in each case is to remember that when the infinite sum in (9.5) is replaced with a finite sum of observable data, the weights from the given expression will now sum to less than one. In the case of small samples, this could make a large difference to the computed EWMA and thus a correction may be necessary. Second, most time series models, such as GARCH (see below), will have forecasts that tend towards the unconditional variance of the series as the prediction horizon increases. This is a good property for a volatility forecasting model to have, since it is well known that volatility series are 'mean-reverting'. This implies that if they are currently at a high level relative to their historic average, they will have a tendency to fall back towards their average level, while if they are at a low level relative to their historic average, they will have a tendency to rise back towards the average. This feature is accounted for in GARCH volatility forecasting models, but not by EWMAs.

9.6 Autoregressive volatility models

Autoregressive volatility models are a relatively simple example from the class of stochastic volatility specifications. The idea is that a time series of observations on some volatility proxy are obtained. The standard Box–Jenkins-type procedures for estimating autoregressive (or ARMA) models can then be applied to this series. If the quantity of interest in the study is a daily volatility estimate, two natural proxies have been employed in the literature: squared daily returns, or daily range estimators. Producing a series of daily squared returns trivially involves taking a column of observed returns and squaring each observation. The squared return at each point in time, t, then becomes the daily volatility estimate for day t. A range estimator typically involves calculating the log of the ratio of the highest observed price to the lowest observed price for trading day t, which then becomes the volatility estimate for day t

$$\sigma_t^2 = \log\left(\frac{high_t}{low_t}\right) \tag{9.6}$$

Given either the squared daily return or the range estimator, a standard autoregressive model is estimated, with the coefficients β_i estimated using OLS (or maximum likelihood – see below). The forecasts are also produced in the usual fashion discussed in chapter 6 in the context of ARMA models

$$\sigma_t^2 = \beta_0 + \sum_{j=1}^{p} \beta_j \sigma_{t-j}^2 + \varepsilon_t \tag{9.7}$$

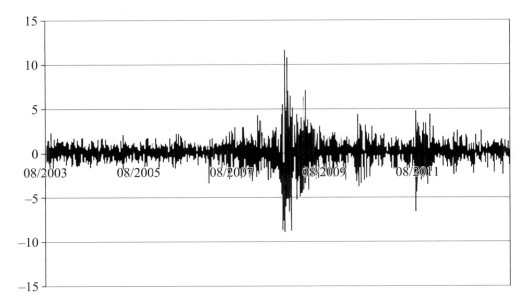

Figure 9.1   Daily S&P returns for August 2003–August 2013

Autoregressive conditionally heteroscedastic (ARCH) models

One particular non-linear model in widespread usage in finance is known as an 'ARCH' model (ARCH stands for 'autoregressive conditionally heteroscedastic'). To see why this class of models is useful, recall that a typical structural model could be expressed by an equation of the form given in (9.1) above with $u_t \sim N(0, \sigma^2)$. The assumption of the CLRM that the variance of the errors is constant is known as *homoscedasticity* (i.e. it is assumed that $\mathrm{var}(u_t) = \sigma^2$). If the variance of the errors is not constant, this would be known as *heteroscedasticity*. As was explained in chapter 5, if the errors are heteroscedastic, but assumed homoscedastic, an implication would be that standard error estimates could be wrong. It is unlikely in the context of financial time series that the variance of the errors will be constant over time, and hence it makes sense to consider a model that does not assume that the variance is constant, and which describes how the variance of the errors evolves.

Another important feature of many series of financial asset returns that provides a motivation for the ARCH class of models, is known as 'volatility clustering' or 'volatility pooling'. Volatility clustering describes the tendency of large changes in asset prices (of either sign) to follow large changes and small changes (of either sign) to follow small changes. In other words, the current level of volatility tends to be positively correlated with its level during the immediately preceding periods. This phenomenon is demonstrated in figure 9.1, which plots daily S&P500 returns for August 2003–August 2013.

The important point to note from figure 9.1 is that *volatility occurs in bursts*. There appears to have been a prolonged period of relative tranquillity in the market during the 2003 to 2008 period until the financial crisis began, evidenced by only relatively small positive and negative returns until that point. On the other hand, during mid-2008 to mid-2009, there was far more volatility, when many large positive and large negative returns were observed during a short space of time. Abusing the terminology slightly, it could be stated that 'volatility is autocorrelated'.

How could this phenomenon, which is common to many series of financial asset returns, be parameterised (modelled)? One approach is to use an ARCH model. To understand how the model works, a definition of the conditional variance of a random variable, u_t, is required. The distinction between the conditional and unconditional variances of a random variable is exactly the same as that of the conditional and unconditional mean. The conditional variance of u_t may be denoted σ_t^2, which is written as

$$\sigma_t^2 = \text{var}(u_t \mid u_{t-1}, u_{t-2}, \ldots) = E[(u_t - E(u_t))^2 \mid u_{t-1}, u_{t-2}, \ldots] \tag{9.8}$$

It is usually assumed that $E(u_t) = 0$, so

$$\sigma_t^2 = \text{var}(u_t \mid u_{t-1}, u_{t-2}, \ldots) = E\left[u_t^2 \mid u_{t-1}, u_{t-2}, \ldots\right] \tag{9.9}$$

Equation (9.9) states that the conditional variance of a zero mean normally distributed random variable u_t is equal to the conditional expected value of the square of u_t. Under the ARCH model, the 'autocorrelation in volatility' is modelled by allowing the conditional variance of the error term, σ_t^2, to depend on the immediately previous value of the squared error

$$\sigma_t^2 = \alpha_0 + \alpha_1 u_{t-1}^2 \tag{9.10}$$

The above model is known as an ARCH(1), since the conditional variance depends on only one lagged squared error. Notice that (9.10) is only a partial model, since nothing has been said yet about the conditional mean. Under ARCH, the conditional mean equation (which describes how the dependent variable, y_t, varies over time) could take almost any form that the researcher wishes. One example of a full model would be

$$y_t = \beta_1 + \beta_2 x_{2t} + \beta_3 x_{3t} + \beta_4 x_{4t} + u_t \qquad u_t \sim N\left(0, \sigma_t^2\right) \tag{9.11}$$

$$\sigma_t^2 = \alpha_0 + \alpha_1 u_{t-1}^2 \tag{9.12}$$

The model given by (9.11) and (9.12) could easily be extended to the general case where the error variance depends on q lags of squared errors, which would be known as an ARCH(q) model:

$$\sigma_t^2 = \alpha_0 + \alpha_1 u_{t-1}^2 + \alpha_2 u_{t-2}^2 + \cdots + \alpha_q u_{t-q}^2 \tag{9.13}$$

Instead of calling the conditional variance σ_t^2, in the literature it is often called h_t, so that the model would be written

$$y_t = \beta_1 + \beta_2 x_{2t} + \beta_3 x_{3t} + \beta_4 x_{4t} + u_t \qquad u_t \sim N(0, h_t) \tag{9.14}$$

$$h_t = \alpha_0 + \alpha_1 u_{t-1}^2 + \alpha_2 u_{t-2}^2 + \cdots + \alpha_q u_{t-q}^2 \tag{9.15}$$

The remainder of this chapter will use σ_t^2 to denote the conditional variance at time t, except for computer instructions where h_t will be used since it is easier not to use Greek letters.

9.7.1 Another way of expressing ARCH models

For illustration, consider an ARCH(1). The model can be expressed in two ways that look different but are in fact identical. The first is as given in (9.11) and (9.12) above. The second way would be as follows

$$y_t = \beta_1 + \beta_2 x_{2t} + \beta_3 x_{3t} + \beta_4 x_{4t} + u_t \tag{9.16}$$

$$u_t = v_t \sigma_t \qquad v_t \sim N(0, 1) \tag{9.17}$$

$$\sigma_t^2 = \alpha_0 + \alpha_1 u_{t-1}^2 \tag{9.18}$$

The form of the model given in (9.11) and (9.12) is more commonly presented, although specifying the model as in (9.16)–(9.18) is required in order to use a GARCH process in a simulation study (see chapter 13). To show that the two methods for expressing the model are equivalent, consider that in (9.17), v_t is normally distributed with zero mean and unit variance, so that u_t will also be normally distributed with zero mean and variance σ_t^2.

9.7.2 Non-negativity constraints

Since h_t is a conditional variance, its value must always be strictly positive; a negative variance at any point in time would be meaningless. The variables on the RHS of the conditional variance equation are all squares of lagged errors, and so by definition will not be negative. In order to ensure that these always result in positive conditional variance estimates, all of the coefficients in the conditional variance are usually required to be non-negative. If one or more of the coefficients were to take on a negative value, then for a sufficiently large lagged squared innovation term attached to that coefficient, the fitted value from the model for the conditional variance could be negative. This would clearly be nonsensical. So, for example, in the case of (9.18), the non-negativity condition would be $\alpha_0 \geq 0$ and $\alpha_1 \geq 0$. More generally, for an ARCH(q) model, all coefficients would be required to be non-negative: $\alpha_i \geq 0 \, \forall \, i = 0, 1, 2, \ldots, q$. In fact, this is a sufficient but not necessary condition for non-negativity of the conditional variance (i.e. it is a slightly stronger condition than is actually necessary).

9.7.3 Testing for 'ARCH effects'

A test for determining whether 'ARCH-effects' are present in the residuals of an estimated model may be conducted using the steps outlined in box 9.1.

Thus, the test is one of a joint null hypothesis that all q lags of the squared residuals have coefficient values that are not significantly different from zero. If

> **Box 9.1　Testing for 'ARCH effects'**
>
> (1) Run any postulated linear regression of the form given in the equation above, e.g.
>
> $$y_t = \beta_1 + \beta_2 x_{2t} + \beta_3 x_{3t} + \beta_4 x_{4t} + u_t \tag{9.19}$$
>
> saving the residuals, $\hat{u}_t$.
>
> (2) Square the residuals, and regress them on q own lags to test for ARCH of order q, i.e. run the regression
>
> $$\hat{u}_t^2 = \gamma_0 + \gamma_1 \hat{u}_{t-1}^2 + \gamma_2 \hat{u}_{t-2}^2 + \cdots + \gamma_q \hat{u}_{t-q}^2 + v_t \tag{9.20}$$
>
> where v_t is an error term.
> Obtain R^2 from this regression.
>
> (3) The test statistic is defined as TR^2 (the number of observations multiplied by the coefficient of multiple correlation) from the last regression, and is distributed as a $\chi^2(q)$.
>
> (4) The null and alternative hypotheses are
>
> $$H_0 : \gamma_1 = 0 \text{ and } \gamma_2 = 0 \text{ and } \gamma_3 = 0 \text{ and} \ldots \text{and } \gamma_q = 0$$
>
> $$H_1 : \gamma_1 \neq 0 \text{ or } \gamma_2 \neq 0 \text{ or } \gamma_3 \neq 0 \text{ or} \ldots \text{or } \gamma_q \neq 0$$

the value of the test statistic is greater than the critical value from the χ^2 distribution, then reject the null hypothesis. The test can also be thought of as a test for autocorrelation in the squared residuals. As well as testing the residuals of an estimated model, the ARCH test is frequently applied to raw returns data.

9.7.4　Testing for 'ARCH effects' in exchange rate returns using EViews

Before estimating a GARCH-type model, it is sensible first to compute the Engle (1982) test for ARCH effects to make sure that this class of models is appropriate for the data. This exercise (and the remaining exercises of this chapter), will employ returns on the daily exchange rates (the file is 'currencies.wf1') where there are 3,988 observations. Models of this kind are inevitably more data intensive than those based on simple linear regressions, and hence, everything else being equal, they work better when the data are sampled daily rather than at a lower frequency.

A test for the presence of ARCH in the residuals is calculated by regressing the squared residuals on a constant and p lags, where p is set by the user. As an example, assume that p is set to 5. The first step is to estimate a linear model so that the residuals can be tested for ARCH. From the main menu, select **Quick** and then select **Estimate Equation**. In the Equation Specification Editor, input **rgbp c ar(1) ma(1)** which will estimate an ARMA(1,1) for the pound-dollar returns.[1] Select the **Least Squares (NLA and ARMA)** procedure to estimate the model, using the whole sample period and press the **OK** button (output not shown).

The next step is to click on **View** from the Equation Window and to select **Residual Diagnostics** and then **Heteroskedasticity Tests . . . .** In the 'Test type' box, choose **ARCH** and the number of lags to include is **5**, and press **OK**. The output below shows the Engle test results. Both the *F*-version and the *LM*-statistic are very significant, suggesting the presence of ARCH in the pound–dollar returns.

Heteroskedasticity Test: ARCH

F-statistic	49.31597	Prob. F(5,1814)	0.0000
Obs*R-squared	232.5277	Prob. Chi-Square(5)	0.0000

Test Equation:
Dependent Variable: RESID^2
Method: Least Squares
Date: 08/06/13 Time: 07:35
Sample (adjusted): 6/06/2002 7/07/2007
Included observations: 3981 after adjustments

	Coefficient	Std. Error	t-Statistic	Prob.
C	0.109478	0.009717	11.26664	0.0000
RESID^2(-1)	0.117137	0.015797	7.414951	0.0000
RESID^2(-2)	0.126761	0.015896	7.974218	0.0000
RESID^2(-3)	0.043690	0.016007	2.729444	0.0064
RESID^2(-4)	0.035868	0.015895	2.256530	0.0241
RESID^2(-5)	0.089178	0.015774	5.653618	0.0000

R-squared	0.058409	Mean dependent var	0.186471
Adjusted R-squared	0.057225	S.D. dependent var	0.536205
S.E. of regression	0.520637	Akaike info criterion	1.533977
Sum squared resid	1077.473	Schwarz criterion	1.543456
Log likelihood	−3047.381	Hannan-Quinn criter.	1.537338
F-statistic	49.31597	Durbin-Watson stat	2.016422
Prob(F-statistic)	0.000020		

---

[1] Note that the (1,1) order has been chosen entirely arbitrarily at this stage. However, it is important to give some thought to the type and order of model used even if it is not of direct interest in the problem at hand (which will later be termed the 'conditional mean' equation), since the variance is measured around the mean and therefore any mis-specification in the mean is likely to lead to a mis-specified variance.

9.7.5 Limitations of ARCH(q) models

ARCH provided a framework for the analysis and development of time series models of volatility. However, ARCH models themselves have rarely been used in the last decade or more, since they bring with them a number of difficulties:

- How should *the value of q*, the number of lags of the squared residual in the model, be decided? One approach to this problem would be the use of a likelihood ratio test, discussed later in this chapter, although there is no clearly best approach.
- The value of q, the number of lags of the squared error that are required to capture all of the dependence in the conditional variance, might be *very large*. This would result in a large conditional variance model that was not parsimonious. Engle (1982) circumvented this problem by specifying an arbitrary linearly declining lag length on an ARCH(4)

$$\sigma_t^2 = \gamma_0 + \gamma_1\left(0.4\hat{u}_{t-1}^2 + 0.3\hat{u}_{t-2}^2 + 0.2\hat{u}_{t-3}^2 + 0.1\hat{u}_{t-4}^2\right) \tag{9.21}$$

such that only two parameters are required in the conditional variance equation (γ_0 and γ_1), rather than the five which would be required for an unrestricted ARCH(4).

- *Non-negativity constraints might be violated.* Everything else equal, the more parameters there are in the conditional variance equation, the more likely it is that one or more of them will have negative estimated values.

A natural extension of an ARCH(q) model which overcomes some of these problems is a GARCH model. In contrast with ARCH, GARCH models are extremely widely employed in practice.

9.8 Generalised ARCH (GARCH) models

The GARCH model was developed independently by Bollerslev (1986) and Taylor (1986). The GARCH model allows the conditional variance to be dependent upon previous own lags, so that the conditional variance equation in the simplest case is now

$$\sigma_t^2 = \alpha_0 + \alpha_1 u_{t-1}^2 + \beta\sigma_{t-1}^2 \tag{9.22}$$

This is a GARCH(1,1) model. σ_t^2 is known as the *conditional variance* since it is a one-period ahead estimate for the variance calculated based on any past information thought relevant. Using the GARCH model it is possible to interpret the current fitted variance, h_t, as a weighted function of a long-term average value (dependent on α_0), information about volatility during the previous period ($\alpha_1 u_{t-1}^2$) and the fitted variance from the model during the previous period ($\beta\sigma_{t-1}^2$). Note that the GARCH model can be expressed in a form that shows that it is effectively an ARMA model for the conditional variance. To see this, consider that the squared return at time t relative to the conditional variance is given by

$$\varepsilon_t = u_t^2 - \sigma_t^2 \tag{9.23}$$

or

$$\sigma_t^2 = u_t^2 - \varepsilon_t \tag{9.24}$$

Using the latter expression to substitute in for the conditional variance in (9.22)

$$u_t^2 - \varepsilon_t = \alpha_0 + \alpha_1 u_{t-1}^2 + \beta\left(u_{t-1}^2 - \varepsilon_{t-1}\right) \tag{9.25}$$

Rearranging

$$u_t^2 = \alpha_0 + \alpha_1 u_{t-1}^2 + \beta u_{t-1}^2 - \beta\varepsilon_{t-1} + \varepsilon_t \tag{9.26}$$

so that

$$u_t^2 = \alpha_0 + (\alpha_1 + \beta)u_{t-1}^2 - \beta\varepsilon_{t-1} + \varepsilon_t \tag{9.27}$$

This final expression is an ARMA(1,1) process for the squared errors.

Why is GARCH a better and therefore a far more widely used model than ARCH? The answer is that the former is more parsimonious, and avoids overfitting. Consequently, the model is less likely to breach non-negativity constraints. In order to illustrate why the model is parsimonious, first take the conditional variance equation in the GARCH(1,1) case, subtract 1 from each of the time subscripts of the conditional variance equation in (9.22), so that the following expression would be obtained

$$\sigma_{t-1}^2 = \alpha_0 + \alpha_1 u_{t-2}^2 + \beta\sigma_{t-2}^2 \tag{9.28}$$

and subtracting 1 from each of the time subscripts again

$$\sigma_{t-2}^2 = \alpha_0 + \alpha_1 u_{t-3}^2 + \beta\sigma_{t-3}^2 \tag{9.29}$$

Substituting into (9.22) for σ_{t-1}^2

$$\sigma_t^2 = \alpha_0 + \alpha_1 u_{t-1}^2 + \beta\left(\alpha_0 + \alpha_1 u_{t-2}^2 + \beta\sigma_{t-2}^2\right) \tag{9.30}$$

$$\sigma_t^2 = \alpha_0 + \alpha_1 u_{t-1}^2 + \alpha_0\beta + \alpha_1\beta u_{t-2}^2 + \beta^2\sigma_{t-2}^2 \tag{9.31}$$

Now substituting into (9.31) for σ_{t-2}^2

$$\sigma_t^2 = \alpha_0 + \alpha_1 u_{t-1}^2 + \alpha_0\beta + \alpha_1\beta u_{t-2}^2 + \beta^2\left(\alpha_0 + \alpha_1 u_{t-3}^2 + \beta\sigma_{t-3}^2\right) \tag{9.32}$$

$$\sigma_t^2 = \alpha_0 + \alpha_1 u_{t-1}^2 + \alpha_0\beta + \alpha_1\beta u_{t-2}^2 + \alpha_0\beta^2 + \alpha_1\beta^2 u_{t-3}^2 + \beta^3\sigma_{t-3}^2 \tag{9.33}$$

$$\sigma_t^2 = \alpha_0(1 + \beta + \beta^2) + \alpha_1 u_{t-1}^2(1 + \beta L + \beta^2 L^2) + \beta^3\sigma_{t-3}^2 \tag{9.34}$$

An infinite number of successive substitutions of this kind would yield

$$\sigma_t^2 = \alpha_0(1 + \beta + \beta^2 + \cdots) + \alpha_1 u_{t-1}^2(1 + \beta L + \beta^2 L^2 + \cdots) + \beta^\infty\sigma_0^2 \tag{9.35}$$

The first expression on the RHS of (9.35) is simply a constant, and as the number of observations tends to infinity, β^∞ will tend to zero. Hence, the GARCH(1,1) model can be written as

$$\sigma_t^2 = \gamma_0 + \alpha_1 u_{t-1}^2 (1 + \beta L + \beta^2 L^2 + \cdots) \tag{9.36}$$

$$= \gamma_0 + \gamma_1 u_{t-1}^2 + \gamma_2 u_{t-2}^2 + \cdots, \tag{9.37}$$

which is a restricted infinite order ARCH model. Thus the GARCH(1,1) model, containing only three parameters in the conditional variance equation, is a very parsimonious model, that allows an infinite number of past squared errors to influence the current conditional variance.

The GARCH(1,1) model can be extended to a GARCH(p,q) formulation, where the current conditional variance is parameterised to depend upon q lags of the squared error and p lags of the conditional variance

$$\sigma_t^2 = \alpha_0 + \alpha_1 u_{t-1}^2 + \alpha_2 u_{t-2}^2 + \cdots + \alpha_q u_{t-q}^2 + \beta_1 \sigma_{t-1}^2$$

$$+ \beta_2 \sigma_{t-2}^2 + \cdots + \beta_p \sigma_{t-p}^2 \tag{9.38}$$

$$\sigma_t^2 = \alpha_0 + \sum_{i=1}^{q} \alpha_i u_{t-i}^2 + \sum_{j=1}^{p} \beta_j \sigma_{t-j}^2 \tag{9.39}$$

But in general a GARCH(1,1) model will be sufficient to capture the volatility clustering in the data, and rarely is any higher order model estimated or even entertained in the academic finance literature.

9.8.1 The unconditional variance under a GARCH specification

The conditional variance is changing, but the unconditional variance of u_t is constant and given by

$$\text{var}(u_t) = \frac{\alpha_0}{1 - (\alpha_1 + \beta)} \tag{9.40}$$

so long as $\alpha_1 + \beta < 1$. For $\alpha_1 + \beta \geq 1$, the unconditional variance of u_t is not defined, and this would be termed 'non-stationarity in variance'. $\alpha_1 + \beta = 1$ would be known as a 'unit root in variance', also termed 'Integrated GARCH' or IGARCH. Non-stationarity in variance does not have a strong theoretical motivation for its existence, as would be the case for non-stationarity in the mean (e.g. of a price series). Furthermore, a GARCH model whose coefficients imply non-stationarity in variance would have some highly undesirable properties. One illustration of these relates to the forecasts of variance made from such models. For stationary GARCH models, conditional variance forecasts converge upon the long-term average value of the variance as the prediction horizon increases (see below). For IGARCH processes, this convergence will not happen, while for $\alpha_1 + \beta > 1$, the conditional variance forecast will tend to infinity as the forecast horizon increases.

> **Box 9.2 Estimating an ARCH or GARCH model**
>
> (1) Specify the appropriate equations for the mean and the variance – e.g. an AR(1)-GARCH(1,1) model
>
> $$y_t = \mu + \phi y_{t-1} + u_t, \; u_t \sim N(0, \sigma_t^2) \tag{9.41}$$
>
> $$\sigma_t^2 = \alpha_0 + \alpha_1 u_{t-1}^2 + \beta \sigma_{t-1}^2 \tag{9.42}$$
>
> (2) Specify the log-likelihood function (LLF) to maximise under a normality assumption for the disturbances
>
> $$L = -\frac{T}{2}\log(2\pi) - \frac{1}{2}\sum_{t=1}^{T}\log\left(\sigma_t^2\right) - \frac{1}{2}\sum_{t=1}^{T}(y_t - \mu - \phi y_{t-1})^2/\sigma_t^2 \tag{9.43}$$
>
> (3) The computer will maximise the function and generate parameter values that maximise the LLF and will construct their standard errors.

9.9 Estimation of ARCH/GARCH models

Since the model is no longer of the usual linear form, OLS cannot be used for GARCH model estimation. There are a variety of reasons for this, but the simplest and most fundamental is that OLS minimises the RSS. The RSS depends only on the parameters in the conditional mean equation, and not the conditional variance, and hence RSS minimisation is no longer an appropriate objective.

In order to estimate models from the GARCH family, another technique known as *maximum likelihood* is employed. Essentially, the method works by finding the most likely values of the parameters given the actual data. More specifically, a log-likelihood function (LLF) is formed and the values of the parameters that maximise it are sought. Maximum likelihood estimation can be employed to find parameter values for both linear and non-linear models. The steps involved in actually estimating an ARCH or GARCH model are shown in box 9.2. The following section will elaborate on points 2 and 3 presented in the box, explaining how the LLF is derived.

9.9.1 Parameter estimation using maximum likelihood

As stated above, under maximum likelihood estimation, a set of parameter values are chosen that are most likely to have produced the observed data. This is done by first forming a *likelihood function*, denoted LF. LF will be a multiplicative function of the actual data, which will consequently be difficult to maximise with respect to the parameters. Therefore, its logarithm is taken in order to turn LF into an additive function of the sample data, i.e. the *LLF*. A derivation of the maximum likelihood (ML) estimator in the context of the simple bivariate regression model with homoscedasticity is given in the appendix to this chapter. Essentially, deriving the ML estimators involves differentiating the *LLF* with respect to the parameters. But how does this help in estimating heteroscedastic models? How can the method outlined in the appendix for homoscedastic models be modified for application to GARCH model estimation?

In the context of conditional heteroscedasticity models, the model is $y_t = \mu + \phi y_{t-1} + u_t$, $u_t \sim N(0, \sigma_t^2)$, so that the variance of the errors has been modified from being assumed constant, σ^2, to being time-varying, σ_t^2, with the equation for the conditional variance as previously. The *LLF* relevant for a GARCH model can be constructed in the same way as for the homoscedastic case by replacing

$$\frac{T}{2} \log \sigma^2$$

with the equivalent for time-varying variance

$$\frac{1}{2} \sum_{t=1}^{T} \log \sigma_t^2$$

and replacing σ^2 in the denominator of the last part of the expression with σ_t^2 (see the appendix to this chapter). Derivation of this result from first principles is beyond the scope of this text, but the log-likelihood function for the above model with time-varying conditional variance and normally distributed errors is given by (9.43) in box 9.2.

Intuitively, maximising the *LLF* involves jointly minimising

$$\sum_{t=1}^{T} \log \sigma_t^2$$

and

$$\sum_{t=1}^{T} \frac{(y_t - \mu - \phi y_{t-1})^2}{\sigma_t^2}$$

(since these terms appear preceded with a negative sign in the *LLF*, and

$$-\frac{T}{2} \log(2\pi)$$

is just a constant with respect to the parameters). Minimising these terms jointly also implies minimising the error variance, as described in chapter 4. Unfortunately, maximising the *LLF* for a model with time-varying variances is trickier than in the homoscedastic case. Analytical derivatives of the *LLF* in (9.43) with respect to the parameters have been developed, but only in the context of the simplest examples of GARCH specifications. Moreover, the resulting formulae are complex, so a numerical procedure is often used instead to maximise the log-likelihood function.

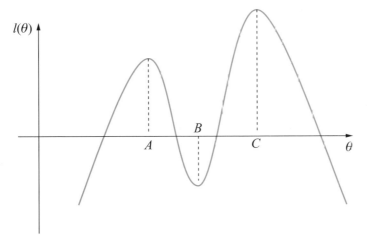

Figure 9.2 The problem of local optima in maximum likelihood estimation

Essentially, all methods work by 'searching' over the parameter-space until the values of the parameters that maximise the log-likelihood function are found. EViews employs an iterative technique for maximising the *LLF*. This means that, given a set of initial guesses for the parameter estimates, these parameter values are updated at each iteration until the program determines that an optimum has been reached. If the *LLF* has only one maximum with respect to the parameter values, any optimisation method should be able to find it – although some methods will take longer than others. A detailed presentation of the various methods available is beyond the scope of this book. However, as is often the case with non-linear models such as GARCH, the *LLF* can have many local maxima, so that different algorithms could find different local maxima of the *LLF*. Hence readers should be warned that different optimisation procedures could lead to different coefficient estimates and especially different estimates of the standard errors (see Brooks, Burke and Persand, 2001 or 2003 for details). In such instances, a good set of initial parameter guesses is essential.

Local optima or multimodalities in the likelihood surface present potentially serious drawbacks with the maximum likelihood approach to estimating the parameters of a GARCH model, as shown in figure 9.2.

Suppose that the model contains only one parameter, θ, so that the log-likelihood function is to be maximised with respect to this one parameter. In figure 9.2, the value of the *LLF* for each value of θ is denoted $l(\theta)$. Clearly, $l(\theta)$ reaches a global maximum when $\theta = C$, and a local maximum when $\theta = A$. This demonstrates the importance of good initial guesses for the parameters. Any initial guesses to the left of *B* are likely to lead to the selection of *A* rather than *C*. The situation is likely to be even worse in practice, since the log-likelihood function will be maximised with respect to several parameters, rather than one, and there could be many local optima. Another possibility that would make optimisation difficult is when the *LLF* is flat around the maximum. So, for example, if the peak corresponding to *C* in figure 9.2, were flat rather than sharp, a range of values

---

Box 9.3   Using maximum likelihood estimation in practice

(1) *Set up* the *LLF*.
(2) Use regression to get *initial estimates* for the mean parameters.
(3) Choose some initial guesses for the *conditional variance parameters*. In most software packages, the default initial values for the conditional variance parameters would be zero. This is unfortunate since zero parameter values often yield a local maximum of the likelihood function. So if possible, set plausible initial values away from zero.
(4) Specify a *convergence criterion* – either by criterion or by value. When 'by criterion' is selected, the package will continue to search for 'better' parameter values that give a higher value of the *LLF* until the change in the value of the *LLF* between iterations is less than the specified convergence criterion. Choosing 'by value' will lead to the software searching until the change in the coefficient estimates are small enough. The default convergence criterion for EViews is 0.001, which means that convergence is achieved and the program will stop searching if the biggest percentage change in any of the coefficient estimates for the most recent iteration is smaller than 0.1%.

---

for θ could lead to very similar values for the *LLF*, making it difficult to choose between them.

So, to explain again in more detail, the optimisation is done in the way shown in box 9.3. The optimisation methods employed by EViews are based on the determination of the first and second derivatives of the log-likelihood function with respect to the parameter values at each iteration, known as the gradient and Hessian (the matrix of second derivatives of the *LLF* w.r.t the parameters), respectively. An algorithm for optimisation due to Berndt, Hall, Hall and Hausman (1974), known as BHHH, is available in EViews. BHHH employs only first derivatives (calculated numerically rather than analytically) and approximations to the second derivatives are calculated. Not calculating the actual Hessian at each iteration at each time step increases computational speed, but the approximation may be poor when the *LLF* is a long way from its maximum value, requiring more iterations to reach the optimum. The Marquardt algorithm, available in EViews, is a modification of BHHH (both of which are variants on the Gauss–Newton method) that incorporates a 'correction', the effect of which is to push the coefficient estimates more quickly to their optimal values. All of these optimisation methods are described in detail in Press *et al.* (1992).

9.9.2   Non-normality and maximum likelihood

Recall that the conditional normality assumption for u_t is essential in specifying the likelihood function. It is possible to test for non-normality using the following representation

$$u_t = v_t \sigma_t, v_t \sim \text{N}(0, 1) \tag{9.44}$$

$$\sigma_t = \sqrt{\alpha_0 + \alpha_1 u_{t-1}^2 + \beta \sigma_{t-1}^2} \tag{9.45}$$

Note that one would not expect u_t to be normally distributed – it is a $\text{N}(0, \sigma_t^2)$ disturbance term from the regression model, which will imply it is likely to have fat tails. A plausible method to test for normality would be to construct the statistic

$$v_t = \frac{u_t}{\sigma_t} \tag{9.46}$$

which would be the model disturbance at each point in time t divided by the conditional standard deviation at that point in time. Thus, it is the v_t that are assumed to be normally distributed, not u_t. The sample counterpart would be

$$\hat{v}_t = \frac{\hat{u}_t}{\hat{\sigma}_t} \tag{9.47}$$

which is known as a standardised residual. Whether the $\hat{v}_t$ are normal can be examined using any standard normality test, such as the Bera–Jarque. Typically, $\hat{v}_t$ are still found to be leptokurtic, although less so than the $\hat{u}_t$. The upshot is that the GARCH model is able to capture some, although not all, of the leptokurtosis in the unconditional distribution of asset returns.

Is it a problem if $\hat{v}_t$ are not normally distributed? Well, the answer is 'not really'. Even if the conditional normality assumption does not hold, the parameter estimates will still be consistent if the equations for the mean and variance are correctly specified. However, in the context of non-normality, the usual standard error estimates will be inappropriate, and a different variance–covariance matrix estimator that is robust to non-normality, due to Bollerslev and Wooldridge (1992), should be used. This procedure (i.e. maximum likelihood with Bollerslev–Wooldridge standard errors) is known as *quasi-maximum likelihood*, or QML.

9.9.3 Estimating GARCH models in EViews

To estimate a GARCH-type model, open the equation specification dialog box by selecting **Quick/Estimate Equation** or by selecting **Object/New Object/Equation . . . .** Select **ARCH** from the 'Estimation Settings Method' selection box. The window in screenshot 9.1 will open.

It is necessary to specify both the mean and the variance equations, as well as the estimation technique and sample.

The mean equation

The specification of the mean equation should be entered in the dependent variable edit box. Enter the specification by listing the dependent variable followed by the regressors. The constant term 'C' should also be included. If your specification includes an ARCH-M term (see later in this chapter), you should click on the

Screenshot 9.1   **Estimating a GARCH-type model**

appropriate button in the upper RHS of the dialog box to select the conditional standard deviation, the conditional variance, or the log of the conditional variance.

The variance equation

The edit box labelled 'Variance regressors' is where variables that are to be included in the variance specification should be listed. Note that EViews will always include a constant in the conditional variance, so that it is not necessary to add 'C' to the variance regressor list. Similarly, it is not necessary to include the ARCH or GARCH terms in this box as they will be dealt with in other parts of the dialog box. Instead, enter here any exogenous variables or dummies that you wish to include in the conditional variance equation, or (as is usually the case), just leave this box blank.

Variance and distribution specification

Under the 'Variance and distribution Specification' label, choose the number of ARCH and GARCH terms. The default is to estimate with one ARCH and one GARCH term (i.e. one lag of the squared errors and one lag of the conditional variance, respectively). To estimate the standard GARCH model, leave the default

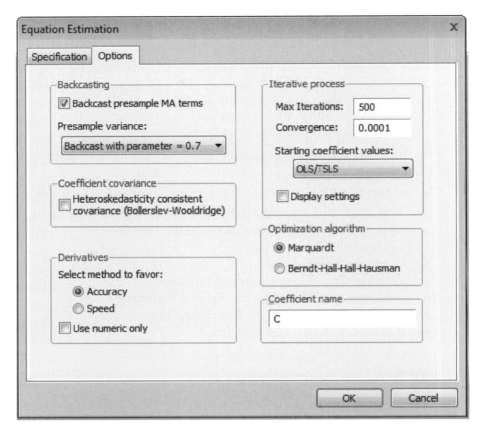

Screenshot 9.2   **GARCH model estimation options**

'GARCH/TARCH'. The other entries in this box describe more complicated variants of the standard GARCH specification, which are described in later sections of this chapter.

Estimation options

EViews provides a number of optional estimation settings. Clicking on the Options tab gives the options in screenshot 9.2 to be filled out as required. The Heteroskedasticity Consistent Covariance option is used to compute the QML covariances and standard errors using the methods described by Bollerslev and Wooldridge (1992). This option should be used if you suspect that the residuals are not conditionally normally distributed. Note that the parameter estimates will be (virtually) unchanged if this option is selected; only the estimated covariance matrix will be altered.

The log-likelihood functions for ARCH models are often not well behaved so that convergence may not be achieved with the default estimation settings. It is possible in EViews to select the iterative algorithm (Marquardt, BHHH/Gauss Newton), to change starting values, to increase the maximum number of iterations or to adjust the convergence criteria. For example, if convergence is not achieved, or implausible parameter estimates are obtained, it is sensible to re-do the estimation using a different set of starting values and/or a different optimisation algorithm.

Once the model has been estimated, EViews provides a variety of pieces of information and procedures for inference and diagnostic checking. For example, the following options are available on the View button:

- Actual, Fitted, Residual
  The residuals are displayed in various forms, such as table, graphs and standardised residuals.
- GARCH graph
  This graph plots the one-step ahead standard deviation, σ_t, or the conditional variance, σ_t^2 for each observation in the sample.
- Covariance Matrix
- Coefficient Tests
- Residual Tests/Correlogram-Q statistics
- Residual Tests/Correlogram Squared Residuals
- Residual Tests/Histogram-Normality Test
- Residual Tests/ARCH LM Test.

ARCH model procedures

These options are all available by pressing the 'Proc' button following the estimation of a GARCH-type model:

- Make Residual Series
- Make GARCH Variance Series
- Forecast.

Estimating the GARCH(1,1) model for the yen–dollar ('rjpy') series using the instructions as listed above, and the default settings elsewhere would yield the results on the following page.

The coefficients on both the lagged squared residual and lagged conditional variance terms in the conditional variance equation are highly statistically significant. Also, as is typical of GARCH model estimates for financial asset returns data, the sum of the coefficients on the lagged squared error and lagged conditional variance is very close to unity (approximately 0.98). This implies that shocks to the conditional variance will be highly persistent. This can be seen by considering the equations for forecasting future values of the conditional variance using a GARCH model given in a subsequent section. A large sum of these coefficients will imply that a large positive or a large negative return will lead future forecasts of the variance to be high for a protracted period. The individual conditional variance coefficients are also as one would expect. The variance intercept term 'C' is very small, and the 'ARCH parameter' is around 0.05 while the coefficient on the lagged conditional variance ('GARCH') is larger at 0.93.

Dependent Variable: RJPY
Method: ML – ARCH (Marquardt) – Normal distribution
Date: 08/06/13 Time: 18:02
Sample (adjusted): 7/08/2002 6/06/2013
Included observations: 3987 after adjustments
Convergence achieved after 24 iterations
Presample variance: backcast (parameter = 0.7)
GARCH = C(2) + C(3)*RESID(−1)^2 + C(4)*GARCH(−1)

	Coefficient	Std. Error	z-Statistic	Prob.
C	0.002664	0.006491	0.410491	0.6814

Variance Equation				
C	0.004404	0.000453	9.713821	0.0000
RESID(−1)^2	0.046623	0.003476	13.41392	0.0000
GARCH(−1)	0.933667	0.005074	184.0124	0.0000

R-squared	−0.000243	Mean depencent var	−0.004699
Adjusted R-squared	−0.000243	S.D. dependent var	0.471950
S.E. of regression	0.472008	Akaike info criterion	1.235623
Sum squared resid	888.0459	Schwarz criterion	1.241935
Log likelihood	−2459.215	Hannan-Quinn criter.	1.237861
Durbin-Watson stat	1.705253		

9.10   Extensions to the basic GARCH model

Since the GARCH model was developed, a huge number of extensions and variants have been proposed. A couple of the most important examples will be highlighted here. Interested readers who wish to investigate further are directed to a comprehensive survey by Bollerslev et al. (1992).

Many of the extensions to the GARCH model have been suggested as a consequence of perceived problems with standard GARCH(p, q) models. First, the non-negativity conditions may be violated by the estimated model. The only way to avoid this for sure would be to place artificial constraints on the model coefficients in order to force them to be non-negative Second, GARCH models cannot account for leverage effects (explained below), although they can account for volatility clustering and leptokurtosis in a series. Finally, the model does not allow for any direct feedback between the conditional variance and the conditional mean.

Some of the most widely used and influential modifications to the model will now be examined. These may remove some of the restrictions or limitations of the basic model.

9.11 Asymmetric GARCH models

One of the primary restrictions of GARCH models is that they enforce a symmetric response of volatility to positive and negative shocks. This arises since the conditional variance in equations such as (9.39) is a function of the magnitudes of the lagged residuals and not their signs (in other words, by squaring the lagged error in (9.39), the sign is lost). However, it has been argued that a negative shock to financial time series is likely to cause volatility to rise by more than a positive shock of the same magnitude. In the case of equity returns, such asymmetries are typically attributed to *leverage effects*, whereby a fall in the value of a firm's stock causes the firm's debt to equity ratio to rise. This leads shareholders, who bear the residual risk of the firm, to perceive their future cashflow stream as being relatively more risky.

An alternative view is provided by the 'volatility-feedback' hypothesis. Assuming constant dividends, if expected returns increase when stock price volatility increases, then stock prices should fall when volatility rises. Although asymmetries in returns series other than equities cannot be attributed to changing leverage, there is equally no reason to suppose that such asymmetries only exist in equity returns.

Two popular asymmetric formulations are explained below: the GJR model, named after the authors Glosten, Jagannathan and Runkle (1993), and the exponential GARCH (EGARCH) model proposed by Nelson (1991).

9.12 The GJR model

The GJR model is a simple extension of GARCH with an additional term added to account for possible asymmetries. The conditional variance is now given by

$$\sigma_t^2 = \alpha_0 + \alpha_1 u_{t-1}^2 + \beta\sigma_{t-1}^2 + \gamma u_{t-1}^2 I_{t-1} \tag{9.48}$$

where $I_{t-1} = 1$ if $u_{t-1} < 0$
$\qquad\quad\; = 0$ otherwise

For a leverage effect, we would see $\gamma > 0$. Notice now that the condition for non-negativity will be $\alpha_0 > 0$, $\alpha_1 > 0$, $\beta \geq 0$, and $\alpha_1 + \gamma \geq 0$. That is, the model is still admissible, even if $\gamma < 0$, provided that $\alpha_1 + \gamma \geq 0$.

Example 9.1

To offer an illustration of the GJR approach, using monthly S&P500 returns from December 1979 until June 1998, the following results would be obtained, with t-ratios in parentheses

$$y_t = 0.172 \tag{9.49}$$

$$(3.198)$$

$$\sigma_t^2 = 1.243 + 0.015u_{t-1}^2 + 0.498\sigma_{t-1}^2 + 0.604u_{t-1}^2 I_{t-1} \tag{9.50}$$

$$(16.372) \quad (0.437) \quad (14.999) \quad (5.772)$$

Note that the asymmetry term, γ, has the correct sign and is significant. To see how volatility rises more after a large negative shock than a large positive one, suppose that $\sigma_{t-1}^2 = 0.823$, and consider $\hat{u}_{t-1} = \pm 0.5$. If $\hat{u}_{t-1} = 0.5$, this implies that $\sigma_t^2 = 1.65$. However, a shock of the same magnitude but of opposite sign, $\hat{u}_{t-1} = -0.5$, implies that the fitted conditional variance for time t will be $\sigma_t^2 = 1.80$.

9.13 The EGARCH model

The exponential GARCH model was proposed by Nelson (1991). There are various ways to express the conditional variance equation, but one possible specification is given by

$$\ln(\sigma_t^2) = \omega + \beta \ln(\sigma_{t-1}^2) + \gamma \frac{u_{t-1}}{\sqrt{\sigma_{t-1}^2}} + \alpha \left[\frac{|u_{t-1}|}{\sqrt{\sigma_{t-1}^2}} - \sqrt{\frac{2}{\pi}} \right] \tag{9.51}$$

The model has several advantages over the pure GARCH specification. First, since the $\log(\sigma_t^2)$ is modelled, then even if the parameters are negative, σ_t^2 will be positive. There is thus no need to artificially impose non-negativity constraints on the model parameters. Second, asymmetries are allowed for under the EGARCH formulation, since if the relationship between volatility and returns is negative, γ, will be negative.

Note that in the original formulation, Nelson assumed a generalised error distribution (GED) structure for the errors. GED is a very broad family of distributions that can be used for many types of series. However, owing to its computational ease and intuitive interpretation, almost all applications of EGARCH employ conditionally normal errors as discussed above rather than using GED.

9.14 GJR and EGARCH in EViews

The main menu screen for GARCH estimation demonstrates that a number of variants on the standard GARCH model are available. Arguably most important of these are asymmetric models, such as the TGARCH ('threshold' GARCH), which is also known as the GJR model, and the EGARCH model. To estimate a GJR model in EViews, from the GARCH model equation specification screen (screenshot 9.1 above), change the 'Threshold Order' number from 0 to 1. To estimate an EGARCH model, **change the 'GARCH/TARCH' model estimation default to 'EGARCH'**.

Coefficient estimates for each of these specifications using the daily Japanese yen–US dollar returns data are given in the next two output tables, respectively. For the GJR specification, the asymmetry term ('(RESID(−1)∧2*RESID(−1)<0)') is positive and highly significant, while for the EGARCH model, the estimate on

'RESID(−1)/SQRT(GARCH(−1))' is highly significant but has a negative sign. So for the GJR model, the estimate indicates that negative shocks imply a higher next period conditional variance than negative shocks of the same sign, whereas the opposite is true for the EGARCH. Clearly, then, we must exercise caution when interpreting the estimates from GARCH-type models since the optimisation routine converged on an optimum in both cases and the estimates appear to be otherwise entirely plausible.

Dependent Variable: RJPY
Method: ML – ARCH (Marquardt) – Normal distribution
Date: 08/06/13   Time: 13:23
Sample (adjusted): 7/08/2002 6/06/2013
Included observations: 3987 after adjustments
Convergence achieved after 21 iterations
Presample variance: backcast (parameter = 0.7)
GARCH = C(2) + C(3)*RESID(−1)^2 + C(4)*RESID(−1)^2*(RESID(−1)<0)
　　　　+ C(5)*GARCH(−1)

	Coefficient	Std. Error	z-Statistic	Prob.
C	−0.001220	0.006679	−0.182713	0.8550
Variance Equation				
C	0.003897	0.000445	8.766881	0.0000
RESID(−1)^2	0.024975	0.003703	6.743803	0.0000
RESID(−1)^2*(RESID(-1)<0)	0.038199	0.004978	7.673294	0.0000
GARCH(−1)	0.938557	0.005137	182.7135	0.0000
R-squared	−0.000054	Mean dependent var		−0.004699
Adjusted R-squared	−0.000054	S.D. dependent var		0.471950
S.E. of regression	0.471963	Akaike info criterion		1.229490
Sum squared resid	887.8779	Schwarz criterion		1.237379
Log likelihood	−2445.989	Hannan-Quinn criter.		1.232287
Durbin-Watson stat	1.705575			

The result for the EGARCH asymmetry term is the opposite to what would have been expected in the case of the application of a GARCH model to a set of stock returns. But arguably, neither the *leverage effect* or *volatility feedback* explanations for asymmetries in the context of stocks apply here. For a positive return shock, this implies more yen per dollar and therefore a strengthening dollar and a weakening yen. Thus the EGARCH results suggest that a strengthening dollar (weakening yen) leads to higher next period volatility than when the yen strengthens by the same amount (vice versa for the GJR).

Dependent Variable: RJPY
Method: ML – ARCH (Marquardt) – Normal distribution
Date: 08/06/13 Time: 13:32
Sample (adjusted): 7/08/2002 6/06/2013
Included observations: 3987 after adjustments
Convergence achieved after 41 iterations
Presample variance: backcast (parameter = 0.7)
LOG(GARCH) = C(2) + C(3)*ABS(RESID(−1)/ SQRT(GARCH(−1)))
    + C(4)*RESID(−1)/ SQRT(GARCH(−1)) + C(5)*LOG(GARCH(−1))

	Coefficient	Std. Error	z-Statistic	Prob.
C	−0.001259	0.006459	−0.194903	0.8455
Variance Equation				
C(2)	−0.107729	0.008416	−12.80063	0.0000
C(3)	0.107247	0.007361	14.56981	0.0000
C(4)	−0.037184	0.004177	−8.903008	0.0000
C(5)	0.979445	0.002483	393.6791	0.0000
R-squared	−0.000053	Mean dependent var		−0.004699
Adjusted R-squared	−0.000053	S.D. dependent var		0.471950
S.E. of regression	0.471963	Akaike info criterion		1.227398
Sum squared resid	887.8769	Schwarz criterion		1.235287
Log likelihood	−2441.818	Hannan-Quinn criter.		1.230195
Durbin-Watson stat	1.705577			

9.15 Tests for asymmetries in volatility

Engle and Ng (1993) have proposed a set of tests for asymmetry in volatility, known as sign and size bias tests. The Engle and Ng tests should thus be used to determine whether an asymmetric model is required for a given series, or whether the symmetric GARCH model can be deemed adequate. In practice, the Engle–Ng tests are usually applied to the residuals of a GARCH fit to the returns data. Define S_{t-1}^- as an indicator dummy that takes the value 1 if $\hat{u}_{t-1} < 0$ and zero otherwise. The test for sign bias is based on the significance or otherwise of ϕ_1 in

$$\hat{u}_t^2 = \phi_0 + \phi_1 S_{t-1}^- + v_t \tag{9.52}$$

where v_t is an iid error term. If positive and negative shocks to $\hat{u}_{t-1}$ impact differently upon the conditional variance, then ϕ_1 will be statistically significant.

It could also be the case that the magnitude or size of the shock will affect whether the response of volatility to shocks is symmetric or not. In this case, a negative size bias test would be conducted, based on a regression where S_{t-1}^- is now used as a slope dummy variable. Negative size bias is argued to be present if ϕ_1 is statistically significant in the regression

$$\hat{u}_t^2 = \phi_0 + \phi_1 S_{t-1}^- u_{t-1} + v_t \tag{9.53}$$

Finally, defining $S_{t-1}^+ = 1 - S_{t-1}^-$, so that S_{t-1}^+ picks out the observations with positive innovations, Engle and Ng propose a joint test for sign and size bias based on the regression

$$\hat{u}_t^2 = \phi_0 + \phi_1 S_{t-1}^- + \phi_2 S_{t-1}^- u_{t-1} + \phi_3 S_{t-1}^+ u_{t-1} + v_t \tag{9.54}$$

Significance of ϕ_1 indicates the presence of sign bias, where positive and negative shocks have differing impacts upon future volatility, compared with the symmetric response required by the standard GARCH formulation. On the other hand, the significance of ϕ_2 or ϕ_3 would suggest the presence of size bias, where not only the sign but the magnitude of the shock is important. A joint test statistic is formulated in the standard fashion by calculating TR^2 from regression (9.54), which will asymptotically follow a χ^2 distribution with three degrees of freedom under the null hypothesis of no asymmetric effects.

9.15.1 News impact curves

A pictorial representation of the degree of asymmetry of volatility to positive and negative shocks is given by the news impact curve introduced by Pagan and Schwert (1990). The news impact curve plots the next-period volatility (σ_t^2) that would arise from various positive and negative values of u_{t-1}, given an estimated model. The curves are drawn by using the estimated conditional variance equation for the model under consideration, with its given coefficient estimates, and with the lagged conditional variance set to the unconditional variance. Then, successive values of u_{t-1} are used in the equation to determine what the corresponding values of σ_t^2 derived from the model would be. For example, consider the GARCH and GJR model estimates given above for the S&P500 data from EViews. Values of u_{t-1} in the range $(-1, +1)$ are substituted into the equations in each case to investigate the impact on the conditional variance during the next period. The resulting news impact curves for the GARCH and GJR models are given in figure 9.3.

As can be seen from figure 9.3, the GARCH news impact curve (the grey line) is of course symmetrical about zero, so that a shock of given magnitude will have the same impact on the future conditional variance whatever its sign. On the other hand, the GJR news impact curve (the black line) is asymmetric, with negative shocks having more impact on future volatility than positive shocks of the same magnitude. It can also be seen that a negative shock of given magnitude will have a bigger impact under GJR than would be implied by a GARCH model, while a positive shock of given magnitude will have more impact under GARCH than GJR. The latter result arises as a result of the reduction in the value of α_1, the coefficient on the lagged squared error, when the asymmetry term is included in the model.

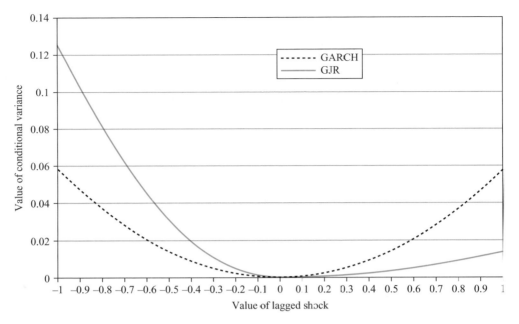

Figure 9.3   News impact curves for S&P500 returns using coefficients implied from GARCH and GJR model estimates

9.16 GARCH-in-mean

Most models used in finance suppose that investors should be rewarded for taking additional risk by obtaining a higher return. One way to operationalise this concept is to let the return of a security be partly determined by its risk. Engle, Lilien and Robins (1987) suggested an ARCH–M specification, where the conditional variance of asset returns enters into the conditional mean equation. Since GARCH models are now considerably more popular than ARCH, it is more common to estimate a GARCH-M model. An example of a GARCH-M model is given by the specification

$$y_t = \mu + \delta\sigma_{t-1} + u_t, \ u_t \sim N\left(0, \sigma_t^2\right) \tag{9.55}$$

$$\sigma_t^2 = \alpha_0 + \alpha_1 u_{t-1}^2 + \beta\sigma_{t-1}^2 \tag{9.56}$$

If δ is positive and statistically significant, then increased risk, given by an increase in the conditional variance, leads to a rise in the mean return. Thus δ can be interpreted as a risk premium. In some empirical applications, the conditional variance term, σ_{t-1}^2, appears directly in the conditional mean equation, rather than in square root form, σ_{t-1}. Also, in some applications the term is contemporaneous, σ_t^2, rather than lagged.

9.16.1 GARCH-M estimation in EViews

The GARCH–M model with the conditional standard deviation term in the mean, estimated using the rjpy data in EViews from the main GARCH menu as described above, with no asymmetries would give the following results:

Dependent Variable: RJPY
Method: ML – ARCH (Marquardt) – Normal distribution
Date: 08/06/13 Time: 16:06
Sample (adjusted): 7/08/2002 6/06/2013
Included observations: 3987 after adjustments
Convergence achieved after 28 iterations
Presample variance: backcast (parameter = 0.7)
GARCH = C(3) + C(4)*RESID(−1)^2 + C(5)*GARCH(−1)

	Coefficient	Std. Error	z-Statistic	Prob.
SQRT(GARCH)	−0.052260	0.076468	−0.683433	0.4943
C	0.024755	0.032632	0.758621	0.4481
Variance Equation				
C	0.004326	0.000457	9.461929	0.0000
RESID(−1)^2	0.046511	0.003485	13.34539	0.0000
GARCH(−1)	0.934156	0.005041	185.3095	0.0000
R-squared	−0.000344	Mean dependent var		−0.004699
Adjusted R-squared	−0.000595	S.D. dependent var		0.471950
S.E. of regression	0.472091	Akaike info criterion		1.236012
Sum squared resid	888.1354	Schwarz criterion		1.243901
Log likelihood	−2458.989	Hannan-Quinn criter.		1.238809
Durbin-Watson stat	1.705155			

In this case, the estimated parameter on the mean equation has a negative sign but is not statistically significant. We would thus conclude that for these currency returns, there is no feedback from the conditional variance to the conditional mean.

9.17 Uses of GARCH-type models including volatility forecasting

Essentially GARCH models are useful because they can be used to model the volatility of a series over time. It is possible to combine together more than one of the time series models that have been considered so far in this book, to obtain more complex 'hybrid' models. Such models can account for a number of important features of financial series at the same time – e.g. an ARMA–EGARCH(1,1)-M model; the potential complexity of the model is limited only by the imagination!

GARCH-type models can be used to forecast volatility. GARCH is a model to describe movements in the conditional variance of an error term, u_t, which may not appear particularly useful. But it is possible to show that

$$\text{var}\,(y_t \mid y_{t-1}, y_{t-2}, \ldots) = \text{var}\,(u_t \mid u_{t-1}, u_{t-2}, \ldots) \tag{9.57}$$

So the conditional variance of y, given its previous values, is the same as the conditional variance of u, given its previous values. Hence, modelling σ_t^2 will give models and forecasts for the variance of y_t as well. Thus, if the dependent variable in a regression, y_t is an asset return series, forecasts of σ_t^2 will be forecasts of the future variance of y_t. So one primary usage of GARCH-type models is in forecasting volatility. This can be useful in, for example, the pricing of financial options where volatility is an input to the pricing model. For example, the value of a 'plain vanilla' call option is a function of the current value of the underlying, the strike price, the time to maturity, the risk free interest rate and volatility. The required volatility, to obtain an appropriate options price, is really the volatility of the underlying asset expected over the lifetime of the option. As stated previously, it is possible to use a simple historical average measure as the forecast of future volatility, but another method that seems more appropriate would be to use a time series model such as GARCH to compute the volatility forecasts. The forecasting ability of various models is considered in a paper by Day and Lewis (1992), discussed in detail below.

Producing forecasts from models of the GARCH class is relatively simple, and the algebra involved is very similar to that required to obtain forecasts from ARMA models. An illustration is given by example 9.2.

Example 9.2

Consider the following GARCH(1,1) model

$$y_t = \mu + u_t,\, u_t \sim \text{N}(0, \sigma_t^2) \tag{9.58}$$

$$\sigma_t^2 = \alpha_0 + \alpha_1 u_{t-1}^2 + \beta \sigma_{t-1}^2 \tag{9.59}$$

Suppose that the researcher had estimated the above GARCH model for a series of returns on a stock index and obtained the following parameter estimates: $\hat{\mu} = 0.0023$, $\hat{\alpha}_0 = 0.0172$, $\hat{\beta} = 0.7811$, $\hat{\alpha}_1 = 0.1251$. If the researcher has data available up to and including time T, write down a set of equations in σ_t^2 and u_t^2 and their lagged values, which could be employed to produce one-, two-, and three-step-ahead forecasts for the conditional variance of y_t.

What is needed is to generate forecasts of $\sigma_{T+1}^2 \mid \Omega_T,\, \sigma_{T+2}^2 \mid \Omega_T, \ldots, \sigma_{T+s}^2 \mid \Omega_T$ where Ω_T denotes all information available up to and including observation T. For time T, the conditional variance equation is given by (9.59). Adding one to each of the time subscripts of this equation, and then two, and then three would yield equations

(9.60)–(9.62)

$$\sigma_{T+1}{}^2 = \alpha_0 + \alpha_1 u_T^2 + \beta \sigma_T^2 \tag{9.60}$$

$$\sigma_{T+2}{}^2 = \alpha_0 + \alpha_1 u_{T+1}^2 + \beta \sigma_{T+1}^2 \tag{9.61}$$

$$\sigma_{T+3}{}^2 = \alpha_0 + \alpha_1 u_{T+2}^2 + \beta \sigma_{T+2}^2 \tag{9.62}$$

Let $\sigma_{1,T}^{f2}$ be the one-step-ahead forecast for σ^2 made at time T. This is easy to calculate since, at time T, the values of all the terms on the RHS are known. $\sigma_{1,T}^{f2}$ would be obtained by taking the conditional expectation of (9.60).

Given $\sigma_{1,T}^{f2}$, how is $\sigma_{2,T}^{f2}$, the two-step-ahead forecast for σ^2 made at time T, calculated?

$$\sigma_{1,T}^{f2} = \alpha_0 + \alpha_1 u_T^2 + \beta \sigma_T^2 \tag{9.63}$$

From (9.61), it is possible to write

$$\sigma_{2,T}^{f2} = \alpha_0 + \alpha_1 \mathrm{E}(u_{T+1}^2 \mid \Omega_T) + \beta \sigma_{1,T}^{f2} \tag{9.64}$$

where $\mathrm{E}(u_{T+1}^2 \mid \Omega_T)$ is the expectation, made at time T, of u_{T+1}^2, which is the squared disturbance term. It is necessary to find $\mathrm{E}(u_{T+1}^2 \mid \Omega_T)$, using the expression for the variance of a random variable u_t. The model assumes that the series u_t has zero mean, so that the variance can be written

$$\mathrm{var}\,(u_t) = \mathrm{E}[(u_t - \mathrm{E}(u_t))^2] = \mathrm{E}\big(u_t^2\big). \tag{9.65}$$

The conditional variance of u_t is σ_t^2, so

$$\sigma_t^2 \mid \Omega_t = \mathrm{E}(u_t)^2 \tag{9.66}$$

Turning this argument around, and applying it to the problem at hand

$$\mathrm{E}(u_{T+1} \mid \Omega_t)^2 = \sigma_{T+1}^2 \tag{9.67}$$

but σ_{T+1}^2 is not known at time T, so it is replaced with the forecast for it, $\sigma_{1,T}^{f2}$, so that (9.64) becomes

$$\sigma_{2,T}^{f2} = \alpha_0 + \alpha_1 \sigma_{1,T}^{f2} + \beta \sigma_{1,T}^{f2} \tag{9.68}$$

$$\sigma_{2,T}^{f2} = \alpha_0 + (\alpha_1 + \beta) \sigma_{1,T}^{f2} \tag{9.69}$$

What about the three-step-ahead forecast?

By similar arguments,

$$\sigma_{3,T}^{f2} = \mathrm{E}_T\big(\alpha_0 + \alpha_1 u_{T+2}^2 + \beta \sigma_{T+2}^2\big) \tag{9.70}$$

$$\sigma_{3,T}^{f2} = \alpha_0 + (\alpha_1 + \beta) \sigma_{2,T}^{f2} \tag{9.71}$$

$$\sigma_{3,T}^{f2} = \alpha_0 + (\alpha_1 + \beta)\big[\alpha_0 + (\alpha_1 + \beta) \sigma_{1,T}^{f2}\big] \tag{9.72}$$

$$\sigma_{3,T}^{f2} = \alpha_0 + \alpha_0(\alpha_1 + \beta) + (\alpha_1 + \beta)^2 \sigma_{1,T}^{f2} \tag{9.73}$$

Any s-step-ahead forecasts would be produced by

$$\sigma_{s,T}^{f2} = \alpha_0 \sum_{i=1}^{s-1} (\alpha_1 + \beta)^{i-1} + (\alpha_1 + \beta)^{s-1} \sigma_{1,T}^{f2} \tag{9.74}$$

for any value of $s \geq 2$.

It is worth noting at this point that variances, and therefore variance forecasts, are additive over time. This is a very useful property. Suppose, for example, that using daily foreign exchange returns, one-, two-, three-, four-, and five-step-ahead variance forecasts have been produced, i.e. a forecast has been constructed for each day of the next trading week. The forecasted variance for the whole week would simply be the sum of the five daily variance forecasts. If the standard deviation is the required volatility estimate rather than the variance, simply take the square root of the variance forecasts. Note also, however, that standard deviations are not additive. Hence, if daily standard deviations are the required volatility measure, they must be squared to turn them to variances. Then the variances would be added and the square root taken to obtain a weekly standard deviation.

9.17.1 Forecasting from GARCH models with EViews

Forecasts from any of the GARCH models that can be estimated using EViews are obtained by using only a sub-sample of available data for model estimation, and then by clicking on the 'Forecast' button that appears after estimation of the required model has been completed. Suppose, for example, we stopped the estimation of the GARCH(1,1) model (with no asymmetries and no GARCH-in-mean term) for the Japanese yen returns at 6 June 2011 so as to keep the last two years of data for forecasting (i.e. the 'Forecast sample' is 6/07/2011 6/06/2013). Then click on the **Forecast** tab above the estimation results and the dialog box in screenshot 9.3 will then appear.

Again, several options are available, including providing a name for the conditional mean and for the conditional variance forecasts, or whether to produce static (a series of rolling single-step-ahead) or dynamic (multiple-step-ahead) forecasts. The dynamic and static forecast plots that would be produced are given in screenshots 9.4 and 9.5.

GARCH(1,1) Dynamic forecasts (up to two years ahead)

The dynamic forecasts show a completely flat forecast structure for the mean (since the conditional mean equation includes only a constant term), while at the end of the in-sample estimation period, the value of the conditional variance was at a historically low level relative to its unconditional average. Therefore, the forecasts converge upon their long-term mean value from below as the forecast horizon increases. Notice also that there are no ± 2-standard error band confidence intervals for the conditional variance forecasts; to compute these would require some kind of estimate of the variance of variance, which is beyond the scope of this book

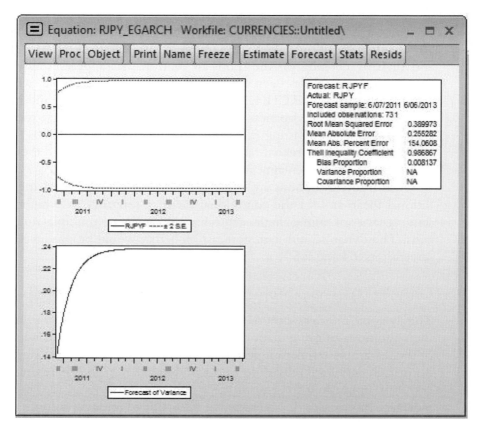

Screenshot 9.3 **Forecasting from GARCH models**

Screenshot 9.4 **Dynamic forecasts of the conditional variance**

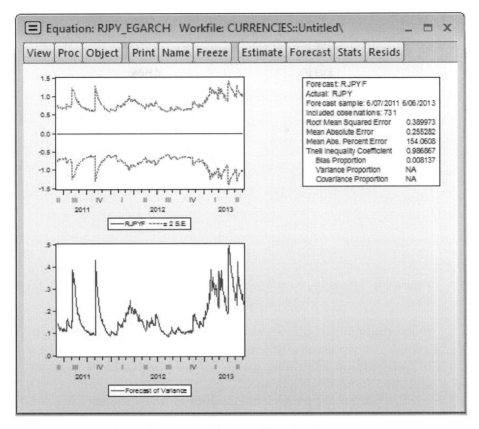

Screenshot 9.5   **Static forecasts of the conditional variance**

(and beyond the capability of the built-in functions of the EViews software). The conditional variance forecasts provide the basis for the standard error bands that are given by the dotted red lines around the conditional mean forecast. Because the conditional variance forecasts rise gradually as the forecast horizon increases, so the standard error bands widen slightly. The forecast evaluation statistics that are presented in the box to the right of the graphs are for the conditional mean forecasts.

GARCH(1,1) Static forecasts (rolling one-day ahead)

It is evident that the variance forecasts have two spikes in mid- and late 2011 but are fairly stable and historically quite low during 2012 before rising again during 2013. Since these are a series of rolling one-step ahead forecasts for the conditional variance, they show much more volatility than for the dynamic forecasts. This volatility also results in more variability in the standard error bars around the conditional mean forecasts. Note that while the forecasts are updated daily based on new information that feeds into the forecasts, the parameter estimates themselves are not updated. Thus, towards the end of the sample the forecasts are based on estimates almost two years old. If we wanted to update the model estimates as we

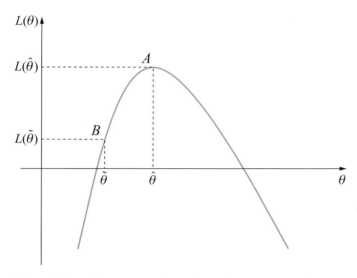

Figure 9.4   Three approaches to hypothesis testing under maximum likelihood

rolled through the sample, we would need to write some code to do this within a loop – it would also run much more slowly as we would be estimating a lot of GARCH models rather than one. See chapter 13 for a discussion of how to construct loops in EViews.

Predictions can be similarly produced for any member of the GARCH family that is estimable with the software.

9.18   Testing non-linear restrictions or testing hypotheses about non-linear models

The usual t- and F-tests are still valid in the context of non-linear models, but they are not flexible enough. For example, suppose that it is of interest to test a hypothesis that $\alpha_1 \beta = 1$. Now that the model class has been extended to non-linear models, there is no reason to suppose that relevant restrictions are only linear.

Under OLS estimation, the F-test procedure works by examining the degree to which the RSS rises when the restrictions are imposed. In very general terms, hypothesis testing under ML works in a similar fashion – that is, the procedure works by examining the degree to which the maximal value of the LLF falls upon imposing the restriction. If the LLF falls 'a lot', it would be concluded that the restrictions are not supported by the data and thus the hypothesis should be rejected.

There are three hypothesis testing procedures based on maximum likelihood principles: Wald, Likelihood ratio and Lagrange Multiplier. To illustrate briefly how each of these operates, consider a single parameter, θ to be estimated, and denote the ML estimate as $\hat{\theta}$ and a restricted estimate as $\tilde{\theta}$. Denoting the maximised value of the LLF by unconstrained ML as $L(\hat{\theta})$ and the constrained optimum as $L(\tilde{\theta})$, the three testing procedures can be illustrated as in figure 9.4.

The tests all require the measurement of the 'distance' between the points A (representing the unconstrained maximised value of the log likelihood function) and B (representing the constrained value). The vertical distance forms the basis of the LR test. Twice this vertical distance is given by $2[L(\hat{\theta}) - L(\tilde{\theta})] = 2\ln[l(\hat{\theta})/l(\tilde{\theta})]$, where L denotes the log-likelihood function, and l denotes the likelihood function. The Wald test is based on the horizontal distance between $\hat{\theta}$ and $\tilde{\theta}$, while the LM test compares the slopes of the curve at A and B. At A, the unrestricted maximum of the log-likelihood function, the slope of the curve is zero. But is it 'significantly steep' at $L(\tilde{\theta})$, i.e. at point B? The steeper the curve is at B, the less likely the restriction is to be supported by the data.

Expressions for LM test statistics involve the first and second derivatives of the log-likelihood function with respect to the parameters at the constrained estimate. The first derivatives of the log-likelihood function are collectively known as the score vector, measuring the slope of the LLF for each possible value of the parameters. The expected values of the second derivatives comprise the information matrix, measuring the peakedness of the LLF, and how much higher the LLF value is at the optimum than in other places. This matrix of second derivatives is also used to construct the coefficient standard errors. The LM test involves estimating only a restricted regression, since the slope of the LLF at the maximum will be zero by definition. Since the restricted regression is usually easier to estimate than the unrestricted case, LM tests are usually the easiest of the three procedures to employ in practice. The reason that restricted regressions are usually simpler is that imposing the restrictions often means that some components in the model will be set to zero or combined under the null hypothesis, so that there are fewer parameters to estimate. The Wald test involves estimating only an unrestricted regression, and the usual OLS t-tests and F-tests are examples of Wald tests (since again, only unrestricted estimation occurs).

Of the three approaches to hypothesis testing in the maximum-likelihood framework, the likelihood ratio test is the most intuitively appealing, and therefore a deeper examination of it will be the subject of the following section; see Ghosh (1991, section 10.3) for further details.

9.18.1   Likelihood ratio tests

Likelihood ratio (LR) tests involve estimation under the null hypothesis and under the alternative, so that two models are estimated: an unrestricted model and a model where the restrictions have been imposed. The maximised values of the LLF for the restricted and unrestricted cases are 'compared'. Suppose that the unconstrained model has been estimated and that a given maximised value of the LLF, denoted L_u, has been achieved. Suppose also that the model has been estimated imposing the constraint(s) and a new value of the LLF obtained, denoted L_r. The LR test statistic asymptotically follows a Chi-squared distribution and is given by

$$LR = -2(L_r - L_u) \sim \chi^2(m) \tag{9.75}$$

where $m =$ number of restrictions. Note that the maximised value of the log-likelihood function will always be at least as big for the unrestricted model as for the restricted model, so that $L_r \leq L_u$. This rule is intuitive and comparable to the effect of imposing a restriction on a linear model estimated by OLS, that $RRSS \geq URSS$. Similarly, the equality between L_r and L_u will hold only when the restriction was already present in the data. Note, however, that the usual F-test is in fact a Wald test, and not a LR test – that is, it can be calculated using an unrestricted model only. The F-test approach based on comparing RSS arises conveniently as a result of the OLS algebra.

Example 9.3

A GARCH model is estimated and a maximised LLF of 66.85 is obtained. Suppose that a researcher wishes to test whether $\beta = 0$ in (9.77)

$$y_t = \mu + \phi y_{t-1} + u_t, \, u_t \sim N(0, \sigma_t^2) \tag{9.76}$$

$$\sigma_t^2 = \alpha_0 + \alpha_1 u_{t-1}^2 + \beta \sigma_{t-1}^2 \tag{9.77}$$

The model is estimated imposing the restriction and the maximised LLF falls to 64.54. Is the restriction supported by the data, which would correspond to the situation where an ARCH(1) specification was sufficient? The test statistic is given by

$$LR = -2(64.54 - 66.85) = 4.62 \tag{9.78}$$

The test follows a $\chi^2(1) = 3.84$ at 5%, so that the null is marginally rejected. It would thus be concluded that an ARCH(1) model, with no lag of the conditional variance in the variance equation, is not quite sufficient to describe the dependence in volatility over time.

9.19 Volatility forecasting: some examples and results from the literature

There is a vast and relatively new literature that attempts to compare the accuracies of various models for producing out-of-sample volatility forecasts. Akgiray (1989), for example, finds the GARCH model superior to ARCH, exponentially weighted moving average and historical mean models for forecasting monthly US stock index volatility. A similar result concerning the apparent superiority of GARCH is observed by West and Cho (1995) using one-step-ahead forecasts of dollar exchange rate volatility, although for longer horizons, the model behaves no better than their alternatives. Pagan and Schwert (1990) compare GARCH, EGARCH, Markov switching regime and three non-parametric models for forecasting monthly US stock return volatilities. The EGARCH followed by the GARCH models perform moderately; the remaining models produce very poor predictions. Franses and van Dijk (1996) compare three members of the GARCH family (standard GARCH, QGARCH and the GJR model) for forecasting the weekly volatility of various European stock market indices. They find that the non-linear GARCH models were unable to beat the standard GARCH model. Finally, Brailsford and Faff (1996) find GJR and GARCH models slightly superior to various simpler models for predicting Australian monthly stock index volatility. The conclusion arising from this growing body of research is that forecasting volatility is a 'notoriously difficult task' (Brailsford and Faff, 1996, p. 419), although it appears that conditional heteroscedasticity models are among the best that are currently available. In particular, more complex non-linear and non-parametric models are inferior in prediction to simpler models, a result echoed in an earlier paper by Dimson and Marsh (1990) in the context of relatively complex versus parsimonious linear models. Finally, Brooks (1998), considers whether measures of market volume can assist in improving volatility forecast accuracy, finding that they cannot.

A particularly clear example of the style and content of this class of research is given by Day and Lewis (1992). The Day and Lewis study will therefore now be examined in depth. The purpose of their paper is to consider the out-of-sample forecasting performance of GARCH and EGARCH models for predicting stock index volatility. The forecasts from these econometric models are compared with those given from an 'implied volatility'. As discussed above, implied volatility is the market's expectation of the 'average' level of volatility of an underlying asset over the life of the option that is implied by the current traded price of the option. Given an assumed model for pricing options, such as the Black–Scholes, all of the inputs to the model except for volatility can be observed directly from the market or are specified in the terms of the option contract. Thus, it is possible, using an iterative search procedure such as the Newton–Raphson method (see, for example, Watsham and Parramore, 2004), to 'back out' the volatility of the underlying asset from the option's price. An important question for research is whether implied or econometric models produce more accurate forecasts of the volatility of the underlying asset. If the options and underlying asset markets are informationally efficient, econometric volatility forecasting models based on past realised values of underlying volatility should have no incremental explanatory power for future values of volatility of the underlying asset. On the other hand, if econometric models do hold additional information useful for forecasting future volatility, it is possible that such forecasts could be turned into a profitable trading rule.

The data employed by Day and Lewis comprise weekly closing prices (Wednesday to Wednesday, and Friday to Friday) for the S&P100 Index option and the underlying index from 11 March 1983–31 December 1989. They employ both mid-week to mid-week returns and Friday to Friday returns to determine whether weekend effects have any significant impact on the latter. They argue that Friday returns contain expiration effects since implied volatilities are seen to jump on the Friday of the week of expiration. This issue is not of direct interest to this book, and consequently only the mid-week to mid-week results will be shown here.

The models that Day and Lewis employ are as follows. First, for the conditional mean of the time series models, they employ a GARCH-M specification for the excess of the market return over a risk-free proxy

$$R_{Mt} - R_{Ft} = \lambda_0 + \lambda_1 \sqrt{h_t} + u_t \tag{9.79}$$

where R_{Mt} denotes the return on the market portfolio, and R_{Ft} denotes the risk-free rate. Note that Day and Lewis denote the conditional variance by h_t^2, while this is modified to the standard h_t here. Also, the notation σ_t^2 will be used to denote implied volatility estimates. For the variance, two specifications are employed: a 'plain vanilla' GARCH(1,1) and an EGARCH

$$h_t = \alpha_0 + \alpha_1 u_{t-1}^2 + \beta_1 h_{t-1} \tag{9.80}$$

or

$$\ln(h_t) = \alpha_0 + \beta_1 \ln(h_{t-1}) + \alpha_1 \left(\theta \frac{u_{t-1}}{\sqrt{h_{t-1}}} + \gamma \left[\left| \frac{u_{t-1}}{\sqrt{h_{t-1}}} \right| - \left(\frac{2}{\pi} \right)^{1/2} \right] \right) \tag{9.81}$$

One way to test whether implied or GARCH-type volatility models perform best is to add a lagged value of the implied volatility estimate (σ_{t-1}^2) to (9.80) and (9.81). A 'hybrid' or 'encompassing' specification would thus result. Equation (9.80) becomes

$$h_t = \alpha_0 + \alpha_1 u_{t-1}^2 + \beta_1 h_{t-1} + \delta \sigma_{t-1}^2 \tag{9.82}$$

and (9.81) becomes

$$\ln(h_t) = \alpha_0 + \beta_1 \ln(h_{t-1})$$
$$+ \alpha_1 \left(\theta \frac{u_{t-1}}{\sqrt{h_{t-1}}} + \gamma \left[\left| \frac{u_{t-1}}{\sqrt{h_{t-1}}} \right| - \left(\frac{2}{\pi} \right)^{1/2} \right] \right) + \delta \ln\left(\sigma_{t-1}^2 \right) \tag{9.83}$$

The tests of interest are given by $H_0 : \delta = 0$ in (9.82) or (9.83). If these null hypotheses cannot be rejected, the conclusion would be that implied volatility contains no incremental information useful for explaining volatility than that derived from a GARCH model. At the same time, $H_0: \alpha_1 = 0$ and $\beta_1 = 0$ in (9.82), and $H_0 : \alpha_1 = 0$ and $\beta_1 = 0$ and $\theta = 0$ and $\gamma = 0$ in (9.83) are also tested. If this second set of restrictions holds, then (9.82) and (9.83) collapse to

$$h_t = \alpha_0 + \delta \sigma_{t-1}^2 \tag{9.82'}$$

and

$$\ln(h_t) = \alpha_0 + \delta \ln\left(\sigma_{t-1}^2 \right) \tag{9.83'}$$

These sets of restrictions on (9.82) and (9.83) test whether the lagged squared error and lagged conditional variance from a GARCH model contain any additional explanatory power once implied volatility is included in the specification. All of these restrictions can be tested fairly easily using a likelihood ratio test. The results of such a test are presented in table 9.1.

It appears from the coefficient estimates and their standard errors under the specification (9.82) that the implied volatility term (δ) is statistically significant, while the GARCH terms (α_1 and β_1) are not. However, the test statistics given in the final column are both greater than their corresponding χ^2 critical values, indicating that both GARCH and implied volatility have incremental power

Table 9.1 GARCH versus implied volatility

$$R_{Mt} - R_{Ft} = \lambda_0 + \lambda_1 \sqrt{h_t} + u_t \tag{9.79}$$

$$h_t = \alpha_0 + \alpha_1 u_{t-1}^2 + \beta_1 h_{t-1} \tag{9.80}$$

$$h_t = \alpha_0 + \alpha_1 u_{t-1}^2 + \beta_1 h_{t-1} + \delta \sigma_{t-1}^2 \tag{9.82}$$

$$h_t = \alpha_0 + \delta \sigma_{t-1}^2 \tag{9.82'}$$

Equation for variance	λ_0	λ_1	$\alpha_0 \times 10^{-4}$	α_1	β_1	δ	Log-L	χ^2
(9.80)	0.0072	0.071	5.428	0.093	0.854	—	767.321	17.77
	(0.005)	(0.01)	(1.65)	(0.84)	(8.17)			
(9.82)	0.0015	0.043	2.065	0.266	−0.068	0.318	776.204	—
	(0.028)	(0.02)	(2.98)	(1.17)	(−0.59)	(3.00)		
(9.82')	0.0056	−0.184	0.993	—	—	0.581	764.394	23.62
	(0.001)	(−0.001)	(1.50)			(2.94)		

Notes: *t*-ratios in parentheses, Log-L denotes the maximised value of the log-likelihood function in each case. χ^2 denotes the value of the test statistic, which follows a $\chi^2(1)$ in the case of (9.82) restricted to (9.80), and a $\chi^2(2)$ in the case of (9.82) restricted to (9.82').
Source: Day and Lewis (1992). Reprinted with the permission of Elsevier.

for modelling the underlying stock volatility. A similar analysis is undertaken in Day and Lewis that compares EGARCH with implied volatility. The results are presented here in table 9.2.

The EGARCH results tell a very similar story to those of the GARCH specifications. Neither the lagged information from the EGARCH specification nor the lagged implied volatility terms can be suppressed, according to the likelihood ratio statistics. In specification (9.83), both the EGARCH terms and the implied volatility coefficients are marginally significant.

However, the tests given above do not represent a true test of the predictive ability of the models, since all of the observations were used in both estimating and testing the models. Hence the authors proceed to conduct an out-of-sample forecasting test. There are a total of 729 data points in their sample. They use the first 410 to estimate the models, and then make a one-step-ahead forecast of the following week's volatility. They then roll the sample forward one observation at a time, constructing a new one-step-ahead forecast at each stage.

They evaluate the forecasts in two ways. The first is by regressing the realised volatility series on the forecasts plus a constant

$$\sigma_{t+1}^2 = b_0 + b_1 \sigma_{ft}^2 + \xi_{t+1} \tag{9.84}$$

Table 9.2 EGARCH versus implied volatility

$$R_{Mt} - R_{Ft} = \lambda_0 + \lambda_1 \sqrt{h_t} + u_t \tag{9.79}$$

$$\ln(h_t) = \alpha_0 + \beta_1 \ln(h_{t-1}) + \alpha_1 \left(\theta \frac{u_{t-1}}{\sqrt{h_{t-1}}} + \gamma \left[\left| \frac{u_{t-1}}{\sqrt{h_{t-1}}} \right| - \left(\frac{2}{\pi} \right)^{1/2} \right] \right) \tag{9.81}$$

$$\ln(h_t) = \alpha_0 + \beta_1 \ln(h_{t-1}) + \alpha_1 \left(\theta \frac{u_{t-1}}{\sqrt{h_{t-1}}} + \gamma \left[\left| \frac{u_{t-1}}{\sqrt{h_{t-1}}} \right| - \left(\frac{2}{\pi} \right)^{1/2} \right] \right) + \delta \ln(\sigma_{t-1}^2) \tag{9.83}$$

$$\ln(h_t) = \alpha_0 + \delta \ln(\sigma_{t-1}^2) \tag{9.83'}$$

Equation for variance	λ_0	λ_1	$\alpha_0 \times 10^{-4}$	β_1	θ	γ	δ	Log-L	χ^2
(9.81)	−0.0026	0.094	−3.62	0.529	0.273	0.357	–	776.436	8.09
	(−0.03)	(0.25)	(−2.90)	(3.26)	(−4.13)	(3.17)			
(9.83)	0.0035	−0.076	−2.28	0.373	−0.282	0.210	0.351	780.480	–
	(0.56)	(−0.24)	(−1.82)	(1.48)	(−4.34)	(1.89)	(1.82)		
(9.83')	0.0047	−0.139	−2.76	–	–	–	0.667	765.034	30.89
	(0.71)	(−0.43)	(−2.30)				(4.01)		

Notes: t-ratios in parentheses, Log-L denotes the maximised value of the log-likelihood function in each case. χ^2 denotes the value of the test statistic, which follows a $\chi^2(1)$ in the case of (9.83) restricted to (9.81), and a $\chi^2(3)$ in the case of (9.83) restricted to (9.83').
Source: Day and Lewis (1992). Reprinted with the permission of Elsevier.

where σ_{t+1}^2 is the 'actual' value of volatility at time $t+1$, and σ_{ft}^2 is the value forecasted for it during period t. Perfectly accurate forecasts would imply $b_0 = 0$ and $b_1 = 1$. The second method is via a set of forecast encompassing tests. Essentially, these operate by regressing the realised volatility on the forecasts generated by several models. The forecast series that have significant coefficients are concluded to encompass those of models whose coefficients are not significant.

But what is volatility? In other words, with what measure of realised or 'ex post' volatility should the forecasts be compared? This is a question that received very little attention in the literature until recently. A common method employed is to assume, for a daily volatility forecasting exercise, that the relevant *ex post* measure is the square of that day's return. For any random variable r_t, its conditional variance can be expressed as

$$\text{var}(r_t) = \text{E}[r_t - \text{E}(r_t)]^2 \tag{9.85}$$

As stated previously, it is typical, and not unreasonable for relatively high frequency data, to assume that $\text{E}(r_t)$ is zero, so that the expression for the variance reduces to

$$\text{var}(r_t) = \text{E}\left[r_t^2\right] \tag{9.86}$$

Andersen and Bollerslev (1998) argue that squared daily returns provide a very noisy proxy for the true volatility, and a much better proxy for the day's variance would be to compute the volatility for the day from intra-daily data. For example, a superior daily variance measure could be obtained by taking hourly returns, squaring them and adding them up. The reason that the use of higher frequency data provides a better measure of *ex post* volatility is simply that it employs more information. By using only daily data to compute a daily volatility measure, effectively only two observations on the underlying price series are employed. If the daily closing price is the same one day as the next, the squared return and therefore the volatility would be calculated to be zero, when there may have been substantial intra-day fluctuations. Hansen and Lunde (2006) go further and suggest that even the ranking of models by volatility forecast accuracy could be inconsistent if the evaluation uses a poor proxy for the true, underlying volatility.

Day and Lewis use two measures of *ex post* volatility in their study (for which the frequency of data employed in the models is weekly):

(1) The square of the weekly return on the index, which they call SR
(2) The variance of the week's daily returns multiplied by the number of trading days in that week, which they call WV.

The Andersen and Bollerslev argument implies that the latter measure is likely to be superior, and therefore that more emphasis should be placed on those results.

The results for the separate regressions of realised volatility on a constant and the forecast are given in table 9.3. The coefficient estimates for b_0 given in table 9.3 can be interpreted as indicators of whether the respective forecasting approaches are biased. In all cases, the b_0 coefficients are close to zero. Only for the historic volatility forecasts and the implied volatility forecast when the *ex post* measure is the squared weekly return, are the estimates statistically significant. Positive coefficient estimates would suggest that on average the forecasts are too low. The estimated b_1 coefficients are in all cases a long way from unity, except for the GARCH (with daily variance *ex post* volatility) and EGARCH (with squared weekly variance as *ex post* measure) models. Finally, the R^2 values are very small (all less than 10%, and most less than 3%), suggesting that the forecast series do a poor job of explaining the variability of the realised volatility measure.

The forecast encompassing regressions are based on a procedure due to Fair and Shiller (1990) that seeks to determine whether differing sets of forecasts contain different sets of information from one another. The test regression is of the form

$$\sigma_{t+1}^2 = b_0 + b_1\sigma_{It}^2 + b_2\sigma_{Gt}^2 + b_3\sigma_{Et}^2 + b_4\sigma_{Ht}^2 + \xi_{t+1} \tag{9.87}$$

with results presented in table 9.4.

The sizes and significances of the coefficients in table 9.4 are of interest. The most salient feature is the lack of significance of most of the forecast series. In the first comparison, neither the implied nor the GARCH forecast series have statistically significant coefficients. When historical volatility is added, its coefficient is positive and statistically significant. An identical pattern emerges when forecasts from implied and EGARCH models are compared: that is, neither forecast series

Table 9.3   Out-of-sample predictive power for weekly volatility forecasts

$$\sigma_{t+1}^2 = b_0 + b_1 \sigma_{ft}^2 + \xi_{t+1} \tag{9.84}$$

Forecasting model	Proxy for *ex post* volatility	b_0	b_1	R^2
Historic	SR	0.0004	0.129	0.094
		(5.60)	(21.18)	
Historic	WV	0.0005	0.154	0.024
		(2.90)	(7.58)	
GARCH	SR	0.0002	0.671	0.039
		(1.02)	(2.10)	
GARCH	WV	0.0002	1.074	0.018
		(1.07)	(3.34)	
EGARCH	SR	0.0000	1.075	0.022
		(0.05)	(2.06)	
EGARCH	WV	−0.0001	1.529	0.008
		(−0.48)	(2.58)	
Implied volatility	SR	0.0022	0.357	0.037
		(2.22)	(1.82)	
Implied volatility	WV	0.0005	0.718	0.026
		(0.389)	(1.95)	

Notes: 'Historic' refers to the use of a simple historical average of the squared returns to forecast volatility; *t*-ratios in parentheses; SR and WV refer to the square of the weekly return on the S&P100, and the variance of the week's daily returns multiplied by the number of trading days in that week, respectively.
Source: Day and Lewis (1992). Reprinted with the permission of Elsevier.

is significant, but when a simple historical average series is added, its coefficient is significant. It is clear from this, and from the last row of table 9.4, that the asymmetry term in the EGARCH model has no additional explanatory power compared with that embodied in the symmetric GARCH model. Again, all of the R^2 values are very low (less than 4%).

The conclusion reached from this study (which is broadly in line with many others) is that within sample, the results suggest that implied volatility contains extra information not contained in the GARCH/EGARCH specifications. But the out-of-sample results suggest that predicting volatility is a difficult task!

Table 9.4 Comparisons of the relative information content of out-of-sample volatility forecasts

$$\sigma_{t+1}^2 = b_0 + b_1\sigma_{It}^2 + b_2\sigma_{Gt}^2 + b_2\sigma_{Gt}^2 + b_3\sigma_{Et}^2 + b_4\sigma_{Ht}^2 + \xi_{t+1} \tag{9.87}$$

Forecast comparisons	b_0	b_1	b_2	b_3	b_4	R^2
Implied versus GARCH	−0.00010	0.601	0.298	–	–	0.027
	(−0.09)	(1.03)	(0.42)			
Implied versus GARCH	0.00018	0.632	−0.243	–	0.123	0.038
versus Historical	(1.15)	(1.02)	(−0.28)		(7.01)	
Implied versus EGARCH	−0.00001	0.695	–	0.176	–	0.026
	(−0.07)	(1.62)		(0.27)		
Implied versus EGARCH	0.00026	0.590	−0.374	–	0.118	0.038
versus Historical	(1.37)	(1.45)	(−0.57)		(7.74)	
GARCH versus EGARCH	0.00005	–	1.070	−0.001	–	0.018
	(0.370)		(2.78)	(−0.00)		

Notes: t-ratios in parentheses; the *ex post* measure used in this table is the variance of the week's daily returns multiplied by the number of trading days in that week.
Source: Day and Lewis (1992). Reprinted with the permission of Elsevier.

9.20 Stochastic volatility models revisited

Autoregressive models were discussed above in section 9.6 and these are special cases of a more general class of models known as stochastic volatility (SV) models. It is a common misconception that GARCH-type specifications are sorts of stochastic volatility models. However, as the name suggests, stochastic volatility models differ from GARCH principally in that the conditional variance equation of a GARCH specification is completely deterministic given all information available up to that of the previous period. In other words, there is no error term in the variance equation of a GARCH model, only in the mean equation.

Stochastic volatility models contain a second error term, which enters into the conditional variance equation. The autoregressive volatility specification is simple to understand and simple to estimate, because it requires that we have an observable measure of volatility which is then simply used as any other variable in an autoregressive model. However, the term 'stochastic volatility' is usually associated with a different formulation, a possible example of which would be

$$y_t = \mu + u_t\sigma_t, \ u_t \sim N(0, 1) \tag{9.88}$$

$$\log\left(\sigma_t^2\right) = \alpha_0 + \beta_1 \log\left(\sigma_{t-1}^2\right) + \sigma_\eta\eta_t \tag{9.89}$$

where η_t is another N(0,1) random variable that is independent of u_t. Here the volatility is latent rather than observed, and so is modelled indirectly.

Stochastic volatility models are closely related to the financial theories used in the options pricing literature. Early work by Black and Scholes (1973) had assumed that volatility is constant through time. Such an assumption was made largely for simplicity, although it could hardly be considered realistic. One unappealing side-effect of employing a model with the embedded assumption that volatility is fixed, is that options deep in-the-money and far out-of-the-money are underpriced relative to actual traded prices. This empirical observation provided part of the genesis for stochastic volatility models, where the logarithm of an unobserved variance process is modelled by a linear stochastic specification, such as an autoregressive model. The primary advantage of stochastic volatility models is that they can be viewed as discrete time approximations to the continuous time models employed in options pricing frameworks (see, for example, Hull and White, 1987). However, such models are hard to estimate. For reviews of (univariate) stochastic volatility models, see Taylor (1994), Ghysels *et al.* (1995) or Shephard (1996) and the references therein.

While stochastic volatility models have been widely employed in the mathematical options pricing literature, they have not been popular in empirical discrete-time financial applications, probably owing to the complexity involved in the process of estimating the model parameters (see Harvey, Ruiz and Shephard, 1994). So, while GARCH-type models are further from their continuous time theoretical underpinnings than stochastic volatility, they are much simpler to estimate using maximum likelihood. A relatively simple modification to the maximum likelihood procedure used for GARCH model estimation is not available, and hence stochastic volatility models are not discussed further here.

9.20.1 Higher moment models

Research over the past two decades has moved from examination purely of the first moment of financial time series (i.e. estimating models for the returns themselves), to consideration of the *second moment* (models for the variance). While this clearly represents a large step forward in the analysis of financial data, it is also evident that conditional variance specifications are not able to fully capture all of the relevant time series properties. For example, GARCH models with normal (0,1) standardised disturbances cannot generate sufficiently fat tails to model the leptokurtosis that is actually observed in financial asset returns series. One proposed approach to this issue has been to suggest that the standardised disturbances are drawn from a Student's t distribution rather than a normal. However, there is also no reason to suppose that the fatness of tails should be constant over time, which it is forced to be by the GARCH-t model.

Another possible extension would be to use a conditional model for the third or fourth moments of the distribution of returns (i.e. the skewness and kurtosis, respectively). Under such a specification, the conditional skewness or kurtosis of the returns could follow a GARCH-type process that allows it to vary through time. Harvey and Siddique (1999, 2000) have developed an autoregressive conditional skewness model, while a conditional kurtosis model was proposed in Brooks, Burke, Heravi and Persand (2005). Such models could have many other applications in finance, including asset allocation (portfolio selection), option pricing, estimation of risk premia, and so on.

An extension of the analysis to moments of the return distribution higher than the second has also been undertaken in the context of the capital asset pricing model, where the conditional co-skewness and co-kurtosis of the asset's returns with the market's are accounted for (e.g. Hung *et al.*, 2004). A recent study by Brooks *et al.* (2012) proposed a utility-based framework for the determination of optimal hedge ratios that can allow for the impact of higher moments on the hedging decision in the context of hedging commodity exposures with futures contracts.

9.20.2 Tail models

It is widely known that financial asset returns do not follow a normal distribution, but rather they are almost always *leptokurtic*, or *fat-tailed*. This observation has several implications for econometric modelling. First, models and inference procedures are required that are robust to non-normal error distributions. Second, the riskiness of holding a particular security is probably no longer appropriately measured by its variance alone. In a risk management context, assuming normality when returns are fat-tailed will result in a systematic underestimation of the riskiness of the portfolio. Consequently, several approaches have been employed to systematically allow for the leptokurtosis in financial data, including the use of a Student's *t* distribution.

Arguably the simplest approach is the use of a mixture of normal distributions. It can be seen that a mixture of normal distributions with different variances will lead to an overall series that is leptokurtic. Second, a Student's *t* distribution can be used, with the usual degrees of freedom parameter estimated using maximum likelihood along with other parameters of the model. The degrees of freedom estimate will control the fatness of the tails fitted from the model. Other probability distributions can also be employed, such as the 'stable' distributions that fall under the general umbrella of extreme value theory (see Brooks, Clare, Dalle Molle and Persand, 2005 for an application of this technique to value at risk modelling and chapter 13 for an alternative approach).

9.21 Forecasting covariances and correlations

A major limitation of the volatility models examined above is that they are entirely univariate in nature – that is, they model the conditional variance of each series entirely independently of all other series. This is potentially an important limitation for two reasons. First, to the extent that there may be 'volatility spillovers' between markets or assets (a tendency for volatility to change in one market or asset following a change in the volatility of another), the univariate model will be misspecified. For instance, using a multivariate model will allow us to determine whether the volatility in one market leads or lags the volatility in others.

Second, it is often the case in finance that the covariances between series are of interest, as well as the variances of the individual series themselves. The calculation of hedge ratios, portfolio value at risk estimates, CAPM betas, and so on, all require covariances as inputs.

Multivariate GARCH models can potentially overcome both of these deficiencies with their univariate counterparts. Multivariate extensions to GARCH models can be used to forecast the volatilities of the component series, just as with univariate models and since the volatilities of financial time series often move together, a joint approach to modelling may be more efficient than treating each separately. In addition, because multivariate models give estimates for the conditional covariances as well as the conditional variances, they have a number of other potentially useful applications.

Several papers have investigated the forecasting ability of various models incorporating correlations. Siegel (1997), for example, finds that implied correlation forecasts from traded options encompass all information embodied in the historical returns (although he does not consider EWMA- or GARCH-based models). Walter and Lopez (2000), on the other hand, find that implied correlation is generally less useful for predicting the future correlation between the underlying assets' returns than forecasts derived from GARCH models. Finally, Gibson and Boyer (1998) find that a diagonal GARCH and a Markov switching approach provide better correlation forecasts than simpler models in the sense that the latter produce smaller profits when the forecasts are employed in a trading strategy.

9.22 Covariance modelling and forecasting in finance: some examples

9.22.1 The estimation of conditional betas

The CAPM beta for asset i is defined as the ratio of the covariance between the market portfolio return and the asset return, to the variance of the market portfolio return. Betas are typically constructed using a set of historical data on market variances and covariances. However, like most other problems in finance, beta estimation conducted in this fashion is backward-looking, when investors should really be concerned with the beta that will prevail in the future over the time that the investor is considering holding the asset. Multivariate GARCH models provide a simple method for estimating conditional (or time-varying) betas. Then forecasts of the covariance between the asset and the market portfolio returns and forecasts of the variance of the market portfolio are made from the model, so that the beta is a forecast, whose value will vary over time

$$\beta_{i,t} = \frac{\sigma_{im,t}}{\sigma_{m,t}^2} \qquad (9.90)$$

where $\beta_{i,t}$ is the time-varying beta estimate at time t for stock i, $\sigma_{im,t}$ is the covariance between market returns and returns to stock i at time t and $\sigma_{m,t}^2$ is the variance of the market return at time t.

9.22.2 Dynamic hedge ratios

Although there are many techniques available for reducing and managing risk, the simplest and perhaps the most widely used, is hedging with futures contracts. A hedge is achieved by taking opposite positions in spot and futures markets simultaneously, so that any loss sustained from an adverse price movement in one market should to some degree be offset by a favourable price movement in the other. The ratio of the number of units of the futures asset that are purchased relative to the number of units of the spot asset is known as the *hedge ratio*. Since risk in this context is usually measured as the volatility of portfolio returns, an intuitively plausible strategy might be to choose that hedge ratio which minimises the variance of the returns of a portfolio containing the spot and futures position; this is known as the *optimal hedge ratio*. The optimal value of the hedge ratio may be determined in the usual way, following Hull (2005) by first defining:

ΔS = change in spot price S, during the life of the hedge ΔF = change in futures price, F, during the life of the hedge σ_s = standard deviation of ΔS σ_F = standard deviation of ΔF p = correlation coefficient between ΔS and ΔF h = hedge ratio

For a short hedge (i.e. long in the asset and short in the futures contract), the change in the value of the hedger's position during the life of the hedge will be given by $(\Delta S - h\Delta F)$, while for a long hedge, the appropriate expression will be $(h\Delta F - \Delta S)$.

The variances of the two hedged portfolios (long spot and short futures or long futures and short spot) are the same. These can be obtained from

$$\text{var}(h\Delta F - \Delta S)$$

Remembering the rules for manipulating the variance operator, this can be written

$$\text{var}(\Delta S) + \text{var}(h\Delta F) - 2\text{cov}(\Delta S, h\Delta F)$$

or

$$\text{var}(\Delta S) + h^2\text{var}(\Delta F) - 2h\text{cov}(\Delta S, \Delta F)$$

Hence the variance of the change in the value of the hedged position is given by

$$v = \sigma_s^2 + h^2\sigma_F^2 - 2hp\sigma_s\sigma_F \tag{9.91}$$

Minimising this expression w.r.t. h would give

$$h = p\frac{\sigma_s}{\sigma_F} \tag{9.92}$$

Again, according to this formula, the optimal hedge ratio is time-invariant, and would be calculated using historical data. However, what if the standard deviations are changing over time? The standard deviations and the correlation between movements in the spot and futures series could be forecast from a multivariate

GARCH model, so that the expression above is replaced by

$$h_t = p_t \frac{\sigma_{s,t}}{\sigma_{F,t}} \qquad (9.93)$$

Various models are available for covariance or correlation forecasting, and several will be discussed below, which are grouped into simple models, multivariate GARCH models, and specific correlation models.

9.23 Simple covariance models

9.23.1 Historical covariance and correlation

In exactly the same fashion as for volatility, the historical covariance or correlation between two series can be calculated in the standard way using a set of historical data.

9.23.2 Implied covariance models

Implied covariances can be calculated using options whose payoffs are dependent on more than one underlying asset. The relatively small number of such options that exist limits the circumstances in which implied covariances can be calculated. Examples include rainbow options, 'crack-spread' options for different grades of oil, and currency options. In the latter case, the implied variance of the cross-currency returns xy is given by

$$\tilde{\sigma}^2(xy) = \tilde{\sigma}^2(x) + \tilde{\sigma}^2(y) - 2\tilde{\sigma}(x, y) \qquad (9.94)$$

where $\tilde{\sigma}^2(x)$ and $\tilde{\sigma}^2(y)$ are the implied variances of the x and y returns, respectively, and $\tilde{\sigma}(x, y)$ is the implied covariance between x and y. By substituting the observed option implied volatilities of the three currencies into (9.94), the implied covariance is obtained via

$$\tilde{\sigma}(x, y) = \frac{\tilde{\sigma}^2(x) + \tilde{\sigma}^2(y) - \tilde{\sigma}^2(xy)}{2} \qquad (9.95)$$

So, for instance, if the implied covariance between USD/DEM and USD/JPY is of interest, then the implied variances of the returns of USD/DEM and USD/JPY, as well as the returns of the cross-currency DEM/JPY, are required so as to obtain the implied covariance using (9.94).

9.23.3 Exponentially weighted moving average model for covariances

Again, as for the case of single series volatility modelling, a EWMA specification is available that gives more weight in the calculation of covariance to recent observations than the estimate based on the simple average. The EWMA model estimates for variances and covariances at time t in the bivariate setup with two returns series x and y may be written as

$$h_{ij,t} = \lambda h_{ij,t-1} + (1 - \lambda)x_{t-1}y_{t-1} \qquad (9.96)$$

where $i \neq j$ for the covariances and $i = j; x = y$ for the variance specifications. As for the univariate case, the fitted values for h also become the forecasts for subsequent periods. $\lambda(0 < \lambda < 1)$ again denotes the decay factor determining the relative weights attached to recent versus less recent observations. this parameter could be estimated (for example, by maximum likelihood), but is often set arbitrarily (– for example, Riskmetrics use a decay factor of 0.97 for monthly data but 0.94 when the data are of daily frequency).

This equation can be rewritten as an infinite order function of only the returns by successively substituting out the covariances

$$h_{ij,t} = (1 - \lambda) \sum_{i=0}^{\infty} \lambda^i x_{t-i} y_{t-i} \tag{9.97}$$

While the EWMA model is probably the simplest way to allow for time-varying variances and covariances, the model is a restricted version of an integrated GARCH (IGARCH) specification, and it does not guarantee the fitted variance-covariance matrix to be positive definite. As a result of the parallel with IGARCH, EWMA models also cannot allow for the observed mean reversion in the volatilities or covariances of asset returns that is particularly prevalent at lower frequencies of observation.

9.24 Multivariate GARCH models

Multivariate GARCH models are in spirit very similar to their univariate counterparts, except that the former also specify equations for how the covariances move over time and are therefore by their nature inherently more complex to specify and estimate. Several different multivariate GARCH formulations have been proposed in the literature, the most popular of which are the *VECH*, the diagonal *VECH* and the *BEKK* models. Each of these and several others is discussed in turn below; for a more detailed discussion, see Kroner and Ng (1998). In each case, there are N assets, whose return variances and covariances are to be modelled.

9.24.1 The VECH model

As with univariate GARCH models, the conditional mean equation may be parameterised in any way desired, although it is worth noting that, since the conditional variances are measured about the mean, misspecification of the latter is likely to imply misspecification of the former. To introduce some notation, suppose, that y_t $(y_{1t} y_{2t} \ldots y_{Nt})$, is an $N \times 1$ vector of time series observations, C is an $N(N + 1)/2$ column vector of conditional variance and covariance intercepts, and A and B are square parameter matrices of order $N(N + 1)/2$. A common specification of the *VECH* model, initially due to Bollerslev, Engle and Wooldridge (1988), is

$$VECH(H_t) = C + A VECH(\Xi_{t-1} \Xi_{t-1}') + B VECH(H_{t-1})$$

$$\Xi_t | \psi_{t-1} \sim N(0, H_t), \tag{9.98}$$

where H_t is a $N \times N$ conditional variance–covariance matrix, Ξ_t is a $N \times 1$ innovation (disturbance) vector, ψ_{t-1} represents the information set at time $t-1$, and $VECH(\cdot)$ denotes the column-stacking operator applied to the upper portion of the symmetric matrix. In the bivariate case (i.e. $N = 2$), C will be a 3×1 parameter vector, and A and B will be 3×3 parameter matrices.

The unconditional variance matrix for the $VECH$ will be given by $C[I - A - B]^{-1}$, where I is an identity matrix of order $N(N+1)/2$. Stationarity of the $VECH$ model requires that the eigenvalues of $[A + B]$ are all less than one in absolute value.

In order to gain a better understanding of how the $VECH$ model works, the elements for $N = 2$ are written out below. Define

$$H_t = \begin{bmatrix} h_{11t} & h_{12t} \\ h_{21t} & h_{22t} \end{bmatrix}, \ \Xi_t = \begin{bmatrix} u_{1t} \\ u_{2t} \end{bmatrix}, \ C = \begin{bmatrix} c_{11} \\ c_{21} \\ c_{31} \end{bmatrix},$$

$$A = \begin{bmatrix} a_{11} & a_{12} & a_{13} \\ a_{21} & a_{22} & a_{23} \\ a_{31} & a_{32} & a_{33} \end{bmatrix}, \ B = \begin{bmatrix} b_{11} & b_{12} & b_{13} \\ b_{21} & b_{22} & b_{23} \\ b_{31} & b_{32} & b_{33} \end{bmatrix},$$

The $VECH$ operator takes the 'upper triangular' portion of a matrix, and stacks each element into a vector with a single column. For example, in the case of $VECH(H_t)$, this becomes

$$VECH(H_t) = \begin{bmatrix} h_{11t} \\ h_{22t} \\ h_{12t} \end{bmatrix}$$

where h_{iit} represent the conditional variances at time t of the two-asset return series $(i = 1, 2)$ used in the model, and h_{ijt} $(i \neq j)$ represent the conditional covariances between the asset returns. In the case of $VECH(\Xi_t \Xi_t')$, this can be expressed as

$$VECH(\Xi_t \Xi_t') = VECH\left(\begin{bmatrix} u_{1t} \\ u_{2t} \end{bmatrix} \begin{bmatrix} u_{1t} & u_{2t} \end{bmatrix}\right)$$

$$= VECH\begin{pmatrix} u_{1t}^2 & u_{1t}u_{2t} \\ u_{1t}u_{2t} & u_{2t}^2 \end{pmatrix}$$

$$= \begin{bmatrix} u_{1t}^2 \\ u_{2t}^2 \\ u_{1t}u_{2t} \end{bmatrix}$$

The *VECH* model in full is given by

$$h_{11t} = c_{11} + a_{11}u_{1t-1}^2 + a_{12}u_{2t-1}^2 + a_{13}u_{1t-1}u_{2t-1} + b_{11}h_{11t-1}$$

$$+ b_{12}h_{22t-1} + b_{13}h_{12t-1} \tag{9.99}$$

$$h_{22t} = c_{21} + a_{21}u_{1t-1}^2 + a_{22}u_{2t-1}^2 + a_{23}u_{1t-1}u_{2t-1} + b_{21}h_{11t-1}$$

$$+ b_{22}h_{22t-1} + b_{23}h_{12t-1} \tag{9.100}$$

$$h_{12t} = c_{31} + a_{31}u_{1t-1}^2 + a_{32}u_{2t-1}^2 + a_{33}u_{1t-1}u_{2t-1} + b_{31}h_{11t-1}$$

$$+ b_{32}h_{22t-1} + b_{33}h_{12t-1} \tag{9.101}$$

Thus, it is clear that the conditional variances and conditional covariances depend on the lagged values of all of the conditional variances of, and conditional covariances between, all of the asset returns in the series, as well as the lagged squared errors and the error cross-products. This unrestricted model is highly parameterised, and it is challenging to estimate. For $N = 2$ there are 21 parameters (C has 3 elements, A and B each have 9 elements), while for $N = 3$ there are 78, and $N = 4$ implies 210 parameters!

9.24.2 The diagonal VECH model

As the number of assets employed increases, estimation of the *VECH* model can quickly become infeasible. Hence the *VECH* model's conditional variance–covariance matrix has been restricted to the form developed by Bollerslev, Engle and Wooldridge (1988), in which A and B are assumed to be diagonal. This restriction implies that there are no direct volatility spillovers from one series to another, which considerably reduces the number of parameters to be estimated to nine in the bivariate case (now A and B each have three elements) and 12 for a trivariate system (i.e. if $N = 3$). The model, known as a diagonal *VECH*, is now characterised by

$$h_{ij,t} = \omega_{ij} + \alpha_{ij}u_{i,t-1}u_{j,t-1} + \beta_{ij}h_{ij,t-1} \quad \text{for } i, j = 1, 2 \tag{9.102}$$

where ω_{ij}, α_{ij} and β_{ij} are parameters.

The diagonal *VECH* multivariate GARCH model could also be expressed as an infinite order multivariate ARCH model, where the covariance is expressed as a geometrically declining weighted average of past cross products of unexpected returns, with recent observations carrying higher weights. An alternative solution to the dimensionality problem would be to use orthogonal GARCH (see, for example, Van der Weide, 2002) or factor GARCH models (see Engle, Ng and Rothschild, 1990). A disadvantage of the *VECH* model is that there is no guarantee of a positive semi-definite covariance matrix.

A variance–covariance or correlation matrix must always be 'positive semi-definite', and in the case where all the returns in a particular series are all the same so that their variance is zero is disregarded, then the matrix will be positive definite. Among other things, this means that the variance–covariance matrix will have all positive numbers on the leading diagonal, and will be symmetrical about this leading diagonal. These properties are intuitively appealing as well as important from a mathematical point of view, for variances can never be negative, and the covariance between two series is the same irrespective of which of the two series is taken first, and positive definiteness ensures that this is the case.

A positive definite correlations matrix is also important for many applications in finance – for example, from a risk management point of view. It is this property which ensures that, whatever the weight of each series in the asset portfolio, an estimated value–at–risk is always positive. Fortunately, this desirable property is automatically a feature of time–invariant correlations matrices which are computed directly using actual data. An anomaly arises when either the correlation matrix is estimated using a non–linear optimisation procedure (as multivariate GARCH models are), or when modified values for some of the correlations are used by the risk manager. The resulting modified correlation matrix may or may not be positive definite, depending on the values of the correlations that are put in, and the values of the remaining correlations. If, by chance, the matrix is not positive definite, the upshot is that for some weightings of the individual assets in the portfolio, the estimated portfolio variance could be negative.

9.24.3 The BEKK model

The *BEKK* model (Engle and Kroner, 1995) addresses the difficulty with *VECH* of ensuring that the H matrix is always positive definite.[2] It is represented by

$$H_t = W'W + A'H_{t-1}A + B'\Xi_{t-1}\Xi'_{t-1}B \tag{9.103}$$

where A, and B are $N \times N$ matrices of parameters and W is an upper triangular matrix of parameters. The positive definiteness of the covariance matrix is ensured owing to the quadratic nature of the terms on the equation's RHS.

9.24.4 Model estimation for multivariate GARCH

Under the assumption of conditional normality, the parameters of the multivariate GARCH models of any of the above specifications can be estimated by maximising the log–likelihood function

$$\ell(\theta) = -\frac{TN}{2}\log 2\pi - \frac{1}{2}\sum_{t=1}^{T}\left(\log|H_t| + \Xi'_t H_t^{-1}\Xi_t\right) \tag{9.104}$$

where θ denotes all the unknown parameters to be estimated, N is the number of assets (i.e. the number of series in the system) and T is the number of observations and all other notation is as above. The maximum–likelihood estimate for θ is asymptotically normal, and thus traditional procedures for statistical inference are applicable. Further details on maximum–likelihood estimation in the context of

---

[2] The BEKK acronym arises from the fact that early versions of the paper also listed Baba and Krafts as co–authors.

multivariate GARCH models are beyond the scope of this book. But suffice to say that the additional complexity and extra parameters involved compared with univariate models make estimation a computationally more difficult task, although the principles are essentially the same.

9.25 Direct correlation models

The VECH and BEKK models specify the dynamics of the covariances between a set of series, and the correlations between any given pair of series at each point in time can be constructed by dividing the conditional covariances by the product of the conditional standard deviations. A subtly different approach would be to model the dynamics for the correlations directly – Bauwens *et al.* (2006) term these 'non-linear combinations of univariate GARCH models' for reasons that will become apparent in the following subsection.

9.25.1 The constant correlation model

An alternative method for reducing the number of parameters in the MGARCH framework is to require the correlations between the disturbances, ϵ_t, (or equivalently between the observed variables, y_t) to be fixed through time. Thus, although the conditional covariances are not fixed, they are tied to the variances as proposed in the constant conditional correlation (CCC) model due to Bollerslev (1990). The conditional variances in the fixed correlation model are identical to those of a set of univariate GARCH specifications (although they are estimated jointly)

$$h_{ii,t} = c_i + a_i\epsilon_{i,t-i}^2 + b_i h_{ii,t-1}, \qquad i = 1, \ldots, N \tag{9.105}$$

The off-diagonal elements of H_i, $h_{ij,t}(i \neq j)$, are defined indirectly via the correlations, denoted ρ_{ij}

$$h_{ij,t} = \rho_{ij} h_{ii,t}^{1/2} h_{jj,t}^{1/2}, \qquad i, j = 1, \ldots, N, i < j \tag{9.106}$$

Is it empirically plausible to assume that the correlations are constant through time? Several tests of this assumption have been developed, including a test based on the information matrix due to Bera and Kim (2002) and a Lagrange Multiplier test due to Tse (2000). The conclusions reached appear dependent on which test is used, but there seems to be non-negligible evidence against constant correlations, particularly in the context of stock returns.

9.25.2 The dynamic conditional correlation model

Several different formulations of the dynamic conditional correlation (DCC) model are available, but a popular specification is due to Engle (2002). The model is related to the CCC formulation described above, but where the correlations are allowed to vary over time. Define the variance-covariance matrix, H_t, as

$$H_t = D_t R_t D_t \tag{9.107}$$

where D_t is a diagonal matrix containing the conditional standard deviations (i.e. the square roots of the conditional variances from univariate GARCH model estimations on each of the N individual series) on the leading diagonal; R_t is the conditional correlation matrix. Forcing R_t to be time-invariant would lead back to the constant conditional correlation model.

Numerous explicit parameterisations of R_t are possible, including an exponential smoothing approach discussed in Engle (2002). More generally, a model of the MGARCH form could be specified as

$$Q_t = S \circ (u' - A - B) + A \circ u_{t-1}u'_{t-1} + B \circ Q_{t-1} \tag{9.108}$$

where S is the unconditional correlation matrix of the vector of standardised residuals (from the first stage estimation – see below), $u_t = D_t^{-1}\epsilon_t$. ι is a vector of ones, and Q_t is an $N \times N$ symmetric positive definite variance-covariance matrix. $\circ$ denotes the *Hadamard* or element-by-element matrix multiplication procedure. This specification for the intercept term simplifies estimation and reduces the number of parameters to be estimated, but is not necessary. Engle (2002) proposes a GARCH-esque formulation for dynamically modelling Q_t with the conditional correlation matrix, R_t, then constructed as

$$R_t = diag\{Q_t^*\}^{-1} Q_t diag\{Q_t^*\}^{-1} \tag{9.109}$$

where $diag(\cdot)$ denotes a matrix comprising the main diagonal elements of $(\cdot)$ and Q^* is a matrix that takes the square roots of each element in Q. This operation is effectively taking the covariances in Q_t and dividing them by the product of the appropriate standard deviations in Q_t^* to create a matrix of correlations.

A slightly different form of the DCC was proposed by Tse and Tsui (2002), and equation (9.108) could also be simplified by specifying A and B each as single scalars so that all the conditional correlations would follow the same process.

The model may be estimated in one single stage using maximum likelihood, although this will still be a difficult exercise in the context of large systems. Consequently, Engle advocates a two-stage estimation procedure where each variable in the system is first modelled separately as a univariate GARCH process. A joint log-likelihood function for this stage could be constructed, which would simply be the sum (over N) of all of the log-likelihoods for the individual GARCH models. Then, in the second stage, the conditional likelihood is maximised with respect to any unknown parameters in the correlation matrix. The log-likelihood function for the second stage estimation will be of the form

$$\ell(\theta_2|\theta_1) = \sum_{t=1}^{T} \left(\log |R_t| + u'_t R_t^{-1} u_t \right) \tag{9.110}$$

where θ_1 denotes all the unknown parameters that were estimated in the first stage and θ_2 denotes all those to be estimated in the second stage. Estimation using this two-step procedure will be consistent but inefficient as a result of any parameter uncertainty from the first stage being carried through to the second.

9.26 Extensions to the basic multivariate GARCH model

Numerous extensions to the univariate specification have been proposed, and many of these carry over to the multivariate case. For example, conditional variance or covariance terms can be included in the conditional mean equation (see Bollerslev et al., 1988, for instance). In the context of financial applications, where the y_t are returns, the parameters on these variables can be loosely interpreted as risk premia.

9.26.1 Asymmetric multivariate GARCH

Asymmetric models have become very popular in empirical applications, where the conditional variances and/or covariances are permitted to react differently to positive and negative innovations of the same magnitude. In the multivariate context, this is usually achieved in the Glosten et al. (1993) framework, rather than the EGARCH specification of Nelson (1991). Kroner and Ng (1998), for example, suggest the following extension to the BEKK formulation (with obvious related modifications for the VECH or diagonal VECH models)

$$H_t = W'W + A'H_{t-1}A + B'\Xi_{t-1}\Xi'_{t-1}B + D'z_{t-1}z'_{t-1}D \qquad (9.111)$$

where z_{t-1} is an N-dimensional column vector with elements taking the value $-\epsilon_{t-1}$ if the corresponding element of ϵ_{t-1} is negative and zero otherwise. The asymmetric properties of time-varying covariance matrix models are analysed by Kroner and Ng (1998), who identify three possible forms of asymmetric behaviour. First, the covariance matrix displays own variance asymmetry if the conditional variance of one series is affected by the sign of the innovation in that series. Second, the covariance matrix displays cross variance asymmetry if the conditional variance of one series is affected by the sign of the innovation of another series. Finally, if the conditional covariance is sensitive to the sign of the innovation in return for either series, then the model is said to display covariance asymmetry.

9.26.2 Alternative distributional assumptions

As was the case for stochastic volatility and univariate GARCH models, an assumption of (multivariate) conditional normality cannot generate sufficiently fat tails to accurately model the distributional properties of financial data. A better approximation to the actual distributions of (especially financial) time series can be obtained using a Student's t distribution. Such a model can still be estimated using maximum likelihood but with a different (and more complex) likelihood function. The standard formulation will involve estimating, as part of the process, a single degree of freedom parameter which applies to all of the series in the system. An additional potential drawback of this approach is that the tail fatness embodied in the degrees of freedom parameter is fixed over time. Brooks, Burke et al. (2005) propose a model where both of these limitations are removed. However, some identifying restrictions are still required. A further issue is the extent to which the unconditional distribution of the shocks is skewed. If this is the case, then a model based on the Student's t will be inadequate, and an alternative such as the multivariate skew Student's t of Bauwens and Laurent (2002) must be used.

Although many other extensions of the basic models may be conceived of, such as periodic or seasonal MGARCH, the range of specifications employed in the existing literature is narrower than for the corresponding univariate models. A major drawback for even the more parsimonious of the models above is that they are too highly parameterised, and yet many potential applications in economics and finance are in the context of high dimensional systems (such as asset allocation among a number of stocks). Thus, an important innovation was the development of orthogonal and factor models referenced above. Both have the same fundamental idea that by forcing some structure on the variance-covariance matrix, a simplification can be achieved.

9.27 A multivariate GARCH model for the CAPM with time-varying covariances

Bollerslev, Engle and Wooldridge (1988) estimate a multivariate GARCH model for returns to US Treasury Bills, gilts and stocks. The data employed comprised calculated quarterly excess holding period returns for six-month US Treasury bills, twenty-year US Treasury bonds and a Center for Research in Security Prices record of the return on the New York Stock Exchange (NYSE) value-weighted index. The data run from 1959Q1 to 1984Q2 – a total of 102 observations.

A multivariate GARCH-M model of the diagonal $VECH$ type is employed, with coefficients estimated by maximum likelihood, and the Berndt et al. (1974) algorithm is used. The coefficient estimates are easiest presented in the following equations for the conditional mean and variance equations, respectively

$$\begin{vmatrix} y_{1t} \\ y_{2t} \\ y_{3t} \end{vmatrix} = \begin{vmatrix} 0.070 \\ {\scriptstyle(0.032)} \\ -4.342 \\ {\scriptstyle(1.030)} \\ -3.117 \\ {\scriptstyle(0.710)} \end{vmatrix} + \underset{{\scriptstyle(0.160)}}{0.499} \sum_j \omega_{jt-1} \begin{vmatrix} h_{1jt} \\ h_{2jt} \\ h_{3jt} \end{vmatrix} + \begin{vmatrix} \varepsilon_{1t} \\ \varepsilon_{2t} \\ \varepsilon_{3t} \end{vmatrix} \tag{9.112}$$

$$\begin{vmatrix} h_{11t} \\ h_{12t} \\ h_{22t} \\ h_{13t} \\ h_{23t} \\ h_{33t} \end{vmatrix} = \begin{vmatrix} 0.011 \\ {\scriptstyle(0.004)} \\ 0.176 \\ {\scriptstyle(0.062)} \\ 13.305 \\ {\scriptstyle(6.372)} \\ 0.018 \\ {\scriptstyle(0.009)} \\ 5.143 \\ {\scriptstyle(2.820)} \\ 2.083 \\ {\scriptstyle(1.466)} \end{vmatrix} + \begin{vmatrix} 0.445\varepsilon_{1t-1}^2 \\ {\scriptstyle(0.105)} \\ 0.233\varepsilon_{1t-1}\varepsilon_{2t-1} \\ {\scriptstyle(0.092)} \\ 0.188\varepsilon_{2t-1}^2 \\ {\scriptstyle(0.113)} \\ 0.197\varepsilon_{1t-1}\varepsilon_{3t-1} \\ {\scriptstyle(0.132)} \\ 0.165\varepsilon_{2t-1}\varepsilon_{3t-1} \\ {\scriptstyle(0.093)} \\ 0.078\varepsilon_{3t-1}^2 \\ {\scriptstyle(0.066)} \end{vmatrix} + \begin{vmatrix} 0.466h_{11t-1} \\ {\scriptstyle(0.056)} \\ 0.598h_{12t-1} \\ {\scriptstyle(0.052)} \\ 0.441h_{22t-1} \\ {\scriptstyle(0.215)} \\ -0.362h_{13t-1} \\ {\scriptstyle(0.361)} \\ -0.348h_{23t-1} \\ {\scriptstyle(0.338)} \\ 0.469h_{33t-1} \\ {\scriptstyle(0.333)} \end{vmatrix} \tag{9.113}$$

Source: Bollerslev, Engle and Wooldridge (1988). Reprinted with the permission of University of Chicago Press.

where y_{jt} are the returns, ω_{jt-1} are a set vector of value weights at time $t-1$, $i = 1, 2, 3$, refers to bills, bonds and stocks, respectively and standard errors are given in parentheses. Consider now the implications of the signs, sizes and significances of the coefficient estimates in (9.112) and (9.113). The coefficient of 0.499 in the conditional mean equation gives an aggregate measure of relative risk aversion, also interpreted as representing the market trade-off between return and risk.

This conditional variance-in-mean coefficient gives the required additional return as compensation for taking an additional unit of variance (risk). The intercept coefficients in the conditional mean equation for bonds and stocks are very negative and highly statistically significant. The authors argue that this is to be expected since favourable tax treatments for investing in longer-term assets encourages investors to hold them even at relatively low rates of return.

The dynamic structure in the conditional variance and covariance equations is strongest for bills and bonds, and very weak for stocks, as indicated by their respective statistical significances. In fact, none of the parameters in the conditional variance or covariance equations for the stock return equations is significant at the 5% level. The unconditional covariance between bills and bonds is positive, while that between bills and stocks, and between bonds and stocks, is negative. This arises since, in the latter two cases, the lagged conditional covariance parameters are negative and larger in absolute value than those of the corresponding lagged error cross-products.

Finally, the degree of persistence in the conditional variance (given by $\alpha_1 + \beta$), which embodies the degree of clustering in volatility, is relatively large for the bills equation, but surprisingly small for bonds and stocks, given the results of other relevant papers in this literature.

9.28 Estimating a time-varying hedge ratio for FTSE stock index returns

A paper by Brooks, Henry and Persand (2002) compared the effectiveness of hedging on the basis of hedge ratios derived from various multivariate GARCH specifications and other, simpler techniques. Some of their main results are discussed below.

9.28.1 Background

There has been much empirical research into the calculation of optimal hedge ratios. The general consensus is that the use of multivariate GARCH (MGARCH) models yields superior performances, evidenced by lower portfolio volatilities, than either time-invariant or rolling OLS hedges. Cecchetti, Cumby and Figlewski (1988), Myers and Thompson (1989) and Baillie and Myers (1991), for example, argue that commodity prices are characterised by time-varying covariance matrices. As news about spot and futures prices arrives to the market in discrete bunches, the conditional covariance matrix, and hence the optimal hedging ratio, becomes time-varying. Baillie and Myers (1991) and Kroner and Sultan (1993), *inter alia*, employ MGARCH models to capture time-variation in the covariance matrix and to estimate the resulting hedge ratio.

9.28.2 Notation

Let S_t and F_t represent the logarithms of the stock index and stock index futures prices, respectively. The actual return on a spot position held from time $t-1$ to t is $\Delta S_t = S_t - S_{t-1}$ similarly, the actual return on a futures position is

$\Delta F_t = F_t - F_{t-1}$. However at time $t-1$ the expected return, $E_{t-1}(R_t)$, of the portfolio comprising one unit of the stock index and β units of the futures contract may be written as

$$E_{t-1}(R_t) = E_{t-1}(\Delta S_t) - \beta_{t-1}E_{t-1}(\Delta F_t) \tag{9.114}$$

where β_{t-1} is the hedge ratio determined at time $t-1$, for employment in period t. The variance of the expected return, $h_{p,t}$, of the portfolio may be written as

$$h_{p,t} = h_{s,t} + \beta_{t-1}^2 h_{F,t} - 2\beta_{t-1}h_{SF,t} \tag{9.115}$$

where $h_{p,t}$, $h_{s,t}$ and $h_{F,t}$ represent the conditional variances of the portfolio and the spot and futures positions, respectively and $h_{SF,t}$ represents the conditional covariance between the spot and futures position. β_{t-1}^*, the optimal number of futures contracts in the investor's portfolio, i.e. the optimal hedge ratio, is given by

$$\beta_{t-1}^* = -\frac{h_{SF,t}}{h_{F,t}} \tag{9.116}$$

If the conditional variance–covariance matrix is time-invariant (and if S_t and F_t are not cointegrated) then an estimate of β^*, the constant optimal hedge ratio, may be obtained from the estimated slope coefficient b in the regression

$$\Delta S_t = a + b\Delta F_t + u_t \tag{9.117}$$

The OLS estimate of the optimal hedge ratio could be given by $b = h_{SF}/h_F$.

9.28.3 Data and results

The data employed in the Brooks, Henry and Persand (2002) study comprises 3,580 daily observations on the FTSE 100 stock index and stock index futures contract spanning the period 1 January 1985–9 April 1999. Several approaches to estimating the optimal hedge ratio are investigated.

The hedging effectiveness is first evaluated in-sample, that is, where the hedges are constructed and evaluated using the same set of data. The out-of-sample hedging effectiveness for a one-day hedging horizon is also investigated by forming one-step-ahead forecasts of the conditional variance of the futures series and the conditional covariance between the spot and futures series. These forecasts are then translated into hedge ratios using (9.116). The hedging performance of a *BEKK* formulation is examined, and also a *BEKK* model including asymmetry terms (in the same style as GJR models). The returns and variances for the various hedging strategies are presented in table 9.5.

The simplest approach, presented in column (2), is that of no hedge at all. In this case, the portfolio simply comprises a long position in the cash market. Such an approach is able to achieve significant positive returns in sample, but with a large variability of portfolio returns. Although none of the alternative strategies generate returns that are significantly different from zero, either in-sample or out-of-sample, it is clear from columns (3)–(5) of table 9.5 that any hedge generates significantly less return variability than none at all.

Table 9.5	Hedging effectiveness: summary statistics for portfolio returns			
		In-sample		
	Unhedged $\beta = 0$	Naive hedge $\beta = -1$	Symmetric time-varying hedge $\beta_t = \dfrac{h_{FS,t}}{h_{F,t}}$	Asymmetric time-varying hedge $\beta_t = \dfrac{h_{FS,t}}{h_{F,t}}$
(1)	(2)	(3)	(4)	(5)
Return	0.0389	−0.0003	0.0061	0.0060
	{2.3713}	{−0.0351}	{0.9562}	{0.9580}
Variance	0.8286	0.1718	0.1240	0.1211
		Out-of-sample		
	Unhedged $\beta = 0$	Naive hedge $\beta = -1$	Symmetric time-varying hedge $\beta_t = \dfrac{h_{FS,t}}{h_{F,t}}$	Asymmetric time-varying hedge $\beta_t = \dfrac{h_{FS,t}}{h_{F,t}}$
Return	0.0819	−0.0004	0.0120	0.0140
	{1.4958}	{0.0216}	{0.7761}	{0.9083}
Variance	1.4972	0.1696	0.1186	0.1188

Note: t-ratios displayed as {.}.
Source: Brooks, Henry and Persand (2002).

The 'naive' hedge, which takes one short futures contract for every spot unit, but does not allow the hedge to time-vary, generates a reduction in variance of the order of 80% in-sample and nearly 90% out-of-sample relative to the unhedged position. Allowing the hedge ratio to be time-varying and determined from a symmetric multivariate GARCH model leads to a further reduction as a proportion of the unhedged variance of 5% and 2% for the in-sample and holdout sample, respectively. Allowing for an asymmetric response of the conditional variance to positive and negative shocks yields a very modest reduction in variance (a further 0.5% of the initial value) in-sample, and virtually no change out-of-sample.

Figure 9.5 graphs the time-varying hedge ratio from the symmetric and asymmetric MGARCH models (source: Brooks, Henry and Persand, 2002). The optimal hedge ratio is never greater than 0.96 futures contracts per index contract, with an average value of 0.82 futures contracts sold per long index contract. The variance of the estimated optimal hedge ratio is 0.0019. Moreover the optimal

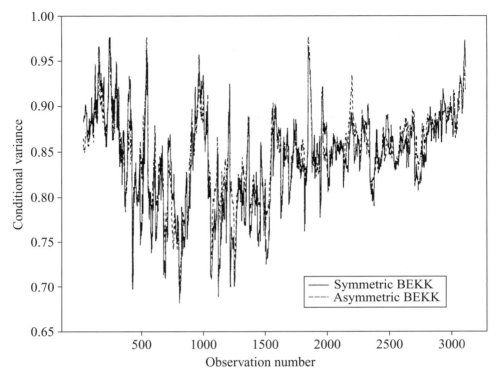

Figure 9.5   Time-varying hedge ratios derived from symmetric and asymmetric BEKK models for FTSE returns

hedge ratio series obtained through the estimation of the asymmetric GARCH model appears stationary. An ADF test of the null hypothesis $\beta^*_{t-1} \sim I(1)$ (i.e. that the optimal hedge ratio from the asymmetric BEKK model contains a unit root) was strongly rejected by the data (ADF statistic $= -5.7215$, 5% Critical value $= -2.8630$). The time-varying hedge requires the sale (purchase) of fewer futures contracts per long (short) index contract and hence would save the firm wishing to hedge a short exposure money relative to the time-invariant hedge. One possible interpretation of the better performance of the dynamic strategies over the naive hedge is that the dynamic hedge uses short-run information, while the naive hedge is driven by long-run considerations and an assumption that the relationship between spot and futures price movements is 1:1.

Brooks, Henry and Persand also investigate the hedging performances of the various models using a modern risk management approach. They find, once again, that the time-varying hedge results in a considerable improvement, but that allowing for asymmetries results in only a very modest incremental reduction in hedged portfolio risk.

9.29 Multivariate stochastic volatility models

As in the univariate case, while the term 'stochastic volatility' is commonly used to describe models from the multivariate GARCH family, strictly they do not fit well under this umbrella because the conditional variance and covariance equations are deterministic given the information set up to the previous period. That is, there is no additional source of noise in the conditional variance (or covariance) equation of a multivariate GARCH model.

The multivariate stochastic volatility (MSV) model was initially proposed by Harvey, Ruiz and Shephard (1994) and the notation here will closely follow theirs. Let y_t be the elements of an $N \times 1$ vector of observations at time t on a series i, with time-varying variance σ_i^2, defined as

$$y_{it} = \epsilon_{it}(\exp\{h_{it}\})^{1/2}, \qquad i = 1, \ldots, N; t = 1, \ldots, T \tag{9.118}$$

where $\epsilon = (\epsilon_{1t}, \ldots, \epsilon_{Nt})$ is a vector of disturbances with zero mean and covariance matrix Σ_ϵ and where

$$h_{it} = \log(\sigma_{it}^2) \tag{9.119}$$

This covariance matrix, Σ_ϵ is defined to have unity on the leading diagonal (and it is therefore also a correlation matrix), while its off-diagonal elements are denoted ρ_{ij}.

Under the stochastic volatility model, the h_{it} can be specified to evolve as an autoregressive (AR) process of order P

$$h_{it} = \gamma_i + \sum_{p=1}^{P} \psi_{ip} h_{i,t-p} + \eta_{it} \qquad i = 1, \ldots, N \tag{9.120}$$

$\eta_t = (\eta_{1t}, \ldots, \eta_{Nt})$ is a vector of disturbances to the conditional variance having zero mean and covariance matrix Σ_η. It is usually further assumed that ϵ_{it} and η_{it} are mutually independent and that each is multivariate normally distributed. Usually, $P = 1$ is deemed sufficient so that the variance dynamics for each series in the system are AR(1). Moving average terms or even exogenous variables could be added to the variance specification but rarely are in practice.

It is worth noting that in this model, the correlations ρ_{ij} between the mean equation disturbances are required to be fixed over time. Thus the covariances across the N series evolve as functions of the variances rather than independently of them. This formulation parallels the constant conditional correlation multivariate GARCH model of Bollerslev (1990) discussed above, and represents an important limitation of the model. It does, however, imply that MSV models are highly parsimonious, and the number of parameters scales directly with the number of variables in the system. For example, in the context of a bivariate MSV model, there are eight parameters to estimate.[3]

Harvey *et al.* (1994) propose estimating the model using quasi-maximum likelihood (QML) via the Kalman filter. However, Danielsson (1998) argues that their QML approach results in inefficient estimation. An alternative approach to estimating MSV models is to make use of Bayesian Markov Chain

---

[3] This compares with nine for a diagonal VECH MGARCH model and 21 for the unrestricted MGARCH.

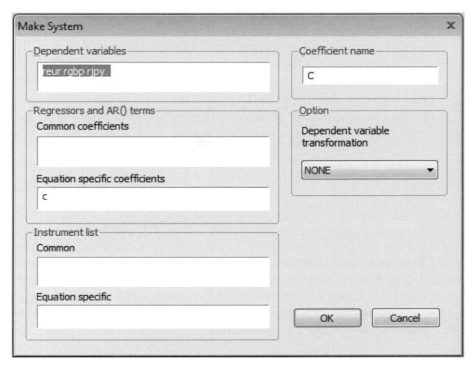

Screenshot 9.6   **Making a system**

Monte Carlo (MCMC) methods, as proposed by Jacquier, Polson and Rossi (1995).[4]

9.30   Estimating multivariate GARCH models using EViews

To estimate such a model, first you need to create a system that contains the variables to be used. **Highlight the three variables 'reur', 'rgbp', and 'rjpy'** and then **right click** the mouse. Choose **Open/as System...,**. Screenshot 9.6 will appear.

Since no explanatory variables will be used in the conditional mean equation, all of the default choices can be retained, so just click **OK**. A system box containing the three equations with just intercepts will be seen. Then click **Proc/Estimate...** for the 'System Estimation' window. Change the 'Estimation method' to **ARCH – Conditional Heteroscedasticity** and screenshot 9.7 will appear.

EViews permits the estimation of three important classes of multivariate GARCH model: the diagonal VECH, the constant conditional correlation and the diagonal BEKK models. For the error distribution, either a multivariate normal or a multivariate Student's t can be used. Additional exogenous variables can be incorporated into the variance equation, and asymmetries can be allowed for.

---

[4] See Chib and Greenberg (1996) for an extensive but very technical discussion of the intricacies of the MCMC technique.

Screenshot 9.7 **Multivariate GARCH estimation options**

Clicking on the Options tab can allow the user to modify the settings used in the optimisation, which can be useful in case there are problems with the model estimation such as non-convergence or convergence to implausible parameter estimates. Leaving all of these options as the defaults and clicking **OK** would yield the results on the following pages.[5]

The first panel of the table presents the conditional mean estimates; in this example, only intercepts were used in the mean equations. The next panel shows the variance equation coefficients, followed by some measures of goodness of fit for the model as a whole and then for each individual mean equation. The final panel presents the transformed variance coefficients, which in this case are identical to the panel of variance coefficients since no transformation is conducted with normal errors (these would only be different if a Student's t specification were used). It is evident that the parameter estimates are all both plausible and statistically significant.

There are a number of useful further steps that can be conducted once the model has been estimated, all of which are available by clicking the 'View' button. For example, we can plot the series of residuals, or estimate the correlations between them. Or by clicking on 'Conditional variance', we can list or plot the values of the conditional variances and covariances or correlations over time. We can also test for autocorrelation and normality of the errors.

---

[5] The complexity of this model means that it takes longer to estimate than any of the univariate GARCH or other models examined previously.

System: UNTITLED
Estimation Method: ARCH Maximum Likelihood (Marquardt)
Covariance specification: Diagonal VECH
Date: 08/06/13 Time: 05:50
Sample: 7/08/2002 6/06/2013
Included observations: 3987
Total system (balanced) observations 11961
Presample covariance: backcast (parameter = 0.7)
Convergence achieved after 15 iterations

	Coefficient	Std. Error	z-Statistic	Prob.
C(1)	−0.014665	0.006099	−2.404605	0.0162
C(2)	−0.010580	0.005707	−1.853937	0.0637
C(3)	0.008758	0.006197	1.413283	0.1576
Variance Equation Coefficients				
C(4)	0.000758	0.000142	5.333032	0.000
C(5)	0.000811	0.000118	6.893582	0.000
C(6)	0.000972	0.000138	7.057098	0.000
C(7)	0.000955	0.000151	6.329567	0.000
C(8)	0.000899	0.000134	6.729971	0.000
C(9)	0.005043	0.000437	11.53342	0.000
C(10)	0.029060	0.001835	15.83992	0.000
C(11)	0.025820	0.001535	16.81733	0.000
C(12)	0.034765	0.002368	14.67968	0.000
C(13)	0.030542	0.001972	15.48565	0.000
C(14)	0.036163	0.002608	13.86502	0.000
C(15)	0.054571	0.003427	15.92236	0.000
C(16)	0.967396	0.001849	523.0839	0.000
C(17)	0.966886	0.001784	542.0472	0.000
C(18)	0.953080	0.003015	316.1549	0.000
C(19)	0.963545	0.002291	420.5394	0.000
C(20)	0.946951	0.003561	265.9424	0.000
C(21)	0.923789	0.004770	193.6745	0.000

Log likelihood	−4949.970	Schwarz criterion	2.526724
Avg. log likelihood	−0.413842	Hannan-Quinn criter.	2.505336
Akaike info criterion	2.493589		

Equation: REUR = C(1)

R-squared	−0.000232	Mean dependent var	−0.007413
Adjusted R-squared	−0.000232	S.D. dependent var	0.476621
S.E. of regression	0.476676	Sum squared resid	905.6991
Prob(F-statistic)	1.694663		

Equation: RGBP = C(2)

R-squared	−0.000548	Mean dependent var	−0.000226
Adjusted R-squared	−0.000548	S.D. dependent var	0.442446
S.E. of regression	0.442568	Sum squared resid	780.7222
Prob(F-statistic)	1.580781		

Equation: RJPY = C(3)

R-squared	−0.000313	Mean dependent var	−0.004699
Adjusted R-squared	−0.000313	S.D. dependent var	0.471950
S.E. of regression	0.472142	Sum squared resid	888.5516
Prob(F-statistic)	1.704282		

Covariance specification: Diagonal VECH
GARCH = M + A1.*RESID(−1)*RESID(−1)` + B1.*GARCH(−1)
M is an indefinite matrix
A1 is an indefinite matrix
B1 is an indefinite matrix

Transformed Variance Coefficients

	Coefficient	Std. Error	z-Statistic	Prob.
M(1,1)	0.000758	0.000142	5.333032	0.000
M(1,2)	0.000811	0.000118	6.893582	0.000
M(1,3)	0.000972	0.000138	7.057098	0.000
M(2,2)	0.000955	0.000151	6.329567	0.000
M(2,3)	0.000899	0.000134	6.729971	0.000
M(3,3)	0.005043	0.000437	11.53342	0.000
A1(1,1)	0.029060	0.001835	15.83992	0.000
A1(1,2)	0.025820	0.001535	16.81733	0.000
A1(1,3)	0.034765	0.002368	14.67968	0.000
A1(2,2)	0.030542	0.001972	15.48565	0.000
A1(2,3)	0.036163	0.002608	13.86502	0.000
A1(3,3)	0.054571	0.003427	15.92236	0.000
B1(1,1)	0.967396	0.001849	523.0839	0.000
B1(1,2)	0.966886	0.001784	542.0472	0.000
B1(1,3)	0.953080	0.003015	316.1549	0.000
B1(2,2)	0.963545	0.002291	420.5394	0.000
B1(2,3)	0.946951	0.003561	265.9424	0.000
B1(3,3)	0.923789	0.004770	193.6745	0.000

∗ Coefficient matrix is not PSD.

The key terms to be able to define and explain from this chapter are

- non-linearity
- conditional variance
- maximum likelihood
- lagrange multiplier test
- asymmetry in volatility
- constant conditional correlation
- diagonal VECH
- news impact curve
- volatility clustering

- GARCH model
- Wald test
- likelihood ratio test
- GJR specification
- exponentially weighted moving average
- BEKK model
- GARCH-in-mean

Appendix   Parameter estimation using maximum likelihood

For simplicity, this appendix will consider by way of illustration the bivariate regression case with homoscedastic errors (i.e. assuming that there is no ARCH and that the variance of the errors is constant over time). Suppose that the linear regression model of interest is of the form

$$y_t = \beta_1 + \beta_2 x_t + u_t \tag{9A.1}$$

Assuming that $u_t \sim N(0, \sigma^2)$, then $y_t \sim N(\beta_1 + \beta_2 x_t, \sigma^2)$ so that the probability density function for a normally distributed random variable with this mean and variance is given by

$$f(y_t \mid \beta_1 + \beta_2 x_t, \sigma^2) = \frac{1}{\sigma\sqrt{2\pi}} \exp\left\{ -\frac{1}{2} \frac{(y_t - \beta_1 - \beta_2 x_t)^2}{\sigma^2} \right\} \tag{9A.2}$$

The probability density is a function of the data given the parameters. Successive values of y_t would trace out the familiar bell-shaped curve of the normal distribution. Since the ys are iid, the joint probability density function (pdf) for all the ys can be expressed as a product of the individual density functions

$$f(y_1, y_2, \ldots, y_T \mid \beta_1 + \beta_2 x_1, \beta_1 + \beta_2 x_2, \ldots, \beta_1 + \beta_2 x_T, \sigma^2)$$

$$= f(y_1 \mid \beta_1 + \beta_2 x_2, \sigma^2) f(y_2 \mid \beta_1 + \beta_2 x_2, \sigma^2) \ldots f(y_T \mid \beta_1 + \beta_2 x_T, \sigma^2)$$

$$= \prod_{t=1}^{T} f(y_t \mid \beta_1 + \beta_2 x_t, \sigma^2) \quad \text{for } t = 1, \ldots, T \tag{9A.3}$$

The term on the LHS of this expression is known as the *joint density* and the terms on the RHS are known as the *marginal densities*. This result follows from the independence of the y values, in the same way as under elementary probability, for three independent events A, B and C, the probability of A, B and C all happening is the probability of A multiplied by the probability of B multiplied by the probability of C. Equation (9A.3) shows the probability of obtaining all of the values of y that did occur. Substituting into (9A.3) for every y_t from (9A.2), and using the result that $Ae^{x_1} \times Ae^{x_2} \times \cdots Ae^{x_T} = A^T(e^{x_1} \times e^{x_2} \times \cdots \times e^{x_T}) = A^T e^{(x_1 + x_2 + \cdots + x_T)}$, the following expression is obtained

$$f(y_1, y_2, \ldots, y_T \mid \beta_1 + \beta_2 x_t, \sigma^2)$$

$$= \frac{1}{\sigma^T(\sqrt{2\pi})^T} \exp\left\{ -\frac{1}{2} \sum_{t=1}^{T} \frac{(y_t - \beta_1 - \beta_2 x_t)^2}{\sigma^2} \right\} \tag{9A.4}$$

This is the joint density of all of the ys given the values of x_t, β_1, β_2 and σ^2. However, the typical situation that occurs in practice is the reverse of the above situation – that is, the x_t and y_t are given and β_1, β_2, σ^2 are to be estimated. If this is the case, then $f(\bullet)$ is known as a likelihood function, denoted $LF(\beta_1, \beta_2, \sigma^2)$, which would be written

$$LF(\beta_1, \beta_2, \sigma^2) = \frac{1}{\sigma^T(\sqrt{2\pi})^T} \exp\left\{ -\frac{1}{2} \sum_{t=1}^{T} \frac{(y_t - \beta_1 - \beta_2 x_t)^2}{\sigma^2} \right\} \tag{9A.5}$$

Maximum likelihood estimation involves choosing parameter values $(\beta_1, \beta_2, \sigma^2)$ that maximise this function. Doing this ensures that the values of the parameters are chosen that maximise the likelihood that we would have actually observed the ys that we did. It is necessary to differentiate (9A.5) w.r.t. β_1, β_2, σ^2, but (9A.5) is a product containing T terms, and so would be difficult to differentiate.

Fortunately, since $\max_x f(x) = \max_x \ln(f(x))$, logs of (9A.5) can be taken, and the resulting expression differentiated, knowing that the same optimal values for the parameters will be chosen in both cases. Then, using the various laws for transforming functions containing logarithms, the log-likelihood function, LLF is obtained

$$LLF = -T \ln \sigma - \frac{T}{2} \ln(2\pi) - \frac{1}{2} \sum_{t=1}^{T} \frac{(y_t - \beta_1 - \beta_2 x_t)^2}{\sigma^2} \tag{9A.6}$$

which is equivalent to

$$LLF = -\frac{T}{2} \ln \sigma^2 - \frac{T}{2} \ln(2\pi) - \frac{1}{2} \sum_{t=1}^{T} \frac{(y_t - \beta_1 - \beta_2 x_t)^2}{\sigma^2} \tag{9A.7}$$

Only the first part of the RHS of (9A.6) has been changed in (9A.7) to make σ^2 appear in that part of the expression rather than σ.

Remembering the result that

$$\frac{\partial}{\partial x}(\ln(x)) = \frac{1}{x}$$

and differentiating (9A.7) w.r.t. β_1, β_2, σ^2, the following expressions for the first derivatives are obtained

$$\frac{\partial LLF}{\partial \beta_1} = -\frac{1}{2} \sum \frac{(y_t - \beta_1 - \beta_2 x_t).2. - 1}{\sigma^2} \tag{9A.8}$$

$$\frac{\partial LLF}{\partial \beta_2} = -\frac{1}{2} \sum \frac{(y_t - \beta_1 - \beta_2 x_t).2. - x_t}{\sigma^2} \tag{9A.9}$$

$$\frac{\partial LLF}{\partial \sigma^2} = -\frac{T}{2}\frac{1}{\sigma^2} + \frac{1}{2} \sum \frac{(y_t - \beta_1 - \beta_2 x_t)^2}{\sigma^4} \tag{9A.10}$$

Setting (9A.8)–(9A.10) to zero to minimise the functions, and placing hats above the parameters to denote the maximum likelihood estimators, from (9A.8)

$$\sum (y_t - \hat{\beta}_1 - \hat{\beta}_2 x_t) = 0 \tag{9A.11}$$

$$\sum y_t - \sum \hat{\beta}_1 - \sum \hat{\beta}_2 x_t = 0 \tag{9A.12}$$

$$\sum y_t - T\hat{\beta}_1 - \hat{\beta}_2 \sum x_t = 0 \tag{9A.13}$$

$$\frac{1}{T} \sum y_t - \hat{\beta}_1 - \hat{\beta}_2 \frac{1}{T} \sum x_t = 0 \tag{9A.14}$$

Recall that

$$\frac{1}{T} \sum y_t = \bar{y}_t$$

the mean of y and similarly for x, an estimator for $\hat{\beta}_1$ can finally be derived

$$\hat{\beta}_1 = \bar{y} - \hat{\beta}_2 \bar{x} \tag{9A.15}$$

From (9A.9)

$$\sum (y_t - \hat{\beta}_1 - \hat{\beta}_2 x_t)x_t = 0 \tag{9A.16}$$

$$\sum y_t x_t - \sum \hat{\beta}_1 x_t - \sum \hat{\beta}_2 x_t^2 = 0 \tag{9A.17}$$

$$\sum y_t x_t - \hat{\beta}_1 \sum x_t - \hat{\beta}_2 \sum x_t^2 = 0 \tag{9A.18}$$

$$\hat{\beta}_2 \sum x_t^2 = \sum y_t x_t - (\bar{y} - \hat{\beta}_2 \bar{x}) \sum x_t \tag{9A.19}$$

$$\hat{\beta}_2 \sum x_t^2 = \sum y_t x_t - T\overline{xy} + \hat{\beta}_2 T\bar{x}^2 \tag{9A.20}$$

$$\hat{\beta}_2\left(\sum x_t^2 - T\bar{x}^2\right) = \sum y_t x_t - T\overline{xy} \tag{9A.21}$$

$$\hat{\beta}_2 = \frac{\sum y_t x_t - T\overline{xy}}{\left(\sum x_t^2 - T\bar{x}^2\right)} \tag{9A.22}$$

From (9A.10)

$$\frac{T}{\hat{\sigma}^2} = \frac{1}{\hat{\sigma}^4}\sum (y_t - \hat{\beta}_1 - \hat{\beta}_2 x_t)^2 \tag{9A.23}$$

Rearranging,

$$\hat{\sigma}^2 = \frac{1}{T}\sum (y_t - \hat{\beta}_1 - \hat{\beta}_2 x_t)^2 \tag{9A.24}$$

But the term in parentheses on the RHS of (9A.24) is the residual for time t (i.e. the actual minus the fitted value), so

$$\hat{\sigma}^2 = \frac{1}{T}\sum \hat{u}_t^2 \tag{9A.25}$$

How do these formulae compare with the OLS estimators? (9A.15) and (9A.22) are identical to those of OLS. So maximum likelihood and OLS will deliver identical estimates of the intercept and slope coefficients. However, the estimate of $\hat{\sigma}^2$ in (9A.25) is different. The OLS estimator was

$$\hat{\sigma}^2 = \frac{1}{T-k}\sum \hat{u}_t^2 \tag{9A.26}$$

and it was also shown that the OLS estimator is unbiased. Therefore, the ML estimator of the error variance must be biased, although it is consistent, since as $T \to \infty$, $T - k \approx T$.

Note that the derivation above could also have been conducted using matrix rather than sigma algebra. The resulting estimators for the intercept and slope coefficients would still be identical to those of OLS, while the estimate of the error variance would again be biased. It is also worth noting that the ML estimator is consistent and asymptotically efficient. Derivation of the ML estimator for the GARCH *LLF* is algebraically difficult and therefore beyond the scope of this book.

Self-study questions

1. (a) What stylised features of financial data cannot be explained using linear time series models?
   (b) Which of these features could be modelled using a GARCH(1,1) process?
   (c) Why, in recent empirical research, have researchers preferred GARCH(1,1) models to pure ARCH(p)?

(d) Describe two extensions to the original GARCH model. What additional characteristics of financial data might they be able to capture?

(e) Consider the following GARCH(1,1) model

$$y_t = \mu + u_t, \qquad u_t \sim N(0, \sigma_t^2) \tag{9.121}$$

$$\sigma_t^2 = \alpha_0 + \alpha_1 u_{t-1}^2 + \beta \sigma_{t-1}^2 \tag{9.122}$$

If y_t is a daily stock return series, what range of values are likely for the coefficients μ, α_0, α_1 and β?

(f) Suppose that a researcher wanted to test the null hypothesis that $\alpha_1 + \beta = 1$ in the equation for part (e). Explain how this might be achieved within the maximum likelihood framework.

(g) Suppose now that the researcher had estimated the above GARCH model for a series of returns on a stock index and obtained the following parameter estimates: $\hat{\mu} = 0.0023$, $\hat{\alpha}_0 = 0.0172$, $\hat{\beta} = 0.9811$, $\hat{\alpha}_1 = 0.1251$. If the researcher has data available up to and including time T, write down a set of equations in σ_t^2 and u_t^2 their lagged values, which could be employed to produce one-, two-, and three-step-ahead forecasts for the conditional variance of y_t.

(h) Suppose now that the coefficient estimate of $\hat{\beta}$ for this model is 0.98 instead. By reconsidering the forecast expressions you derived in part (g), explain what would happen to the forecasts in this case.

2. (a) Discuss briefly the principles behind maximum likelihood.

(b) Describe briefly the three hypothesis testing procedures that are available under maximum likelihood estimation. Which is likely to be the easiest to calculate in practice, and why?

(c) OLS and maximum likelihood are used to estimate the parameters of a standard linear regression model. Will they give the same estimates? Explain your answer.

3. (a) Distinguish between the terms 'conditional variance' and 'unconditional variance'. Which of the two is more likely to be relevant for producing:
   i. one-step-ahead volatility forecasts
   ii. twenty-step-ahead volatility forecasts.

(b) If u_t follows a GARCH(1,1) process, what would be the likely result if a regression of the form (9.121) were estimated using OLS and assuming a constant conditional variance?

(c) Compare and contrast the following models for volatility, noting their strengths and weaknesses:
   i. Historical volatility
   ii. EWMA
   iii. GARCH(1,1)
   iv. Implied volatility.

4. Suppose that a researcher is interested in modelling the correlation between the returns of the NYSE and LSE markets.

(a) Write down a simple diagonal VECH model for this problem. Discuss the values for the coefficient estimates that you would expect.

(b) Suppose that weekly correlation forecasts for two weeks ahead are required. Describe a procedure for constructing such forecasts from a set of daily returns data for the two market indices.

(c) What other approaches to correlation modelling are available?

(d) What are the strengths and weaknesses of multivariate GARCH models relative to the alternatives that you propose in part (c)?

5. (a) What is a news impact curve? Using a spreadsheet or otherwise, construct the news impact curve for the following estimated EGARCH and GARCH models, setting the lagged conditional variance to the value of the unconditional variance (estimated from the sample data rather than the mode parameter estimates), which is 0.096

$$\sigma_t^2 = \alpha_0 + \alpha_1 u_{t-1}^2 + \alpha_2 \sigma_{t-1}^2 \tag{9.123}$$

$$\log\left(\sigma_t^2\right) = \alpha_0 + \alpha_1 \frac{u_{t-1}}{\sqrt{\sigma_{t-1}^2}} + \alpha_2 \log\left(\sigma_{t-1}^2\right) + \alpha_3 \left[\frac{|u_{t-1}|}{\sqrt{\sigma_{t-1}^2}} - \sqrt{\frac{2}{\pi}} \right] \tag{9.124}$$

	GARCH	EGARCH
μ	−0.0130	−0.0278
	(0.0669)	(0.0855)
α_0	0.0019	0.0823
	(0.0017)	(0.5728)
α_1	0.1022**	−0.0214
	(0.0333)	(0.0332)
α_2	0.9050**	0.9639**
	(0.0175)	(0.0136)
α_3	—	0.2326**
		(0.0795)

(b) In fact, the models in part (a) were estimated using daily foreign exchange returns. How can financial theory explain the patterns observed in the news impact curves?

6. Using EViews, estimate a multivariate GARCH model for the spot and futures returns series in 'sandphedge.wf1'. Note that these series are somewhat short for multivariate GARCH model estimation. Save the fitted conditional variances and covariances, and then use these to construct the time-varying optimal hedge ratios. Compare this plot with the unconditional hedge ratio calculated in chapter 3.

10 Switching models

Learning outcomes

In this chapter, you will learn how to
- Use intercept and slope dummy variables to allow for seasonal behaviour in time series
- Motivate the use of regime switching models in financial econometrics
- Specify and explain the logic behind Markov switching models
- Compare and contrast Markov switching and threshold autoregressive models
- Describe the intuition behind the estimation of regime switching models

10.1 Motivations

Many financial and economic time series seem to undergo episodes in which the behaviour of the series changes quite dramatically compared to that exhibited previously. The behaviour of a series could change over time in terms of its mean value, its volatility, or to what extent its current value is related to its previous value. The behaviour may change once and for all, usually known as a 'structural break' in a series. Or it may change for a period of time before reverting back to its original behaviour or switching to yet another style of behaviour, and the latter is typically termed a 'regime shift' or 'regime switch'.

10.1.1 What might cause one-off fundamental changes in the properties of a series?

Usually, very substantial changes in the properties of a series are attributed to large-scale events, such as wars, financial panics – e.g. a 'run on a bank', significant changes in government policy, such as the introduction of an inflation target, or the removal of exchange controls, or changes in market microstructure – e.g. the 'Big Bang', when trading on the London Stock Exchange (LSE) became electronic, or

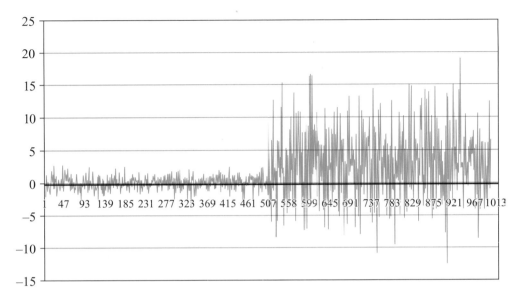

Figure 10.1   Sample time series plot illustrating a regime shift

a change in the market trading mechanism, such as the partial move of the LSE from a quote-driven to an order-driven system in 1997.

However, it is also true that regime shifts can occur on a regular basis and at much higher frequency. Such changes may occur as a result of more subtle factors, but still leading to statistically important modifications in behaviour. An example would be the intraday patterns observed in equity market bid–ask spreads (see chapter 7). These appear to start with high values at the open, gradually narrowing throughout the day, before widening again at the close.

To give an illustration of the kind of shifts that may be seen to occur, figure 10.1 gives an extreme example. As can be seen from the figure, the behaviour of the series changes markedly at around observation 500. Not only does the series become much more volatile than previously, its mean value is also substantially increased. Although this is a severe case that was generated using simulated data, clearly, in the face of such 'regime changes' a linear model estimated over the whole sample covering the change would not be appropriate. One possible approach to this problem would be simply to split the data around the time of the change and to estimate separate models on each portion. It would be possible to allow a series, y_t to be drawn from two or more different generating processes at different times. For example, if it was thought an AR(1) process was appropriate to capture the relevant features of a particular series whose behaviour changed at observation 500, say, two models could be estimated:

$$y_t = \mu_1 + \phi_1 y_{t-1} + u_{1t} \quad \text{before observation 500} \tag{10.1}$$

$$y_t = \mu_2 + \phi_2 y_{t-1} + u_{2t} \quad \text{after observation 500} \tag{10.2}$$

In the context of figure 10.1, this would involve focusing on the mean shift only. These equations represent a very simple example of what is known as a piecewise linear model – that is, although the model is globally (i.e. when it is taken as a whole) non-linear, each of the component parts is a linear model.

This method may be valid, but it is also likely to be wasteful of information. For example, even if there were enough observations in each sub-sample to estimate separate (linear) models, there would be an efficiency loss in having fewer observations in each of two samples than if all the observations were collected together. Also, it may be the case that only one property of the series has changed – for example, the (unconditional) mean value of the series may have changed, leaving its other properties unaffected. In this case, it would be sensible to try to keep all of the observations together, but to allow for the particular form of the structural change in the model-building process. Thus, what is required is a set of models that allow all of the observations on a series to be used for estimating a model, but also that the model is sufficiently flexible to allow different types of behaviour at different points in time. Two classes of regime switching models that potentially allow this to occur are *Markov switching models* and *threshold autoregressive models*.

A first and central question to ask is: How can it be determined where the switch(es) occurs? The method employed for making this choice will depend upon the model used. A simple type of switching model is one where the switches are made deterministically using dummy variables. One important use of this in finance is to allow for 'seasonality' in financial data. In economics and finance generally, many series are believed to exhibit seasonal behaviour, which results in a certain element of partly predictable cycling of the series over time. For example, if monthly or quarterly data on consumer spending are examined, it is likely that the value of the series will rise rapidly in late November owing to Christmas-related expenditure, followed by a fall in mid-January, when consumers realise that they have spent too much before Christmas and in the January sales! Consumer spending in the UK also typically drops during the August vacation period when all of the sensible people have left the country. Such phenomena will be apparent in many series and will be present to some degree at the same time every year, whatever else is happening in terms of the long-term trend and short-term variability of the series.

10.2 Seasonalities in financial markets: introduction and literature review

In the context of financial markets, and especially in the case of equities, a number of other 'seasonal effects' have been noted. Such effects are usually known as 'calendar anomalies' or 'calendar effects'. Examples include open- and close-of-market effects, 'the January effect', weekend effects and bank holiday effects. Investigation into the existence or otherwise of 'calendar effects' in financial markets has been the subject of a considerable amount of recent academic research. Calendar effects may be loosely defined as the tendency of financial asset returns to display systematic patterns at certain times of the day, week, month or year. One example of the most important such anomalies is the *day-of-the-week effect*, which results in average returns being significantly higher on some days of the week than others. Studies by French (1980), Gibbons and Hess (1981) and Keim and Stambaugh (1984), for example, have found that the average market close-to-close return in the US is significantly negative on Monday and significantly positive on Friday. By contrast, Jaffe and Westerfield (1985) found that the lowest mean returns for the Japanese and Australian stock markets occur on Tuesdays.

At first glance, these results seem to contradict the efficient markets hypothesis, since the existence of calendar anomalies might be taken to imply that investors could develop trading strategies which make abnormal profits on the basis of such patterns. For example, holding all other factors constant, equity purchasers may wish to sell at the close on Friday and to buy at the close on Thursday in order to take advantage of these effects. However, evidence for the predictability of stock returns does not necessarily imply market inefficiency, for at least two reasons. First, it is likely that the small average excess returns documented by the above papers would not generate net gains when employed in a trading strategy once the costs of transacting in the markets has been taken into account. Therefore, under many 'modern' definitions of market efficiency (e.g. Jensen, 1978), these markets would not be classified as inefficient. Second, the apparent differences in returns on different days of the week may be attributable to time-varying stock market risk premiums.

If any of these calendar phenomena are present in the data but ignored by the model-building process, the result is likely to be a misspecified model. For example, ignored seasonality in y_t is likely to lead to residual autocorrelation of the order of the seasonality – e.g. fifth order residual autocorrelation if y_t is a series of daily returns.

10.3 Modelling seasonality in financial data

As discussed above, seasonalities at various different frequencies in financial time series data are so well documented that their existence cannot be doubted, even if there is argument about how they can be rationalised. One very simple method for coping with this and examining the degree to which seasonality is present is the inclusion of dummy variables in regression equations. The number of dummy variables that could sensibly be constructed to model the seasonality would depend on the frequency of the data. For example, four dummy variables would be created for quarterly data, twelve for monthly data, five for daily data and so on. In the case of quarterly data, the four dummy variables would be defined as follows:

$D1_t = 1$ in quarter 1 and zero otherwise
$D2_t = 1$ in quarter 2 and zero otherwise
$D3_t = 1$ in quarter 3 and zero otherwise
$D4_t = 1$ in quarter 4 and zero otherwise

How many dummy variables can be placed in a regression model? If an intercept term is used in the regression, the number of dummies that could also be included would be one less than the 'seasonality' of the data. To see why this is the case, consider what happens if all four dummies are used for the quarterly series. The following gives the values that the dummy variables would take for a period

Box 10.1   How do dummy variables work?

The dummy variables as described above operate by *changing the intercept*, so that the average value of the dependent variable, given all of the explanatory variables, is permitted to change across the seasons. This is shown in figure 10.2.

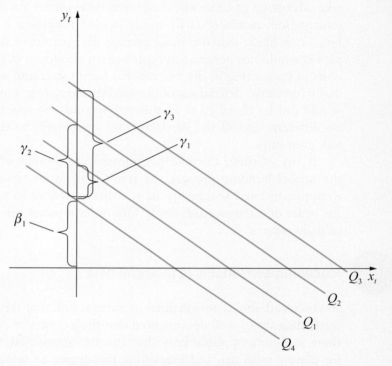

Figure 10.2   Use of intercept dummy variables for quarterly data

Consider the following regression

$$y_t = \beta_1 + \gamma_1 D1_t + \gamma_2 D2_t + \gamma_3 D3_t + \beta_2 x_{2t} + \cdots + u_t \qquad (10.3)$$

During each period, the intercept will be changed. The intercept will be:

- $\hat{\beta}_1 + \hat{\gamma}_1$ in the first quarter, since $D1 = 1$ and $D2 = D3 = 0$ for all quarter 1 observations
- $\hat{\beta}_1 + \hat{\gamma}_2$ in the second quarter, since $D2 = 1$ and $D1 = D3 = 0$ for all quarter 2 observations.
- $\hat{\beta}_1 + \hat{\gamma}_3$ in the third quarter, since $D3 = 1$ and $D1 = D2 = 0$ for all quarter 3 observations
- $\hat{\beta}_1$ in the fourth quarter, since $D1 = D2 = D3 = 0$ for all quarter 4 observations.

during the mid–1980s, together with the sum of the dummies at each point in time, presented in the last column:

		D1	D2	D3	D4	Sum
1986	Q1	1	0	0	0	1
	Q2	0	1	0	0	1
	Q3	0	0	1	0	1
	Q4	0	0	0	1	1
1987	Q1	1	0	0	0	1
	Q2	0	1	0	0	1
	Q3	0	0	1	0	1
			etc.			

The sum of the four dummies would be 1 in every time period. Unfortunately, this sum is of course identical to the variable that is implicitly attached to the intercept coefficient. Thus, if the four dummy variables and the intercept were both included in the same regression, the problem would be one of perfect multi-collinearity so that $(X'X)^{-1}$ would not exist and none of the coefficients could be estimated. This problem is known as the *dummy variable trap*. The solution would be either to just use three dummy variables plus the intercept, or to use the four dummy variables with no intercept.

The seasonal features in the data would be captured using either of these, and the residuals in each case would be identical, although the interpretation of the coefficients would be changed. If four dummy variables were used (and assuming that there were no explanatory variables in the regression), the estimated coefficients could be interpreted as the average value of the dependent variable during each quarter. In the case where a constant and three dummy variables were used, the interpretation of the estimated coefficients on the dummy variables would be that they represented the average deviations of the dependent variables for the included quarters from their average values for the excluded quarter, as discussed in box 10.1.

Example 10.1 •

Brooks and Persand (2001a) examine the evidence for a day-of-the-week effect in five Southeast Asian stock markets: South Korea, Malaysia, the Philippines, Taiwan and Thailand. The data, obtained from Primark Datastream, are collected on a daily close-to-close basis for all weekdays (Mondays to Fridays) falling in the period 31 December 1989 to 19 January 1996 (a total of 1,581 observations). The first regressions estimated, which constitute the simplest tests for day-of-the-week effects, are of the form

$$r_t = \gamma_1 D1_t + \gamma_2 D2_t + \gamma_3 D3_t + \gamma_4 D4_t + \gamma_5 D5_t + u_t \qquad (10.4)$$

where r_t is the return at time t for each country examined separately, $D1_t$ is a dummy variable for Monday, taking the value 1 for all Monday observations and zero otherwise, and so on. The coefficient estimates can be interpreted as the average

Table 10.1 Values and significances of days of the week coefficients

	Thailand	Malaysia	Taiwan	South Korea	Philippines
Monday	0.49E-3	0.00322	0.00185	0.56E-3	0.00119
	(0.6740)	(3.9804)**	(2.9304)**	(0.4321)	(1.4369)
Tuesday	−0.45E-3	−0.00179	−0.00175	0.00104	−0.97E-4
	(−0.3692)	(−1.6834)	(−2.1258)**	(0.5955)	(−0.0916)
Wednesday	−0.37E-3	−0.00160	0.31E-3	−0.00264	−0.49E-3
	(−0.5005)	(−1.5912)	(0.4786)	(−2.107)**	(−0.5637)
Thursday	0.40E-3	0.00100	0.00159	−0.00159	0.92E-3
	(0.5468)	(1.0379)	(2.2886)**	(−1.2724)	(0.8908)
Friday	−0.31E-3	0.52E-3	0.40E-4	0.43E-3	0.00151
	(−0.3998)	(0.5036)	(0.0536)	(0.3123)	(1.7123)

Notes: Coefficients are given in each cell followed by t-ratios in parentheses; * and ** denote significance at the 5% and 1% levels, respectively.
Source: Brooks and Persand (2001a).

sample return on each day of the week. The results from these regressions are shown in table 10.1.

Briefly, the main features are as follows. Neither Thailand nor the Philippines have significant calendar effects; both Taiwan and Malaysia have significant positive Monday average returns and significant negative Tuesday returns; Taiwan has a significant Thursday effect.

Dummy variables could also be used to test for other calendar anomalies, such as the January effect, etc. as discussed above, and a given regression can include dummies of different frequencies at the same time. For example, a new dummy variable $D6_t$ could be added to (10.4) for 'April effects', associated with the start of the new tax year in the UK. Such a variable, even for a regression using daily data, would take the value 1 for all observations falling in April and zero otherwise.

If we choose to omit one of the dummy variables and to retain the intercept, then the omitted dummy variable becomes the reference category against which all the others are compared. For example consider a model such as the one above, but where the Monday dummy variable has been omitted

$$r_t = \alpha + \gamma_2 D2_t + \gamma_3 D3_t + \gamma_4 D4_t + \gamma_5 D5_t + u_t \tag{10.5}$$

The estimate of the intercept will be $\hat{\alpha}$ on Monday, $\hat{\alpha} + \hat{\gamma}_{21}$ on Tuesday and so on. $\hat{\gamma}_2$ will now be interpreted as the difference in average returns between Monday and

Tuesday. Similarly, $\hat{\gamma}_3, \ldots, \hat{\gamma}_5$ can also be interpreted as the differences in average returns between Wednesday, ..., Friday, and Monday.

This analysis should hopefully have made it clear that by thinking carefully about which dummy variable (or the intercept) to omit from the regression, we can control the interpretation to test naturally the hypothesis that is of most interest. The same logic can also be applied to slope dummy variables, which are described in the following section.

10.3.1 Slope dummy variables

As well as, or instead of, intercept dummies, slope dummy variables can also be used. These operate by changing the slope of the regression line, leaving the intercept unchanged. Figure 10.3 gives an illustration in the context of just one slope dummy (i.e. two different 'states'). Such a setup would apply if, for example, the data were bi-annual (twice yearly) or bi-weekly or observations made at the open and close of markets. Then D_t would be defined as $D_t = 1$ for the first half of the year and zero for the second half.

A slope dummy changes the slope of the regression line, leaving the intercept unchanged. In the above case, the intercept is fixed at α, while the slope varies over time. For periods where the value of the dummy is zero, the slope will be β, while for periods where the dummy is one, the slope will be $\beta + \gamma$.

Of course, it is also possible to use more than one dummy variable for the slopes. For example, if the data were quarterly, the following setup could be used, with $D1_t \ldots D3_t$ representing quarters 1–3.

$$y_t = \alpha + \beta x_t + \gamma_1 D1_t x_t + \gamma_2 D2_t x_t + \gamma_3 D3_t x_t + u_t \tag{10.6}$$

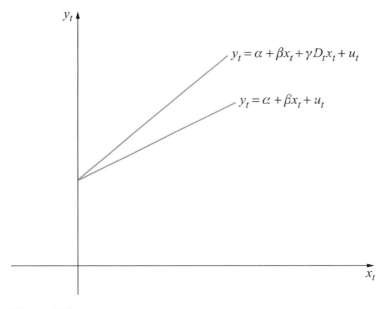

Figure 10.3   Use of slope dummy variables

In this case, since there is also a term in x_t with no dummy attached, the interpretation of the coefficients on the dummies (γ_1, etc.) is that they represent the deviation of the slope for that quarter from the average slope over all quarters. On the other hand, if the four slope dummy variables were included (and not βx_t), the coefficients on the dummies would be interpreted as the average slope coefficients during each quarter. Again, it is important not to include four quarterly slope dummies and the βx_t in the regression together, otherwise perfect multicollinearity would result.

Example 10.2

Returning to the example of day-of-the-week effects in Southeast Asian stock markets, although significant coefficients in (10.4) will support the hypothesis of seasonality in returns, it is important to note that risk factors have not been taken into account. Before drawing conclusions on the potential presence of arbitrage opportunities or inefficient markets, it is important to allow for the possibility that the market can be more or less risky on certain days than others. Hence, low (high) significant returns in (10.4) might be explained by low (high) risk. Brooks and Persand thus test for seasonality using the empirical market model, whereby market risk is proxied by the return on the FTA World Price Index. Hence, in order to look at how risk varies across the days of the week, interactive (i.e. slope) dummy variables are used to determine whether risk increases (decreases) on the day of high (low) returns. The equation, estimated separately using time series data for each country can be written

$$r_t = \left(\sum_{i=1}^{5} \alpha_i D_{it} + \beta_i D_{it} RWM_t \right) + u_t \qquad (10.7)$$

where α_i and β_i are coefficients to be estimated, D_{it} is the ith dummy variable taking the value 1 for day $t = i$ and zero otherwise, and RWM_t is the return on the world market index. In this way, when considering the effect of market risk on seasonality, both risk and return are permitted to vary across the days of the week. The results from estimation of (10.7) are given in table 10.2. Note that South Korea and the Philippines are excluded from this part of the analysis, since no significant calendar anomalies were found to explain in table 10.1.

As can be seen, significant Monday effects in the Bangkok and Kuala Lumpur stock exchanges, and a significant Thursday effect in the latter, remain even after the inclusion of the slope dummy variables which allow risk to vary across the week. The t-ratios do fall slightly in absolute value, however, indicating that the day-of-the-week effects become slightly less pronounced. The significant negative average return for the Taiwanese stock exchange, however, completely disappears. It is also clear that average risk levels vary across the days of the week. For example, the betas for the Bangkok stock exchange vary from a low of 0.36 on Monday to a high of over unity on Tuesday. This illustrates that not only is there a significant positive Monday effect in this market, but also that the responsiveness of Bangkok market movements to changes in the value of the general world stock market is considerably lower on this day than on other days of the week.

Table 10.2 Day-of-the-week effects with the inclusion of interactive dummy variables with the risk proxy

	Thailand	Malaysia	Taiwan
Monday	0.00322	0.00185	0.544E-3
	(3.3571)**	(2.8025)**	(0.3945)
Tuesday	−0.00114	−0.00122	0.00140
	(−1.1545)	(−1.8172)	(1.0163)
Wednesday	−0.00164	0.25E-3	−0.00263
	(−1.6926)	(0.3711)	(−1.9188)
Thursday	0.00104	0.00157	−0.00166
	(1.0913)	(2.3515)*	(−1.2116)
Friday	0.31E-4	−0.3752	−0.13E-3
	(0.03214)	(−0.5680)	(−0.0976)
Beta-Monday	0.3573	0.5494	0.6330
	(2.1987)*	(4.9284)**	(2.7464)**
Beta-Tuesday	1.0254	0.9822	0.6572
	(8.0035)**	(11.2708)**	(3.7078)**
Beta-Wednesday	0.6040	0.5753	0.3444
	(3.7147)**	(5.1870)**	(1.4856)
Beta-Thursday	0.6662	0.8163	0.6055
	(3.9313)**	(6.9846)**	(2.5146)*
Beta-Friday	0.9124	0.8059	1.0906
	(5.8301)**	(7.4493)**	(4.9294)**

Notes: Coefficients are given in each cell followed by *t*-ratios in parentheses; * and ** denote significance at the 5% and 1%, levels respectively.
Source: Brooks and Persand (2001a).

10.3.2 Dummy variables for seasonality in EViews

The most commonly observed calendar effect in monthly data is a *January effect*. In order to examine whether there is indeed a January effect in a monthly time series regression, a dummy variable is created that takes the value 1 only in the months of January. This is easiest achieved by creating a new dummy variable called JANDUM containing zeros everywhere, and then editing the variable entries manually, changing all of the zeros for January months to ones. Returning to the Microsoft stock price example in the 'macro.wf1' workfile of chapters 4 and 5, **create this variable** using the methodology described above, and run the regression again including this new dummy variable as well. The results of this regression are in the following table.

Dependent Variable: ERMSOFT
Method: Least Squares
Date: 07/08/13 Time: 06:30
Sample (adjusted): 1986M05 2013M04
Included observations: 324 after adjustments

	Coefficient	Std. Error	t-Statistic	Prob.
C	−0.222940	0.897978	−0.248269	0.8041
ERSANDP	1.386384	0.143283	9.675858	0.0000
DPROD	−1.242103	1.206216	−1.029752	0.3039
DCREDIT	−3.18E-05	6.97E-05	−0.456415	0.6484
DINFLATION	1.962921	2.242415	0.875360	0.3820
DMONEY	−0.003737	0.034398	−0.108637	0.9136
DSPREAD	4.281578	6.333687	0.676001	0.4995
RTERM	4.622120	2.287478	2.020619	0.0442
FEB98DUM	−65.65307	11.59806	−5.660694	0.0000
FEB03DUM	−66.80029	11.57405	−5.771558	0.0000
JANDUM	4.127243	2.834769	1.455936	0.1464
R-squared	0.350457	Mean dependent var		−0.311466
Adjusted R-squared	0.329705	S.D. dependent var		14.05871
S.E. of regression	11.51008	Akaike info criterion		7.757685
Sum squared resid	41466.86	Schwarz criterion		7.886043
Log likelihood	−1245.745	Hannan-Quinn criter.		7.886043
F-statistic	16.88775	Durbin-Watson stat		2.153722
Prob(F-statistic)	0.000000			

As can be seen, the dummy is just outside being statistically significant at the 10% level, and it has the expected positive sign. The coefficient value of 4.127, suggests that on average and holding everything else equal, Microsoft stock returns are around 4% higher in January than the average for other months of the year.

10.4 Estimating simple piecewise linear functions

The piecewise linear model is one example of a general set of models known as *spline techniques*. Spline techniques involve the application of polynomial functions in a piecewise fashion to different portions of the data. These models are widely used to fit yield curves to available data on the yields of bonds of different maturities (see, for example, Shea, 1984).

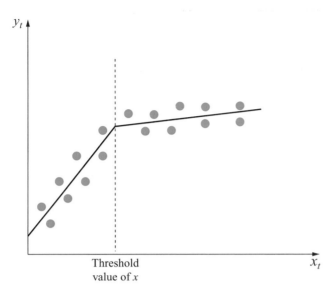

Figure 10.4   Piecewise linear model with threshold x^*

A simple piecewise linear model could operate as follows. If the relationship between two series, y and x, differs depending on whether x is smaller or larger than some threshold value x^*, this phenomenon can be captured using dummy variables. A dummy variable, D_t, could be defined, taking values

$$D_t = \begin{cases} 0 & \text{if } x_t < x^* \\ 1 & \text{if } x_t \geq x^* \end{cases} \qquad (10.8)$$

To offer an illustration of where this may be useful, it is sometimes the case that the tick size limits vary according to the price of the asset. For example, according to George and Longstaff (1993, see also chapter 6 of this book), the Chicago Board of Options Exchange (CBOE) limits the tick size to be \$(1/8) for options worth \$3 or more, and \$(1/16) for options worth less than \$3. This means that the minimum permissible price movements are \$(1/8) and (\$1/16) for options worth \$3 or more and less than \$3, respectively. Thus, if y is the bid–ask spread for the option, and x is the option price, used as a variable to partly explain the size of the spread, the spread will vary with the option price partly in a piecewise manner owing to the tick size limit. The model could thus be specified as

$$y_t = \beta_1 + \beta_2 x_t + \beta_3 D_t + \beta_4 D_t x_t + u_t \qquad (10.9)$$

with D_t defined as above. Viewed in the light of the above discussion on seasonal dummy variables, the dummy in (10.8) is used as both an intercept and a slope dummy. An example showing the data and regression line is given by figure 10.4.

Note that the value of the threshold or 'knot' is assumed known at this stage. Throughout, it is also possible that this situation could be generalised to the case where y_t is drawn from more than two regimes or is generated by a more complex model.

10.5 Markov switching models

Although a large number of more complex, non-linear threshold models have been proposed in the econometrics literature, only two kinds of model have had any noticeable impact in finance (aside from threshold GARCH models of the type alluded to in chapter 8). These are the Markov regime switching model associated with Hamilton (1989, 1990), and the threshold autoregressive model associated with Tong (1983, 1990). Each of these formulations will be discussed below.

10.5.1 Fundamentals of Markov switching models

Under the Markov switching approach, the universe of possible occurrences is split into m states of the world, denoted s_i, $i = 1, \ldots, m$, corresponding to m regimes. In other words, it is assumed that y_t switches regime according to some unobserved variable, s_t, that takes on integer values. In the remainder of this chapter, it will be assumed that $m = 1$ or 2. So if $s_t = 1$, the process is in regime 1 at time t, and if $s_t = 2$, the process is in regime 2 at time t. Movements of the state variable between regimes are governed by a Markov process. This Markov property can be expressed as

$$P[a < y_t \leq b \,|\, y_1, y_2, \ldots, y_{t-1}] = P[a < y_t \leq b \,|\, y_{t-1}] \qquad (10.10)$$

In plain English, this equation states that the probability distribution of the state at any time t depends only on the state at time $t-1$ and not on the states that were passed through at times $t-2$, $t-3$, ... Hence Markov processes are not path-dependent. The model's strength lies in its flexibility, being capable of capturing changes in the variance between state processes, as well as changes in the mean.

The most basic form of Hamilton's model, also known as 'Hamilton's filter' (see Hamilton, 1989), comprises an unobserved state variable, denoted z_t, that is postulated to evaluate according to a first order Markov process

$$\text{prob}[z_t = 1 | z_{t-1} = 1] = p_{11} \qquad (10.11)$$

$$\text{prob}[z_t = 2 | z_{t-1} = 1] = 1 - p_{11} \qquad (10.12)$$

$$\text{prob}[z_t = 2 | z_{t-1} = 2] = p_{22} \qquad (10.13)$$

$$\text{prob}[z_t = 1 | z_{t-1} = 2] = 1 - p_{22} \qquad (10.14)$$

where p_{11} and p_{22} denote the probability of being in regime 1, given that the system was in regime 1 during the previous period, and the probability of being in regime 2, given that the system was in regime 2 during the previous period, respectively. Thus $1 - p_{11}$ defines the probability that y_t will change from state 1 in period $t-1$ to state 2 in period t, and $1 - p_{22}$ defines the probability of a shift from state 2 to state 1 between times $t-1$ and t. It can be shown that under this specification, z_t evolves as an AR(1) process

$$z_t = (1 - p_{11}) + \rho z_{t-1} + \eta_t \qquad (10.15)$$

where $\rho = p_{11} + p_{22} - 1$. Loosely speaking, z_t can be viewed as a generalisation of the dummy variables for one-off shifts in a series discussed above. Under the Markov switching approach, there can be multiple shifts from one set of behaviour to another.

In this framework, the observed returns series evolves as given by (10.15)

$$y_t = \mu_1 + \mu_2 z_t + (\sigma_1^2 + \phi z_t)^{1/2} u_t \tag{10.16}$$

where $u_t \sim N(0, 1)$. The expected values and variances of the series are μ_1 and σ_1^2, respectively in state 1, and $(\mu_1 + \mu_2)$ and $\sigma_1^2 + \phi$ in respectively, state 2. The variance in state 2 is also defined, $\sigma_2^2 = \sigma_1^2 + \phi$. The unknown parameters of the model $(\mu_1, \mu_2, \sigma_1^2, \sigma_2^2, p_{11}, p_{22})$ are estimated using maximum likelihood. Details are beyond the scope of this book, but are most comprehensively given in Engel and Hamilton (1990).

If a variable follows a Markov process, all that is required to forecast the probability that it will be in a given regime during the next period is the current period's probability and a set of transition probabilities, given for the case of two regimes by (10.11)–(10.14). In the general case where there are m states, the transition probabilities are best expressed in a matrix as

$$P = \begin{bmatrix} P_{11} & P_{12} & \cdots & P_{1m} \\ P_{21} & P_{22} & \cdots & P_{2m} \\ \cdots & \cdots & \cdots & \cdots \\ P_{m1} & P_{m2} & \cdots & P_{mm} \end{bmatrix} \tag{10.17}$$

where P_{ij} is the probability of moving from regime i to regime j. Since, at any given time, the variable must be in one of the m states, it must be true that

$$\sum_{j=1}^{m} P_{ij} = 1 \quad \forall \quad i \tag{10.18}$$

A vector of current state probabilities is then defined as

$$\pi_t = \begin{bmatrix} \pi_1 & \pi_2 & \cdots & \pi_m \end{bmatrix} \tag{10.19}$$

where π_i is the probability that the variable y is currently in state i. Given π_t and P, the probability that the variable y will be in a given regime next period can be forecast using

$$\pi_{t+1} = \pi_t P \tag{10.20}$$

The probabilities for S steps into the future will be given by

$$\pi_{t+s} = \pi_t P^s \tag{10.21}$$

10.6 A Markov switching model for the real exchange rate

There have been a number of applications of the Markov switching model in finance. Clearly, such an approach is useful when a series is thought to undergo shifts from one type of behaviour to another and back again, but where the 'forcing variable' that causes the regime shifts is unobservable.

One such application is to modelling the real exchange rate. As discussed in chapter 8, purchasing power parity (PPP) theory suggests that the law of one price should always apply in the long run such that the cost of a representative basket of goods and services is the same wherever it is purchased, after converting it into a common currency. Under some assumptions, one implication of PPP is that the real exchange rate (that is, the exchange rate divided by a general price index such as the consumer price index (CPI)) should be stationary. However, a number of studies have failed to reject the unit root null hypothesis in real exchange rates, indicating evidence against the PPP theory.

It is widely known that the power of unit root tests is low in the presence of structural breaks as the ADF test finds it difficult to distinguish between a stationary process subject to structural breaks and a unit root process. In order to investigate this possibility, Bergman and Hansson (2005) estimate a Markov switching model with an AR(1) structure for the real exchange rate, which allows for multiple switches between two regimes. The specification they use is

$$y_t = \mu_{s_t} + \phi y_{t-1} + \epsilon_t \tag{10.22}$$

where y_t is the real exchange rate, s_t, $(t = 1, 2)$ are the two states, and $\epsilon_t \sim N(0, \sigma^2)$.[1] The state variable s_t is assumed to follow a standard 2-regime Markov process as described above.

Quarterly observations from 1973Q2 to 1997Q4 (99 data points) are used on the real exchange rate (in units of foreign currency per US dollar) for the UK, France, Germany, Switzerland, Canada and Japan. The model is estimated using the first seventy-two observations (1973Q2–1990Q4) with the remainder retained for out-of-sample forecast evaluation. The authors use 100 times the log of the real exchange rate, and this is normalised to take a value of one for 1973Q2 for all countries. The Markov switching model estimates obtained using maximum likelihood estimation are presented in table 10.3.

As the table shows, the model is able to separate the real exchange rates into two distinct regimes for each series, with the intercept in regime 1 (μ_1) being positive for all countries except Japan (resulting from the phenomenal strength of the yen over the sample period), corresponding to a rise in the log of the number of units of the foreign currency per US dollar, i.e. a depreciation of the domestic currency against the dollar. μ_2, the intercept in regime 2, is negative for all countries, corresponding to a domestic currency appreciation against the dollar. The probabilities of remaining within the same regime during the following period (p_{11} and p_{22}) are fairly low for the UK, France, Germany and Switzerland, indicating fairly frequent switches from one regime to another for those countries' currencies.

Interestingly, after allowing for the switching intercepts across the regimes, the AR(1) coefficient, ϕ, in table 10.3 is a considerable distance below unity, indicating that these real exchange rates are stationary. Bergman and Hansson simulate data from the stationary Markov switching AR(1) model with the estimated parameters

---

[1] The authors also estimate models that allow ϕ and σ^2 to vary across the states, but the restriction that the parameters are the same across the two states cannot be rejected and hence the values presented in the study assume that they are constant.

Table 10.3	Estimates of the Markov switching model for real exchange rates					
Parameter	UK	France	Germany	Switzerland	Canada	Japan
μ_1	3.554 (0.550)	6.131 (0.604)	6.569 (0.733)	2.390 (0.726)	1.693 (0.230)	−0.370 (0.681)
μ_2	−5.096 (0.549)	−2.845 (0.409)	−2.676 (0.487)	−6.556 (0.775)	−0.306 (0.249)	−8.932 (1.157)
ϕ	0.928 (0.027)	0.904 (0.020)	0.888 (0.023)	0.958 (0.027)	0.922 (0.021)	0.871 (0.027)
σ^2	10.118 (1.698)	7.706 (1.293)	10.719 (1.799)	13.513 (2.268)	1.644 (0.276)	15.879 (2.665)
p_{11}	0.672	0.679	0.682	0.792	0.952	0.911
p_{22}	0.690	0.833	0.830	0.716	0.944	0.817

Note: Standard errors in parentheses.
Source: Bergman and Hansson (2005).
Reprinted with the permission of Elsevier.

but they assume that the researcher conducts a standard ADF test on the artificial data. They find that for none of the cases can the unit root null hypothesis be rejected, even though clearly this null is wrong as the simulated data are stationary. It is concluded that a failure to account for time-varying intercepts (i.e. structural breaks) in previous empirical studies on real exchange rates could have been the reason for the finding that the series are unit root processes when the financial theory had suggested that they should be stationary.

Finally, the authors employ their Markov switching AR(1) model for forecasting the remainder of the exchange rates in the sample in comparison with the predictions produced by a random walk and by a Markov switching model with a random walk. They find that for all six series, and for forecast horizons up to four steps (quarters) ahead, their Markov switching AR model produces predictions with the lowest mean squared errors; these improvements over the pure random walk are statistically significant.

10.7 A Markov switching model for the gilt–equity yield ratio

As discussed below, a Markov switching approach is also useful for modelling the time series behaviour of the gilt–equity yield ratio (GEYR), defined as the ratio of the income yield on long-term government bonds to the dividend yield on equities. It has been suggested that the current value of the GEYR might be a useful tool for investment managers or market analysts in determining whether to invest in equities or whether to invest in gilts. Thus the GEYR is purported to contain information useful for determining the likely direction of future equity market trends. The GEYR is assumed to have a long-run equilibrium level, deviations from which are taken to signal that equity prices are at an unsustainable level. If the GEYR becomes high relative to its long-run level, equities are viewed as being expensive relative to bonds. The expectation, then, is that for given levels of bond yields, equity yields must rise, which will occur via a fall in equity prices. Similarly, if the GEYR is well below its long-run level, bonds are considered expensive relative to stocks, and by the same analysis, the price of the latter is expected to increase. Thus, in its crudest form, an equity trading rule based on the GEYR would say, 'if the GEYR is low, buy equities; if the GEYR is high, sell equities'. The paper by Brooks and Persand (2001b) discusses the usefulness of the Markov switching approach in this context, and considers whether profitable trading rules can be developed on the basis of forecasts derived from the model.

Brooks and Persand (2001b) employ monthly stock index dividend yields and income yields on government bonds covering the period January 1975 until August 1997 (272 observations) for three countries – the UK, the US and Germany. The series used are the dividend yield and index values of the FTSE100 (UK), the S&P500 (US) and the DAX (Germany). The bond indices and redemption yields are based on the clean prices of UK government consols, and US and German ten-year government bonds.

As an example, figure 10.5 presents a plot of the distribution of the GEYR for the US (in blue), together with a normal distribution having the same mean

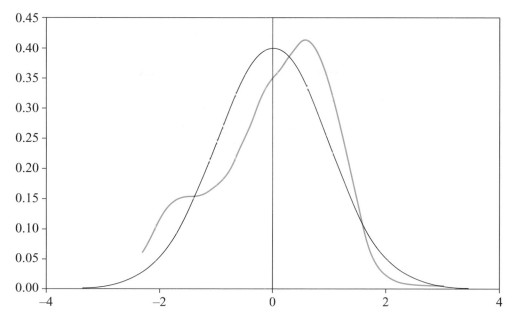

Figure 10.5   Unconditional distribution of US GEYR together with a normal distribution with the same mean and variance

and variance (source: Brooks and Persand, 2001b). Clearly, the distribution of the GEYR series is not normal, and the shape suggests two separate modes: one upper part of the distribution embodying most of the observations, and a lower part covering the smallest values of the GEYR.

Such an observation, together with the notion that a trading rule should be developed on the basis of whether the GEYR is 'high' or 'low', and in the absence of a formal econometric model for the GEYR, suggests that a Markov switching approach may be useful. Under the Markov switching approach, the values of the GEYR are drawn from a mixture of normal distributions, where the weights attached to each distribution sum to one and where movements between series are governed by a Markov process. The Markov switching model is estimated using a maximum likelihood procedure (as discussed in chapter 9), based on GAUSS code supplied by James Hamilton. Coefficient estimates for the model are presented in table 10.4.

The means and variances for the values of the GEYR for each of the two regimes are given in columns headed (1)–(4) of table 10.4 with standard errors associated with each parameter in parentheses. It is clear that the regime switching model has split the data into two distinct samples – one with a high mean (of 2.43, 2.46 and 3.03 for the UK, US and Germany, respectively) and one with a lower mean (of 2.07, 2.12, and 2.16), as was anticipated from the unconditional distribution of returns. Also apparent is the fact that the UK and German GEYR are more variable at times when it is in the high mean regime, evidenced by their higher variance (in fact, it is around four and twenty times higher than for the low GEYR state, respectively). The number of observations for which the probability

	μ_1	μ_2	σ_1^2	σ_2^2	p_{11}	p_{22}	N_1	N_2
Statistic	(1)	(2)	(3)	(4)	(5)	(6)	(7)	(8)
UK	2.4293	2.0749	0.0624	0.0142	0.9547	0.9719	102	170
	(0.0301)	(0.0367)	(0.0092)	(0.0018)	(0.0726)	(0.0134)		
US	2.4554	2.1218	0.0294	0.0395	0.9717	0.9823	100	172
	(0.0181)	(0.0623)	(0.0604)	(0.0044)	(0.0171)	(0.0106)		
Germany	3.0250	2.1563	0.5510	0.0125	0.9816	0.9328	200	72
	(0.0544)	(0.0154)	(0.0569)	(0.0020)	(0.0107)	(0.0323)		

Table 10.4   Estimated parameters for the Markov switching models

Notes: Standard errors in parentheses; N_1 and N_2 denote the number of observations deemed to be in regimes 1 and 2, respectively.
Source: Brooks and Persand (2001b).

that the GEYR is in the high mean state exceeds 0.5 (and thus when the GEYR is actually deemed to be in this state) is 102 for the UK (37.5% of the total), while the figures for the US are 100 (36.8%) and for Germany 200 (73.5%). Thus, overall, the GEYR is more likely to be in the low mean regime for the UK and US, while it is likely to be high in Germany.

The columns marked (5) and (6) of table 10.4 give the values of p_{11} and p_{22}, respectively, that is the probability of staying in state 1 given that the GEYR was in state 1 in the immediately preceding month, and the probability of staying in state 2 given that the GEYR was in state 2 previously, respectively. The high values of these parameters indicates that the regimes are highly stable with less than a 10% chance of moving from a low GEYR to a high GEYR regime and vice versa for all three series. Figure 10.6 presents a 'q-plot', which shows the value of GEYR and probability that it is in the high GEYR regime for the UK at each point in time (source: Brooks and Persand, 2001b).

As can be seen, the probability that the UK GEYR is in the 'high' regime (the dotted line) varies frequently, but spends most of its time either close to zero or close to one. The model also seems to do a reasonably good job of specifying which regime the UK GEYR should be in, given that the probability seems to match the broad trends in the actual GEYR (the full line).

Engel and Hamilton (1990) show that it is possible to give a forecast of the probability that a series y_t, which follows a Markov switching process, will be in a particular regime. Brooks and Persand (2001b) use the first sixty observations (January 1975–December 1979) for in-sample estimation of the model parameters (μ_1, μ_2, σ_1^2, σ_2^2, p_{11}, p_{22}). Then a one step–ahead forecast is produced of the

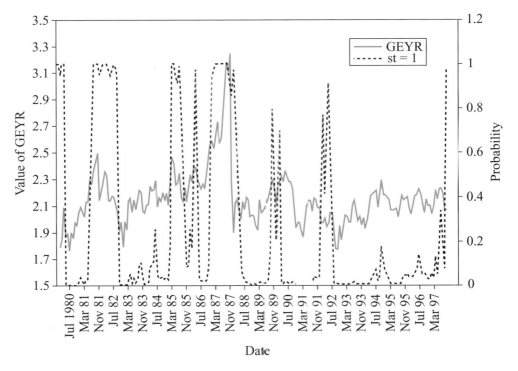

Figure 10.6 Value of GEYR and probability that it is in the High GEYR regime for the UK

probability that the GEYR will be in the high mean regime during the next period. If the probability that the GEYR will be in the low regime during the next period is forecast to be more that 0.5, it is forecast that the GEYR will be low and hence equities are bought or held. If the probability that the GEYR is in the low regime is forecast to be less than 0.5, it is anticipated that the GEYR will be high and hence gilts are invested in or held. The model is then rolled forward one observation, with a new set of model parameters and probability forecasts being constructed. This process continues until 212 such probabilities are estimated with corresponding trading rules.

The returns for each out-of-sample month for the switching portfolio are calculated, and their characteristics compared with those of buy-and-hold equities and buy-and-hold gilts strategies. Returns are calculated as continuously compounded percentage returns on a stock (the FTSE in the UK, the S&P500 in the US, the DAX in Germany) or on a long-term government bond. The profitability of the trading rules generated by the forecasts of the Markov switching model are found to be superior in gross terms compared with a simple buy-and-hold equities strategy. In the UK context, the former yields higher average returns and lower standard deviations. The switching portfolio generates an average return of 0.69% per month, compared with 0.43% for the pure bond and 0.62% for the pure equity portfolios. The improvements are not so clear-cut for the US and Germany. The Sharpe ratio for the UK Markov switching portfolio is almost twice that of the buy-and-hold equities portfolio, suggesting that, after allowing for risk, the switching model provides a superior trading rule. The improvement in the Sharpe ratio for the other two countries is, on the contrary, only very modest.

To summarise:

- The Markov switching approach can be used to model the gilt–equity yield ratio
- The resulting model can be used to produce forecasts of the probability that the GEYR will be in a particular regime
- Before transactions costs, a trading rule derived from the model produces a better performance than a buy-and-hold equities strategy, in spite of inferior predictive accuracy as measured statistically
- Net of transactions costs, rules based on the Markov switching model are not able to beat a passive investment in the index for any of the three countries studied.

10.8 Estimating Markov switching models in EViews

Markov switching models can now be estimated easily in EViews.[2] The example we will consider relates to the changes in house prices series used previously. So **Reopen the 'UKHP.wf1' file**, click **Quick/Estimate Equation** and then under 'Estimation Settings, Method', **Change LS Least squares (NLS and ARMA)** to the last option, **SWITCHREG – Switching Regression** and complete the dialog box as in screenshot 10.1.

The first box will include the dependent variable followed by a list of regressors that are allowed to vary across regimes. To estimate a simple switching model with just a varying intercept in each state, include only the constant. Any variables whose associated parameters should not be allowed to vary across regimes should be listed in the second box. To allow the variances to be different across the regimes, **tick the 'Regime specific error variances' box**. We could choose more regimes but for now **select '2'**. As usual, there is an 'Options' tab which allows the user to specify how the estimation and computation of standard errors is conducted. However, this can be left at the default options so click **OK** and the results will appear as in the following table.

Examining the results, it is clear that the model has successfully captured the features of the data. Two distinct regimes have been identified: regime 1 has a high average price increase of 0.96% per month and a low standard deviation, whereas regime 2 has a negative mean return (corresponding to a price fall of 0.20% per month) and a much higher volatility. To see the transition

---

[2] However, threshold autoregressive models with observed threshold variables of the type described below cannot be estimated using the built-in procedures of EViews 8.

Screenshot 10.1   **Estimating a Markov switching model**

probability matrix, click **View/Regime Results/Transition Results...** and then select **Summary** and click **OK**. The regimes are fairly stable, with probabilities of around 97% of remaining in a given regime in the next period. The average durations are forty months for regime 1 and thirty-five months for regime 2, which is again indicative of the stability of the regimes. To examine the fitted states over time, select View/Regime Results/Regime Probabilities. It is then possible to choose the one-step ahead probabilities, or the filtered or smoothed probabilities. The smoothed probabilities are estimated using the entire sample whereas the filtered probabilities use a recursive approach using only information available at time t to compute the probability of being in each regime at time t. Selecting the smoothed probabilties on multiple graphs gives the plots in screenshot 10.2.

The first thing to note is that of course the two figures are mirror images of one another since the probabilities of being in regime 1 and in regime 2 must

Dependent Variable: DHP
Method: Switching Regression (Markov Switching)
Date: 08/13/13 Time: 06:37
Sample (adjusted): 1991M02 2013M05
Included observations: 268 after adjustments
Number of states: 2
Initial probabilities obtained from ergodic solution
Ordinary standard errors & covariance using numeric Hessian
Random search: 25 starting values with 10 iterations using 1 standard
          deviation (rng=kn, seed=151806152)
Convergence achieved after 8 iterations

Variable	Coefficient	Std. Error	z-Statistic	Prob.
Regime 1				
C	0.958845	0.109325	8.770593	0.0000
LOG(SIGMA)	−0.066307	0.063072	−1.051297	0.2931
Regime 2				
C	−0.204681	0.136676	−1.497556	0.1342
LOG(SIGMA)	0.160707	0.075853	2.118648	0.0341
Transition Matrix Parameters				
P11-C	3.669935	0.809152	4.535532	0.0000
P21-C	−3.528586	0.885610	−3.984359	0.0001
Mean of dependent var	0.437995	S.D. dependent var		1.200502
S.E. of regression	1.102850	Sum squared resid		321.0977
Durbin-Watson stat	1.708086	Log likelihood		−404.3894
Akaike info criterion	3.062607	Schwarz criterion		3.143003
Hannan-Quinn criter.	3.094898			

always sum to one. Examining how the graphs move over time, the probability of being in regime 1 was close to zero until the mid-1990s, corresponding to a period of low or negative house price growth. The behaviour then changed and the probability of being in the low and negative growth state (regime 2) fell to zero and the housing market enjoyed a period of good performance until around 2005 when the regimes became less stable but tending increasingly towards regime 2 until early 2013 when the market again appeared to have turned a corner.

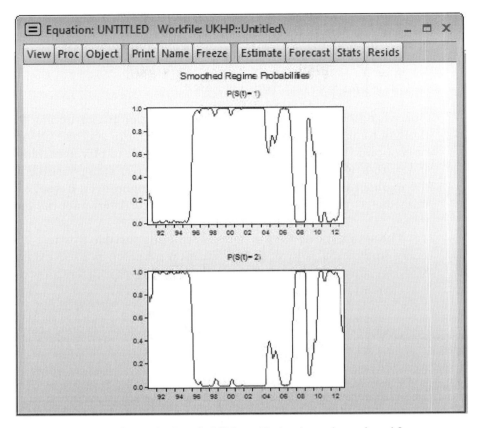

Screenshot 10.2   **Smoothed probabilities of being in regimes 1 and 2**

10.9 Threshold autoregressive models

Threshold autoregressive (TAR) models are one class of non-linear autoregressive models. Such models are a relatively simple relaxation of standard linear autoregressive models that allow for a locally linear approximation over a number of states. According to Tong (1990, p. 99), the threshold principle 'allows the analysis of a complex stochastic system by decomposing it into a set of smaller sub-systems'. The key difference between TAR and Markov switching models is that, under the former, the state variable is assumed known and observable, while it is latent under the latter. A very simple example of a threshold autoregressive model is given by (10.23). The model contains a first order autoregressive process in each of two regimes, and there is only one threshold. Of course, the number of thresholds will always be the number of regimes minus one. Thus, the dependent variable y_t is purported to follow an autoregressive process with intercept coefficient μ_1 and autoregressive coefficient ϕ_1 if the value of the state-determining variable lagged k periods, denoted s_{t-k} is lower than some threshold value r. If the value of the state-determining variable lagged k periods, is equal to or greater than that threshold value r, y_t is specified to follow a different autoregressive process, with intercept coefficient μ_2 and autoregressive coefficient ϕ_2. The model would be written

$$
y_t = \begin{cases} \mu_1 + \phi_1 y_{t-1} + u_{1t} & \text{if } s_{t-k} < r \\ \mu_2 + \phi_2 y_{t-1} + u_{2t} & \text{if } s_{t-k} \geq r \end{cases} \tag{10.23}
$$

But what is s_{t-k}, the state-determining variable? It can be any variable that is thought to make y_t shift from one set of behaviour to another. Obviously, financial or economic theory should have an important role to play in making this decision. If $k = 0$, it is the current value of the state-determining variable that influences the regime that y is in at time t, but in many applications k is set to 1, so that the immediately preceding value of s is the one that determines the current value of y.

The simplest case for the state determining variable is where it is the variable under study, i.e. $s_{t-k} = y_{t-k}$. This situation is known as a self-exciting TAR, or a SETAR, since it is the lag of the variable y itself that determines the regime that y is currently in. The model would now be written

$$
y_t = \begin{cases} \mu_1 + \phi_1 y_{t-1} + u_{1t} \text{ if } y_{t-k} < r \\ \mu_2 + \phi_2 y_{t-1} + u_{2t} \text{ if } y_{t-k} \geq r \end{cases} \tag{10.24}
$$

The models of (10.23) or (10.24) can of course be extended in several directions. The number of lags of the dependent variable used in each regime may be higher than one, and the number of lags need not be the same for both regimes. The number of states can also be increased to more than two. A general threshold autoregressive model, that notationally permits the existence of more than two regimes and more than one lag, may be written

$$
x_t = \sum_{j=1}^{J} I_t^{(j)} \left(\phi_0^{(j)} + \sum_{i=1}^{p_j} \phi_i^{(j)} x_{t-i} + u_t^{(j)} \right), \quad r_{j-1} \leq z_{t-d} \leq r_j \tag{10.25}
$$

where $I_t^{(j)}$ is an indicator function for the jth regime taking the value one if the underlying variable is in state j and zero otherwise. z_{t-d} is an observed variable determining the switching point and $u_t^{(j)}$ is a zero-mean independently and identically distributed error process. Again, if the regime changes are driven by own lags of the underlying variable, x_t (i.e. $z_{t-d} = x_{t-d}$), then the model is a self-exciting TAR (SETAR).

It is also worth re-stating that under the TAR approach, the variable y is either in one regime or another, given the relevant value of s, and there are discrete transitions between one regime and another. This is in contrast with the Markov switching approach, where the variable y is in both states with some probability at each point in time. Another class of threshold autoregressive models, known as smooth transition autoregressions (STAR), allows for a more gradual transition between the regimes by using a continuous function for the regime indicator rather than an on–off switch (see Franses and van Dijk, 2000, chapter 3).

10.10 Estimation of threshold autoregressive models

Estimation of the model parameters (ϕ_i, r_j, d, p_j) is considerably more difficult than for a standard linear autoregressive process, since in general they cannot be determined simultaneously in a simple way, and the values chosen for one parameter are likely to influence estimates of the others. Tong (1983, 1990) suggests a complex non-parametric lag regression procedure to estimate the values of the thresholds (r_j) and the delay parameter (d).

Ideally, it may be preferable to endogenously estimate the values of the threshold(s) as part of the non-linear least squares (NLS) optimisation procedure, but this is not feasible. The underlying functional relationship between the variables is discontinuous in the thresholds, such that the thresholds cannot be estimated at the same time as the other components of the model. One solution to this problem that is sometimes used in empirical work is to use a grid search procedure that seeks the minimal residual sum of squares over a range of values of the threshold(s) for an assumed model. Some sample code to achieve this is presented later in this chapter.

10.10.1 Threshold model order (lag length) determination

A simple, although far from ideal, method for determining the appropriate lag lengths for the autoregressive components for each of the regimes would be to assume that the same number of lags are required in all regimes. The lag length is then chosen in the standard fashion by determining the appropriate lag length for a linear autoregressive model, and assuming that the lag length for all states of the TAR is the same. While it is easy to implement, this approach is clearly not a good one, for it is unlikely that the lag lengths for each state when the data are drawn from different regimes would be the same as that appropriate when a linear functional form is imposed. Moreover, it is undesirable to require the lag lengths to be the same in each regime. This conflicts with the notion that the data behave differently in different states, which was precisely the motivation for considering threshold models in the first place.

An alternative and better approach, conditional upon specified threshold values, would be to employ an information criterion to select across the lag lengths in each regime simultaneously. A drawback of this approach, that Franses and van Dijk (2000) highlight, is that in practice it is often the case that the system will be resident in one regime for a considerably longer time overall than the others. In such situations, information criteria will not perform well in model selection for the regime(s) containing few observations. Since the number of observations is small in these cases, the overall reduction in the residual sum of squares as more parameters are added to these regimes will be very small. This leads the criteria to always select very small model orders for states containing few observations. A solution, therefore, is to define an information criterion that does not penalise the whole model for additional parameters in one state. Tong (1990) proposes a modified version of Akaike's information criterion (AIC) that weights $\hat{\sigma}^2$ for each regime by the number of observations in that regime. For the two-regime case, the modified AIC would be written

$$AIC\,(p_1, p_2) = T_1 \ln \hat{\sigma}_1^2 + T_2 \ln \hat{\sigma}_2^2 + 2(p_1 + 1) + 2(p_2 + 1) \tag{10.26}$$

where T_1 and T_2 are the number of observations in regimes 1 and 2, respectively, p_1 and p_2 are the lag lengths and $\hat{\sigma}_1^2$ and $\hat{\sigma}_2^2$ are the residual variances. Similar modifications can of course be developed for other information criteria.

10.10.2 Determining the delay parameter, *d*

The delay parameter, d, can be decided in a variety of ways. It can be determined along with the lag orders for each of the regimes by an information criterion, although of course this added dimension greatly increases the number of candidate models to be estimated. In many applications, however, it is typically set to one on theoretical grounds. It has been argued (see, for example, Kräger and Kugler, 1993) that in the context of financial markets, it is most likely that the most recent past value of the state-determining variable would be the one to determine the current state, rather than that value two, three, . . . periods ago.

Estimation of the autoregressive coefficients can then be achieved using NLS. Further details of the procedure are discussed in Franses and van Dijk (2000, chapter 3).

10.11 Specification tests in the context of Markov switching and threshold autoregressive models: a cautionary note

In the context of both Markov switching and TAR models, it is of interest to determine whether the threshold models represent a superior fit to the data relative to a comparable linear model. A tempting, but incorrect, way to examine this issue would be to do something like the following: estimate the desired threshold model and the linear counterpart, and compare the residual sums of squares using an F-test. However, such an approach is not valid in this instance owing to unidentified nuisance parameters under the null hypothesis. In other words, the null hypothesis for the test would be that the additional parameters in the regime switching model were zero so that the model collapsed to the linear specification, but under the linear model, there is no threshold. The upshot is that the conditions required to show that the test statistics follow a standard asymptotic distribution do not apply. Hence analytically derived critical values are not available, and critical values must be obtained via simulation for each individual case. Hamilton (1994) provides substitute hypotheses for Markov switching model evaluation that can validly be tested using the standard hypothesis testing framework, while Hansen (1996) offers solutions in the context of TAR models.

This chapter will now examine two applications of TAR modelling in finance: one to the modelling of exchange rates within a managed floating environment, and one to arbitrage opportunities implied by the difference between spot and futures prices for a given asset. For a (rather technical) general survey of several TAR applications in finance, see Yadav, Pope and Paudyal (1994).

10.12 A SETAR model for the French franc–German mark exchange rate

During the 1990s, European countries which were part of the Exchange Rate Mechanism (ERM) of the European Monetary System (EMS), were required to constrain their currencies to remain within prescribed bands relative to other ERM currencies. This seemed to present no problem by early in the new millennium since European Monetary Union (EMU) was already imminent and conversion rates of domestic currencies into euros were already known. However, in the early 1990s, the requirement that currencies remain within a certain band around their central parity forced central banks to intervene in the markets to effect either an appreciation or a depreciation in their currency. A study by Chappell *et al.* (1996) considered the effect that such interventions might have on the dynamics and time series properties of the French franc–German mark (hereafter FRF–DEM) exchange rate. 'Core currency pairs', such as the FRF–DEM were allowed to move up to ±2.25% either side of their central parity within the ERM. The study used daily data from 1 May 1990 until 30 March 1992. The first 450 observations are used for model estimation, with the remaining 50 being retained for out-of-sample forecasting.

A SETAR model was employed to allow for different types of behaviour according to whether the exchange rate is close to the ERM boundary. The argument is that, close to the boundary, the respective central banks will be required to intervene in opposite directions in order to drive the exchange rate back towards its central parity. Such intervention may be expected to affect the usual market dynamics that ensure fast reaction to news and the absence of arbitrage opportunities.

Let E_t denote the log of the FRF–DEM exchange rate at time t. Chappell *et al.* (1996) estimate two models: one with two thresholds and one with one threshold. The former was anticipated to be most appropriate for the data at hand since exchange rate behaviour is likely to be affected by intervention if the exchange rate comes close to either the ceiling or the floor of the band. However, over the sample period employed, the mark was never a weak currency, and therefore the FRF–DEM exchange rate was either at the top of the band or in the centre, never close to the bottom. Therefore, a model with one threshold is more appropriate since any second estimated threshold was deemed likely to be spurious.

The authors show, using DF and ADF tests, that the exchange rate series is not stationary. Therefore, a threshold model in the levels is not strictly valid for analysis. However, they argue that an econometrically valid model in first difference would lose its intuitive interpretation, since it is the *value* of the exchange rate that is targeted by the monetary authorities, not its change. In addition, if the currency bands are working effectively, the exchange rate is constrained to lie within them, and hence in some senses of the word, it must be stationary, since it cannot wander without bound in either direction. The model orders for each regime are determined using *AIC*, and the estimated model is given in table 10.5.

Table 10.5 SETAR model for FRF–DEM		
Model	For regime	Number of observations
$\hat{E}_t = 0.0222 + 0.9962E_{t-1}$ (0.0458) (0.0079)	$E_{t-1} < 5.8306$	344
$\hat{E}_t = 0.3486 + 0.4394E_{t-1} + 0.3057E_{t-2} + 0.1951E_{t-3}$ (0.2391) (0.0889) (0.1098) (0.0866)	$E_{t-1} \geq 5.8306$	103

Source: Chappell et al. (1996). Reprinted with permission of John Wiley and Sons.

As can be seen, the two regimes comprise a random walk with drift under normal market conditions, where the exchange rate lies below a certain threshold, and an AR(3) model corresponding to much slower market adjustment when the exchange rate lies on or above the threshold. The (natural log of) the exchange rate's central parity over the period was 5.8153, while the (log of the) ceiling of the band was 5.8376. The estimated threshold of 5.8306 is approximately 1.55% above the central parity, while the ceiling is 2.25% above the central parity. Thus, the estimated threshold is some way below the ceiling, which is in accordance with the authors' expectations since the central banks are likely to intervene before the exchange rate actually hits the ceiling.

Forecasts are then produced for the last fifty observations using the threshold model estimated above, the SETAR model with two thresholds, a random walk and an AR(2) (where the model order was chosen by in-sample minimisation of AIC). The results are presented here in table 10.6.

For the FRF–DEM exchange rate, the one-threshold SETAR model is found to give lower mean squared errors than the other three models for one-, two-, three-, five- and ten-step-ahead forecasting horizons. Under the median squared forecast error measure, the random walk is marginally superior to the one threshold SETAR one and two steps ahead, while it has regained its prominence by three steps ahead.

However, in a footnote, the authors also argue that the SETAR model was estimated and tested for nine other ERM exchange rate series, but in every one of these other cases, the SETAR models produced less accurate forecasts than a random walk model. A possible explanation for this phenomenon is given in section 10.14.

Brooks (2001) extends the work of Chappell et al. to allow the conditional variance of the exchange rate series to be drawn from a GARCH process which itself contains a threshold, above which the behaviour of volatility is different to that below. He finds that the dynamics of the conditional variance are quite different from one regime to the next, and that models allowing for different regimes can provide superior volatility forecasts compared to those which do not.

Table 10.6   FRF–DEM forecast accuracies

	Steps ahead				
	1	*2*	*3*	*5*	*10*
Panel A: mean squared forecast error					
Random walk	1.84E-07	3.49E-07	4.33E-07	8.03E-07	1.83E-06
AR(2)	3.96E-07	1.19E-06	2.33E-06	6.15E-06	2.19E-05
One-threshold SETAR	1.80E-07	2.96E-07	3.63E-07	5.41E-07	5.34E-07
Two-threshold SETAR	1.80E-07	2.96E-07	3.63E-07	5.74E-07	5.61E-07
Panel B: Median squared forecast error					
Random walk	7.80E-08	1.04E-07	2.21E-07	2.49E-07	1.00E-06
AR(2)	2.29E-07	9.00E-07	1.77E-06	5.34E-06	1.37E-05
One-threshold SETAR	9.33E-08	1.22E-07	1.57E-07	2.42E-07	2.34E-07
Two-threshold SETAR	1.02E-07	1.22E-07	1.87E-07	2.57E-07	2.45E-07

Source: Chappell *et al.* (1996). Reprinted with permission of John Wiley and Sons.

10.13 Threshold models and the dynamics of the FTSE 100 index and index futures markets

One of the examples given in chapter 8 discussed the implications for the effective functioning of spot and futures markets of a lead–lag relationship between the two series. If the two markets are functioning effectively, it was also shown that a cointegrating relationship between them would be expected.

If stock and stock index futures markets are functioning properly, price movements in these markets should be best described by a first order vector error correction model (VECM) with the error correction term being the price differential between the two markets (the basis). The VECM could be expressed as

$$\begin{bmatrix} \Delta f_t \\ \Delta s_t \end{bmatrix} = \begin{bmatrix} \pi_{11} \\ \pi_{21} \end{bmatrix} [\, f_{t-1} - s_{t-1} \,] + \begin{bmatrix} u_{1t} \\ u_{2t} \end{bmatrix} \tag{10.27}$$

where Δf_t and Δs_t are changes in the log of the futures and spot prices, respectively, π_{11} and π_{21} are coefficients describing how changes in the spot and futures prices occur as a result of the basis. Writing these two equations out in full, the following would result

$$f_t - f_{t-1} = \pi_{11}[\, f_{t-1} - s_{t-1} \,] + u_{1t} \tag{10.28}$$

$$s_t - s_{t-1} = \pi_{21}[\, f_{t-1} - s_{t-1} \,] + u_{2t} \tag{10.29}$$

Subtracting (10.29) from (10.28) would give the following expression

$$(f_t - f_{t-1}) - (s_t - s_{t-1}) = (\pi_{11} - \pi_{21})[f_{t-1} - s_{t-1}] + (u_{1t} - u_{2t}) \qquad (10.30)$$

which can also be written as

$$(f_t - s_t) - (f_{t-1} - s_{t-1}) = (\pi_{11} - \pi_{21})[f_{t-1} - s_{t-1}] + (u_{1t} - u_{2t}) \qquad (10.31)$$

or, using the result that $b_t = f_t - s_t$

$$b_t - b_{t-1} = (\pi_{11} - \pi_{21})b_{t-1} + \varepsilon_t \qquad (10.32)$$

where $\varepsilon_t = u_{1t} - u_{2t}$. Taking b_{t-1} from both sides

$$b_t = (\pi_{11} - \pi_{21} - 1)b_{t-1} + \varepsilon_t \qquad (10.33)$$

If the first order VECM is appropriate, then it is not possible to identify structural equations for returns in stock and stock index futures markets with the obvious implications for predictability and the two markets are indeed efficient. Hence, for efficient markets and no arbitrage, there should be only a first order autoregressive process describing the basis and no further patterns. Recent evidence suggests, however, that there are more dynamics present than should be in effectively functioning markets. In particular, it has been suggested that the basis up to three trading days prior carries predictive power for movements in the FTSE 100 cash index, suggesting the possible existence of unexploited arbitrage opportunities. The paper by Brooks and Garrett (2002) analyses whether such dynamics can be explained as the result of different regimes within which arbitrage is not triggered and outside of which arbitrage will occur. The rationale for the existence of different regimes in this context is that the basis (adjusted for carrying costs if necessary), which is very important in the arbitrage process, can fluctuate within bounds determined by transaction costs without actually triggering arbitrage. Hence an autoregressive relationship between the current and previous values of the basis could arise and persist over time within the threshold boundaries since it is not profitable for traders to exploit this apparent arbitrage opportunity. Hence there will be thresholds within which there will be no arbitrage activity but once these thresholds are crossed, arbitrage should drive the basis back within the transaction cost bounds. If markets are functioning effectively then irrespective of the dynamics of the basis within the thresholds, once the thresholds have been crossed the additional dynamics should disappear.

The data used by Brooks and Garrett (2002) are the daily closing prices for the FTSE 100 stock index and stock index futures contract for the period January 1985–October 1992. The October 1987 stock market crash occurs right in the middle of this period, and therefore Brooks and Garrett conduct their analysis on a 'pre-crash' and a 'post-crash' sample as well as the whole sample. This is necessary since it has been observed that the normal spot/futures price relationship broke down around the time of the crash (see Antoniou and Garrett, 1993). Table 10.7 shows the coefficient estimates for a linear AR(3) model for the basis.

The results for the whole sample suggest that all of the first three lags of the basis are significant in modelling the current basis. This result is confirmed (although less strongly) for the pre-crash and post-crash sub-samples. Hence, a linear specification

Table 10.7   Linear AR(3) model for the basis

$$b_t = \phi_0 + \phi_1 b_{t-1} + \phi_2 b_{t-2} + \phi_3 b_{t-3} + \varepsilon_t$$

Parameter	Whole sample	Pre-crash sample	Post-crash sample
ϕ_1	0.7051**	0.7174**	0.6791**
	(0.0225)	(0.0377)	(0.0315)
ϕ_2	0.1268**	0.0946*	0.1650**
	(0.0274)	(0.0463)	(0.0378)
ϕ_3	0.0872**	0.1106**	0.0421
	(0.0225)	(0.0377)	(0.0315)

Notes: Figures in parentheses are heteroscedasticity-robust standard errors; * and ** denote significance at the 5% and 1% levels, respectively.
Source: Brooks and Garrett (2002).

would seem to suggest that the basis is to some degree predictable, indicating possible arbitrage opportunities.

In the absence of transactions costs, deviations of the basis away from zero in either direction will trigger arbitrage. The existence of transactions costs, however, means that the basis can deviate from zero without actually triggering arbitrage. Thus, assuming that there are no differential transactions costs, there will be upper and lower bounds within which the basis can fluctuate without triggering arbitrage. Brooks and Garrett (2002) estimate a SETAR model for the basis, with two thresholds (three regimes) since these should correspond to the upper and lower boundaries within which the basis can fluctuate without causing arbitrage. Under efficient markets, profitable arbitrage opportunities will not be present when $r_0 \leq b_{t-1} < r_1$ where r_0 and r_1 are the thresholds determining which regime the basis is in. If these thresholds are interpreted as transactions costs bounds, when the basis falls below the lower threshold (r_0), the appropriate arbitrage transaction is to buy futures and short stock. This applies in reverse when the basis rises above r_1. When the basis lies within the thresholds, there should be no arbitrage transactions. Three lags of the basis enter into each equation and the thresholds are estimated using a grid search procedure. The one-period lag of the basis is chosen as the state-determining variable. The estimated model for each sample period is given in table 10.8.

The results show that, to some extent, the dependence in the basis is reduced when it is permitted to be drawn from one of three regimes rather than a single linear model. For the post-crash sample, and to some extent for the whole sample and the pre-crash sample, it can be seen that there is considerably slower adjustment, evidenced by the significant second and third order autoregressive terms, between the thresholds than outside them. There still seems to be some

Table 10.8 A two-threshold SETAR model for the basis

$$
b_t = \begin{cases}
\phi_0^1 + \sum_{i=1}^{3} \phi_i^1 b_{t-i} + \varepsilon_t^1 & \text{if } b_{t-1} < r_0 \\[2mm]
\phi_0^2 + \sum_{i=1}^{3} \phi_i^2 b_{t-i} + \varepsilon_t^2 & \text{if } r_0 \leq b_{t-1} < r_1 \\[2mm]
\phi_0^3 + \sum_{i=1}^{3} \phi_i^3 b_{t-i} + \varepsilon_t^3 & \text{if } b_{t-1} \geq r_1
\end{cases}
$$

	$b_{t-1} < r_0$	$r_0 \leq b_{t-1} < r_1$	$b_{t-1} \geq r_1$
	Panel A: whole sample		
ϕ_1	0.5743**	−0.6395	0.8380**
	(0.0415)	(0.7549)	(0.0512)
ϕ_2	0.2088**	−0.0594	0.0439
	(0.0401)	(0.0846)	(0.0462)
ϕ_3	0.1330**	0.2267**	0.0415
	(0.0355)	(0.0811)	(0.0344)
$\hat{r}_0$		0.0138	
$\hat{r}_1$		0.0158	
	Panel B: pre-crash sample		
ϕ_1	0.4745**	0.4482*	0.8536**
	(0.0808)	(0.1821)	(0.0720)
ϕ_2	0.2164**	0.2608**	−0.0388
	(0.0781)	(0.0950)	(0.0710)
ϕ_3	0.1142	0.2309**	0.0770
	(0.0706)	(0.0834)	(0.0531)
$\hat{r}_0$		0.0052	
$\hat{r}_1$		0.0117	
	Panel C: post-crash sample		
ϕ_1	0.5019**	0.7474**	0.8397**
	(0.1230)	(0.1201)	(0.0533)
ϕ_2	0.2011*	0.2984**	0.0689
	(0.0874)	(0.0691)	(0.0514)
ϕ_3	0.0434	0.1412	0.0461
	(0.0748)	(0.0763)	(0.0400)
$\hat{r}_0$		0.0080	
$\hat{r}_1$		0.0140	

Notes: Figures in parentheses are heteroscedasticity-robust standard errors, * and ** denote significance at the 5% and at 1% levels, respectively.
Source: Brooks and Garrett (2002).

evidence of slow adjustment below the lower threshold, where the appropriate trading strategy would be to go long the futures and short the stock. Brooks and Garrett (2002) attribute this in part to restrictions on and costs of short-selling the stock that prevent adjustment from taking place more quickly. Short-selling of futures contracts is easier and less costly, and hence there is no action in the basis beyond an AR(1) when it is above the upper threshold.

Such a finding is entirely in accordance with expectations, and suggests that, once allowance is made for reasonable transactions costs, the basis may fluctuate with some degree of flexibility where arbitrage is not profitable. Once the basis moves outside the transactions costs-determined range, adjustment occurs within one period as the theory predicted.

10.14 A note on regime switching models and forecasting accuracy

Several studies have noted the inability of threshold or regime switching models to generate superior out-of-sample forecasting accuracy than linear models or a random walk in spite of their apparent ability to fit the data better in sample. A possible reconciliation is offered by Dacco and Satchell (1999), who suggest that regime switching models may forecast poorly owing to the difficulty of forecasting the regime that the series will be in. Thus, any gain from a good fit of the model within the regime will be lost if the model forecasts the regime wrongly. Such an argument could apply to both the Markov switching and TAR classes of models.

Key concepts

The key terms to be able to define and explain from this chapter are
- seasonality
- slope dummy variable
- regime switching
- self-exciting TAR
- Markov process

- intercept dummy variable
- dummy variable trap
- threshold autoregression (TAR)
- delay parameter
- transition probability

Self-study questions

1. A researcher is attempting to form an econometric model to explain daily movements of stock returns. A colleague suggests that she might want to see whether her data are influenced by daily seasonality.
   (a) How might she go about doing this?
   (b) The researcher estimates a model with the dependent variable as the daily returns on a given share traded on the London stock exchange, and various macroeconomic variables and accounting ratios as independent variables. She attempts to estimate this model, together with five daily dummy variables (one for each day of the week), and a constant term, using EViews. EViews then tells her that it cannot estimate the

parameters of the model. Explain what has probably happened, and how she can fix it.

(c) A colleague estimates instead the following model for asset returns, r_t is as follows (with standard errors in parentheses)

$$\hat{r}_t = 0.0034 - 0.0183D1_t + 0.0155D2_t - 0.0007D3_t$$

$$(0.0146)\ (0.0068) \qquad (0.0231) \qquad (0.0179)$$

$$-0.0272D4_t + \text{other variables}$$

$$(0.0193)$$

The model is estimated using 500 observations. Is there significant evidence of any 'day-of-the-week effects' after allowing for the effects of the other variables?

(d) Distinguish between intercept dummy variables and slope dummy variables, giving an example of each.

(e) A financial researcher suggests that many investors rebalance their portfolios at the end of each financial year to realise losses and consequently reduce their tax liabilities. Develop a procedure to test whether this behaviour might have an effect on equity returns.

2. (a) What is a switching model? Describe briefly and distinguish between threshold autoregressive models and Markov switching models. How would you decide which of the two model classes is more appropriate for a particular application?

(b) Describe the following terms as they are used in the context of Markov switching models
   (i) The Markov property
   (ii) A transition matrix.

(c) What is a SETAR model? Discuss the issues involved in estimating such a model.

(d) What problem(s) may arise if the standard information criteria presented in chapter 6 were applied to the determination of the orders of each equation in a TAR model? How do suitably modified criteria overcome this problem?

(e) A researcher suggests a reason that many empirical studies find that PPP does not hold is the existence of transactions costs and other rigidities in the goods markets. Describe a threshold model procedure that may be used to evaluate this proposition in the context of a single good.

(f) A researcher estimates a SETAR model with one threshold and three lags in both regimes using maximum likelihood. He then estimates a linear AR(3) model by maximum likelihood and proceeds to use a likelihood ratio test to determine whether the non-linear threshold model is necessary. Explain the flaw in this approach.

(f) 'Threshold models are more complex than linear autoregressive models. Therefore, the former should produce more accurate forecasts since they should capture more relevant features of the data.' Discuss.

3. A researcher suggests that the volatility dynamics of a set of daily equity returns are different:

   - on Mondays relative to other days of the week
   - if the previous day's return volatility was bigger than 0.1% relative to when the previous day's return volatility was less than 0.1%.

   Describe models that could be used to capture these reported features of the data.

4. (a) Re-open the exchange rate returns series and test them for day-of-the-week effects.

   (b) Re-open the house price changes series and determine whether there is any evidence of seasonality.

11 Panel data

Learning outcomes

In this chapter, you will learn how to

- Describe the key features of panel data and outline the advantages and disadvantages of working with panels rather than other structures
- Explain the intuition behind seemingly unrelated regressions and propose examples of where they may be usefully employed
- Contrast the fixed effect and random effect approaches to panel model specification, determining which is the more appropriate in particular cases
- Estimate and interpret the results from panel unit root and cointegration tests
- Construct and estimate panel models in EViews

11.1 Introduction – what are panel techniques and why are they used?

The situation often arises in financial modelling where we have data comprising both time series and cross-sectional elements, and such a dataset would be known as a panel of data or longitudinal data. A panel of data will embody information across both time and space. Importantly, a panel keeps the same individuals or objects (henceforth we will call these 'entities') and measures some quantity about them over time.[1] This chapter will present and discuss the important features of panel analysis, and will describe the techniques used to model such data.

Econometrically, the setup we may have is as described in the following equation

$$y_{it} = \alpha + \beta x_{it} + u_{it} \tag{11.1}$$

---

[1] Hence, strictly, if the data are not on the same entities (for example, different firms or people) measured over time, then this would not be panel data.

where y_{it} is the dependent variable, α is the intercept term, β is a $k \times 1$ vector of parameters to be estimated on the explanatory variables, and x_{it} is a $1 \times k$ vector of observations on the explanatory variables, $t = 1, \ldots, T; i = 1, \ldots, N.$[2]

The simplest way to deal with such data would be to estimate a pooled regression, which would involve estimating a single equation on all the data together, so that the dataset for y is stacked up into a single column containing all the cross-sectional and time series observations, and similarly all of the observations on each explanatory variable would be stacked up into single columns in the x matrix. Then this equation would be estimated in the usual fashion using OLS.

While this is indeed a simple way to proceed, and requires the estimation of as few parameters as possible, it has some severe limitations. Most importantly, pooling the data in this way implicitly assumes that the average values of the variables and the relationships between them are constant over time and across all of the cross-sectional units in the sample. We could, of course, estimate separate time series regressions for each of objects or entities, but this is likely to be a sub-optimal way to proceed since this approach would not take into account any common structure present in the series of interest. Alternatively, we could estimate separate cross-sectional regressions for each of the time periods, but again this may not be wise if there is some common variation in the series over time. If we are fortunate enough to have a panel of data at our disposal, there are important advantages to making full use of this rich structure:

- First, and perhaps most importantly, we can address a broader range of issues and tackle more complex problems with panel data than would be possible with pure time series or pure cross-sectional data alone.
- Second, it is often of interest to examine how variables, or the relationships between them, change dynamically (over time). To do this using pure time series data would often require a long run of data simply to get a sufficient number of observations to be able to conduct any meaningful hypothesis tests. But by combining cross-sectional and time series data, one can increase the number of degrees of freedom, and thus the power of the test, by employing information on the dynamic behaviour of a large number of entities at the same time. The additional variation introduced by combining the data in this way can also help to mitigate problems of multicollinearity that may arise if time series are modelled individually.
- Third, as will become apparent below, by structuring the model in an appropriate way, we can remove the impact of certain forms of omitted variables bias in regression results.

[2] Note that k is defined slightly differently in this chapter compared with others in the book. Here, k represents the number of slope parameters to be estimated (rather than the total number of parameters as it is elsewhere), which is equal to the number of explanatory variables in the regression model.

One approach to making more full use of the structure of the data would be to use the *seemingly unrelated regression* (SUR) framework initially proposed by Zellner (1962). This has been used widely in finance where the requirement is to model several closely related variables over time.[3] A SUR is so called because the dependent variables may seem unrelated across the equations at first sight, but a more careful consideration would allow us to conclude that they are in fact related after all. One example would be the flow of funds (i.e. net new money invested) to portfolios (mutual funds) operated by two different investment banks. The flows could be related since they are, to some extent, substitutes (if the manager of one fund is performing poorly, investors may switch to the other). The flows are also related because the total flow of money into all mutual funds will be affected by a set of common factors (for example, related to people's propensity to save for their retirement). Although we could entirely separately model the flow of funds for each bank, we may be able to improve the efficiency of the estimation by capturing at least part of the common structure in some way. Under the SUR approach, one would allow for the contemporaneous relationships between the error terms in the two equations for the flows to the funds in each bank by using a generalised least squares (GLS) technique. The idea behind SUR is essentially to transform the model so that the error terms become uncorrelated. If the correlations between the error terms in the individual equations had been zero in the first place, then SUR on the system of equations would have been equivalent to running separate OLS regressions on each equation. This would also be the case if all of the values of the explanatory variables were the same in all equations – for example, if the equations for the two funds contained only macroeconomic variables.

However, the applicability of the technique is limited because it can be employed only when the number of time series observations, T, per cross-sectional unit i is at least as large as the total number of such units, N. A second problem with SUR is that the number of parameters to be estimated in total is very large, and the variance-covariance matrix of the errors (which will be a phenomenal $NT \times NT$) also has to be estimated. For these reasons, the more flexible full panel data approach is much more commonly used.

There are broadly two classes of panel estimator approaches that can be employed in financial research: *fixed effects* models and *random effects* models. The simplest types of fixed effects models allow the intercept in the regression model to differ cross-sectionally but not over time, while all of the slope estimates are fixed both cross-sectionally and over time. This approach is evidently more parsimonious than a SUR (where each cross-sectional unit would

---

[3] For example, the SUR framework has been used to test the impact of the introduction of the euro on the integration of European stock markets (Kim *et al.*, 2005), in tests of the CAPM, and in tests of the forward rate unbiasedness hypothesis (Hodgson *et al.*, 2004).

have different slopes as well), but it still requires the estimation of $(N + k)$ parameters.[4]

A first distinction we must draw is between a *balanced panel* and an *unbalanced panel*. A balanced panel has the same number of time series observations for each cross-sectional unit (or equivalently but viewed the other way around, the same number of cross-sectional units at each point in time), whereas an unbalanced panel would have some cross-sectional elements with fewer observations or observations at different times to others. The same techniques are used in both cases, and while the presentation below implicitly assumes that the panel is balanced, missing observations should be automatically accounted for by the software package used to estimate the model.

11.3 The fixed effects model

To see how the fixed effects model works, we can take equation (11.1) above, and decompose the disturbance term, u_{it}, into an individual specific effect, μ_i, and the 'remainder disturbance', v_{it}, that varies over time and entities (capturing everything that is left unexplained about y_{it}).

$$u_{it} = \mu_i + v_{it} \tag{11.2}$$

So we could rewrite equation (11.1) by substituting in for u_{it} from (11.2) to obtain

$$y_{it} = \alpha + \beta x_{it} + \mu_i + v_{it} \tag{11.3}$$

We can think of μ_i as encapsulating all of the variables that affect y_{it} cross-sectionally but do not vary over time – for example, the sector that a firm operates in, a person's gender, or the country where a bank has its headquarters, etc. This model could be estimated using dummy variables, which would be termed the least squares dummy variable (LSDV) approach

$$y_{it} = \beta x_{it} + \mu_1 D1_i + \mu_2 D2_i + \mu_3 D3_i + \cdots + \mu_N DN_i + v_{it} \tag{11.4}$$

where $D1_i$ is a dummy variable that takes the value 1 for all observations on the first entity (e.g. the first firm) in the sample and zero otherwise, $D2_i$ is a dummy variable that takes the value 1 for all observations on the second entity (e.g. the second firm) and zero otherwise, and so on. Notice that we have removed the intercept term (α) from this equation to avoid the 'dummy variable trap' described in chapter 10 where we have perfect multicollinearity between the dummy variables and the intercept. When the fixed effects model is written in this way, it is relatively easy to see how to test for whether the panel approach is really necessary at all. This test would be a slightly modified version of the Chow test described in

---

[4] It is important to recognise this limitation of panel data techniques that the relationship between the explained and explanatory variables is assumed constant both cross-sectionally and over time, even if the varying intercepts allow the average values to differ. The use of panel techniques rather than estimating separate time series regressions for each object or estimating separate cross-sectional regressions for each time period thus implicitly assumes that the efficiency gains from doing so outweigh any biases that may arise in the parameter estimation.

chapter 5, and would involve incorporating the restriction that all of the intercept dummy variables have the same parameter (i.e. $H_0 : \mu_1 = \mu_2 = \cdots = \mu_N$). If this null hypothesis is not rejected, the data can simply be pooled together and OLS employed. If this null is rejected, however, then it is not valid to impose the restriction that the intercepts are the same over the cross-sectional units and a panel approach must be employed.

Now the model given by equation (11.4) has $N + k$ parameters to estimate, which would be a challenging problem for any regression package when N is large. In order to avoid the necessity to estimate so many dummy variable parameters, a transformation is made to the data to simplify matters. This transformation, known as the *within transformation*, involves subtracting the time-mean of each entity away from the values of the variable.[5] So define $\overline{y}_i = \frac{1}{T}\sum_{t=1}^{T} y_{it}$ as the time-mean of the observations on y for cross-sectional unit i, and similarly calculate the means of all of the explanatory variables. Then we can subtract the time-means from each variable to obtain a regression containing demeaned variables only. Note that again, such a regression does not require an intercept term since now the dependent variable will have zero mean by construction. The model containing the demeaned variables is

$$y_{it} - \overline{y}_i = \beta(x_{it} - \overline{x}_i) + u_{it} - \overline{u}_i \tag{11.5}$$

which we could write as

$$\ddot{y}_{it} = \beta \ddot{x}_{it} + \ddot{u}_{it} \tag{11.6}$$

where the double dots above the variables denote the demeaned values.

An alternative to this demeaning would be to simply run a cross-sectional regression on the time-averaged values of the variables, which is known as the *between estimator*.[6] A further possibility is that instead, the first difference operator could be applied to equation (11.1) so that the model becomes one for explaining the change in y_{it} rather than its level. When differences are taken, any variables that do not change over time (i.e. the μ_i) will again cancel out. Differencing and the within transformation will produce identical estimates in situations where there are only two time periods; when there are more, the choice between the two approaches will depend on the assumed properties of the error term. Wooldridge (2010) describes this issue in considerable detail.

Equation (11.6) can now be routinely estimated using OLS on the pooled sample of demeaned data, but we do need to be aware of the number of degrees of freedom which this regression will have. Although estimating the equation will use only k degrees of freedom from the NT observations, it is important to recognise that we also used a further N degrees of freedom in constructing the demeaned variables (i.e. we lost a degree of freedom for every one of the N explanatory

---

[5] It is known as the *within transformation* because the subtraction is made within each cross-sectional object.

[6] An advantage of running the regression on average values (the *between estimator*) over running it on the demeaned values (the *within estimator*) is that the process of averaging is likely to reduce the effect of measurement error in the variables on the estimation process.

variables for which we were required to estimate the mean). Hence the number of degrees of freedom that must be used in estimating the standard errors in an unbiased way and when conducting hypothesis tests is $NT - N - k$. Any software packages used to estimate such models should take this into account automatically.

The regression on the time-demeaned variables will give identical parameters and standard errors as would have been obtained directly from the LSDV regression, but without the hassle of estimating so many parameters! A major disadvantage of this process, however, is that we lose the ability to determine the influences of all of the variables that affect y_{it} but do not vary over time.

11.4 Time-fixed effects models

It is also possible to have a time-fixed effects model rather than an entity-fixed effects model. We would use such a model where we thought that the average value of y_{it} changes over time but not cross-sectionally. Hence with time-fixed effects, the intercepts would be allowed to vary over time but would be assumed to be the same across entities at each given point in time. We could write a time-fixed effects model as

$$y_{it} = \alpha + \beta x_{it} + \lambda_t + v_{it} \tag{11.7}$$

where λ_t is a time-varying intercept that captures all of the variables that affect y_{it} and that vary over time but are constant cross-sectionally. An example would be where the regulatory environment or tax rate changes part-way through a sample period. In such circumstances, this change of environment may well influence y, but in the same way for all firms, which could be assumed to all be affected equally by the change.

Time variation in the intercept terms can be allowed for in exactly the same way as with entity-fixed effects. That is, a least squares dummy variable model could be estimated

$$y_{it} = \beta x_{it} + \lambda_1 D1_t + \lambda_2 D2_t + \lambda_3 D3_t + \cdots + \lambda_T DT_t + v_{it} \tag{11.8}$$

where $D1_t$, for example, denotes a dummy variable that takes the value 1 for the first time period and zero elsewhere, and so on.

The only difference is that now, the dummy variables capture time variation rather than cross-sectional variation. Similarly, in order to avoid estimating a model containing all T dummies, a within transformation can be conducted to subtract the cross-sectional averages from each observation

$$y_{it} - \overline{y}_t = \beta(x_{it} - \overline{x}_t) + u_{it} - \overline{u}_t \tag{11.9}$$

where $\overline{y}_t = \frac{1}{N}\sum_{i=1}^{N} y_{it}$ as the mean of the observations on y across the entities for each time period. We could write this equation as

$$\ddot{y}_{it} = \beta \ddot{x}_{it} + \ddot{u}_{it} \tag{11.10}$$

where the double dots above the variables denote the demeaned values (but now cross-sectionally rather than temporally demeaned).

Finally, it is possible to allow for both entity-fixed effects and time-fixed effects within the same model. Such a model would be termed a two-way error component model, which would combine equations (11.3) and (11.7), and the LSDV equivalent model would contain both cross-sectional and time dummies

$$y_{it} = \beta x_{it} + \mu_1 D1_i + \mu_2 D2_i + \mu_3 D3_i + \cdots + \mu_N DN_i + \lambda_1 D1_t$$

$$+ \lambda_2 D2_t + \lambda_3 D3_t + \cdots + \lambda_T DT_t + v_{it} \tag{11.11}$$

However, the number of parameters to be estimated would now be $k + N + T$, and the within transformation in this two-way model would be more complex.

11.5 Investigating banking competition using a fixed effects model

The UK retail banking sector has been subject to a considerable change in structure over the past thirty years as a result of deregulation, merger waves and new technology. The relatively high concentration of market share in retail banking among a modest number of fairly large banks, combined with apparently phenomenal profits that appear to be recurrent, have led to concerns that competitive forces in British banking are not sufficiently strong.[7] This is argued to go hand in hand with restrictive practices, barriers to entry and poor value for money for consumers. A study by Matthews, Murinde and Zhao (2007) investigates competitive conditions in the UK between 1980 and 2004 using the 'new empirical industrial organisation' approach pioneered by Panzar and Rosse (1982, 1987). The model posits that if the market is *contestable*, entry to and exit from the market will be easy (even if the concentration of market share among firms is high), so that prices will be set equal to marginal costs. The technique used to examine this conjecture is to derive testable restrictions upon the firm's reduced form revenue equation.

The empirical investigation consists of deriving an index (the Panzar–Rosse H-statistic) of the sum of the elasticities of revenues to factor costs (input prices). If this lies between 0 and 1, we have monopolistic competition or a partially contestable equilibrium, whereas $H < 0$ would imply a monopoly and $H = 1$ would imply perfect competition or perfect contestability. The key point is that if the market is characterised by perfect competition, an increase in input prices will not affect the output of firms, while it will under monopolistic competition. The model Matthews *et al.* investigate is given by

$$lnREV_{it} = \alpha_0 + \alpha_1 lnPL_{it} + \alpha_2 lnPK_{it} + \alpha_3 lnPF_{it} + \beta_1 lnRISKASS_{it}$$

$$+ \beta_2 lnASSET_{it} + \beta_3 lnBR_{it} + \gamma_1 GROWTH_t + \mu_i + v_{it} \tag{11.12}$$

where 'REV_{it}' is the ratio of bank revenue to total assets for firm i at time t ($i = 1, \ldots, N; t = 1, \ldots, T$); 'PL' is personnel expenses to employees (the unit price of labour); 'PK' is the ratio of capital assets to fixed assets (the unit price of capital); and 'PF' is the ratio of annual interest expenses to total loanable funds (the unit price of funds). The model also includes several variables that capture

---

[7] Interestingly, while many casual observers believe that concentration in UK retail banking has grown considerably, it actually fell slightly between 1986 and 2002.

time-varying bank-specific effects on revenues and costs, and these are 'RISKASS', the ratio of provisions to total assets; 'ASSET' is bank size, as measured by total assets; 'BR' is the ratio of the bank's number of branches to the total number of branches for all banks. Finally, 'GROWTH$_t$' is the rate of growth of GDP, which obviously varies over time but is constant across banks at a given point in time; μ_i are bank-specific fixed effects and v_{it} is an idiosyncratic disturbance term. The contestability parameter, H, is given as $\alpha_1 + \alpha_2 + \alpha_3$.

Unfortunately, the Panzar–Rosse approach is valid only when applied to a banking market in long-run equilibrium. Hence the authors also conduct a test for this, which centres on the regression

$$lnROA_{it} = \alpha'_0 + \alpha'_1 lnPL_{it} + \alpha'_2 lnPK_{it} + \alpha'_3 lnPF_{it} + \beta'_1 lnRISKASS_{it}$$
$$+ \beta'_2 lnASSET_{it} + \beta'_3 lnBR_{it} + \gamma'_1 GROWTH_t + \eta_i + w_{it} \qquad (11.13)$$

The explanatory variables for the equilibrium test regression (11.13) are identical to those of the contestability regression (11.12), but the dependent variable is now the log of the return on assets ('lnROA'). Equilibrium is argued to exist in the market if $\alpha'_1 + \alpha'_2 + \alpha'_3 = 0$.

The UK market is argued to be of particular international interest as a result of its speed of deregulation and the magnitude of the changes in market structure that took place over the sample period and therefore the study by Matthews *et al.* focuses exclusively on the UK. They employ a fixed effects panel data model which allows for differing intercepts across the banks, but assumes that these effects are fixed over time. The fixed effects approach is a sensible one given the data analysed here since there is an unusually large number of years (twenty-five) compared with the number of banks (twelve), resulting in a total of 219 bank-years (observations). The data employed in the study are obtained from banks' annual reports and the Annual Abstract of Banking Statistics from the British Bankers Association. The analysis is conducted for the whole sample period, 1980–2004, and for two sub-samples, 1980–91 and 1992–2004. The results for tests of equilibrium are given first, in table 11.1.

The null hypothesis that the bank fixed effects are jointly zero ($H_0 : \eta_i = 0$) is rejected at the 1% significance level for the full sample and for the second sub-sample but not at all for the first sub-sample. Overall, however, this indicates the usefulness of the fixed effects panel model that allows for bank heterogeneity. The main focus of interest in table 11.1 is the equilibrium test, and this shows slight evidence of disequilibrium (E is significantly different from zero at the 10% level) for the whole sample, but not for either of the individual sub-samples. Thus the conclusion is that the market appears to be sufficiently in a state of equilibrium that it is valid to continue to investigate the extent of competition using the Panzar–Rosse methodology. The results of this are presented in table 11.2.[8]

The value of the contestability parameter, H, which is the sum of the input elasticities, is given in the last row of table 11.2 and falls in value from 0.78 in the

---

[8] A Chow test for structural stability reveals a structural break between the two sub-samples. No other commentary on the results of the equilibrium regression is given by the authors.

Table 11.1   Tests of banking market equilibrium with fixed effects panel models

Variable	1980–2004	1980–91	1992–2004
Intercept	0.0230***	0.1034*	0.0252
	(3.24)	(1.87)	(2.60)
lnPL	−0.0002	0.0059	0.0002
	(0.27)	(1.24)	(0.37)
lnPK	−0.0014*	−0.0020	−0.0016*
	(1.89)	(1.21)	(1.81)
lnPF	−0.0009	−0.0034	0.0005
	(1.03)	(1.01)	(0.49)
lnRISKASS	−0.6471***	−0.5514***	−0.8343***
	(13.56)	(8.53)	(5.91)
lnASSET	−0.0016***	−0.0068**	−0.0016**
	(2.69)	(2.07)	(2.07)
lnBR	−0.0012*	0.0017	−0.0025
	(1.91)	(0.97)	(1.55)
GROWTH	0.0007***	0.0004	0.0006*
	(4.19)	(1.54)	(1.71)
R^2 within	0.5898	0.6159	0.4706
$H_0 : \eta_i = 0$	$F(11, 200) = 7.78^{***}$	$F(9, 66) = 1.50$	$F(11, 117) = 11.28^{***}$
$H_0 : E = 0$	$F(1, 200) = 3.20^{*}$	$F(1, 66) = 0.01$	$F(1, 117) = 0.28$

Notes: t-ratios in parentheses; *, ** and *** denote significance at the 10%, 5% and 1% levels respectively.
Source: Matthews *et al.* (2007). Reprinted with the permission of Elsevier.

first sub-sample to 0.46 in the second, suggesting that the degree of competition in UK retail banking weakened over the period. However, the results in the two rows above that show that the null hypotheses $H = 0$ and $H = 1$ can both be rejected at the 1% significance level for both sub-samples, showing that the market is best characterised by monopolistic competition rather than either perfect competition (perfect contestability) or pure monopoly. As for the equilibrium regressions, the null hypothesis that the fixed effects dummies (μ_i) are jointly zero is strongly rejected, vindicating the use of the fixed effects panel approach and suggesting that the base levels of the dependent variables differ.

Table 11.2 Tests of competition in banking with fixed effects panel models

Variable	1980–2004	1980–91	1992–2004
Intercept	−3.083	1.1033**	−0.5455
	(1.60)	(2.06)	(1.57)
lnPL	−0.0098	0.164***	−0.0164
	(0.54)	(3.57)	(0.64)
lnPK	0.0025	0.0026	−0.0289
	(0.13)	(0.16)	(0.91)
lnPF	0.5788***	0.6119***	0.5096***
	(23.12)	(18.97)	(12.72)
lnRISKASS	2.9886**	1.4147**	5.8986
	(2.30)	(2.26)	(1.17)
lnASSET	−0.0551***	−0.0963***	−0.0676**
	(3.34)	(2.89)	(2.52)
lnBR	0.0461***	0.00094	0.0809
	(2.70)	(0.57)	(1.43)
GROWTH	−0.0082*	−0.0027	−0.0121
	(1.91)	(1.17)	(1.00)
R^2 within	0.9209	0.9181	0.8165
$H_0 : \eta_i = 0$	$F(11, 200) = 23.94^{***}$	$F(9, 66) = 21.97^{***}$	$F(11, 117) = 11.95^{***}$
$H_0 : H = 0$	$F(1, 200) = 229.46^{***}$	$F(1, 66) = 205.89^{***}$	$F(1, 117) = 71.25^{***}$
$H_1 : H = 1$	$F(1, 200) = 128.99^{***}$	$F(1, 66) = 16.59^{***}$	$F(1, 117) = 94.76^{***}$
H	0.5715	0.7785	0.4643

Notes: t-ratios in parentheses; *, ** and ***, denote significance at the 10%, 5% and 1% levels respectively. The final set of asterisks in the table was added by the present author.
Source: Matthews et al. (2007). Reprinted with the permission of Elsevier.

Finally, the additional bank control variables all appear to have intuitively appealing signs. The risk assets variable has a positive sign, so that higher risks lead to higher revenue per unit of total assets; the asset variable has a negative sign and is statistically significant at the 5% level or below in all three periods, suggesting that smaller banks are relatively more profitable; the effect of having more branches is to reduce profitability; and revenue to total assets is largely unaffected by macroeconomic conditions – if anything, the banks appear to have been more profitable when GDP was growing more slowly.

11.6 The random effects model

An alternative to the fixed effects model described above is the random effects model, which is sometimes also known as the error components model. As with fixed effects, the random effects approach proposes different intercept terms for each entity and again these intercepts are constant over time, with the relationships between the explanatory and explained variables assumed to be the same both cross-sectionally and temporally.

However, the difference is that under the random effects model, the intercepts for each cross-sectional unit are assumed to arise from a common intercept α (which is the same for all cross-sectional units and over time), plus a random variable ϵ_i that varies cross-sectionally but is constant over time. ϵ_i measures the random deviation of each entity's intercept term from the 'global' intercept term α. We can write the random effects panel model as

$$y_{it} = \alpha + \beta x_{it} + \omega_{it}, \quad \omega_{it} = \epsilon_i + v_{it} \tag{11.14}$$

where x_{it} is still a $1 \times k$ vector of explanatory variables, but unlike the fixed effects model, there are no dummy variables to capture the heterogeneity (variation) in the cross-sectional dimension. Instead, this occurs via the ϵ_i terms. Note that this framework requires the assumptions that the new cross-sectional error term, ϵ_i, has zero mean, is independent of the individual observation error term (v_{it}), has constant variance σ_ϵ^2 and is independent of the explanatory variables (x_{it}).

The parameters (α and the β vector) are estimated consistently but inefficiently by OLS, and the conventional formulae would have to be modified as a result of the cross-correlations between error terms for a given cross-sectional unit at different points in time. Instead, a generalised least squares procedure is usually used. The transformation involved in this GLS procedure is to subtract a weighted mean of the y_{it} over time (i.e. part of the mean rather than the whole mean, as was the case for fixed effects estimation). Define the 'quasi-demeaned' data as $y_{it}^* = y_{it} - \theta \bar{y}_i$ and $x_{it}^* = x_{it} - \theta \bar{x}_i$, where $\bar{y}_i$ and $\bar{x}_i$ are the means over time of the observations on y_{it} and x_{it}, respectively.[9] θ will be a function of the variance of the observation error term, σ_v^2, and of the variance of the entity-specific error term, σ_ϵ^2

$$\theta = 1 - \frac{\sigma_v}{\sqrt{T\sigma_\epsilon^2 + \sigma_v^2}} \tag{11.15}$$

This transformation will be precisely that required to ensure that there are no cross-correlations in the error terms, but fortunately it should automatically be implemented by standard software packages.

Just as for the fixed effects model, with random effects it is also conceptually no more difficult to allow for time variation than it is to allow for cross-sectional variation. In the case of time variation, a time period-specific error term is included

$$y_{it} = \alpha + \beta x_{it} + \omega_{it}, \quad \omega_{it} = \epsilon_t + v_{it} \tag{11.16}$$

[9] The notation used here is a slightly modified version of Kennedy (2003, p. 315).

> ### Box 11.1   Fixed or random effects?
>
> It is often said that the random effects model is more appropriate when the entities in the sample can be thought of as having been randomly selected from the population, but a fixed effect model is more plausible when the entities in the sample effectively constitute the entire population (for instance, when the sample comprises all of the stocks traded on a particular exchange). More technically, the transformation involved in the GLS procedure under the random effects approach will not remove the explanatory variables that do not vary over time, and hence their impact on y_{it} can be enumerated. Also, since there are fewer parameters to be estimated with the random effects model (no dummy variables or within transformation to perform) and therefore degrees of freedom are saved, the random effects model should produce more efficient estimation than the fixed effects approach.
>
> However, the random effects approach has a major drawback which arises from the fact that it is valid only when the composite error term ω_{it} is uncorrelated with all of the explanatory variables. This assumption is more stringent than the corresponding one in the fixed effects case, because with random effects we thus require both ϵ_i and v_{it} to be independent of all of the x_{it}. This can also be viewed as a consideration of whether any unobserved omitted variables (that were allowed for by having different intercepts for each entity) are uncorrelated with the included explanatory variables. If they are uncorrelated, a random effects approach can be used; otherwise the fixed effects model is preferable.
>
> A test for whether this assumption is valid for the random effects estimator is based on a slightly more complex version of the Hausman test described in section 7.6. If the assumption does not hold, the parameter estimates will be biased and inconsistent. To see how this arises, suppose that we have only one explanatory variable, x_{2it}, that varies positively with y_{it} and also with the error term, ω_{it}. The estimator will ascribe all of any increase in y to x when in reality some of it arises from the error term, resulting in biased coefficients.

and again, a two-way model could be envisaged to allow the intercepts to vary both cross-sectionally and over time. Box 11.1 discusses the choice between fixed effects and random effects models.

11.7   Panel data application to credit stability of banks in Central and Eastern Europe

Banking has become increasingly global over the past two decades, with domestic markets in many countries being increasingly penetrated by foreign-owned competitors. Foreign participants in the banking sector may improve competition and efficiency to the benefit of the economy that they enter, and they may have a stabilising effect on credit provision since they will probably be better diversified than domestic banks and will therefore be more able to continue to lend when the host economy is performing poorly. But it is also argued that foreign banks may alter the credit supply to suit their own aims rather than those of the host economy, and they may act more pro-cyclically than local banks, since they have alternative markets to withdraw their credit supply to when host market activity falls. Moreover, worsening conditions in the home country may force the repatriation of funds to support a weakened parent bank.

There may be differences in policies for credit provision dependent upon the nature of the formation of the subsidiary abroad. If the subsidiary's existence results from a take-over of a domestic bank, it is likely that the subsidiary will continue to operate the policies of, and in the same manner as, and with the same management as, the original separate entity, albeit in a diluted form. However, when the foreign bank subsidiary results from the formation of an entirely new startup operation (a 'greenfield investment'), the subsidiary is more likely to reflect the aims and objectives of the parent institution from the outset, and may be more willing to rapidly expand credit growth in order to obtain a sizeable foothold in the credit market as quickly as possible.

A study by de Haas and van Lelyveld (2006) employs a panel regression using a sample of around 250 banks from ten Central and East European countries to examine whether domestic and foreign banks react differently to changes in home or host economic activity and banking crises.

The data cover the period 1993–2000 and are obtained from BankScope. The core model is a random effects panel regression of the form

$$gr_{it} = \alpha + \beta_1 \textit{Takeover}_{it} + \beta_2 \textit{Greenfield}_i + \beta_3 \textit{Crisis}_{it} + \beta_4 \textit{Macro}_{it}$$
$$+ \beta_5 \textit{Contr}_{it} + (\mu_i + \epsilon_{it}) \tag{11.17}$$

where the dependent variable, 'gr_{it}', is the percentage growth in the credit of bank i in year t; '$\textit{Takeover}_{it}$' is a dummy variable taking the value 1 for foreign banks resulting from a takeover at time t and zero otherwise; '$\textit{Greenfield}_i$' is a dummy taking the value 1 if bank i is the result of a foreign firm making a new banking investment rather than taking over an existing one; 'crisis' is a dummy variable taking the value 1 if the host country for bank i was subject to a banking disaster in year t. 'Macro' is a vector of variables capturing the macroeconomic conditions in the home country (the lending rate and the change in GDP for the home and host countries, the host country inflation rate, and the differences in the home and host country GDP growth rates and the differences in the home and host country lending rates). 'Contr' is a vector of bank-specific control variables that may affect the dependent variable irrespective of whether it is a foreign or domestic bank, and these are: 'weakness parent bank', defined as loan loss provisions made by the parent bank; 'solvency', the ratio of equity to total assets; 'liquidity', the ratio of liquid assets to total assets; 'size', the ratio of total bank assets to total banking assets in the given country; 'profitability', return on assets; and 'efficiency', net interest margin. α and the βs are parameters (or vectors of parameters in the cases of β_4 and β_5), $\mu_i \sim IID(0, \sigma_\mu^2)$ is the unobserved random effect that varies across banks but not over time, and $\epsilon_{it} \sim IID(0, \sigma_\epsilon^2)$ is an idiosyncratic error term, $i = 1, \ldots, N; t = 1, \ldots, T_i$.

de Haas and van Lelyveld discuss the various techniques that could be employed to estimate such a model. OLS is considered to be inappropriate since it does not allow for differences in average credit market growth rates at the bank level. A model allowing for entity-specific effects (i.e. a fixed effects model that effectively allowed for a different intercept for each bank) would have been preferable to OLS (used to estimate a pooled regression), but is ruled out on the grounds that there are many more banks than time periods and thus too many parameters would be required to be estimated. They also argue that these bank-specific effects are not of interest to the problem at hand, which leads them to select the random effects panel model, that essentially allows for a different error structure for each bank. A Hausman test is conducted and shows that the random effects model is valid since the bank-specific effects (μ_i) are found, 'in most cases not to be significantly correlated with the explanatory variables'.

The results of the random effects panel estimation are presented in table 11.3. Five separate regressions are conducted, with the results displayed in columns 2–6 of the table.[10] The regression is conducted on the full sample of banks and separately on the domestic and foreign bank sub-samples. The specifications allow in separate regressions for differences between host and home variables (denoted 'I', columns 2 and 5) and the actual values of the variables rather than the differences (denoted 'II', columns 3 and 6).

The main result is that during times of banking disasters, domestic banks significantly reduce their credit growth rates (i.e. the parameter estimate on the *crisis* variable is negative for domestic banks), while the parameter is close to zero and not significant for foreign banks. There is a significant negative relationship between home country GDP growth, but a positive relationship with host country GDP growth and credit change in the host country. This indicates that, as the authors expected, when foreign banks have fewer viable lending opportunities in their own countries and hence a lower opportunity cost for the loanable funds, they may switch their resources to the host country. Lending rates, both at home and in the host country, have little impact on credit market share growth. Interestingly, the greenfield and takeover variables are not statistically significant (although the parameters are quite large in absolute value), indicating that the method of investment of a foreign bank in the host country is unimportant in determining its credit growth rate or that the importance of the method of investment varies widely across the sample, leading to large standard errors. A weaker parent bank (with higher loss provisions) leads to a statistically significant contraction of credit in the host country as a result of the reduction in the supply of available funds.

---

[10] de Haas and van Lelyveld employ corrections to the standard errors for heteroscedasticity and autocorrelation. They additionally conduct regressions including interactive dummy variables, although these are not discussed here.

Table 11.3 Results of random effects panel regression for credit stability of Central and East European banks

Explanatory variables	Full sample I	Full sample II	Domestic banks	Foreign banks I	Foreign banks II
Takeover	−11.58	−5.65			
	(1.26)	(0.29)			
Greenfield	14.99	29.59		12.39	8.11
	(1.29)	(1.55)		(0.88)	(0.65)
Crisis	−19.79***	−14.42***	−19.36***	0.31	−4.13
	(4.30)	(2.93)	(3.43)	(0.03)	(0.33)
Host − home ΔGDP	8.08***			8.86***	
	(4.18)			(4.11)	
Host ΔGDP		6.68***	6.74***		8.64***
		(7.39)	(6.98)		(2.93)
Home ΔGDP		−6.04*			−8.62***
		(1.89)			(2.78)
Host − home lending rate	1.12**			0.85	
	(1.97)			(0.88)	
Host lending rate		0.28	0.34		1.50
		(1.08)	(1.36)		(1.11)
Home lending rate		2.97***			1.11
		(4.03)			(1.15)
Host inflation	−0.01	0.03	0.03	0.08	0.07
	(0.37)	(1.01)	(0.12)	(0.61)	(0.44)
Weakness parent bank	−0.19***	−0.16***		−0.23***	−0.19***
	(4.37)	(3.04)		(7.00)	(4.27)
Solvency	1.29***	1.25***	0.85***	3.33***	3.18***
	(5.34)	(4.77)	(3.24)	(5.53)	(5.30)
Liquidity	−0.05**	0.02	0.02	−0.53	−0.43
	(2.09)	(0.78)	(0.70)	(1.40)	(1.14)
Size	−34.65**	−29.14	−21.93	−108.00	−136.19
	(1.96)	(1.56)	(1.16)	(0.54)	(0.72)
Profitability	1.09**	1.09**	1.21***	2.16	0.91
	(2.18)	(2.14)	(2.81)	(0.75)	(0.29)
Interest margin	1.66***	1.90***	2.71***	−3.42	−2.84
	(2.90)	(3.41)	(4.96)	(1.18)	(0.94)
Observations	1003	1003	770	233	233
No. of banks	247	247	184	82	82
Hausman test statistic	0.66	0.94	0.76	0.58	0.92
R^2	0.28	0.33	0.30	0.46	0.47

Notes: *t*-ratios in parentheses. Intercept and country dummy parameter estimates are not shown. Empty cells occur when a particular variable is not included in a regression.
Source: de Haas and van Lelyveld (2006). Reprinted with the permission of Elsevier.

Overall, both home-related ('push') and host-related ('pull') factors are found to be important in explaining foreign bank credit growth.

11.8 Panel data with EViews

The estimation of panel models, both fixed and random effects, is very easy with EViews; the harder part is organising the data so that the software can recognise that you have a panel of data and can apply the techniques accordingly. While there are a number of different ways to construct a panel workfile in EViews, the simplest way, which will be adopted in this example, is to use three stages:

(1) Set up a new workfile to hold the data with the appropriate number of cross-sectional observations, the appropriate time period and the appropriate frequency.
(2) Import the data as pooled variables with all observations on a given series in a single column and with each column representing a separate variable.
(3) Structure the data within EViews so that the full panel framework is available.

The application to be considered here is that of a variant on an early test of the capital asset pricing model due to Fama and MacBeth (1973), discussed in greater detail in chapter 14. Their test involves a two-step estimation procedure: first, the betas are estimated in separate time series regressions for each firm, and second, for each separate point in time, a cross-sectional regression of the excess returns on the betas is conducted

$$R_{it} - R_{ft} = \lambda_0 + \lambda_m \beta_{Pi} + u_i \tag{11.18}$$

where the dependent variable, $R_{it} - R_{ft}$, is the excess return of the stock i at time t and the independent variable is the estimated beta for the portfolio (P) that the stock has been allocated to. The betas of the firms themselves are not used on the RHS, but rather, the betas of portfolios formed on the basis of firm size. If the CAPM holds, then λ_0 should not be significantly different from zero and λ_m should approximate the (time average) equity market risk premium, $R_m - R_f$. Fama and MacBeth proposed estimating this second stage (cross-sectional) regression separately for each time period, and then taking the average of the parameter estimates to conduct hypothesis tests. However, one could also achieve a similar objective using a panel approach. We will use an example in the spirit of Fama–MacBeth comprising the annual returns and 'second pass betas' for eleven years on 2,500 UK firms.[11]

As described above, the first stage is to construct a workfile to hold the data, so **Open EViews** and select **File/New/Workfile**. Then, in the 'Workfile structure

---

[11] Computation by Keith Anderson and the author. There would be some severe limitations of this analysis if it purported to be a piece of original research, but the range of freely available panel datasets is severely limited and so hopefully it will suffice as an example of how to estimate panel models with EViews. No doubt readers, with access to a wider range of data, will be able to think of much better applications.

Screenshot 11.1   **Panel workfile create window**

type' box, select **Balanced Panel** with **Annual data**, starting in **1996** and ending in **2006** with **2500** cross-sections. The Workfile create window will appear and should be completed as in screenshot 11.1.

Next, import the Excel file entitled 'panelex.xls' by selecting **File/Import/Read**. Don't forget to change the file type to Excel (∗.xls). Read the data **By Observation**, with the data starting in Cell **A2**. In the 'Name for Series or Number . . . ' box, enter **4** and click **OK**. This will import the data with the four variables in columns. It is obvious what two of the variables are: the returns series and the beta series, but for panel data, we also need time (a variable that I have called 'year') and cross-sectional ('firm_ident') identifiers.

The final stage is now to structure the panel correctly. This can be achieved by **double clicking on the word 'Range'** in the upper panel of the workfile window, which will make the 'Workfile structure' window open; this window should be filled in as in screenshot 11.2.

So in the 'Cross section ID series:' box, enter **firm_ident** and in the 'Date series:' box, enter **year** and then click **OK**. The panel is now set up and ready for use. To estimate panel regressions, click **Quick/Estimate Equation. . .** and then the Equation Estimation window will open. For the variables, enter **return c beta** in the Equation Specification window. If you click on the **Panel Options** tab, you will see a number of options specific to panel data models are available. The most important of these is the first box, where either fixed or random effects can be chosen. The default is for neither, which would effectively imply a simple pooled

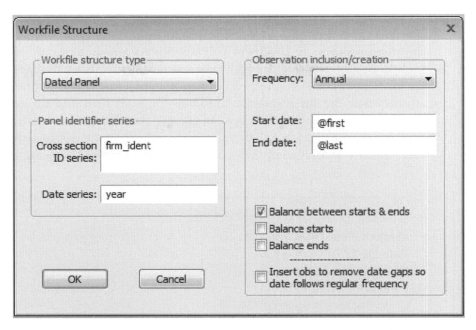

Screenshot 11.2   **Panel workfile structure window**

regression, so **estimate a model with neither fixed nor random effects** first. The results would be as in the following table.

Dependent Variable: RETURN
Method: Panel Least Squares
Date: 08/15/13   Time: 06:41
Sample: 1996 2006
Periods included: 11
Cross-sections included: 1734
Total panel (unbalanced) observations: 8856

	Coefficient	Std. Error	t-Statistic	Prob.
C	0.001843	0.003075	0.599274	0.5490
BETA	0.000454	0.002735	0.166156	0.8680

R-squared	0.000003	Mean dependent var		0.002345
Adjusted R-squared	−0.000110	S.D. dependent var		0.052282
S.E. of regression	0.052285	Akaike info criterion		−3.063986
Sum squared resid	24.20443	Schwarz criterion		−3.062385
Log likelihood	13569.33	Hannan-Quinn criter.		−3.063441
F-statistic	0.027608	Durbin-Watson stat		1.639308
Prob(F-statistic)	0.868038			

We can see that neither the intercept nor the slope is statistically significant. The returns in this regression are in proportion terms rather than percentages, so the slope estimate of 0.000454 corresponds to a risk premium of 0.0454% per month, or around 0.5% per year, whereas the (unweighted average) excess return for all firms in the sample is around −2% per year. But this pooled regression assumes that the intercepts are the same for each firm and for each year. This may be an inappropriate assumption, and we could instead estimate a model with firm fixed and time-fixed effects, which will allow for latent firm-specific and time-specific heterogeneity respectively, as shown in the following table.

Dependent Variable: RETURN
Method: Panel Least Squares
Date: 09/23/07 Time: 21:37
Sample: 1996 2006
Periods included: 11
Cross-sections included: 1734
Total panel (unbalanced) observations: 8856

	Coefficient	Std. Error	t-Statistic	Prob.
C	0.015393	0.004406	3.493481	0.0005
BETA	−0.011800	0.003957	−2.981904	0.0029

Effects specification

Cross-section fixed (dummy variables)
Period fixed (dummy variables)

R-squared	0.303743	Mean dependent var	0.002345
Adjusted R-squared	0.132984	S.D. dependent var	0.052282
S.E. of regression	0.048682	Akaike info criterion	−3.032388
Sum squared resid	16.85255	Schwarz criterion	−1.635590
Log likelihood	15172.42	Hannan-Quinn criter.	−2.556711
F-statistic	1.778776	Durbin-Watson stat	2.067530
Prob(F-statistic)	0.000000		

We can see that the estimate on the beta parameter is now negative and statistically significant, while the intercept is positive and statistically significant. If we wish to see the fixed effects (i.e. to see the values of the dummy variables for each firm and for each point in time), we could click on View/Fixed/Random Effects and then either Cross-Section Effects or Period Effects (the latter are what EViews calls time-fixed effects).

Next, it is worth determining whether the fixed effects are necessary or not by running a redundant fixed effects test. To do this, click **View/Fixed/Random**

Effects Testing and then **Redundant Fixed Effects – Likelihood Ratio Test**. The output in the following table will be seen.

Redundant Fixed Effects Tests Equation: Untitled Test cross-section and period fixed effects			
Effects test	Statistic	d.f.	Prob.
Cross-section F	1.412242	(1733,7111)	0.0000
Cross-section Chi-square	2619.419	1733	0.0000
Period F	63.16944	(10,7111)	0.0000
Period Chi-square	753.7063	10	0.0000
Cross-Section/Period F	1.779779	(1743,7111)	0.0000
Cross-Section/Period Chi-square	3206.169	1743	0.0000

Note that EViews will also present the results for a restricted model where only cross-sectional fixed effects and no period fixed effects are allowed for, and then a restricted model where only period fixed effects are allowed for.[12] Interestingly, the cross-sectional only fixed effects model parameters are not qualitatively different from those of the initial pooled regression, so it is the period fixed effects that make a difference. Three different redundant fixed effects tests are employed, each in both χ^2 and F-test versions, for: (1) restricting the cross-section fixed effects to zero; (2) restricting the period fixed effects to zero; and (3) restricting both types of fixed effects to zero. In all three cases, the p-values associated with the test statistics are zero to four decimal places, indicating that the restrictions are not supported by the data and that a pooled sample could not be employed.

Next, estimate a **random effects** model by selecting this from the panel estimation option tab. As for fixed effects, the random effects could be along either the cross-sectional or period dimensions, but select random effects **for the firms** (i.e. cross-sectional) but not **over time**. The results are observed as in the table at the top of the next page.

The slope estimate is again of a different order of magnitude compared with both the pooled and the fixed effects regressions. It is of interest to determine whether the random effects model passes the Hausman test for the random effects being uncorrelated with the explanatory variables. To do this, click **View/Fixed/Random Effects Testing/Correlated Random Effects – Hausman Test**. The results at the bottom of the next page are observed,

---

[12] These models are not shown to preserve space.

Dependent Variable: RETURN
Method: Panel EGLS (Cross-section random effects)
Date: 09/23/07 Time: 21:55
Sample: 1996 2006
Periods included: 11
Cross-sections included: 1734
Total panel (unbalanced) observations: 8856
Swamy and Arora estimator of component variances

	Coefficient	Std. Error	t-Statistic	Prob.
C	0.003281	0.003267	1.004366	0.3152
BETA	−0.001499	0.002894	−0.518160	0.6044

Effects specification			
		S.D.	Rho
Cross-section random		0.012366	0.0560
Idiosyncratic random		0.050763	0.9440

Weighted statistics			
R-squared	0.000030	Mean dependent var	0.001663
Adjusted R-squared	−0.000083	S.D. dependent var	0.051095
S.E. of regression	0.051106	Sum squared resid	23.12475
F-statistic	0.264896	Durbin-Watson stat	1.683253
Prob(F-statistic)	0.606781		

Unweighted statistics			
R-squared	−0.000245	Mean dependent var	0.002345
Sum squared resid	24.21044	Durbin-Watson stat	1.638922

with only the top panel that reports the Hausman test results being displayed here.

Correlated Random Effects – Hausman Test
Equation: Untitled
Test cross-section random effects

Test summary	Chi-Sq. Statistic	Chi-Sq. d.f.	Prob.
Cross-section random	12.633579	1	0.0004

The p-value for the test is less than 1%, indicating that the random effects model is not appropriate and that the fixed effects specification is to be preferred.

11.9 Panel unit root and cointegration tests

11.9.1 Background and motivation

The principle of unit root testing in the panel context is very similar to that employed in single equations framework discussed in chapter 8. We noted there that unit root tests of the Dickey–Fuller and Phillips–Perron types have low power, especially for modest sample sizes. This provides a key motivation for using a panel – the hope that more powerful versions of the tests can be employed when time series and cross-sectional information is combined – as a result of the increase in sample size. Of course, it would be easier to increase the number of observations by simply increasing the length of the sample period, but this data may not be available, or may be of limited use because of structural breaks in the time series.

While the single series and panel approaches to unit root and stationarity testing appear very similar on the surface, in fact a valid construction and application of the test statistics is much more complex for panels than for single series. One complication arises since different asymptotic distributions for the test statistics may result depending on whether N is fixed and T tends to infinity, or vice versa, or both T and N increase simultaneously in a fixed ratio.

Two important issues to consider are first, that the design and interpretation of the null and alternative hypotheses needs careful thought in the panel arena and second, there may be a problem of cross-sectional dependence in the errors across the unit root testing regressions. Some of the literature refers to the early studies that assumed cross-sectional independence as 'first generation' panel unit root tests, while the more recent approaches that allow for some form of dependence are termed 'second generation' tests.

A perhaps obvious starting point for unit root tests when one has a panel of data would be to run separate regressions over time for each series but to use Zellner's SUR approach, which we might term the multivariate ADF (MADF) test. This method can only be employed if $T >> N$, and Taylor and Sarno (1998) provide an early application to tests for purchasing power parity. However, it is fair to say that technique is now rarely used, researchers preferring instead to make use of the full panel structure.

A key consideration is the dimensions of the panel – is the situation that T is large or that N is large or both? If T is large and N small, the MADF approach can be used, although as Breitung and Pesaran (2008) note, in such a situation one may question whether it is worthwhile to adopt a panel approach at all, since for sufficiently large T, separate ADF tests ought to be reliable enough to render the panel approach hardly worth the additional complexity.

11.9.2   Tests with common alternative hypotheses

Levin, Lin and Chu (2002) – LLC hereafter – develop a test based on the equation

$$\Delta y_{i,t} = \alpha_i + \theta_t + \delta_i t + \rho_i y_{i,t-1} + \sum \gamma_j \Delta y_{t-j} + v_{i,t}$$

$$t = 1, 2, \ldots, T; i = 1, 2, \ldots, N. \tag{11.19}$$

The model is very general since it allows for both entity-specific and time-specific effects through α_i and θ_t respectively as well as separate deterministic trends in each series through $\delta_i t$, and the lag structure to mop up autocorrelation in Δy. Of course, as for the Dickey–Fuller tests, any or all of these deterministic terms can be omitted from the regression. The null hypothesis is $H_0 : \rho_i \equiv \rho = 0 \ \forall \ i$ and the alternative is $H_1 : \rho < 0 \ \forall \ i$.

One of the reasons that unit root testing is more complex in the panel framework in practice is due to the plethora of 'nuisance parameters' in the equation which are necessary to allow for the fixed effects (i.e. the α_i, θ_t, $\delta_i t$). These nuisance parameters will affect the asymptotic distribution of the test statistics and hence LLC propose that two auxiliary regressions are run to remove their impacts. First, Δy_{it} is regressed on its lags, Δy_{it-j}, $j = 1, \ldots, p_i$ and on the exogenous variables (any or all from α_i, θ_t, and $\delta_i t$ as desired); the residuals, u_{1it} are obtained. Note that the numbers of lags of the dependent variables, p_i, need not be the same for each series in the panel. Next, the lagged level of y, y_{it-1}, is regressed on the same variables to get the residuals, u_{2it}. Then the residuals from both regressions are standardised by dividing them by the regression standard error, s_i, which is obtained from the augmented Dickey–Fuller regression (11.19)

$$\tilde{u}_{1it} = u_{1it}/s_i \tag{11.20}$$

and

$$\tilde{u}_{2it} = u_{2it}/s_i \tag{11.21}$$

Thus $\tilde{u}_{1it}$ will be equivalent to Δy_{it} but with the effects of the deterministic components removed, and $\tilde{u}_{2it}$ will be equivalent to y_{it-1} but with the effects of the deterministic components removed. Finally, $\tilde{u}_{1it}$ is regressed on $\tilde{u}_{2it}$, and the slope estimate from this test regression is then used to construct a test statistic which is asymptotically distributed as a standard normal variate. The test statistic will approach this 'limiting' normal distribution as T tends to infinity and as N tends to infinity, although the convergence is faster for the former than the latter.

Breitung (2000) develops a modified version of the LLC test which does not include the deterministic terms (i.e. the fixed effects and/or a deterministic trend), and which standardises the residuals from the auxiliary regression in a more sophisticated fashion.

It should be clear that under the LLC and Breitung approaches, only evidence against the non-stationary null in one series is required before the joint null will be rejected. Breitung and Pesaran (2008) suggest that the appropriate conclusion when the null is rejected is that 'a significant proportion of the cross-sectional units are stationary'. Especially in the context of large N, this might not be very helpful since no information is provided on how many of the N series are stationary. Often, the homogeneity assumption is not economically meaningful either, since there is no theory suggesting that all of the series have the same autoregressive dynamics and thus the same value of ρ.

11.9.3 Panel unit root tests with heterogeneous processes

The difficulty described at the end of the previous sub-section led Im, Pesaran and Shin (2003) – hereafter IPS – to propose an alternative approach where, given equation (11.19) as above, the null and alternative hypotheses are now $H_0 : \rho_i = 0 \ \forall \ i$ and $H_1 : \rho_i < 0, i = 1, 2, \ldots, N_1; \rho_i = 0, i = N_1 + 1, N_1 + 2, \ldots, N$.

So the null hypothesis still specifies all series in the panel as non-stationary, but under the alternative, a proportion of the series (N_1/N) are stationary, and the remaining proportion $((N - N_1)/N)$ are non-stationary. But it is clear that no restriction where all of the ρ are identical is imposed. The statistic for the panel test in this case is constructed by conducting separate unit root tests for each series in the panel, calculating the ADF t-statistic for each one in the standard fashion, and then taking their cross-sectional average. This average is then transformed into a standard normal variate under the null hypothesis of a unit root in all the series; IPS develop an LM-test approach as well as the more familiar t-test.[13] If the time series dimension is sufficiently large, it is then possible to run separate unit root tests on each series in order to determine the proportion for which the individual tests cause a rejection, and thus how strong is the weight of evidence against the joint null hypothesis.

It should be noted that while IPS's heterogeneous panel unit root tests are superior to the homogeneous case when N is modest relative to T, they may not be sufficiently powerful when N is large and T is small, in which case the LLC approach may be preferable.

Maddala and Wu (1999) and Choi (2001) developed a slight variant on the IPS approach based on an idea dating back to Fisher (1932), where unit root tests are again conducted separately on each series in the panel, and the p-values associated with the test statistics are then combined. If we call these p-values $pv_i, i = 1, 2, \ldots, N$, then under the null hypothesis of a unit root in each series, each pv_i will be distributed uniformly over the $[0,1]$ interval and hence the following will hold for given N as $T \to \infty$

$$\lambda = -2 \sum_{i=1}^{N} ln(pv_i) \sim \chi^2_{2N}. \tag{11.22}$$

The number of observations per series can differ in this case as the regressions are run separately for each series and then only their p-values are combined in the test statistic. Notice that the cross-sectional independence assumption is crucial here for this sum to follow a χ^2 distribution. Since the distribution of the ADF test statistic

---

[13] Both tests presume that there is a balanced panel – that is, the number of time series observations is the same for each cross-sectional entity.

is non-standard and is dependent upon the inclusion of the nuisance parameters, unfortunately the p-values for inclusion in this equation must be obtained from a Monte Carlo simulation. Moreover, if the series under consideration have different lag lengths for Δy_{it} or there are different numbers of observations, each will require a separate Monte Carlo!

As well as the χ^2 statistic, Choi (2001) develops a variant of the test, still based on the p-values, that is asymptotically standard normally distributed. It should be evident that, like IPS, the Maddala-Wu-Choi approach does not require the same parameter, ρ, to apply to all of the series since the ADF test is run separately on each series in the panel.

11.9.4 Panel stationarity tests

The approaches described above are non-stationarity tests, and analogous to the Dickey–Fuller approach, they have non-stationarity under the null hypothesis. It is also possible, however, to construct a test where the null hypothesis is of stationarity for all series in the panel, analogous to the KPSS test of Kwaitkowski *et al.* (1992). In this case, the null hypothesis is that all of the series are stationary, which is rejected if at least one of them is non-stationary. This approach in the panel context was developed by Hadri (2000), and leads to a test statistic that is asymptotically normally distributed. As in the univariate case, stationarity tests can be useful as a way to check for the robustness of the conclusions from unit root tests.

11.9.5 Allowing for cross-sectional heterogeneity

The assumption of cross-sectional independence of the error terms in the panel regression is highly unrealistic and likely to be violated in practice. For example, in the context of testing for whether purchasing power parity holds, there are likely to be important unspecified factors that affect all exchange rates or groups of exchange rates in the sample, and will result in correlated residuals. O'Connell (1998) demonstrates the considerable size distortions that can arise when such cross-sectional dependencies are present but not accounted for – that is, the null hypothesis is rejected far too frequently when it is correct than should arise by chance alone if the distributional assumption holds for the test statistic. If the critical values employed in the tests are adjusted to remove the impacts of these size distortions, then the power of the tests will fall such that in extreme cases the benefit of using a panel structure could disappear completely. According to Maddala and Wu (1999), tests based on the Fisher statistic are more robust in the presence of unparameterised cross-sectional dependence than the IPS approach.

O'Connell proposes a feasible GLS estimator for ρ where an assumed non-zero form for the correlations between the disturbances is employed. To overcome the limitation that the correlation matrix must be specified (and this may be troublesome because it is not clear what form it should take), Bai and Ng (2004) propose an approach based on separating the data into a common factor component that is highly correlated across the series and a specific part that is idiosyncratic; a further approach is to proceed with OLS but to employ modified standard errors – so-called 'panel corrected standard errors' (PCSEs) – see, for example Breitung and Das (2005).

Overall, however, it is clear that satisfactorily dealing with cross-sectional dependence makes an already complex issue considerable harder still. In the presence of such dependencies, the test statistics are affected in a non-trivial way by the nuisance parameters. As a result, despite their inferiority in theory, the first generation approaches that ignore cross-sectional dependence are still widely employed in the empirical literature.

11.9.6 Panel cointegration

It is often remarked in the literature that the development of the techniques for panel cointegration modelling is still in its infancy, while that for panel unit root testing is already quite mature. Testing for cointegration in panels is a rather complex issue, since one must consider the possibility of cointegration across groups of variables (what we might term 'cross-sectional cointegration') as well as within the groups. It is also possible that the parameters in the cointegrating series and even the number of cointegrating relationships could differ across the panel.

Most of the work so far has relied upon a generalisation of the single equation methods of the Engle–Granger type following the pioneering work by Pedroni (1999, 2004). His setup is very general and allows for separate intercepts for each group of potentially cointegrating variables and separate deterministic trends. For a set of variables y_{it} and $x_{m,i,t}$ that are individually integrated of order one and thought to be cointegrated

$$y_{it} = \alpha_i + \delta_i t + \beta_{1i} x_{1i,t} + \beta_{2i} x_{2i,t} + \ldots + \beta_{Mi} x_{Mi,t} + u_{i,t} \tag{11.23}$$

where $m = 1, \ldots, M$ are the explanatory variables in the potentially cointegrating regression; $t = 1, \ldots, T$ and $i = 1, \ldots, N$.

The residuals from this regression, $\hat{u}_{i,t}$ are then subjected to separate Dickey–Fuller or augmented Dickey–Fuller type regressions for each group of variables to determine whether they are I(1) – for example

$$\hat{u}_{i,t} = \rho_i \hat{u}_{i,t-1} + \sum_{j=1}^{p_i} \psi_{i,j} \Delta \hat{u}_{i,t-j} + v_{i,t} \tag{11.24}$$

The null hypothesis is that the residuals from all of the test regressions are unit root processes ($H_0 : \rho_i = 1$), and therefore that there is no cointegration. Pedroni proposes two possible alternative hypotheses – first, that all of the autoregressive dynamics are the same stationary process ($H_1 : \rho_i = \rho < 1 \ \forall \ i$) and second, that the dynamics from each test equation follow a different stationary process ($H_1 : \rho_i < 1 \ \forall \ i$). Hence, in the first case no heterogeneity is permitted, while in the second it is – analogous to the difference between LLC and IPS as described above. Pedroni then constructs a raft of different test statistics based on standardised versions of the usual t-ratio from equation (11.24). The standardisation required is a function of whether an intercept or trend is included in (11.24), and the value of M. These standardised test statistics are each asymptotically standard normally distributed.

Kao (1999) essentially develops a restricted version of Pedroni's approach, where the slope parameters in equation (11.23) are assumed to be fixed across the groups, although the intercepts are still permitted to vary. Then the DF or ADF test regression is run on a pooled sample assuming homogeneity in the value of ρ. These restrictions allow some simplification in the testing approach.

As well as testing for cointegration using the residuals following these extensions of Engle and Granger, it is also possible, although in general more complicated, to use a generalisation of the Johansen technique. This approach is deployed by Larsson *et al.* (2001), but a simpler alternative is to apply the Johansen approach to each group of series separately, collect the p-values for the trace test and then take -2 times the sum of their logs following Maddala and Wu (1999) as in (11.22) above. A full systems approach based on a 'global VAR' is possible but with considerable additional complexity – see Breitung and Pesaran (2008) and the many references therein for further details.

11.9.7 An illustration of the use of panel unit root and cointegration tests: the link between financial development and GDP growth

An important issue for developing countries from a policy perspective is the extent to which economic growth and the sophistication of the country's financial markets are linked. It has been argued in the relevant literature that excessive government regulations (such as limits on lending, restrictions on lending and borrowing interest rates, the barring of foreign banks, etc.) may impede the development of the financial markets and consequently economic growth will be slower than if the financial markets were more vibrant. On the other hand, if economic agents are able to borrow at reasonable rates of interest or raise funding easily on the capital markets, this can increase the viability of real investment opportunities and allow for a more efficient allocation of capital.

Both the theoretical and empirical research in this area has led to mixed conclusions; the theoretical models arrive at different findings dependent upon the framework employed and the assumptions made. And on the empirical side, many existing studies in this area are beset by two issues: first, the direction of causality between economic and financial development could go the other way: if an economy grows, then the demand for financial products will itself increase. Thus it is possible that economic growth leads to financial market development rather than the other line of causality. Second, given that long time series are typically unavailable for developing economies, traditional unit root and cointegration tests that examine the link between these two variables suffer from low power. In particular, while research has been able to identify a link between economic growth and stock market development, such an effect could not be identified for the sophistication of the banking sector. This provides a strong motivation for the use of panel techniques, which are more powerful, and which constitute the approach adopted by Christopoulos and Tsionas (2004). Some of the key methodologies and findings of their paper will now be discussed.

Table 11.4   Panel unit root test results for economic growth and financial development

Variables	Levels		First differences	
	IPS	Maddala–Wu	IPS	Maddala–Wu
Output (y)	−0.18	27.12	−4.52***	58.33***
Financial depth (F)	2.71	14.77	−6.63***	83.64***
Investment share (S)	−0.04	30.37	−5.81***	62.98***
Inflation ($\dot{p}$)	−0.47	26.37	−5.19***	74.29***

Notes: The critical value for the Maddala–Wu test is 37.57 at the 1% level. *** denotes rejection of the null hypothesis of a unit root at the 1% level.
Source: Christopoulos and Tsionas (2004). Reprinted with the permission of Elsevier.

Defining real output for country i as y_{it}, financial 'depth' as F, the proportion of total output that is investment as S, and the rate of inflation as $\dot{p}$, the core model they employ is

$$y_{it} = \beta_{0i} + \beta_{1i}F_{it} + \beta_{2i}S_{it} + \beta_{3i}\dot{p}_{it} + u_{it}. \tag{11.25}$$

Financial depth, F, is proxied using the ratio of total bank liabilities to GDP. Christopoulos and Tsionas obtain data from the IMF's *International Financial Statistics* for ten countries (Colombia, Paraguay, Peru, Mexico, Ecuador, Honduras, Kenya, Thailand, the Dominican Republic and Jamaica) over the period 1970–2000.

The regression in equation (11.25) has national output as the dependent variable, and financial development as one of the independent variables, but Christopoulos and Tsionas also investigate the reverse causality with F as the dependent variable and y as one of the independent variables. They first apply unit root tests to each of the individual series (output, financial depth, investment share in GDP, and inflation) separately for the ten countries. The findings are mixed, but show that most series are best characterised by unit root processes in levels but are stationary in first differences. They then employ the panel unit root tests of Im, Pesaran and Shin, and the Maddala–Wu chi-squared test separately for each variable, but now using a panel comprising all ten countries. The number of lags of Δy_{it} is determined using AIC. The null hypothesis in all cases is that the process is a unit root. Now the results, presented here in table 11.4, are much stronger and show conclusively that all four series are non-stationary in levels but stationary in differences.

The next stage is to test whether the series are cointegrated, and again this is first conducted separately for each country and then using a panel approach. Focusing on the latter, the LLC approach is used along with the Harris–Tzavalis technique, which is broadly the same as LLC but has slightly different correction

Table 11.5 Panel cointegration test results for economic growth and financial development

	LLC		Harris–Tzavalis	
	Fixed effects	Fixed effects + trend	Fixed effects	Fixed effects + trend
Dep. var.: y	−8.36***	0.89	−77.13***	−5.57***
Dep. var.: F	−1.2	0.5	−0.85	−1.65
	$r = 0$	$r \leq 1$	$r \leq 2$	$r \leq 3$
Fisher χ^2	76.09***	30.73	28.91	23.26

Notes: 'Dep. var.' denotes the dependent variable; *** denotes rejection of the null hypothesis of no cointegration at the 2% level. The critical values for the Fisher test are 37.57 and 31.41 at the 1% and 5% levels respectively.
Source: Christopoulos and Tsionas (2004). Reprinted with the permission of Elsevier.

factors in the limiting distribution owing to its assumption that T is fixed as N tends to infinity. As discussed in the previous sub-section, these techniques are based on a unit root test on the residuals from the potentially cointegrating regression, and Christopoulos and Tsionis investigate the use of panel cointegration tests with fixed effects, and with both fixed effects and a deterministic trend in the test regressions. These are applied to the regressions both with y, and separately F, as the dependent variables.

The results in table 11.5 quite strongly demonstrate that when the dependent variable is output, the LLC approach rejects the null hypothesis of a unit root in the potentially cointegrating regression residuals when fixed effects only are included in the test regression, but not when a trend is also included. In the context of the Harris–Tzavalis variant of the residuals-based test, for both the fixed effects and the fixed effects + trend regressions, the null is rejected. When financial depth is instead used as the dependent variable, none of these tests reject the null hypothesis. Thus, the weight of evidence from the residuals-based tests is that cointegration exists when output is the dependent variable, but it does not when financial depth is. The authors interpret this result as implying that causality runs from output to financial depth but not the other way around.

In the final row of table 11.5, a systems approach to testing for cointegration, based on the sum of the logs of the p-values from the Johansen test, shows that the null hypothesis of no cointegrating vectors ($H_0 : r = 0$) is rejected, while ($H_0 : r \leq 1$) and above are all not rejected. Thus the conclusion is that one cointegrating relationship exists between the four variables across the panel. Note that in this case, since cointegration is tested within a VAR system, all variables are treated in parallel, and hence there are not separate results for different dependent variables.

11.9.8   Testing for unit roots and cointegration in panels using EViews

EViews provides a range of tests for unit roots within a panel structure, but all are based on the assumption of cross-sectional independence. Given that all of the approaches can be simultaneously employed at the click of a mouse, it seems preferable to do so in order to evaluate the sensitivity of the findings to the methodology employed. This illustration will use the Treasury bill/bond yields in 'macro.wf1' so **re-open this workfile**. We have already created a group to conduct the Johansen tests (I called this 'tbill_johansen'). If you did not name and save the group in the workfile, you will need to create a group again containing the yields on the Treasury instruments for all maturities – 3-month, 6-month, 1-year, 3-year, 5-year and 10-year. You could do this by highlighting the six series, then select Object/New Object/Group. The six series will already be included in the box and you can simply name the group and save the workfile.

Before running any panel unit root or cointegration tests, it is useful to start by examining the results of individual unit root tests on each series, so **run an augmented Dickey–Fuller test** on the levels of each yield series using a regression with an intercept but no deterministic trend, and use SIC to select the lag lengths in each case. You should find that all of the test statistics are around -0.1, with p-values of around 0.7-0.8, thus indicating that the unit root null hypothesis cannot be rejected.

As we know from the discussion above, unit root tests have low power in the presence of small samples, and so the panel unit root tests may provide different results. To run these in EViews is easy, **double click on the group** that you created so that the spreadsheet view containing the six series appears. Then **click View/Unit Root Test...** and screenshot 11.3 will appear.

The default options can be retained, and include printing a summary of the results from a range of panel unit root tests. Changing the test type box will enable the selection of a specific type of test and in that case the results will be shown with more detail including the test regression. If we simply examine the summary results for now, just click **OK**, and we will see the results on the following page.

Two lags were chosen on the basis of SIC for the ADF test including an intercept but no trend. Several tests are presented – first, the LLC test that assumes a common ρ for each series. The test statistic is 1.28 with p-value 0.9 and thus the unit root null is not rejected. Second, three tests that permit separate values of ρ for each series are presented. These are the IPS test and then two variants of the Fisher test proposed by Maddala and Wu (1999) and Choi (2001) – one for the ADF test and one for the Phillips–Perron test. In all cases, the test statistics are well below the critical values, indicating that the series contain unit roots. Thus the conclusions from the panel unit root test are the same as those of the individual ones – in this case using the panel did not make any difference, perhaps because $N = 6$ is quite small, while $T = 326$ for each series, is quite large and so the additional benefits from using a panel are minimal.

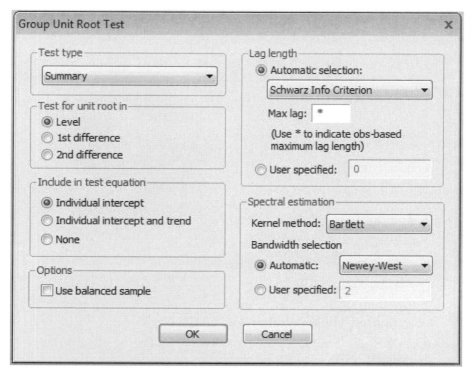

Screenshot 11.3   **Panel unit root test window**

Group unit root test: Summary
Series: USTB10Y, USTB1Y, USTB3M, USTB3Y, USTB5Y, USTB6M
Date: 08/15/13 Time: 06:41
Sample: 1986M03 2013M04
Exogenous variables: individual effects
Automatic selection of maximum lags
Automatic lag selection based on SIC: 0 to 2
Newey-West automatic bandwidth selection and Bartlett kernel

Method	Statistic	Prob.**	Cross-sections	Obs
Null: Unit root (assumes common unit root process)				
Levin, Lin & Chu t*	1.28778	0.9011	6	1943
Null: Unit root (assumes individual unit root process)				
Im, Pesaran and Shin W-stat	1.55966	0.9406	6	1943
ADF - Fisher Chi-square	3.27867	0.9932	6	1943
PP - Fisher Chi-square	4.13585	0.9809	6	1950

** Probabilities for Fisher tests are computed using an asymptotic Chi-square distribution. All other tests assume asymptotic normality.

If we wanted to run a panel cointegration test, this could be done simply by selecting **View/Cointegration Test** from the group spreadsheet view. Then either a Johansen-based system approach or a single equation approach can be chosen.

11.10 Further reading

Some readers may feel that further instruction in this area could be useful. If so, the classic specialist references to panel data techniques are Baltagi (2005) and Hsiao (2003) and further references are Arellano (2003) and Wooldridge (2010). All four are extremely detailed and have excellent referencing to recent developments in the theory of panel model specification, estimation and testing. However, all also require a high level of mathematical and econometric ability on the part of the reader. A more intuitive and accessible, but less detailed, treatment is given in Kennedy (2003, chapter 17). Some examples of financial studies that employ panel techniques and outline the methodology sufficiently descriptively to be worth reading as aids to learning are given in the examples above. The book by Maddala and Kim (1999) provides a fairly accessible treatment of unit roots and cointegration generally, although the time of publication implies that the most recent developments are excluded. Breitung and Pesaran (2008) is a more recent survey and is comprehensive, but at a higher technical level.

Key concepts

The key terms to be able to define and explain from this chapter are

- pooled data
- fixed effects
- random effects
- within transform
- between estimation
- panel cointegration test

- seemingly unrelated regression
- least squares dummy variable estimation
- Hausman test
- time-fixed effects
- panel unit root test

Self-study questions

1. (a) What are the advantages of constructing a panel of data, if one is available, rather than using pooled data?
   (b) What is meant by the term 'seemingly unrelated regression'? Give examples from finance of where such an approach may be used.
   (c) Distinguish between balanced and unbalanced panels, giving examples of each.

2. (a) Explain how fixed effects models are equivalent to an ordinary least squares regression with dummy variables.

(b) How does the random effects model capture cross-sectional heterogeneity in the intercept term?

(c) What are the relative advantages and disadvantages of the fixed versus random effects specifications and how would you choose between them for application to a particular problem?

3. Find a further example of where panel regression models have been used in the academic finance literature and do the following:

   ● Explain why the panel approach was used.
   ● Was a fixed effects or random effects model chosen and why?
   ● What were the main results of the study and is any indication given about whether the results would have been different had a pooled regression been employed instead in this or in previous studies?

4. (a) What are the advantages and disadvantages of conducting unit root tests within a panel framework rather than series by series?

   (b) Explain the differences between panel unit root tests based on a common alternative hypothesis and those based on heterogeneous processes.

12 Limited dependent variable models

Learning outcomes

In this chapter, you will learn how to

- Compare between different types of limited dependent variables and select the appropriate model
- Interpret and evaluate logit and probit models
- Distinguish between the binomial and multinomial cases
- Deal appropriately with censored and truncated dependent variables
- Estimate limited dependent variable models using maximum likelihood in EViews

12.1 Introduction and motivation

Chapters 5 and 10 have shown various uses of dummy variables to numerically capture the information qualitative variables – for example, day-of-the-week effects, gender, credit ratings, etc. When a dummy is used as an explanatory variable in a regression model, this usually does not give rise to any particular problems (so long as one is careful to avoid the *dummy variable trap* – see chapter 10). However, there are many situations in financial research where it is the explained variable, rather than one or more of the explanatory variables, that is qualitative. The qualitative information would then be coded as a dummy variable and the situation would be referred to as a *limited dependent variable* and needs to be treated differently. The term refers to any problem where the values that the dependent variables may take are limited to certain integers (e.g. 0, 1, 2, 3, 4) or even where it is a binary number (only 0 or 1). There are numerous examples of instances where this may arise, for example where we want to model:

- Why firms choose to list their shares on the NASDAQ rather than the NYSE
- Why some stocks pay dividends while others do not
- What factors affect whether countries default on their sovereign debt

- Why some firms choose to issue new stock to finance an expansion while others issue bonds
- Why some firms choose to engage in stock splits while others do not.

It is fairly easy to see in all these cases that the appropriate form for the dependent variable would be a 0–1 dummy variable since there are only two possible outcomes. There are, of course, also situations where it would be more useful to allow the dependent variable to take on other values, but these will be considered later in section 12.9. We will first examine a simple and obvious, but unfortunately flawed, method for dealing with binary dependent variables, known as the *linear probability model*.

12.2　The linear probability model

The linear probability model (LPM) is by far the simplest way of dealing with binary dependent variables, and it is based on an assumption that the probability of an event occurring, P_i, is linearly related to a set of explanatory variables x_{2i}, $x_{3i}, \ldots, x_{ki}$

$$P_i = p(y_i = 1) = \beta_1 + \beta_2 x_{2i} + \beta_3 x_{3i} + \cdots + \beta_k x_{ki} + u_i, \quad i = 1, \ldots, N$$

(12.1)

The actual probabilities cannot be observed, so we would estimate a model where the outcomes, y_i (the series of zeros and ones), would be the dependent variable. This is then a linear regression model and would be estimated by OLS. The set of explanatory variables could include either quantitative variables or dummies or both. The fitted values from this regression are the estimated probabilities for $y_i = 1$ for each observation i. The slope estimates for the linear probability model can be interpreted as the change in the probability that the dependent variable will equal 1 for a one-unit change in a given explanatory variable, holding the effect of all other explanatory variables fixed. Suppose, for example, that we wanted to model the probability that a firm i will pay a dividend ($y_i = 1$) as a function of its market capitalisation (x_{2i}, measured in millions of US dollars), and we fit the following line:

$$\hat{P}_i = -0.3 + 0.012 x_{2i}$$

(12.2)

where $\hat{P}_i$ denotes the fitted or estimated probability for firm i. This model suggests that for every $1m increase in size, the probability that the firm will pay a dividend increases by 0.012 (or 1.2%). A firm whose stock is valued at $50m will have a $-0.3 + 0.012 \times 50 = 0.3$ (or 30%) probability of making a dividend payment. Graphically, this situation may be represented as in figure 12.1.

While the linear probability model is simple to estimate and intuitive to interpret, the diagram should immediately signal a problem with this setup. For any firm whose value is less than $25m, the model-predicted probability of dividend payment is negative, while for any firm worth more than $88m, the probability is greater than one. Clearly, such predictions cannot be allowed to stand, since the probabilities should lie within the range (0,1). An obvious solution is to truncate

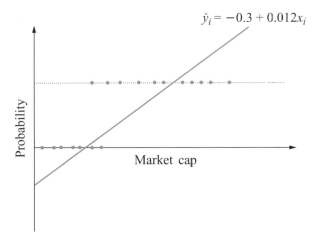

$$\hat{y}_i = -0.3 + 0.012x_i$$

Figure 12.1   The fatal flaw of the linear probability model

the probabilities at 0 or 1, so that a probability of -0.3, say, would be set to zero, and a probability of, say, 1.2 would be set to 1. However, there are at least two reasons why this is still not adequate:

(1) The process of truncation will result in too many observations for which the estimated probabilities are exactly zero or one.

(2) More importantly, it is simply not plausible to suggest that the firm's probability of paying a dividend is either exactly zero or exactly one. Are we really certain that very small firms will definitely never pay a dividend and that large firms will always make a payout? Probably not, so a different kind of model is usually used for binary dependent variables – either a *logit* or a *probit* specification. These approaches will be discussed in the following sections. But before moving on, it is worth noting that the LPM also suffers from a couple of more standard econometric problems that we have examined in previous chapters. First, since the dependent variable takes only one of two values, for given (fixed in repeated samples) values of the explanatory variables, the disturbance term will also take on only one of two values.[1] Consider again equation (12.1). If $y_i = 1$, then by definition

$$u_i = 1 - \beta_1 - \beta_2 x_{2i} - \beta_3 x_{3i} - \cdots - \beta_k x_{ki};$$

but if $y_i = 0$, then

$$u_i = -\beta_1 - \beta_2 x_{2i} - \beta_3 x_{3i} - \cdots - \beta_k x_{ki}.$$

Hence the error term cannot plausibly be assumed to be normally distributed. Since u_i changes systematically with the explanatory variables, the disturbances will also be heteroscedastic. It is therefore essential that heteroscedasticity-robust standard errors are always used in the context of limited dependent variable models.

---

[1] N.B. The discussion refers to the disturbance, u_i, rather than the residual, $\hat{u}_i$.

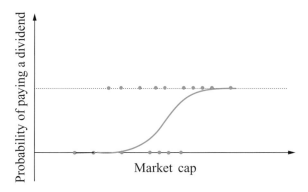

Figure 12.2   The logit model

12.3   The logit model

Both the logit and probit model approaches are able to overcome the limitation of the LPM that it can produce estimated probabilities that are negative or greater than one. They do this by using a function that effectively transforms the regression model so that the fitted values are bounded within the (0,1) interval. Visually, the fitted regression model will appear as an S-shape rather than a straight line, as was the case for the LPM. This is shown in figure 12.2.

The logistic function F, which is a function of any random variable, z, would be

$$F\left(z_i\right) = \frac{e^{z_i}}{1 + e^{z_i}} = \frac{1}{1 + e^{-z_i}} \tag{12.3}$$

where e is the exponential under the logit approach. The model is so called because the function F is in fact the cumulative logistic distribution. So the logistic model estimated would be

$$P_i = \frac{1}{1 + e^{-(\beta_1 + \beta_2 x_{2i} + \cdots + \beta_k x_{ki} + u_i)}} \tag{12.4}$$

where again P_i is the probability that $y_i = 1$.

With the logistic model, 0 and 1 are asymptotes to the function and thus the probabilities will never actually fall to exactly zero or rise to one, although they may come infinitesimally close. In equation (12.3), as z_i tends to infinity, e^{-z_i} tends to zero and $1/(1 + e^{-z_i})$ tends to 1; as z_i tends to minus infinity, e^{-z_i} tends to infinity and $1/(1 + e^{-z_i})$ tends to 0.

Clearly, this model is not linear (and cannot be made linear by a transformation) and thus is not estimable using OLS. Instead, maximum likelihood is usually used – this is discussed in section 12.7 and in more detail in the appendix to this chapter.

12.4 ## Using a logit to test the pecking order hypothesis

This section examines a study of the pecking order hypothesis due to Helwege and Liang (1996). The theory of firm financing suggests that corporations should use the cheapest methods of financing their activities first (i.e. the sources of funds that require payment of the lowest rates of return to investors) and switch to more expensive methods only when the cheaper sources have been exhausted. This is known as the 'pecking order hypothesis', initially proposed by Myers (1984). Differences in the relative cost of the various sources of funds are argued to arise largely from information asymmetries since the firm's senior managers will know the true riskiness of the business, whereas potential outside investors will not.[2] Hence, all else equal, firms will prefer internal finance and then, if further (external) funding is necessary, the firm's riskiness will determine the type of funding sought. The more risky the firm is perceived to be, the less accurate will be the pricing of its securities.

Helwege and Liang (1996) examine the pecking order hypothesis in the context of a set of US firms that had been newly listed on the stock market in 1983, with their additional funding decisions being tracked over the 1984–92 period. Such newly listed firms are argued to experience higher rates of growth, and are more likely to require additional external funding than firms which have been stock market listed for many years. They are also more likely to exhibit information asymmetries due to their lack of a track record. The list of initial public offerings (IPOs) came from the Securities Data Corporation and the Securities and Exchange Commission with data obtained from Compustat.

A core objective of the paper is to determine the factors that affect the probability of raising external financing. As such, the dependent variable will be binary – that is, a column of 1s (firm raises funds externally) and 0s (firm does not raise any external funds). Thus OLS would not be appropriate and hence a logit model is used. The explanatory variables are a set that aims to capture the relative degree of information asymmetry and degree of riskiness of the firm. If the pecking order hypothesis is supported by the data, then firms should be more likely to raise external funding the less internal cash they hold. Hence variable 'deficit' measures (capital expenditures + acquisitions + dividends − earnings). 'Positive deficit' is a variable identical to deficit but with any negative deficits (i.e. surpluses) set to zero; 'surplus' is equal to the negative of deficit for firms where deficit is negative; 'positive deficit × operating income' is an interaction term where the two variables are multiplied together to capture cases where firms have strong investment opportunities but limited access to internal funds; 'assets' is used as a measure of firm size; 'industry asset growth' is the average rate of growth of assets in that firm's industry over the 1983–92 period; 'firm's growth of sales' is the growth rate of sales averaged over the previous five years; 'previous financing' is a dummy

---

[2] 'Managers have private information regarding the value of assets in place and investment opportunities that cannot credibly be conveyed to the market. Consequently, any risky security offered by the firm will not be priced fairly from the manager's point of view' (Helwege and Liang, p. 438).

Variable	(1)	(2)	(3)
Table 12.1 Logit estimation of the probability of external financing			
Intercept	−0.29	−0.72	−0.15
	(−3.42)	(−7.05)	(−1.58)
Deficit	0.04	0.02	
	(0.34)	(0.18)	
Positive deficit			−0.24
			(−1.19)
Surplus			−2.06
			(−3.23)
Positive deficit × operating income			−0.03
			(−0.59)
Assets	0.0004	0.0003	0.0004
	(1.99)	(1.36)	(1.99)
Industry asset growth	−0.002	−0.002	−0.002
	(−1.70)	(−1.35)	(−1.69)
Previous financing		0.79	
		(8.48)	

Note: a blank cell implies that the particular variable was not included in that regression; *t*-ratios in parentheses; only figures for all years in the sample are presented.
Source: Helwege and Liang (1996). Reprinted with the permission of Elsevier.

variable equal to 1 for firms that obtained external financing in the previous year. The results from the logit regression are presented in table 12.1.

The key variable, 'deficit,' has a parameter that is not statistically significant and hence the probability of obtaining external financing does not depend on the size of a firm's cash deficit.[3] The parameter on the 'surplus' variable has the correct negative sign, indicating that the larger a firm's surplus, the less likely it is to seek external financing, which provides some limited support for the pecking order hypothesis. Larger firms (with larger total assets) are more likely to use the capital markets, as are firms that have already obtained external financing during the previous year.

---

[3] Or an alternative explanation, as with a similar result in the context of a standard regression model, is that the probability varies widely across firms with the size of the cash deficit so that the standard errors are large relative to the point estimate.

12.5 The probit model

Instead of using the cumulative logistic function to transform the model, the cumulative normal distribution is sometimes used instead. This gives rise to the probit model. The function F in equation (12.3) is replaced by

$$F(z_i) = \frac{1}{\sqrt{2\pi}} \int_{-\infty}^{z_i} e^{-\frac{z_i^2}{2}} dz \qquad (12.5)$$

This function is the cumulative distribution function for a standard normally distributed random variable. As for the logistic approach, this function provides a transformation to ensure that the fitted probabilities will lie between zero and one. Also as for the logit model, the marginal impact of a unit change in an explanatory variable, x_{4i} say, will be given by $\beta_4 F(z_i)$, where β_4 is the parameter attached to x_{4i} and $z_i = \beta_1 + \beta_2 x_{2i} + \beta_3 x_{3i} + \cdots + u_i$.

12.6 Choosing between the logit and probit models

For the majority of the applications, the logit and probit models will give very similar characterisations of the data because the densities are very similar. That is, the fitted regression plots (such as figure 12.2) will be virtually indistinguishable and the implied relationships between the explanatory variables and the probability that $y_i = 1$ will also be very similar. Both approaches are much preferred to the linear probability model. The only instance where the models may give non-negligibility different results occurs when the split of the y_i between 0 and 1 is very unbalanced – for example, when $y_i = 1$ occurs only 10% of the time.

Stock and Watson (2006) suggest that the logistic approach was traditionally preferred since the function does not require the evaluation of an integral and thus the model parameters could be estimated faster. However, this argument is no longer relevant given the computational speeds now achievable and the choice of one specification rather than the other is now usually arbitrary.

12.7 Estimation of limited dependent variable models

Given that both logit and probit are non-linear models, they cannot be estimated by OLS. While the parameters could, in principle, be estimated using non-linear least squares (NLS), maximum likelihood (ML) is simpler and is invariably used in practice. As discussed in chapter 9, the principle is that the parameters are chosen to jointly maximise a log-likelihood function (LLF). The form of this LLF will depend upon whether the logit or probit model is used, but the general principles for parameter estimation described in chapter 9 will still apply. That is, we form the appropriate log-likelihood function and then the software package will find the values of the parameters that jointly maximise it using an iterative search procedure. A derivation of the ML estimator for logit and probit models is given in the appendix to this chapter. Box 12.1 shows how to interpret the estimated parameters from probit and logit models.

Box 12.1   Parameter interpretation for probit and logit models

Standard errors and t-ratios will automatically be calculated by the econometric software package used, and hypothesis tests can be conducted in the usual fashion. However, interpretation of the coefficients needs slight care. It is tempting, but incorrect, to state that a 1-unit increase in x_{2i}, for example, causes a $\beta_2\%$ increase in the probability that the outcome corresponding to $y_i = 1$ will be realised. This would have been the correct interpretation for the linear probability model.

However, for logit models, this interpretation would be incorrect because the form of the function is not $P_i = \beta_i + \beta_2 x_i + u_i$, for example, but rather $P_i = F(\beta_i + \beta_2 x_i + u_i)$, where F represents the (non-linear) logistic function. To obtain the required relationship between changes in x_{2i} and P_i, we would need to differentiate F with respect to x_{2i} and it turns out that this derivative is $\beta_2 F(x_{2i})(1 - F(x_{2i}))$. So in fact, a 1-unit increase in x_{2i} will cause a $\beta_2 F(x_{2i})(1 - F(x_{2i}))$ increase in probability. Usually, these impacts of incremental changes in an explanatory variable are evaluated by setting each of them to their mean values. For example, suppose we have estimated the following logit model with three explanatory variables using maximum likelihood

$$\hat{P}_i = \frac{1}{1 + e^{-(0.1 + 0.3x_{2i} - 0.6x_{3i} + 0.9x_{4i})}} \tag{12.6}$$

Thus we have $\hat{\beta}_1 = 0.1$, $\hat{\beta}_2 = 0.3$, $\hat{\beta}_3 = -0.6$, $\hat{\beta}_4 = 0.9$. We now need to calculate $F(z_i)$, for which we need the means of the explanatory variables, where z_i is defined as before. Suppose that these are $\bar{x}_2 = 1.6$, $\bar{x}_3 = 0.2$, $\bar{x}_4 = 0.1$, then the estimate of $F(z_i)$ will be given by

$$\hat{P}_i = \frac{1}{1 + e^{-(0.1 + 0.3 \times 1.6 - 0.6 \times 0.2 + 0.9 \times 0.1)}} = \frac{1}{1 + e^{-0.55}} = 0.63 \tag{12.7}$$

Thus a 1-unit increase in x_2 will cause an increase in the probability that the outcome corresponding to $y_i = 1$ will occur by $0.3 \times 0.63 \times 0.37 = 0.07$. The corresponding changes in probability for variables x_3 and x_4 are $-0.6 \times 0.63 \times 0.37 = -0.14$ and $0.9 \times 0.63 \times 0.37 = 0.21$, respectively. These estimates are sometimes known as the *marginal effects*.

There is also another way of interpreting discrete choice models, known as the random utility model. The idea is that we can view the value of y that is chosen by individual i (either 0 or 1) as giving that person a particular level of utility, and the choice that is made will obviously be the one that generates the highest level of utility. This interpretation is particularly useful in the situation where the person faces a choice between more than two possibilities as in section 12.9 below.

Once the model parameters have been estimated, standard errors can be calculated and hypothesis tests conducted. While t-test statistics are constructed in the usual way, the standard error formulae used following the ML estimation are valid asymptotically only. Consequently, it is common to use the critical values from a normal distribution rather than a t distribution with the implicit assumption that the sample size is sufficiently large.

12.8 Goodness of fit measures for linear dependent variable models

While it would be possible to calculate the values of the standard goodness of fit measures such as RSS, R^2 or $\bar{R}^2$ for linear dependent variable models, these cease to have any real meaning. The objective of ML is to maximise the value of the LLF, not to minimise the RSS. Moreover, R^2 and adjusted R^2, if calculated in the usual fashion, will be misleading because the fitted values from the model can take on any value but the actual values will be only either 0 and 1. To illustrate, suppose that we are considering a situation where a bank either grants a loan ($y_i = 1$) or it refuses ($y_i = 0$). Does, say, $\hat{P}_i = 0.8$ mean the loan is offered or not? In order to answer this question, sometimes, any value of $\hat{P}_i > 0.5$ would be rounded up to one and any value <0.5 rounded down to zero. However, this approach is unlikely to work well when most of the observations on the dependent variable are one or when most are zero. In such cases, it makes more sense to use the unconditional probability that $y = 1$ (call this $\bar{y}$) as the threshold rather than 0.5. So if, for example, only 20% of the observations have $y = 1$ (so $\bar{y} = 0.2$), then we would deem the model to have correctly predicted the outcome concerning whether the bank would grant the loan to the customer where $\hat{P}_i > 0.2$ and $y_i = 1$ and where $\hat{P}_i < 0.2$ and $y_i = 0$.

Thus if $y_i = 1$ and $\hat{P}_i = 0.8$, the model has effectively made the correct prediction (either the loan is granted or refused – we cannot have any outcome in between), whereas R^2 and $\bar{R}^2$ will not give it full credit for this. Two goodness of fit measures that are commonly reported for limited dependent variable models are as follows.

(1) The percentage of y_i values correctly predicted, defined as $100 \times$ the number of observations predicted correctly divided by the total number of observations:

$$\text{Percent correct predictions} = \frac{100}{N} \sum_{i=1}^{N} y_i I(\hat{P}_i) + (1 - y_i)(1 - I(\hat{P}_i))$$

(12.8)

where $I(\hat{y}_i) = 1$ if $\hat{y}_i > \bar{y}$ and 0 otherwise.

Obviously, the higher this number, the better the fit of the model. Although this measure is intuitive and easy to calculate, Kennedy (2003) suggests that it is not ideal, since it is possible that a 'nave predictor' could do better than any model if the sample is unbalanced between 0 and 1. For example, suppose that $y_i = 1$ for 80% of the observations. A simple rule that the prediction is always 1 is likely to outperform any more complex model on this measure but is unlikely to be very useful. Kennedy (2003, p. 267) suggests measuring goodness of fit as the percentage of $y_i = 1$ correctly predicted plus the percentage of $y_i = 0$ correctly predicted. Algebraically, this can be calculated as

$$\text{Percent correct predictions} = 100 \times \left[\frac{\sum y_i I(\hat{P}_i)}{\sum y_i} + \frac{\sum (1 - y_i)(1 - I(\hat{P}_i))}{N - \sum y_i} \right]$$

(12.9)

Again, the higher the value of the measure, the better the fit of the model.
(2) A measure known as 'pseudo-R^2', defined as

$$\text{pseudo} - R^2 = 1 - \frac{LLF}{LLF_0}$$

(12.10)

where LLF is the maximised value of the log-likelihood function for the logit and probit model and LLF_0 is the value of the log-likelihood function for a restricted model where all of the slope parameters are set to zero (i.e. the model contains only an intercept). Pseudo-R^2 will have a value of zero for the restricted model, as with the traditional R^2, but this is where the similarity ends. Since the likelihood is essentially a joint probability, its value must be between zero and one, and therefore taking its logarithm to form the LLF must result in a negative number. Thus, as the model fit improves, LLF will become less negative and therefore pseudo-R^2 will rise. The maximum value of one could be reached only if the model fitted perfectly (i.e. all the $\hat{P}_i$ were either exactly zero or one corresponding to the actual values). This could never occur in reality and therefore pseudo-R^2 has a maximum value less than one. We also lose the simple interpretation of the standard R^2 that it measures the proportion of variation in the dependent variable that is explained by the model. Indeed, pseudo-R^2 does not have any intuitive interpretation.

This definition of pseudo-R^2 is also known as McFadden's R^2, but it is also possible to specify the metric in other ways. For example, we could define pseudo-R^2 as $[1 - (RSS/TSS)]$ where RSS is the residual sum of squares from the fitted model and TSS is the total sum of squares of y_i.

12.9 Multinomial linear dependent variables

All of the examples that have been considered so far in this chapter have concerned situations where the dependent variable is modelled as a binary (0,1) choice. But there are also many instances where investors or financial agents are faced with more alternatives. For example, a company may be considering listing on the NYSE, the NASDAQ or the AMEX markets; a firm that is intending to take over another may choose to pay by cash, with shares, or with a mixture of both; a retail investor may be choosing between five different mutual funds; a credit ratings agency could assign one of sixteen (AAA to B3/B−) different ratings classifications to a firm's debt.

Notice that the first three of these examples are different from the last one. In the first three cases, there is no natural ordering of the alternatives: the choice is simply made between them. In the final case, there is an obvious ordering, because a score of 1, denoting a AAA-rated bond, is better than a score of 2, denoting a AA1/AA+-rated bond, and so on (see section 5.15 in chapter 5). These two situations need to be distinguished and a different approach used in each case. In the first (when there is no natural ordering), a multinomial logit or probit would be used, while in the second (where there is an ordering), an ordered logit or probit would be used. This latter situation will be discussed in the next section, while multinomial models will be considered now.

When the alternatives are unordered, this is sometimes called a *discrete choice* or *multiple choice* problem. The models used are derived from the principles of utility maximisation – that is, the agent chooses the alternative that maximises his utility relative to the others. Econometrically, this is captured using a simple generalisation of the binary setup discussed earlier. When there were only two choices (0,1), we required just one equation to capture the probability that one or the other would be chosen. If there are now three alternatives, we would need two equations; for four alternatives, we would need three equations. In general, if there are m possible alternative choices, we need $m - 1$ equations.

The situation is best illustrated by first examining a multinomial linear probability model. This still, of course, suffers from the same limitations as it did in the binary case (i.e. the same problems as the LPM), but it nonetheless serves as a simple example by way of introduction.[4] The multiple choice example most commonly used is that of the selection of the mode of transport for travel to work.[5] Suppose that the journey may be made by car, bus, or bicycle (three alternatives), and suppose that the explanatory variables are the person's income (I), total hours worked (H), their gender (G) and the distance travelled (D).[6] We could set up two equations

$$BUS_i = \alpha_1 + \alpha_2 I_i + \alpha_3 H_i + \alpha_4 G_i + \alpha_5 D_i + u_i \tag{12.11}$$

$$CAR_i = \beta_1 + \beta_2 I_i + \beta_3 H_i - \beta_4 G_i + \beta_5 D_i + v_i \tag{12.12}$$

where $BUS_i = 1$ if person i travels by bus and 0 otherwise; $CAR_i = 1$ if person i travels by car and 0 otherwise.

There is no equation for travel by bicycle and this becomes a sort of reference point, since if the dependent variables in the two equations are both zero, the person must be travelling by bicycle.[7] In fact, we do not need to estimate the third equation (for travel by bicycle) since any quantity of interest can be inferred from the other two. The fitted values from the equations can be interpreted as probabilities and so, together with the third possibility, they must sum to unity. Thus, if, for a particular

---

[4] Multinomial models are clearly explained with intuitive examples in Halcoussis (2005, chapter 12).
[5] This illustration is used in Greene (2002) and Kennedy (2003), for example.
[6] Note that the same variables must be used for all equations for this approach to be valid.
[7] We are assuming that the choices are exhaustive and mutually exclusive – that is, one and only one method of transport can be chosen!

individual i, the probability of travelling by car is 0.4 and by bus is 0.3, then the possibility that she will travel by bicycle must be 0.3 (1−0.4−0.3). Also, the intercepts for the three equations (the two estimated equations plus the missing one) must sum to zero across the three modes of transport.

While the fitted probabilities will always sum to unity by construction, as with the binomial case, there is no guarantee that they will all lie between 0 and 1 − it is possible that one or more will be greater than 1 and one or more will be negative. In order to make a prediction about which mode of transport a particular individual will use, given that the parameters in equations (12.11) and (12.12) have been estimated and given the values of the explanatory variables for that individual, the largest fitted probability would be set to 1 and the others set to 0. So, for example, if the estimated probabilities of a particular individual travelling by car, bus and bicycle are 1.1, 0.2 and −0.3, these probabilities would be rounded to 1, 0, and 0. So the model would predict that this person would travel to work by car.

Exactly as the LPM has some important limitations that make logit and probit the preferred models, in the multiple choice context multinomial logit and probit models should be used. These are direct generalisations of the binary cases, and as with the multinomial LPM, $m − 1$ equations must be estimated where there are m possible outcomes or choices. The outcome for which an equation is not estimated then becomes the reference choice, and thus the parameter estimates must be interpreted slightly differently. Suppose that travel by bus (B) or by car (C) have utilities for person i that depend on the characteristics described above (I_i, H_i, G_i, D_i), then the car will be chosen if

$$(\beta_1 + \beta_2 I_i + \beta_3 H_i + \beta_4 G_i + \beta_5 D_i + v_i)$$
$$> (\alpha_1 + \alpha_2 I_i + \alpha_3 H_i + \alpha_4 G_i + \alpha_5 D_i + u_i) \tag{12.13}$$

That is, the probability that the car will be chosen will be greater than that of the bus being chosen if the utility from going by car is greater. Equation (12.13) can be rewritten as

$$(\beta_1 - \alpha_1) + (\beta_2 - \alpha_2) I_i + (\beta_3 - \alpha_3) H_i$$
$$+ (\beta_4 - \alpha_4) G_i + (\beta_5 - \alpha_5) D_i > (u_i - v_i) \tag{12.14}$$

If it is assumed that u_i and v_i independently follow a particular distribution, then the difference between them will follow a logistic distribution.[8] Thus we can write

$$P(C_i/B_i) = \frac{1}{1 + e^{-z_i}} \tag{12.15}$$

where z_i is the function on the left hand side of (12.14), i.e. $(\beta_1 - \alpha_1) + (\beta_2 - \alpha_2) I_i + \cdots$ and travel by bus becomes the reference category. $P(C_i/B_i)$ denotes the probability that individual i would choose to travel by car rather than by bus.

Equation (12.15) implies that the probability of the car being chosen in pref‐erence to the bus depends upon the logistic function of the differences in the

[8] In fact, they must follow independent log Weibull distributions.

parameters describing the relationship between the utilities from travelling by each mode of transport. Of course, we cannot recover both β_2 and α_2 for example, but only the difference between them (call this $\gamma_2 = \beta_2 - \alpha_2$). These parameters measure the impact of marginal changes in the explanatory variables on the probability of travelling by car relative to the probability of travelling by bus. Note that a unit increase in I_i will lead to a $\gamma_2 F(I_i)$ increase in the probability and not a γ_2 increase – see equations (12.5) and (12.6) above. For this trinomial problem, there would need to be another equation – for example, based on the difference in utilities between travelling by bike and by bus. These two equations would be estimated simultaneously using maximum likelihood.

For the multinomial logit model, the error terms in the equations (u_i and v_i in the example above) must be assumed to be independent. However, this creates a problem whenever two or more of the choices are very similar to one another. This problem is known as the 'independence of irrelevant alternatives'. To illustrate how this works, Kennedy (2003, p. 270) uses an example where another choice to travel by bus is introduced and the only thing that differs is the colour of the bus. Suppose that the original probabilities for the car, bus and bicycle were 0.4, 0.3 and 0.3. If a new green bus were introduced in addition to the existing red bus, we would expect that the overall probability of travelling by bus should stay at 0.3 and that bus passengers should split between the two (say, with half using each coloured bus). This result arises since the new colour of the bus is irrelevant to those who have already chosen to travel by car or bicycle. Unfortunately, the logit model will not be able to capture this and will seek to preserve the relative probabilities of the old choices (which could be expressed as $\frac{4}{10}$, $\frac{3}{10}$ and $\frac{3}{10}$ respectively). These will become $\frac{4}{13}$, $\frac{3}{13}$, $\frac{3}{13}$ and $\frac{3}{13}$ for car, green bus, red bus and bicycle respectively – a long way from what intuition would lead us to expect.

Fortunately, the multinomial probit model, which is the multiple choice generalisation of the probit model discussed in section 12.5 above, can handle this. The multinomial probit model would be set up in exactly the same fashion as the multinomial logit model, except that the cumulative normal distribution is used for $(u_i - v_i)$ instead of a cumulative logistic distribution. This is based on an assumption that u_i and v_i are multivariate normally distributed but unlike the logit model, they can be correlated. A positive correlation between the error terms can be employed to reflect a similarity in the characteristics of two or more choices. However, such a correlation between the error terms makes estimation of the multinomial probit model using maximum likelihood difficult because multiple integrals must be evaluated. Kennedy (2003, p. 271) suggests that this has resulted in continued use of the multinomial logit approach despite the independence of irrelevant alternatives problem.

12.10 The pecking order hypothesis revisited – the choice between financing methods

In section 12.4, a logit model was used to evaluate whether there was empirical support for the pecking order hypothesis where the hypothesis boiled down to a consideration of the probability that a firm would seek external financing or not. But suppose that we wish to examine not only whether a firm decides to issue external funds but also which method of funding it chooses when there are a number of alternatives available. As discussed above, the pecking order hypothesis suggests that the least costly methods, which, everything else equal, will arise where there is least information asymmetry, will be used first, and the method used will also depend on the riskiness of the firm. Returning to Helwege and Liang's study, they argue that if the pecking order is followed, low-risk firms will issue public debt first, while moderately risky firms will issue private debt and the most risky companies will issue equity. Since there is more than one possible choice, this is a multiple choice problem and consequently, a binary logit model is inappropriate and instead, a multinomial logit is used. There are three possible choices here: bond issue, equity issue and private debt issue. As is always the case for multinomial models, we estimate equations for one fewer than the number of possibilities, and so equations are estimated for equities and bonds, but not for private debt. This choice then becomes the reference point, so that the coefficients measure the probability of issuing equity or bonds rather than private debt, and a positive parameter estimate in, say, the equities equation implies that an increase in the value of the variable leads to an increase in the probability that the firm will choose to issue equity rather than private debt.

The set of explanatory variables is slightly different now given the different nature of the problem at hand. The key variable measuring risk is now the 'unlevered Z score', which is Altman's Z score constructed as a weighted average of operating earnings before interest and taxes, sales, retained earnings and working capital. All other variable names are largely self-explanatory and so are not discussed in detail, but they are divided into two categories – those measuring the firm's level of risk (unlevered Z-score, debt, interest expense and variance of earnings) and those measuring the degree of information asymmetry (R&D expenditure, venture-backed, age, age over fifty, plant property and equipment, industry growth, non-financial equity issuance, and assets). Firms with heavy R&D expenditure, those receiving venture capital financing, younger firms, firms with less property, plant and equipment, and smaller firms are argued to suffer from greater information asymmetry. The parameter estimates for the multinomial logit are presented in table 12.2, with equity issuance as a (0,1) dependent variable in the second column and bond issuance as a (0,1) dependent variable in the third column.

Overall, the results paint a very mixed picture about whether the pecking order hypothesis is validated or not. The positive (significant) and negative (insignificant) estimates on the unlevered Z-score and interest expense variables respectively suggest that firms in good financial health (i.e. less risky firms) are more likely to issue equities or bonds rather than private debt. Yet the positive sign of the parameter on the debt variable is suggestive that riskier firms are more likely to issue equities or bonds; the variance of earnings variable has the wrong sign but is not statistically significant. Almost all of the asymmetric information variables have statistically insignificant parameters. The only exceptions are that firms having venture backing are more likely to seek capital market financing of either type,

Table 12.2 Multinomial logit estimation of the type of external financing

Variable	Equity equation	Bonds equation
Intercept	−4.67	−4.68
	(−6.17)	(−5.48)
Unlevered Z-score	0.14	0.26
	(1.84)	(2.86)
Debt	1.72	3.28
	(1.60)	(2.88)
Interest expense	−9.41	−4.54
	(−0.93)	(−0.42)
Variance of earnings	−0.04	−0.14
	(−0.55)	(−1.56)
R&D	0.61	0.89
	(1.28)	(1.59)
Venture-backed	0.70	0.86
	(2.32)	(2.50)
Age	−0.01	−0.03
	(−1.10)	(−1.85)
Age over fifty	1.58	1.93
	(1.44)	(1.70)
Plant, property and equipment	(0.62)	0.34
	(0.94)	(0.50)
Industry growth	0.005	0.003
	(1.14)	(0.70)
Non-financial equity issuance	0.008	0.005
	(3.89)	(2.65)
Assets	−0.001	0.002
	(−0.59)	(4.11)

Notes: t-ratios in parentheses; only figures for all years in the sample are presented.
Source: Helwege and Liang (1996). Reprinted with the permission of Elsevier.

as are non-financial firms. Finally, larger firms are more likely to issue bonds (but not equity). Thus the authors conclude that the results 'do not indicate that firms strongly avoid external financing as the pecking order predicts' and 'equity is not the least desirable source of financing since it appears to dominate bank loans' (Helwege and Liang (1996), p. 458).

12.11 Ordered response linear dependent variables models

Some limited dependent variables can be assigned numerical values that have a natural ordering. The most common example in finance is that of credit ratings, as discussed previously, but a further application is to modelling a security's bid–ask spread (see, for example, ap Gwilym et al., 1998). In such cases, it would not be appropriate to use multinomial logit or probit since these techniques cannot take into account any ordering in the dependent variables. Notice that ordinal variables are still distinct from the usual type of data that were employed in the early chapters in this book, such as stock returns, GDP, interest rates, etc. These are examples of cardinal numbers, since additional information can be inferred from their actual values relative to one another. To illustrate, an increase in house prices of 20% represents twice as much growth as a 10% rise. The same is not true of ordinal numbers, where (returning to the credit ratings example) a rating of AAA, assigned a numerical score of 16, is not 'twice as good' as a rating of Baa2/BBB, assigned a numerical score of 8. Similarly, for ordinal data, the difference between a score of, say, 15 and of 16 cannot be assumed to be equivalent to the difference between the scores of 8 and 9. All we can say is that as the score increases, there is a monotonic increase in the credit quality. Since only the ordering can be interpreted with such data and not the actual numerical values, OLS cannot be employed and a technique based on ML is used instead. The models used are generalisations of logit and probit, known as *ordered logit* and *ordered probit*.

Using the credit rating example again, the model is set up so that a particular bond falls in the AA+ category (using Standard and Poor's terminology) if its unobserved (latent) creditworthiness falls within a certain range that is too low to classify it as AAA and too high to classify it as AA. The boundary values between each rating are then estimated along with the model parameters.

12.12 Are unsolicited credit ratings biased downwards? An ordered probit analysis

Modelling the determinants of credit ratings is one of the most important uses of ordered probit and logit models in finance. The main credit ratings agencies construct what may be termed *solicited* ratings, which are those where the issuer of the debt contacts the agency and pays them a fee for producing the rating. Many firms globally do not seek a rating (because, for example, the firm believes that the ratings agencies are not well placed to evaluate the riskiness of debt in their country or because they do not plan to issue any debt or because they believe that they would be awarded a low rating), but the agency may produce a rating anyway.

Such 'unwarranted and unwelcome' ratings are known as *unsolicited* ratings. All of the major ratings agencies produce unsolicited ratings as well as solicited ones, and they argue that there is a market demand for this information even if the issuer would prefer not to be rated.

Companies in receipt of unsolicited ratings argue that these are biased downwards relative to solicited ratings and that they cannot be justified without the level of detail of information that can be provided only by the rated company itself. A study by Poon (2003) seeks to test the conjecture that unsolicited ratings are biased after controlling for the rated company's characteristics that pertain to its risk.

The data employed comprise a pooled sample of all companies that appeared on the annual 'issuer list' of S&P during the years 1998–2000. This list contains both solicited and unsolicited ratings covering 295 firms over fifteen countries and totalling 595 observations. In a preliminary exploratory analysis of the data, Poon finds that around half of the sample ratings were unsolicited, and indeed the unsolicited ratings in the sample are on average significantly lower than the solicited ratings.[9] As expected, the financial characteristics of the firms with unsolicited ratings are significantly weaker than those for firms that requested ratings. The core methodology employs an ordered probit model with explanatory variables comprising firm characteristics and a dummy variable for whether the firm's credit rating was solicited or not

$$R_i^* = X_i \beta + \epsilon_i \tag{12.16}$$

with

$$R_i = \begin{cases} 1 & \text{if } R_i^* \le \mu_0 \\ 2 & \text{if } \mu_0 < R_i^* \le \mu_1 \\ 3 & \text{if } \mu_1 < R_i^* \le \mu_2 \\ 4 & \text{if } \mu_2 < R_i^* \le \mu_3 \\ 5 & \text{if } R_i^* > \mu_3 \end{cases}$$

where R_i are the observed ratings scores that are given numerical values as follows: AA or above $= 6$, A $= 5$, BBB $= 4$, BB $= 3$, B $= 2$ and CCC or below $= 1$; R_i^* is the unobservable 'true rating' (or 'an unobserved continuous variable representing S&P's assessment of the creditworthiness of issuer i'), X_i is a vector of variables that explains the variation in ratings; β is a vector of coefficients; μ_i are the threshold parameters to be estimated along with β; and ϵ_i is a disturbance term that is assumed normally distributed.

The explanatory variables attempt to capture the creditworthiness using publicly available information. Two specifications are estimated: the first includes the variables listed below, while the second additionally incorporates an interaction of the main financial variables with a dummy variable for whether the firm's rating was solicited (SOL) and separately with a dummy for whether the firm is based in

---

[9] We are assuming here that the broader credit rating categories, of which there are six (AAA, AA, A, BBB, BB, B), are being used rather than the finer categories used by Cantor and Packer (1996).

Japan.[10] The financial variables are ICOV − interest coverage (i.e. earnings interest), ROA − return on assets, DTC − total debt to capital, and SDTD − short-term debt to total debt. Three variables − SOVAA, SOVA and SOVBBB − are dummy variables that capture the debt issuer's sovereign credit rating.[11] Table 12.3 presents the results from the ordered probit estimation.

The key finding is that the SOL variable is positive and statistically significant in Model 1 (and it is positive but insignificant in Model 2), indicating that even after accounting for the financial characteristics of the firms, unsolicited firms receive ratings on average 0.359 units lower than an otherwise identical firm that had requested a rating. The parameter estimate for the interaction term between the solicitation and Japanese dummies (SOL*JP) is positive and significant in both specifications, indicating strong evidence that Japanese firms soliciting ratings receive higher scores. On average, firms with stronger financial characteristics (higher interest coverage, higher return on assets, lower debt to total capital, or a lower ratio of short-term debt to long-term debt) have higher ratings.

A major flaw that potentially exists within the above analysis is the *self-selection bias* or *sample selection bias* that may have arisen if firms that would have received lower credit ratings (because they have weak financials) elect not to solicit a rating. If the probit equation for the determinants of ratings is estimated ignoring this potential problem and it exists, the coefficients will be inconsistent. To get around this problem and to control for the sample selection bias, Heckman (1979) proposed a two–step procedure that in this case would involve first estimating a 0–1 probit model for whether the firm chooses to solicit a rating and second estimating the ordered probit model for the determinants of the rating. The first-stage probit model is

$$Y_i^* = Z_i\gamma + \xi_i \tag{12.17}$$

where $Y_i = 1$ if the firm has solicited a rating and 0 otherwise, and Y_i^* denotes the latent propensity of issuer i to solicit a rating, Z_i are the variables that explain the choice to be rated or not, and γ are the parameters to be estimated. When this equation has been estimated, the rating R_i as defined above in equation (12.16) will be observed only if $Y_i = 1$. The error terms from the two equations, ϵ_i and ξ_i, follow a bivariate standard normal distribution with correlation $\rho_{\epsilon\xi}$. Table 12.4 shows the results from the two-step estimation procedure, with the estimates from the binary probit model for the decision concerning whether to solicit a rating in panel A and the determinants of ratings for rated firms in panel B.

A positive parameter value in panel A indicates that higher values of the associated variable increases the probability that a firm will elect to be rated. Of the four financial variables, only the return on assets and the short-term debt as a

---

[10] The Japanese dummy is used since a disproportionate number of firms in the sample are from this country.

[11] So SOVAA = 1 if the sovereign (i.e. the government of that country) has debt with a rating of AA or above and 0 otherwise; SOVA has a value 1 if the sovereign has a rating of A; and SOVBBB has a value 1 if the sovereign has a rating of BBB; any firm in a country with a sovereign whose rating is below BBB is assigned a zero value for all three sovereign rating dummies.

Table 12.3 Ordered probit model results for the determinants of credit ratings

Explanatory variables	Model 1		Model 2	
	Coefficient	Test statistic	Coefficient	Test statistic
Intercept	2.324	8.960***	1.492	3.155***
SOL	0.359	2.105**	0.391	0.647
JP	−0.548	−2.949***	1.296	2.441**
JP*SOL	1.614	7.027***	1.487	5.183***
SOVAA	2.135	8.768***	2.470	8.975***
SOVA	0.554	2.552**	0.925	3.968***
SOVBBB	−0.416	−1.480	−0.181	−0.601
ICOV	0.023	3.466***	−0.005	−0.172
ROA	0.104	10.306***	0.194	2.503**
DTC	−1.393	−5.736***	−0.522	−1.130
SDTD	−1.212	−5.228***	0.111	0.171
SOL*ICOV	–	–	0.005	0.163
SOL*ROA	–	–	−0.116	−1.476
SOL*DTC	–	–	0.756	1.136
SOL*SDTD	–	–	−0.887	−1.290
JP*ICOV	–	–	0.009	0.275
JP*ROA	–	–	0.183	2.200**
JP*DTC	–	–	−1.865	−3.214***
JP*SDTD	–	–	−2.443	−3.437***
AA or above	>5.095		>5.578	
A	>3.788 and ≤5.095	25.278***	>4.147 and ≤5.578	23.294***
BBB	>2.550 and ≤3.788	19.671***	>2.803 and ≤4.147	19.204***
BB	>1.287 and ≤2.550	14.342***	>1.432 and ≤2.803	14.324***
B	>0 and ≤1.287	7.927***	>0 and ≤1.432	7.910***
CCC or below	≤0		≤0	

Note: *, ** and *** denote significance at the 10%, 5% and 1% levels respectively.
Source: Poon (2003). Reprinted with the permission of Elsevier.

Table 12.4 Two-step ordered probit model allowing for selectivity bias in the determinants of credit ratings

Explanatory variable	Coefficient	Test statistic
Panel A: Decision to be rated		
Intercept	1.624	3.935***
JP	−0.776	−4.951***
SOVAA	−0.959	−2.706***
SOVA	−0.614	−1.794*
SOVBBB	−1.130	−2.899***
ICOV	−0.005	−0.922
ROA	0.051	6.537***
DTC	0.272	1.019
SDTD	−1.651	−5.320***
Panel B: Rating determinant equation		
Intercept	1.368	2.890***
JP	2.456	3.141***
SOVAA	2.315	6.121***
SOVA	0.875	2.755***
SOVBBB	0.306	0.768
ICOV	0.002	0.118
ROA	0.038	2.408**
DTC	−0.330	−0.512
SDTD	0.105	0.303
JP*ICOV	0.038	1.129
JP*ROA	0.188	2.104**
JP*DTC	−0.808	−0.924
JP*SDTD	−2.823	−2.430**
Estimated correlation	−0.836	−5.723***
AA or above	>4.275	
A	>2.841 and ≤4.275	8.235***
BBB	>1.748 and ≤2.841	9.164***
BB	>0.704 and ≤1.748	6.788***
B	>0 and ≤0.704	3.316***
CCC or below	≤0	

Note: *, ** and *** denote significance at the 10%, 5% and 1% levels respectively.
Source: Poon (2003). Reprinted with the permission of Elsevier.

proportion of total debt have correctly signed and significant (positive and negative respectively) impacts on the decision to be rated. The parameters on the sovereign credit rating dummy variables (SOVAA, SOVA and SOVB) are all significant and negative in sign, indicating that any debt issuer in a country with a high sovereign rating is less likely to solicit its own rating from S&P, other things equal.

These sovereign rating dummy variables have the opposite sign in the ratings determinant equation (panel B) as expected, so that firms in countries where government debt is highly rated are themselves more likely to receive a higher rating. Of the four financial variables, only ROA has a significant (and positive) effect on the rating awarded. The dummy for Japanese firms is also positive and significant, and so are three of the four financial variables when interacted with the Japan dummy, indicating that S&P appears to attach different weights to the financial variables when assigning ratings to Japanese firms compared with comparable firms in other countries.

Finally, the estimated correlation between the error terms in the decision to be rated equation and the ratings determinant equation, $\rho_{\epsilon\xi}$, is significant and negative (-0.836), indicating that the results in table 12.3 above would have been subject to self-selection bias and hence the results of the two-stage model are to be preferred. The only disadvantage of this approach, however, is that by construction it cannot answer the core question of whether unsolicited ratings are on average lower after allowing for the debt issuer's financial characteristics, because only firms with solicited ratings are included in the sample at the second stage!

12.13 Censored and truncated dependent variables

Censored or truncated variables occur when the range of values observable for the dependent variables is limited for some reason. Unlike the types of limited dependent variables examined so far in this chapter, censored or truncated variables may not necessarily be dummies. A standard example is that of charitable donations by individuals. It is likely that some people would actually prefer to make negative donations (that is, to receive from the charity rather than to donate to it), but since this is not possible, there will be many observations at exactly zero. So suppose, for example, that we wished to model the relationship between donations to charity and people's annual income, in pounds. The situation we might face is illustrated in figure 12.3.

Given the observed data, with many observations on the dependent variable stuck at zero, OLS would yield biased and inconsistent parameter estimates. An obvious but flawed way to get around this would be just to remove all of the zero observations altogether, since we do not know whether they should be truly zero or negative. However, as well as being inefficient (since information would be discarded), this would still yield biased and inconsistent estimates. This arises because the error term, u_i, in such a regression would not have an expected value of zero, and it would also be correlated with the explanatory variable(s), violating the assumption that $Cov(u_i, x_{ki}) = 0 \ \forall \ k$.

The key differences between censored and truncated data are highlighted in box 12.2. For both censored and truncated data, OLS will not be appropriate, and

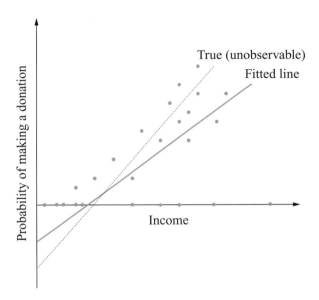

Figure 12.3   Modelling charitable donations as a function of income

an approach based on maximum likelihood must be used, although the model in each case would be slightly different. In both cases, we can work out the marginal effects given the estimated parameters, but these are now more complex than in the logit or probit cases.

12.13.1   Censored dependent variable models

The approach usually used to estimate models with censored dependent variables is known as tobit analysis, named after Tobin (1958). To illustrate, suppose that we wanted to model the demand for privatisation IPO shares, as discussed above, as a function of income (x_{2i}), age (x_{3i}), education (x_{4i}) and region of residence (x_{5i}). The model would be

$$y_i^* = \beta_1 + \beta_2 x_{2i} + \beta_3 x_{3i} + \beta_4 x_{4i} + \beta_5 x_{5i} + u_i$$

$$y_i = y_i^* \quad \text{for } y_i^* < 250 \tag{12.18}$$

$$y_i = 250 \quad \text{for } y_i^* \geq 250$$

y_i^* represents the true demand for shares (i.e. the number of shares requested) and this will be observable only for demand less than 250. It is important to note in this model that β_2, β_3, etc. represent the impact on the number of shares demanded (of a unit change in x_{2i}, x_{3i}, etc.) and not the impact on the actual number of shares that will be bought (allocated).

An interesting financial application of the tobit approach is due to Haushalter (2000), who employs it to model the determinants of the extent of hedging by oil and gas producers using futures or options over the 1992–4 period. The dependent variable used in the regression models, the proportion of production hedged, is clearly censored because around half of all of the observations are exactly zero

Box 12.2   The differences between censored and truncated dependent variables

Although at first sight the two words might appear interchangeable, when the terms are used in econometrics, censored and truncated data are different.

- Censored data occur when the dependent variable has been '*censored*' at a certain point so that values above (or below) this cannot be observed. Even though the dependent variable is censored, the corresponding values of the independent variables are still observable.
- As an example, suppose that a privatisation IPO is heavily oversubscribed, and you were trying to model the demand for the shares using household income, age, education and region of residence as explanatory variables. The number of shares allocated to each investor may have been capped at, say, 250, resulting in a truncated distribution.
- In this example, even though we are likely to have many share allocations at 250 and none above this figure, all of the observations on the independent variables are present and hence the dependent variable is censored, not truncated.
- A truncated dependent variable, meanwhile, occurs when the observations for both the dependent and the independent variables are missing when the dependent variable is above (or below) a certain threshold. Thus the key difference from censored data is that we cannot observe the x_is either, and so some observations are completely cut out or *truncated* from the sample. For example, suppose that a bank were interested in determining the factors (such as age, occupation and income) that affected a customer's decision as to whether to undertake a transaction in a branch or online. Suppose also that the bank tried to achieve this by encouraging clients to fill in an online questionnaire when they log on. There would be no data at all for those who opted to transact in person since they probably would not have even logged on to the bank's web-based system and so would not have the opportunity to complete the questionnaire. Thus, dealing with truncated data is really a sample selection problem because the sample of data that can be observed is not representative of the population of interest – the sample is biased, very likely resulting in biased and inconsistent parameter estimates. This is a common problem, which will result whenever data for buyers or users only can be observed while data for non-buyers or non-users cannot. Of course, it is possible, although unlikely, that the population of interest is focused only on those who use the internet for banking transactions, in which case there would be no problem.

(i.e. the firm does not hedge at all).[12] The censoring of the proportion of production hedged may arise because of high fixed costs that prevent many firms from being able to hedge even if they wished to. Moreover, if companies expect the price of oil or gas to rise in the future, they may wish to increase rather than reduce their exposure to price changes (i.e. 'negative hedging'), but this would not be observable given the way that the data are constructed in the study.

The main results from the study are that the proportion of exposure hedged is negatively related to creditworthiness, positively related to indebtedness, to the firm's marginal tax rate, and to the location of the firm's production facility. The extent of hedging is not, however, affected by the size of the firm as measured by its total assets.

Before moving on, two important limitations of tobit modelling should be noted. First, such models are much more seriously affected by non-normality and heteroscedasticity than are standard regression models (see Amemiya, 1984), and biased and inconsistent estimation will result. Second, as Kennedy (2003, p. 283) argues, the tobit model requires it to be plausible that the dependent variable can have values close to the limit. There is no problem with the privatisation IPO example discussed above since the demand could be for 249 shares. However, it would not be appropriate to use the tobit model in situations where this is not the case, such as the number of shares issued by each firm in a particular month. For most companies, this figure will be exactly zero, but for those where it is not, the number will be much higher and thus it would not be feasible to issue, say, one or three or fifteen shares. In this case, an alternative approach should be used.

12.13.2 Truncated dependent variable models

For truncated data, a more general model is employed that contains two equations – one for whether a particular data point will fall into the observed or constrained categories and another for modelling the resulting variable. The second equation is equivalent to the tobit approach. This two-equation methodology allows for a different set of factors to affect the sample selection (for example, the decision to set up internet access to a bank account) from the equation to be estimated (for example, to model the factors that affect whether a particular transaction will be conducted online or in a branch). If it is thought that the two sets of factors will be the same, then a single equation can be used and the tobit approach is sufficient. In many cases, however, the researcher may believe that the variables in the sample selection and estimation equations should be different. Thus the equations could be

$$a_i^* = \alpha_1 + \alpha_2 z_{2i} + \alpha_3 z_{3i} + \cdots + \alpha_m z_{mi} + \varepsilon_i \qquad (12.19)$$

$$y_i^* = \beta_1 + \beta_2 x_{2i} + \beta_3 x_{3i} + \cdots + \beta_k x_{ki} + u_i \qquad (12.20)$$

[12] Note that this is an example of a *censored* rather than a *truncated* dependent variable because the values of all of the explanatory variables are still available from the annual accounts even if a firm does not hedge at all.

where $y_i = y_i^*$ for $a_i^* > 0$ and, y_i is unobserved for $a_i^* \leq 0$. a_i^* denotes the relative 'advantage' of being in the observed sample relative to the unobserved sample.

The first equation determines whether the particular data point i will be observed or not, by regressing a proxy for the latent (unobserved) variable a_i^* on a set of factors, z_i. The second equation is similar to the tobit model. Ideally, the two equations (12.19) and (12.20) will be fitted jointly by maximum likelihood. This is usually based on the assumption that the error terms, ε_i and u_i, are multivariate normally distributed and allowing for any possible correlations between them. However, while joint estimation of the equations is more efficient, it is computationally more complex and hence a two-stage procedure popularised by Heckman (1976) is often used. The Heckman procedure allows for possible correlations between ε_i and u_i while estimating the equations separately in a clever way – see Maddala (1983).

12.14 Limited dependent variable models in EViews

Estimating limited dependent variable models in EViews is very simple. The example that will be considered here concerns whether it is possible to determine the factors that affect the likelihood that a student will fail his/her MSc. The data comprise a sample from the actual records of failure rates for five years of MSc students in finance at the ICMA Centre, University of Reading contained in the spreadsheet 'MSc_fail.xls'. While the values in the spreadsheet are all genuine, only a sample of 100 students is included for each of five years who completed (or not as the case may be!) their degrees in the years 2003 to 2007 inclusive. Therefore, the data should not be used to infer actual failure rates on these programmes. The idea for this example is taken from a study by Heslop and Varotto (2007) which seeks to propose an approach to preventing systematic biases in admissions decisions.[13]

The objective here is to analyse the factors that affect the probability of failure of the MSc. The dependent variable ('fail') is binary and takes the value 1 if that particular candidate failed at first attempt in terms of his/her overall grade and 0 elsewhere. Therefore, a model that is suitable for limited dependent variables is required, such as a logit or probit.

The other information in the spreadsheet that will be used includes the age of the student, a dummy variable taking the value 1 if the student is female, a dummy variable taking the value 1 if the student has work experience, a dummy variable taking the value 1 if the student's first language is English, a country code variable that takes values from 1 to 10,[14] a dummy variable that takes the value 1 if the student already has a postgraduate degree, a dummy variable that takes the value 1 if the student achieved an A-grade at the undergraduate level

---

[13] Note that since this book uses only a sub-set of their sample and variables in the analysis, the results presented below may differ from theirs. Since the number of fails is relatively small, I deliberately retained as many fail observations in the sample as possible, which will bias the estimated failure rate upwards relative to the true rate.

[14] The exact identities of the countries involved are not revealed in order to avoid any embarrassment for students from countries with high relative failure rates, except that Country 8 is the UK!

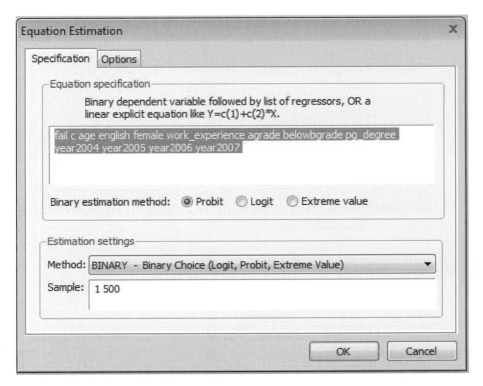

Screenshot 12.1　**Equation estimation window for limited dependent variables**

(i.e. a first-class honours degree or equivalent), and a dummy variable that takes the value 1 if the undergraduate grade was less than a B-grade (i.e. the student received the equivalent of a lower second-class degree). The B-grade (or upper second-class degree) is the omitted dummy variable and this will then become the reference point against which the other grades are compared – see chapter 10. The reason why these variables ought to be useful predictors of the probability of failure should be fairly obvious and is therefore not discussed. To allow for differences in examination rules and in average student quality across the five-year period, year dummies for 2004, 2005, 2006 and 2007 are created and thus the year 2003 dummy will be omitted from the regression model.

First, **open a new workfile** that can accept 'unstructured/undated' series of length 500 observations and then **import the 13 variables**. The data are **organised by observation** and start in cell **A2**. The country code variable will require further processing before it can be used but the others are already in the appropriate format, so to begin, suppose that we estimate an LPM of fail on a constant, age, English, female and work experience. This would be achieved simply by running a linear regression in the usual way. While this model has a number of very undesirable features as discussed above, it would nonetheless provide a useful benchmark with which to compare the more appropriate models estimated below.

Next, estimate a probit model and a logit model using the same dependent and independent variables as above. Choose **Quick** and then **Equation**

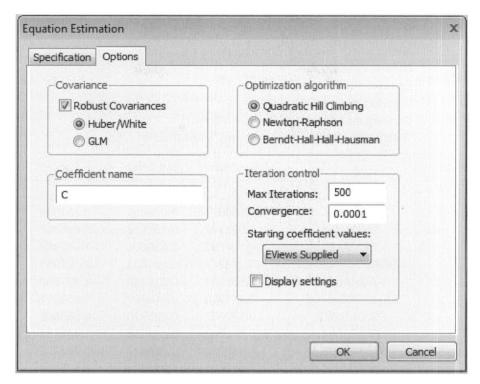

Screenshot 12.2   **Equation estimation options for limited dependent variables**

Estimation. Then type the dependent variable followed by the explanatory variables

FAIL C AGE ENGLISH FEMALE WORK_EXPERIENCE AGRADE BELOWBGRADE PG_DEGREE YEAR2004 YEAR2005 YEAR2006 YEAR2007

and then in the second window, marked 'Estimation settings', select **BINARY – Binary Choice (Logit, Probit, Extreme Value)** with the whole sample 1 500. The screen will appear as in screenshot 12.1.

You can then choose either the probit or logit approach. Note that EViews also provides support for truncated and censored variable models and for multiple choice models, and these can be selected from the drop-down menu by choosing the appropriate method under 'estimation settings'. Suppose that here we wish to choose a probit model (the default). Click on the **Options** tab at the top of the window and this enables you to select **Robust Covariances** and **Huber/White**. This option will ensure that the standard error estimates are robust to heteroscedasticity (see screenshot 12.2).

There are other options to change the optimisation method and convergence criterion, as discussed in chapter 9. We do not need to make any modifications from the default here, so click **OK** and the results will appear. **Freeze and name this table** and then, for completeness, **estimate a logit model**. The results that you should obtain for the probit model are in the following table.

Dependent Variable: FAIL
Method: ML – Binary Probit (Quadratic hill climbing)
Date: 08/04/07 Time: 19:10
Sample: 1 500
Included observations: 500
Convergence achieved after 5 iterations
QML (Huber/White) standard errors & covariance

	Coefficient	Std. Error	z-Statistic	Prob.
C	−1.287210	0.609503	−2.111901	0.0347
AGE	0.005677	0.022559	0.251648	0.8013
ENGLISH	−0.093792	0.156226	−0.600362	0.5483
FEMALE	−0.194107	0.186201	−1.042460	0.2972
WORK_EXPERIENCE	−0.318247	0.151333	−2.102956	0.0355
AGRADE	−0.538814	0.231148	−2.331038	0.0198
BELOWBGRADE	0.341803	0.219301	1.558601	0.1191
PG_DEGREE	0.132957	0.225925	0.588502	0.5562
YEAR2004	0.349663	0.241450	1.448181	0.1476
YEAR2005	−0.108330	0.268527	−0.403422	0.6866
YEAR2006	0.673612	0.238536	2.823944	0.0047
YEAR2007	0.433785	0.24793	1.749630	0.0802

McFadden R-squared	0.088870	Mean dependent var		0.134000
S.D. dependent var	0.340993	S.E. of regression		0.333221
Akaike info criterion	0.765825	Sum squared resid		54.18582
Schwarz criterion	0.866976	Log likelihood		−179.4563
Hannan-Quinn criter.	0.805517	Restr. log likelihood		−196.9602
LR statistic	35.00773	Avg. log likelihood		−0.358913
Prob(LR statistic)	0.000247			

Obs with Dep=0	433	Total obs	500
Obs with Dep=1	67		

As can be seen, the pseudo-R^2 values are quite small at just below 9%, although this is often the case for limited dependent variable models. Only the work experience and A-grade variables and two of the year dummies have parameters that are statistically significant, and the Below B-grade dummy is almost significant at the 10% level in the probit specification (although less so in the logit). As the final two rows of the tables note, the proportion of fails in this sample is quite small, which makes it harder to fit a good model than if the proportions of passes and fails had been more evenly balanced. Various goodness of fit statistics can be examined by (from the logit or probit estimation output window) clicking **View/Goodness-of-fit Test (Hosmer-Lemeshow)**. A further check on model adequacy is to produce a set of 'in-sample forecasts' – in other words, to construct the fitted values. To do this, click on the **Forecast** tab after estimating the probit model

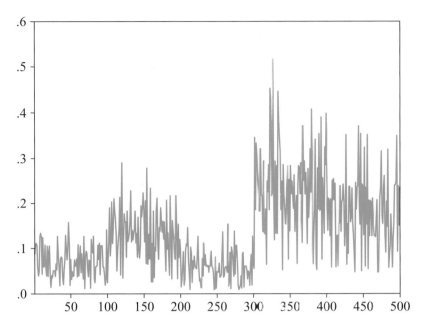

Figure 12.4   Fitted values from the failure probit regression

and then **uncheck the forecast evaluation box** in the 'Output' window as the evaluation is not relevant in this case. All other options can be left as the default settings and then the plot of the fitted values shown on figure 12.4 results.

The unconditional probability of failure for the sample of students we have is only 13.4% (i.e. only 67 out of 500 failed), so an observation should be classified as correctly fitted if either $y_i = 1$ and $\hat{y}_i > 0.134$ or $y_i = 0$ and $\hat{y}_i < 0.134$. The easiest way to evaluate the model in EViews is to click **View/Actual,Fitted,Residual Table** from the logit or probit output screen. Then from this information we can identify that of the 67 students that failed, the model correctly predicted 46 of them to fail (and it also incorrectly predicted that 21 would pass). Of the 433 students who passed, the model incorrectly predicted 155 to fail and correctly predicted the remaining 278 to pass. Eviews can construct an 'expectation-prediction classification table' automatically by clicking on **View/Expectation–Prediction Evaluation** and then entering the unconditional probability of failure as the cutoff when prompted (**0.134**). Overall, we could consider this a reasonable set of (in sample) predictions with 64.8% of the total predictions correct, comprising 64.2% of the passes correctly predicted as passes and 68.66% of the fails correctly predicted as fails.

It is important to note that, as discussed above, we cannot interpret the parameter estimates in the usual way. In order to be able to do this, we need to calculate the marginal effects. Unfortunately, EViews does not do this automatically, so the procedure is probably best achieved in a spreadsheet using the approach described in box 12.1 for the logit model and analogously for the probit model. If we did this, we would end up with the statistics displayed in table 12.5, which are interestingly quite similar in value to those obtained from the linear probability model.

Table 12.5   Marginal effects for logit and probit models for probability of MSc failure

Parameter	Logit	Probit
C	−0.2433	−0.1646
AGE	0.0012	0.0007
ENGLISH	−0.0178	−0.0120
FEMALE	−0.0360	−0.0248
WORK_EXPERIENCE	−0.0613	−0.0407
AGRADE	−0.1170	−0.0689
BELOWBGRADE	0.0606	0.0437
PG_DEGREE	0.0229	0.0170
YEAR2004	0.0704	0.0447
YEAR2005	−0.0198	−0.0139
YEAR2006	0.1344	0.0862
YEAR2007	0.0917	0.0555

This table presents us with values that can be intuitively interpreted in terms of how the variables affect the probability of failure. For example, an age parameter value of 0.0012 implies that an increase in the age of the student by one year would increase the probability of failure by 0.12%, holding everything else equal, while a female student is around 2.5–3% (depending on the model) less likely than a male student with otherwise identical characteristics to fail. Having an A-grade (first class) in the bachelors degree makes a candidate either 6.89% or 12.7% (depending on the model) less likely to fail than an otherwise identical student with a B-grade (upper second-class degree). Finally, since the year 2003 dummy has been omitted from the equations, this becomes the reference point. So students were more likely in 2004, 2006 and 2007, but less likely in 2005, to fail the MSc than in 2003.

Key concepts

The key terms to be able to define and explain from this chapter are

- limited dependent variables
- probit
- truncated variables
- multinomial logit
- pseudo-R^2
- logit
- censored variables
- ordered response
- marginal effects

Self-study questions

1. Explain why the linear probability model is inadequate as a specification for limited dependent variable estimation.
2. Compare and contrast the probit and logit specifications for binary choice variables.
3. (a) Describe the intuition behind the maximum likelihood estimation technique used for limited dependent variable models.
   (b) Why do we need to exercise caution when interpreting the coefficients of a probit or logit model?
   (c) How can we measure whether a logit model that we have estimated fits the data well or not?
   (d) What is the difference, in terms of the model setup, in binary choice versus multiple choice problems?
4. (a) Explain the difference between a censored variable and a truncated variable as the terms are used in econometrics.
   (b) Give examples from finance (other than those already described in this book) of situations where you might meet each of the types of variable described in part (a) of this question.
   (c) With reference to your examples in part (b), how would you go about specifying such models and estimating them?
5. Re-open the 'fail_xls' spreadsheet for modelling the probability of MSc failure and do the following:
   (a) Take the country code series and construct separate dummy variables for each country. Re-run the probit and logit regression above with all of the other variables plus the country dummy variables. Set up the regression so that the UK becomes the reference point against which the effect on failure rate in other countries is measured. Is there evidence that any countries have significantly higher or lower probabilities of failure than the UK, holding all other factors in the model constant? In the case of the logit model, use the approach given in box 12.1 to evaluate the differences in failure rates between the UK and each other country.
   (b) Suppose that a fellow researcher suggests that there may be a non-linear relationship between the probability of failure and the age of the student. Estimate a probit model with all of the same variables as above plus an additional one to test this. Is there indeed any evidence of such a nonlinear relationship?

Appendix   The maximum likelihood estimator for logit and probit models

Recall that under the logit formulation, the estimate of the probability that $y_i = 1$ will be given from equation (12.4), which was

$$P_i = \frac{1}{1 + e^{-(\beta_1 + \beta_2 x_{2i} + \ldots + \beta_k x_{ki} + u_i)}} \tag{12A.1}$$

Set the error term, u_i, to its expected value for simplicity and again, let $z_i = \beta_1 + \beta_2 x_{2i} + \cdots + \beta_k x_{ki}$, so that we have

$$P_i = \frac{1}{1 + e^{-z_i}} \tag{12A.2}$$

We will also need the probability that $y_i \neq 1$ or equivalently the probability that $y_i = 0$. This will be given by 1 minus the probability in (12A.2).[15] Given that we can have actual zeros and ones only for y_i rather than probabilities, the likelihood function for each observation y_i will be

$$L_i = \left(\frac{1}{1 + e^{-z_i}}\right)^{y_i} \times \left(\frac{1}{1 + e^{z_i}}\right)^{(1-y_i)} \tag{12A.3}$$

The likelihood function that we need will be based on the joint probability for all N observations rather than an individual observation i. Assuming that each observation on y_i is independent, the joint likelihood will be the product of all N marginal likelihoods. Let $L(\theta \mid x_{2i}, x_{3i}, \ldots, x_{ki}; i = 1, N)$ denote the likelihood function of the set of parameters $(\beta_1, \beta_2, \ldots, \beta_k)$ given the data. Then the likelihood function will be given by

$$L(\theta) = \prod_{i=1}^{N} \left(\frac{1}{1 + e^{-z_i}}\right)^{y_i} \times \left(\frac{1}{1 + e^{z_i}}\right)^{(1-y_i)} \tag{12A.4}$$

As for maximum likelihood estimator of GARCH models, it is computationally much simpler to maximise an additive function of a set of variables than a multiplicative function, so long as we can ensure that the parameters required to achieve this will be the same. We thus take the natural logarithm of equation (12A.4) and this log-likelihood function is maximised

$$LLF = -\sum_{i=1}^{N} [y_i \ln(1 + e^{-z_i}) + (1 - y_i) \ln(1 + e^{z_i})] \tag{12A.5}$$

Estimation for the probit model will proceed in exactly the same way, except that the form for the likelihood function in (12A.4) will be slightly different. It will instead be based on the familiar normal distribution function described in the appendix to chapter 9.

---

[15] We can use the rule that

$$1 - \frac{1}{1 + e^{-z_i}} = \frac{1 + e^{-z_i} - 1}{1 + e^{-z_i}} = \frac{e^{-z_i}}{1 + e^{-z_i}} = \frac{e^{-z_i}}{1 + \frac{1}{e^{z_i}}} = \frac{e^{-z_i} \times e^{z_i}}{1 + e^{z_i}} = \frac{1}{1 + e^{z_i}}.$$

13 Simulation methods

Learning outcomes

In this chapter, you will learn how to

- Design simulation frameworks to solve a variety of problems in finance
- Explain the difference between pure simulation and bootstrapping
- Describe the various techniques available for reducing Monte Carlo sampling variability
- Implement a simulation analysis in EViews

13.1 Motivations

There are numerous situations, in finance and in econometrics, where the researcher has essentially no idea what is going to happen! To offer one illustration, in the context of complex financial risk measurement models for portfolios containing large numbers of assets whose movements are dependent on one another, it is not always clear what will be the effect of changing circumstances. For example, following full European Monetary Union (EMU) and the replacement of member currencies with the euro, it is widely believed that European financial markets have become more integrated, leading the correlation between movements in their equity markets to rise. What would be the effect on the properties of a portfolio containing equities of several European countries if correlations between the markets rose to 99%? Clearly, it is probably not possible to be able to answer such a question using actual historical data alone, since the event (a correlation of 99%) has not yet happened.

The practice of econometrics is made difficult by the behaviour of series and inter-relationships between them that render model assumptions at best questionable. For example, the existence of fat tails, structural breaks and bi-directional causality between dependent and independent variables, etc. will make the process of parameter estimation and inference less reliable. Real data is messy, and no one really knows all of the features that lurk inside it. Clearly, it is important for researchers to have an idea of what the effects of such phenomena will be for model estimation and inference.

By contrast, simulation is the econometrician's chance to behave like a 'real scientist', conducting experiments under controlled conditions. A simulations experiment enables the econometrician to determine what the effect of changing one factor or aspect of a problem will be, while leaving all other aspects unchanged. Thus, simulations offer the possibility of complete flexibility. Simulation may be defined as an approach to modelling that seeks to mimic a functioning system as it evolves. The simulations model will express in mathematical equations the assumed form of operation of the system. In econometrics, simulation is particularly useful when models are very complex or sample sizes are small.

13.2　Monte Carlo simulations

Simulations studies are usually used to investigate the properties and behaviour of various statistics of interest. The technique is often used in econometrics when the properties of a particular estimation method are not known. For example, it may be known from asymptotic theory how a particular test behaves with an infinite sample size, but how will the test behave if only fifty observations are available? Will the test still have the desirable properties of being correctly sized and having high power? In other words, if the null hypothesis is correct, will the test lead to rejection of the null 5% of the time if a 5% rejection region is used? And if the null is incorrect, will it be rejected a high proportion of the time?

Examples from econometrics of where simulation may be useful include:

- Quantifying the simultaneous equations bias induced by treating an endogenous variable as exogenous
- Determining the appropriate critical values for a Dickey–Fuller test
- Determining what effect heteroscedasticity has upon the size and power of a test for autocorrelation.

Simulations are also often extremely useful tools in finance, in situations such as:

- The pricing of exotic options, where an analytical pricing formula is unavailable
- Determining the effect on financial markets of substantial changes in the macroeconomic environment
- 'Stress-testing' risk management models to determine whether they generate capital requirements sufficient to cover losses in all situations.

In all of these instances, the basic way that such a study would be conducted (with additional steps and modifications where necessary) is shown in box 13.1.

A brief explanation of each of these steps is in order. The first stage involves *specifying the model* that will be used to generate the data. This may be a pure time series model or a structural model. Pure time series models are usually simpler to implement, as a full structural model would also require the researcher to specify a data generating process for the explanatory variables as well. Assuming that a time series model is deemed appropriate, the next choice to be made is of the

> **Box 13.1   Conducting a Monte Carlo simulation**
>
> (1) Generate the data according to the desired data generating process (DGP), with the errors being drawn from some given distribution
> (2) Do the regression and calculate the test statistic
> (3) Save the test statistic or whatever parameter is of interest
> (4) Go back to stage 1 and repeat N times.

probability distribution specified for the errors. Usually, standard normal draws are used, although any other empirically plausible distribution (such as a Student's t) could also be used.

The second stage involves estimation of the parameter of interest in the study. The parameter of interest might be, for example, the value of a coefficient in a regression, or the value of an option at its expiry date. It could instead be the value of a portfolio under a particular set of scenarios governing the way that the prices of the component assets move over time.

The quantity N is known as the number of replications, and this should be as large as is feasible. The central idea behind Monte Carlo is that of random sampling from a given distribution. Therefore, if the number of replications is set too small, the results will be sensitive to 'odd' combinations of random number draws. It is also worth noting that asymptotic arguments apply in Monte Carlo studies as well as in other areas of econometrics. That is, the results of a simulation study will be equal to their analytical counterparts (assuming that the latter exist) asymptotically.

13.3 Variance reduction techniques

Suppose that the value of the parameter of interest for replication i is denoted x_i. If the average value of this parameter is calculated for a set of, say, $N = 1,000$ replications, and another researcher conducts an otherwise identical study with different sets of random draws, a different average value of x is almost certain to result. This situation is akin to the problem of selecting only a sample of observations from a given population in standard regression analysis. The sampling variation in a Monte Carlo study is measured by the standard error estimate, denoted S_x

$$S_x = \sqrt{\frac{\text{var}(x)}{N}} \tag{13.1}$$

where $\text{var}(x)$ is the variance of the estimates of the quantity of interest over the N replications. It can be seen from this equation that to reduce the Monte Carlo standard error by a factor of 10, the number of replications must be increased by a factor of 100. Consequently, in order to achieve acceptable accuracy, the number of replications may have to be set at an infeasibly high level. An alternative way to reduce Monte Carlo sampling error is to use a variance reduction technique. There are many variance reduction techniques available. Two of the intuitively simplest and most widely used methods are the method of *antithetic variates* and the method of *control variates*. Both of these techniques will now be described.

13.3.1 Antithetic variates

One reason that a lot of replications are typically required of a Monte Carlo study is that it may take many, many repeated sets of sampling before the entire probability space is adequately covered. By their very nature, the values of the random draws are random, and so after a given number of replications, it may be the case that not the whole range of possible outcomes has actually occurred.[1] What is really required is for successive replications to cover different parts of the probability space − that is, for the random draws from different replications to generate outcomes that span the entire spectrum of possibilities. This may take a long time to achieve naturally.

The antithetic variate technique involves taking the complement of a set of random numbers and running a parallel simulation on those. For example, if the driving stochastic force is a set of $TN(0, 1)$ draws, denoted u_t, for each replication, an additional replication with errors given by $-u_t$ is also used. It can be shown that the Monte Carlo standard error is reduced when antithetic variates are used. For a simple illustration of this, suppose that the average value of the parameter of interest across two sets of Monte Carlo replications is given by

$$\bar{x} = (x_1 + x_2)/2 \tag{13.2}$$

where x_1 and x_2 are the average parameter values for replications sets 1 and 2, respectively. The variance of $\bar{x}$ will be given by

$$\text{var}(\bar{x}) = \frac{1}{4} \left(\text{var}(x_1) + \text{var}(x_2) + 2\text{cov}(x_1, x_2) \right) \tag{13.3}$$

If no antithetic variates are used, the two sets of Monte Carlo replications will be independent, so that their covariance will be zero, i.e.

$$\text{var}(\bar{x}) = \frac{1}{4} \left(\text{var}(x_1) + \text{var}(x_2) \right) \tag{13.4}$$

However, the use of antithetic variates would lead the covariance in (13.3) to be negative, and therefore the Monte Carlo sampling error to be reduced.

It may at first appear that the reduction in Monte Carlo sampling variation from using antithetic variates will be huge since, by definition, $\text{corr}(u_t, -u_t) = \text{cov}(u_t, -u_t) = -1$. However, it is important to remember that the relevant covariance is between the simulated quantity of interest for the standard replications and

---

[1] Obviously, for a continuous random variable, there will be an infinite number of possible values. In this context, the problem is simply that if the probability space is split into arbitrarily small intervals, some of those intervals will not have been adequately covered by the random draws that were actually selected.

those using the antithetic variates. But the perfect negative covariance is between the random draws (i.e. the error terms) and their antithetic variates. For example, in the context of option pricing (discussed below), the production of a price for the underlying security (and therefore for the option) constitutes a non-linear transformation of u_t. Therefore the covariances between the terminal prices of the underlying assets based on the draws and based on the antithetic variates will be negative, but not -1.

Several other variance reduction techniques that operate using similar principles are available, including stratified sampling, moment-matching and low-discrepancy sequencing. The latter are also known as *quasi-random sequences* of draws. These involve the selection of a specific sequence of representative samples from a given probability distribution. Successive samples are selected so that the unselected gaps left in the probability distribution are filled by subsequent replications. The result is a set of random draws that are appropriately distributed across all of the outcomes of interest. The use of low-discrepancy sequences leads the Monte Carlo standard errors to be reduced in direct proportion to the number of replications rather than in proportion to the square root of the number of replications. Thus, for example, to reduce the Monte Carlo standard error by a factor of 10, the number of replications would have to be increased by a factor of 100 for standard Monte Carlo random sampling, but only 10 for low-discrepancy sequencing. Further details of low-discrepancy techniques are beyond the scope of this text, but can be seen in Boyle (1977) or Press *et al.* (1992). The former offers a detailed and relevant example in the context of options pricing.

13.3.2 Control variates

The application of control variates involves employing a variable similar to that used in the simulation, but whose properties are known prior to the simulation. Denote the variable whose properties are known by y, and that whose properties are under simulation by x. The simulation is conducted on x and also on y, with the same sets of random number draws being employed in both cases. Denoting the simulation estimates of x and y by $\hat{x}$ and $\hat{y}$, respectively, a new estimate of x can be derived from

$$x^* = y + (\hat{x} - \hat{y}) \tag{13.5}$$

Again, it can be shown that the Monte Carlo sampling error of this quantity, x^*, will be lower than that of x provided that a certain condition holds. The control variates help to reduce the Monte Carlo variation owing to particular sets of random draws by using the same draws on a related problem whose solution is known. It is expected that the effects of sampling error for the problem under study and the known problem will be similar, and hence can be reduced by calibrating the Monte Carlo results using the analytic ones.

It is worth noting that control variates succeed in reducing the Monte Carlo sampling error only if the control and simulation problems are very closely related. As the correlation between the values of the control statistic and the statistic of interest is reduced, the variance reduction is weakened. Consider again (13.5), and take the variance of both sides

$$\text{var}(x^*) = \text{var}(y + (\hat{x} - \hat{y})) \tag{13.6}$$

$\text{var}(y) = 0$ since y is a quantity which is known analytically and is therefore not subject to sampling variation, so (13.6) can be written

$$\text{var}(x^*) = \text{var}(\hat{x}) + \text{var}(\hat{y}) - 2\text{cov}(\hat{x}, \hat{y}) \tag{13.7}$$

The condition that must hold for the Monte Carlo sampling variance to be lower with control variates than without is that $\text{var}(x^*)$ is less than $\text{var}(\hat{x})$. Taken from (13.7), this condition can also be expressed as

$$\text{var}(\hat{y}) - 2\text{cov}(\hat{x}, \hat{y}) < 0$$

or

$$\text{cov}(\hat{x}, \hat{y}) > \frac{1}{2}\text{var}(\hat{y})$$

Divide both sides of this inequality by the products of the standard deviations, i.e. by $(\text{var}(\hat{x}), \text{var}(\hat{y}))^{1/2}$, to obtain the correlation on the LHS

$$\text{corr}(\hat{x}, \hat{y}) > \frac{1}{2}\sqrt{\frac{\text{var}(\hat{y})}{\text{var}(\hat{x})}}$$

To offer an illustration of the use of control variates, a researcher may be interested in pricing an arithmetic Asian option using simulation. Recall that an arithmetic Asian option is one whose payoff depends on the arithmetic average value of the underlying asset over the lifetime of the averaging; at the time of writing, an analytical (closed-form) model is not yet available for pricing such options. In this context, a control variate price could be obtained by finding the price via simulation of a similar derivative whose value is known analytically – e.g. a vanilla European option. Thus, the Asian and vanilla options would be priced using simulation, as shown below, with the simulated price given by P_A and P^*_{BS}, respectively. The price of the vanilla option, P_{BS} is also calculated using an analytical formula, such as Black–Scholes. The new estimate of the Asian option price, P^*_A, would then be given by

$$P^*_A = (P_A - P_{BS}) + P^*_{BS} \tag{13.8}$$

13.3.3 Random number re-usage across experiments

Although of course it would not be sensible to re-use sets of random number draws within a Monte Carlo experiment, using the same sets of draws across experiments can greatly reduce the variability of the difference in the estimates across those experiments. For example, it may be of interest to examine the power of the Dickey–Fuller test for samples of size 100 observations and for different values of ϕ (to use the notation of chapter 8). Thus, for each experiment involving a different value of ϕ, the same set of standard normal random numbers could be used to reduce the sampling variation across experiments. However, the accuracy of the actual estimates in each case will not be increased, of course.

Another possibility involves taking long series of draws and then slicing them up into several smaller sets to be used in different experiments. For example, Monte Carlo simulation may be used to price several options of different times to maturity, but which are identical in all other respects. Thus, if six-month, three-month and one-month horizons were of interest, sufficient random draws to cover six months would be made. Then the six-months' worth of draws could be used to construct two replications of a three-month horizon, and six replications for the one-month horizon. Again, the variability of the simulated option prices across maturities would be reduced, although the accuracies of the prices themselves would not be increased for a given number of replications.

Random number re-usage is unlikely to save computational time, for making the random draws usually takes a very small proportion of the overall time taken to conduct the whole experiment.

13.4 Bootstrapping

Bootstrapping is related to simulation, but with one crucial difference. With simulation, the data are constructed completely artificially. Bootstrapping, on the other hand, is used to obtain a description of the properties of empirical estimators by using the sample data points themselves, and it involves sampling repeatedly with replacement from the actual data. Many econometricians were initially highly sceptical of the usefulness of the technique, which appears at first sight to be some kind of magic trick − creating useful additional information from a given sample. Indeed, Davison and Hinkley (1997, p. 3), state that the term 'bootstrap' in this context comes from an analogy with the fictional character Baron Munchhausen, who got out from the bottom of a lake by pulling himself up by his bootstraps.

Suppose a sample of data, $\mathbf{y} = y_1, y_2, \ldots, y_T$ are available and it is desired to estimate some parameter θ. An approximation to the statistical properties of $\hat{\theta}_T$ can be obtained by studying a sample of bootstrap estimators. This is done by taking N samples of size T with replacement from $\mathbf{y}$ and re-calculating $\hat{\theta}$ with each new sample. A series of $\hat{\theta}$ estimates is then obtained, and their distribution can be considered.

The advantage of bootstrapping over the use of analytical results is that it allows the researcher to make inferences without making strong distributional assumptions, since the distribution employed will be that of the actual data. Instead of imposing a shape on the sampling distribution of the $\hat{\theta}$ value, bootstrapping involves empirically estimating the sampling distribution by looking at the variation of the statistic within-sample.

A set of new samples is drawn with replacement from the sample and the test statistic of interest calculated from each of these. Effectively, this involves sampling from the sample, i.e. treating the sample as a population from which samples can be drawn. Call the test statistics calculated from the new samples $\hat{\theta}^*$. The samples are likely to be quite different from each other and from the original $\hat{\theta}$ value, since some observations may be sampled several times and others not at all. Thus a distribution of values of $\hat{\theta}^*$ is obtained, from which standard errors or some other statistics of interest can be calculated.

Along with advances in computational speed and power, the number of bootstrap applications in finance and in econometrics have increased rapidly in previous years. For example, in econometrics, the bootstrap has been used in the context of unit root testing. Scheinkman and LeBaron (1989) also suggest that the bootstrap can be used as a 'shuffle diagnostic', where as usual the original data are sampled with replacement to form new data series. Successive applications of this procedure should generate a collection of data sets with the same distributional properties, on average, as the original data. But any kind of dependence in the original series (e.g. linear or non-linear autocorrelation) will, by definition, have been removed. Applications of econometric tests to the shuffled series can then be used as a benchmark with which to compare the results on the actual data or to construct standard error estimates or confidence intervals.

In finance, an application of bootstrapping in the context of risk management is discussed below. Another important recent proposed use of the bootstrap is as a method for detecting data snooping (data mining) in the context of tests of the profitability of technical trading rules. Data snooping occurs when the same set of data is used to construct trading rules and also to test them. In such cases, if a sufficient number of trading rules are examined, some of them are bound, purely by chance alone, to generate statistically significant positive returns. Intra-generational data snooping is said to occur when, over a long period of time, technical trading rules that 'worked' in the past continue to be examined, while the ones that did not fade away. Researchers are then made aware of only the rules that worked, and not the other, perhaps thousands, of rules that failed.

Data snooping biases are apparent in other aspects of estimation and testing in finance. Lo and MacKinlay (1990) find that tests of financial asset pricing models (CAPM) may yield misleading inferences when properties of the data are used to construct the test statistics. These properties relate to the construction of portfolios based on some empirically motivated characteristic of the stock, such as market capitalisation, rather than a theoretically motivated characteristic, such as dividend yield.

Sullivan, Timmermann and White (1999) and White (2000) propose the use of a bootstrap to test for data snooping. The technique works by placing the rule under study in the context of a 'universe' of broadly similar trading rules. This gives some empirical content to the notion that a variety of rules may have been examined before the final rule is selected. The bootstrap is applied to each trading rule, by sampling with replacement from the time series of observed returns for that rule. The null hypothesis is that there does not exist a superior technical trading rule. Sullivan, Timmermann and White show how a p-value of the 'reality check' bootstrap-based test can be constructed, which evaluates the significance of the returns (or excess returns) to the rule after allowing for the fact that the whole universe of rules may have been examined.

> **Box 13.2   Re-sampling the data**
>
> (1)   Generate a sample of size T from the original data by sampling with replacement from the whole rows taken together (that is, if observation 32 is selected, take y_{32} and all values of the explanatory variables for observation 32).
> (2)   Calculate $\hat{\beta}^*$, the coefficient matrix for this bootstrap sample.
> (3)   Go back to stage 1 and generate another sample of size T. Repeat these stages a total of N times. A set of N coefficient vectors, $\hat{\beta}^*$, will thus be obtained and in general they will all be different, so that a distribution of estimates for each coefficient will result.

13.4.1   An example of bootstrapping in a regression context

Consider a standard regression model

$$y = X\beta + u \tag{13.9}$$

The regression model can be bootstrapped in two ways.

Re-sample the data

This procedure involves taking the data, and sampling the entire rows corresponding to observation i together. The steps would then be as shown in box 13.2.

A methodological problem with this approach is that it entails sampling from the regressors, and yet under the CLRM, these are supposed to be fixed in repeated samples, which would imply that they do not have a sampling distribution. Thus, resampling from the data corresponding to the explanatory variables is not in the spirit of the CLRM.

As an alternative, the only random influence in the regression is the errors, u, so why not just bootstrap from those?

Re-sampling from the residuals

This procedure is 'theoretically pure' although harder to understand and to implement. The steps are shown in box 13.3.

13.4.2   Situations where the bootstrap will be ineffective

There are at least two situations where the bootstrap, as described above, will not work well.

> ### Box 13.3 Re-sampling from the residuals
>
> (1) Estimate the model on the actual data, obtain the fitted values $\hat{y}$, and calculate the residuals, $\hat{u}$
> (2) Take a sample of size T with replacement from these residuals (and call these $\hat{u}^*$), and generate a bootstrapped-dependent variable by adding the fitted values to the bootstrapped residuals
>
> $$y^* = \hat{y} + \hat{u}^* \qquad (13.10)$$
>
> (3) Then regress this new dependent variable on the original X data to get a bootstrapped coefficient vector, $\hat{\beta}^*$
> (4) Go back to stage 2, and repeat a total of N times.

Outliers in the data

If there are *outliers* in the data, the conclusions of the bootstrap may be affected. In particular, the results for a given replication may depend critically on whether the outliers appear (and how often) in the bootstrapped sample.

Non-independent data

Use of the bootstrap implicitly assumes that the data are *independent of one another*. This would obviously not hold if, for example, there were autocorrelation in the data. A potential solution to this problem is to use a 'moving block bootstrap'. Such a method allows for the dependence in the series by sampling whole blocks of observations at a time. These, and many other issues relating to the theory and practical usage of the bootstrap are given in Davison and Hinkley (1997); see also Efron (1979, 1982).

It is also worth noting that variance reduction techniques are also available under the bootstrap, and these work in a very similar way to those described above in the context of pure simulation.

13.5 Random number generation

Most econometrics computer packages include a random number generator. The simplest class of numbers to generate are from a uniform (0,1) distribution. A uniform (0,1) distribution is one where only values between zero and one are drawn, and each value within the interval has an equal chance of being selected. Uniform draws can be either discrete or continuous. An example of a discrete uniform number generator would be a die or a roulette wheel. Computers generate continuous uniform random number draws.

Numbers that are a continuous uniform $(0,1)$ can be generated according to the following recursion

$$y_{i+1} = (ay_i + c) \text{ modulo } m, i = 0, 1, \ldots, T \tag{13.11}$$

then

$$R_{i+1} = y_{i+1}/m \text{ for } i = 0, 1, \ldots, T \tag{13.12}$$

for T random draws, where y_0 is the seed (the initial value of y), a is a multiplier and c is an increment. All three of these are simply constants. The 'modulo operator' simply functions as a clock, returning to one after reaching m.

Any simulation study involving a recursion, such as that described by (13.11) to generate the random draws, will require the user to specify an initial value, y_0, to get the process started. The choice of this value will, undesirably, affect the properties of the generated series. This effect will be strongest for $y_1, y_2, \ldots$, but will gradually die away. For example, if a set of random draws is used to construct a time series that follows a GARCH process, early observations on this series will behave less like the GARCH process required than subsequent data points. Consequently, a good simulation design will allow for this phenomenon by generating more data than are required and then dropping the first few observations. For example, if 1,000 observations are required, 1,200 observations might be generated, with observations 1 to 200 subsequently deleted and 201 to 1,200 used to conduct the analysis.

These computer-generated random number draws are known as *pseudo-random numbers*, since they are in fact not random at all, but entirely deterministic, since they have been derived from an exact formula! By carefully choosing the values of the user-adjustable parameters, it is possible to get the pseudo-random number generator to meet all the statistical properties of true random numbers. Eventually, the random number sequences will start to repeat, but this should take a long time to happen. See Press *et al.* (1992) for more details and Fortran code, or Greene (2002) for an example.

The U(0,1) draws can be transformed into draws from any desired distribution – for example a normal or a Student's t. Usually, econometric software packages with simulations facilities would do this automatically.

13.6 Disadvantages of the simulation approach to econometric or financial problem solving

- *It might be computationally expensive*

  That is, the number of replications required to generate precise solutions may be very large, depending upon the nature of the task at hand. If each replication is relatively complex in terms of estimation issues, the problem might be computationally infeasible, such that it could take days, weeks or even years to run the experiment. Although CPU time is becoming ever cheaper as faster computers are brought to market, the technicality of the problems studied seems to accelerate just as quickly!

- *The results might not be precise*
  Even if the number of replications is made very large, the simulation experiments will not give a precise answer to the problem if some unrealistic assumptions have been made of the data generating process. For example, in the context of option pricing, the option valuations obtained from a simulation will not be accurate if the data generating process assumed normally distributed errors while the actual underlying returns series is fat-tailed.

- *The results are often hard to replicate*
  Unless the experiment has been set up so that the sequence of random draws is known and can be reconstructed, which is rarely done in practice, the results of a Monte Carlo study will be somewhat specific to the given investigation. In that case, a repeat of the experiment would involve different sets of random draws and therefore would be likely to yield different results, particularly if the number of replications is small.

- *Simulation results are experiment-specific*
  The need to specify the data generating process using a single set of equations or a single equation implies that the results could apply to only that exact type of data. Any conclusions reached may or may not hold for other data generating processes. To give one illustration, examining the power of a statistical test would, by definition, involve determining how frequently a wrong null hypothesis is rejected. In the context of DF tests, for example, the power of the test as determined by a Monte Carlo study would be given by the percentage of times that the null of a unit root is rejected. Suppose that the following data generating process is used for such a simulation experiment

$$y_t = 0.99y_{t-1} + u_t, \qquad u_t \sim N(0, 1) \tag{13.13}$$

Clearly, the null of a unit root would be wrong in this case, as is necessary to examine the power of the test. However, for modest sample sizes, the null is likely to be rejected quite infrequently. It would not be appropriate to conclude from such an experiment that the DF test is generally not powerful, since in this case the null ($\phi = 1$) is not very wrong! This is a general problem with many Monte Carlo studies. The solution is to run simulations using as many different and relevant data generating processes as feasible. Finally, it should be obvious that the Monte Carlo data generating process should match the real-world problem of interest as far as possible.

To conclude, simulation is an extremely useful tool that can be applied to an enormous variety of problems. The technique has grown in popularity over the past decade, and continues to do so. However, like all tools, it is dangerous in the wrong hands. It is very easy to jump into a simulation experiment without thinking about whether such an approach is valid or not.

An example of Monte Carlo simulation in econometrics: deriving a set of critical values for a Dickey–Fuller test

Recall, that the equation for a Dickey–Fuller (DF) test applied to some series y_t is the regression

$$y_t = \phi y_{t-1} + u_t \tag{13.14}$$

so that the test is one of H_0: $\phi = 1$ against H_1: $\phi < 1$. The relevant test statistic is given by

$$\tau = \frac{\hat{\phi} - 1}{SE(\hat{\phi})} \tag{13.15}$$

Under the null hypothesis of a unit root, the test statistic does not follow a standard distribution, and therefore a simulation would be required to obtain the relevant critical values. Obviously, these critical values are well documented, but it is of interest to see how one could generate them. A very similar approach could then potentially be adopted for situations where there has been less research and where the results are relatively less well known.

The simulation would be conducted in the four steps shown in box 13.4. Some EViews code for conducting such a simulation is given below. The objective is to develop a set of critical values for Dickey–Fuller test regressions. The simulation framework considers sample sizes of 1,000, 500 and 100 observations. For each of these sample sizes, regressions with no constant or trend, a constant but no trend, and a constant and trend are conducted. 50,000 replications are used in each case, and the critical values for a one-sided test at the 1%, 5% and 10% levels are determined. The code can be found pre-written in a file entitled 'dfcv.prg'.

EViews programs are simply sets of instructions saved as plain text, so that they can be written from within EViews, or using a word processor or text editor. EViews program files must have a '.PRG' suffix. There are several ways to run the programs once written, but probably the simplest is to write all of the instructions first, and to save them. Then open the EViews software and choose **File, Open and Programs. . .** , and when prompted select the directory and file for the instructions. The program containing the instructions will then appear on the screen. To run the program, click on the **Run** button. EViews will then open a dialog box with several options, including whether to run the program in 'Verbose' or 'Quiet' mode. Choose Verbose mode to see the instruction line that is being run at each point in its execution (i.e. the screen is continually updated). This is useful for debugging programs or for running short programs. Choose Quiet to run the program without updating the screen display as it is running, which will make it execute (considerably) more quickly. The screen would appear as in screenshot 13.1.

Then click **OK** and off it goes! The following lists the instructions that are contained in the program, and the discussion below explains what each line does.

Box 13.4   Setting up a Monte Carlo simulation

(1) Construct the data generating process under the null hypothesis – that is, obtain a series for y that follows a unit root process. This would be done by:

- Drawing a series of length T, the required number of observations, from a normal distribution. This will be the error series, so that $u_t \sim N(0,1)$.
- Assuming a first value for y, i.e. a value for y at time $t = 1$.
- Constructing the series for y recursively, starting with y_2, y_3, and so on

$$y_2 = y_1 + u_2$$
$$y_3 = y_2 + u_3$$ (13.16)
$$\cdots$$
$$y_T = y_{T-1} + u_T$$

(2) Calculating the test statistic, τ.

(3) Repeating steps 1 and 2 N times to obtain N replications of the experiment. A distribution of values for τ will be obtained across the replications.

(4) Ordering the set of N values of τ from the lowest to the highest. The relevant 5% critical value will be the 5th percentile of this distribution.

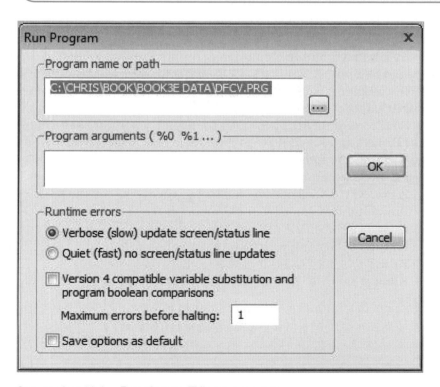

Screenshot 13.1   **Running an EViews program**

```
'NEW WORKFILE CREATED CALLED DF_CV, UNDATED
'WITH 50000 OBSERVATIONS
    WORKFILE DF_CV U 50000
    RNDSEED 12345
    SERIES T1
    SERIES T2
    SERIES T3
    SCALAR K1
    SCALAR K2
    SCALAR K3
    SCALAR K4
    SCALAR K5
    SCALAR K6
    SCALAR K7
    SCALAR K8
    SCALAR K9
    !NREPS=50000
    !NOBS=1000
    FOR !REPC=1 TO !NREPS
    SMPL @FIRST @FIRST
    SERIES Y1=0
    SMPL @FIRST+1   !NOBS+200
    SERIES Y1=Y1(-1)+NRND
    SERIES DY1=Y1-Y1(-1)
    SMPL @FIRST+200   !NOBS+200
    EQUATION EQ1.LS DY1 Y1(-1)
    T1(!REPC)=@TSTATS(1)
    EQUATION EQ2.LS DY1 C Y1(-1)
    T2(!REPC)=@TSTATS(2)
    EQUATION EQ3.LS DY1 C @TREND Y1(-1)
    T3(!REPC)=@TSTATS(3)
    NEXT
    SMPL @FIRST !NREPS
    K1=@QUANTILE(T1,0.01)
    K2=@QUANTILE(T1,0.05)
    K3=@QUANTILE(T1,0.1)
    K4=@QUANTILE(T2,0.01)
    K5=@QUANTILE(T2,0.05)
    K6=@QUANTILE(T2,0.1)
    K7=@QUANTILE(T3,0.01)
    K8=@QUANTILE(T3,0.05)
    K9=@QUANTILE(T3,0.1)
```

Although there are probably more efficient ways to structure the program than that given above, this sample code has been written in a style to make it easy to follow. The program would be run in the way described above. That is, it would be opened from within EViews, and then the Run button would be pressed and the mode of execution (Verbose or Quiet) chosen.

A first point to note is that comment lines are denoted by a ' symbol in EViews. The first line of code, 'WORKFILE DF_CV U 50000' will set up a new EViews workfile called DF_CV.WK1, which will be undated (U) and will contain series of length 50,000. This step is required for EViews to have a place to put the output series since no other workfile will be opened by this program! In situations where the program requires an already existing workfile containing data to be opened, this line would not be necessary since any new results and objects created would be appended to the original workfile. RNDSEED 12345 sets the random number seed that will be used to start the random draws.

'SERIES T1' creates a new series T1 that will be filled with NA elements. The series T1, T2 and T3, will hold the Dickey–Fuller test statistics for each replication, for the three cases (no constant or trend, constant but no trend, constant and trend, respectively). 'SCALAR K1' sets up a scalar (single number) K1. K1, ..., K9 will be used to hold the 1%, 5% and 10% critical values for each of the three cases. !NREPS=50000 and !NOBS=1000 set the number of replications that will be used to 50,000 and the number of observations to be used in each time series to 1,000. The exclamation marks enable the scalars to be used without previously having to define them using the SCALAR instruction. Of course, these values can be changed as desired. Loops in EViews are defined as FOR at the start and NEXT at the end, in a similar way to visual basic code. Thus FOR !REPC=1 TO !NREPS starts the main replications loop, which will run from 1 to NREPS.

```
SMPL @FIRST @FIRST
SERIES Y1=0
```

The two lines above set the first observation of a new series Y1 to zero (so @FIRST is EViews method of denoting the first observation in the series, and the final observation is denoted by, you guessed it, @LAST). Then

```
SMPL @FIRST+1 !NOBS+200
SERIES Y1=Y1(−1)+NRND
SERIES DY1=Y1-Y1(−1)
```

will set the sample to run from observation 2 to observation !NOBS+200 (1200). This enables the program to generate 200 additional startup observations. It is very easy in EViews to construct a series following a random walk process, and this is done by the second of the above three lines. The current value of Y1 is set to the previous value plus a standard normal random draw (NRND). In EViews, draws can be taken from a wide array of distributions (see the User Guide). SERIES DY1 . . . creates a new series called DY1 that contains the first difference of Y.

```
SMPL @FIRST+200 !NOBS+200
EQUATION EQ1.LS DY1 Y1(−1)
```

The first of the two lines above sets the sample to run from observation 201 to observation 1200, thus dropping the 200 startup observations. The following line actually conducts an OLS estimation ('.LS'), in the process creating an equation object called EQ1. The dependent variable is DY1 and the independent variable is the lagged value of Y, Y(−1).

Following the equation estimation, several new quantities will have been created. These quantities are denoted by a '@' in EViews. So the line 'T1(!REPC)=@TSTATS(1)' will take the t-ratio of the coefficient on the first (and in this case only) independent variable, and will place it in the !REPC row of the series T1. Similarly, the t-ratios on the lagged value of Y will be placed in T2 and T3 for the regressions with constant and constant and trend respectively. Finally, NEXT will finish the replications loop and SMPL @FIRST !NREPS will set the sample to run from 1 to 50,000, and the 1%, 5%, and 10% critical values for the no constant or trend case will then be found in K1, K2 and K3. The '@QUANTILE(T1,0.01)' instruction will take the 1% quantile from the series T1, which avoids sorting the series.

The critical value obtained by running the above instructions, which are virtually identical to those found in the statistical tables at the end of this book, are (to two decimal places)

	1%	5%	10%
No constant or trend	−2.58	−1.95	−1.63
Constant but no trend	−3.45	−2.85	−2.56
Constant and trend	−3.93	−3.41	−3.43

This is to be expected, for the use of 50,000 replications should ensure that an approximation to the asymptotic behaviour is obtained. For example, the 5% critical value for a test regression with no constant or trend and 500 observations is −1.945 in this simulation, and −1.95 in Fuller (1976). Although the Dickey–Fuller simulation was unnecessary in the sense that the critical values for the resulting test statistics are already well known and documented, a very similar procedure could be adopted for a variety of problems. For example, a similar approach could be used for constructing critical values or for evaluating the performance of statistical tests in various situations.

13.8 An example of how to simulate the price of a financial option

A simple example of how to use a Monte Carlo study for obtaining a price for a financial option is shown below. Although the option used for illustration here is just a plain vanilla European call option which could be valued analytically using the standard Black–Scholes (1973) formula, again, the method is sufficiently general that only relatively minor modifications would be required to value more complex options. Boyle (1977) gives an excellent and highly readable introduction to the pricing of financial options using Monte Carlo. The steps involved are shown in box 13.5.

> ## Box 13.5 Simulating the price of an Asian option
>
> (1) *Specify a data generating process for the underlying asset.* A random walk with drift model is usually assumed. Specify also the assumed size of the drift component and the assumed size of the volatility parameter. Specify also a strike price K, and a time to maturity, T.
> (2) Draw a series of length T, the required number of observations for the life of the option, from a normal distribution. This will be the *error series*, so that $\varepsilon_t \sim N(0, 1)$.
> (3) Form a series of observations of length T on the *underlying asset.*
> (4) *Observe the price of the underlying asset at maturity observation T.* For a call option, if the value of the underlying asset on maturity date, $P_T \leq K$, the option expires worthless for this replication. If the value of the underlying asset on maturity date, $P_T > K$, the option expires in the money, and has value on that date equal to $P_T - K$, which should be discounted back to the present day using the risk-free rate. Use of the risk-free rate relies upon risk-neutrality arguments (see Duffie, 1996).
> (5) Repeat steps 1 to 4 a total of N times, and take the average value of the option over the N replications. This average will be the *price of the option.*

13.8.1 Simulating the price of a financial option using a fat-tailed underlying process

A fairly limiting and unrealistic assumption in the above methodology for pricing options is that the underlying asset returns are normally distributed, whereas in practice, it is well know that asset returns are fat-tailed. There are several ways to remove this assumption. First, one could employ draws from a fat-tailed distribution, such as a Student's t, in step 2 above. Another method, which would generate a distribution of returns with fat tails, would be to assume that the errors and therefore the returns follow a GARCH process. To generate draws from a GARCH process, do the steps shown in box 13.6.

13.8.2 Simulating the price of an Asian option

An Asian option is one whose payoff depends upon the average value of the underlying asset over the averaging horizon specified in the contract. Most Asian options contracts specify that arithmetic rather than geometric averaging should be employed. Unfortunately, the arithmetic average of a unit root process with a drift is not well defined. Additionally, even if the asset prices are assumed to be log-normally distributed, the arithmetic average of them will not be. Consequently, a closed-form analytical expression for the value of an Asian option has yet to

---

Box 13.6 Generating draws from a GARCH process

(1) Draw a series of length T, the required number of observations for the life of the option, from a normal distribution. This will be the error series, so that $\varepsilon_t \sim N(0, 1)$.

(2) Recall that one way of expressing a GARCH model is

$$r_t = \mu + u_t \qquad u_t = \varepsilon_t \sigma_t \qquad \varepsilon_t \sim N(0, 1) \tag{13.17}$$

$$\sigma_t^2 = \alpha_0 + \alpha_1 u_{t-1}^2 + \beta \sigma_{t-1}^2 \tag{13.18}$$

A series of ε_t, have been constructed and it is necessary to specify initialising values y_1 and σ_1^2 and plausible parameter values for α_0, α_1, β. Assume that y_1 and σ_1^2 are set to μ and one, respectively, and the parameters are given by $\alpha_0 = 0.01$, $\alpha_1 = 0.15$, $\beta = 0.80$. The equations above can then be used to generate the model for r_t as described above.

---

be developed. Thus, the pricing of Asian options represents a natural application for simulations methods. Determining the value of an Asian option is achieved in almost exactly the same way as for a vanilla call or put. The simulation is conducted identically, and the only difference occurs in the very last step where the value of the payoff at the date of expiry is determined.

13.8.3 Pricing Asian options using EViews

A sample of EViews code for determining the value of an Asian option is given below. The example is in the context of an arithmetic Asian option on the FTSE 100, and two simulations will be undertaken with different strike prices (one that is out of the money forward and one that is in the money forward). In each case, the life of the option is six months, with daily averaging commencing immediately, and the option value is given for both calls and puts in terms of index points. The parameters are given as follows, with dividend yield and risk-free rates expressed as percentages:

Simulation 1: strike=6500, risk-free=6.24, dividend yield=2.42, 'today's' FTSE=6289.70, forward price=6405.35, implied volatility=26.52
Simulation 2: strike=5500, risk-free=6.24, dividend yield=2.42, 'today's' FTSE=6289.70, forward price=6405.35, implied volatility=34.33

Any other programming language or statistical package would be equally applicable, since all that is required is a Gaussian random number generator, the ability to store in arrays and to loop. Since no actual estimation is performed, differences between packages are likely to be negligible. All experiments are based on 25,000 replications and their antithetic variates (total: 50,000 sets of draws) to reduce Monte Carlo sampling error.

Some sample code for pricing an ASIAN option for normally distributed errors using EViews is given as follows:

```
'UNDATED WORKFILE CREATED CALLED ASIAN_P
'WITH 50000 OBSERVATIONS
WORKFILE ASIAN_P U 50000
RNDSEED 12345
!N=125
!TTM=0.5
!NREPS=50000
!IV=0.28
!RF=0.0624
!DY=0.0242
!DT=!TTM / !N
!DRIFT=(!RF-!DY-(!IV^2/2.0))*!DT
!VSQRDT=!IV*(!DT^0.5)
!K=5500
!S0=6289.7
SERIES APVAL
SERIES ACVAL
SERIES SPOT
SCALAR AV
SCALAR CALLPRICE
SCALAR PUTPRICE
SERIES RANDS
'GENERATES THE DATA
FOR !REPC=1 TO !NREPS STEP 2
RANDS=NRND
SERIES SPOT=0
SMPL @FIRST @FIRST
SPOT(1)=!S0*EXP(!DRIFT+!VSQRDT*RANDS(1))
SMPL 2 !N
SPOT=SPOT(-1)*EXP(!DRIFT+!VSQRDT*RANDS(!N))
'COMPUTE THE DAILY AVERAGE
SMPL @FIRST !N
AV=@MEAN(SPOT)
IF AV>!K THEN
    ACVAL(!REPC)=(AV-!K)*EXP(-!RF*!TTM)
ELSE
    ACVAL(!REPC)=0
ENDIF
IF AV<!K THEN
    APVAL(!REPC)=(!K-AV)*EXP(-!RF*!TTM)
```

```
ELSE
    APVAL(!REPC)=0
ENDIF
RANDS=-RANDS
SERIES SPOT=0
SMPL @FIRST @FIRST
SPOT(1)=!S0*EXP(!DRIFT+!VSQRDT*RANDS(1))
SMPL 2 !N
SPOT=SPOT(-1)*EXP(!DRIFT+!VSQRDT*RANDS(!N))
'COMPUTE THE DAILY AVERAGE
SMPL @FIRST !N
AV=@MEAN(SPOT)
IF AV>!K THEN
    ACVAL(!REPC+1)=(AV-!K)*EXP(-!RF*!TTM)
ELSE
    ACVAL(!REPC+1)=0
ENDIF
IF AV<!K THEN
    APVAL(!REPC+1)=(!K-AV)*EXP(-!RF*!TTM)
ELSE
    APVAL(!REPC+1)=0
ENDIF
NEXT
SMPL @FIRST !NREPS
CALLPRICE=@MEAN(ACVAL)
PUTPRICE=@MEAN(APVAL)
```

Many parts of the program above use identical instructions to those given for the DF critical value simulation, and so annotation will now focus on the construction of the program and on previously unseen commands. The first block of commands set up a new workfile called 'ASIAN_P' that will hold all of the objects and output. Then the following lines specify the parameters for the simulation of the path of the price of the underlying asset (the drift, the implied volatility, etc.).

'!=DT=!TTM/!N' splits the time to maturity (0.5 years) into N discrete time periods. Since daily averaging is required, it is easiest to set N = 125 (the approximate number of trading days in half a year), so that each time period DT represents one day. The model assumes under a risk-neutral measure that the underlying asset price follows a geometric Brownian motion, which is given by

$$dS = (rf - dy) \, Sdt + \sigma Sdz \tag{13.19}$$

where dz is the increment of a Brownian motion. Further details of this continuous time representation of the movement of the underlying asset over time are beyond the scope of this book. A treatment of this and many other useful option pricing formulae and computer code are given in Haug (1998), and an accessible discussion is given in Hull (2011). The discrete time approximation to this for a time step of one can be written

$$S_t = S_{t-1} \exp\left[\left(rf - dy - \frac{1}{2}\sigma^2 \right) dt + \sigma \sqrt{dt}\, u_t \right] \tag{13.20}$$

where u_t is a white noise error process. The following instructions set up the arrays for the underlying spot price (called 'SPOT'), and for the discounted values of the put ('APVAL') and call ('ACVAL'). Note that by default, arrays of the length given by the 'workfile' definition statement (50000) will be created.

The command 'FOR !REPC=1 TO !NREPS DO REPC=1, NREPS,2' starts the main do loop for the simulation, looping up to the number of replications, in steps of 2. The loop ends at 'END DO REPC'. Steps of 2 are used because antithetic variates are also used for each replication, which will create another simulated path for the underlying asset prices and option value.

The random N(0,1) draws are made, which are then constructed into a series of future prices of the underlying asset for the next 125 days. 'AV=@MEAN(SPOT)' will compute the average price of the underlying over the lifetime of the option (125 days). The following two statements construct the terminal payoffs for the call and the put options respectively. For the call, 'ACVAL' is set to the average underlying price less the strike price if the average is greater than the strike (i.e. if the option expires in the money), and zero otherwise. Vice versa for the put. The payoff at expiry is discounted back to the present using the risk-free rate, and placed in the REPC row of the 'ACVAL' or 'APVAL' array for the calls and puts, respectively.

The process then repeats using the antithetic variates, constructed using 'RANDS=-RANDS'. The call and put present values for these paths are put in the even rows of 'ACVAL' and 'APVAL'.

This completes one cycle of the REPC loop, which starts again with REPC=3, then 5, 7, 9, ..., 49999. The result will be two arrays 'ACVAL' and 'APVAL', which will contain 50,000 rows comprising the present value of the call and put option for each simulated path. The option prices would then simply be given by the averages over the 50,000 replications.

Note that both call values and put values can be calculated easily from a given simulation, since the most computationally expensive step is in deriving the path of simulated prices for the underlying asset. The results are given in table 10.1, along with the values derived from an analytical approximation to the option price, derived by Levy, and estimated using VBA code in Haug (1998, pp. 97–100).

The main difference between the way that the simulation is conducted here and the method used for EViews simulation of the Dickey–Fuller critical values is that here, the random numbers are generated by opening a new series called 'RANDS' and filling it with the random number draws. The reason that this must be done is so that the negatives of the elements of RANDS can later be taken to form the antithetic variates. Finally, for each replication, the IF clause will set out of the money call prices (where K>AV) and out of the money put prices (K<AV) to zero. Then the call and put prices for each replication are discounted back to the present using the risk-free rate, and outside the replications loop,

the options prices are the averages of these discounted prices across the 50,000 replications.

The workfile 'ASIAN_P' will contain quite a few objects by the end of the simulation, including the scalars CALLPRICE and PUTPRICE, which will be the call and put prices. Also, the series ACVAL and APVAL will contain the current value of the option for each of the 50,000 simulated paths. Having the whole series across all replications can be useful for constructing standard errors, and for checking that the program appears to have been working correctly.

Applying the instructions above (with K = 5500, and implied volatility at 28%) gives simulated call and put prices as given in the following table.

Strike = 6500, IV = 26.52		Strike = 5500, IV = 34.33	
CALL	Price	CALL	Price
Analytical Approximation	203.45	Analytical Approximation	888.55
Monte Carlo Normal	204.22	Monte Carlo Normal	885.29
PUT	Price	PUT	Price
Analytical Approximation	348.7	Analytical Approximation	64.52
Monte Carlo Normal	349.43	Monte Carlo Normal	61.52

In both cases, the simulated options prices are quite close to the analytical approximations, although the Monte Carlo seems to overvalue the out-of-the-money call and to undervalue the out-of-the-money put. Some of the errors in the simulated prices relative to the analytical approximation may result from the use of a discrete-time averaging process using only 125 points.

13.9 An example of bootstrapping to calculate capital risk requirements

13.9.1 Financial motivation

Risk management modelling has, in this author's opinion, been one of the most rapidly developing areas of application of econometric techniques over the past decade or so. One of the most popular approaches to risk measurement is by calculating what is known as an institution's 'value-at-risk', denoted VaR. Broadly speaking, value-at-risk is an estimation of the *probability of likely losses which could arise from changes in market prices*. More precisely, it is defined as the money-loss of a portfolio that is expected to occur over a pre-determined horizon and with a pre-determined degree of confidence. The roots of VaR's popularity stem from the simplicity of its calculation, its ease of interpretation and from the fact that VaR can be suitably aggregated across an entire firm to produce a single number which broadly encompasses the risk of the positions of the firm as a whole. The value-at-risk estimate is also often known as the position risk requirement or minimum capital risk requirement (MCRR); the three terms will be used interchangeably in the exposition below. There are various methods available for calculating value-at-risk, including the 'delta-normal' method; historical simulation, involving the estimation of the quantile of returns of the portfolio; and structured Monte Carlo simulation; see Dowd (1998) or Jorion (2006) for thorough introductions to value-at-risk.

The *Monte Carlo* approach involves two steps. First, a data generating process is specified for the underlying assets in the portfolio. Second, possible future paths are simulated for those assets over given horizons, and the value of the portfolio at the end of the period is examined. Thus the returns for each simulated path are obtained, and from this distribution across the Monte Carlo replications, the VaR as a percentage of the initial value of the portfolio can be measured as the first or fifth percentile.

The Monte Carlo method is clearly a very powerful and flexible method for generating VaR estimates, since any stochastic process for the underlying assets can be specified. The effect of increasing variances or correlations, etc. can easily be incorporated into the simulation design. However, there are at least two drawbacks with the use of Monte Carlo simulation for estimating VaR. First, for a large portfolio, the computational time required to compute the VaR may be excessively great. Second, and more fundamentally, the calculated VaR may be inaccurate if the stochastic process that has been assumed for the underlying asset is inappropriate. In particular, asset prices are often assumed to follow a random walk or a random walk with drift, where the driving disturbances are random draws from a normal distribution. Since it is well known that asset returns are fat-tailed, the use of Gaussian draws in the simulation is likely to lead to a systematic underestimate of the VaR, as extremely large positive or negative returns are more likely in practice than would arise under a normal distribution. Of course, the normal random draws could be replaced by draws from a *t*-distribution, or the returns could be assumed to follow a GARCH process, both of which would generate an unconditional distribution of returns with fat tails. However, there is still some concern as to whether the distribution assumed in designing the simulations framework is really appropriate.

An alternative approach, that could potentially overcome this criticism, would be to use bootstrapping rather than Monte Carlo simulation. In this context, the future simulated prices are generated using random draws with replacement from the actual returns themselves, rather than artificially generating the disturbances from an assumed distribution. Such an approach is used in calculating MCRRs by Hsieh (1993) and by Brooks, Clare and Persand (2000). The methodology proposed by Hsieh will now be examined.

Hsieh (1993) employs daily log returns on foreign currency (against the US dollar) futures series from 22 February 1985 until 9 March 1990 (1,275 observations) for the British pound (denoted BP), the German mark (DM), the Japanese yen (JY) and the Swiss franc (SF). The first stage in setting up the bootstrapping framework is to form a model that fits the data and adequately describes its features. Hsieh employs the BDS test (discussed briefly in chapter 9) to determine an appropriate class of models. An application of the test to the raw returns data shows that the data are not random, and that there is some structure in the data. The dependence in the series, shown in the rejection of randomness by the test implies that there is either:

- a linear relationship between y_t and $y_{t-1}, y_{t-2}, \ldots$ or
- a non-linear relationship between y_t and $y_{t-1}, y_{t-2}, \ldots$

The Box–Pierce Q test is applied to test for both, on the returns for the former, and on the squared or absolute values of the returns for the latter. The results of this test are not shown but effectively rule out the possibility of linear dependence (so that, for example, an ARMA model would not be appropriate for the returns), but there appears to be evidence of non-linear dependence in the series. Therefore, a second question, is whether the non-linearity is in-mean or in-variance (see chapter 8 for elucidation). Hsieh uses a bicorrelation test to show that there is no evidence for non-linearity in-mean. Therefore, the most appropriate class of models for the returns series is a model which has time-varying (conditional) variances. Hsieh employs two types of model: EGARCH and autoregressive volatility (ARV) models. The coefficient estimates for the EGARCH model are reported in table 13.1.

Several features of the EGARCH estimates are worth noting. First, as one may anticipate for a set of currency futures returns, the asymmetry terms (i.e. the estimated values of γ) are not significant for any of the four series. The high estimated values of β suggest a high degree of persistence in volatility in all cases except the Japanese yen. Brooks, Clare and Persand (2000) suggest that such persistence may be excessive in the sense that the volatility implied by the estimated conditional variance is too persistent to reproduce the profile of the volatility of the actual returns series. Such excessive volatility persistence could lead to an overestimate of the VaR. Leaving this issue aside, Hsieh continues to evaluate the effectiveness of the EGARCH models in capturing all of the non-linear dependence in the data. This is achieved by reapplying the BDS test to the standardised residuals, constructed by taking the residuals from the estimated models, and dividing them by their respective conditional standard deviations. If the model has captured all of the important features of the data, the standardised residual series should be completely random. It is observed that the EGARCH model cannot capture all of the non-linear dependence in the mark or franc series.

A second approach to modelling volatility is derived from a high/low volatility estimator. A daily volatility series is thus constructed using a re-scaled estimate of the range over the trading day

$$\sigma_{P,t} = (0.361 \times 1440/M)^{1/2} \log(High_t/Low_t) \tag{13.21}$$

where $High_t$ and Low_t are the highest and lowest transacted prices on day t and M is the number of trading minutes during the day. The volatility series, $\sigma_{P,t}$ can now be modelled as any other series. A natural model to propose, given the dependence

$$x_t = \mu + \sigma_t \eta_t$$

$$\eta_t \sim N(0, 1)$$

$$\log \sigma_t^2 = \alpha + \beta \log \sigma_{t-1}^2 + \phi(|\eta_{t-1}| - (2/\pi)^{1/2}) + \gamma \eta_{t-1}$$

Coefficient	BP	DM	JY	SF
μ	0.000319	0.000377	0.000232	0.000239
	(0.000208)	(0.000214)	(0.000189)	(0.000235)
α	−0.688127	−1.072229	−4.438289	−0.993241
	(0.030088)	(0.041828)	(0.756704)	(0.032479)
β	0.928780	0.889511	0.550707	0.895527
	(0.002995)	(0.004386)	(0.075851)	(0.003508)
ϕ	0.135854	0.187005	0.282167	0.157669
	(0.019961)	(0.028388)	(0.093357)	(0.024013)
γ	−0.110718	0.084173	0.313274	0.129035
	(0.177458)	(0.147279)	(0.201531)	(0.166507)

Notes: Standard errors in parentheses.
Source: Hsieh (1993). Reprinted with the permission of School of Business Administration, University of Washington.

(or persistence) in volatility over time, is an autoregressive model in the volatility. The formulation used for the price series is known as an autoregressive volatility (ARV) model

$$x_t = \sigma_{P,t} u_t \tag{13.22}$$

$$\ln \sigma_{P,t} = \alpha + \sum_i \beta_i \ln \sigma_{P,t-i} + v_t \tag{13.23}$$

where v_t is an error term. The appropriate lag length for the ARV model is determined using Schwarz's information criterion, which suggests that 8, 8, 5 and 8 lags should be used for the pound, mark, yen and franc series, respectively. The coefficient estimates for the ARV models are given in table 13.2.

The degrees of persistence for each exchange rate series implied by the ARV estimates is given by the sums of the β coefficients, which are 0.78, 0.76, 0.62, 0.74, respectively. These figures are high, although less so than under the EGARCH formulation. The standardised residuals from this model are given by $x_t / \hat{\sigma}_{P,t}$, where $\hat{\sigma}_{P,t}$ are the fitted values of volatility. An application of the BDS test to these standardised residuals shows no evidence of further structure apart from

Table 13.2 Autoregressive volatility estimates for currency futures returns

$$x_t = \sigma_{P,t} u_t$$

$$\ln \sigma_{P,t} = \alpha + \sum_i \beta_i \ln \sigma_{P,t-i} + v_t$$

Coefficient	BP	DM	JY	SF
α	−1.037	−1.139	−1.874	−1.219
	(0.171)	(0.187)	(0.199)	(0.193)
β_1	0.192	0.153	0.208	0.115
	(0.028)	(0.028)	(0.028)	(0.028)
β_2	0.134	0.111	0.137	0.106
	(0.029)	(0.028)	(0.028)	(0.028)
β_3	0.062	0.052	0.058	0.068
	(0.029)	(0.028)	(0.029)	(0.028)
β_4	0.069	0.092	0.109	0.091
	(0.029)	(0.028)	(0.028)	(0.028)
β_5	0.137	0.091	0.112	0.118
	(0.028)	(0.028)	(0.028)	(0.028)
β_6	0.027	0.072		0.074
	(0.029)	(0.028)		(0.028)
β_7	0.073	0.110		0.086
	(0.028)	(0.028)		(0.028)
β_8	0.088	0.079		0.078
	(0.028)	(0.028)		(0.028)
$\bar{R}^2$	0.274	0.227	0.170	0.193

Source: Hsieh (1993). Reprinted with the permission of School of Business Administration, University of Washington.

in the Swiss franc case, where the test statistics are marginally significant. Thus, since these standardised residuals are iid, it is valid to sample from them using the bootstrap technique.

To summarise, it is concluded that both the EGARCH and ARV models present reasonable descriptions of the futures returns series, which are then employed in conjunction with the bootstrap to estimate the value at risk estimates.

This is achieved by simulating the future values of the futures price series, using the parameter estimates from the two models, and using disturbances obtained by sampling with replacement from the standardised residuals $(\hat{\eta}_t / \hat{h}_t^{1/2})$ for the EGARCH model and from u_t and v_t for ARV models. In this way, 10,000 possible future paths of the series are simulated (i.e. 10,000 replications are used), and in each case, the maximum drawdown (loss) can be calculated over a given holding period by

$$Q = (P_0 - P_1) \times number\ of\ contracts \tag{13.24}$$

where P_0 is the initial value of the position, and P_1 is the lowest simulated price (for a long position) or highest simulated price (for a short position) over the holding period. The maximum loss is calculated assuming holding periods of 1, 5, 10, 15, 20, 25, 30, 60, 90 and 180 days. It is assumed that the futures position is opened on the final day of the sample used to estimate the models, 9 March 1990.

The ninetieth percentile of these 10,000 maximum losses can be taken to obtain a figure for the amount of capital required to cover losses on 90% of days. It is important for firms to consider the maximum daily losses arising from their futures positions, since firms will be required to post additional funds to their margin accounts to cover such losses. If funds are not made available to the margin account, the firm is likely to have to liquidate its futures position, thus destroying any hedging effects that the firm required from the futures contracts in the first place.

However, Hsieh (1993) uses a slightly different approach to the final stage, which is as follows. Assuming (without loss of generality) that the number of contracts held is 1, the following can be written for a long position

$$\frac{Q}{x_0} = \left(1 - \frac{x_1}{x_0}\right) \tag{13.25}$$

or

$$\frac{Q}{x_0} = \left(\frac{x_1}{x_0} - 1\right) \tag{13.26}$$

for a short position. x_1 is defined as the minimum price for a long position (or the maximum price for a short position) over the horizon that the position is held. In either case, since x_0 is a constant, the distribution of Q will depend on the distribution of x_1. Hsieh (1993) assumes that prices are lognormally distributed, i.e. that the logs of the ratios of the prices,

$$\ln\left(\frac{x_1}{x_0}\right)$$

are normally distributed. This being the case, an alternative estimate of the fifth percentile of the distribution of returns can be obtained by taking the relevant critical value from the normal statistical tables, multiplying it by the standard deviation and adding it to the mean of the distribution.

The MCRRs estimated using the ARV and EGARCH models are compared with those estimated by bootstrapping from the price changes themselves, termed the 'unconditional density model'. The estimated MCRRs are given in table 13.3.

The entries in table 13.3 refer to the amount of capital required to cover 90% of expected losses, as percentages of the initial values of the positions. For example, according to the EGARCH model, approximately 14% of the initial value of a long position should be held in the case of the yen to cover 90% of expected losses for a 180-day horizon. The results contain several interesting features. First, the MCRRs derived from bootstrapping the price changes themselves (the 'unconditional approach') are in most cases higher than those generated from the other two methods, especially at short investment horizons. This is argued to have occurred owing to the fact that the level of volatility at the start of the MCRR calculation period was low relative to its historical level. Therefore, the conditional estimation methods (EGARCH and ARV) will initially forecast volatility to be lower than the historical average. As the holding period increases from 1 towards 180 days, the MCRR estimates from the ARV model converge upon those of the unconditional densities. On the other hand, those of the EGARCH model do not converge, even after 180 days (in fact, in some cases, the EGARCH MCRR seems oddly to diverge from the unconditionally estimated MCRR as the horizon increases). It is thus argued that the EGARCH model may be inappropriate for MCRR estimation in this application.

It can also be observed that the MCRRs for short positions are larger than those of comparative long positions. This could be attributed to an upward drift in the futures returns over the sample period, suggesting that on average an upwards move in the futures price was slightly more likely than a fall.

A further step in the analysis, which Hsieh did not conduct, but which is shown in Brooks, Clare and Persand (2000), is to evaluate the performance of the MCRR estimates in an out-of-sample period. Such an exercise would evaluate the models by assuming that the MCRR estimated from the model had been employed, and by tracking the change in the value of the position over time. If the MCRR is adequate, the 90% nominal estimate should be sufficient to cover losses on 90% of out-of-sample testing days. Any day where the MCRR is insufficient to cover losses is termed an 'exceedence' or an 'exception'. A model that leads to more than 10% exceptions for a nominal 90% coverage is deemed unacceptable on the grounds that on average, the MCRR was insufficient. Equally, a model that leads to considerably less than the expected 10% exceptions would also be deemed unacceptable on the grounds that the MCRR has been set at an inappropriately high level, leading capital to be unnecessarily tied up in a liquid and unprofitable form. Brooks, Clare and Persand (2000) observe, as Hsieh's results forewarn, that the MCRR estimates from GARCH-type models are too high, leading to considerably fewer exceedences than the nominal proportion.

13.9.2 VaR estimation using bootstrapping in EViews

Following the discussion above concerning the Hsieh (1993) and Brooks, Clare and Persand (2000) approaches to calculating minimum capital risk requirements, the following EViews code can be used to calculate the MCRR for a ten-day holding

Table 13.3 Minimum capital risk requirements for currency futures as a percentage of the initial value of the position

	No. of days	Long position			Short position		
		AR	Unconditional density	EGARCH	AR	Unconditional density	EGARCH
BP	1	0.73	0.91	0.93	0.80	0.98	1.05
	5	1.90	2.30	2.61	2.18	2.76	3.00
	10	2.83	3.27	4.19	3.38	4.22	4.88
	15	3.54	3.94	5.72	4.45	5.48	6.67
	20	4.10	4.61	6.96	5.24	6.33	8.43
	25	4.59	5.15	8.25	6.20	7.36	10.46
	30	5.02	5.58	9.08	7.11	8.33	12.06
	60	7.24	7.44	14.50	11.64	12.87	20.71
	90	8.74	8.70	17.91	15.45	16.90	28.03
	180	11.38	10.67	24.25	25.81	27.36	48.02
DM	1	0.72	0.87	0.83	0.89	1.00	0.95
	5	1.89	2.18	2.34	2.23	2.70	2.91
	10	2.77	3.14	3.93	3.40	4.12	5.03
	15	3.52	3.86	5.37	4.36	5.30	6.92
	20	4.05	4.45	6.54	5.19	6.14	8.91
	25	4.55	4.90	7.86	6.14	7.21	10.69
	30	4.93	5.37	8.75	7.02	7.88	12.36
	60	7.16	7.24	13.14	11.36	12.38	20.86
	90	8.87	8.39	16.06	14.68	16.16	27.75
	180	11.38	10.35	21.69	24.25	26.25	45.68
JY	1	0.56	0.74	0.72	0.68	0.87	0.86
	5	1.61	1.99	2.22	1.92	2.36	2.73
	10	2.59	2.82	3.46	3.06	3.53	4.41
	15	3.30	3.46	4.37	4.11	4.60	5.79
	20	3.95	4.10	5.09	5.13	5.45	6.77
	25	4.42	4.58	5.78	5.91	6.30	7.98
	30	4.95	4.92	6.34	6.58	6.85	8.81
	60	6.99	6.84	8.72	10.53	10.74	13.58
	90	8.43	8.00	10.51	13.61	14.00	17.63
	180	10.97	10.27	13.99	21.86	22.21	27.39

Table 13.3 *(cont.)*

	No. of days	Long position			Short position		
		AR	Unconditional density	EGARCH	AR	Unconditional density	EGARCH
SF	1	0.82	0.97	0.89	0.93	1.12	0.98
	5	1.99	2.51	2.48	2.23	2.93	2.98
	10	2.87	3.60	4.12	3.37	4.53	5.09
	15	3.67	4.35	5.60	4.22	5.67	7.03
	20	4.24	5.10	6.82	5.09	6.69	8.86
	25	4.81	5.65	8.12	5.90	7.77	10.93
	30	5.23	6.20	9.12	6.70	8.47	12.50
	60	7.69	8.41	13.73	10.55	13.10	21.27
	90	9.23	9.93	16.89	13.60	17.06	27.80
	180	12.18	12.57	22.92	21.72	27.45	45.47

Source: Hsieh (1993). Reprinted with the permission of School of Business Administration, University of Washington.

period (the length that regulators require banks to employ) using daily S&P500 data, which is found in the file 'sp500.wf1'. The code is presented, followed by an annotated copy of some of the key lines.

```
'THIS PROGRAM APPLIES THE BOOTSTRAP TO THE
'CALCULATION OF
'MCRR FOR A 10-DAY HORIZON PERIOD
'LOAD WORKFILE
LOAD "D:\CHRIS\BOOK\SP500.WF1"
RNDSEED 12345
!NREPS=10000
SERIES RT
SERIES U
SERIES H
SERIES MIN
SERIES MAX
SERIES L1
SERIES S1
SCALAR MCRRL
SCALAR MCRRS
RT=LOG(SP500/SP500(−1))
EQUATION EQ1.ARCH(M=100,C=1E-5) RT C
```

```
EQ1.MAKEGARCH H
EXPAND 1 10000
SERIES HSQ=H^0.5
SERIES RESI=RT-@COEFS(1)
SERIES SRES=RESI/HSQ
EQ1.FORECAST RTF YSE HF
'BOOTSTRAP LOOP
FOR !Z=1 TO !NREPS
    SMPL 3 2610
    GROUP G1 SRES
    G1.RESAMPLE
    SMPL 2611 2620
    RT=@COEFS(1)+@SQRT(HF(-2610))*SRES_B(-10)
    SP500=SP500(-1)*EXP(RT)
MIN(!Z)=@MIN(SP500)
MAX(!Z)=@MAX(SP500)
NEXT
SMPL 1 10000
'LONG POSITION
L1=LOG(MIN/1138.73)
MCRRL=1-(EXP((-1.645*@STDEV(L1))+@MEAN(L1)))
'SHORT POSITION
S1=LOG(MAX/1138.73)
MCRRS=(EXP((1.645*@STDEV(S1))+@MEAN(S1)))-1
```

Again, annotation of the EViews code above will concentrate on commands that have not been discussed previously. The 'SERIES...' and 'SCALAR...' statements set up the arrays that will hold the series and the scalars (i.e. single numbers) respectively.

Then 'EQUATION EQ1.ARCH(M=100,C=1E-5) RT C' estimates an ARCH model, denoting the equation object created by 'EQ1', and allowing the process to perform up to 100 iterations with a convergence criterion of 10^{-5}, with the dependent variable RT (which is the returns series) and the conditional mean equation containing a constant only. The line 'EQ1.MAKEGARCH H' will generate a series of fitted conditional variance values, denoted by H. The 'EXPAND 1 10000' instruction will increase the size of the arrays in the workfile to 10000 from the original length of the S&P series (2,610 observations).

The three lines SERIES HSQ=H^0.5, SERIES RESI=RT-@COEFS(1) and SERIES SRES=RESI/HSQ will construct a set of standardised residuals.

The next step is to forecast the conditional variances for ten observations 2611 to 2620 using the command 'EQ1.FORECAST RTF YSE HF', which will construct forecasts of the conditional mean (placed into RTF), the conditional standard deviation (YSE) and the conditional variance (HF), respectively.

Next follows the core of the program, which is the bootstrap loop, Z. The number of replications '!NREPS' has been defined as 10,000. The instructions GROUP G1 SRES and G1.RESAMPLE construct a group (in this case, containing only one element SRES), which is then resampled. The re-sampled series is then placed in SRES_B. The future paths of the series over the ten-day holding period are then constructed, and the maximum and minimum price achieved over that period (observations 2611 to 2620) are saved in the arrays MAX and MIN, respectively. Finally, NEXT finishes the bootstrapping loop.

The following SMPL instruction is necessary to reset the sample period used to cover all observation numbers from 1 to 10,000 (i.e. to incorporate all of the 10,000 bootstrap replications). By default, if this statement was not included, EViews would have continued to use the most recent sample statement, conducting analysis using only observations 2611 to 2620:

SMPL   1   10000

The following block of two commands generates the MCRR for the long position. The first stage is to construct the log returns for the maximum loss over the ten-day holding period. Notice that the command will automatically do this calculation for every element of the 'MIN' array – i.e. for all 10,000 replications. In order to use information from all of the replications, and under the assumption that the L1 statistic is normally distributed across the replications, the MCRR can be calculated using the command given (rather than using the fifth percentile of the empirical distribution). This works as follows. Assuming that $\ln(\frac{x_1}{x_0})$ is normally distributed with some mean m and standard deviation sd, a standard normal variable can be constructed by subtracting the mean and dividing by the standard deviation

$$\frac{\ln\left(\frac{x_1}{x_0}\right) - m}{sd} \sim N(0, 1).$$

The 5% lower tail critical value for a standard normal is -1.645, so to find the fifth percentile

$$\frac{\ln\left(\frac{x_1}{x_0}\right) - m}{sd} = -1.645 \tag{13.27}$$

Rearranging (13.27)

$$\frac{x_1}{x_0} = \exp\left[-1.645sd + m\right] \tag{13.28}$$

From (13.25), (13.28) can also be written

$$\frac{Q}{x_0} = 1 - \exp\left[-1.645sd + m\right] \tag{13.29}$$

which will give the maximum loss or draw down on a long position over the simulated ten days. The maximum draw down for a short position will be given by

$$\frac{Q}{x_0} = \exp\left[-1.645sd + m\right] - 1 \tag{13.30}$$

The following two lines then repeat the above procedure, but replacing the 'MIN' array with 'MAX' to calculate the MCRR for a short position: The results that would be generated by running the above program are approximately:

$$MCRR = 0.04035$$

$$MCRR = 0.04814$$

These figures represent the minimum capital risk requirement for a long and short position, respectively, as a percentage of the initial value of the position for 95% coverage over a ten-day horizon. This means that, for example, approximately 4% of the value of a long position held as liquid capital will be sufficient to cover losses on 95% of days if the position is held for ten days. The required capital to cover 95% of losses over a ten-day holding period for a short position in the S&P500 index would be around 4.8%. This is as one would expect since the index had a positive drift over the sample period. Therefore, the index returns are not symmetric about zero as positive returns are slightly more likely than negative returns. Higher capital requirements are thus necessary for a short position since a loss is more likely than for a long position of the same magnitude.

Key concepts

The key terms to be able to define and explain from this chapter are

- simulation
- Monte Carlo sampling variability
- antithetic variates

- bootstrapping
- pseudo-random number
- control variates

Self-study questions

1. (a) Present two examples in finance and two in econometrics (ideally other than those listed in this chapter!) of situations where a simulation approach would be desirable. Explain in each case why simulations are useful.
    (b) Distinguish between pure simulation methods and bootstrapping. What are the relative merits of each technique? Therefore, which situations would benefit more from one technique than the other?
    (c) What are variance reduction techniques? Describe two such techniques and explain how they are used.
    (d) Why is it desirable to conduct simulations using as many replications of the experiment as possible?
    (e) How are random numbers generated by a computer?
    (f) What are the drawbacks of simulation methods relative to analytical approaches, assuming that the latter are available?

2. A researcher tells you that she thinks the properties of the Ljung–Box test (i.e. the size and power) will be adversely affected by ARCH in the data. Design a simulations experiment to test this proposition.

3. (a) Consider the following AR(1) model

$$y_t = \phi y_{t-1} + u_t$$

Design a simulation experiment (with code for EViews) to determine the effect of increasing the value of ϕ from 0 to 1 on the distribution of the t-ratios.

(b) Consider again the AR(1) model from part (a) of this question. As stated in chapter 4, the explanatory variables in a regression model are assumed to be non-stochastic, and yet y_{t-1} is stochastic. The result is that the estimator for ϕ will be biased in small samples. Design a simulation experiment to investigate the effect of the value of ϕ and the sample size on the extent of the bias.

4. A barrier option is a path-dependent option whose payoff depends on whether the underlying asset price traverses a barrier. A knock-out call is a call option that ceases to exist when the underlying price falls below a given barrier level H. Thus the payoff is given by

$$\begin{aligned} \max[0, S_T - K] \quad &\text{if } S_t > H \, \forall \, t \leq T \\ 0 \quad &\text{if } S_t \leq H \text{ for any } t \leq T. \end{aligned}$$

where S_T is the underlying price at expiry date T, and K is the exercise price. Suppose that a knock-out call is written on the FTSE 100 Index. The current index value, $S_0 = 5000$, $K = 5100$, time to maturity $= 1$ year, $H = 4900$, $IV = 25\%$, risk-free rate $= 5\%$, dividend yield $= 2\%$.

Design a Monte Carlo simulation to determine the fair price to pay for this option. Using the same set of random draws, what is the value of an otherwise identical call without a barrier? Design computer code in EViews to test your experiment.

14 Conducting empirical research or doing a project or dissertation in finance

Learning outcomes

In this chapter, you will learn how to
- Choose a suitable topic for an empirical research project in finance
- Draft a research proposal
- Find appropriate sources of literature and data
- Determine a sensible structure for the dissertation
- Set up and conduct a valid event study
- Employ the Fama–MacBeth and Fama–French approaches to testing asset pricing models and explaining the variation in asset returns

14.1 What is an empirical research project and what is it for?

Many courses, at both the undergraduate and postgraduate levels, require or allow the student to conduct a project. This may vary from being effectively an extended essay to a full-scale dissertation or thesis of 10,000 words or more.

Students often approach this part of their degree with much trepidation, although in fact doing a project gives students a unique opportunity to select a topic of interest and to specify the whole project themselves from start to finish. The purpose of a project is usually to determine whether students can define and execute a piece of fairly original research within given time, resource and report-length constraints. In terms of econometrics, conducting empirical research is one of the best ways to get to grips with the theoretical material, and to find out what practical difficulties econometricians encounter when conducting research. Conducting the research gives the investigator the opportunity to solve a puzzle and potentially to uncover something that nobody else has; it can be a highly rewarding experience. In addition, the project allows students to select a topic of direct interest or relevance to them, and is often useful in helping students to develop time-management and report-writing skills. The final document can in many cases provide a platform for discussion at job interviews, or act as a springboard to further study at the taught postgraduate or doctoral level.

This chapter seeks to give suggestions on how to go about the process of conducting empirical research in finance. Only general guidance is given, and following this advice cannot necessarily guarantee high marks, for the objectives and required level of the project will vary from one institution to another.[1]

14.2 Selecting the topic

Following the decision or requirement to do a project, the first stage is to determine an appropriate *subject area*. This is, in many respects, one of the most difficult and most crucial parts of the whole exercise. Some students are immediately able to think of a precise topic, but for most, it is a process that starts with specifying a very general and very broad subject area, and subsequently narrowing it down to a much smaller and manageable problem.

Inspiration for the choice of topic may come from a number of sources. A good approach is to think rationally about your own interests and areas of expertise. For example, you may have worked in the financial markets in some capacity, or you may have been particularly interested in one aspect of a course unit that you have studied. It is worth spending time talking to some of your instructors in order to gain their advice on what are interesting and plausible topics in their subject areas. At the same time, you may feel very confident at the quantitative end of finance, pricing assets or estimating models for example, but you may not feel comfortable with qualitative analysis where you are asked to give an opinion on particular issues (e.g. 'should financial markets be more regulated?'). In that case, a highly technical piece of work may be appropriate.

Equally, many students find econometrics both difficult and uninteresting. Such students may be better suited to more qualitative topics, or topics that involve only elementary statistics, but where the rigour and value added comes from some other aspect of the problem. A case-study approach that is not based on any quantitative analysis may be entirely acceptable and indeed an examination of a set of carefully selected case studies may be more appropriate for addressing particular problems, especially in situations where hard data are not readily available, or where each entity is distinct so that generalising from a model estimated on one set of data may be inadvisable. Case studies are useful when the case itself is unusual or unique or when each entity under study is very heterogeneous. They involve more depth of study than quantitative approaches. Highly mathematical work that has little relevance and which has been applied inappropriately may be much weaker than a well constructed and carefully analysed case study.

Combining all of these inputs to the choice of topic should enable you at the least to determine whether to conduct quantitative or non-quantitative work, and to select a general subject area (e.g. pricing securities, market microstructure, risk management, asset selection, operational issues, international finance, financial

---

[1] Note that there is only one review question for this chapter and that is to write an excellent research project.

> ## Box 14.1   Possible types of research project
>
> - An empirical piece of work involving quantitative analysis of data
> - A survey of business practice in the context of a financial firm
> - A new method for pricing a security, or the theoretical development of a new method for hedging an exposure
> - A critical review of an area of literature
> - An analysis of a new market or new asset class.
>
> Each of these types of project requires a slightly different approach, and is conducted with varying degrees of success. The remainder of this chapter focuses upon the type of study which involves the formulation of an empirical model using the tools developed in this book. This type of project seems to be the one most commonly selected. It also seems to be a lower risk strategy than others. For example, projects which have the bold ambition to develop a new financial theory, or a whole new model for pricing options, are likely to be unsuccessful and to leave the student with little to write about. Also, critical reviews often lack rigour and are not critical enough, so that an empirical application involving estimating an econometric model appears to be a less risky approach, since the results can be written up whether they are 'good' or not.

econometrics, etc.). The project may take one of a number of forms as illustrated in box 14.1.

A good project or dissertation must have an element of *originality*, i.e. a 'contribution to knowledge'. It should add, probably a very small piece, to the overall picture in that subject area, so that the body of knowledge is larger at the end than before the project was started. This statement often scares students, for they are unsure from where the originality will arise. In empirically based projects, this usually arises naturally. For example, a project may employ standard techniques on data from a different country or a new market or asset, or a project may develop a new technique or apply an existing technique to a different area. Interesting projects can often arise when ideas are taken from another field and applied to finance – for example, you may be able to identify ideas or approaches from the material that you studied from a different discipline as part of your undergraduate degree.

A good project will also contain an in-depth analysis of the issues at hand, rather than a superficial, purely descriptive presentation, as well as an individual contribution. A good project will be interesting, and it will have relevance for one or more user groups (although the user group may be other academic researchers and not necessarily practitioners); it may or may not be on a currently fashionable and newsworthy topic. The best research challenges prior beliefs and changes the way that the reader thinks about the problem under investigation. Good projects can be primarily of interest to other academics and they do not necessarily have to be of direct practical applicability. On the other hand, highly practical work must also be well grounded in the academic approach to doing research.

The next stage is to transform this broad direction into a workably sized topic that can be tackled within the constraints laid down by the institution. It is important to ensure that the aims of the research are not so broad or substantive that the questions cannot be addressed within the constraints on available time and word limits. The objective of the project is usually not to solve the entire world's financial puzzles, but rather to form and address a small problem.

It is often advisable at this stage to browse through recent issues of the main journals relevant to the subject area. This will show which ideas are relatively fashionable, and how existing research has tackled particular problems. A list of relevant journals is presented in table 14.1. They can be broadly divided into two categories: practitioner-oriented and academic journals. Practitioner-oriented journals are usually very focused in a particular area, and articles in these often centre on very practical problems, and are typically less mathematical in nature and less theory-based, than are those in academic journals. Of course, the divide between practitioner and academic journals is not a total one, for many articles in practitioner journals are written by academics and vice versa! The list given in table 14.1 is by no means exhaustive and, particularly in finance, new journals appear on a monthly basis.

Many web sites contain lists of journals in finance or links to finance journals. Some useful ones are:

- www.cob.ohio-state.edu/dept/fin/overview.htm – the Virtual Finance Library, with good links and a list of finance journals
- www.helsinki.fi/WebEc/journals.html – provides a list of journals in the economics area, including finance, plus a number of finance-related resources
- www.people.hbs.edu/pgompers/finjourn.htm – provides a list of links to finance journals
- www.numa.com/ref/journals.htm – the Numa directory of derivatives journals – lots of useful links and contacts for academic and especially practitioner journals on derivatives
- www.aeaweb.org/econlit/journal_list.php – provides a comprehensive list of journals in the economics area, including finance

14.3 Sponsored or independent research?

Some business schools are sufficiently well connected with industry that they are able to offer students the opportunity to work on a specific research project with a 'sponsor'. The sponsor may choose the topic and offer additional expert guidance from a practical perspective. Sponsorship may give the student an insight into the kind of research problems that are of interest to practitioners, and will probably ensure that the work is practically focused and of direct relevance in the private sector. The sponsor may be able to provide access to proprietary or confidential data, which will broaden the range of topics that could be tackled. Most importantly, many students hope that if they impress the firm that they are working with, a permanent job offer will follow.

Table 14.1   Journals in finance and econometrics

Journals in finance	Journals in econometrics and related fields
Applied Financial Economics	Biometrika
Applied Mathematical Finance	Econometrica
European Financial Management	Econometric Reviews
European Journal of Finance	Econometric Theory
Finance and Stochastics	Econometrics Journal
Financial Analysts Journal	International Journal of Forecasting
Financial Management	Journal of Applied Econometrics
Financial Review	Journal of Business and Economic Statistics
Global Finance Journal	Journal of Econometrics
International Journal of Finance & Economics	Journal of Forecasting
International Journal of Theoretical	Journal of the American Statistical Association
and Applied Finance	Journal of Financial Econometrics
Journal of Applied Corporate Finance	Journal of the Royal Statistical Society (A to C)
International Review of Financial Analysis	Journal of Time Series Analysis
Journal of Applied Finance	Society for Nonlinear Dynamics and Econometrics
Journal of Asset Management	
Journal of Banking and Finance	
Journal of Business	
Journal of Business Finance & Accounting	
Journal of Computational Finance	
Journal of Corporate Finance	
Journal of Derivatives	
Journal of Empirical Finance	
Journal of Finance	
Journal of Financial & Quantitative Analysis	
Journal of Financial Economics	
Journal of Financial Markets	
Journal of Financial Research	
Journal of Fixed Income	
Journal of Futures Markets	
Journal of International Financial	
Markets, Institutions and Money	
Journal of International Money and Finance	
Journal of Money, Credit, and Banking	
Journal of Portfolio Management	
Journal of Risk	
Journal of Risk and Insurance	
Journal of Risk and Uncertainty	
Mathematical Finance	
Pacific Basin Finance Journal	
Quarterly Review of Economics and Finance	
Review of Asset Pricing Studies	
Review of Behavioural Finance	
Review of Corporate Finance Studies	
Review of Finance	
Review of Financial Studies	
Risk	

The chance to work on a sponsored project is usually much sought after by students but it is very much a double-edged sword, so that there are also a number of disadvantages. First, most schools are not able to offer such sponsorships, and even those that can are usually able to provide them to only a fraction of the class. Second, the disappointing reality is that the problems of most interest and relevance to practitioners are often (although admittedly not always) of less interest to an academic audience – fundamentally, the objectives of the sponsor and of a university may be divergent. For example, a stereotypical investment bank might like to see a project that compares a number of technical trading rules and evaluates their profitability; but many academics would argue that this area has been well researched before and that finding a highly profitable rule does not constitute a contribution to knowledge and is therefore weak as a research project. So if you have the opportunity to undertake a sponsored project, ensure that your research is of academic as well as practical value – after all, it will almost certainly be the academic who grades the work.

14.4 The research proposal

Some schools will require the submission of a research proposal which will be evaluated and used to determine the appropriateness of the ideas and to select a suitable supervisor. While the requirements for the proposal are likely to differ widely from one institution to another, there are some general points that may be universally useful. In some ways, the proposal should be structured as a miniature version of the final report, but without the results or conclusions!

- The required length of the proposal will vary, but will usually be between one and six sides of A4, typed with page numbering.
- The proposal should start by briefly motivating the topic – why is it interesting or useful?
- There should be a **brief** review of the relevant literature, but this should not cover more than around a third to one half of the total length of the proposal.
- The research questions or hypotheses to be tested should then be clearly stated.
- There should be a discussion of the data and methodology that you intend to use.
- Some proposals also include a time-scale – i.e. which parts of the project do you expect to have completed by what dates?

14.5 Working papers and literature on the internet

Unfortunately, the lag between a paper being written and it actually being published in a journal is often two–three years (and increasing fast), so that research in even the most recent issues of the published journals will be somewhat dated. Additionally, many securities firms, banks and central banks across the world, produce high quality research output in report form, which they often do not bother to try to publish. Much of this is now available on the internet, so it is worth conducting searches with keywords using readily available web search engines. A few suggestions for places to start are given in table 14.2.

Table 14.2　Useful internet sites for financial literature

Universities

Almost all universities around the world now make copies of their discussion papers available electronically.

A few examples from finance departments are:

w4.stern.nyu.edu/finance – Department of Finance, Stern School, New York University

fic.wharton.upenn.edu/fic/papers.html – Wharton Financial Institutions Center

haas.berkeley.edu/finance/WP/rpf.html – University of California at Berkeley

www.icmacentre.ac.uk/research/discussion-papers – ICMA Centre, University of Reading, of course!

US Federal Reserve Banks and the Bank of England

www.bankofengland.co.uk – Bank of England – containing their working papers, news and discussion

www.frbatlanta.org – Federal Reserve Bank of Atlanta – including information on economic and research data and publications

www.stls.frb.org/fred – Federal Reserve Bank of St. Louis – a great deal of useful US data, including monetary, interest rate, and financial data, available daily, weekly, or monthly, including long time histories of data

www.chicagofed.org – Federal Reserve Bank of Chicago – including interest data and useful links

www.dallasfed.org – Federal Reserve Bank of Dallas – including macroeconomic, interest rate, monetary and bank data

www.federalreserve.gov/pubs/ifdp – Federal Reserve Board of Governors International Finance Discussion Papers

www.ny.frb.org/research – Federal Reserve Bank of New York

International bodies

dsbb.imf.org – the International Monetary Fund (IMF) – including working papers, forecasts, and IMF primary commodity price series

www.worldbank.org/reference – World Bank working papers in finance

www.oecd-ilibrary.org – Organisation for Economic Cooperation and Development (OECD) working papers, data etc., searchable

Table 14.2 (cont.)

Miscellaneous

www.nber.org – National Bureau of Economic Research (NBER) – huge database
of discussion papers and links including data sources

econpapers.repec.org – Econpapers (formerly WoPEc) – huge database of
working papers in areas of economics, including finance

www.ssrn.com – The Social Science Research Network – a huge and rapidly
growing searchable database of working papers and the abstracts of
published papers

The free data sources used in this book

www.nationwide.co.uk/default.htm – UK house price index, quarterly back to
1952, plus house prices by region and by property type

www.oanda.com/convert/fxhistory – historical exchange rate series for
an incredible range of currency pairs

www.bls.gov – US Bureau of Labor Statistics – US macroeconomic series

www.federalreserve.gov/econresdata/default.htm – US Federal Reserve Board
– more US macroeconomic series, interest rates, etc. and working papers

research.stlouisfed.org/fred2 – a vast array of US macroeconomic series

finance.yahoo.com – Yahoo! Finance – an incredible range of free
financial data, information, research and commentary

14.6 Getting the data

Although there is more work to be done before the data are analysed, it is important
to think prior to doing anything further about *what data are required* to complete
the project. Many interesting and sensible ideas for projects fall flat owing to a lack
of availability of relevant data. For example, the data required may be confidential,
they may be available only at great financial cost, they may be too time-consuming
to collect from a number of different paper sources, and so on. So before finally
deciding on a particular topic, make sure that the data are going to be available.

The data may be available at your institution, either in paper form (for example, from the IMF or World Bank reports), or preferably electronically. Many
universities have access to Reuters, Datastream or the Bloomberg. Many of the
URLs listed above include extensive databases and furthermore, many markets and
exchanges have their own web pages detailing data availability. One needs to be
slightly careful, however, in ensuring the accuracy of freely available data; 'free'
data also sometimes turn out not to be!

14.7   Choice of computer software

Clearly, the choice of computer software will depend on the tasks at hand. Projects that seek to offer opinions, to synthesise the literature and to provide a review, may not require any specialist software at all. However, even for those conducting highly technical research, project students rarely have the time to learn a completely new programming language from scratch while conducting the research. Therefore, it is usually advisable, if possible, to use a standard software package. It is also worth stating that marks will hardly ever be awarded for students who 'reinvent the wheel'. Therefore, learning to program a multivariate GARCH model estimation routine in C++ may be a valuable exercise for career development for those who wish to be quantitative researchers, but is unlikely to attract high marks as part of a research project unless there is some other value added. The best approach is usually to conduct the estimation as quickly and accurately as possible to leave time free for other parts of the work.

14.8   Methodology

Good research is rarely purely empirical – the empirical model should arise from an economic or financial *theory* and this theory should be presented and discussed before the investigative work begins. We could define a theory as a system of statements that encompass a number of hypotheses. Theory shows what features in the data and what relationships would be expected based on some underlying principles. Theory can give order and meaning to empirical results, and can ensure that the findings are not the result of a data-mining exercise.

Assuming that the project is empirical in nature (i.e. it seeks to test a theory or answer a particular question using actual data), then an important question will concern the type of model to employ. This chapter will now discuss two of the most important approaches to conducting research in finance that have emerged over the past two or three decades: the event study methodology and the Fama–French approach. Although neither of these requires any new econometric tools that were not covered in previous chapters, the terminology employed is quite specific to this part of the literature and thus a focused discussion of how to implement these techniques may prove useful.

14.9   Event studies

Event studies are very useful in finance research and as a result they are extremely commonly employed in the literature. In essence, they represent an attempt to gauge the effect of an identifiable *event* on a financial variable, usually stock returns. So, for example, research has investigated the impact of various types of announcements (e.g. dividends, stock splits, entry into or deletion from a stock index) on the returns of the stocks concerned. Event studies are often considered to be tests for market efficiency: if the financial markets are informationally efficient, there should be an immediate reaction to the event on the announcement date and no further reaction on subsequent trading days.

MacKinlay (1997) argues that conducting event studies initially appears difficult but is in fact easy; my view is that exactly the reverse is true: in principle, event studies are simple to understand and to conduct, but to do so in a rigorous manner requires a great deal of thought. There is a bewildering array of approaches that can be deployed, and at first blush it is not at all clear which of them is appropriate or optimal. The main groundwork for conducting modern event studies was established by Ball and Brown (1968) and by Fama et al. (1969), but as MacKinlay notes, something like them was conducted more than three decades earlier.

While there are now many useful survey papers that describe the various aspects of event studies in considerable detail, unfortunately each has its own notation and approach which can be confusing. Corrado (2011) is a recent example, although Armitage (1995) and MacKinlay (1997) are particularly clearly explained and more closely resemble the treatment given here. A similar discussion is offered by Campbell et al. (1997) but using matrix notation.

14.9.1 Some notation and a description of the basic approach

We of course need to be able to define precisely the dates on which the events occur, and the sample data are usually aligned with respect to this date. If we have N events in the sample, we usually specify an 'event window', which is the period of time over which we investigate the impact of the event. The length of this window will be set depending on whether we wish to investigate the short- or long-run effects of the event. It is common to examine a period comprising, say, ten trading days before the event up to ten trading days after as a short-run event window, while long-run windows can cover a month, a year, or even several years after the event.

A first question to ask once the event has been identified is what frequency of data should be employed in the analysis. MacKinlay (1997) shows that the power of event studies to detect abnormal performance is much greater when daily data are employed rather than weekly or monthly observations, so that the same power can be achieved with a much smaller N, or for given N, the power will be much larger. Although it would in some cases be possible to use intra-daily data, these are harder to collect and may bring additional problems including nuisance microstructure effects; this is perhaps why daily observations are the frequency of choice for most studies in the literature.[2]

Define the return for each firm i on each day t during the event window as R_{it}. We can conduct the following approach separately for each day within the event window − for example, we might investigate it for all of ten days before the event up to ten days after (where $t = 0$ represents the date of the event and $t = -10, -9, -8, \ldots, -1, 0, 1, 2, \ldots, 8, 9, 10$). Note that we will need to

---

[2] We need to be aware of the potential impacts that thin trading of stocks may have, leading to stale prices and unrepresentative abnormal returns; however, this issue is not discussed further here.

exercise care in the definition of the reference day $t = 0$ if the announcement is made after the close of the market.

In most cases, we need to be able to separate the impact of the event from other, unrelated movements in prices. For example, if it is announced that a firm will become a member of a widely followed stock index and its share price that day rises by 4%, but on average the prices of all other stocks also rise by 4%, it would be unwise to conclude that all of the increase in the price of the stock under study is attributable to the announcement. This motivates the idea of constructing abnormal returns, denoted AR_{it}, which are calculated by subtracting an expected return from the actual return

$$AR_{it} = R_{it} - E(R_{it}) \tag{14.1}$$

There are numerous ways that the expected returns can be calculated, but usually this is achieved using a sample of data before the event window so that the nature of the event is not allowed to 'contaminate' estimation of the expected returns. Armitage (1995) suggests that estimation periods can comprise anything from 100 to 300 days for daily observations and 24 to 60 months when the analysis is conducted on a monthly basis. Longer estimation windows will in general increase the precision of parameter estimation, although with it the likelihood of a structural break and so there is a trade-off.

If the event window is very short (e.g. a day or a few days), then we need be far less concerned about constructing an expected return since it is likely to be very close to zero over such a short horizon. In such circumstances, it will probably be acceptable to simply use the actual returns in place of abnormal returns.

It is further often the case that a gap is left between the estimation period and the event window, to be completely sure that anticipation (i.e. 'leakage') of the event does not affect estimation of the expected return equation. However, it might well be the case that in practice we do not have the luxury of doing this since the sample period available is insufficient. Clearly, what we would like to do is to calculate the return that would have been expected for that stock if the event did not happen at all so that we can isolate the impact of the event from any unrelated incidents that may be occurring at the same time.

The simplest method for constructing expected returns (apart from setting them to zero) is to assume a constant mean return, so that the expected return is simply the average return for each stock i calculated at the same frequency over the estimation window, which we might term $\bar{R}_i$. Brown and Warner (1980, 1985) conduct a simulation experiment to compare methods of estimating expected returns for event studies. They find that an approach simply using historical return averages outperforms many more complicated approaches because of the estimation error that comes with the latter.

A second, slightly more sophisticated approach, is to subtract the return on a proxy for the market portfolio that day t from the individual return. This will certainly overcome the impact of general market movements in a rudimentary way, and is equivalent to the assumption that the stock's beta in the market model or the CAPM is unity.

Probably the most common approach to constructing expected returns, however, is to use the market model. This in essence works by constructing the expected return using a regression of the return to stock i on a constant and the return to the market portfolio

$$R_{it} = \alpha_i + \beta_i R_{mt} + u_{it} \tag{14.2}$$

The expected return for firm i on any day t during the event window would then be calculated as the beta estimate from this regression multiplied by the actual market return on day t.

An interesting question is whether the expected return should incorporate the α from the estimation period in addition to β multiplied by the market return. Most applications of event studies include this, and indeed the original study by Fama *et al.* includes an alpha. However, we need to exercise caution when doing so since if – either because of some unrelated incident affecting the price of the stock or in anticipation of the event – the alpha is particularly high (particularly low) during the estimation period, it will push up (down) the expected return. Thus it may be preferable to assume an expected value of zero for the alpha and to exclude it from the event period abnormal return calculation.

In most applications, a broad stock index such as the FTSE All–Share or the S&P500 would be employed to proxy for the market portfolio. This equation can be made as complicated as desired – for example, by allowing for firm size or other characteristics – these would be included as additional factors in the regression with the expected return during the event window being calculated in a similar fashion. An approach based on the arbitrage pricing models of Chen *et al.* (1986) or of Fama and French (1993) could also be employed – more discussion is made of this issue in the following section.

A final further approach would be to set up a 'control portfolio' of firms that have characteristics as close as possible to those of the event firm – for example, matching on firm size, beta, industry, book–to–market ratio, etc. – and then using the returns on this portfolio as the expected returns. Armitage (1995) reports the results of several Monte Carlo simulations that compare the results of various model frameworks that can be used for event studies.

The hypothesis testing framework is usually set up so that the null to be examined is of the event having no effect on the stock price (i.e. an abnormal return of zero). Under the null of no abnormal performance for firm i on day t during the event window, we can construct test statistics based on the standardised abnormal performance. These test statistics will be asymptotically normally distributed (as the length of the estimation window, T, increases)

$$AR_{it} \sim N(0, \sigma^2(AR_{it}))$$

where $\sigma^2(AR_{it})$ is the variance of the abnormal returns, which can be estimated in various ways. A simple method, used by Brown and Warner (1980) among others, is to use the time series of data from the estimation of the expected returns separately for each stock. So we could define $\hat{\sigma}^2(AR_{it})$ as being the equal to the variance of the residuals from the market model, which could be calculated for example using

$$\hat{\sigma}^2(AR_{it}) = \frac{1}{T-2} \sum_{t=2}^{T} \hat{u}_{it}^2 \qquad (14.3)$$

where T is the number of observations in the estimation period. If instead the expected returns had been estimated using historical average returns, we would simply use the variance of those.

Sometimes, an adjustment is made to $\hat{\sigma}^2(AR_{it})$ that reflects the errors arising from estimation of α and β in the market model. Including the adjustment, the variance in the previous equation becomes

$$\hat{\sigma}^2(AR_{it}) = \frac{1}{T-2} \sum_{t=2}^{T} \left(\hat{u}_{it}^2 + \frac{1}{T} \left[1 + \frac{R_{mt} - \bar{R}_m}{\hat{\sigma}_m^2} \right] \right) \qquad (14.4)$$

where $\bar{R}_m$ and $\hat{\sigma}_m^2$ are the average and variance of the returns on the market portfolio respectively during the estimation window. It should be clear that as the length of the estimation period, T, increases, this adjustment will gradually shrink to zero.

We can then construct a test statistic by taking the abnormal return and dividing it by its corresponding standard error, which will asymptotically follow a standard normal distribution[3]

$$S\hat{A}R_{it} = \frac{\hat{A}R_{it}}{[\hat{\sigma}^2(AR_{it})]^{1/2}} \sim N(0, 1) \qquad (14.5)$$

where $S\hat{A}R_{it}$ stands for the standardised abnormal return, which is the test statistic for each firm i and for each event day t.

It is likely that there will be quite a bit of variation of the returns across the days within the event window, with the price rising on some days and then falling on others. As such, it would be hard to identify the overall patterns. We may therefore consider computing the time series cumulative average return over a multi-period event window (for example, over ten trading days) by summing the average returns over several periods, say from time T_1 to T_2

$$C\hat{A}R_i(T_1, T_2) = \sum_{t=T_1}^{T_2} \hat{A}R_{it} \qquad (14.6)$$

Note that the time from T_1 to T_2 may constitute the entire event window or it might just be a sub-set of it. The variance of this $C\hat{A}R$ will be given by the number

---

[3] Note that in some studies, since the sample variance has to be estimated, the test statistic is assumed to follow a Student's t distribution with $T - k$ degrees of freedom in finite samples, where k is the number of parameters estimated in constructing the measure of expected returns ($k = 2$ for the market model). Provided that the estimation window is of a reasonable length (e.g. six months of trading days or more), it will be inconsequential whether the t or normal distributions are employed.

of observations in the event window plus one multiplied by the daily abnormal return variance calculated in equation (14.4) above

$$\hat{\sigma}^2(CAR_i(T_1, T_2)) = (T_2 - T_1 + 1)\hat{\sigma}^2(\hat{AR}_{it}) \tag{14.7}$$

This expression is essentially the sum of the individual daily variances over the days in T_1 to T_2 inclusive.[4]

We can now construct a test statistic for the cumulative abnormal return in the same way as we did for the individual dates, which will again be standard normally distributed

$$S\hat{CAR}_i(T_1, T_2) = \frac{\hat{CAR}_i(T_1, T_2)}{[\hat{\sigma}^2(CAR_i(T_1, T_2))]^{1/2}} \sim N(0, 1) \tag{14.8}$$

It is common to examine a pre-event window (to consider whether there is any anticipation of the event) and a post-event window – in other words, we sum the daily returns for a given firm i for days $t - 10$ to $t - 1$, say, and separately from $t + 1$ to $t + 10$, with the actual day of the event, t, being considered on its own.

Typically, some of the firms will show a negative abnormal return around the event when a positive figure was expected, and this is probably not very useful. But if we have N firms or N events, it is usually of more interest whether the return averaged across all firms is statistically different from zero than whether this is the case for any specific individual firm. We could define this average across firms for each separate day t during the event window as

$$\hat{AR}_t = \frac{1}{N} \sum_{i=1}^{N} \hat{AR}_{it} \tag{14.9}$$

This firm–average abnormal return, $\hat{AR}_t$ will have variance given by $1/N$ multiplied by the average of the variances of the individual firm returns

$$\hat{\sigma}^2(AR_t) = \frac{1}{N^2} \sum_{i=1}^{N} \hat{\sigma}^2(AR_{it}) \tag{14.10}$$

Thus the test statistic (the standardised return) for testing the null hypothesis that the average (across the N firms) return on day t is zero will be given by

$$S\hat{AR}_t = \frac{\hat{AR}_t}{[\hat{\sigma}^2(AR_t)]^{1/2}} = \frac{\frac{1}{N}\sum_{i=1}^{N} \hat{AR}_{it}}{[\frac{1}{N^2}\sum_{i=1}^{N} \hat{\sigma}^2(AR_{it})]^{1/2}} \sim N(0, 1) \tag{14.11}$$

Finally, we can aggregate both across firms and over time to form a single test statistic for examining the null hypothesis that the average multi-horizon (i.e. cumulative) return across all firms is zero. We would get an equivalent statistic whether we first aggregated over time and then across firms or the other way

[4] The number of days during the period T_1 to T_2 including both the end points is $T_2 - T_1 + 1$.

around. The CAR calculated by averaging across firms first and then cumulating over time could be written

$$\hat{CAR}(T_1, T_2) = \sum_{t=T_1}^{T_2} \hat{AR}_t \tag{14.12}$$

Or equivalently, if we started with the $CAR_i(T_1, T_2)$ separately for each firm, we would take the average of these over the N firms

$$\hat{CAR}(T_1, T_2) = \frac{1}{N} \sum_{i=1}^{N} \hat{CAR}_i(T_1, T_2) \tag{14.13}$$

To obtain the variance of this $\hat{CAR}(T_1, T_2)$ we could take $1/N$ multiplied by the average of the variances of the individual $\hat{CAR}_i$.

$$\hat{\sigma}^2(CAR(T_1, T_2)) = \frac{1}{N^2} \sum_{i=1}^{N} \hat{\sigma}^2(CAR_i(T_1, T_2)) \tag{14.14}$$

And again we can construct a standard normally distributed test statistic as

$$\hat{SCAR}(T_1, T_2) = \frac{\hat{CAR}(T_1, T_2)}{[\hat{\sigma}^2(CAR(T_1, T_2))]^{1/2}} \sim N(0, 1) \tag{14.15}$$

14.9.2 Cross-sectional regressions

The methodologies and formulae presented above provide various tools for examining whether abnormal returns are statistically significant or not. However, it will often be the case that we are interested in allowing for differences in the characteristics of a sub-section of the events and also examining the link between the characteristics and the magnitude of the abnormal returns. For example, does the event have a bigger impact on small firms? Or on firms which are heavily traded etc.? The simplest way to achieve this would be to calculate the abnormal returns as desired using something like equation (14.2) above and then to use these as the dependent variable in a cross-sectional regression of the form

$$AR_i = \gamma_0 + \gamma_1 x_{1i} + \gamma_2 x_{2i} + \ldots + \gamma_M x_{Mi} + w_i \tag{14.16}$$

where AR_i is the abnormal return for firm i measured over some horizon, and x_{ji}, $(j = 1, \ldots, M)$ are a set of M characteristics that are thought to influence the abnormal returns, γ_j measures the impact of the corresponding variable j on the abnormal return, and w_i is an error term. We can examine the sign, size and statistical significance of γ_0 as a test for whether the average abnormal return is significantly different from zero after allowing for the impacts of the M characteristics. MacKinlay (1997) advocates the use of heteroscedasticity-robust standard errors in the regression.

The abnormal return used in this equation would typically be measured over several days (or perhaps even the whole event window), but it could also be based on a single day.

14.9.3 Complications when conducting event studies and their resolution

The above discussion presents the standard methodology that is commonly employed when conducting event studies, and most of the time it will provide appropriate inferences. However, as always in econometrics, the use of test statistics requires a number of assumptions about the nature of the data and models employed. Some of these assumptions will now be highlighted and their implications explored.

Cross-sectional dependence

A key assumption when the returns are aggregated across firms is that the events are independent of one another. Often, this will not be the case, particularly when the events are clustered through time. For example, if we were investigating the impact of index recompositions on the prices of the stocks concerned, these index constituents generally only change at specific times of the year. So, typically, a bunch of stocks will enter into an index on the same day, and then there may be no further such events for three or six months.

The impact of this clustering is that we cannot assume the returns to be independent across firms, and as a result the variances in the aggregates across firms (equations (14.10) and (14.14)) will not apply since these derivations have effectively assumed the returns to be independent across firms so that all of the covariances between returns across firms can be set to zero. An obvious solution to this would be not to aggregate the returns across firms, but simply to construct the test statistics on an event-by-event basis and then to undertake a summary analysis of them (e.g. reporting their means, variances, percentage of significant events, etc.).

A second solution would be to construct portfolios of firms having the event at the same time and then the analysis would be done on each of the portfolios. The standard deviation would be calculated using the cross-section of those portfolios' returns on day t (or on days T_1 to T_2, as desired). This approach will allow for cross-correlations since they will automatically be taken into account in constructing the portfolio returns and the standard deviations of those returns. But a disadvantage of this technique is that it cannot allow for different variances for each firm as all are equally weighted within the portfolio; the standard method described above would do so, however.

Changing variances of returns

It has been argued in the literature that often the variance of returns will increase over the event window, but the variance figure used in the testing procedure will have been calculated based on the estimation window, which is usually some time before the event. Either the event itself or the factors that led to it are likely to increase uncertainty and with it the volatility of returns. As a result, the measured variance will be too low and the null hypothesis of no abnormal return during the event will be rejected too often. To deal with this, Boehmer et al. (1991), among others, suggest estimating the variance of abnormal returns by employing the cross-sectional variance of returns across firms during the *event* window. Clearly, if we adopt this procedure we cannot estimate separate test statistics for each firm (although arguably these are usually of little interest anyway). The variance estimator in equation (14.10) would be replaced by

$$\hat{\sigma}^2(AR_t) = \frac{1}{N^2} \sum_{i=1}^{N} (\hat{AR}_{it} - \hat{AR}_t)^2 \qquad (14.17)$$

with the test statistic following as before. A similar adjustment could be made for the variance of the cumulative abnormal return

$$\sigma^2(CAR(T_1, T_2)) = \frac{1}{N^2} \sum_{i=1}^{N} \left(\hat{CAR}_i(T_1, T_2) - \hat{CAR}(T_1, T_2) \right) \qquad (14.18)$$

While this test statistic will allow for the variance to change over time, a drawback is that it does not allow for differences in return variances across firms and nor does it allow for cross-correlations in returns caused by event clustering.

Weighting the stocks

Another issue is that the approach as stated above will not give equal weight to each stock's return in the calculation. The steps outlined above construct the cross-firm aggregate return (in equation (14.9)) and then standardise this using the aggregate standard deviation (in equation (14.11)). An alternative method would be to first standardise each firm's abnormal return (dividing by its appropriate standard deviation) and then aggregating these standardised abnormal returns. If we take the standardised abnormal return for each firm, $\hat{SAR}_{i,t}$, from equation (14.5), we can calculate the average of these across the N firms

$$\hat{SAR}_t = \frac{1}{N} \sum_{i=1}^{N} \hat{SAR}_{it} \qquad (14.19)$$

These SARs have already been standardised so there is no need to divide them by the square root of the variance. If we take this SAR_t and multiply it by $\sqrt{N}$, we will get a test statistic that is asymptotically normally distributed and which, by construction, will give equal weight to each SAR (because we have taken an unweighted average of them)

$$\sqrt{N} SAR_t \sim N(0, 1)$$

We could similarly take an unweighted average of the standardised cumulative abnormal returns ($SCAR$)

$$\hat{SCAR}(T_1, T_2) = \frac{1}{N} \sum_{i=1}^{N} \hat{SCAR}_i(T_1, T_2) \qquad (14.20)$$

and

$$\sqrt{N}SCAR(T_1, T_2) \sim N(0, 1)$$

If the true abnormal return is similar across securities, we would be better to equally weight the abnormal returns in calculating the test statistics (as in equations (14.19) and (14.20)), but if the abnormal return varies positively with its variance measure, then it would be better to give more weight to stocks with lower return variances (as in equation (14.15) for example).

Long event windows

Event studies are joint tests of whether the event-induced abnormal return is zero and whether the model employed to construct expected returns is correct. If we wish to examine the impact of an event over a long period (say, more than a few months), we need to be more careful about the design of the model for expected returns and also to ensure that this model appropriately allows for risk. Over short windows, discrepancies between models are usually small and any errors in model specification are almost negligible. But over the longer run, small errors in setting up the asset pricing model can lead to large errors in the calculation of abnormal returns and therefore the impact of the event.

A key question in conducting event studies to measure long-run impacts is whether to use cumulative abnormal returns (CARs), as described above, or buy-and-hold abnormal returns (BHARs). There are several important differences between the two. First, BHARs employ geometric returns rather than arithmetic returns (used in computing CARs) in calculating the overall return over the event period of interest. Thus the BHAR can allow for compounding whereas the CAR does not. The formula for calculating the BHAR is usually given by

$$\hat{BHAR}_i = [\Pi_{t=T_1}^{T_2}(1 + R_{it}) - 1] - [\Pi_{t=T_1}^{T_2}(1 + E(R_{it})) - 1] \tag{14.21}$$

where $E(R_{it})$ is the expected return. Usually, when constructing BHARs the expected return is based on a non-event firm or portfolio of firms that is matched in some way to the event firm (e.g. based on size, industry, etc.). Alternatively, although less desirably, it could be obtained from a benchmark such as a stock market index.

If desired, we can then sum the $BHAR_i$ across the N firms to construct an aggregate measure. BHARs have been advocated, among others, by Barber and Lyon (1997) and Lyon et al. (1999) because they better match the 'investor experience' than CARs given the former's use of geometric rather than arithmetic averaging. CARs represent biased estimates of the actual returns received by investors. However, by contrast, Fama (1998) in particular argues in favour of the use of CARs rather than BHARs. The latter seem to be more adversely affected by skewness in the sample of abnormal returns than the former because of the impact of compounding in BHARs.[5] In addition, Fama indicates that the average CAR

---

[5] Although Lyon et al. (1999) propose a skewness-adjusted t-statistic with bootstrapping to mitigate this problem.

increases at a rate of $(T_2 - T_1)$ with the number of months included in the sum, whereas its standard error increases only at a rate $\sqrt{(T_2 - T_1)}$. This is not true for BHARs where the standard errors grow at the faster rate $(T_2 - T_1)$ rather than its square root. Hence any inaccuracies in measuring expected returns will be more serious for BHARs as another consequence of compounding.

Event time versus calendar time analysis

All of the procedures discussed above have involved conducting analysis in *event time*. There is, however, an alternative approach that involves using *calendar time*, advocated by Fama (1998) and Mitchell and Stafford (2000) among others. In essence, using a calendar time methodology involves running a time series regression and examining the intercept from that regression. The dependent variable is a series of portfolio returns, which measure the average returns at each point in time of the set of firms that have undergone the event of interest within a pre-defined measurement period before that time. So, for example, we might choose to examine the returns of firms for a year after the event that they announce cessation of their dividend payments. Then, for each observation t, the dependent variable will be the average return on all firms that stopped paying dividends at any point during the past year. One year after the event, by construction the firm will drop out of the portfolio. Hence the number of firms within the portfolio will vary over time (as the number of firms ceasing dividend payment varies) and the portfolio will effectively be rebalanced each month. The explanatory variables may be risk measures from the Carhart (1997) four-factor model for example – this will be discussed in detail below.

The calendar time approach will weight each time period equally and thus the weight on each individual firm in the sample will vary inversely with the number of other firms that have undergone the event during the observation period. This may be problematic and will result in a loss of power to detect an effect if managers time their events to take advantage of misvaluations.

Small samples and non-normality

The test statistics presented in the previous section are all asymptotic, and problems may arise either if the estimation window (T) is too short, or if the number of firms (N) is too small when the firm-aggregated statistic is used. As we discussed earlier in the book, it is well known that stock returns are leptokurtic and tend to have longer lower tails than upper tails. And particularly with small samples, the presence of outliers – for example, very large returns during the estimation window affecting the market model parameter estimation or the residual variance estimates – may also be problematic. One possible remedy would be to use a bootstrap approach to computing the test statistics.

A second strategy for dealing with non-normality would be to use a non-parametric test. Such tests are robust in the presence of non-normal distributions, although they are usually less powerful than their parametric counterparts. In the present context, we could test the null hypothesis that the proportion of positive abnormal returns is not affected by the event. In other words, the proportion of positive abnormal returns across firms remains at the expected level. We could then use the test statistic, Z_p

$$Z_p = \frac{[p - p^*]}{[p^*(1 - p^*)/N]^{1/2}}$$

(14.22)

where p is the actual proportion of negative abnormal returns during the event window and p^* is the expected proportion of negative abnormal returns. Under the null hypothesis, the test statistic follows a binomial distribution, which can be approximated by the standard normal distribution. Sometimes p^* is set to 0.5, but this may not be appropriate if the return distribution is skewed, which is typically the case. Instead, it is better to calculate p^* based on the proportion of negative abnormal returns during the estimation window. The Wilcoxon signed-rank test can also be used.

Event studies – some further issues

A further implicit assumption in the standard event test methodology is that the events themselves occur involuntarily. In practice, however, firms often have discretion about the extent, timing and presentational forms of the announcements that they make. Thus they are likely to use any discretion they have to make announcements when market reactions are going to be the most favourable. For example, where the local regulatory rules allow discretion, firms may release bad news when the markets are closed or when the media and investors are preoccupied with other significant news items. Prabhala (1997) discusses the implications of and solutions to the endogeneity of the firm's decision about when (and perhaps even whether) to make an announcement. When a firm chooses not to announce at a particular time, we have a sort of truncated sample since we can observe events only for firms who choose to make an announcement.

A way of simultaneously dealing with a number of the issues highlighted above (i.e. differing return variances across firms, changing return variances over time, and clustering of events across firms) is to use what has been termed generalised least squares (GLS) in constructing the test statistics. In essence this works by constructing a variance-covariance matrix from the abnormal returns and using this to weight the returns in computing the aggregate test statistic – see Armitage (1995) for further details.

We can see from the above that a range of procedures exists for conducting event studies. The core of the approach is the same in each case, but they differ according to how the aggregation is performed over time and across firms and this affects the method of calculation of the standard deviations. So how do we choose which approach to use? Hopefully, given the context and the nature of the events under consideration, we can gain a reasonable idea of which approach is likely to be the most justifiable. For example, is clustering an issue? Is it expectable that the return variances will have changed over time? Is it important to allow for the variances of returns to vary between firms? By answering these questions, we can usually select the appropriate procedure. But if in doubt, it is always advisable to examine a range of methods and to compare the results as a robustness check. With luck, the various calculation techniques will lead to the same conclusion.

14.9.4 Conducting an event study using Excel

This section will now use the core of the approaches described above in order to conduct an event study. While this ought to be enough to get started and to obtain some indicative results, it is important to note that there is far more that can be done with event studies to make them more rigorous than the approach presented here and readers are encouraged to consult the papers cited above for further details.

The first step would be to decide which event to consider the impact of, and there is certainly no shortage of possibilities (dividend announcements; stock spit announcements; index composition changes; merger announcements; CEO turnover; new contract announcements; macroeconomic announcements, etc.). Once this is done and the data are collected, the time-consuming part is to then organise them in a way to make them easy to work with. It would be possible to conduct the analysis in any software package for data analysis, including EViews. However, since the bulk of the task involves data arrangement and the econometric part is usually not sophisticated (in most cases, a regression will not even be conducted), it probably makes sense to revert back to Microsoft Excel or a similar spreadsheet package.[6]

The starting point for the analysis conducted here are the abnormal returns for $N = 20$ firms, which are given in the Excel file 'Event.xls', and have already been calculated using the market model using equations (14.1) and (14.2). The returns are given for days -259 to $+263$. The raw data are on the sheet 'abnormal returns'. The spreadsheet has been set up with the data aligned on the event day, so while the firms underwent the event on different days, the spreadsheet is constructed so that day '0' is the event day in the same row for all firms. The estimation period is from day -259 to day -10 inclusive (249 days), while the event periods examined are $(T - 10, T - 1)$, day T itself, $(T + 1, T + 10)$ and $(T + 1, T + 250)$. The first of these windows allows us to examine whether there was any leakage of information that affected stock returns prior to the event. Whether there is an immediate effect on the day that the event occurs will depend on whether the announcement is made in advance or it is a 'surprise' to the markets. If the event was known in advance to be happening on day T then the impact on the markets that day may be muted since it could have already been reflected in prices. Note that in this case the adjustment in equation (14.4) is not employed since the estimation period ($T = 249$) is quite long and would render the adjustment term negligible.

We first calculate the average return across all twenty firms for each day during the estimation and event windows in column V of the 'abnormal returns' sheet using the Excel AVERAGE formula in the usual way. All of the calculations of the

---

[6] The example below uses a small sample of real data from a real event, but no details are given as to the nature of the event so that they can be distributed freely with the book.

key statistics are done on a separate sheet which I have called 'summary stats'. The sheet first calculates the AR for day T and the CARs for the date ranges using equations (14.1) and (14.6) respectively for each individual firm and also for the average across all firms.

The next step is to calculate the variances of the abnormal returns or cumulative abnormal returns. For day T, this is done using equation (14.3), which is simply the time series variance of returns during the estimation window and placed in row 2 (and copied directly into row 11). For the multi-day event windows, the one-day variance from (14.3) is scaled up by the number of days in the event window (10 or 250) using equation (14.7). Then the test statistics are calculated by dividing the AR by its respective standard deviation (i.e. the square root of the variance) using (14.5) or its CAR equivalent in (14.8). Finally, the easiest way to obtain p-values for the tests is to use the TDIST function in Excel for a two-sided test and with a large number of degrees of freedom (say, 1,000), so that it approximates the normal distribution.

As discussed in the previous section, there are several potential issues with the fairly simple event study methodology just described. So, for robustness, it is a good idea to examine different ways of tackling the problem, and two possible checks are given in columns X and Y of the 'summary stats' sheet. Both of these procedures can only be undertaken based on the average across firms and not at the individual firm level. The first tweak is to calculate the standard deviation used in the test statistics cross-sectionally in order to allow for the possibility that the return variances may have changed (typically, risen) around the time of the event. Thus we simply take the variance across firms for the abnormal return or cumulative abnormal return of interest, divide this by N (i.e. 20) and then proceed in the usual way.

A further possibility examined in column Y is to equally weight firms by calculating the average of the standardised abnormal returns as in equation (14.19) or (14.20). Then the test statistic is simply this average multiplied by the square root of the N.

If we now consider the results on this sheet, it is clear that there is little evidence of a short-term reaction to the event. During the two trading weeks before the event, $(T - 10$ to $T - 1)$, only one firm has a significant abnormal return at the 5% level (firm 20 has a CAR of 15.43% with a test statistic of 2.02). None of the individual firms have significant returns on the event date (T), and neither do any of them show significance in the short post-event window $(T + 1$ to $T + 10)$. It is over the longer term – the next trading year – where there is some action. Now five firms have statistically significant returns together with economically quite large cumulative abnormal returns of 20% to 55%.

Examining the aggregate-level results, it is reassuring that the three slightly different approaches in columns W to Y yield very similar conclusions. Here the null hypothesis is that the average abnormal return (or average cumulative abnormal return) is zero. There is again no discernible market reaction before, on, or in the short-run after, the event. However, the long-run abnormal return is positive and highly statistically significant whichever of the three approaches is considered. Interestingly, the variance estimates before the event (at times $t - 10$

to $T - 1$) are higher for the cross-sectional approach in (14.18), although they are lower for cross-sectional approach during and after the event.

Finally, in the third sheet of the Event.xls workbook, labelled 'non-parametric test', the non-parametric statistic Z_p of equation (14.22) is calculated and then the p-value is obtained using the TDIST function as above. This examines the null hypothesis that the proportion of abnormal returns around the event is the same as it was during the estimation window. So the first calculation row of the sheet (row 2) calculates p^*, the expected proportion of negative returns based on data from the estimation window. Then for each event period range, we calculate p, the actual proportion of negative returns.[7]

The expected proportion of negative returns varies from 0.43 for firm 18 to 0.55 for firm 8, but the actual proportions for the short pre- and post-event windows are often much lower than that. For example, for firm 1, p was 0.3 (i.e. negative returns on only three days from ten) before the event. Pre-event, six of the twenty firms have significant differences between p and p^*, while for the two weeks immediately after the event, only three of them show significant differences. Over the long-run, however, there are no significant differences between the expected and actual proportions of negative return days – either for any of the individual firms or for the average.

14.10 Tests of the CAPM and the Fama–French Methodology

14.10.1 Testing the CAPM

The basics

Before moving on to the more sophisticated multi-factor models, it may be useful to review the standard approach that was developed for testing the CAPM. This is not the place for a detailed discussion of the motivation for the CAPM or its derivation – such a discussion can be found at an accessible level in Bodie *et al.* (2011) or most other finance textbooks; alternatively, see Campbell *et al.* (1997) for a more technical treatment. A good introduction to the general area of asset pricing tests is given in the book by Cuthbertson and Nitzsche (2004).

The most commonly quoted equation for the CAPM is

$$E(R_i) = R_f + \beta_i[E(R_m) - R_f] \tag{14.23}$$

So the CAPM states that the expected return on any stock i is equal to the risk-free rate of interest, R_f, plus a risk premium. This risk premium is equal to the risk premium per unit of risk, also known as the market risk premium, $[E(R_m) - R_f]$, multiplied by the measure of how risky the stock is, known as 'beta', β_i. Beta is not observable from the market and must be calculated, and hence tests of the CAPM are usually done in two steps – first, estimating the stock betas and second, actually testing the model. It is important to note that the CAPM is an equilibrium model,

---

[7] Note of course that it is not possible to calculate Z for the event date by itself since the proportion of negative returns, p would be either exactly zero or exactly one.

or a model in terms of expectations. Thus, we would not expect the CAPM to hold in every time period for every stock. But if it is a good model, then it should hold 'on average'. Usually, we will use a broad stock market index as a proxy for the market portfolio and the yield on short-term Treasury bills as the risk-free rate.

A stock's beta can be calculated in two ways – one approach is to calculate it directly as the covariance between the stock's *excess* return and the excess return on the market portfolio, divided by the variance of the excess returns on the market portfolio

$$\beta_i = \frac{Cov(R_i^e, R_m^e)}{Var(R_m^e)} \qquad (14.24)$$

where the ^{e} superscript denotes excess returns (i.e. the return with the risk-free rate subtracted from it). Alternatively, and equivalently, we can run a simple *time series* regression of the excess stock returns on the excess returns to the market portfolio separately for each stock, and the slope estimate will be the beta

$$R_{i,t}^e = \alpha_i + \beta_i R_{m,t}^e + u_{i,t}, \qquad i = 1, \ldots, N; \quad t = 1, \ldots, T \qquad (14.25)$$

where N is the total number of stocks in the sample and T is the number of time series observations on each stock.

The intercept estimate $(\hat{\alpha}_i)$ from this regression would be 'Jensen's alpha' for the stock, which would measure how much the stock underperformed or outperformed what would have been expected given its level of market risk. It is probably not very interesting to examine the alpha for an individual stock, but we could use exactly the same regression to test the performance of portfolios, trading strategies and so on – all we would do would be to replace the excess returns that comprise the dependent variable with those from the portfolio or trading rule.

Returning to testing the CAPM, suppose that we had a sample of 100 stocks ($N = 100$) and their returns using five years of monthly data ($T = 60$). The first step would be to run 100 time series regressions (one for each individual stock), the regressions being run with the sixty monthly data points. Then the second stage would involve a single cross-sectional regression of the average (over time) of the stock returns on a constant and the betas

$$\bar{R}_i = \lambda_0 + \lambda_1 \beta_i + v_i, \qquad i = 1, \ldots, N \qquad (14.26)$$

where $\bar{R}_i$ is the return for stock i averaged over the sixty months. Notice that, unlike the first stage, this second stage regression now involves the actual returns and not excess returns. Essentially, the CAPM says that stocks with higher betas are more risky and therefore should command higher average returns to compensate investors for that risk.

If the CAPM is a valid model, two key predictions arise which can be tested using this second stage regression: $\lambda_0 = R_f$ and $\lambda_1 = [R_m - R_f]$. So, to find support for the CAPM, we would expect to see the intercept estimate being close to the risk-free rate of interest and the slope being close to the market risk premium.

Two further implications of the CAPM being valid are first, that there is a linear relationship between a stock's return and its beta and second, that no other variables should help to explain the cross-sectional variation in returns. So, in other words, any additional variable we add to the second stage regression (14.26) should not have a statistically significant parameter estimate attached to it. We could thus for example run the augmented regression

$$\bar{R}_i = \lambda_0 + \lambda_1 \beta_i + \lambda_2 \beta_i^2 + \lambda_3 \sigma_i^2 + v_i \tag{14.27}$$

where β_i^2 is the squared beta for stock i and σ_i^2 is the variance of the residuals from the first stage regression, which is a measure of idiosyncratic risk for stock i. The squared beta term can capture whether there is any non-linearity in the relationship between returns and beta. If the CAPM is a valid and complete model, then we should see that $\lambda_2 = 0$ and $\lambda_3 = 0$.

However, research has indicated that the CAPM is not a complete model of stock returns. In particular, it has been found that returns are systematically higher for small capitalisation stocks than the CAPM would predict, and similarly, returns are systematically higher for 'value' stocks (those with low market-to-book or price-to-earnings ratios) than the CAPM would predict. We can test this directly using a different augmented second stage regression

$$\bar{R}_i = \lambda_0 + \lambda_1 \beta_i + \lambda_2 MV_i + \lambda_3 BTM_i + v_i \tag{14.28}$$

where MV_i is the market capitalisation for stock i and BTM_i is the ratio of its book value to its market value of equity.[8] This is the kind of model employed by Fama and French (1992), as discussed below. As for equation (14.27), the test for the CAPM to be supported by the data would be $\lambda_2 = 0$ and $\lambda_3 = 0$.

Unfortunately, returns data are beset by problems that can render the results from tests of the CAPM dubious or possibly even invalid. First, the familiar non-normality of returns can lead to problems with tests in finite samples – while normality is not a specific theoretical requirement of the CAPM, it is required for valid hypothesis testing. Second, there is also likely to be heteroscedasticity in the returns. More recent research testing the CAPM has used the generalised method of moments (GMM), where estimators can be constructed that are robust to these issues – see for, example, Cochrane (2005). A final important problem is the measurement error in beta discussed extensively in section 5.13 of this book. In order to minimise such measurement errors, the beta estimates can be based on portfolios rather than individual securities. Alternatively, the Shanken (1992) correction can be applied, where the standard deviation in the test statistic is multiplied by a factor to adjust for the measurement error.

The Fama–MacBeth approach

Fama and MacBeth (1973) used the two stage approach to testing the CAPM outlined above, but using a *time series of cross-sections*. The basics are exactly as described above, but instead of running a single time-series regression for each

---

[8] Note that many studies use the market-to-book ratio, which is simply one divided by the book-to-market ratio – so value stocks have a low number for the former and a high number for the latter.

stock and then a single cross-sectional regression, the estimation is conducted with a rolling window.

Fama and MacBeth employ five years of observations to estimate the CAPM betas and the other risk measures (i.e. the standard deviation and squared beta) and these are used as the explanatory variables in a set of cross-sectional regressions each month for the following four years. The estimation period is then rolled forward four years and the process continues until the end of the sample period is reached.[9] To illustrate, their initial time series estimation period for the betas is January 1930 to December 1934. The cross-sectional regressions are run with monthly returns on each stock as the dependent variable for January 1935, and then separately for February 1935, ..., to December 1938. The sample is then rolled forward with the beta estimation from January 1934 to December 1938 and the cross-sectional regressions now beginning January 1939. In this way, they end up with a cross-sectional regression for every month in the sample (except for the first five years used for the initial beta estimations).

Since we will have one estimate of the lambdas, $\hat{\lambda}_{j,t}$ ($j = 1, 2, 3, 4$), for each time period t, we can form a t-ratio for each of these as being the average over t, denoted $\hat{\lambda}_j$, divided by its standard error (which is the standard deviation over time divided by the square root of the number of time series estimates of the $\hat{\lambda}_{j,t}$).

Thus the average value over t of $\hat{\lambda}_{j,t}$ can be calculated as

$$\hat{\lambda}_j = \frac{1}{T_{FMB}} \sum_{t=1}^{T_{FMB}} \hat{\lambda}_{j,t}, \quad j = 1, 2, 3, 4 \tag{14.29}$$

where T_{FMB} is the number of cross-sectional regressions used in the second stage of the test, and the standard deviation is

$$\hat{\sigma}_j = \sqrt{\frac{1}{T_{FMB} - 1} \sum_{t=1}^{T_{FMB}} (\hat{\lambda}_{j,t} - \hat{\lambda}_j)^2} \tag{14.30}$$

The test statistic is then simply $\sqrt{T_{FMB}}\hat{\lambda}_j/\hat{\sigma}_j$, which is asymptotically standard normal, or follows a t distribution with $T_{FME} - 1$ degrees of freedom in finite samples. The key results from Fama and MacBeth corroborate other early evidence by Black, Jensen and Scholes (1972), and are summarised in table 14.3.

We can compare the estimated values of the intercept and slope with the actual values of the risk-free rate (R_f) and the market risk premium [$\bar{R}_m - \bar{R}_f$], which are, for the full-sample corresponding to the results presented in the table, 0.013 and 0.143 respectively. The parameter estimates $\hat{\lambda}_0$ and $\hat{\lambda}_1$ have the correct signs (both are positive). Thus the implied risk-free rate is positive and so is the relationship between returns and beta – both parameters are significantly different from zero, although they become insignificant when the other risk measures are

---

[9] The main reason that the updating was only undertaken every four years was due to the lack of computing power available at that time. More recent studies would do this annually or even monthly.

Table 14.3   Fama and MacBeth's results on testing the CAPM

Model	$\hat{\lambda}_0$	$\hat{\lambda}_1$	$\hat{\lambda}_2$	$\hat{\lambda}_3$
Model 1: CAPM	0.0061*	0.0085*		
	(3.24)	(2.57)		
Model 2: Augmented CAPM	0.0020	0.0114	−0.0026	0.0516
	(0.55)	(1.85)	(−0.86)	(1.11)

Notes: t-ratios in parentheses; * denotes significance at the 5% level.
Source: Fama and MacBeth (1973), numbers extracted from their Table 3.

included as in the second row of the table. Hence it has been argued that there is *qualitative* support for the CAPM but not *quantitative* support as the intercept and slope are not of the appropriate sizes, although the differences between the estimated parameters and their expected values are not statistically significant for Fama and MacBeth's whole sample. It is also worth noting from the second row of the table that squared beta and idiosyncratic risk have parameters that are even less significant than beta itself in explaining the cross-sectional variation in returns.

14.10.2   Asset pricing tests – the Fama–French approach

Of all of the approaches to asset pricing tests that have been developed, the range of techniques pioneered by Fama and French in a series of papers is by far the most commonly employed. The 'Fama–French methodology' is not really a single technique but rather a family of related approaches based on the notion that market risk is insufficient to explain the cross-section of stock returns – in other words, why some stocks generate higher average returns than others.

The Fama–French and Carhart models, described in detail below, seek to measure abnormal returns after allowing for the impact of the characteristics of the firms or portfolios under consideration. It is well-established in the finance literature that certain types of stocks yield, on average, considerably higher returns than others. For example, the stocks of small companies, value stocks (those with low price-to-earnings ratios), and stocks with momentum (that have experienced recent price increases), typically yield higher returns than those having the opposite characteristics. This has important implications for asset pricing and for the way that we think about risk and expected returns. If, for example, we wanted to evaluate the performance of a fund manager, it would be important to take the characteristics of these portfolios into account to avoid incorrectly labelling a manager as having stock-picking skills when he routinely followed a strategy of buying small, value stocks with momentum, which will on average outperform the equity market as a whole.

Fama–French (1992)

The Fama–French (1992) approach, like Fama and MacBeth (1973), is based on a time series of cross-sections model. Here, we run a set of cross-sectional regressions of the form

$$R_{i,t} = \alpha_{0,t} + \alpha_{1,t}\beta_{i,t} + \alpha_{2,t}MV_{i,t} + \alpha_{3,i}BTM_{i,t} + u_{i,t} \tag{14.31}$$

where $R_{i,t}$ are again the monthly returns, $\beta_{i,t}$ are the CAPM betas, $MV_{i,t}$ are the market capitalisations, and $BTM_{i,t}$ are the book-to-price ratios, each for firm i and month t. So the explanatory variables in the regressions here are the firm characteristics themselves. Fama and French show that when we employ size and book-to-market in the cross-sectional regressions, these are highly significantly related to returns (with negative and positive signs respectively) so that small and value stocks earn higher returns all else equal than growth or large stocks. They also show that market beta is not significant in the regression (and even has the wrong sign), providing very strong evidence against the CAPM.

Fama–French (1993)

Fama and French (1993) use a factor-based model in the context of a time series regression which is now run separately on each portfolio i

$$R_{i,t} = \alpha_i + \beta_{i,M}RMRF_t + \beta_{i,S}SMB_t + \beta_{i,V}HML_t + \epsilon_{i,t} \tag{14.32}$$

where $R_{i,t}$ is the return on stock or portfolio i at time t, $RMRF$, SMB, and HML are the *factor mimicking portfolio* returns for market excess returns, firm size, and value respectively.[10]

The factor mimicking portfolios are designed to have unit exposure to the factor concerned and zero exposure to all other factors. In more detail, the factors in the Fama and French (1993) model are constructed as follows. The excess market return is measured as the difference in returns between the S&P500 index and the yield on Treasury bills ($RMRF$); SMB is the difference in returns between a portfolio of small stocks and a portfolio of large stocks, termed 'small minus big' portfolio returns; HML is the difference in returns between a portfolio of value stocks with high book-value to market-value ratios and a portfolio of growth stocks with low book-value to market-value ratios, termed 'high minus low' portfolio returns. One of the main reasons they use factor-mimicking portfolios rather than continuing their (1992) approach is that they want to also include bonds in the set of asset returns considered, and these do not have obvious analogues to market capitalisation or the book-to-market ratio.

In Fama and French's (1993) case, these time series regressions are run on portfolios of stocks that have been two-way sorted according to their book-to-market ratios and their market capitalisations. It is then possible to compare the parameter estimates qualitatively across the portfolios i. The parameter estimates from these time series regressions are known as *factor loadings* that measure the

---

[10] While this model could be applied to individual stocks, it makes more sense in the context of portfolios, although the principles are the same.

sensitivity of each individual portfolio to each of the factors. We will obtain a separate set of factor loadings for each portfolio i since each portfolio is the subject of a different time series regression and will have different sensitivities to the risk factors. Fama and French (1993) qualitatively compare these factor loadings across a set of twenty-five portfolios that have been two-way sorted on their size and book-to-market ratios.

Then, the second stage in this approach is to use the factor loadings from the first stage as explanatory variables in a cross-sectional regression

$$\bar{R}_i = \alpha + \lambda_M \beta_{i,M} + \lambda_S \beta_{i,S} + \lambda_V \beta_{i,V} + e_i \tag{14.33}$$

We can interpret the second stage regression parameters, $\lambda_M, \lambda_S, \lambda_V$ as *factor risk premia* − in other words, they show the amount of extra return that is generated on average from taking on an additional unit of that source of risk.

Since the factor loadings and risk premia have a tendency to vary over time, the model is estimated using a rolling window. For example, the time series model in equation (14.32) is typically estimated using five years of monthly data, and then the λs would be estimated from equation (14.33) using separate cross-sectional regressions with a monthly return for each of the following twelve months. The sample would then be rolled forward by a year with a new set of βs being estimated from (14.32) and then a new set of twelve estimates of λ produced and so on. Alternatively, the rolling update could occur monthly. Either way, there will be one estimate of each of the λs for every month after the initial five-year beta estimation window, which we would then average to get the overall estimates of the risk premia.

Fama and French (1993) apply the model to their twenty-five size- and value-sorted portfolios and argue that the statistical significance of the lambdas in the second stage regressions and the high R^2 values are indicative of the importance of size and value as explanators of the cross-sectional variation in returns.

Carhart (1997)

Since Carhart's (1997) study on mutual fund performance persistence, it has become customary to add a fourth factor to the equations above based on momentum, measured as the difference between the returns on the best performing stocks over the past year and the worst performing stocks − this factor is known as UMD − 'up-minus-down'. Equation (14.32) then becomes

$$R_{i,t} = \alpha_i + \beta_{i,M} RMRF_t + \beta_{i,S} SMB_t + \beta_{i,V} HML_t + \beta_{i,U} UMD_t + \epsilon_{i,t} \tag{14.34}$$

And, if desired, equation (14.33) becomes[11]

$$\bar{R}_i = \alpha + \lambda_M \beta_{i,M} + \lambda_S \beta_{i,S} + \lambda_V \beta_{i,V} + \lambda_U \beta_{i,U} + e_i \tag{14.35}$$

---

[11] Note that Carhart's paper does not use this second-stage cross-sectional regression containing the factor sensitivities.

Carhart forms decile portfolios of mutual funds based on their one-year lagged performance and runs the time series regression of equation (14.34) on each of them. He finds that the mutual funds which performed best last year (in the top decile) also had positive exposure to the momentum factor (UMD) while those which performed worst had negative exposure. Hence a significant portion of the momentum that exists at the fund level arises from momentum in the stocks that those funds are holding.

14.10.3   The Fama–MacBeth procedure in EViews

It should be clear from the discussion above that there is nothing particularly complex about the two-stage procedure – it only involves two sets of standard linear regressions. The hard part is really in collecting and organising the data. If we wished to do a more sophisticated study – for example, using a bootstrapping procedure or using the Shanken correction, this would require more analysis than is conducted in the illustration below. However, hopefully the EViews code and explanation will be sufficient to demonstrate how to apply the procedures to any set of data.

The example employed here is taken from the study by Gregory, Tharyan and Chistidis (2013) that examines the performance of several different variants of the Fama–French and Carhart models using the Fama–MacBeth methodology in the UK following several earlier studies showing that these approaches appear to work far less well for the UK than the US. The data required are provided by Gregory *et al.* on their web site.[12] Note that their data have been refined and further cleaned since their paper was written (i.e. the web site data are not identical to those used in the paper) and as a result the parameter estimates presented here deviate slightly from theirs. However, given that the motivation for this exercise is to demonstrate how the Fama–MacBeth approach can be used in EViews, this difference should not be consequential. The two data files used are 'monthlyfactors.csv' and 'vw_sizebm_25groups.csv'. The former file includes the time series of returns on all of the factors (SMB, HML, UMD, RMRF, the return on the market portfolio (RM) and the return on the risk-free asset (RF)), while the latter includes the time series of returns on twenty-five value-weighted portfolios formed from a large universe of stocks, two-way sorted according to their sizes and book-to-market ratios.

The first step in this analysis for conducting the Fama–French or Carhart procedures using the methodology developed by Fama and MacBeth is to create a new EViews workfile which I have called 'ff_example.wf1' and to import the two csv data files into it. The data in both cases run from October 1980 to December 2012, making a total of 387 data points. However, in order to obtain results as close as possible to those of the original paper, when running the regressions, the period is from October 1980 to December 2010 (363 data points). We then need to set up a program file along the lines of those set up in the previous chapter – I have called mine 'FF_PROG.prg'.

---

[12] http://business-school.exeter.ac.uk/research/areas/centres/xfi/research/famafrench/files.

The full code to run the tests is as follows, and annotated below.

```
'READ DATA
LOAD C:\ CHRIS\ BOOK\ BOOK3E\ DATA\ FF_EXAMPLE.WF1

'TRANSFORM ACTUAL RETURNS INTO EXCESS RETURNS
SL=SL-RF
S2=S2-RF
S3=S3-RF
S4=S4-RF
SH=SH-RF
S2L=S2L-RF
S22=S22-RF
S23=S23-RF
S24=S24-RF
S2H=S2H-RF
M3L=M3L-RF
M32=M32-RF
M33=M33-RF
M34=M34-RF
M3H=M3H-RF
B4L=B4L-RF
B42=B42-RF
B43=B43-RF
B44=B44-RF
B4H=B4H-RF
BL=BL-RF
B2=B2-RF
B3=B3-RF
B4=B4-RF
BH=BH-RF

'DEFINE THE NUMBER OF TIME SERIES OBSERVATIONS
!NOBS=363

'CREATE SERIES TO PUT BETAS FROM STAGE 1
'AND LAMBDAS FROM STAGE 2 INTO
SERIES BETA_C
SERIES BETA_RMRF
SERIES BETA_UMD
SERIES BETA_HML
SERIES BETA_SMB
SERIES LAMBDA_C
SERIES LAMBDA_RMRF
SERIES LAMBDA_UMD
SERIES LAMBDA_HML
SERIES LAMBDA_SMB
SERIES LAMBDA_R2
SCALAR LAMBDA_C_MEAN
```

```
SCALAR LAMBDA_C_TRATIO
SCALAR LAMBDA_RMRF_MEAN
SCALAR LAMBDA_RMRF_TRATIO
SCALAR LAMBDA_UMD_MEAN
SCALAR LAMBDA_UMD_TRATIO
SCALAR LAMBDA_HML_MEAN
SCALAR LAMBDA_HML_TRATIO
SCALAR LAMBDA_SMB_MEAN
SCALAR LAMBDA_SMB_TRATIO
SCALAR LAMBDA_R2_MEAN
'THIS LOOP CREATES THE SERIES TO PUT THE
'CROSS-SECTIONAL DATA IN
FOR !M = 1 TO 387
SERIES TIME{%M}
NEXT


'NOW RUN THE FIRST STAGE TIME-SERIES REGRESSIONS
'SEPARATELY FOR EACH PORTFOLIO AND
'PUT THE BETAS INTO THE APPROPRIATE SERIES
SMPL 1980:10 2010:12
!J=1
FOR %Y SL S2 S3 S4 SH S2L S22 S23 S24 S2H M3L M32 M33 M34 M3H
   B4L B42 B43 B44 B4H BL B2 B3 B4 BH
'THE PREVIOUS COMMAND WITH VARIABLE NAMES
'NEEDS TO ALL GO ON ONE LINE
EQUATION EQ1.LS {%Y} C RMRF UMD HML SMB
BETA_C(!J)=@COEFS(1)
BETA_RMRF(!J)=@COEFS(2)
BETA_UMD(!J)=@COEFS(3)
BETA_HML(!J)=@COEFS(4)
BETA_SMB(!J)=@COEFS(5)
!J=!J+1
NEXT


'NOW RESORT THE DATA SO THAT EACH COLUMN IS A
'MONTH AND EACH ROW IS RETURNS ON PORTFOLIOS
FOR !K=1 TO 387
TIME!K(1)=SL(!K)
TIME!K(2)=S2(!K)
TIME!K(3)=S3(!K)
TIME!K(4)=S4(!K)
TIME!K(5)=SH(!K)
TIME!K(6)=S2L(!K)
TIME!K(7)=S22(!K)
TIME!K(8)=S23(!K)
TIME!K(9)=S24(!K)
TIME!K(10)=S2H(!K)
TIME!K(11)=M3L(!K)
TIME!K(12)=M32(!K)
```

```
TIME!K(13)=M33(!K)
TIME!K(14)=M34(!K)
TIME!K(15)=M3H(!K)
TIME!K(16)=B4L(!K)
TIME!K(17)=B42(!K)
TIME!K(18)=B43(!K)
TIME!K(19)=B44(!K)
TIME!K(20)=B4H(!K)
TIME!K(21)=BL(!K)
TIME!K(22)=B2(!K)
TIME!K(23)=B3(!K)
TIME!K(24)=B4(!K)
TIME!K(25)=BH(!K)
NEXT


'RUN 2ND STAGE CROSS-SECTIONAL REGRESSIONS
FOR !Z = 1 TO !NOBS
EQUATION EQ1.LS TIME!Z C BETA_RMRF BETA_UMD BETA_HML BETA_SMB
LAMBDA_C(!Z)=@COEFS(1)
LAMBDA_RMRF(!Z)=@COEFS(2)
LAMBDA_UMD(!Z)=@COEFS(3)
LAMBDA_HML(!Z)=@COEFS(4)
LAMBDA_SMB(!Z)=@COEFS(5)
LAMBDA_R2(!Z)=@R2
NEXT


'FINALLY, ESTIMATE THE MEANS AND T-RATIOS
'FOR THE LAMBDA ESTIMATES IN THE SECOND STAGE
LAMBDA_C_MEAN =@MEAN(LAMBDA_C)
LAMBDA_C_TRATIO=@SQRT(!NOBS)*@MEAN(LAMBDA_C)/@STDEV(LAMBDA_C)
LAMBDA_RMRF_MEAN=@MEAN(LAMBDA_RMRF)
LAMBDA_RMRF_TRATIO=@SQRT(!NOBS)*@MEAN(LAMBDA_RMRF)/@STDEV(LAMBDA_RMRF)
LAMBDA_UMD_MEAN=@MEAN(LAMBDA_UMD)
LAMBDA_UMD_TRATIO=@SQRT(!NOBS)*@MEAN(LAMBDA_UMD)/@STDEV(LAMBDA_UMD)
LAMBDA_HML_MEAN=@MEAN(LAMBDA_HML)
LAMBDA_HML_TRATIO=@SQRT(!NOBS)*@MEAN(LAMBDA_HML)/@STDEV(LAMBDA_HML)
LAMBDA_SMB_MEAN=@MEAN(LAMBDA_SMB)
LAMBDA_SMB_TRATIO=@SQRT(!NOBS)*@MEAN(LAMBDA_SMB)/@STDEV(LAMBDA_SMB)
LAMBDA_R2_MEAN=@MEAN(LAMBDA_R2)
```

We can think of this program as comprising of several sections. The first step is to transform all of the raw portfolio returns into excess returns which are required to compute the betas in the first stage of Fama–MacBeth. This is fairly simple to do and writes over the original series with their excess return counterparts.

The line (!NOBS=363) ensures that the same sample period as the paper by Gregory *et al.* is employed throughout. The next stage involves creating the arrays to put the betas and lambdas in. These are set up as series since there will be one entry for each regression. Then we also need the final estimates for each of the lambda parameters, which will be the time series averages of the cross-sections.

We need to first run a set of time series regressions to estimate the betas but we will later need to estimate a set of cross-sectional regressions. This presents a problem because the data can only be organised in one way or the other in EViews. So the following three lines

```
FOR !M = 1 TO 387
SERIES TIME{M}
NEXT
```

set up a set of 387 new series called TIME1, TIME2, ..., TIME387 which we will subsequently organise as cross-sectional data. !M in curly brackets is what tells EViews to add the numbers 1, 2, ..., onto the word TIME to create the names for the new series. These three lines of code very efficiently replace 387 separate lines of code that we would otherwise have had to have written such as SERIES TIME1 etc.

Then we set up and run all of the first-stage time series regressions. We want to run the Carhart 4-factor model separately for each of the twenty-five portfolios. It would be possible to have twenty-five separate regression statements, but it seems easier and more efficient to set these up in a loop. SMPL 1980:10 2010:12 runs the regressions for the period 1980:10 to 2010:12 only rather than on the whole sample period.

The statements

```
FOR %Y followed by the list of variable names
...
NEXT
```

constitute the main loop that runs over all the twenty-five series. Then the line

```
EQUATION EQ1.LS {%Y} C RMRF UMD HML SMB
```

runs an OLS time series regression for each of the twenty-five series in the loop defined in the previous line on a constant and the four variables RMRF UMD HML SMB. This effectively uses equation (14.34) from above. We need to store the estimates from these regressions into separate series for each parameter. The lines beginning BETA_C(!J)=@COEFS(1) do this. The letter J is an index which is defined outside the loop to start with a value of 1 (the statement !J=1) and then as each regression is run, the value of J is increased by 1 (the statement !J=!J+1 does this). So, the loop starts off with J=1 and the regression will be run with the series SL as the dependent variable. Then the intercept (i.e. the alpha) from this regression will be placed as the first entry in BETA_C (i.e. it will be BETA_C(1)), the parameter estimate on the RMRF term will be placed in BETA_RMRF(1) and so on. Then the value of J will be increased by 1 to 2, and the second regression will have dependent variable S2. Its intercept estimate will be placed in BETA_C(2), the slope estimate on RMRF will be placed in BETA_RMRF(2) and so on. This will continue until the final regression is run on the twenty-fifth series, which will be BH, with its intercept estimate being placed in BETA_C(25). We should thus note that while these BETA_ series were set up with the total number of observations in the workfile (i.e. they will have 387 rows), only the first twenty-five of those rows will be filled and the remainder will contain NA.

So now we have run the first step of the Fama–MacBeth methodology – we have estimated all of the betas, also known as the factor exposures. The slope parameter estimates for the regression of a given portfolio will show how sensitive the returns on that portfolio are to the factors and the intercepts will be Jensen's alpha estimates. These intercept estimates in BETA_C should be comparable to those in the second panel of Table 6 in Gregory *et al.* – their column headed '*Simple 4F*'. Since the parameter estimates in all of their tables are expressed as percentages, we need to multiply all of the figures given from the EViews output by 100 to make them on the same scale. If the 4-factor model is a good one, we should find that all of these alphas are statistically insignificant. We could test this individually if we wished by adding an additional line of code in the loop to save the *t*-ratios in the regressions (something like BETA_T_C(!J)=@TSTATS(2) should do it). It would also be possible to test the joint null hypothesis that all of the alphas are jointly zero using a test developed by Gibbons, Ross and Shanken (1989) – the GRS test, but this is beyond the scope of this book.

The second stage of Fama–MacBeth is to run a separate cross-sectional regression for each point in time. An easy way to do this is to, effectively, rearrange the data so that each column (while still in a time series workfile) is a set of cross-sectional data. So the loop over K takes the observations in the twenty-five portfolios and arranges them cross-sectionally. Thus TIME1 will contain twenty-five data points (one for each portfolio) – all the observations for the first month, October 1980; TIME2 will contain all twenty-five observations for the portfolios in the second month, November 1980; . . . ; TIME387 will contain all twenty-five portfolio observations for December 2012.

We are now in a position to run the second-stage cross-sectional regressions corresponding to equation (14.35) above – note that this runs from 1 to NOBS, which was defined as Gregory *et al.*'s sample to run to December 2010 and not on all the data available up to December 2012. Again, it is more efficient to run these in a loop (since there will be 363 of them!) rather than individually. The Z index will loop over each of the months to produce a set of parameter estimates (lambdas) for each one, each time running a regression on the corresponding parameter estimates from the first stage.

Thus the first regression will be of TIME1 on a constant, BETA_RMRF, BETA_UMD, BETA_HML, and BETA_SMB with the estimates being put in new series as before. LAMBDA_C will contain all of the intercepts from the second stage regressions, LAMBDA_RMRF will contain all of the parameter estimates

Table 14.4 Results from Fama–MacBeth procedure using EViews

Parameter	Estimate	t-ratio
Cons	0.34	0.89
λ_M	0.21	0.62
λ_S	0.08	0.50
λ_V	0.42	2.23
λ_U	0.32	0.50

on the market risk premium betas and so on. We also collect the R^2 for each regression as it is of interest to examine the cross-sectional average.

The final stage is to estimate the averages and standard errors of these estimates using something equivalent to equations (14.29) and (14.30) respectively for each parameter. The mean is calculated simply using the @MEAN object, and the standard deviation is calculated using @STDEV. So LAMBDA_C_MEAN will contain the mean of the cross-sectional intercept estimates, and the corresponding t-ratio will be in LAMBDA_C_TRATIO and so on.

Once the program is run, we can double click on each of these objects to examine the contents. The lambda parameter estimates should be comparable with the results in the column headed '*Simple 4F Single*' from Panel A of Table 9 in Gregory *et al.* Note that they use γ to denote the parameters which have been called λ in this text. The parameter estimates obtained from this simulation and their corresponding t-ratios are given in table 14.4. Note that the latter do not use the Shanken correction as Gregory *et al.* do. These parameter estimates are the prices of risk for each of the factors (again, the coefficients from EViews need to be multiplied by 100 to turn them into percentages), and interestingly only the price of risk for value is significantly different from zero. While Gregory *et al.* additionally conduct a range of closely related but more sophisticated tests, their conclusion that further research is required to discover more convincing asset pricing model for the UK is identical to this one using the standard approach.

14.11 How might the finished project look?

Different projects will of course require different structures, but it is worth outlining at the outset the form that a good project or dissertation will take. Unless there are good reasons for doing otherwise (for example, because of the nature of the subject), it is advisable to follow the format and structure of a full-length article in

Table 14.5   Suggested structure for a typical dissertation or project
Title page
Abstract or executive summary
Acknowledgements
Table of contents
Section 1: Introduction
Section 2: Literature review
Section 3: Data
Section 4: Methodology
Section 5: Results
Section 6: Conclusions
References
Appendices

a scholarly journal. In fact, many journal articles are, at approximately 5,000 words long, roughly the same length as a student research project. A suggested outline for an empirical research project in finance is presented in table 14.5. We shall examine each component in table 14.5 in turn.

The title page

The *title page* is usually not numbered, and will contain only the title of the project, the name of the author, and the name of the department, faculty, or centre in which the research is being undertaken.

The abstract

The *abstract* is usually a short summary of the problem being addressed and of the main results and conclusions of the research. The maximum permissible length of the abstract will vary, but as a general guide, it should not be more than 300 words in total. The abstract should usually not contain any references or quotations, and should not be unduly technical, even if the subject matter of the project is.

Acknowledgements

The *acknowledgements* page is a list of people whose help you would like to note. For example, it is courteous to thank your instructor or project supervisor (even if he/she was useless and didn't help at all), any agency that gave you the data, friends who read and checked or commented upon the work, etc. It is also 'academic etiquette' to put a disclaimer after the acknowledgements, worded something like 'Responsibility for any remaining errors lies with the author(s) alone'. This also seems appropriate for a dissertation, for it symbolises that the student is completely responsible for the topic chosen, and for the contents and the structure of the project. It is your project, so you cannot blame anyone else, either deliberately or inadvertently, for anything wrong with it! The disclaimer should also remind project authors that it is not valid to take the work of others and to pass it off as one's own. Any ideas taken from other papers should be adequately referenced as such, and any sentences lifted directly from other research should be placed in quotations and attributed to their original author(s).

The table of contents

The *table of contents* should list the sections and sub-sections contained in the report. The section and sub-section headings should reflect accurately and concisely the subject matter that is contained within those sections. It should also list the page number of the first page of each section, including the references and any appendices.

The abstract, acknowledgements and table of contents pages are usually numbered with lower case Roman numerals (e.g. i, ii, iii, iv, etc.), and the introduction then starts on page 1 (reverting back to Arabic numbers), with page numbering being consecutive thereafter for the whole document, including references and any appendices.

The introduction

The *introduction* should give some very general background information on the problem considered, and why it is an important area for research. A good introductory section will also give a description of what is *original* in the study – in other words, how does this study help to advance the literature on this topic or how does it address a new problem, or an old problem in a new way? What are the aims and objectives of the research? If these can be clearly and concisely expressed, it usually demonstrates that the project is well defined. The introduction should be sufficiently non-technical that the intelligent non-specialist should be able to understand what the study is about, and it should finish with an outline of the remainder of the report.

The literature review

Before commencing any empirical work, it is essential to thoroughly review the existing literature, and the relevant articles that are found can be summarised in the *literature review* section. This will not only help to give ideas and put the proposed research in a relevant context, but may also highlight potential problem areas. Conducting a careful review of existing work will ensure that up-to-date techniques are used and that the project is not a direct (even if unintentional) copy of an already existing work.

The literature review should follow the style of an extended literature review in a scholarly journal, and should always be *critical in nature*. It should comment on the relevance, value, advantages and shortcomings of the cited articles. Do not simply provide a list of authors and contributions – the review should be written in continuous prose and not in note form. It is important to demonstrate understanding of the work and to provide a critical assessment – i.e. to point out important weaknesses in existing studies. Being 'critical' is not always easy but is a delicate balance; the tone of the review should remain polite. The review should synthesise existing work into a summary of what is and is not known and should identify trends, gaps and controversies.

Some papers in the literature are *seminal*: they change the way that people have thought about a problem or have had a major influence on policy or practice They might be introducing a new idea or an idea new to that subject area. Reviews can sometimes be organised around such papers and certainly any literature review should cite the seminal works in the field.

The process of writing a literature review can be made much easier if there exists a closely related *survey* or *review* paper. Review papers are published and (usually) high quality and detailed reports on a particular area of research. However, it goes without saying that you should not simply copy the review for several reasons. First, your topic may not match exactly that of the survey paper. Second, there may be more recent studies that are not included in the review paper. Third, you may wish to have a different emphasis and a wider perspective.

An interesting question is whether papers from low ranking journals, poorly written papers, those that are methodologically weak, and so on, be included in the review? This is, again, a difficult balance. In general the answer is probably not, but they should be included if they are directly relevant to your own work, but you should be sure to highlight the weaknesses of the approaches used.

The data

The *data* section should describe the data in detail – the source, the format, the features of the data and any limitations which are relevant for later analysis (for example, are there missing observations? Is the sample period short? Does the sample include large potential structural breaks, e.g. caused by a stock market crash?). If there are a small number of series which are being primarily investigated, it is common to plot the series, noting any interesting features, and to supply summary statistics – such as the mean, variance, skewness, kurtosis, minimum and maximum values of each series, tests for non-stationarity, measures of autocorrelation, etc.

Methodology

'*Methodology*' should describe the estimation technique(s) used to compute estimates of the parameters of the model or models. The models should be outlined and explained, using equations where appropriate. Again, this description should be written *critically*, noting any potential weaknesses in the approach and, if relevant, why more robust or up-to-date techniques were not employed. If the methodology employed does not require detailed descriptions, this section may usefully be combined with the data section.

Results

The *results* will usually be tabulated or graphed, and each table or figure should be described, noting any interesting features – whether expected or unexpected, and in particular, inferences should relate to the original aims and objectives of the research outlined in the introduction. Results should be *discussed and analysed*, not simply presented blandly. Comparisons should also be drawn with the results of similar existing studies if relevant – do your results confirm or contradict those of previous research? Each table or figure should be mentioned explicitly in the text (e.g. 'Results from estimation of equation (11) are presented in Table 4'). Do not include in the project any tables or figures which are not discussed in the text. It is also worth trying to present the results in as interesting and varied a way as possible – for example, including figures and charts as well as just tables

Conclusions

The *conclusions* section should re-state the original aim of the dissertation and outline the most important results. Any weaknesses of the study as a whole should be highlighted, and finally some suggestions for further research in the area should be presented.

References

A list of *references* should be provided, in alphabetical order by author. Note that a list of *references* (a list of all the papers, books or web pages referred to in the study, irrespective of whether you read them, or found them cited in other studies), as opposed to a bibliography (a list of items that you read, irrespective of whether you referred to them in the study), is usually required.

Although there are many ways to show citations and to list references, one possible style is the following. The citations given in the text can be given as 'Brooks (1999) demonstrated that . . .' or 'A number of authors have concluded that . . . (see, for example, Brooks, 1999).'

All works cited can be listed in the references section using the following style:

Books

Harvey, A. C. (1993) *Time Series Models*, second edition, Harvester Wheatsheaf, Hemel Hempstead, England

Published articles

Hinich, M. J. (1982) Testing for Gaussianity and Linearity of a Stationary Time Series, *Journal of Time Series Analysis* 3(3), 169–176

Unpublished articles or theses

Bera, A. K. and Jarque, C. M. (1981) An Efficient Large-Sample Test for Normality of Observations and Regression Residuals, *Australian National University Working Papers in Econometrics* 40, Canberra.

Appendices

Finally, an *appendix* or *appendices* can be used to improve the structure of the study as a whole when placing a specific item in the text would interrupt the flow of the document. For example, if you want to outline how a particular variable was constructed, or you had to write some computer code to estimate the models, and you think this could be interesting to readers, then it can be placed in an appendix. The appendices should not be used as a dumping ground for irrelevant material, or for padding, and should not be filled with printouts of raw output from computer packages!

14.12 Presentational issues

There is little sense in making the final report longer than it needs to be. Even if you are not in danger of exceeding the word limit, superfluous material will generate no additional credit and may be penalised. Assessors are likely to take into account the presentation of the document, as well as its content. Hence students should ensure that the structure of their report is orderly and logical, that equations are correctly specified, and that there are no spelling or other typographical mistakes, or grammatical errors.

Some students find it hard to know when to stop the investigative part of their work and get to the tidying up stage. Of course, it is always possible to make a piece of work better by working longer on it but there comes a point when further work on the project seems counterproductive because the remaining time is better spent on improving the writing and presentational aspects. It is definitely worth reserving a week at the end of the allocated project time if possible to read the draft paper carefully at least twice. Also, your supervisor or advisor may be willing to read through the draft and to offer comments upon it prior to final submission. If not, maybe friends who have done similar courses can give suggestions. All comments are useful – after all, any that you do not like or agree with can be ignored!

Appendix 1
Sources of data used in this book

I am grateful to the following people and organisations, who all kindly agreed to allow their data to be used as examples in this book and for it to be copied onto the book's web site: Alan Gregory/Rajesh Tharyan, the Bureau of Labor Statistics, Federal Reserve Board, Federal Reserve Bank of St. Louis, Nationwide, Oanda, and Yahoo! Finance. The following table gives details of the data used and of the provider's web site.

Provider	Data	Web
Alan Gregory/Rajesh Tharyan	Size/value-sorted portfolios and Fama–French factors	business-school.exeter.ac.uk/research/areas/centres/xfi/research/famafrench
Bureau of Labor Statistics	CPI	www.bls.gov
Federal Reserve Board	US T-bill yields, money supply, industrial production, consumer credit	www.federalreserve.gov
Federal Reserve Bank of St. Louis	average AAA & BAA corporate bond yields	research.stlouisfed.org/fred2
Nationwide	UK average house prices	www.nationwide.co.uk/hpi/datadownload/data_download.htm
Oanda	euro–dollar, pound–dollar & yen–dollar exchange rates	www.oanda.com/convert/fxhistory
Yahoo! Finance	S&P500 and various US stock and futures prices	finance.yahoo.com

Appendix 2
Tables of statistical distributions

Table A2.1	Normal critical values for different values of α								
α	0.4	0.25	0.2	0.15	0.1	0.05	0.025	0.01	0.005	0.001
Z_α	.2533	.6745	.8416	1.0364	1.2816	1.6449	1.9600	2.3263	2.5758	3.0902

Source: Author's computation using the NORMDIST function in Excel.

Table A2.2 Critical values of Student's t-distribution for different probability levels, α and degrees of freedom, ν

α	0.4	0.25	0.15	0.1	0.05	0.025	0.01	0.005	0.001	0.0005
ν										
1	0.3249	1.0000	1.9626	3.0777	6.3138	12.7062	31.8205	63.6567	318.3087	636.6189
2	0.2887	0.8165	1.3862	1.8856	2.9200	4.3027	6.9646	9.9248	22.3271	31.5991
3	0.2767	0.7649	1.2498	1.6377	2.3534	3.1824	4.5407	5.8409	10.2145	12.9240
4	0.2707	0.7407	1.1896	1.5332	2.1318	2.7764	3.7469	4.6041	7.1732	8.6103
5	0.2672	0.7267	1.1558	1.4759	2.0150	2.5706	3.3649	4.0321	5.8934	6.8688
6	0.2648	0.7176	1.1342	1.4398	1.9432	2.4469	3.1427	3.7074	5.2076	5.9588
7	0.2632	0.7111	1.1192	1.4149	1.8946	2.3646	2.9980	3.4995	4.7853	5.4079
8	0.2619	0.7064	1.1081	1.3968	1.8595	2.3060	2.8965	3.3554	4.5008	5.0413
9	0.2610	0.7027	1.0997	1.3830	1.8331	2.2622	2.8214	3.2498	4.2968	4.7809
10	0.2602	0.6998	1.0931	1.3722	1.8125	2.2281	2.7638	3.1693	4.1437	4.5869
11	0.2596	0.6974	1.0877	1.3634	1.7959	2.2010	2.7181	3.1058	4.0247	4.4370
12	0.2590	0.6955	1.0832	1.3562	1.7823	2.1788	2.6810	3.0545	3.9296	4.3178
13	0.2586	0.6938	1.0795	1.3502	1.7709	2.1604	2.6503	3.0123	3.8520	4.2208
14	0.2582	0.6924	1.0763	1.3450	1.7613	2.1448	2.6245	2.9768	3.7874	4.1405
15	0.2579	0.6912	1.0735	1.3406	1.7531	2.1314	2.6025	2.9467	3.7328	4.0728
16	0.2576	0.6901	1.0711	1.3368	1.7459	2.1199	2.5835	2.9208	3.6862	4.0150
17	0.2573	0.6892	1.0690	1.3334	1.7396	2.1098	2.5669	2.8982	3.6458	3.9651
18	0.2571	0.6884	1.0672	1.3304	1.7341	2.1009	2.5524	2.8784	3.6105	3.9216
19	0.2569	0.6876	1.0655	1.3277	1.7291	2.0930	2.5395	2.8609	3.5794	3.8834
20	0.2567	0.6870	1.0640	1.3253	1.7247	2.0860	2.5280	2.8453	3.5518	3.8495
21	0.2566	0.6864	1.0627	1.3232	1.7207	2.0796	2.5176	2.8314	3.5272	3.8193
22	0.2564	0.6858	1.0614	1.3212	1.7171	2.0739	2.5083	2.8188	3.5050	3.7921
23	0.2563	0.6853	1.0603	1.3195	1.7139	2.0687	2.4999	2.8073	3.4850	3.7676
24	0.2562	0.6848	1.0593	1.3178	1.7109	2.0639	2.4922	2.7969	3.4668	3.7454
25	0.2561	0.6844	1.0584	1.3163	1.7081	2.0595	2.4851	2.7874	3.4502	3.7251
26	0.2560	0.6840	1.0575	1.3150	1.7056	2.0555	2.4786	2.7787	3.4350	3.7066
27	0.2559	0.6837	1.0567	1.3137	1.7033	2.0518	2.4727	2.7707	3.4210	3.6896
28	0.2558	0.6834	1.0560	1.3125	1.7011	2.0484	2.4671	2.7633	3.4082	3.6739
29	0.2557	0.6830	1.0553	1.3114	1.6991	2.0452	2.4620	2.7564	3.3962	3.6594
30	0.2556	0.6828	1.0547	1.3104	1.6973	2.0423	2.4573	2.7500	3.3852	3.6460
35	0.2553	0.6816	1.0520	1.3062	1.6896	2.0301	2.4377	2.7238	3.3400	3.5911
40	0.2550	0.6807	1.0500	1.3031	1.6839	2.0211	2.4233	2.7045	3.3069	3.5510
45	0.2549	0.6800	1.0485	1.3006	1.6794	2.0141	2.4121	2.6896	3.2815	3.5203
50	0.2547	0.6794	1.0473	1.2987	1.6759	2.0086	2.4033	2.6778	3.2614	3.4960
60	0.2545	0.6786	1.0455	1.2958	1.6706	2.0003	2.3901	2.6603	3.2317	3.4602
70	0.2543	0.6780	1.0442	1.2938	1.6669	1.9944	2.3808	2.6479	3.2108	3.4350
80	0.2542	0.6776	1.0432	1.2922	1.6641	1.9901	2.3739	2.6387	3.1953	3.4163
90	0.2541	0.6772	1.0424	1.2910	1.6620	1.9867	2.3685	2.6316	3.1833	3.4019
100	0.2540	0.6770	1.0418	1.2901	1.6602	1.9840	2.3642	2.6259	3.1737	3.3905
120	0.2539	0.6765	1.0409	1.2886	1.6577	1.9799	2.3578	2.6174	3.1595	3.3735
150	0.2538	0.6761	1.0400	1.2872	1.6551	1.9759	2.3515	2.6090	3.1455	3.3566
200	0.2537	0.6757	1.0391	1.2858	1.6525	1.9719	2.3451	2.6006	3.1315	3.3398
300	0.2536	0.6753	1.0382	1.2844	1.6499	1.9679	2.3388	2.5923	3.1176	3.3233
∞	0.2533	0.6745	1.0364	1.2816	1.6449	1.9600	2.3263	2.5758	3.0902	3.2905

Source: Author's own computation using the TINV function in Excel.

Table A2.3 Upper 5% critical values for F-distribution

Degrees of freedom for numerator (m)

Degrees of freedom for denominator $(T - k)$	1	2	3	4	5	6	7	8	9	10	12	15	20	24	30	40	60	120	∞
1	161	200	216	225	230	234	237	239	241	242	244	246	248	249	250	251	252	253	254
2	18.5	19.0	19.2	19.2	19.3	19.3	19.4	19.4	19.4	19.4	19.4	19.4	19.4	19.5	19.5	19.5	19.5	19.5	19.5
3	10.1	9.55	9.28	9.12	9.01	8.94	8.89	8.85	8.81	8.79	8.74	8.70	8.66	8.64	8.62	8.59	8.57	8.55	8.53
4	7.71	6.94	6.59	6.39	6.26	6.16	6.09	6.04	6.00	5.96	5.91	5.86	5.80	5.77	5.75	5.72	5.69	5.66	5.63
5	6.61	5.79	5.41	5.19	5.05	4.95	4.88	4.82	4.77	4.74	4.68	4.62	4.56	4.53	4.50	4.46	4.43	4.40	4.37
6	5.99	5.14	4.76	4.53	4.39	4.28	4.21	4.15	4.10	4.06	4.00	3.94	3.87	3.84	3.81	3.77	3.74	3.70	3.67
7	5.59	4.74	4.35	4.12	3.97	3.87	3.79	3.73	3.68	3.64	3.57	3.51	3.44	3.41	3.38	3.34	3.30	3.27	3.23
8	5.32	4.46	4.07	3.84	3.69	3.58	3.50	3.44	3.39	3.35	3.28	3.22	3.15	3.12	3.08	3.04	3.01	2.97	2.93
9	5.12	4.26	3.86	3.63	3.48	3.37	3.29	3.23	3.18	3.14	3.07	3.01	2.94	2.90	2.86	2.83	2.79	2.75	2.71
10	4.96	4.10	3.71	3.48	3.33	3.22	3.14	3.07	3.02	2.98	2.91	2.85	2.77	2.74	2.70	2.66	2.62	2.58	2.54
11	4.84	3.98	3.59	3.36	3.20	3.09	3.01	2.95	2.90	2.85	2.79	2.72	2.65	2.61	2.57	2.53	2.49	2.45	2.40
12	4.75	3.89	3.49	3.26	3.11	3.00	2.91	2.85	2.80	2.75	2.69	2.62	2.54	2.51	2.47	2.43	2.38	2.34	2.30
13	4.67	3.81	3.41	3.18	3.03	2.92	2.83	2.77	2.71	2.67	2.60	2.53	2.46	2.42	2.38	2.34	2.30	2.25	2.21
14	4.60	3.74	3.34	3.11	2.96	2.85	2.76	2.70	2.65	2.60	2.53	2.46	2.39	2.35	2.31	2.27	2.22	2.18	2.13
15	4.54	3.68	3.29	3.06	2.90	2.79	2.71	2.64	2.59	2.54	2.48	2.40	2.33	2.29	2.25	2.20	2.16	2.11	2.07
16	4.49	3.63	3.24	3.01	2.85	2.74	2.66	2.59	2.54	2.49	2.42	2.35	2.28	2.24	2.19	2.15	2.11	2.06	2.01
17	4.45	3.59	3.20	2.96	2.81	2.70	2.61	2.55	2.49	2.45	2.38	2.31	2.23	2.19	2.15	2.10	2.06	2.01	1.96
18	4.41	3.55	3.16	2.93	2.77	2.66	2.58	2.51	2.46	2.41	2.34	2.27	2.19	2.15	2.11	2.06	2.02	1.97	1.92
19	4.38	3.52	3.13	2.90	2.74	2.63	2.54	2.48	2.42	2.38	2.31	2.23	2.16	2.11	2.07	2.03	1.98	1.93	1.88
20	4.35	3.49	3.10	2.87	2.71	2.60	2.51	2.45	2.39	2.35	2.28	2.20	2.12	2.08	2.04	1.99	1.95	1.90	1.84
21	4.32	3.47	3.07	2.84	2.68	2.57	2.49	2.42	2.37	2.32	2.25	2.18	2.10	2.05	2.01	1.96	1.92	1.87	1.81
22	4.30	3.44	3.05	2.82	2.66	2.55	2.46	2.40	2.34	2.30	2.23	2.15	2.07	2.03	1.98	1.94	1.89	1.84	1.78
23	4.28	3.42	3.03	2.80	2.64	2.53	2.44	2.37	2.32	2.27	2.20	2.13	2.05	2.01	1.96	1.91	1.86	1.81	1.76
24	4.26	3.40	3.01	2.78	2.62	2.51	2.42	2.36	2.30	2.25	2.18	2.11	2.03	1.98	1.94	1.89	1.84	1.79	1.73
25	4.24	3.39	2.99	2.76	2.60	2.49	2.40	2.34	2.28	2.24	2.16	2.09	2.01	1.96	1.92	1.87	1.82	1.77	1.71
30	4.17	3.32	2.92	2.69	2.53	2.42	2.33	2.27	2.21	2.16	2.09	2.01	1.93	1.89	1.84	1.79	1.74	1.68	1.62
40	4.08	3.23	2.84	2.61	2.45	2.34	2.25	2.18	2.12	2.08	2.00	1.92	1.84	1.79	1.74	1.69	1.64	1.58	1.51
60	4.00	3.15	2.76	2.53	2.37	2.25	2.17	2.10	2.04	1.99	1.92	1.84	1.75	1.70	1.65	1.59	1.53	1.47	1.39
120	3.92	3.07	2.68	2.45	2.29	2.18	2.09	2.02	1.96	1.91	1.83	1.75	1.66	1.61	1.55	1.50	1.43	1.35	1.25
∞	3.84	3.00	2.60	2.37	2.21	2.10	2.01	1.94	1.88	1.83	1.75	1.67	1.57	1.52	1.46	1.39	1.32	1.22	1.00

Table A2.4 Upper 1% critical values for F-distribution

	Degrees of freedom for numerator (m)																		
	1	2	3	4	5	6	7	8	9	10	12	15	20	24	30	40	60	120	∞
Degrees of freedom for denominator $(T-k)$																			
1	4,052	5,000	5,403	5,625	5,764	5,859	5,928	5,982	6,023	6,056	6,106	6,157	6,209	6,235	6,261	6,287	6,313	6,339	6,366
2	98.5	99.0	99.2	99.3	99.3	99.3	99.4	99.4	99.4	99.4	99.4	99.4	99.5	99.5	99.5	99.5	99.5	99.5	99.5
3	34.1	30.8	29.5	28.7	28.2	27.9	27.7	27.5	27.3	27.2	27.1	26.9	26.7	26.6	26.5	26.4	26.4	26.2	26.1
4	21.2	18.0	16.7	16.0	15.5	15.2	15.0	14.8	14.7	14.5	14.4	14.2	14.0	13.9	13.8	13.7	13.7	13.6	13.5
5	16.3	13.3	12.1	11.4	11.0	10.7	10.5	10.3	10.2	10.1	9.89	9.72	9.55	9.47	9.38	9.29	9.20	9.11	9.02
6	13.7	10.9	9.78	9.15	8.75	8.47	8.26	8.10	7.98	7.87	7.72	7.56	7.40	7.31	7.23	7.14	7.06	6.97	6.88
7	12.2	9.55	8.45	7.85	7.46	7.19	6.99	6.84	6.72	6.62	6.47	6.31	6.16	6.07	5.99	5.91	5.82	5.74	5.65
8	11.3	8.65	7.59	7.01	6.63	6.37	6.18	6.03	5.91	5.81	5.67	5.52	5.36	5.28	5.20	5.12	5.03	4.95	4.86
9	10.6	8.02	6.99	6.42	6.06	5.80	5.61	5.47	5.35	5.26	5.11	4.96	4.81	4.73	4.65	4.57	4.48	4.40	4.31
10	10.0	7.56	6.55	5.99	5.64	5.39	5.20	5.06	4.94	4.85	4.71	4.56	4.41	4.33	4.25	4.17	4.08	4.00	3.91
11	9.65	7.21	6.22	5.67	5.32	5.07	4.89	4.74	4.63	4.54	4.40	4.25	4.10	4.02	3.94	3.86	3.78	3.69	3.60
12	9.33	6.93	5.95	5.41	5.06	4.82	4.64	4.50	4.39	4.30	4.16	4.01	3.86	3.78	3.70	3.62	3.54	3.45	3.36
13	9.07	6.70	5.74	5.21	4.86	4.62	4.44	4.30	4.19	4.10	3.96	3.82	3.66	3.59	3.51	3.43	3.34	3.25	3.17
14	8.86	6.51	5.56	5.04	4.70	4.46	4.28	4.14	4.03	3.94	3.80	3.66	3.51	3.43	3.35	3.27	3.18	3.09	3.00
15	8.68	6.36	5.42	4.89	4.56	4.32	4.14	4.00	3.89	3.80	3.67	3.52	3.37	3.29	3.21	3.13	3.05	2.96	2.87
16	8.53	6.23	5.29	4.77	4.44	4.20	4.03	3.89	3.78	3.69	3.55	3.41	3.26	3.18	3.10	3.02	2.93	2.84	2.75
17	8.40	6.11	5.19	4.67	4.34	4.10	3.93	3.79	3.68	3.59	3.46	3.31	3.16	3.08	3.00	2.92	2.83	2.75	2.65
18	8.29	6.01	5.09	4.58	4.25	4.01	3.84	3.71	3.60	3.51	3.37	3.23	3.08	3.00	2.92	2.84	2.75	2.66	2.57
19	8.19	5.93	5.01	4.50	4.17	3.94	3.77	3.63	3.52	3.43	3.30	3.15	3.00	2.92	2.84	2.76	2.67	2.58	2.49
20	8.10	5.85	4.94	4.43	4.10	3.87	3.70	3.56	3.46	3.37	3.23	3.09	2.94	2.86	2.78	2.69	2.61	2.52	2.42
21	8.02	5.78	4.87	4.37	4.04	3.81	3.64	3.51	3.40	3.31	3.17	3.03	2.88	2.80	2.72	2.64	2.55	2.46	2.36
22	7.95	5.72	4.82	4.31	3.99	3.76	3.59	3.45	3.35	3.26	3.12	2.98	2.83	2.75	2.67	2.58	2.50	2.40	2.31
23	7.88	5.66	4.76	4.26	3.94	3.71	3.54	3.41	3.30	3.21	3.07	2.93	2.78	2.70	2.62	2.54	2.45	2.35	2.26
24	7.82	5.61	4.72	4.22	3.90	3.67	3.50	3.36	3.26	3.17	3.03	2.89	2.74	2.66	2.58	2.49	2.40	2.31	2.21
25	7.77	5.57	4.68	4.18	3.86	3.63	3.46	3.32	3.22	3.13	2.99	2.85	2.70	2.62	2.53	2.45	2.36	2.27	2.17
30	7.56	5.39	4.51	4.02	3.70	3.47	3.30	3.17	3.07	2.98	2.84	2.70	2.55	2.47	2.39	2.30	2.21	2.11	2.01
40	7.31	5.18	4.31	3.83	3.51	3.29	3.12	2.99	2.89	2.80	2.66	2.52	2.37	2.29	2.20	2.11	2.02	1.92	1.80
60	7.08	4.98	4.13	3.65	3.34	3.12	2.95	2.82	2.72	2.63	2.50	2.35	2.20	2.12	2.03	1.94	1.84	1.73	1.60
120	6.85	4.79	3.95	3.48	3.17	2.96	2.79	2.66	2.56	2.47	2.34	2.19	2.03	1.95	1.86	1.76	1.66	1.53	1.38
∞	6.63	4.61	3.78	3.32	3.02	2.80	2.64	2.51	2.41	2.32	2.18	2.04	1.88	1.79	1.70	1.59	1.47	1.32	1.00

Source: Author's own computation using the Excel FINV function.

Table A2.5 Chi-squared critical values for different values of α and degrees of freedom. υ

υ	0.995	0.990	0.975	0.950	0.900	0.750	0.500	0.250	0.100	0.050	0.025	0.010	0.005
1	0.00004	0.00016	0.00098	0.00393	0.01579	0.1015	0.4549	1.323	2.706	3.841	5.024	6.635	7.879
2	0.01003	0.02010	0.05065	0.1026	0.2107	0.5754	1.386	2.773	4.605	5.991	7.378	9.210	10.597
3	0.07172	0.1148	0.2158	0.3518	0.5844	1.213	2.366	4.108	6.251	7.815	9.348	11.345	12.838
4	0.2070	0.2971	0.4844	0.7107	1.064	1.923	3.357	5.385	7.779	9.488	11.143	13.277	14.860
5	0.4117	0.5543	0.8312	1.145	1.610	2.675	4.351	6.626	9.236	11.070	12.833	15.086	16.750
6	0.6757	0.8721	1.237	1.635	2.204	3.455	5.348	7.841	10.645	12.592	14.449	16.812	18.548
7	0.9893	1.239	1.690	2.167	2.833	4.255	6.346	9.037	12.017	14.067	16.013	18.475	20.278
8	1.344	1.646	2.180	2.733	3.490	5.071	7.344	10.219	13.362	15.507	17.535	20.090	21.955
9	1.735	2.088	2.700	3.325	4.168	5.899	8.343	11.389	14.684	16.919	19.023	21.666	23.589
10	2.156	2.558	3.247	3.940	4.865	6.737	9.342	12.549	15.987	18.307	20.483	23.209	25.188
11	2.603	3.053	3.816	4.575	5.578	7.584	10.341	13.701	17.275	19.675	21.920	24.725	26.757
12	3.074	3.571	4.404	5.226	6.304	8.438	11.340	14.845	18.54	21.026	23.337	26.217	28.300
13	3.565	4.107	5.009	5.892	7.041	9.299	12.340	15.984	19.812	22.362	24.736	27.688	29.819
14	4.075	4.660	5.629	6.571	7.790	10.165	13.339	17.117	21.064	23.685	26.119	29.141	31.319
15	4.601	5.229	6.262	7.261	8.547	11.036	14.339	18.245	22.307	24.996	27.488	30.578	32.801
16	5.142	5.812	6.908	7.962	9.312	11.912	15.338	19.369	23.542	26.296	28.845	32.000	34.267
17	5.697	6.408	7.564	8.672	10.085	12.792	16.338	20.489	24.769	27.587	30.191	33.409	35.718
18	6.265	7.015	8.231	9.390	10.865	13.675	17.338	21.605	25.989	28.869	31.526	34.805	37.156
19	6.844	7.633	8.907	10.117	11.651	14.562	18.338	22.718	27.204	30.143	32.852	36.191	38.582
20	7.434	8.260	9.591	10.851	12.443	15.452	19.337	23.828	28.412	31.410	34.170	37.566	39.997
21	8.034	8.897	10.283	11.591	13.240	16.344	20.337	24.935	29.615	32.670	35.479	38.932	41.401
22	8.643	9.542	10.982	12.338	14.041	17.240	21.337	26.039	30.813	33.924	36.781	40.289	42.796

Table A2.5 (cont.)

df													
23	9.260	10.196	11.688	13.090	14.848	18.137	22.337	27.141	32.007	35.172	38.076	41.638	44.181
24	9.886	10.856	12.401	13.848	15.659	19.037	23.337	28.241	33.196	36.415	39.364	42.080	45.558
25	10.520	11.524	13.120	14.611	16.473	19.939	24.337	29.339	34.382	37.652	40.646	44.314	46.928
26	11.160	12.198	13.844	15.379	17.292	20.843	25.336	30.434	35.563	38.885	41.923	45.642	48.290
27	11.808	12.879	14.573	16.151	18.114	21.749	26.336	31.528	36.741	40.113	43.194	46.963	49.645
28	12.461	13.565	15.308	16.928	18.939	22.657	27.336	32.620	37.916	41.337	44.461	48.278	50.993
29	13.121	14.256	16.047	17.708	19.768	23.567	28.336	33.711	39.087	42.557	45.722	49.588	52.336
30	13.787	14.954	16.791	18.493	20.599	24.478	29.336	34.800	40.256	43.773	46.979	50.892	53.672
35	17.192	18.509	20.569	22.465	24.797	29.054	34.336	40.223	46.059	49.802	53.203	57.342	60.275
40	20.707	22.164	24.433	26.509	29.050	33.660	39.335	45.616	51.805	55.758	59.342	63.691	66.766
45	24.311	25.901	28.366	30.612	33.350	38.291	44.335	50.985	57.505	61.656	65.410	69.957	73.166
50	27.991	29.707	32.357	34.764	37.689	42.942	49.335	56.334	63.167	67.505	71.420	76.154	79.490
55	31.735	33.571	36.398	38.958	42.060	47.611	54.335	61.665	68.796	73.311	77.381	82.292	85.749
60	35.535	37.485	40.482	43.158	46.459	52.294	59.335	66.981	74.397	79.082	83.298	85.379	91.952
70	43.275	45.442	48.758	51.739	55.329	61.698	69.334	77.577	85.527	90.531	95.023	100.425	104.215
80	51.172	53.540	57.153	60.391	64.278	71.144	79.334	88.130	96.578	101.879	106.629	112.329	116.321
90	59.196	61.754	65.647	69.126	73.291	80.625	89.334	98.650	107.565	113.145	118.136	124.116	128.299
100	67.328	70.065	74.222	77.929	82.358	90.133	99.334	109.141	118.498	124.342	129.561	135.807	140.169
120	83.829	86.909	91.568	95.705	100.627	109.224	119.335	130.051	140.228	146.565	152.214	158.963	163.670
150	109.122	112.655	117.980	122.692	126.278	137.987	149.334	161.258	172.577	179.579	185.803	193.219	198.380
200	152.224	156.421	162.724	168.279	174.825	186.175	199.334	213.099	226.018	233.993	241.060	249.455	255.281
250	196.145	200.929	208.095	214.392	221.809	234.580	249.334	264.694	279.947	287.889	295.691	304.948	311.361

Source: Author's own computation using the Excel CHIINV function.

Table A2.6 Lower and upper 1% critical values for Durbin–Watson statistic

T	$k'=1$ d_L	d_U	$k'=2$ d_L	d_U	$k'=3$ d_L	d_U	$k'=4$ d_L	d_U	$k'=5$ d_L	d_U
15	0.81	1.07	0.70	1.25	0.59	1.46	0.49	1.70	0.39	1.96
16	0.84	1.09	0.74	1.25	0.63	1.44	0.53	1.66	0.44	1.90
17	0.87	1.10	0.77	1.25	0.67	1.43	0.57	1.63	0.48	1.85
18	0.90	1.12	0.80	1.26	0.71	1.42	0.61	1.60	0.52	1.80
19	0.93	1.13	0.83	1.26	0.74	1.41	0.65	1.58	0.56	1.77
20	0.95	1.15	0.86	1.27	0.77	1.41	0.68	1.57	0.60	1.74
21	0.97	1.16	0.89	1.27	0.80	1.41	0.72	1.55	0.63	1.71
22	1.00	1.17	0.91	1.28	0.83	1.40	0.75	1.54	0.66	1.69
23	1.02	1.19	0.94	1.29	0.86	1.40	0.77	1.53	0.70	1.67
24	1.04	1.20	0.96	1.30	0.88	1.41	0.80	1.53	0.72	1.66
25	1.05	1.21	0.98	1.30	0.90	1.41	0.83	1.52	0.75	1.65
26	1.07	1.22	1.00	1.31	0.93	1.41	0.85	1.52	0.78	1.64
27	1.09	1.23	1.02	1.32	0.95	1.41	0.88	1.51	0.81	1.63
28	1.10	1.24	1.04	1.32	0.97	1.41	0.90	1.51	0.83	1.62
29	1.12	1.25	1.05	1.33	0.99	1.42	0.92	1.51	0.85	1.61
30	1.13	1.26	1.07	1.34	1.01	1.42	0.94	1.51	0.88	1.61
31	1.15	1.27	1.08	1.34	1.02	1.42	0.96	1.51	0.90	1.60
32	1.16	1.28	1.10	1.35	1.04	1.43	0.98	1.51	0.92	1.60
33	1.17	1.29	1.11	1.36	1.05	1.43	1.00	1.51	0.94	1.59
34	1.18	1.30	1.13	1.36	1.07	1.43	1.01	1.51	0.95	1.59
35	1.19	1.31	1.14	1.37	1.08	1.44	1.03	1.51	0.97	1.59
36	1.21	1.32	1.15	1.38	1.10	1.44	1.04	1.51	0.99	1.59
37	1.22	1.32	1.16	1.38	1.11	1.45	1.06	1.51	1.00	1.59
38	1.23	1.33	1.18	1.39	1.12	1.45	1.07	1.52	1.02	1.58
39	1.24	1.34	1.19	1.39	1.14	1.45	1.09	1.52	1.03	1.58
40	1.25	1.34	1.20	1.40	1.15	1.46	1.10	1.52	1.05	1.58
45	1.29	1.38	1.24	1.42	1.20	1.48	1.16	1.53	1.11	1.58
50	1.32	1.40	1.28	1.45	1.24	1.49	1.20	1.54	1.16	1.59
55	1.36	1.43	1.32	1.47	1.28	1.51	1.25	1.55	1.21	1.59
60	1.38	1.45	1.35	1.48	1.32	1.52	1.28	1.56	1.25	1.60
65	1.41	1.47	1.38	1.50	1.35	1.53	1.31	1.57	1.28	1.61
70	1.43	1.49	1.40	1.52	1.37	1.55	1.34	1.58	1.31	1.61
75	1.45	1.50	1.42	1.53	1.39	1.56	1.37	1.59	1.34	1.62
80	1.47	1.52	1.44	1.54	1.42	1.57	1.39	1.60	1.36	1.62
85	1.48	1.53	1.46	1.55	1.43	1.58	1.41	1.60	1.39	1.63
90	1.50	1.54	1.47	1.56	1.45	1.59	1.43	1.61	1.41	1.64
95	1.51	1.55	1.49	1.57	1.47	1.60	1.45	1.62	1.42	1.64
100	1.52	1.56	1.50	1.58	1.48	1.60	1.46	1.63	1.44	1.65

Note: T, number of observations; k', number of explanatory variables (excluding a constant term).
Source: Durbin and Watson (1951): 159–77. Reprinted with the permission of Oxford University Press.

Table A2.7 Dickey–Fuller critical values for different significance levels, α

Sample size T	0.01	0.025	0.05	0.10
		τ		
25	−2.66	−2.26	−1.95	−1.60
50	−2.62	−2.25	−1.95	−1.61
100	−2.60	−2.24	−1.95	−1.61
250	−2.58	−2.23	−1.95	−1.62
500	−2.58	−2.23	−1.95	−1.62
∞	−2.58	−2.23	−1.95	−1.62
		τ_μ		
25	−3.75	−3.33	−3.00	−2.63
50	−3.58	−3.22	−2.93	−2.60
100	−3.51	−3.17	−2.89	−2.58
250	−3.46	−3.14	−2.88	−2.57
500	−3.44	−3.13	−2.87	−2.57
∞	−3.43	−3.12	−2.86	−2.57
		τ_τ		
25	−4.38	−3.95	−3.60	−3.24
50	−4.15	−3.80	−3.50	−3.18
100	−4.04	−3.73	−3.45	−3.15
250	−3.99	−3.69	−3.43	−3.13
500	−3.98	−3.68	−3.42	−3.13
∞	−3.96	−3.66	−3.41	−3.12

Source: Fuller (1976). Reprinted with the permission of John Wiley and Sons.

Table A2.8   Critical values for the Engle–Granger cointegration test on regression residuals with no constant in test regression

Number of variables in system	Sample size T	0.01	0.05	0.10
	50	−4.32	−3.67	−3.28
2	100	−4.07	−3.37	−3.03
	200	−4.00	−3.37	−3.02
	50	−4.84	−4.11	−3.73
3	100	−4.45	−3.93	−3.59
	200	−4.35	−3.78	−3.47
	50	−4.94	−4.35	−4.02
4	100	−4.75	−4.22	−3.89
	200	−4.70	−4.18	−3.89
	50	−5.41	−4.76	−4.42
5	100	−5.18	−4.58	−4.26
	200	−5.02	−4.48	−4.18

Source: Engle and Yoo (1987). Reprinted with the permission of Elsevier.

Table A2.9 Quantiles of the asymptotic distribution of the Johansen cointegration rank test statistics (constant in cointegrating vectors only)

$p - r$	50%	80%	90%	95%	97.5%	99%	Mean	Var
λ_{max}								
1	3.40	5.91	7.52	9.24	10.80	12.97	4.03	7.07
2	8.27	11.54	13.75	15.67	17.63	20.20	8.86	13.08
3	13.47	17.40	19.77	22.00	24.07	26.81	14.02	19.24
4	18.70	22.95	25.56	28.14	30.32	33.24	19.23	23.83
5	23.78	28.76	31.66	34.40	36.90	39.79	24.48	29.26
6	29.08	34.25	37.45	40.30	43.22	46.82	29.72	34.63
7	34.73	40.13	43.25	46.45	48.99	51.91	35.18	38.35
8	39.70	45.53	48.91	52.00	54.71	57.95	40.35	41.98
9	44.97	50.73	54.35	57.42	60.50	63.71	45.55	44.13
10	50.21	56.52	60.25	63.57	66.24	69.94	50.82	49.28
11	55.70	62.38	66.02	69.74	72.64	76.63	56.33	54.99
λ_{Trace}								
1	3.40	5.91	7.52	9.24	10.80	12.97	4.03	7.07
2	11.25	15.25	17.85	19.96	22.05	24.60	11.91	18.94
3	23.28	28.75	32.00	34.91	37.61	41.07	23.84	37.98
4	38.84	45.65	49.65	53.12	56.06	60.16	39.50	59.42
5	58.46	66.91	71.86	76.07	80.06	84.45	59.16	91.65
6	81.90	91.57	97.18	102.14	106.74	111.01	82.49	126.94
7	109.17	120.35	126.58	131.70	136.49	143.09	109.75	167.91
8	139.83	152.56	159.48	165.58	171.28	177.20	140.57	208.09
9	174.88	198.08	196.37	202.92	208.81	215.74	175.44	257.84
10	212.93	228.08	236.54	244.15	251.30	257.68	213.53	317.24
11	254.84	272.82	282.45	291.40	298.31	307.64	256.15	413.35

Source: Osterwald-Lenum (1992, table 1*). Reprinted with the permission of Blackwell Publishers.

Table A2.10 Quantiles of the asymptotic distribution of the Johansen cointegration rank test statistics (constant, i.e. a drift only in VAR and in cointegrating vector)

$p - r$	50%	80%	90%	95%	97.5%	99%	Mean	Var
λ_{max}								
1	0.44	1.66	2.69	3.76	4.95	6.65	0.99	2.04
2	6.85	10.04	12.07	14.07	16.05	18.63	7.47	12.42
3	12.34	16.20	18.60	20.97	23.09	25.52	12.88	18.67
4	17.66	21.98	24.73	27.07	28.98	32.24	18.26	23.47
5	23.05	27.85	30.90	33.46	35.71	38.77	23.67	28.82
6	28.45	33.67	36.76	39.37	41.86	45.10	29.06	33.57
7	33.83	39.12	42.32	45.28	47.96	51.57	34.37	37.41
8	39.29	45.05	48.33	51.42	54.29	57.69	39.85	42.90
9	44.58	50.55	53.98	57.12	59.33	62.80	45.10	44.93
10	49.66	55.97	59.62	62.81	65.44	69.09	50.29	49.41
11	54.99	61.55	65.38	68.83	72.11	75.95	55.63	54.92
λ_{Trace}								
1	0.44	1.66	2.69	3.76	4.95	6.65	0.99	2.04
2	7.55	11.07	13.33	15.41	17.52	20.04	8.23	14.38
3	18.70	23.64	26.79	29.68	32.56	35.65	19.32	32.43
4	33.60	40.15	43.95	47.21	50.35	54.46	34.24	52.75
5	52.30	60.29	64.84	68.52	71.80	76.07	52.95	79.25
6	75.26	84.57	89.48	94.15	98.33	103.18	75.74	114.65
7	101.22	112.30	118.50	124.24	128.45	133.57	101.91	158.78
8	131.62	143.97	150.53	156.00	161.32	168.36	132.09	201.82
9	165.11	178.90	186.39	192.89	198.82	204.95	165.90	246.45
10	202.58	217.81	225.85	233.13	239.46	247.18	203.39	300.80
11	243.90	260.82	269.96	277.71	284.87	293.44	244.66	379.56

Source: Osterwald-Lenum (1992, table 1). Reprinted with the permission of Blackwell Publishers.

Table A2.11   Quantiles of the asymptotic distribution of the Johansen cointegration rank test statistics (constant in cointegrating vector and VAR, trend in cointegrating vector)

$p - r$	50%	80%	90%	95%	97.5%	99%	Mean	Var
λ_{max}								
1	5.55	8.65	10.49	12.25	14.21	16.26	6.22	10.11
2	10.90	14.70	16.85	18.96	21.14	23.65	11.51	16.38
3	16.24	20.45	23.11	25.54	27.68	30.34	16.82	22.01
4	21.50	26.30	29.12	31.46	33.60	36.65	22.08	27.74
5	26.72	31.72	34.75	37.52	40.01	42.36	27.32	31.36
6	32.01	37.50	40.91	43.97	46.84	49.51	32.68	37.91
7	37.57	43.11	46.32	49.42	51.94	54.71	38.06	39.74
8	42.72	48.56	52.16	55.50	58.08	62.46	43.34	44.83
9	48.17	54.34	57.87	61.29	64.12	67.88	48.74	49.20
10	53.21	59.49	63.18	66.23	69.56	73.73	53.74	52.64
11	58.54	64.97	69.26	72.72	75.72	79.23	59.15	56.97
λ_{Trace}								
1	5.55	8.65	10.49	12.25	14.21	16.26	6.22	10.11
2	15.59	20.19	22.76	25.32	27.75	30.45	16.20	24.90
3	29.53	35.56	39.06	42.44	45.42	48.45	30.15	45.68
4	47.17	54.80	59.14	62.99	66.25	70.05	47.79	74.48
5	68.64	77.83	83.20	87.31	91.06	96.58	69.35	106.56
6	94.05	104.73	110.42	114.90	119.29	124.75	94.67	143.33
7	122.87	134.57	141.01	146.76	152.52	158.49	123.51	182.85
8	155.40	169.10	176.67	182.82	187.91	196.08	156.41	234.11
9	192.37	207.25	215.17	222.21	228.05	234.41	193.03	288.30
10	231.59	247.91	256.72	263.42	270.33	279.07	232.25	345.23
11	276.34	294.12	303.13	310.81	318.02	327.45	276.88	416.98

Source: Osterwald-Lenum (1992, table 2*). Reprinted with the permission of Blackwell Publishers.

Glossary

This glossary gives brief definitions of all the key terms used in the book. For more details, go back and read the chapters or the references therein!

adjusted R^2: a measure of how well a model fits the sample data that automatically penalises models with large numbers of parameters.

Akaike information criterion (AIC): a metric that can be used to select the best fitting from a set of competing models and that incorporates a weak penalty term for including additional parameters.

alternative hypothesis: a formal expression as part of a hypothesis testing framework that encompasses all of the remaining outcomes of interest aside from that incorporated into the null hypothesis.

arbitrage: a concept from finance that refers to the situation where profits can be made without taking any risk (and without using any wealth).

asymptotic: a property that applies as the sample size tends to infinity.

autocorrelation: a standardised measure, which must lie between -1 and $+1$, of the extent to which the current value of a series is related to its own previous values.

autocorrelation function: a set of estimated values showing the strength of association between a variable and its previous values as the lag length increases.

autocovariance: an unstandardised measure of the extent to which the current value of a series is related to its own previous values.

autoregressive conditional heteroscedasticity (ARCH) model: a time series model for volatilities.

autoregressive (AR) model: a time series model where the current value of a series is fitted with its previous values.

autoregressive moving average (ARMA) model: a time series model where the current value of a series is fitted with its previous values (the autoregressive part) and the current and previous values of an error term (the moving average part).

autoregressive volatility (ARV) model: a time series model where the current volatility is fitted with its previous values.

auxiliary regression: a second stage regression that is usually not of direct interest in its own right, but rather is conducted in order to test the statistical adequacy of the original regression model.

balanced panel: a dataset where the variables have both time series and cross-sectional dimensions, and where there are equally long samples for each cross-sectional entity (i.e. no missing data).

Bayes information criterion: *see* Schwarz's Bayesian information criterion (SBIC).

BDS test: a test for whether there are patterns in a series, predominantly used for determining whether there is evidence for non-linearities.

BEKK model: a multivariate model for volatilities and covariances between series that ensures the variance–covariance matrix is positive definite.

BHHH algorithm: a technique that can be used for solving optimisation problems including maximum likelihood.

backshift operator: *see* lag operator.

Bera–Jarque test: a widely employed test for determining whether a series closely approximates a normal distribution.

best linear unbiased estimator (BLUE): is one that provides the lowest sampling variance and which is also unbiased.

between estimator: is used in the context of a fixed effects panel model, involving running a cross-sectional regression on the time-averaged values of all the variables in order to reduce the number of parameters requiring estimation.

biased estimator: where the expected value of the parameter to be estimated is not equal to the true value.

bid–ask spread: the difference between the amount paid for an asset (the ask or offer price) when it is purchased and the amount received if it is sold (the bid).

binary choice: a discrete choice situation with only two possible outcomes.

bivariate regression: a regression model where there are only two variables – the dependent variable and a single independent variable.

bootstrapping: a technique for constructing standard errors and conducting hypothesis tests that requires no distributional assumptions and works by resampling from the data.

Box–Jenkins approach: a methodology for estimating ARMA models.

Box–Pierce Q-statistic: a general measure of the extent to which a series is autocorrelated.

break date: the date at which a structural change occurs in a time series or in a model's parameters.

Breusch–Godfrey test: a test for autocorrelation of any order in the residuals from an estimated regression model, based on an auxiliary regression of the residuals on the original explanatory variables plus lags of the residuals.

broken trend: a process which is a deterministic trend with a structural break.

calendar effects: the systematic tendency for a series, especially stock returns, to be higher at certain times than others.

capital asset pricing model (CAPM): a financial model for determining the expected return on stocks as a function of their level of market risk.

capital market line (CML): a straight line showing the risks and returns of all combinations of a risk-free asset and an optimal portfolio of risky assets.

Carhart model: a time series model for explaining the performance of mutual funds or trading rules based on four factors: excess market returns, size, value and momentum.

causality tests: a way to examine whether one series leads or lags another.

censored dependent variable: where values of the dependent variable above or below a certain threshold cannot be observed, while the corresponding values for the independent variables are still available.

central limit theorem: the mean of a sample of data having any distribution converges upon a normal distribution as the sample size tends to infinity.

chaos theory: an idea taken from the physical sciences whereby although a series may appear completely random to the naked eye or to many statistical tests, in fact there is an entirely deterministic set of non-linear equations driving its behaviour.

Chow test: an approach to determine whether a regression model contains a change in behaviour (structural break) part-way through based on splitting the sample into two parts, assuming that the break-date is known.

Cochrane–Orcutt procedure: an iterative approach that corrects standard errors for a specific form of autocorrelation.

coefficient of multiple determination: *see* R^2.

cointegration: a concept whereby time series have a fixed relationship in the long run.

cointegrating vector: the set of parameters that describes the long-run relationship between two or more time series.

common factor restrictions: these are the conditions on the parameter estimates that are implicitly assumed when an iterative procedure such as Cochrane–Orcutt is employed to correct for autocorrelation.

conditional expectation: the value of a random variable that is expected for time $t + s$ ($s = 1, 2, \ldots$) given information available until time t.

conditional mean: the mean of a series at a point in time t fitted given all information available until the previous point in time $t - 1$.

conditional variance: the variance of a series at a point in time t fitted given all information available until the previous point in time $t - 1$.

confidence interval: a range of values within which we are confident to a given degree (e.g. 95% confident) that the true value of a given parameter lies.

confidence level: one minus the significance level (expressed as a proportion rather than a percentage) for a hypothesis test.

consistency: the desirable property of an estimator whereby the calculated value of a parameter converges upon the true value as the sample size increases.

contemporaneous terms: those variables that are measured at the same time as the dependent variable – i.e. both are at time t.

continuous variable: a random variable that can take on any value (possibly within a given range).

convergence criterion: a pre-specified rule that tells an optimiser when to stop looking further for a solution and to stick with the best one it has already found.

copulas: a flexible way to link together the distributions for individual series in order to form joint distributions.

correlation: a standardised measure, bounded between -1 and $+1$, of the strength of association between two variables.

correlogram: *see* autocorrelation function.

cost of carry (COC) model: shows the equilibrium relationship between spot and corresponding futures prices where the spot price is adjusted for the cost of 'carrying' the spot asset forward to the maturity date.

covariance matrix: *see* variance–covariance matrix.

covariance stationary process: *see* weakly stationary process.

covered interest parity (CIP): states that exchange rates should adjust so that borrowing funds in one currency and investing them in another would not be expected to earn abnormal profits.

credit rating: an evaluation made by a ratings agency of the ability of a borrower to meet its obligations to meet interest costs and to make capital repayments when due.

critical values (CV): key points in a statistical distribution that determine whether, given a calculated value of a test statistic, the null hypothesis will be rejected or not.

cross-equation restrictions: a set of restrictions needed for a hypothesis test that involves more than one equation within a system.

cross-sectional regression: a regression involving series that are measured only at a single point in time but across many entities.

cumulative distribution: a function giving the probability that a random variable will take on a value lower than some pre-specified value.

CUSUM and CUSUMSQ tests: tests for parameter stability in an estimated model based on the cumulative sum of residuals (CUSUM) or cumulative sum of squared residuals (CUSUMSQ) from a recursive regression.

daily range estimator: a crude measure of volatility calculated as the difference between the day's lowest and highest observed prices.

damped sine wave: a pattern, especially in an autocorrelation function plot, where the values cycle from positive to negative in a declining manner as the lag length increases.

data generating process (DGP): the true relationship between the series in a model.

data mining: looking very intensively for patterns in data and relationships between series without recourse to financial theory, possibly leading to spurious findings.

data revisions: changes to series, especially macroeconomic variables, that are made after they are first published.

data snooping: *see* data mining.

day-of-the-week effect: the systematic tendency for stock returns to be higher on some days of the week than others.

degrees of freedom: a parameter that affects the shape of a statistical distribution and therefore its critical values. Some distributions have one degree of freedom parameter, while others have more.

degree of persistence: the extent to which a series is positively related to its previous values.

dependent variable: the variable, usually denoted by y that the model tries to explain.

deterministic: a process that has no random (stochastic) component.

Dickey–Fuller (DF) test: an approach to determining whether a series contains a unit root, based on a regression of the change in that variable on the lag of the level of that variable.

differencing: a technique used to remove a (stochastic) trend from a series that involves forming a new series by taking the lagged value of the original series away from the current one.

differentiation: a mathematical technique to find the derivative, which is the slope of a function, or in other words the rate at which y changes in response to changes in x.

discrete choice: a model where the key variable takes only integer values that capture the selections made between alternatives – for example, between modes of transport for a particular journey.

discrete variable: a random variable that can only take specific values.

distributed lag models: contain lags of the explanatory variables but no lags of the explained variable.

disturbance term: *see* error term.

double logarithmic form: a specification of a model where logarithms are taken of both the dependent variable (y) and the independent variable(s) (x).

dummy variables: artificially constructed variables that capture qualitative information – for example, for male/female, days of the week, emerging/developed markets, etc. They are usually binary variables (0 or 1).

Durbin–Watson (DW) statistic: a test for first order autocorrelation, i.e. a test for whether a (residual) series is related to its immediately preceding values.

dynamic conditional correlation: a model that explicitly models correlations in a time-varying, autoregressive fashion.

dynamic model: a model that includes lagged or differenced terms of the dependent or independent variables (or both).

efficient estimator: an approach to parameter estimation that is optimal in some sense. In econometrics, this is usually taken to mean a formula for calculating the parameters that leads to minimum sampling variance; in other words, the estimates vary as little as possible from one sample to another.

efficient frontier: a curve that traces out all possible optimal portfolios.

efficient market hypothesis: the notion that asset prices will rapidly reflect all relevant and available information.

eigenvalues: the characteristic roots of a matrix.

eigenvectors: a set of vectors that, when multiplied by a square matrix, give a set of vectors that differ from the originals by a multiplicative scalar.

elasticities: the responsiveness of a percentage change in one variable to percentage changes in another.

encompassing principle: the notion that a good model will be able to explain all that competing models can and more.

encompassing regression: a hybrid model that incorporates the variables contained in two or more competing models as a method of selecting which is the best between them. The parameters of the best model will be significant in the hybrid model.

endogenous variable: a variable whose value is determined within the system of equations under study. In the context of a simultaneous system, each endogenous variable has its own equation specifying how it is generated.

Engle–Granger (EG) test: a unit root test applied to the residuals of a potentially cointegrating regression.

Engle–Ng test: a test for appropriate specification of a GARCH model in terms of whether there are any uncaptured asymmetries.

equilibrium correction model: *see* error correction model.

error correction model (ECM): a model constructed using variables that are employed in stationary, first-differenced forms together with a term that captures movements back towards long run equilibrium.

error term: part of a regression model that sweeps up any influences on the dependent variable that are not captured by the independent variables.

errors-in-variables regression: a valid approach to estimating the parameters of a regression when the explanatory variables are measured with error and are thus stochastic.

estimate: the calculated value of a parameter obtained from the sample data.

estimator: an equation that is employed together with the data in order to calculate the parameters that describe the regression relationship.

exogeneity: the extent to which a variable is determined outside of the model under study.

event study: an approach to financial research where the impact of an identifiable event (e.g. a dividend announcement) is measured on a firm characteristic (e.g. its stock price) to evaluate the market reaction to the event.

exogenous variables: variables whose values are taken as given and are determined outside of the equation or system of equations under study and are thus not correlated with the error term.

expectations hypothesis: related particularly to the term structure of interest rates. It states that the expected return from investing in a long term bond will be equal to the return from investing in a series of short-term bonds plus a risk premium. In other words, the long term interest rate is a geometric average of the current and expected future short term rates (plus a risk premium).

explained sum of squares (ESS): the part of the variation in y that is explained by the model.

explained variable: *see* dependent variable.

explanatory variables: those variables which are on the right hand side of an equation, whose values are usually taken as fixed, and which are purported to be explaining the values of the dependent variable y.

exponential (EGARCH): a model where volatility is modelled in an exponential form so that no non-negativity conditions need to be applied to the parameters. This specification also that allows for asymmetries in the relationship between volatility and returns of different signs.

exponential growth model: a model where the dependent variable is an exponential function of one or more independent variables.

exponential smoothing: a simple approach to modelling and forecasting where the current smoothed value is a geometrically declining function of all previous values of the series.

exponentially weighted moving average (EWMA) model: a simple method for modelling and forecasting volatility where the current estimate is simply a weighted combination of previous values, with the weightings exponentially declining back through time.

F-statistic: a measure that follows an F-distribution used for testing multiple hypotheses.

factor loading: has several meanings but in particular in the context of principal component analysis, it gives the amount of a variable that appears in each component.

Fama–MacBeth procedure: a two-step procedure for testing asset pricing models such as the CAPM. In the first stage the betas are estimated in a set of time series regressions and then a second stage cross-sectional regression examines the explanatory power of these betas.

financial options: securities that give the holder the right but not the obligation to buy or sell another asset at a pre-specified price on a pre-specified date.

first differences: new series constructed by taking the immediately previous value of a series from its current value.

fitted value: the value of y that the model fits for a given data point, i.e. for given values of the explanatory variable.

fixed effects: most commonly a type of model used for panel data that employs dummies to account for variables that affect the dependent variable y cross-sectionally but do not vary over time. Alternatively, the dummies can capture variables that affect y over time but do not vary cross-sectionally.

forcing variable: sometimes used synonymously with explanatory variable; alternatively it can mean the unobservable state-determining variable that governs the regime in a Markov switching regression model.

forecast encompassing test: a regression of the actual values of a series on several corresponding sets of forecasts. The idea is that if a parameter estimate is statistically significant, then the forecasts from the corresponding model encompass (i.e. contain more information than) those of the other model(s).

forecast error: the difference between the actual value of a series and the value that has been forecast for it.

forward rate unbiasedness (FRU): the hypothesis that the forward rate of foreign exchange should be an unbiased prediction of the future spot rate of interest.

fractionally integrated models: a way to represent series that are stationary but highly persistent and thus have long memory.

functional form misspecification: *see* RESET test.

futures prices: the price of a specific quantity of a good or asset for delivery at some pre-specified date in the future.

GARCH-in-mean (GARCH-M): a dynamic model for volatility where the standard deviation (or variance) enters into the generating process for returns.

Gauss–Markov theorem: a derivation using algebra showing that, providing a certain set of assumptions hold, the OLS estimator is the best linear unbiased estimator (BLUE).

general-to-specific methodology: a philosophical approach to constructing econometric models where the researcher commences with a very broad model and then, through hypothesis testing, reduces the model down to a smaller one.

generalised autoregressive conditional heteroscedasticity (GARCH) models: a common specification of dynamic model for volatility.

generalised least squares (GLS): an approach to the estimation of econometric models that is more flexible than ordinary least squares and can be used to relax one or more of its limiting assumptions.

generalised unrestricted model (GUM): the initial, broad model that is specified as the first step of the general-to-specific approach to model construction.

gilt–equity yield ratio (GEYR): the ratio of the yield on long term Treasury bonds to the dividend yield on stocks.

GJR model: a model for time-varying volatilities developed by Glosten, Jaganathan and Runkle to allow for asymmetries in the relationship between volatility and returns of different signs.

Goldfeld–Quandt test for heteroscedasticity: one of several available tests for whether the residuals from an estimated model have constant variance.

goodness of fit statistic: a measure of how well the model that has been estimated fits the sample data.

Granger representation theorem: states that if there exists a dynamic linear model with stationary disturbances but where the component variables are non-stationary, then they must be cointegrated.

Hamilton's filter: a form of Markov-switching model where an unobservable state variable switches between discrete regimes via a first-order Markov process.

Hannan–Quinn information criterion: a metric that can be used to select the best fitting from a set of competing models and that incorporates a moderate penalty term for including additional parameters.

Hausman test: a test for whether a variable can be treated as exogenous or whether in fact the researcher needs to specify a separate structural equation for that variable. It can also refer to a test for whether a random effects approach to panel regression is valid or whether a fixed effects model is necessary.

Heckman procedure: a two-step method that corrects for the selection bias that can be observed in the context of samples not selected randomly.

hedge ratios: in the context of hedging with futures contracts, this is the number of futures contracts that are sold per unit of the spot asset held.

hedonic pricing models: a modelling approach where the price of a physical asset is modelled as a function of its characteristics.

heteroscedasticity: where the variance of a series is not constant throughout the sample.

heteroscedasticity-robust: a set of standard errors (or test statistics) that have been calculated using an approach that is valid in the presence of heteroscedastic residuals.

hypothesis test: a framework for considering plausible values of the true population parameters given the sample estimates.

identification: a condition for whether all of the structural parameters in a particular equation from a simultaneous system can be retrieved from estimating the corresponding reduced form equation.

identity matrix: a square matrix containing ones on the main diagonal and zeros everywhere else.

implied volatility models: an approach whereby the volatility of an underlying asset is calculated from the traded price of an option and a pricing formula.

impulse responses: an examination of the impact of a unit shock to one variable on the other variables in a vector autoregressive (VAR) system.

independent variables: *see* explanatory variables.

information criteria: a family of methods for selecting between competing models that incorporate automatic correction penalties when larger numbers of parameters are included.

instrumental variables (instruments): can be used to replace endogenous variables on the right hand side of a regression equation. The instruments are correlated with the variables they replace but not with the error term in the regression.

integrated GARCH (IGARCH): a model where the variance process is non-stationary so that the impact of shocks on volatility persists indefinitely.

integrated variable: one which requires differencing to make it stationary.

interactive dummy variable: when a dummy variable is multiplied by an explanatory variable to allow the regression slope to change according to the value of the dummy.

intercept: the point where a regression line crosses the y-axis, also known sometimes as 'the coefficient on the constant term', or sometimes just 'the constant term'.

inverse (of a matrix): a transformed matrix which, when multiplied by the original matrix, yields the identity matrix.

invertibility: a condition for a moving average (MA) model to be representable as a valid infinite-order autoregressive model.

irrelevant variables: variables that are included in a regression equation but in fact have no impact on the dependent variable.

Jensen's alpha: the intercept estimate in a regression model of the returns to a portfolio or strategy on a risk factor or set of risk factors, especially in the context of the CAPM. Alpha measures the degree to which there was abnormally bad or good performance.

Johansen test: an approach to determining whether a set of variables is cointegrated – i.e. if they have a long-run equilibrium relationship.

joint hypothesis: a multiple hypothesis that involves making more than one restriction simultaneously.

just identified equation: occurs when the parameters in a structural equation from a system can be uniquely obtained by substitution from the reduced form estimates

KPSS test: a test for stationarity – in other words, a test where the null hypothesis is that a series is stationary against an alternative hypothesis that it is not.

kurtosis: the standardised fourth moment of a series; a measure of whether a series has 'fat tails'.

lag length: the number of lagged values of a series used in a model.

lag operator: an algebraic notation for taking the current value of a series and turning it into a past value of that series.

Lagrange multiplier (LM) test: used in the context of maximum-likelihood estimation, an LM test involves estimation of a restricted regression only. In practice, an LM test is often employed via the calculation of R^2 from an auxiliary regression to construct a test statistic that follows a χ^2 distribution.

law of large numbers: a theorem stating that the mean from a sample will approach the true population mean (i.e. the expected value) as the sample size increases.

least squares: *see* ordinary least squares.

least squares dummy variables (LSDV): an approach to estimating panel data models using 0–1 intercept dummy variables for each cross-sectional unit.

leptokurtosis: a phenomenon whereby a series has a higher peak at the mean and fatter tails than a normal distribution with the same mean and variance.

leverage effects: the tendency for stock volatility to rise more following a large stock price fall than a price rise of the same magnitude owing to the consequent impact on the firm's debt-to-equity (leverage) ratio.

likelihood function: a mathematical expression that relates to the data and the parameters. A likelihood function is constructed given an assumption about the distribution of the errors, and then the values of the parameters that maximise it are chosen.

likelihood ratio (LR) test: an approach to hypothesis testing arising from maximum likelihood estimation that revolves around a comparison of the maximised values of the log-likelihood functions for the restricted and unrestricted models.

limited dependent variable: when the values that the dependent variable can take are restricted in some way. In such cases, OLS cannot be validly used to estimate the model parameters.

linear probability model: a simple but flawed model for use when the dependent variable in a regression model is binary (0 or 1).

linearity: the extent to which a relationship between variables can be represented by a (possibly multi-dimensional) straight line.

Ljung–Box test: a general test for autocorrelation in a variable or residual series.

log-likelihood function (LLF): the natural logarithm of the likelihood function.

log-log model: *see* double logarithmic form.

logit model: an approach for use when the dependent variable in a regression model is binary (0 or 1), and which ensures that the estimated probabilities are bounded by 0 and 1.

long-memory models: *see* fractionally integrated models.

long-run static solution: the algebraic manipulation of a dynamic equation to construct the long-run relationship between the variables.

longitudinal data: *see* panel data.

loss function: is constructed in order to evaluate the accuracy of a model fit or of forecasts. The parameters of a model are usually estimated by minimising or maximising a loss function.

Lyapunov exponent: a characteristic that can be used to determine whether a series can be described as chaotic.

marginal effects: the impacts of changes in the explanatory variables on changes in the probabilities for probit and logit models. They are calculated in order to intuitively interpret the models.

marginal probability: the probability of a single random variable.

market microstructure: a financial term, concerned with the way that markets work and the impact that the design and structure of the market can have on the outcomes of trade, including prices, volumes and execution costs.

market risk premium: the amount of additional return that an investor requires for accepting an additional unit of market risk, often calculated as the difference between the returns on a broad portfolio of stocks and a proxy for the risk free rate of interest.

market timing: the extent to which investors are able to select the optimal times to invest in different asset classes.

Markov switching model: a time series approach based on a dependent variable that alternates between regimes according to the value of an unobservable state variable that follows a Markov process.

Marquardt algorithm: an approach to optimisation that can be used, for example, as part of the procedure to estimate the parameter values in maximum likelihood estimation.

matrix: a two-dimensional array of numbers constructed in rows and columns.

maximum likelihood (ML): an approach that can be used for parameter estimation based on the construction and maximisation of a likelihood function, which is particularly useful for non-linear models.

minimum capital risk requirement (MCRR): *see* value-at-risk.

misspecification error: occurs when the model estimated is incorrect – for example, if the true relationship between the variables is non-linear but a linear model is adopted.

misspecification tests: are diagnostic tests that can provide the researcher with information concerning whether a model has desirable statistical properties, particularly regarding the residuals.

model interpretation: the examination of an estimated model in terms of whether the signs of the parameters (i.e. positive or negative) and sizes of the parameters (i.e. their values) make sense intuitively.

moments: the moments of a distribution describe its shape. The first moment of a distribution is the mean, the second moment is the variance, the third (standardised) moment is the skewness and the fourth (standardised) moment is the kurtosis. The fifth moments and higher are harder to interpret and in general are not calculated.

moving average (MA) process: a model where the dependent variable depends upon the current and past values of a white noise (error) process.

multicollinearity: a phenomenon where two or more of the explanatory variables used in a regression model are highly related to one another.

multimodal: a characteristic of a distribution whereby it does not have a single peak at the mean, but rather reaches a maximum in more than one place.

multinomial logit or probit: classes of models that are used for discrete choice problems, where we wish to explain how individuals make choices between more than two alternatives.

multivariate generalised autoregressive conditionally heteroscedastic (GARCH) models: a family of dynamic models for time-varying variances and covariances.

neural network models: a class of statistical models whose structure is loosely based on how computation is performed by the brain. They have been employed for time series modelling and for classification purposes.

Newey–West estimator: a procedure that can be employed to adjust standard errors to allow for heteroscedasticity and/or autocorrelation in the residuals from a regression model.

news impact curve: a pictorial representation of the responsiveness of volatility to positive and negative shocks of different magnitudes.

Newton–Raphson procedure: an iterative approach to optimisation – in other words, for finding the values of a parameter or set of parameters that maximise or minimise a function.

nominal series: a series that has not been deflated (i.e. not been adjusted for inflation).

non-linear least squares (NLS): an estimation technique for use on non-linear models (models that are non-linear in the parameters) based on minimising the sum of the squared residuals.

non-negativity constraints: the conditions that it is sometimes necessary to impose on the parameter estimates from non-linear models to ensure that they are not negative in situations where it would not make sense for them to be so.

non-nested models: where there are at least two models, neither of which is a special (i.e. restricted) case of the other.

non-normality: not following a normal or Gaussian distribution.

non-stationarity: a characteristic of a time series whereby it does not have a constant mean, a constant variance, and a constant autocovariance structure.

null hypothesis: a formal expression of the statement actually being tested as part of a hypothesis test.

observations: another name for the data points available for analysis.

omitted variable: a relevant variable for explaining the dependent variable has been left out of the estimated regression equation, leading to biased inferences on the remaining parameters.

one-sided hypothesis test: used when theory suggests that the alternative hypothesis should be of the greater than form only or of the less than form only (and not both).

optimal portfolio: a combination of risky assets that maximises return for a given risk or minimises risk for a given return.

order of integration: the number of times that a stochastically non-stationary series must be differenced to make it stationary.

ordered response variable: usually a situation where the dependent variable in a model is limited to only certain values but where there is a natural ordering of those values – for example, where the values represent sovereign credit rating assignments.

ordinal scale: where a variable is limited so that its values define a position or ordering only, and thus the precise values that the variable takes have no direct interpretation.

ordinary least squares (OLS): the standard and most common approach that is used to estimate linear regression models.

out-of-sample: sometimes, not all observations are employed to estimate the model (in-sample data), but instead some are retained for forecasting (the out-of-sample data).

outliers: data points that do not fit in with the pattern of the other observations and that are a long way from the fitted model.

overfitting: estimating too large a model with too many parameters.

overidentified equation: occurs when more than one estimate of each parameter in the structural equation from a system can be obtained by substitution from the reduced form estimates.

overreaction effect: the tendency for asset (especially stock) prices to overshoot their new equilibrium prices when news is released.

oversized test: a statistical test that rejects the null hypothesis too often when it is in fact correct.

p-value: the exact significance level, or the marginal significance level which would make us indifferent between rejecting and not rejecting the null hypothesis.

panel data analysis: the use of data having both cross-sectional and time series dimensions.

parsimonious model: one that describes the data accurately while using as few parameters as possible.

partial autocorrelation function (pacf): measures the correlation of a variable with its value k periods ago ($k = 1, 2, \ldots$) after removing the effects of observations at all intermediate lags.

pecking order hypothesis: the notion from corporate finance that firms will select the cheapest method of financing (usually retained earnings) first before switching to increasingly more expensive forms.

perfect multicollinearity: occurs when an explanatory variable used in a regression model is a precise linear combination of one or more other explanatory variables from that model.

period effects: *see* time fixed effects.

piecewise linear model: a model that is linear (i.e. can be represented by a straight line) within restricted ranges of the data, but where taken overall the model is non-linear.

pooled sample: where there is a panel of data (i.e. having both time series and cross-sectional dimensions), but where all of the observations are employed together without regard for the panel structure.

population: the collection of all objects or entities that are relevant to the idea being tested in a model.

population regression function (PRF): embodies the true but unobservable relationship between the dependent and independent variables.

portmanteau tests: general tests for non-linear patterns or model-misspecification; in other words, tests that have power over a broad range of alternative structures.

position risk requirement: *see* value-at-risk.

power of a test: the ability of a test to correctly reject a wrong null hypothesis.

pre-determined variables: are uncorrelated with past or current values of the error term in a regression equation but may be correlated with future values of the error term.

predicted value: *see* fitted value.

predictive failure test: a test for parameter stability or structural change in a regression model, which is based on estimating an auxiliary regression for a sub-sample of the data and then evaluating how well that model can 'predict' the other observations.

price deflator: a series that measures the general level of prices in an economy, used to adjust a nominal series to a real one.

principal components analysis (PCA): a technique that is sometimes used where a set of variables are highly correlated. More specifically, it is a mathematical operation that converts a set of correlated series into a new set of linearly independent series.

probability density function (pdf): a relationship or mapping that describes how likely it is that a random variable will take on a value within a given range.

probit model: an appropriate model for binary (0 or 1) dependent variables where the underlying function used to transform the model is a cumulative normal distribution.

pseudo-random numbers: a set of artificial random-looking numbers generated using a purely deterministic sequence (e.g. using a computer).

purchasing power parity (PPP): the hypothesis that, in equilibrium, exchange rates should adjust so that a representative basket of goods and services should cost the same when converted into a common currency irrespective of where it was purchased.

qualitative variables: *see* dummy variables.

Quandt likelihood ratio test: a test for structural breaks in a regression model, based on the Chow test but where the break date is assumed unknown.

quantile: the position (within the 0–1 interval) in an ordered series where an observation falls.

quantile regression: an approach to model specification that involves constructing a family of regression models, each for different quantiles of the distribution of the dependent variable.

R^2: a standardised measure, bounded between zero and one, of how well a sample regression model fits the data.

R-bar^2: *see* adjusted R^2.

random effects model: a particular type of panel data model specification where the intercepts vary cross-sectionally as a result of each cross-sectional entity having a different error term.

random walk: a simple model where the current value of a series is simply the previous value perturbed by a white noise (error) term. Therefore the optimal forecast for a variable that follows a random walk is the most recently observed value of that series.

random walk with drift: a random walk model that also includes an intercept, so that changes in the variable are not required to average zero.

rank (of a matrix): a measure of whether all the rows and columns of a matrix are independent of one another.

real series: a series that has been deflated (adjusted for inflation).

recursive model: an approach to estimation where a set of time series regressions are estimated using sub-samples of increasing length. After the first model is estimated, an additional observation is added to the end of the sample so that the sample size increases by one observation. This continues until the end of the sample is reached.

reduced form equations: the equations with no endogenous variables on the right-hand side that have been derived algebraically from the structural forms in the context of a simultaneous system.

redundant fixed effects test: a test for whether a fixed effects panel regression approach must be employed, or whether the data can simply be pooled and estimated using a standard ordinary least squares regression model.

regressand: *see* dependent variable.

regressor: *see* explanatory variable.

rejection region: if a test statistic falls within this area plotted onto a statistical distribution function then the null hypothesis under study is rejected.

re-sampling: creating a simulated distribution for computing standard errors or critical values via sampling with replacement from the original data.

RESET test: a non-linearity test, or a test for misspecification of functional form, i.e. a situation where the shape of the regression model estimated is incorrect – for example, where the model estimated is linear but it should have been non-linear.

residual diagnostics: an examination of the residuals for whether they have any patterns remaining that were present in the dependent variable and not captured by the fitted model.

residual sum of squares (RSS): the addition of all of the squared values of the differences between the actual data points and the corresponding model fitted values.

residual terms: the differences between the actual values of the dependent variable and the values that the model estimated for them – in other words, the parts of the dependent variable that the model could not explain.

restricted model: a regression where the parameters cannot be freely determined by the data, but instead some restrictions have been placed on the values that can be taken by one or more of the parameters.

risk premium: the additional return that investors expect for bearing risk.

riskless arbitrage opportunities: *see* arbitrage.

rolling window: an approach to estimation where a set of time series regressions are estimated using sub-samples of fixed length. After the first model is estimated, the first observation is removed from the sample and one observation is added to the end. This continues until the end of the sample is reached.

sample: a selection of some entities from the population which are then used to estimate a model.

sample regression function (SRF): the regression model that has been estimated from the actual data.

sample size: the number of observations or data points per series in the sample.

sampling error: the inaccuracy in parameter estimation that arises as a result of having only a sample and not the whole population; as a consequence of sampling error, the estimates vary from one sample to another.

Schwarz's Bayesian information criterion (SBIC): a metric that can be used to select the best fitting from a set of competing models and that incorporates a strict penalty term for including additional parameters.

second moment: the moments of a distribution define its shape; the second moment is another term for the variance of the data.

seemingly unrelated regression (SUR): a time series regression approach for modelling the movements of several highly related dependent variables. The approach allows for the correlation between the error terms of the regressions, hence improving the efficiency of the estimation.

self-exciting threshold autoregression (SETAR): a TAR model where the state-determining variable is the same as the variable under study.

semi-interquartile range: a measure of the spread of a set of data (an alternative to the variance) that is based on the difference between the quarter- and three-quarter points of the ordered data.

sensitive dependence on initial conditions (SDIC): this is the defining characteristic of a chaotic system that the impact on a system of an infinitesimally small change in the initial values will grow exponentially over time.

serial correlation: see autocorrelation.

Sharpe ratio: in finance, this is a risk-adjusted performance measure calculated by subtracting the risk-free return from the portfolio return, and then dividing this by the portfolio standard deviation.

shocks: another name for the disturbances in a regression model.

short-selling: selling a financial asset that you do not own, in anticipation of repurchasing it at a later date when the price has fallen.

significance level: the size of the rejection region for a statistical test, also equal to the probability that the null hypothesis will be rejected when it is correct.

sign and size bias tests: tests for asymmetries in volatility – i.e. tests for whether positive and negative shocks of a given size have the same effect on volatility.

simultaneous equations: a set of interlinked equations each comprising several variables.

size of test: see significance level.

skewness: the standardised third moment of a distribution that shows whether it is symmetrical around its mean value.

slippage time: the amount of time that it is assumed to take to execute a trade after a rule is computer-generated.

slope: the gradient of a straight (regression) line, measured by taking the change in the dependent variable, y between two points, and dividing it by the change in the independent variable, x between the same points.

sovereign credit ratings: are assessments of the riskiness of debts issued by governments.

sovereign yield spreads: usually defined as the difference between the yield on the bonds of a government under study and the yield on US Treasury bonds.

specific-to-general modelling: a philosophical approach to building econometric models that involves starting with a specific model as indicated by theory and then sequentially adding to it or modifying it so that it gradually becomes a better description of reality.

spline techniques: piecewise linear models that involve the application of polynomial functions in a piecewise fashion to different portions of the data.

spot price: the price of a specific quantity of a good or asset for immediate delivery.

spurious regressions: if a regression involves two or more independent non-stationary variables, the slope estimate(s) may appear highly significant to standard statistical tests and may have highly significant t-ratios even though in reality there is no relationship between the variables.

standard deviation: a measure of the spread of the data about their mean value, which has the same units as the data.

standard errors: measure the precision or reliability of the regression estimates.

stationary variable: one that does not contain a unit or explosive root and can thus be validly used directly in a regression model.

statistical inference: the process of drawing conclusions about the likely characteristics of the population from the sample estimates.

statistically significant: a result is statistically significant if the null hypothesis is rejected (usually using a 5% significance level).

stochastic regressors: it is usually assumed when using regression models that the regressors are non-stochastic or fixed; in practice, however, they may be random or stochastic – for example, if there are lagged dependent variables or endogenous regressors.

stochastic trend: some levels time series possess a stochastic trend, meaning that they can be characterised as unit root processes, which are non-stationary.

stochastic volatility (SV) model: a less common alternative to GARCH models, where the conditional variance is explicitly modelled using an equation containing an error term.

strictly exogenous variable: one that is uncorrelated with past, present and future values of the error term.

strictly stationary process: one where the entire probability distribution is constant over time.

structural break: a situation where the properties of a time series or of a model exhibit a substantial long-term shift in behaviour.

structural equations: the original equations describing a simultaneous system, which contain endogenous variables on the right hand side.

sum of squared residuals: *see* residual sum of squares.

switching model: an econometric specification for a variable whose behaviour alternates between two or more different states.

t-ratio: the ratio of a parameter estimate to its standard error, forming a statistic to test the null hypothesis that the true value of the parameter is one.

Theil's U-statistic: a metric to evaluate forecasts, where the mean squared error of the forecasts from the model under study is divided by the mean squared error of the forecasts from a benchmark model. A U-statistic of less than one implies that the model is superior to the benchmark.

threshold autoregressive (TAR) models: a class of time series models where the series under study switches between different types of autoregressive dynamics when an underlying (observable) variable exceeds a certain threshold.

time fixed effects: a panel data model that allows the regression intercept to vary over time and is useful when the average value of the variable under study changes over time but not cross-sectionally.

time series regressions: models built using time series data – i.e. data collected for a period of time for one or more variables.

tobit regression: a model that is appropriate when the dependent variable is censored – that is, where the values of the variable beyond a specific threshold cannot be observed, even though the corresponding values of the independent variables are observable.

total sum of squares (TSS): the sum of the squared deviations of the dependent variable about its mean value.

transition probabilities: a square matrix of estimates of the likelihood that a Markov switching variable will move from a given regime to each other regime.

truncated dependent variable: a situation where the values of this variable beyond a certain threshold cannot be observed, and neither can the corresponding values of the independent variables.

two-stage least squares (TSLS or 2SLS): an approach to parameter estimation that is valid for use on simultaneous equations systems.

unbalanced panel: a set of data having both time series and cross-sectional elements, but where some data are missing – i.e. where the number of time series observations available is not the same for all cross-sectional entities.

unbiased estimator: a formula or set of formulae that, when applied, will give estimates that are on average equal to the corresponding true population parameter values.

uncovered interest parity (UIP): holds if covered interest parity and forward rate unbiasedness both apply.

underidentified or unidentified equation: occurs when estimates of the parameters in the structural equation from a system cannot be obtained by substitution from the reduced form estimates as there is insufficient information in the latter.

unit root process: a series follows a unit root process if it is non-stationary but becomes stationary by taking first differences.

unparameterised: if a feature of the dependent variable y is not captured by the model, it is unparameterised.

unrestricted regression: a model that is specified without any restrictions being imposed so that the estimation technique can freely determine the parameter estimates.

value-at-risk (VaR): an approach to measuring risk based on the loss on a portfolio that may be expected to occur with a given probability over a specific horizon.

variance–covariance matrix: an array of numbers that comprises each of the variances of a set of random variables on the leading diagonal of the matrix and their covariances as the off-diagonal elements.

variance decomposition: a way to examine the importance of each variable in a vector autoregressive (VAR) model by calculating how much of the forecast error variance (for 1, 2, . . . , periods ahead) for each dependent variable can be explained by innovations in each independent variable.

variance reduction techniques: are employed in the context of Monte Carlo simulations in order to reduce the number of replications required to achieve a given level of standard errors of the estimates.

VECH model: a relatively simple multivariate approach that allows for the estimation of time-varying volatilities and covariances that are stacked into a vector.

vector autoregressive (VAR) model: a multivariate time series specification where lagged values of (all) the variables appear on the right hand side in (all) the equations of the (unrestricted) model.

vector autoregressive moving average (VARMA) model: a VAR model where there are also lagged values of the error terms appearing in each equation.

vector error correction model (VECM): an error correction model that is embedded into a VAR framework so that the short- and long-run relationships between a set of variables can be modelled simultaneously.

vector moving average (VMA) model: a multivariate time series model where a series is expressed as a combination of lagged values of a vector of white noise processes.

volatility: the extent to which a series is highly variable over time, usually measured by its standard deviation or variance.

volatility clustering: the tendency for the variability of asset returns to occur 'in bunches', so that there are prolonged periods when volatility is high and other prolonged periods when it is low.

Wald test: an approach to testing hypotheses where estimation is undertaken only under the alternative hypothesis; most common forms of hypothesis tests (e.g. t- and F-tests) are Wald tests.

weakly exogenous variables: *see* predetermined variables.

weakly stationary process: has a constant mean, constant variance and constant autocovariances for each given lag.

weighted least squares (WLS): *see* generalised least squares.

white noise process: has a fixed mean and variance but no other structure (e.g. it has zero

autocorrelations for all lags). The error term in a regression model is usually assumed to be white noise.

White's correction: an adjustment to the standard errors of regression parameters that allows for heteroscedasticity in the residuals from the estimated equation.

White's test: an approach to determining whether the assumption of homoscedastic errors in a model is valid, based on estimating an auxiliary regression of the squared residuals on the regressors, their squared values, and their cross-products.

within transformation: used in the context of a fixed effects panel model, involving the subtraction of the time series mean from each variable to reduce the number of dummy variable parameters requiring estimation.

Wold's decomposition theorem: states that any stationary series can be decomposed into the sum of two unrelated processes, a purely deterministic part and a purely stochastic part.

yield curves: show how the yields on bonds vary as the term to maturity increases.

Yule–Walker equations: a set of formulae that can be used to calculate the autocorrelation function coefficients for an autoregressive model.

References

Akaike, H. (1974) A New Look at the Statistical Model Identification, *IEEE Transactions on Automatic Control* AC-19(6), 716–23

Akgiray, V. (1989) Conditional Heteroskedasticity in Time Series of Stock Returns: Evidence and Forecasts, *Journal of Business* 62(1), 55–80

Amemiya, T. (1984) Tobit Models: A Survey, *Journal of Econometrics* 24, 3–61

Andersen, T. and Bollerslev, T. (1998) Answering the Skeptics: Yes, Standard Volatility Models do Provide Accurate Forecasts, *International Economic Review* 39, 885–905

Anselin, L. (1988) *Spatial Econometrics: Methods and Models*, Kluwer Academic, Dordrecht

Antoniou, A. and Garrett, I. (1993) To What Extent Did Stock Index Futures Contribute to the October 1987 Stock Market Crash?, *Economic Journal* 103, 1444–61

ap Gwilym, O., Clare, A. and Thomas, S. (1998) The Bid–Ask Spread on Stock Index Options: An Ordered Probit Analysis, *Journal of Futures Markets* 18(4), 467–85

Arellano, M. (2003) *Panel Data Econometrics*, Oxford University Press, Oxford

Armitage, S. (1995) Event Study Methods and Evidence on their Performance, *Journal of Economic Surveys* 8(4), 25–52

Bai, J. and Ng, S. (2004) A Panic Attack on Unit Roots and Cointegration, *Econometrica* 72, 1127–77

Baillie, R. T. (1989) Tests of Rational Expectations and Market Efficiency, *Econometric Reviews* 8, 151–86

Baillie, R. T. and Bollerslev, T. (1989) The Message in Daily Exchange Rates: A Conditional-Variance Tale, *Journal of Business and Economic Statistics* 7(3), 297–305

Baillie, R. T. and Myers, R. J. (1991) Bivariate GARCH Estimation of the Optimal Commodity Futures Hedge, *Journal of Applied Econometrics* 6, 109–24

Baks, K., Metrick, A. and Wachter, J. A. (2001) Should Investors Avoid All Actively Managed Mutual Funds? A Study in Bayesian Performance Evaluation, *Journal of Finance* 56(1), 45–85

Ball, R. and Brown, P. (1968) An Empirical Evaluation of Accounting Numbers, *Journal of Accounting Research* 6(2), 159–78

Ball, R. and Kothari, S. P. (1989) Nonstationary Expected Returns: Implications for Tests of Market Efficiency and Serial Correlation in Returns, *Journal of Financial Economics* 25, 51–74

Baltagi, B. H. (2005) *Econometric Analysis of Panel Data*, John Wiley, Chichester

Banerjee, A., Lumsdaine, R. L. and Stock, J. H. (1992) Recursive and Sequential Tests of the Unit-root and Trend-break Hypotheses: Theory and International Evidence, *Journal of Business and Economic Statistics* 10, 271–87

Barber, B. and Lyon, J. (1997) Detecting Long-run Abnormal Stock Returns: the Empirical Power and Specifications of Test Statistics, *Journal of Financial Economics* 43, 341–72

Bassett, G. W. and Chen, H-L. (2001) Portfolio Style: Return-based Attribution using Quantile Regression, *Empirical Economics* 26, 293–305

Bauwens, L. and Laurent, S. (2002) A New Class of Multivariate Skew Densities with Application to GARCH Models, *CORE discussion paper* 2002/20

Bauwens, L., Laurent, S. and Rombouts, J. V. K. (2006) Multivariate GARCH Models: A Survey, *Journal of Applied Econometrics* 21, 79–109

Bauwens, L. and Lubrano, M. (1998) Bayesian Inference on GARCH Models using the Gibbs Sampler, *Econometrics Journal* 1(1), 23–46

Benninga, S. (2011) *Principles of Finance with Microsoft Excel*, 2nd edn, Oxford University Press, New York

Bera, A. K. and Jarque, C. M. (1981) An Efficient Large-sample Test for Normality of Observations and Regression Residuals, *Australian National University Working Papers in Econometrics* 40, Canberra

Bera, A. K. and Kim, S. (2002) Testing Constancy of Correlation and other Specifications of the BGARCH Model with an Application to International Equity Returns, *Journal of Empirical Finance* 9, 171–95

Bergman, U. M. and Hansson, J. (2005) Real Exchange Rates and Switching Regimes, *Journal of International Money and Finance* 24, 121–38

Berndt, E. K., Hall, B. H., Hall, R. E. and Hausman, J. A. (1974) Estimation and Inference in Nonlinear Structural Models, *Annals of Economic and Social Measurement* 4, 653–65

Black, F., Jensen, M. C. and Scholes, M. (1972) The Capital Asset Pricing Model: Some Empirical Tests, in M. C. Jensen (ed.) *Studies in the Theory of Capital Markets*, Praeger, New York

Black, F. and Scholes, M. (1973) The Pricing of Options and Corporate Liabilities, *Journal of Political Economy* 81(3), 637–54

Bodie, Z., Kane, A. and Marcus, A. J. (2011) *Investments and Portfolio Management* 9th edn, McGraw-Hill, New York

Boehmer, E., Musumeci, J. and Poulsen, A. (1991) Event Study Methodology under Conditions of Event Induced Variance, *Journal of Financial Economics* 30, 253–72

Bollerslev, T. (1986) Generalised Autoregressive Conditional Heteroskedasticity, *Journal of Econometrics* 31, 307–27

(1990) Modelling the Coherence in Short-run Nominal Exchange Rates: a Multivariate Generalised ARCH Model, *Review of Economics and Statistics* 72, 498–505

Bollerslev, T., Chou, R. Y. and Kroner, K. F. (1992) ARCH Modelling in Finance: a Review of the Theory and Empirical Evidence, *Journal of Econometrics* 52(5), 5–59

Bollerslev, T., Engle, R. F. and Wooldridge, J. M. (1988) A Capital-asset Pricing Model with Time-varying Covariances, *Journal of Political Economy* 96(1), 116–31

Bollerslev, T. and Mikkelsen, H. O. (1996) Modelling and Pricing Long Memory in Stock Market Volatility, *Journal of Econometrics* 73, 151–84

Bollerslev, T. and Wooldridge, J. M. (1992) Quasi-maximum Likelihood Estimation and Inference in Dynamic Models with Time-varying Covariances, *Econometric Reviews* 11(2), 143–72

Box, G. E. P. and Jenkins, G. M. (1976) *Time Series Analysis: Forecasting and Control*, 2nd edn, Holden-Day, San Francisco

Box, G. E. P. and Pierce, D. A. (1970) Distributions of Residual Autocorrelations in Autoregressive Integrated Moving Average Models, *Journal of the American Statistical Association* 65, 1509–26

Boyle, P. P. (1977) Options: a Monte Carlo Approach, *Journal of Financial Economics* 4(3), 323–38

Brailsford, T. J. and Faff, R. W. (1996) An Evaluation of Volatility Forecasting Techniques, *Journal of Banking and Finance* 20, 419–38

Brealey, R. A. and Myers, S. C. (2013) *Principles of Corporate Finance*, Global edn, McGraw-Hill, New York

Breitung, J. (2000) The Local Power of Some Unit Root Tests for Panel Data, in B. Baltagi (ed.) *Nonstationary Panels, Panel Cointegration and Dynamic Panels*, Advances in Econometrics 15, 161–78, JAI Press, Amsterdam

Breitung, J. and Das, S. (2005) Panel Unit Root Tests under Cross-sectional Dependence, *Statistica Neerlandica* 59, 414–33

Breitung, J. and Pesaran, M. H. (2008) Unit Roots and Cointegration in Panels, in L. Matyas and P. Sevestre (eds.) *The Econometrics of Panel Data*, 3rd edn, Springer-Verlag, Berlin

Brock, W. A., Dechert, D., Scheinkman, H. and LeBaron, B. (1996) A Test for Independence Based on the Correlation Dimension, *Econometric Reviews* 15, 197–235

Brock, W. A., Hsieh, D. A. and LeBaron, B. (1991) *Nonlinear Dynamics, Chaos, and Instability: Statistical Theory and Economic Evidence*, MIT Press, Cambridge, MA

Brooks, C. (1996) Testing for Nonlinearity in Daily Pound Exchange Rates, *Applied Financial Economics* 6, 307–17

(1997) GARCH Modelling in Finance: a Review of the Software Options, *Economic Journal* 107(443), 1271–6

(1998) Forecasting Stock Return Volatility: Does Volume Help?, *Journal of Forecasting* 17, 59–80

(2001) A Double Threshold GARCH Model for the French Franc/German Mark Exchange Rate, *Journal of Forecasting* 20, 135–43

Brooks, C., Burke, S. P. and Persand, G. (2001) Benchmarks and the Accuracy of GARCH Model Estimation, *International Journal of Forecasting* 17, 45–56

(2003) Multivariate GARCH Models: Software Choice and Estimation Issues, *Journal of Applied Econometrics* 18, 725–34

Brooks, C., Burke, S. P., Heravi, S. and Persand, G. (2005) Autoregressive Conditional Kurtosis, *Journal of Financial Econometrics* 3(3), 399–421

Brooks, C., Černý, A. and Miffre, J. (2012) Optimal Hedging with Higher Moments, *Journal of Futures Markets* 32, 909–44

Brooks, C., Clare, A. D., Dalle Molle, J. W. and Persand, G. (2005) A Comparison of Extreme Value Approaches for Determining Value at Risk, *Journal of Empirical Finance* 12, 339–52

Brooks, C., Clare, A. D. and Persand, G. (2000) A Word of Caution on Calculating Market-based Minimum Capital Risk Requirements, *Journal of Banking and Finance* 14(10), 1557–74

Brooks, C. and Garrett, I. (2002) Can We Explain the Dynamics of the UK FTSE 100 Stock and Stock Index Futures Markets?, *Applied Financial Economics* 12(1), 25–31

Brooks, C. and Henry, O. T. (2000) Can Portmanteau Model Nonlinearity Tests Serve as General Model Mis-specification Diagnostics? Evidence from Symmetric and Asymmetric GARCH Models, *Economics Letters* 67, 245–51

Brooks, C., Henry, O. T. and Persand, G. (2002) Optimal Hedging and the Value of News, *Journal of Business* 75(2), 333–52

Brooks, C. and Heravi, S. (1999) The Effect of Mis-specified GARCH Filters on the Finite Sample Distribution of the BDS Test, *Computational Economics* 13, 147–62

Brooks, C. and Hinich, M. J. (1999) Cross-correlations and Cross-bicorrelations in Sterling Exchange Rates, *Journal of Empirical Finance* 6(4), 385–404

Brooks, C. and Persand, G. (2001a) Seasonality in Southeast Asian Stock Markets: Some New Evidence on Day-of-the-week Effect, *Applied Economics Letters* 8, 155–8

(2001b) The Trading Profitability of Forecasts of the Gilt–Equity Yield Ratio, *International Journal of Forecasting* 17, 11–29

Brooks, C. and Rew, A. G. (2002) Testing for Non-stationarity and Cointegration Allowing for the Possibility of a Structural Break: an Application to EuroSterling Interest Rates, *Economic Modelling* 19, 65–90

Brooks, C., Rew, A. G. and Ritson, S. (2001) A Trading Strategy Based on the Lead–Lag Relationship Between the FTSE 100 Spot Index and the LIFFE Traded FTSE Futures Contract, *International Journal of Forecasting* 17, 31–44

Brooks, C. and Tsolacos, S. (1999) The Impact of Economic and Financial Factors on UK Property Performance, *Journal of Property Research* 16(2), 139–52

Brown, S. J. and Warner, J. B. (1980) Measuring Security Price Performance, *Journal of Financial Economics* 8, 205–58

(1985) Using Daily Stock Returns: the Case of Event Studies, *Journal of Financial Economics* 14, 3–31

Campbell, J. Y., Lo, A. W. and MacKinlay, A. C. (1997) *The Econometrics of Financial Markets*, Princeton University Press, Princeton, NJ

Campbell, J. Y. and Shiller, R. J. (1988) Interpreting Cointegrated Models, *Journal of Economic Dynamics and Control* 12, 503–22

(1991) Yield Spreads and Interest Rate Movements: a Bird's Eye View, *Review of Economic Studies* 58, 495–514

Cantor, R. and Packer, F. (1996) Determinants and Impacts of Sovereign Credit Ratings, *Journal of Fixed Income* 6, 76–91

Carhart, M. (1997) On Persistence in Mutual Fund Performance, *Journal of Finance* 52, 57–82

Cecchetti, S. G., Cumby, R. E. and Figlewski, S. (1988) Estimation of the Optimal Futures Hedges, *Review of Economics and Statistics* 70(4), 623–30

Chappel, D., Padmore, J., Mistry, P. and Ellis, C. (1996) A Threshold Model for the French Franc/Deutschmark Exchange Rate, *Journal of Forecasting* 15, 155–64

Chen, B. (1995) Long-run Purchasing Power Parity: Evidence from Some European Monetary System Countries, *Applied Economics* 27, 377–83

Chen, N-F., Roll, R. and Ross, S. A. (1986) Economic Forces and the Stock Market, *Journal of Business* 59(3), 383–403

Chernozhukov, V. and Umantsev, L. (2001) Conditional Value-at-risk: Aspects of Modelling and Estimation, *Empirical Economics* 26(1), 271–92

Chib, S. and Greenberg, E. (1996) Markov Chain Monte Carlo Simulation Methods in Econometrics, *Econometric Theory* 12, 409–31

Choi, I. (2001) Unit Root Tests for Panel Data, *Journal of International Money and Finance* 20, 249–72

Christiano, L. J. (1992) Searching for a Break in GNP, *Journal of Business and Economic Statistics* 10, 237–50

Christopoulos, D. K. and Tsionas, E. G. (2004) Financial Development and Economic growth: Evidence from Panel Unit Root and Cointegration Tests, *Journal of Development Economics* 73, 55–74

Chu, K.-Y. (1978) Short-run Forecasting of Commodity Prices: an Application of Autoregressive Moving Average Models, *IMF Staff Papers* 25, 90–111

Chu, S.-H. and Freund, S. (1996) Volatility Estimation for Stock Index Options: a GARCH Approach, *Quarterly Review of Economics and Finance* 36(4), 431–50

Clare, A. D., Maras, M. and Thomas, S. H. (1995) The Integration and Efficiency of International Bond Markets, *Journal of Business Finance and Accounting* 22(2), 313–22

Clare, A. D. and Thomas, S. H. (1995) The Overreaction Hypothesis and the UK Stock Market, *Journal of Business Finance and Accounting* 22(7), 961–73

Cochrane, D. and Orcutt, G. H. (1949) Application of Least Squares Regression to Relationships Containing Autocorrelated Error Terms, *Journal of the American Statistical Association* 44, 32–61

Cochrane, J. H. (2005) *Asset Pricing*, Princeton University Press, Princeton, NJ

Corrado, C. J. (2011) Event Studies: a Methodology Review, *Accounting and Finance* 51, 207–34

Cuthbertson, K. and Nitzsche, D. (2004) *Quantitative Financial Economics*, 2nd edn, John Wiley, Chichester, UK

Dacco, R. and Satchell, S. E. (1999) Why do Regime Switching Models Forecast so Badly?, *Journal of Forecasting* 18, 1–16

Danielsson, J. (1998) Multivariate Stochastic Volatility Models: Estimation and Comparison with VGARCH Models, *Journal of Empirical Finance* 5, 155–73

Davidson, R. and MacKinnon, J. G. (1981) Several Tests For Model Specification in the Presence of Alternative Hypotheses, *Econometrica* 49(3), 781–94

Davison, A. C. and Hinkley, D. V. (1997) *Bootstrap Methods and their Application*, Cambridge University Press, Cambridge, UK

Day, T. E. and Lewis, C. M. (1992) Stock Market Volatility and the Information Content of Stock Index Options, *Journal of Econometrics* 52, 267–87

DeBondt, W. F. M. and Thaler, R. H. (1985) Does the Stock Market Overreact?, *Journal of Finance* 40, 793–805

(1987) Further Evidence on Investor Overreaction and Stock Market Seasonality, *Journal of Finance* 42, 567–80

de Haas, R. and van Lelyveld, I. (2006) Foreign Banks and Credit Stability in Central and Eastern Europe. A Panel Data Analysis, *Journal of Banking and Finance* 30, 1927–52

Des Rosiers, F. and Thériault, M. (1996) Rental Amenities and the Stability of Hedonic Prices: a Comparative Analysis of Five Market Segments, *Journal of Real Estate Research* 12(1), 17–36

Dickey, D. A. and Fuller, W. A. (1979) Distribution of Estimators for Time Series Regressions with a Unit Root, *Journal of the American Statistical Association* 74, 427–31

(1981) Likelihood Ratio Statistics for Autoregressive Time Series with a Unit Root, *Econometrica* 49(4), 1057–72

Dickey, D. A. and Pantula, S. (1987) Determining the Order of Differencing in Autoregressive Processes, *Journal of Business and Economic Statistics* 5, 455–61

Dielman, T. E. (1986) A Comparison of Forecasts from Least Absolute Value and Least Squares Regression, *Journal of Forecasting* 5, 189–95

Dimson, E. and Marsh, P. (1990) Volatility Forecasting without Data-snooping, *Journal of Banking and Finance* 14, 399–421

Ding, Z., Granger, C. W. J. and Engle, R. F. (1993) A Long Memory Property of Stock Market Returns and a New Model, *Journal of Empirical Finance* 1, 83–106

Doan, T. (1994) *Regression Analysis of Time Series User Manual*, 4th edn, Estima, Evanston, IL

Dougherty, C. (1992) *Introduction to Econometrics*, Oxford University Press, Oxford

Dowd, K. (1998) *Beyond Value at Risk: the New Science of Risk Management*, Wiley, Chichester, UK

Duffie, D. (1996) *Dynamic Asset Pricing Theory*, 2nd edn, Princeton University Press, Princeton, NJ

Dufour, A. and Engle, R. F. (2000) Time and the Price Impact of a Trade, *Journal of Finance* 55(6), 2467–98

Durbin, J. and Watson, G. S. (1951) Testing for Serial Correlation in Least Squares Regression, *Biometrika* 38, 159–71

Efron, B. (1979) Bootstrap Methods: Another Look at the Jackknife, *Annals of Statistics* 7(1), 1–26

(1982) *The Jackknife, the Bootstrap and other Resampling Plans*, Society for Industrial and Applied Mathematics, Philadelphia

Embrechts, P., Lindskog, P. and McNeil, A. J. (2003) Modelling Dependence with Copulas amd Applications to Risk Management, in S. T. Rachev (ed.) *Handbook of Heavy Tailed Distributions in Finance*, Elsevier, Amsterdam

Engel, C. and Hamilton, J. D. (1990) Long Swings in the Dollar: Are they in the Data and Do Markets Know It?, *American Economic Review* 80(4), 689–713

Engle, R. F. (1982) Autoregressive Conditional Heteroskedasticity with Estimates of the Variance of United Kingdom Inflation, *Econometrica* 50(4), 987–1007

(2002) Dynamic Conditional Correlation – A Simple Class of Multivariate GARCH Models, *Journal of Business and Economic Statistics* 20, 339–50

Engle, R. F. and Granger, C. W. J. (1987) Co-integration and Error Correction: Representation, Estimation and Testing, *Econometrica* 55, 251–76

Engle, R. F. and Kroner, K. F. (1995) Multivariate Simultaneous Generalised GARCH, *Econometric Theory* 11, 122–50

Engle, R. F., Lilien, D. M. and Robins, R. P. (1987) Estimating Time Varying Risk Premia in the Term Structure: the ARCH-M Model, *Econometrica* 55(2), 391–407

Engle, R. F. and Manganelli, S. (2004) CAViaR: Conditional Autoregressive Value at Risk by Regression Quantile, *Journal of Business and Economic Statistics* 22(4), 367–81

Engle, R. F. and Ng, V. K. (1993) Measuring and Testing the Impact of News on Volatility, *Journal of Finance* 48, 1749–78

Engle, R. F., Ng, V. K. and Rothschild, M. (1990) Asset Pricing with a Factor-ARCH Covariance Structure: Empirical Estimates for Treasury Bills, *Journal of Econometrics* 45, 213–38

Engle, R. F. and Russell, J. R. (1998) Autoregressive Conditional Duration: a New Model for Irregularly Spaced Transaction Data, *Econometrica* 66(5), 1127–62

Engle, R. F. and Yoo, B. S. (1987) Forecasting and Testing in Cointegrated Systems, *Journal of Econometrics* 35, 143–59

Fabozzi, F. J. and Francis, J. C. (1980) Heteroscedasticity in the Single Index Model, *Journal of Economics and Business* 32, 243–8

Fair, R. C. and Shiller, R. J. (1990) Comparing Information in Forecasts from Econometric Models, *American Economic Review* 80, 375–89

Fama, E. F. (1998) Market Efficiency, Long-term Returns and Behavioral Finance, *Journal of Financial Economics* 49, 283–306

Fama, E. F., Fisher, L., Jensen, M. C. and Roll, R. (1969) The Adjustment of Stock Prices to New Information, *International Economic Review* 10, 1–21

Fama, E. F. and French, K. R. (1992) The Cross-section of Expected Stock Returns, *Journal of Finance* 47, 427–65

(1993) Common Risk Factors in the Returns on Stocks and Bonds, *Journal of Financial Economics* 33, 3–53

Fama, E. F. and MacBeth, J. D. (1973) Risk, Return and Equilibrium: Empirical Tests, *Journal of Political Economy* 81(3), 607–36

Fase, M. M. G. (1973) A Principal Components Analysis of Market Interest Rates in the Netherlands, 1962–1970, *European Economic Review* 4(2), 107–34

Fisher, R. A. (1932) *Statistical Methods for Research Workers*, 4th edn, Oliver and Boyd, Edinburgh

Franses, P. H. and van Dijk, D. (1996) Forecasting Stock Market Volatility Using Non-Linear GARCH Models, *Journal of Forecasting* 15, 229–35

(2000) *Non-linear Time Series Models in Empirical Finance*, Cambridge University Press, Cambridge, UK

French, K. R. (1980) Stock Returns and the Weekend Effect, *Journal of Financial Economics* 8(1), 55–69

Fuller, W. A. (1976) *Introduction to Statistical Time Series*, Wiley, New York

George, T. J. and Longstaff, F. A. (1993) Bid–Ask Spreads and Trading Activity in the S&P 100 Index Options Market, *Journal of Financial and Quantitative Analysis* 28, 381–97

Gerlow, M. E., Irwin, S. H. and Liu, T.-R. (1993) Economic Evaluation of Commodity Price Forecasting Models, *International Journal of Forecasting* 9, 387–97

Ghosh, S. K. (1991) *Econometrics: Theory and Applications*, Prentice-Hall, Englewood Cliffs, NJ

Ghysels, E., Harvey, A. C. and Renault, E. (1995) Stochastic Volatility, in G. S. Maddala and C. R. Rao (eds.) *Handbook of Statistics Volume 14*, Elsevier, Amsterdam, 119–91

Gibbons, M. R. and Hess, P. (1981) Day of the Week Effects and Asset Returns, *Journal of Business* 54(4), 579–96

Gibbons, M. R., Ross, S. A. and Shanken, J. (1989) A Test of the Efficiency of a Given Portfolio, *Econometrica* 57(5), 121–52

Gibson, M. S. and Boyer, B. H. (1998) Evaluating Forecasts of Correlation Using Option Pricing, *Journal of Derivatives*, Winter, 18–38

Gilbert, C. (1986) Professor Hendry's Methodology, *Oxford Bulletin of Economics and Statistics* 48, 283–307

Glosten, L. R., Jagannathan, R. and Runkle, D. E. (1993) On the Relation Between the Expected Value and the Volatility of the Nominal Excess Return on Stocks, *The Journal of Finance* 48(5), 1779–801

Goldfeld, S. M. and Quandt, R. E. (1965) Some Tests for Homoskedasticity, *Journal of the American Statistical Association* 60, 539–47

Granger, C. W. J. (1969) Investigating Causal Relations by Econometric Models and Cross-spectral Methods, *Econometrica* 37, 424–38

Granger, C. W. J. and Newbold, P. (1986) *Forecasting Economic Time Series* 2nd edn, Academic Press, San Diego, CA

Greene, W. H. (2002) *Econometric Analysis*, 5th edn, Prentice-Hall, Upper Saddle River, NJ

Gregory, A. Tharyan, R. and Chistidis, A. (2013) Constructing and Testing Alternative Versions of the Fama-French and Carhart Models in the UK, *Journal of Business Finance and Accounting* 40(1) and (2), 172–214

Gregory, A. W. and Hansen, B. E. (1996) A Residual-based Test for Cointegration in Models with Regime Shifts, *Journal of Econometrics* 70, 99–126

Gujarati, D. N. (2003) *Basic Econometrics*, 4th edn, McGraw-Hill, New York

Hadri, K. (2000) Testing for Stationarity in Heterogeneous Panel Data, *Econometrics Journal* 3, 148–61

Halcoussis, D. (2005) *Understanding Econometrics*, Thomson South Western, Mason, OH

Hamilton, J. D. (1989) A New Approach to the Economic Analysis of Nonstationary Time Series and the Business Cycle, *Econometrica* 57(2), 357–84

(1990) Analysis of Time Series Subject to Changes in Regime, *Journal of Econometrics* 45, 39–70

(1994) *Time Series Analysis*, Princeton University Press, Princeton, NJ

Handa, P. and Tiwari, A. (2006) Does Stock Return Predictability Imply Improved Asset Allocation and Performance? Evidence from the US Stock Market (1954–2002), *Journal of Business* 79, 2423–68

Hansen, B. E. (1996) Inference When a Nuisance Parameter is not Identified under the Null Hypothesis, *Econometrica* 64, 413–30

Hansen, L. P. (1982) Large Sample Properties of Generalised Method of Moments Estimators, *Econometrica* 50, 1029–54

Hansen, P. R. and Lunde, A. (2006) Consistent Ranking of Volatility Models, *Journal of Econometrics* 131, 97–21

Harris, L. (2002) *Trading and Exchanges: Market Microstructure for Practitioners*, Oxford University Press, New York

Harris, R. I. D. (1995) *Cointegration Analysis in Econometric Modelling*, Prentice-Hall, Harlow, UK

Harris, R. D. F. and Tzavalis, E. (1999) Inference for Unit Roots in Dynamic Panels where the Time Dimension is Fixed, *Journal of Econometrics* 91, 201–26

Harvey, A., Ruiz, E. and Shephard, N. (1994) Multivariate Stochastic Variance Models, *Review of Economic Studies* 61, 247–64

Harvey, C. R. and Siddique, A. (1999) Autoregressive Conditional Skewness, *Journal of Financial and Quantitative Analysis* 34(4), 465–77

   (2000) Conditional Skewness in Asset Pricing Tests, *Journal of Finance* 55, 1263–95

Hasbrouck, J. (2007) *Empirical Market Microstructure: the Institutions, Economics, and Econometrics of Securities Trading*, Oxford University Press, New York

Haug, E. G. (1998) *The Complete Guide to Options Pricing Formulas*, McGraw-Hill, New York

Haushalter, G. D. (2000) Financing Policy, Basis Risk and Corporate Hedging: Evidence from Oil and Gas Producers, *Journal of Finance* 55(1), 107–52

Heckman, J. J. (1976) The Common Structure of Statistical Models of Truncation, Sample Selection and Limited Dependent Variables and a Simple Estimator for Such Models, *Annals of Economic and Social Measurement* 5, 475–92

   (1979) Sample Selection Bias as a Specification Error, *Econometrica* 47(1), 153–61

Helwege, J. and Liang, N. (1996) Is there a Pecking Order? Evidence from a Panel of IPO Firms, *Journal of Financial Economics* 40, 429–58

Hendry, D. F. (1980) Econometrics – Alchemy or Science?, *Economica* 47, 387–406

Hendry, D. F. and Juselius, K. (2000) Explaining Cointegration Analysis: Part I, *Energy Journal* 21, 1–42

Hendry, D. F. and Mizon, G. E. (1978) Serial Correlation as a Convenient Simplification, not a Nuisance: a Comment on a Study of the Demand for Money by The Bank of England, *Economic Journal* 88, 549–63

Hendry, D. F. and Richard, J. F. (1982) On the Formulation of Empirical Models in Dynamic Econometrics, *Journal of Econometrics* 20, 3–33

Heslop, S. and Varotto, S. (2007) Admissions of International Graduate Students: Art or Science? A Business School Experience, *ICMA Centre Discussion Papers in Finance* 2007–8

Hill, C. W., Griffiths, W. and Judge, G. (1997) *Undergraduate Econometrics*, Wiley, New York

Hinich, M. J. (1982) Testing for Gaussianity and Linearity of a Stationary Time Series, *Journal of Time Series Analysis* 3(3), 169–76

   (1996) Testing for Dependence in the Input to a Linear Time Series Model, *Journal of Nonparametric Statistics* 6, 205–21

Hinich, M. J. and Patterson, D. M. (1985) Evidence of Nonlinearity in Daily Stock Returns, *Journal of Business and Economic Statistics* 3(1), 69–77

Hodgson, D. J., Linton, O. B. and Vorkink, K. (2004) Testing Forward Exchange Rate Unbiasedness Efficiently: a Semiparametric Approach, *Journal of Applied Economics* 7, 325–53

Hsiao, C. (2003) *Analysis of Panel Data*, 2nd edn, Cambridge University Press, Cambridge, UK

Hsieh, D. A. (1993) Implications of Nonlinear Dynamics for Financial Risk Management, *Journal of Financial and Quantitative Analysis* 28(1), 41–64

Hull, J. C. (2011) *Options, Futures and Other Derivatives*, 8th edn, Prentice-Hall, NJ

Hull, J. C. and White, A. D. (1987) The Pricing of Options on Assets with Stochastic Volatilities, *Journal of Finance* 42(2), 281–300

Hung, C.-H., Shackleton, M. and Xu, X. (2004) CAPM, Higher Co-moment and Factor Models of UK Stock Returns, *Journal of Business Finance and Accounting* 31(1–2), 87–112

Im, K. S., Pesaran, M. H. and Shin, Y. (2003) Testing for Unit Roots in Heterogeneous Panels, *Journal of Econometrics* 115, 53–74

Ito, T. (1988) Use of (Time-Domain) Vector Autoregressions to Test Uncovered Interest Parity, *Review of Economics and Statistics* 70(2), 296–305

Jacquier, E., Polson, N. G. and Rossi, P. (1995) Stochastic Volatility: Univariate and Multivariate Extensions, *Mimeo*, Cornell University

Jaffe, J. and Westerfield, R. (1985) Patterns in Japanese Common Stock Returns: Day of the Week and Turn of the Year Effects, *Journal of Financial and Quantitative Analysis* 20(2), 261–72

Jensen, M. C. (1968) The Performance of Mutual Funds in the Period 1945–1964, *Journal of Finance* 23, 389–416

(1978) Some Anomalous Evidence Regarding Market Efficiency, *Journal of Financial Economics* 6, 95–101

Johansen, S. (1988) Statistical Analysis of Cointegrating Vectors, *Journal of Economic Dynamics and Control* 12, 231–54

Johansen, S. and Juselius, K. (1990) Maximum Likelihood Estimation and Inference on Cointegration with Applications to the Demand for Money, *Oxford Bulletin of Economics and Statistics* 52, 169–210

Jorion, P. (2006) *Value at Risk*, 3rd edn, McGraw-Hill, New York

Kao, C. D. (1999) Spurious Regression and Residual-based Tests for Cointegration in Panel Data, *Journal of Econometrics* 90, 1–44

Keim, D. B. and Stambaugh, R. F. (1984) A Further Investigation of the Weekend Effect in Stock Returns, *Journal of Finance* 39(3), 819–35

Kennedy, P. (2003) *Guide to Econometrics*, 5th edn, Blackwell, Malden, MA

Kim, S.-J., Moshirian, F. and Wu, E. (2005) Dynamic Stock Market Integration Driven by the European Monetary Union: an Empirical Analysis, *Journal of Banking and Finance* 29(10), 2475–502

Koenker, R. (2005) *Quantile Regression*, Cambridge University Press, Cambridge, UK

Koenker, R. and Bassett, G. (1978) Regression Quantiles, *Econometrica* 46, 33–50

Koenker, R. and Hallock, K. F. (2001) Quantile Regression, *Journal of Economic Perspectives* 15(4), 143–56

Koopmans, T. C. (1937) *Linear Regression Analysis of Economic Time Series*, Netherlands Economics Institute, Haarlem

Kräger, H. and Kugler, P. (1993) Nonlinearities in Foreign Exchange Markets: a Different Perspective, *Journal of International Money and Finance* 12, 195–208

Kroner, K. F. and Ng, V. K. (1998) Modelling Asymmetric Co-movements of Asset Returns, *Review of Financial Studies* 11, 817–44

Kroner, K. F. and Sultan, S. (1993) Time-varying Distributions and Dynamic Hedging with Foreign Currency Futures, *Journal of Financial and Quantitative Analysis* 28(4), 535–51

Kwaitkowski, D., Phillips, P. C. B., Schmidt, P. and Shin, Y. (1992) Testing the Null Hypothesis of Stationarity Against the Alternative of a Unit Root, *Journal of Econometrics* 54, 159–78

Larsson, R., Lyhagen, J. and Lothgren, M. (2001) Likelihood-based Cointegration Tests in Heterogeneous Panels, *Econometrics Journal* 4, 109–42

Leamer, E. E. (1978) *Specification Searches*, John Wiley, New York

    (1985) Vector Autoregressions for Causal Interference, in K. Brunner and A. Meltzer (eds.) *Understanding Monetary Regimes*, Cambridge University Press, Cambridge, UK, 255–304

Leitch, G. and Tanner, J. E. (1991) Economic Forecast Evaluation: Profit Versus the Conventional Error Measures, *American Economic Review* 81(3), 580–90

Levin, A., Lin, C. and Chu, C. (2002) Unit Root Tests in Panel Data: Asymptotic and Finite-sample Properties, *Journal of Econometrics* 108, 1–24

Leybourne, S. J., Mills, T. C. and Newbold, P. (1998) Spurious Rejections by Dickey–Fuller Tests in the Presence of a Break under the Null, *Journal of Econometrics* 87, 191–203

Ljung, G. M. and Box, G. E. P. (1978) On a Measure of Lack of Fit in Time Series Models, *Biometrika* 65(2), 297–303

Lo, A. W. and MacKinlay, C. A. (1990) Data-snooping Biases in Tests of Financial Asset Pricing Models, *Review of Financial Studies* 3, 431–67

Lumsdaine, R. L. and Papell, D. H. (1997) Multiple Trend Breaks and the Unit Root Hypothesis, *Review of Economics and Statistics* 79 (2), 212–18

Lütkepohl, H. (1991) *Introduction to Multiple Time Series Analysis*, Springer-Verlag, Berlin

Lyon, J., Barber, B. and Tsai, C. (1999) Improved Methods of Tests of Long-horizon Abnormal Stock Returns, *Journal of Finance* 54, 165–201

MacKinlay, A. C. (1997) Event Studies in Economics and Finance, *Journal of Economic Literature* 55, 13–39

MacKinnon, J. G. (1996) Numerical Distribution Functions for Unit Root and Cointegration Tests, *Journal of Applied Econometrics* 11, 601–18

MacKinnon, J. G., Haug, A. and Michelis, L. (1999) Numerical Distribution Functions of Likelihood Ratio Tests for Cointegration, *Journal of Applied Econometrics* 14(5), 563–77

Maddala, G. S. (1983) *Limited-dependent and Quantitative Variables in Econometrics*, Cambridge University Press, Cambridge, UK

Maddala, G. S. and Kim, I-M. (1999) *Unit Roots, Cointegration and Structural Change*, Cambridge University Press, Cambridge

Maddala, G. S. and Wu, S. (1999) A Comparative Study of Unit Root Tests with Panel Data and a New Simple Test, *Oxford Bulletin of Economics and Statistics* 61, 631–52

Madhavan, A. (2000) Market Microstructure: a Survey, *Journal of Financial Markets* 3, 205–58

Makridakis, S. (1993) Accuracy Measures: Theoretical and Practical Concerns, *International Journal of Forecasting* 9, 527–9

Makridakis, S. and Hibon, M. (1995) Evaluating Accuracy (or Error) Measures, *INSEAD Working Paper* 95/18/TM

Matthews, K., Murinde, V. and Zhao, T. (2007) Competitive Conditions among the Major British Banks, *Journal of Banking and Finance* 31(7), 2025–42

McCue, T. E. and Kling, J. L. (1994) Real Estate Returns and the Macroeconomy: Some Empirical Evidence from Real Estate Investment Trust Data, 1972–1991, *Journal of Real Estate Research* 9(3), 277–87

McCulloch, J. H. (1987) US Government Term Structure Data, Ohio State University, mimeo

McNees, S. K. (1986) Forecasting Accuracy of Alternative Techniques: a Comparison of US Macroeconomic Forecasts, *Journal of Business and Economic Statistics* 4(1), 5–15

Mills, T. C. and Markellos, R. N. (2008) *The Econometric Modelling of Financial Time Series*, 3rd edn, Cambridge University Press, Cambridge, UK

Mills, T. C. and Mills, A. G. (1991) The International Transmission of Bond Market Movements, *Bulletin of Economic Research* 43, 273–82

Mitchell, M. and Stafford, E. (2000) Managerial Decisions and Long-term Stock Price Performance, *Journal of Business* 73, 287–329

Myers, R. J. and Thompson, S. R. (1989) Generalized Optimal Hedge Ratio Estimation, *American Journal of Agricultural Economics* 71(4), 858–68

Myers, S. C. (1984) The Capital Structure Puzzle, *Journal of Finance* 39, 575–92

Nelsen, R. B. (2006) *An Introduction to Copulas*, Springer-Verlag, New York

Nelson, C. R. and Plosser, C. I. (1982) Trends and Random Walks in Macroeconomic Time Series, *Journal of Monetary Economics* 10, 139–62

Nelson, D. B. (1991) Conditional Heteroskedasticity in Asset Returns: a New Approach, *Econometrica* 59(2), 347–70

Newey, W. K. and West, K. D. (1987) A Simple Positive-definite Heteroskedasticity and Autocorrelation-consistent Covariance Matrix, *Econometrica* 55, 703–8

O'Connell, P. G. J. (1998) The Overvaluation of Purchasing Power Parity, *Journal of International Economics* 44, 1–20

O'Hara, M. (1995) *Market Microstructure Theory*, Blackwell, Malden, MA

Osborn, D. (1990) A survey of seasonality in UK macroeconomic variables, *International Journal of Forecasting* 6(3), 327–36

Osterwald-Lenum, M. (1992) A Note with Quantiles of the Asymptotic Distribution of the ML Cointegration Rank Test Statistics, *Oxford Bulletin of Economics and Statistics* 54, 461–72

Pagan, A. R. and Schwert, G. W. (1990) Alternative Models for Conditional Stock Volatilities, *Journal of Econometrics* 45, 267–90

Panzar, J. C. and Rosse, J. N. (1982) Structure, Conduct and Comparative Statistics, *Bell Laboratories Economics Discussion Paper*

(1987) Testing for 'Monopoly' Equilibrium, *Journal of Industrial Economics* 35(4), 443–56

Pedroni, P. (1999) Critical Values for Cointegration Tests in Heterogeneous Panels with Multiple Regressors, *Oxford Bulletin of Economics and Statistics* 61, 653–70

(2004) Panel Cointegration: Asymptotic and Finite Sample Properties of Pooled Time Series Tests with an Application to the PPP Hypothesis, *Econometric Theory* 20, 597–625

Perron. P. (1989) The Great Crash, the Oil Price Shock and the Unit Root Hypothesis, *Econometrica* 57, 1361–401

(1997) Further Evidence on Breaking Trend Functions in Macroeconomic Variables, *Journal of Econometrics* 80, 355–85

Pesaran, M. H. and Timmerman, A. (1992) A Simple Non-parametric Test of Predictive Performance, *Journal of Business and Economic Statistics* 10(4), 461–5

Poon, W. P. H. (2003) Are Unsolicited Credit Ratings Biased Downward?, *Journal of Banking and Finance* 27, 593–614

Prabhala, N. R. (1997) Conditional Methods in Event-studies and an Equilibrium Justification for Standard Event-study Procedures, *Review of Financial Studies* 10(1), 1–38

Press, W. H., Teukolsy, S. A., Vetterling, W. T. and Flannery, B. P. (1992) *Numerical Recipes in Fortran*, Cambridge University Press, Cambridge, UK

Quandt, R. (1960) Tests of the Hypothesis that a Linear Regression System Obeys Two Different Regimes, *Journal of the American Statistical Association* 55, 324–30

Ramanathan, R. (1995) *Introductory Econometrics with Applications*, 3rd edn, Dryden Press, Fort Worth, TX

Ramsey, J. B. (1969) Tests for Specification Errors in Classical Linear Least-squares Regression Analysis, *Journal of the Royal Statistical Society B* 31(2), 350–71

Refenes, A.-P. (1995) *Neural Networks in the Capital Markets*, John Wiley, Chichester, UK

Ross, S. A. (1976) The Arbitrage Theory of Capital Asset Pricing, *Journal of Economic Theory* 13(3), 341–60

Runkle, D. E. (1987) Vector Autoregressions and Reality, *Journal of Business and Economic Statistics* 5(4), 437–42

Scheinkman, J. A. and LeBaron, B. (1989) Nonlinear Dynamics and Stock Returns, *Journal of Business* 62(3), 311–37

Schwarz, G. (1978) Estimating the Dimension of a Model, *Annals of Statistics* 6, 461–4

Shaffer, S. and DiSalvo, J. (1994) Conduct in a Banking Duopoly, *Journal of Banking and Finance* 18, 1063–82

Shanken, J. (1992) On the Estimation of Beta-pricing Models, *Review of Financial Studies* 5, 1–33

Shea, G. (1984) Pitfalls in Smoothing Interest Rate Term Structure Data: Equilibrium Models and Spline Approximations, *Journal of Financial and Quantitative Analysis* 19(3), 253–69

(1992) Benchmarking the Expectations Hypothesis of the Interest Rate Term Structure: an Analysis of Cointegrating Vectors, *Journal of Business and Economic Statistics* 10(3), 347–66

Shephard, N. (1996) Statistical aspects of ARCH and Stochastic Volatility, in D. R. Cox, D. V. Hinkley and O. E. Barndorff-Nielsen (eds.) *Time Series Models: in Econometrics, Finance, and Other Fields*, Chapman and Hall, London 1–67

Siegel, A. F. (1997) International Currency Relationship Information Revealed by Cross-option Prices, *Journal of Futures Markets* 17, 369–84

Sims, C. A. (1972) Money, Income, and Causality, *American Economic Review* 62(4), 540–52

(1980) Macroeconomics and Reality, *Econometrica* 48, 1–48

Stock, J. H. and Watson, M. W. (1988) Testing for Common Trends, *Journal of the American Statistical Association* 83, 1097–107

(2011) *Introduction to Econometrics*, 3rd edn, Pearson, Boston, MA

Sullivan, R., Timmermann, A. and White, H. (1999) Data-snooping, Technical Trading Rule Performance, and the Bootstrap, *Journal of Finance* 54, 1647–91

Sutcliffe, C. (1997) *Stock Index Futures: Theories and International Evidence*, 2nd edn, International Thompson Business Press, London

Taylor, M. P. (1987) Risk Premia and Foreign Exchange – A Multiple Time Series Approach to Testing Uncovered Interest Parity, *Weltwirtschaftliches Archiv* 123(4), 579–91

(1989) Covered Interest Arbitrage and Market Turbulence, *Economic Journal* 99, 376–91

Taylor, M. P. and Sarno, L. (1998) The Behavior of Real Exchange Rates during the Post-Bretton Woods Period, *Journal of International Economics* 46(2), 281–312

Taylor, M. P. and Tonks, I. (1989) The Internationalisation of Stock Markets and the Abolition of UK Exchange Controls, *Review of Economics and Statistics* 71, 332–6

Taylor, S. J. (1986) Forecasting the Volatility of Currency Exchange Rates, *International Journal of Forecasting* 3, 159–70

(1994) Modelling Stochastic Volatility: a Review and Comparative Study, *Mathematical Finance* 4, 183–204

Theil, H. (1966) *Applied Economic Forecasting*, North-Holland, Amsterdam

Tobin, J. (1958) Estimation of Relationships for Limited Dependent Variables, *Econometrica* 26(1), 24–36

Tong, H. (1983) *Threshold Models in Nonlinear Time Series Analysis*, Springer-Verlag, New York

(1990) *Nonlinear Time Series: a Dynamical Systems Approach*, Oxford University Press, Oxford

Trippi, R. R. and Turban, E. (1993) *Neural Networks in Finance and Investing*, McGraw-Hill, New York

Tse, Y. K. (1995) Lead–Lag Relationship between Spot Index and Futures Price of the Nikkei Stock Average, *Journal of Forecasting* 14, 553–63

(2000) A Test for Constant Correlations in a Multivariate GARCH Model, *Journal of Econometrics* 98, 107–27

Tse, Y. K. and Tsui, A. K. C. (2002) A Multivariate GARCH Model with Time-varying Correlations, *Journal of Business and Economic Statistics* 20, 351–62

Van der Weide, R. (2002) GO-GARCH: a Multivariate Generalised Orthogonal GARCH Model, *Journal of Applied Econometrics* 17, 549–64

Van Eyden, R. J. (1996) *The Application of Neural Networks in the Forecasting of Share Prices*, Finance and Technology Publishing, Haymarket

Vrontos, I. D., Dellaportas, P. and Politis, D. N. (2000) Full Bayesian Inference for GARCH and EGARCH Models, *Journal of Business and Economic Statistics* 18(2), 187–98

Walter, C. and Lopez, J. (2000) Is Implied Correlation Worth Calculating? Evidence from Foreign Exchange Options, *Journal of Derivatives*, Spring, 65–81

Wang, G. H. K. and Yau, J. (2000) Trading Volume, Bid–Ask Spread and Price Volatility in Futures Markets, *Journal of Futures Markets* 20(10), 943–70

Wang, G. H. K., Yau, J. and Baptiste, T. (1997) Trading Volume, Transactions Costs in Futures Markets, *Journal of Futures Markets* 17(7), 757–80

Watsham, T. J. and Parramore, K. (2004) *Quantitative Methods in Finance*, 2nd edn, International Thompson Business Press, London

West, K. D. and Cho, D. (1995) The Predictive Ability of Several Models of Exchange Rate Volatility, *Journal of Econometrics* 69, 367–91

White, H. (1980) A Heteroskedasticity-consistent Covariance Matrix Estimator and a Direct Test for Heteroskedasticity, *Econometrica* 48, 817–38

(1992) *Artificial Neural Networks: Approximation and Learning Theory*, Blackwell, Malden, MA

(2000) A Reality Check for Data Snooping, *Econometrica* 68, 1097–126

Wooldridge, J. M. (2010) *Econometric Analysis of Cross-section and Panel Data*, 2nd edn, MIT Press, MA

Yadav, P. K., Pope, P. F. and Paudyal, K. (1994) Threshold Autoregressive Modelling in Finance: the Price Difference of Equivalent Assets, *Mathematical Finance* 4, 205–21

Zarowin, P. (1990) Size, Seasonality and Stock Market Overreaction, *Journal of Financial and Quantitative Analysis* 25, 113–25

Zellner, A. (1962) An Efficient Method of Estimating Seemingly Unrelated Regressions and Tests for Aggregation Bias, *Journal of the American Statistical Association* 57, 348–68

Zivot, E. and Andrews, K. (1992) Further Evidence on the Great Crash, the Oil Price Shock, and the Unit Root Hypothesis, *Journal of Business and Economic Statistics* 10, 251–70

Index

Hadamard product, 472
Hamilton's filter, 502
Hausman test, 312, 537, 539
Heckman procedure, 583
hedge ratios, 86, 465, 475
hedonic pricing models, 156
heteroscedasticity, 34, 181, 423
    conditional, 432
historical covariance, 466
homoscedasticity, 181, 423, 432, 484
hypothesis testing, 99, 111
    confidence interval, 106
    error classification, 110
    Lagrange multiplier (LM) test, 180, 184, 452
    likelihood ratio (LR) test, 330, 453
    under maximum likelihood, 317, 431, 434,
        452, 484, 583
    significance level, 102, 110, 120, 340
    test of significance approach, 102
    Wald test, 121, 144, 145, 180, 452

identification, 273, 275
    order condition, 309
    rank condition, 309
implied covariance, 466
implied volatility models, 421, 454
impulse responses, 336, 342, 344, 396
independence of irrelevant alternatives, 571
information criteria, 160, 278, 331
    adjusted R^2, 275
    Akaike's (AIC), 275
    Hannan–Quinn (HQIC), 275
    Schwartz's Bayesian (SBIC), 275
intercept, 28, 129, 136, 494, 501, 528, 529, 531,
    536, 551, 555, 644, 649, 651
interest rates, 172, 281, 339, 368
    term structure of, 204, 398
invertibility, 267

Jensen's alpha, 113, 649, 660
Johansen test, 379, 386, 389, 393, 399, 400, 551,
    554
jumps, 455, 602

KPSS test, 365, 370, 550
kurtosis, 66, 209, 210, 216, 462

lag lengths, 201, 260, 329, 330, 331, 340, 363,
    370, 383, 386, 402, 515, 555, 616
lag operator, 256, 260, 361
lagged regressors, 205
lagged value, 189, 203, 205, 206, 283, 328, 340,
    456
Lagrange multiplier (LM) test, 180, 184, 452, 471

lags number of, 203, 205, 206, 283, 328, 456
large sample property, 92, 199
laws of logs, 35, 85
lead-lag relationships, 344, 380, 519
least squares dummy variables (LSDV), 529, 531
leptokurtosis, 416, 435, 439, 462, 463
leverage effects, 416, 439
likelihood function, 317, 431, 452, 473, 485,
    488
likelihood ratio (LR) test, 330, 453
linear models, 75, 85, 90, 134
linear probability model, 560, 565
linearity, 85
Ljung–Box test, 254, 277
log-likelihood function (LLF), 431, 453, 470,
    471, 485, 565, 568, 589
log-return formulation, 8
logit model, 562, 563, 574, 583
    comparison with probit, 565
    estimation of, 572, 589
    measuring goodness of fit, 567
    parameter interpretation, 566
long-memory models, 411
long-run static solution, 46, 204
loss function, see residual sum of squares
Lyapunov exponent, 419

macroeconomic indicators, 3, 145, 170, 186, 241,
    244, 323, 338, 418, 538
marginal distribution, 70
marginal effects, 566, 587
market microstructure, 3, 203, 311, 318, 490
market reaction, 645
market returns, 145, 339, 459, 464, 653
market risk premium, 76, 82, 119, 493, 541, 648,
    651, 661
market timing, 383
Markov switching regime, 492, 502, 516, 523
Marquardt algorithm, 434
matrices, 41
    eigenvalues of, 46
matrix notation, 50
maximum likelihood, 317, 431, 434, 452, 484,
    583, 589
measurement error, 3, 236, 650
median, 62, 64, 66, 162
minimum capital risk requirement (MCRR), see
    value-at-risk
misspecification error, 204, 220, 467
misspecification tests, 15, 180
misspecified dynamics, 201
mode, 62, 66
model construction, 11, 276
model interpretation, 332